Introduction to Law

The West Legal Studies Series

Your options keep growing with West Legal Studies

Each year our list continues to offer you more options for every area of the law to meet your course or on-the-job reference requirements. We now have over 140 titles from which to choose in the following areas:

Administrative Law	Family Law
Alternative Dispute Resolution	Federal Taxation
Bankruptcy	Intellectual Property
Business Organizations/Corporations	Introduction to Law
Civil Litigation and Procedure	Introduction to Paralegalism
CLA Exam Preparation	Law Office Management
Client Accounting	Law Office Procedures
Computer in the Law Office	Legal Research, Writing, and Analysis
Constitutional Law	Legal Terminology
Contract Law	Paralegal Employment
Criminal Law and Procedure	Real Estate Law
Document Preparation	Reference Materials
Environmental Law	Torts and Personal Injury Law
Ethics	Will, Trusts, and Estate Administration

You will find unparalleled, practical support

Each book is augmented by instructor and student supplements to ensure the best learning experience possible. We also offer custom publishing and other benefits such as West's Student Achievement Award. In addition, our sales representatives are ready to provide you with dependable service.

We want to hear from you

Our best contributions for improving the quality of our books and instructional materials are feedback from the people who use them. If you have a question, concern, or observation about any of our materials, or you have a product proposal or manuscript, we want to hear from you. Please contact your local representative or write us at the following address:

West Legal Studies, 3 Columbia Circle, P.O. Box 15015, Albany, NY 12212-5015

For additional information point your browser at
www.westlegalstudies.com

West Legal Studies
an imprint of Delmar Publishers

an International Thomson Publishing company I(T)P

Introduction to Law

THIRD EDITION

Beth Walston-Dunham

MIDLAND LUTHERAN COLLEGE
FREMONT, NEBRASKA

WEST LEGAL STUDIES

an International Thomson Publishing company I(T)P®

Albany • Bonn • Boston • Cincinnati • Detroit • London • Madrid
Melbourne • Mexico City • Minneapolis/St. Paul • New York • Pacific Grove
Paris • San Francisco • Singapore • Tokyo • Toronto • Washington

Cover Design: Susan Mathews, Stillwater Studio
Cover Image: Stock Studios Photography

Delmar Staff

Publisher: Susan Simpfenderfer
Acquisitions Editor: Joan Gill
Developmental Editor: Rhonda Dearborn
Editorial Assistant: Lisa H. Flatley

Marketing Manager: Katherine M.S. Hans
Production Manager: Wendy Troeger
Production Editor: Laurie A. Boyce

Carlisle Publishers Services
Project management
and composition

COPYRIGHT © 1999
By West Publishing
an imprint of Delmar Publishers
a division of International Thomson Publishing

The ITP logo is a trademark under license.

Printed in the United States of America

For more information, contact:

Delmar Publishers
3 Columbia Circle, Box 15015
Albany, New York 12212-5015

**International Thomson
Publishing Europe**
Berkshire House
168-173 High Holborn
London, WC1V7AA
United Kingdom

Nelson ITP, Australia
102 Dodds Street
South Melbourne,
Victoria, 3205 Australia

Nelson Canada
1120 Birchmont Road
Scarborough, Ontario
M1K 5G4, Canada

**International Thomson
Publishing France**
Tour Maine-Montparnasse
33 Avenue du Maine
75755 Paris Cedex 15, France

International Thomson Editores
Seneca 53
Colonia Polanco
11560 Mexico D. F. Mexico

**International Thomson Publishing
GmbH**
Königswinterer Straße 418
53227 Bonn
Germany

**International Thomson
Publishing Asia**
60 Albert Street
#15-01 Albert Complex
Singapore 189969

**International Thomson
Publishing Japan**
Hirakawa-cho Kyowa Building, 3F
2-2-1 Hirakawa-cho, Chiyoda-ku,
Tokyo 102, Japan

ITE Spain/Paraninfo
Calle Magallanes, 25
28015-Madrid, Espana

1 2 3 4 5 6 7 8 9 10 XXX 03 02 01 00 99 98

Library of Congress Cataloging-in-Publication Data

Walston-Dunham, Beth.
    Introduction to law / Beth Walston-Dunham.—3rd ed.
      p. cm.
    Includes bibliographical references and index.
    ISBN 0-314-12938-3
    1. Law—United States. I. Title
  KF385.W35 1998
  349.73—dc21
                              98-42223
                                CIP

To the Memory of
M. George Dunham, M.D.
1948–1996

You taught me the meaning of courage, the importance of focus and always striving to put forth your best effort, and ultimately true grace and dignity in the face of all adversity. You were and remain my partner, my inspiration, and my best friend.

Table of Cases

Preface

The purpose of this book is not to answer all of one's questions about the law but to generate questions. The goal of this book as an introductory text is to create an awareness and appreciation for the effect that law has on virtually every facet of life and society. The chapters guide the student from a basic introduction of the rationale behind the structure of the American system of government to a discussion of each major area of law in the legal system. Regardless of the initial reason for picking up this book, the intended outcome of reading it remains the same: to gain a better understanding of not only how but also why law is such an integral part of our professional and personal lives and to gain some sense of the order and stability law provides while remaining adaptive to the ever-changing face of American society.

This text is aimed at the student who is studying law for the first time. Each chapter is designed to introduce the student to fundamental legal concepts and principles. Chapters 1 to 6 provide an introduction to the American legal system, the manner in which law is created and administered, and certain considerations that affect legal disputes. Most of the remaining chapters (Chapters 7 to 14) concentrate on different areas of law by exploring basic principles and terminology. The areas covered include property, business, estates, tort, family, contract, and criminal law and procedure. Chapter 15 addresses the roles of legal professionals and their support staff. Throughout the text, and specifically in Chapter 15, discussion is given to the ethical considerations that affect legal professionals and subjects of law.

CHANGES TO THE THIRD EDITION

The third edition of *Introduction to Law* is an updated version of the prior texts. In this edition, new cases are included to reflect the current trends of the courts in the areas of law presented. A section on bankruptcy (Chapter 10) has been added to introduce the student to the basic concepts and principals of this growing area of practice. The employment section of the chapter on torts has been expanded to touch on actions based on nonphysical injuries such as sexual harassment. Finally, many assignments have been modified to reflect the changes in the text. They will provide more opportunity for the student to analytically process the information. The intent of these changes is to provide the student with the opportunity to obtain an understanding at an introductory level of the current state of the American legal system.

CHAPTER FORMAT

Recent case law has been incorporated to provide a better view of the current position of courts across the nation. Chapter features include the following:

- Chapter objectives open each chapter to focus the student's attention on the main elements the student will learn.
- Hypothetical applications are interspersed through each chapter to illustrate chapter concepts. Points for Discussion follow the applications and provide a springboard for class discussion.
- Longer edited cases, many new to this edition, are followed by questions that encourage students to consider the major issues in each case.
- Assignments throughout each chapter test students' knowledge by asking them to apply the chapter material.
- Key terms are set in **boldface** type and defined in the margin where they first appear within the chapter. Also, for easy review, each chapter ends with a list of the key terms found in the chapter.
- A chapter summary ends each chapter with a brief review of the main points covered.
- Review questions follow the chapter material, which allow the student yet another opportunity to review the chapter content.

SUPPORT MATERIAL

This edition is accompanied by a support package that will assist students in learning and aid instructors in teaching:

- A study guide by Beth Walston-Dunham accompanies this edition and parallels all major concepts in the text. It is a practical tool to assist the student in extracting important information and reviewing the materials. The format of the study guide allows the student to take an active but structured role in the learning process. Initially, short-answer questions require the student to examine the text by identifying and explaining major concepts. Next, a matching section allows the student to reinforce comprehension of terminology. Finally, a true/false series of questions provides a self-test of concepts and terms. Because of the variety and depth of the subjects addressed, the study guide should allow the student to maximize the level of understanding in the time available for study outside the classroom.
- An instructor's manual and test bank by Beth Walston-Dunham accompanies this edition and has been greatly expanded to incorporate all changes in the text and to provide comprehensive teaching support. It includes such items as sample syllabi, a lecture key consisting of a synopsis of all major concepts, answers to all applications, information to guide classroom discussion in the Points for Discussion following applications, assignment and review questions, and answers. Also included are case briefs for all cases found in the text. A comprehensive test bank provides 450 objective test

questions and answers. The test bank consists of questions that have already been successfully class tested.

◆ Westest Computerized Testing provides the entire test bank on disk.

ACKNOWLEDGMENTS

Thanks and appreciation are extended to the manuscript reviewers, instructors, and others who provided invaluable suggestions and support in the preparation of the third edition:

Jane Bennett
ORANGE COAST COLLEGE
COSTA MESA, CA

Oliver N. Blaise, III, Esq.
BINGHAMTON, NY

Terry Breden
GODFREY, IL

Cindy Burns
FREMONT, NE

Linda S. Corvallis
SANFORD-BROWN COLLEGE
NORTH KANSAS CITY, MO

Elizabeth Hannan
ST. PAUL, MN

Mary Louis Kurr
UNIVERSITY COLLEGE OF BANGOR
BANGOR, ME

Scott Michalec
MIDSTATE COLLEGE
PEORIA, IL

Laura Morrison-Dombrowski, atty.
CHICAGO, IL

Timothy W. Murphy
USAF ACADEMY
COLORADO SPRINGS, CO

Scott F. Myers
MARIST COLLEGE
POUGHKEEPSIE, NY

Rebecca Parker
ARAPAHOE COMMUNITY COLLEGE
LITTLETON, CO

Kathleen Mercer Reed
UNIVERSITY OF OHIO
TOLEDO, OH

Lisa Rothanzl
FREMONT, NE

Marilyn R. Tayler
MONTCLAIR STATE COLLEGE
UPPER MONTCLAIR, NJ

Sandra Thornton
GEORGIA INSTITUTE OF TECHNOLOGY
ATLANTA, GA

Keith, Betty, and Eric Walston
EAST ALTON, IL

Lee Weinberg
UNIVERSITY OF PITTSBURGH
PITTSBURGH, PA

Susan Wilbanks
ITAWAMBA COMMUNITY COLLEGE
FULTON, MS

Norma Wooten
JOHNSON COUNTY COMMUNITY COLLEGE
OVERLAND PARK, KS

I would also like to thank Elizabeth Hannan, formerly of West Publishing Company, for the years of tremendous support and patience as I undertook these projects under what were often less than ideal circumstances.

Beth Walston-Dunham

Contents

CHAPTER   9

Torts   241

CHAPTER   10

The Law of Business   289

CHAPTER   11

Estates and Probate   335

CHAPTER   12

Criminal Law   355

CHAPTER   13

Criminal Procedure   389

CHAPTER 1

The Historical Basis and Current Structure of the American Legal System

CHAPTER OBJECTIVES

After reading this chapter, you should be able to

- *Distinguish the positivist, naturalist, and sociological theories.*

- *Explain the role of the political theories in the present system of American government.*

- *Discuss the weaknesses of the Articles of Confederation.*

- *Describe the function of each branch of government under the Constitution.*

- *Explain the differences between legislative, judicial, and administrative law.*

- *Distinguish the traditional and modern balance of application of laws.*

- *List the hierarchy of law and explain the exception to the rule of the hierarchy.*

THE HISTORICAL BASIS OF AMERICAN LAW

Before the Government

The American legal system was not developed hastily. The first settlers in the New World had no intention of creating an entirely new legal system. Rather, for more than a century, these people clung to the methods of law and order that they or their ancestors had known in Europe, predominately in England. Not only did the colonists adhere to many of the laws of England, but they also accepted and sanctioned the prevailing attitudes toward religion under which people were charged and punished by the government for committing acts regarded as sinful and thus illegal. However, as the American population grew, the British and other European governments increased their efforts to establish a formal and permanent influence in America. These attempts included establishment of all aspects of the foreign governments in the colonies. Although the colonists were willing to adopt many legal principles from England, they were not interested in adopting a governmental structure that they felt was not responsive to the will of the people, especially since this was the very structure they had sought to avoid by coming to America.

During the revolutionary era, the colonists realized that they had to establish some form of permanent governmental structure if they were to avoid rule by another country. The present-day structure derives from a combination of factors that influenced those responsible for establishing the American government. The founders' foresight is evidenced by many of the laws and procedures they established that are still in place over two centuries later.

Initially, the colonists' primary legal concern was to deter and punish criminal acts as a means of maintaining order. The founders sought to prosecute and punish those who committed crimes against the morals of the predominantly religious population. Since what was considered morally and religiously right was usually determined by members of the aristocracy, it is no coincidence that the aristocrats were rarely found guilty of immoral or criminal acts. The focus of law in early American society thus was an attempt by the aristocracy to impress its perception of right and wrong upon the working classes and to punish those who the wealthy and powerful perceived to be improper or sinful.

The original system of justice in America was a simplistic theory of right and wrong. For some time, the colonists saw no need for written statutes, because this theory, also known as the **naturalist theory,**[1] was based on the belief that all persons inherently knew the difference between right and wrong and should conduct themselves accordingly. However, as the population increased and industry advanced and expanded, vast numbers of individuals with differing opinions of right and wrong made simple aristocratic beliefs obsolete. The people required a more detailed legal system that included written legal principles applicable to the entire population.

Almost simultaneously with the increase in population and industry came direct attempts by other nations to control the colonies. Initially, each colony fought this control as an individual government without ties to the other colonies. But the colonists quickly realized that if any of the colonies were to succeed against the attempts of the British and others to take control, the colonies must become unified.

Naturalist Theory
Philosophy that all persons know inherently the difference between right and wrong.

The Results of the Revolution

At the time of the Revolution, the colonies came together and issued their Declaration of Independence. To enforce such a document was not an easy task for a largely unsophisticated, poorly armed, and disorganized band of citizens who were matched against Great Britain's army and navy. Nevertheless, the people succeeded and formed a central government made up of individual states.

This new government was guided by a document known as the Articles of Confederation. The Constitution was not passed until eleven years later in September of 1787. The Articles bore little resemblance to the current Constitution. Under the Articles, each state sent delegates as members of Congress who then nominated and elected a president among themselves. The delegates passed laws, acted as judges in disputes among the states, negotiated treaties, and served as the government for the new nation. The duties assigned the president were to preside over sessions of Congress and act as an ambassador to and receive representatives of other governments. All legal disputes with respect to individuals continued to be dealt with by each state's own system of justice.

In a short time, the colonists considered the Articles of Confederation and Congress largely ineffective. The national government had no "enforcement power": it had no judges, no jails, and no way to force collection of the monies each state was supposed to contribute. Moreover, there was no money or organization to support a national army. Nor was there a staff of government employees to operate the government when Congress was not in session. The president was only the head of a small group of delegates, not the leader of the nation. Clearly, if such a nation was to succeed, a much more organized system would have to be created.

Assignment 1.1

> Prepare a list of ten modern government functions, services, or guarantees that would not be possible if the national government had no judiciary for citizen disputes and no enforcement power over the states. It may be helpful to refer to the Constitution in Appendix A. Be prepared to discuss your answers.

Interestingly, the first real issue in creating a permanent government was whether to allow the states to continue in existence. Several delegates, including some from the South, believed that the individual states should be abolished and that all people and all legal issues should be governed by a central authority. But this idea failed to win popular support, and a government comprising separate state governments and a national government with separate functions was created. The states were left intact because they could respond effectively and quickly to the needs of their citizens and their individual economies. The national government was formed to protect the fundamental rights of all citizens and ensure that the state governments would not prohibit individual rights. The national government would also handle national issues such as interstate commerce, Indian affairs and immigration, and international issues such as treaties for trade and nonaggression.

Establishment of branches of government.   Once the issue of statehood was decided, the Constitutional Congress convened in Philadelphia to create a structure for the new federal government. The Constitutional Congress drafted the Constitution, which clearly defined the powers and limitations of the national and state governments with respect to each other and to individual citizens. The members of the Constitutional Congress agreed that there would be three distinct branches of government, each with separate duties and all with the obligation to cooperate with and monitor the other branches to ensure that no one branch obtained too much power.

The first branch of government created by the Constitutional Congress was the legislative branch, to be called Congress. Congress would be elected by the people (directly for the House of Representatives, indirectly for the Senate, which was elected by the state legislatures until the Seventeenth Amendment was ratified in 1913). Congress would retain the sole authority to make statutory law. In this way, the people as a whole would always have significant influence in making the laws that all persons were required to follow. As delegated by the Constitution, only Congress, and no other branch, has the power to create statutory law. In the past, when any other governmental source attempted to create statutory law, the law was struck down as being in violation of what is known as the delegation doctrine. The delegation doctrine is based on the legal principle that Congress cannot delegate or give away its authority to make statutory law. The doctrine has been applied most often in the creation of regulatory law by administrative agencies under the executive branch. Chapter 4, which covers administrative law specifically, discusses the delegation doctrine more fully.

The second branch of government created was the executive branch. The president heads the executive branch at the national level, while each state executive branch is headed by a governor. Under the Constitution, the president is elected indirectly by the people through the electoral college. Each state is entitled to appoint a number of electors equal to the state's total number of senators and representatives to Congress. A person cannot serve as both a member of Congress and an elector. Each state legislature determines the manner in which the electors are appointed. The electors vote and elect the president by a majority. Generally, the electoral vote reflects the popular vote. In the event there is no one person with a majority, the House of Representatives is responsible for electing the president. The details of the electoral process can be found in Article II of the Constitution (Appendix A). Chapter 4 further discusses the executive branch.

The president has power to approve or reject acts of Congress; however, the power is not absolute, and the president cannot deny the authority of Congress to enact law if it is in fact the will of the majority that such law be enacted. Rejection by the president of a law enacted by Congress is known as the veto power and can be overridden by a significant majority of Congress. The president also has several important functions with respect to foreign affairs and has the ultimate duty to enforce the laws of the United States. Consequently, federal law enforcement agencies are considered part of the executive branch. A similar structure is in place at the state level between the governor and state law enforcement personnel. The various powers and functions of the executive branch are discussed further in Chapter 4.

Finally, the Constitutional Convention determined that a third and separate branch of government was needed to serve as mediator of disputes. Thus, the judicial branch was established. The judiciary has the authority to interpret laws and protect the Constitution from violation by Congress, the president, or the states. Although the Constitution vests the ultimate authority to enforce laws in the president, in practice, the judiciary also assists in enforcement when the courts apply law to specific cases.

The Bill of Rights.   The three separate but related branches of government were designed to offer protection from a small number of persons gaining power over the entire population. By independent operation of the branches but with the power of the branches to influence one another, the people are better protected from one branch obtaining too much power or using its power unwisely. Through this system of checks and balances, each branch can use its specially designated powers to make sure the other branches act within their constitutionally prescribed limits.

In addition to framing the Constitution, Congress, with the approval of the people, subsequently passed the Bill of Rights, which protects essential fundamental human freedoms. The Bill of Rights protects all citizens from government infringement on those matters presumed to be inherently personal and a matter of choice for all human beings. The following rights are specifically protected:

- Freedom of speech, religion, and press; peaceable assembly; petitions for governmental change.
- Right to bear arms.
- Freedom from unreasonable invasion of home by the government for purposes of search and seizure of persons or property.
- Right to have an independent judicial magistrate determine if probable cause exists before a search or arrest warrant can be issued.
- Right not to be tried twice for the same crime.
- Right not to have persons or property seized without due process.
- Right to a speedy and public trial.
- Right to an impartial jury in the jurisdiction where the alleged crime occurred.
- Freedom from forced self-incrimination.
- Right to counsel in criminal prosecutions.
- Right of the accused to know of the crime alleged.
- Right of the accused to confront the witnesses for the prosecution.
- Right not to be subjected to excessive bail.
- Freedom from cruel or unusual punishment.
- Right of the states to govern on matters not addressed in the Constitution or its amendments.

The Bill of Rights establishes the standards of fundamental fairness by which the government must deal with its citizens. The standards of fairness established by the Bill of Rights have been and continue to be protected by the U.S. Supreme Court. (See *Texas v. Johnson*, 491 U.S. 397, 109 S.Ct. 2533, 105 L.Ed.2d 342 [1989], near the end of the chapter as an example of the protection of personal rights.)

Additional individual rights.   In recent years, the Supreme Court has been increasingly asked to resolve issues that determine the rights of persons to be free from governmental intrusion into their private lives. Issues have ranged from abortion to the rights of law enforcement to search and seize persons and evidence of criminal activity. Frequently, news reports will discuss opinions of the Supreme Court that define the boundaries between the government obligations and individual freedoms with respect to the Bill of Rights. From time to time, additional language regarding these freedoms has been added through amendments to the Constitution as Congress and the people have deemed appropriate.

Not only are the Constitution and its amendments documents created over 200 years ago to establish a new government, but they are also the foundations of present-day law. Every time Congress passes a statute, the executive branch enforces the law or the judiciary interprets law to be applicable to a situation or an individual, such action must be taken in accordance with the requirements of the Constitution and its amendments. All law created in this country must be consistent with, and embody the spirit of, the rights guaranteed in the Constitution and its amendments. The Constitution and its amendments continue to be responsible for giving definition to the rights of citizens and government alike. In recent years, the courts have used the Constitution and its amendments to prevent police from invading the privacy of individuals without a warrant, to allow people the right to publicly express their religious and political beliefs, and to encourage the public to take an active role in government through elections, petitions, and peaceful protests.

Assignment 1.2

> Prepare a list of ten specific types of conduct in which anyone is entitled to engage based on the Bill of Rights. An example might be the right to attend the church of one's choice without persecution. In formulating your list, it may be helpful to think of activities that are not allowed in nondemocratic nations. Be prepared to discuss your answers.

The Influence of Political Theories

The functioning of the branches of government and the manner in which issues between government and citizens are decided are the product of distinct philosophies that have influenced the American legal system since its inception. As Congress structured the new government, the naturalist theory became inadequate to deal with the complexity of legal issues that arose. As a result, other theories regarding the establishment of an orderly society were incorporated into the U.S. system of government and law. One influential theory was the **positivist theory,** which proposes that a government should have a single entity to determine what is right and wrong as a matter of law.[2] The law cannot be questioned or challenged. If a law is violated, punishment will automatically follow. This theory is evident in the court of last resort—the U.S. Supreme Court. Short of a constitutional amendment, the decisions of the Supreme Court are not subject to any other authority.

Positivist Theory
Political belief that there should be a superior governmental entity that is not subject to question or challenge.

Another political theory of law that has become an integral part of American law is rooted in social consciousness. This sociological view suggests that people as a group determine what is and is not acceptable, based on the needs of society at the time. **Sociological theory** holds that the law is in a constant state of change and adjusts accordingly to the needs of society. Society as a whole decides what is right and what is wrong.[3] In conjunction with the naturalist theory, the positivist and sociological theories provide the components for a successful and durable government. Today the majority of law is created by representatives elected to Congress by the population. If citizens believe a law is wrong, they can lobby to have it changed. If they believe their elected representatives are not enacting laws that embody the beliefs of the people, they can elect new legislators. If the legislature passes a law that appears to violate the Constitution, citizens can challenge the law in the courts that have the power to resolve the issue by upholding the statute or invalidating it as unconstitutional.

Sociological Theory
Doctrine that follows the principle that government should adapt laws to reflect the current needs and beliefs of society.

Balance as the Key to Success

In some respects, the U.S. government is a product of each of the three philosophies previously discussed. The naturalist theory is reflected in the language of the Constitution and the Bill of Rights, which (especially the Bill of Rights) state what was and continues to be considered fundamentally fair. The Constitution and the Bill of Rights also contain statements indicative of the positivist idea of an ultimate authority that interprets the laws and decides in what circumstances they apply and how they should be enforced. The ultimate rule has been embodied in the judiciary. Although laws can be challenged, in such cases, the Supreme Court is generally the final authority on legal issues. A decision by this court can be affected only by a congressional constitutional enactment or in a decision wherein the Court revises a previous position (both are relatively rare occurrences). The Supreme Court helps ensure that the laws are applied consistently to all people. The duty of the Court is to guarantee that each individual's rights will be protected against government, persons, or entities that might violate those rights.

The sociological theory plays an important role in our governmental structure, because society can influence the government and laws in a number of ways. The people have the right to periodically elect representatives to Congress and to select the president. They even have the right to approve or reject constitutional amendments and certain other laws. If society's needs change, the flexible system of government allows passage of laws or election of representatives who will enact laws suited to the changing times or both. Evidence of this can be seen in any governmental election. Senators and representatives are elected by a majority who share similar political beliefs. Theoretically, the members of Congress elected by the majority represent the beliefs of the people with regard to the law.

As a practical matter, citizens have more frequent personal contact with the judicial branch than with any other branch of government. Judges hear everything from traffic cases to domestic disputes to claims that Congress has exceeded the limits of its authority by passing laws that are in violation of the Constitution. Since the beginning of the current system of government, courts have continually faced the task of balancing competing interests. These interests might be called the **traditional balance** and the **modern balance,** both of which judges employ when determining legal claims.

The traditional balance arose from the very heart of our governmental system. The people no longer wanted strictly positivist rule from a single source but wanted to have input into the laws they had to live by. However, not everyone agrees as to what the law should be in a given situation. Under majority rule, laws are enacted based on what the majority thinks is necessary to protect the rights of the public as a whole. But some individuals may maintain that they have a valid right to disobey a particular law or that the law as written does not apply to their particular situation. In that case, the judiciary must examine the broadly written laws and apply them to individual circumstances. The challenge facing every judge is to enforce the laws to the extent necessary to protect the rights of the public while permitting the greatest amount of personal freedom possible for the individual. Simply stated, the traditional balance equals The Rights of the People versus The Rights of the Individual.

Traditional Balance

Goal of the judiciary to allow maximum personal freedom without detracting from the welfare of the general public.

Modern Balance

Goal of lawmaking authorities to balance the need for consistency and stability against the need for a flexible and adaptive government.

 APPLICATION 1.1

Vivian Brady lives in a house near a large metropolitan airport. She is the fourth generation of her family to live in the home and wants very much to stay there. However, the airport is badly in need of expansion to meet the increasing demands of the growing city. The city wants to purchase Vivian's house to enable the expansion. Vivian does not want to sell. The city takes Vivian to court to force the sale based on laws that allow the state to reclaim property for public use. The traditional balance of the court is to weigh the right of the public to support growth of the city against the right of Vivian to stay in her home and continue four generations of tradition.

Brad Schmidt is the owner of a condominium unit. He is hard of hearing, and to hear his stereo he must turn up the volume. Headphones do not work because they limit Brad's movement around his home. Brad's neighbors object to the noise and take Brad to court for creating a nuisance. The judge must determine which right is more important to protect: the legal rights of the neighbors to enjoy peace and quiet or the legal right of Brad to do as he pleases on his own property. The traditional balance would be the right of Brad, the individual, versus the right of the neighbors, the public.

Points for Discussion
1. How do you think each of the preceding situations should be resolved?
2. What are the reasons for your answer?

Initially, judges had only to balance individual freedoms against the good of the nation as a whole. But over the course of time, American society became increasingly complex. People from many different cultures, races, and religions came to this country in large numbers. The industrial revolution reached full force, followed by the age of advanced technology. The government withstood a civil war, two world wars, and numerous conflicts with other countries of different political structures. Many other governments and societies have crumbled under much less stress. The longevity of the American government is largely the result of the willingness of the judiciary and the other branches of government to develop and employ the modern balance in conjunction with the traditional balance.

The modern balance is a very delicate one. In essence, it is the need to enforce existing legal principles based on the Constitution versus the need to adopt legal principles more reflective of current society. To write laws that would envision all the potential situations and changes in society for hundreds of years to come is an impossible task. Thus, the judiciary, with the help of the executive branch and Congress, must be able to recognize those situations where modifications in the existing system were warranted. This balance has been accomplished without ever disturbing the fundamental structure set forth in the Constitution. Indeed, the modern balance is the ability to enforce law consistently while retaining enough flexibility to adapt to changes in societal standards.

 APPLICATION 1.2

For more than 100 years, the law of State X has been that a person could not sue and recover for the emotional injury suffered by merely witnessing injury to a family member. Nancy Du Four watched as a drunken motorist deliberately ran down and killed Nancy's child, who was walking on the sidewalk in front of her home. Nancy sued the driver for the death of her child and for the emotional trauma of witnessing this accident, which cost her thousands of dollars in psychiatric services to help her deal with the memory of the accident. The court must determine whether it should (to promote consistency in the law) follow the law established in the 1800s that witnesses cannot recover or allow for the first time—and thereby establish new precedent—a bystander to recover for the trauma incurred by witnessing injury to a family member. The court must evaluate what the majority of present-day society would deem appropriate.

The law in State A has been clear for 200 years that the natural father of an illegitimate child has no rights with regard to placement for adoption of the child at birth. Burt Donovan is a 22-year-old man who has fathered a child. The birth mother has indicated her intention to place the child for adoption. Burt wants very much to have custody of the child and has filed a petition to prevent the adoption. The court is faced with the issue of following the existing law, which would preclude Burt from stopping the adoption, or changing the law to allow Burt to seek legal rights of paternity. The court must make its decision based on societal changes with respect to the role of the father in American culture.

Points for Discussion
1. How should this issue be resolved?
2. What are the reasons for your answer?

Assignment 1.3

For each type of balance, describe a situation that reflects the basic elements. Explain how the facts of the situation reflect the elements of the balance.

THE MODERN LEGAL SYSTEM

The present U.S. government that enacts and administers federal law in the United States is far more sophisticated and much larger than the first government that took office under the Constitution in 1789. The first government was made up of a single Congress comprising senators and representatives from the thirteen colonies (the Senate with two senators elected by each state legislature and the House of Representatives with members proportionate to the population of each state), a president whose role was still not well defined beyond basic duties listed in Article II of the Constitution, and a single court to serve as the judiciary for an entire nation.

Today, that same Congress includes senators and representatives elected by the population of each of the fifty states. The presidency has developed into a complicated office that not only represents this country in foreign affairs but also oversees the administrative agencies of government and approves or rejects all acts of Congress. The federal judiciary has grown to include three separate levels: the Supreme Court, thirteen U.S. Circuit Courts of Appeals, and more than ninety U.S. District Courts. Interestingly, all three branches still follow the same basic purposes outlined in the Constitution. The manner in which each of these branches operates today is discussed in greater detail in subsequent chapters.

The Sources of Law

The primary source of all law in this country is the U.S. Constitution. Added to that are the state constitutions for each of the fifty states. From these flow the other sources of law. A common misconception is that legislatures—either state or federal (Congress)—are the source of all laws. In reality, legislatures are only one source of law. Law, also known as a **legal standard** or legal principle, comes in different forms and from different sources. It can apply to people in general, a particular group of citizens, or a specific person or entity such as a corporation.

Legal Standard
Legal principle, point of law. May appear in the form of statutory, judicial, or administrative law.

Each branch of government plays an active role in creating the law of the nation. In addition, each state has a system of government very similar to the federal structure, and law at the state level is created in much the same way as at the federal level. The distinction is that state governments are responsible for dealing with those issues not addressed by the U.S. Constitution. The following discussion examines the sources of law as well as their relationship to each other and the hierarchy of law.

Statutory law. As just noted, the most familiar law is **statutory** (legislative) **law.** Such laws are enacted by a state legislature or by Congress.[4] If a state legislature enacts a law, all persons and entities present in the state must obey it. If Congress enacts a federal law, all persons in the nation are required to follow it. (Chapter 3 addresses the manner in which legislative laws are created.) Once approved by the legislature, a statute will generally continue indefinitely as law until either the legislature repeals (deactivates) it or the high court of the state or federal government rules it unconstitutional. Federal laws must be consistent with the U.S. Constitution, whereas state laws must be in accordance with both the state and the federal constitutions. Similarly, no state constitution can conflict with the U.S. Constitution.[5] The provision of the U.S. Constitution declaring that federal laws take precedence over conflicting state laws is known as the supremacy clause.

Statutory Law
A statute. Law created by the legislature.

The language of statutes is fairly broad. Such language is necessary because the legislature wants to include as many potential situations as possible when it sets down a legal standard of what is right and what is wrong. However, if a court determines that a law is written so vaguely that citizens cannot determine exactly what is and is not acceptable conduct, the law will not be upheld as valid. The Constitution guarantees the right to fair notice of what is considered illegal conduct. Thus, courts have stricken statutes for being unconstitutional because of overly broad language.[6] The legislature has a particularly difficult but necessary task in establishing laws that apply to all intended persons and situations but that are also specific enough to warn an individual of what is required in a particular situation. Figure 1.1 is an example of statutory law.

FIGURE 1.1

Vermont Statute
(T.9 § 4452 on
p 1–23A)

VERMONT STATUTES ANNOTATED
TITLE NINE. COMMERCE AND TRADE
PART 7. LANDLORD AND TENANT
CHAPTER 137. RESIDENTIAL RENTAL AGREEMENTS

§ 4452. Exclusions
    Unless created to avoid the application of this chapter, this chapter does not apply to:
(1) occupancy at a public or private institution, operated for the purpose of providing medical, geriatric, educational, counseling, religious or similar service;
(2) occupancy under a contract of sale of a dwelling unit or the property of which it is a part, if the occupant is the purchaser or a person who succeeds to the interest of the purchaser;
(3) occupancy by a member of a fraternal, social or religious organization in the portion of a building operated for the benefit of the organization;
(4) transient occupancy in a hotel, motel, or lodging during the time the occupancy is subject to a tax levied under chapter 225 of Title 32;
(5) occupancy by the owner of a condominium unit or the holder of a proprietary lease in a co-operative;
(6) rental of a mobile home lot governed by chapter 153 of Title 10.

Judicial Law

Opinions that have the effect of law and that are issued by members of the judiciary in legal disputes.

Stare Decisis

"Let the decision stand." Method used by the judiciary when applying precedent to current situations.

Precedent

Existing legal standards that courts look to for guidance when making a determination of a legal issue.

Judicial law.   A second type of law is **judicial law.** The judiciary interprets law from other sources but also on occasion creates legal standards. Judges may consider a statute and determine whether it was meant to apply to the circumstances of a particular case. Persons in similar situations may then look to the judge's decision to guide their own conduct. Furthermore, the legislature cannot possibly enact laws to apply to every conceivable circumstance. Therefore, when no law exists, judges are responsible for making law or extending decisions of judges in previous similar cases.

The tradition of judges looking to previous rulings in similar past cases is an integral part of the American system of justice. The continuation of existing legal standards is the stability element in the modern balance. This process is commonly referred to as **stare decisis** (literally, "let the decision stand"). The doctrine of stare decisis basically holds that following the same legal principles in similar cases gives our legal system consistency. People can look to the past for guidance in what to expect from the courts in the future. The wisdom of past judges is utilized to achieve fair and consistent treatment of persons involved in similar cases.

When a court applies stare decisis and follows the same type of ruling as issued in a previous similar case, it is following a **precedent**—a previously established legal standard. Courts generally attempt to apply stare decisis with respect to precedents unless the prior case is too dissimilar in facts or issues or unless societal standards have changed since the precedent was established, making the former legal principle of the precedent impractical. In such a case, the court does not employ stare decisis but rules on the case based on new societal standards and establishes a new precedent for future reference. Chapter 2 presents more information on the way in which precedents are created.

Over the years, countless disputes have arisen that required a decision of law for resolution. The legal issues involved in such cases are not considered significant or common enough to require a legislative act, and the courts are left to issue rulings to resolve the disputes. In this way, the judiciary frequently serves as a valuable bridge between the people and the legislature when it interprets statutory legal standards in very specific circumstances or creates legal standards where none exist. For example, José Martinez intends to repair his roof. José is seriously injured when the ladder he is climbing collapses. José wants the ladder company to pay for his injuries, but there is no statute that requires ladder companies to pay for injuries caused by faulty ladders. The court, however, may look to prior cases that require manufacturers to be careful in the design and construction of products. Relying on precedent such as those prior cases, the court can apply stare decisis and require the ladder company to pay for José's injuries.

Judicial law has indirectly provided guidance to the state and federal legislatures as to the type of laws needed to be enacted. A perfect example of this involves the advent of the automobile. At first, many people were skeptical, and certainly most people never envisioned that motor-driven vehicles would become such an essential part of life. However, as more and more automobiles were placed on the roads, accidents happened, the need for roadways and traffic control developed, an overwhelming source of jobs was discovered, and mass transit became a reality. For the first time in history, the world became very mobile with unlimited travel that was convenient and fast. Rules were needed so that people could make, sell, and buy vehicles efficiently and travel in them in safety and comfort.

Until the issues of automobile travel and its accompanying disputes became so significant as to warrant legislation, the judiciary handled them. As the number of automobiles and related legal issues increased, the legislature stepped in and established broad legal standards for the manufacture, sale, and operation of motor vehicles.

Many concepts of today's statutory standards are consistent with the initial judicial legal standards. In *Texas v. Johnson*, the judiciary examines the law of previous decisions interpreting a statute and applies them to a current similar set of facts.

 CASE

TEXAS v. JOHNSON

491 U.S. 397, 109
S.Ct. 2533, 105
L.Ed.2d 342 (1989).

Justice **BRENNAN** delivered the opinion of the Court. After publicly burning an American flag as a means of political protest, Gregory Lee Johnson was convicted of desecrating a flag in violation of Texas law. This case presents the question whether his conviction is consistent with the First Amendment. We hold that it is not.

I

While the Republican National Convention was taking place in Dallas in 1984, respondent Johnson participated in a political demonstration dubbed the "Republican War Chest Tour." As explained in literature distributed by the demonstrators and in speeches made by them, the purpose of this event was to protest the policies of the Reagan administration and of certain Dallas-based corporations. . . . [Johnson] accept[ed] an American flag handed to him by a fellow protestor who had taken it from a flag pole outside one of the targeted buildings.

The demonstration ended in front of Dallas City Hall, where Johnson unfurled the American flag, doused it with kerosene, and set it on fire. While the flag burned, the protestors chanted, "America, the red, white, and blue, we spit on you." . . . No one was physically injured or threatened with injury, though several witnesses testified that they had been seriously offended by the flag burning. Of the approximately 100 demonstrators, Johnson alone was charged with a crime. The only criminal offense with which he was charged was the desecration of a venerated object in violation of Tex.Penal Code Ann. § 42.09(a)(3)(1989). After a trial, he was convicted, sentenced to one year in prison, and fined $2,000. The Court of Appeals for the Fifth District of Texas at Dallas affirmed Johnson's conviction, 706 S.W.2d 120 (1986), but the Texas Court of Criminal Appeals reversed, 755 S.W.2d 92 (1988), holding that the State could not, consistent with the First Amendment, punish Johnson for burning the flag in these circumstances. . . .

The Court of Criminal Appeals began by recognizing that Johnson's conduct was symbolic speech protected by the First Amendment: "Given the context of an organized demonstration, speeches, slogans, and the distribution of literature, anyone who observed appellant's act would have understood the message that appellant intended to convey. The act for which appellant was convicted was clearly 'speech' contemplated by the First Amendment." To justify Johnson's conviction for engaging in symbolic speech, the State asserted two interests: preserving the flag as a symbol of national unity and preventing breaches of the peace. The Court of Criminal Appeals held that neither interest supported his conviction. . . .

Because it reversed Johnson's conviction on the ground that 42.09 was unconstitutional as applied to him, the state court did not address Johnson's argument that the statute was, on its face, unconstitutionally vague and overbroad. We granted certiorari, 488 U.S. 907, 109 S.Ct. 257, 102 L.Ed.2d 245 (1988), and now affirm.

II

Johnson was convicted of flag desecration for burning the flag rather than for uttering insulting words. This fact somewhat complicates our consideration of his conviction under the First Amendment. We must first determine whether Johnson's burning of the flag constituted expressive conduct, permitting him to invoke the First Amendment in challenging his conviction. See, e.g., Spence v. Washington, 418 U.S. 405, 409–411, 94 S.Ct. 2727, 2729–31 (1974). If his conduct was expressive, we next decide whether the State's regulation is related to the suppression of free expression. See, e.g., United States v. O'Brien, 391 U.S. 367, 377, 88 S.Ct. 1673, 1679, 20 L.Ed.2d 672 (1968); Spence, supra, at 414, n. 8, 94 S.Ct., at 2732, n. 8. If the State's regulation is not related to expression, then the less stringent standard we announced in United States v. O'Brien for regulations of noncommunicative conduct controls. See O'Brien, supra, at 377, 88 S.Ct., at 1679. If it is, then we are outside of O'Brien's test, and we must ask whether this interest justifies Johnson's conviction under a more demanding standard. See Spence, supra, at 411, 94 S.Ct., at 2730. A third possibility is that the State's asserted interest is simply not implicated on these facts, and in that event the interest drops out of the picture. See 418 U.S., at 414, n. 8, 94 S.Ct., at 2732, n. 8.

Because the prosecutor's closing argument observed that Johnson had led the protestors in chants denouncing the flag while it burned, Johnson suggests that he may have been convicted for uttering critical words rather than for burning the flag. . . . He relies on Street v. New York, 394 U.S. 576, 578, 89 S.Ct. 1354, 1358, 22 L.Ed.2d 572 (1969), in which we reversed a conviction obtained under a New York statute that prohibited publicly defying or casting contempt on the flag "either by words or act" because we were persuaded that the defendant may have been convicted for his words alone. Unlike the law we faced in Street, however, the Texas flag-desecration statute does not on its face permit conviction for remarks critical of the flag, as Johnson himself admits. . . . Nor was the jury in this case told that it could convict Johnson of flag desecration if it found only that he had uttered words critical of the flag and its referents. . . .

Although Johnson has raised a facial challenge to Texas' flag-desecration statute, we choose to resolve this case on the basis of his claim that the statute as applied to him violates the First Amendment. Section 42.09 regulates only physical conduct with respect to the flag, not the written or spoken word, and although one violates the statute only if one "knows" that one's physical treatment of the flag "will seriously offend one or more persons likely to observe or discover his action," Tex.Penal Code Ann. § 42.09(b) (1989), this fact does not necessarily mean that the statute applies only to expressive conduct protected by the First Amendment. Cf. Smith v. Goguen, 415 U.S. 566, 588, 94 S.Ct. 1242, 1254, 39 L.Ed.2d 605 (1974) (WHITE, J., concurring in judgment) (statute prohibiting "contemptuous" treatment of flag encompasses only expressive conduct). A tired person might, for example, drag a flag through the mud, knowing that this conduct is likely to offend others, and yet have no thought of expressing any idea; neither the language nor the Texas courts' interpretations of the statute precludes the possibility that such a person would be prosecuted for flag desecration. Because the prosecution of a person who had not engaged in expressive conduct would pose a different case, and because this case may be disposed of on narrower grounds, we address only Johnson's claim at § 42.09 as applied to political expression like his violates the First Amendment.

The First Amendment literally forbids the abridgment only of "speech," but we have long recognized that its protection does not end at the spoken or written word. While we have rejected "the view that an apparently limitless variety of conduct can be labeled 'speech' whenever the person engaging in the conduct intends thereby to express an idea," United States v. O'Brien, supra, at 376, 88 S.Ct., at 1678, we have acknowledged that conduct may be "sufficiently imbued with elements of communication to fall within the scope of the First and Fourteenth Amendments," Spence, supra, at 409, 94 S.Ct., at 2730.

In deciding whether particular conduct possesses sufficient communicative elements to bring the First Amendment into play, we have asked whether "[a]n intent to convey a particularized message was present, and [whether] the likelihood was great that the message would be understood by those who viewed it." 418 U.S., at 410–411, 94 S.Ct., at 2730. . . .

Especially pertinent to this case are our decisions recognizing the communicative nature of conduct relating to flags. Attaching a peace sign to the flag, Spence, supra, at 409–410, 94 S.Ct., at 2729–30; refusing to salute the flag, Barnette, 319 U.S., at 632, 63 S.Ct., at 1182; and displaying a red flag, Stromberg v. California, 283 U.S. 359, *405 368–369, 51 S.Ct. 532, 535–36, 75 L.Ed. 1117 (1931), we have held, all may find shelter under the First Amendment. See also Smith v. Goguen, 415 U.S. 566, 588, 94 S.Ct. 1242, 1254, 39 L.Ed.2d 605 (1974) (WHITE, J., concurring in judgment) (treating flag "contemptuously" by wearing pants with small flag sewn into their seat is expressive conduct). That we have had little difficulty identifying an expressive element in conduct relating to flags should not be surprising. The very purpose of a national flag is to serve as a symbol of our country; it is, one might say, "the one visible manifestation of two hundred years of nationhood." Id., at 603, 94 S.Ct., at 1262 (REHNQUIST, J., dissenting). Thus, we have observed:

"[T]he flag salute is a form of utterance. Symbolism is a primitive but effective way of communicating ideas. The use of an emblem or flag to symbolize some system, idea, institution, or personality, is a short cut from mind to mind. Causes and nations, political parties, lodges and ecclesiastical groups seek to knit the loyalty of their followings to a flag or banner, a color or design." Barnette, supra, at 632, 63 S.Ct., at 1182.

Pregnant with expressive content, the flag as readily signifies this Nation as does the combination of letters found in "America."

We have not automatically concluded, however, that any action taken with respect to our flag is expressive. Instead, in characterizing such action for First Amendment purposes, we have considered the context in which it occurred. In Spence, for example, we emphasized that Spence's taping of a peace sign to his flag was "roughly simultaneous with and concededly triggered by the Cambodian incursion and the Kent State tragedy." 418 U.S., at 410, 94 S.Ct., at 2730. The State of Washington had conceded, in fact, that Spence's conduct was a form of communication, and we stated that "the State's concession is inevitable on this record." Id., at 409, 94 S.Ct., at 2730.

The State of Texas conceded for purposes of its oral argument in this case that Johnson's conduct was expressive conduct . . . and this concession seems to us as prudent as was Washington's in Spence. Johnson burned an American flag as part—indeed, as the culmination—of a political demonstration that coincided with the convening of the Republican Party and its renomination of Ronald Reagan for President. The expressive, overtly political nature of this conduct was both intentional and overwhelmingly apparent. At his trial, Johnson explained his reasons for burning the flag as follows: "The American Flag was burned as Ronald Reagan was being renominated as President. And a more powerful statement of symbolic speech, whether you agree with it or not, couldn't have been made at that time. It's quite a just position [juxtaposition]. We had new patriotism and no patriotism." 5 Record 656. In these circumstances, Johnson's burning of the flag was conduct "sufficiently imbued with elements of communication," Spence, 418 U.S., at 409, 94 S.Ct., at 2730, to implicate the First Amendment.

III

The government generally has a freer hand in restricting expressive conduct than it has in restricting the written or spoken word. See O'Brien, 391 U.S. at 376–377, 88 S.Ct., at 1678–1679; Clark v. Community for Creative Non-Violence, 468 U.S. 288, 293, 104 S.Ct. 3065, 3068, 82 L.Ed.2d 221 (1984); Dallas v. Stanglin, 490 U.S. 19, 25, 109 S.Ct. 1591, 1594, 104 L.Ed.2d 18 (1989). It may not, however, proscribe particular conduct because it has expressive elements. "[W]hat might be termed the more generalized guarantee of freedom of expression makes the communicative nature of conduct an inadequate basis for singling out that conduct for proscription. A law directed at the communicative nature of conduct must, like a law directed at speech itself, be justified by the substantial showing of need that the First Amendment requires." Community for Creative Non-Violence v. Watt, 227 U.S.App.D.C. 19, 55–56, 703 F.2d 586, 622–623 (1983). . . .

It is, in short, not simply the verbal or nonverbal nature of the expression, but the governmental interest at stake, that helps to determine whether a restriction on that expression is valid.

Thus, although we have recognized that where " 'speech' and 'nonspeech' elements are combined in the same course of conduct, a sufficiently important governmental interest in regulating the nonspeech element can justify incidental limitations on First Amendment freedoms," O'Brien, supra, at 376, 88 S.Ct., at 1678, we have limited the applicability of O'Brien's relatively lenient standard to those cases in which "the governmental interest is unrelated to the suppression of free expression." Id., at 377, 88 S.Ct., at 1679; see also Spence, 418 U.S., at 414, n. 8, 94 S.Ct., at 2732, n. 8. In stating, moreover, that O'Brien's test "in the last analysis is little, if any, different from the standard applied to time, place, or manner restrictions," Clark, supra, at 298, 104 S.Ct., at 3071, we have highlighted the requirement that the governmental interest in question be unconnected to expression in order to come under O'Brien's less demanding rule.

In order to decide whether O'Brien's test applies here, therefore, we must decide whether Texas has asserted an interest in support of Johnson's conviction that is unrelated to the suppression of expression. If we find that an interest asserted by the State is simply not implicated on the facts before us, we need not ask whether O'Brien's test applies. See Spence, supra, at 414, n. 8, 94 S.Ct., at 2732, n. 8. The State offers two separate interests to justify this conviction: preventing breaches of the peace and preserving the flag as a symbol of nationhood and national unity. We hold that the first interest is not implicated on this record and that the second is related to the suppression of expression.

A

Texas claims that its interest in preventing breaches of the peace justifies Johnson's conviction for flag desecration. However, no disturbance of the peace actually occurred or threatened to occur because of Johnson's burning of the flag. Although the State stresses the disruptive behavior of the protestors during their march toward City Hall, Brief for Petitioner 34–36, it admits that "no actual breach of the peace occurred at the time of the flagburning or in response to the flagburning." Id., at 34. The State's emphasis on the protestors' disorderly actions prior to arriving at City Hall is not only somewhat surprising given that no charges were brought on the basis of this conduct, but it also fails to show that a disturbance of the peace was a likely reaction to Johnson's conduct. The only evidence offered by the State at trial to show the reaction to Johnson's actions was the testimony of several persons who had been seriously offended by the flag burning. Id., at 6–7.

Relying on our decision in Boos v. Barry, 485 U.S. 312, 108 S.Ct. 1157, 99 L.Ed.2d 333 (1988), Johnson argues that this state interest is related to the suppression of free expression within the meaning of United States v. O'Brien, 391 U.S. 367, 88 S.Ct. 1673, 20 L.Ed.2d 672 (1968). He reasons that the violent reaction to flag burnings feared by Texas would be the result of the message conveyed by them, and that this fact connects the State's interest to the suppression of expression. Brief for Respondent 12, n. 11. This view has found some favor in the lower courts. See Monroe v. State Court of Fulton County, 739 F.2d 568, 574–575 (CA11 1984). Johnson's theory may overread Boos insofar as it suggests that a desire to prevent a violent audience reaction is "related to expression" in the same way that a desire to prevent an audience from being offended is "related to expression." Because we find that the State's interest in preventing breaches of the peace is not implicated on these facts, however, we need not venture further into this area.

The State's position, therefore, amounts to a claim that an audience that takes serious offense at particular expression is necessarily likely to disturb the peace and that the expression may be prohibited on this basis. Our precedents do not countenance such a presumption. On the contrary, they recognize that a principal "function of free speech under our system of government is to invite dispute. It may indeed best serve its high purpose when it induces a condition of unrest, creates dissatisfaction with conditions as they are, or even stirs people to anger." Terminiello v. Chicago, 337 U.S. 1, 4, 69 S.Ct. 894, 896, 93 L.Ed. 1131 (1949). . . . It would be odd indeed to conclude both that "if it is the speaker's opinion that gives offense, that consequence is a reason for according it constitutional protection," FCC v. Pacifica Foundation, 438 U.S. 726, 745, 98 S.Ct.

3026, 3038, 57 L.Ed.2d 1073 (1978) . . . and that the Government may ban the expression of certain disagreeable ideas on the unsupported presumption that their very disagreeableness will provoke violence. . . .

Thus, we have not permitted the Government to assume that every expression of a provocative idea will incite a riot, but have instead required careful consideration of the actual circumstances surrounding such expression, asking whether the expression "is directed to inciting or producing imminent lawless action and is likely to incite or produce such action." Brandenburg v. Ohio, 395 U.S. 444, 447, 89 S.Ct. 1827, 1829, 23 L.Ed.2d 430 (1969) (reviewing circumstances surrounding rally and speeches by Ku Klux Klan). To accept Texas' arguments that it need only demonstrate "the potential for a breach of the peace," Brief for Petitioner 37, and that every flag burning necessarily possesses that potential, would be to eviscerate our holding in Brandenburg. This we decline to do.

Nor does Johnson's expressive conduct fall within that small class of "fighting words" that are "likely to provoke the average person to retaliation, and thereby cause a breach of the peace." Chaplinsky v. New Hampshire, 315 U.S. 568, 574, 62 S.Ct. 766, 770, 86 L.Ed. 1031 (1942). No reasonable onlooker would have regarded Johnson's generalized expression of dissatisfaction with the policies of the Federal Government as a direct personal insult or an invitation to exchange fisticuffs. See id., at 572–573, 62 S.Ct., at 769–770; Cantwell v. Connecticut, 310 U.S. 296, 309, 60 S.Ct. 900, 905–06, 84 L.Ed. 1213 (1940); FCC v. Pacifica Foundation, supra, at 745, 98 S.Ct., at 3038.

We thus conclude that the State's interest in maintaining order is not implicated on these facts. The State need not worry that our holding will disable it from preserving the peace. We do not suggest that the First Amendment forbids a State to prevent "imminent lawless action." Brandenburg, supra, at 447, 89 S.Ct., at 1829. And, in fact, Texas already has a statute specifically prohibiting breaches of the peace, Tex.Penal Code Ann. § 42.01 (1989), which tends to confirm that Texas need not punish this flag desecration in order to keep the peace. See Boos v. Barry, 485 U.S., at 327–329.

B

The State also asserts an interest in preserving the flag as a symbol of nationhood and national unity. In Spence, we acknowledged that the government's interest in preserving the flag's special symbolic value "is directly related to expression in the context of activity" such as affixing a peace symbol to a flag. 418 U.S., at 414, n. 8, 94 S.Ct., at 2732, n. 8. We are equally persuaded that this interest is related to expression in the case of Johnson's burning of the flag. The State, apparently, is concerned that such conduct will lead people to believe either that the flag does not stand for nationhood and national unity, but instead reflects other, less positive concepts, or that the concepts reflected in the flag do not in fact exist, that is, that we do not enjoy unity as a Nation. These concerns blossom only when a person's treatment of the flag communicates some message, and thus are related "to the suppression of free expression" within the meaning of O'Brien. We are thus outside of O'Brien's test altogether. . . .

Whether Johnson's treatment of the flag violated Texas law thus depended on the likely communicative impact of his expressive conduct. Our decision in Boos v. Barry, supra, tells us that this restriction on Johnson's expression is content based. In Boos, we considered the constitutionality of a law prohibiting "the display of any sign within 500 feet of a foreign embassy if that sign tends to bring that foreign government into 'public odium' or 'public disrepute.' " Id., at 315, 108 S.Ct., at 1160. Rejecting the argument that the law was content neutral because it was justified by "our international law obligation to shield diplomats from speech that offends their dignity," id., at 320, 108 S.Ct., at 1163, we held that "[t]he emotive impact of speech on its audience is not a 'secondary effect' " unrelated to the content of the expression itself. Id., at 321, 108 S.Ct., at 1164. . . .

Texas suggests that Johnson's conviction did not depend on the onlookers' reaction to the flag burning because § 42.09 is violated only when a person physically mistreats the flag in a way that he "knows will seriously offend one or more persons likely to observe or discover his action." Tex.Penal Code Ann. § 42.09(b) (1969) (emphasis added). "The 'serious offense' language of the statute," Texas argues, "refers to an individual's

intent and to the manner in which the conduct is effectuated, not to the reaction of the crowd." Brief for Petitioner 44. If the statute were aimed only at the actor's intent and not at the communicative impact of his actions, however, there would be little reason for the law to be triggered only when an audience is "likely" to be present. At Johnson's trial, indeed, the State itself seems not to have seen the distinction between knowledge and actual communicative impact that it now stresses; it proved the element of knowledge by offering the testimony of persons who had in fact been seriously offended by Johnson's conduct. Id., at 6–7. In any event, we find the distinction between Texas' statute and one dependent on actual audience reaction too precious to be of constitutional significance. Both kinds of statutes clearly are aimed at protecting onlookers from being offended by the ideas expressed by the prohibited activity.

According to the principles announced in Boos, Johnson's political expression was restricted because of the content of the message he conveyed. We must therefore subject the State's asserted interest in preserving the special symbolic character of the flag to "the most exacting scrutiny." Boos v. Barry, 485 U.S., at 321, 108 S.Ct., at 1164. . . .

Texas argues that its interest in preserving the flag as a symbol of nationhood and national unity survives this close analysis. Quoting extensively from the writings of this Court chronicling the flag's historic and symbolic role in our society, the State emphasizes the " 'special place' " reserved for the flag in our Nation. Brief for Petitioner 22, quoting Smith v. Goguen, 415 U.S., at 601, 94 S.Ct., at 1261 (REHNQUIST, J., dissenting). The State's argument is not that it has an interest simply in maintaining the flag as a symbol of something, no matter what it symbolizes; indeed, if that were the State's position, it would be difficult to see how that interest is endangered by highly symbolic conduct such as Johnson's. Rather, the State's claim is that it has an interest in preserving the flag as a symbol of nationhood and national unity, a symbol with a determinate range of meanings. Brief for Petitioner 20–24. According to Texas, if one physically treats the flag in a way that would tend to cast doubt on either the idea that nationhood and national unity are the flag's referents or that national unity actually exists, the message conveyed thereby is a harmful one and therefore may be prohibited.

Texas claims that "Texas is not endorsing, protecting, avowing or prohibiting any particular philosophy." Brief for Petitioner 29. If Texas means to suggest that its asserted interest does not prefer Democrats over Socialists, or Republicans over Democrats, for example, then it is beside the point, for Johnson does not rely on such an argument. He argues instead that the State's desire to maintain the flag as a symbol of nationhood and national unity assumes that there is only one proper view of the flag. Thus, if Texas means to argue that its interest does not prefer any viewpoint over another, it is mistaken; surely one's attitude toward the flag and its referents is a viewpoint.

If there is a bedrock principle underlying the First Amendment, it is that the government may not prohibit the expression of an idea simply because society finds the idea itself offensive or disagreeable. See, e.g., Hustler Magazine v. Falwell, 485 U.S., at 55–56. . . .

We have not recognized an exception to this principle even where our flag has been involved. In Street v. New York, 394 U.S. 576, 89 S.Ct. 1354, 22 L.Ed.2d 572 (1969), we held that a State may not criminally punish a person for uttering words critical of the flag. Rejecting the argument that the conviction could be sustained on the ground that Street had "failed to show the respect for our national symbol which may properly be demanded of every citizen," we concluded that "the constitutionally guaranteed 'freedom to be intellectually . . . diverse or even contrary,' and the 'right to differ as to things that touch the heart of the existing order,' encompass the freedom to express publicly one's opinions about our flag, including those opinions which are defiant or contemptuous." Id., at 593, 89 S.Ct., at 1366, quoting Barnette, 319 U.S., at 642, 63 S.Ct., at 1187. Nor may the government, we have held, compel conduct that would evince respect for the flag. "To sustain the compulsory flag salute we are required to say that a Bill of Rights which guards the individual's right to speak his own mind, left it open to public authorities to compel him to utter what is not in his mind." Id., at 634, 63 S.Ct., at 1183. . . .

In short, nothing in our precedents suggests that a State may foster its own view of the flag by prohibiting expressive conduct relating to it. To bring its argument outside our precedents, Texas attempts to convince us that even if its interest in preserving the flag's symbolic role does not allow it to prohibit words or some expressive conduct critical of the flag, it does permit it to forbid the outright destruction of the flag. The State's argument cannot depend here on the distinction between written or spoken words and nonverbal conduct. That distinction, we have shown, is of no moment where the nonverbal conduct is expressive, as it is here, and where the regulation of that conduct is related to expression, as it is here. See supra, at 2538–2539. In addition, both Barnette and Spence involved expressive conduct, not only verbal communication, and both found that conduct protected.

L.Ed. 696 (1907), addressing the validity of a state law prohibiting certain commercial uses of the flag, is not to the contrary. That case was decided "nearly 20 years before the Court concluded that the First Amendment applies to the States by virtue of the Fourteenth Amendment." Spence v. Washington, 418 U.S. 405, 413, n. 7, 94 S.Ct. 2727, 2731, n. 7, 41 L.Ed.2d 842 (1974). . . .

We never before have held that the Government may ensure that a symbol be used to express only one view of that symbol or its referents. Indeed, in Schacht v. United States, we invalidated a federal statute permitting an actor portraying a member of one of our armed forces to " 'wear the uniform of that armed force if the portrayal does not tend to discredit that armed force.' " 398 U.S., at 60, 90 S.Ct., at 1557, quoting 10 U.S.C. § 772(f). This proviso, we held, "which leaves Americans free to praise the war in Vietnam but can send persons like Schacht to prison for opposing it, cannot survive in a country which has the First Amendment." Id., at 63, 90 S.Ct., at 1559.

We perceive no basis on which to hold that the principle underlying our decision in Schacht does not apply to this case. To conclude that the government may permit designated symbols to be used to communicate only a limited set of messages would be to enter territory having no discernible or defensible boundaries. Could the government, on this theory, prohibit the burning of state flags? Of copies of the Presidential seal? Of the Constitution? In evaluating these choices under the First Amendment, how would we decide which symbols were sufficiently special to warrant this unique status? To do so, we would be forced to consult our own political preferences, and impose them on the citizenry, in the very way that the First Amendment forbids us to do. See Carey v. Brown, 447 U.S., at 466–467, 100 S.Ct., at 2293–2294.

There is, moreover, no indication—either in the text of the Constitution or in our cases interpreting it—that a separate juridical category exists for the American flag alone. Indeed, we would not be surprised to learn that the persons who framed our Constitution and wrote the Amendment that we now construe were not known for their reverence for the Union Jack. The First Amendment does not guarantee that other concepts virtually sacred to our Nation as a whole—such as the principle that discrimination on the basis of race is odious and destructive—will go unquestioned in the marketplace of ideas. See Brandenburg v. Ohio, 395 U.S. 444, 89 S.Ct. 1827, 23 L.Ed.2d 430 (1969). We decline, therefore, to create for the flag an exception to the joust of principles protected by the First Amendment.

It is not the State's ends, but its means, to which we object. It cannot be gainsaid that there is a special place reserved for the flag in this Nation, and thus we do not doubt that the government has a legitimate interest in making efforts to "preserv[e] the national flag as an unalloyed symbol of our country." Spence, 418 U.S., at 412, 94 S.Ct., at 2731. We reject the suggestion, urged at oral argument by counsel for Johnson, that the government lacks "any state interest whatsoever" in regulating the manner in which the flag may be displayed. Tr. of Oral Arg. 38. Congress has, for example, enacted precatory regulations describing the proper treatment of the flag, see 36 U.S.C. § § 173–177, and we cast no doubt on the legitimacy of its interest in making such recommendations. To say that the government has an interest in encouraging proper treatment of the flag, however, is not to say that it may criminally punish a person for burning a flag as a means of political protest. "National unity as an end which officials may foster by persuasion and example is not in question. The problem is whether under our Constitution compulsion as here employed is a permissible means for its achievement." Barnette, 319 U.S., at 640, 63 S.Ct., at 1186.

We are fortified in today's conclusion by our conviction that forbidding criminal punishment for conduct such as Johnson's will not endanger the special role played by our flag or the feelings it inspires. To paraphrase Justice Holmes, we submit that nobody can suppose that this one gesture of an unknown man will change our Nation's attitude towards its flag. See Abrams v. United States, 250 U.S. 616, 628, 40 S.Ct. 17, 21, 63 L.Ed. 1173 (1919) (HOLMES, J., dissenting). Indeed Texas' argument that the burning of an American flag " 'is an act having a high likelihood to cause a breach of the peace,' " Brief for Petitioner 31, quoting Sutherland v. DeWulf, 323 F.Supp. 740, 745 (SD Ill.1971) (citation omitted), and its statute's implicit assumption that physical mistreatment of the flag will lead to "serious offense," tend to confirm that the flag's special role is not in danger; if it were, no one would riot or take offense because a flag had been burned.

We are tempted to say, in fact, that the flag's deservedly cherished place in our community will be strengthened, not weakened, by our holding today. Our decision is a reaffirmation of the principles of freedom and inclusiveness that the flag best reflects, and of the conviction that our toleration of criticism such as Johnson's is a sign and source of our strength. Indeed, one of the proudest images of our flag, the one immortalized in our own national anthem, is of the bombardment it survived at Fort McHenry. It is the Nation's resilience, not its rigidity, that Texas sees reflected in the flag—and it is that resilience that we reassert today.

The way to preserve the flag's special role is not to punish those who feel differently about these matters. It is to persuade them that they are wrong. "To courageous, self-reliant men, with confidence in the power of free and fearless reasoning applied through the processes of popular government, no danger flowing from speech can be deemed clear and present, unless the incidence of the evil apprehended is so imminent that it may befall before there is opportunity for full discussion. If there be time to expose through discussion the falsehood and fallacies, to avert the evil by the processes of education, the remedy to be applied is more speech, not enforced silence." Whitney v. California, 274 U.S. 357, 377, 47 S.Ct. 641, 649, 71 L.Ed. 1095 (1927) (BRANDEIS, J., concurring). And, precisely because it is our flag that is involved, one's response to the flag burner may exploit the uniquely persuasive power of the flag itself. We can imagine no more appropriate response to burning a flag than waving one's own, no better way to counter a flag burner's message than by saluting the flag that burns, no surer means of preserving the dignity even of the flag that burned than by—as one witness here did—according its remains a respectful burial. We do not consecrate the flag by punishing its

desecration, for in doing so we dilute the freedom that this cherished emblem represents.

V

Johnson was convicted for engaging in expressive conduct. The State's interest in preventing breaches of the peace does not support his conviction because Johnson's conduct did not threaten to disturb the peace. Nor does the State's interest in preserving the flag as a symbol of nationhood and national unity justify his criminal conviction for engaging in political expression. The judgment of the Texas Court of Criminal Appeals is therefore Affirmed.

Case Question

Would the result change if the defendant had simply used the flag on a routine basis to light his barbeque because of the flag's petroleum-based cloth?

Administrative law. Although the legislature attempts to arrive at legal principles that apply to all persons, the judiciary deals with individual circumstances. Over the years, however, it became increasingly clear that an additional source of law that could tailor rules for specific groups of citizens or subjects was necessary. In many sectors of our society and economy, large numbers of people or areas of commerce needed specific guidelines. Such an area is the air transportation industry, which is overseen by the Federal Aviation Administration (FAA). It is impractical for Congress or even state legislatures to attempt to deal with all of the questions raised by this massive industry. At the same time, it would be unduly burdensome and increase the likelihood of inconsistent decisions from different judges in different areas if the judiciary had to handle all cases that arose. The response to dilemmas of this sort has been the advent of **administrative law.**

The Constitution gives the duty for enforcement of law to the executive branch. Therefore, the executive branch has the primary responsibility to determine when a law has been violated or whether the law is even applicable to a particular situation. Administrative agencies are overseen by the executive branch with direct influence by the Congress and the judiciary. At the federal level, the president is assisted by administrative agencies in carrying out the law enacted by Congress.

Administrative law is primarily made up of two elements: administrative regulations (sometimes called rules) and administrative decisions. Administrative agencies issue regulations or rules that more specifically define the broadly written statutes. Administrative decisions issued for very specific cases have the same effect of law as judicial or legislative law. These cases usually involve persons or entities that challenge the authority of the agency to issue or enforce a particular regulation.

Administrative Law

Regulations and decisions that explain and detail statutes. Such regulations and decisions are issued by administrative agencies.

Administrative law is an extension of statutory law established by the Congress. Failure to obey administrative law can result in penalties or even criminal prosecution.

Administrative law is quite complex and is discussed further in Chapter 4.

The Hierarchy of Law

Although the sources of American law are the legislature, the judiciary, and the executive branch, they are all interrelated. If the sources of law were completely independent, the potential for deadlock would exist if the sources conflicted with regard to the law.

American law is governed by a distinct hierarchy. First in the hierarchy is the U.S. Constitution. Although technically the Constitution and its amendments are statutory law, they are considered superior to all other law, since they established the governmental structure and the process for creating all other law. One concept that has remained consistent throughout the legal history of this country is that all branches of state and federal government and all persons in the United States must function within the parameters of the U.S. Constitution. If at any time the will of the people is in conflict with the Constitution, the Constitution can be amended through the proper process, which is designed to guarantee that the amendment does in fact reflect the will of the majority. Chapter 3 discusses further the process for amendment of the Constitution.

Next in the hierarchy of laws are the legislative (statutory) acts of Congress. Statutes have greater weight than judicial or administrative law, since statutes are enacted by Congress and state legislatures, which are composed of people elected by the people. Thus, statutes are most likely to represent the laws intended for and desired by the majority.

The judiciary has the authority to interpret legislation and to fill in gray areas where the law is unclear or nonexistent. The judiciary is also obligated to ensure that the law is consistent with the Constitution. We might think of the judiciary as the protectors of the Constitution. In any case when the judiciary determines that the law does not meet the requirements of the Constitution, it has the authority to declare the law invalid and thereby supersede the ordinarily superior statutory law. Constitutionality is the only basis for judicial rather than statutory law controlling an issue. A prime example of this would be a law that is vague or overbroad. Such a law is unconstitutional because it would not provide fair and clear notice to persons of what is illegal conduct. Such notice is a requirement of the Constitution and its amendments. Thus, the court would have the authority to strike down the statute and dismiss charges against anyone who is alleged to have violated the statute.

Last in the hierarchy is administrative law. Administrative agencies assist Congress by issuing regulations and decisions that clarify and aid in the enforcement of statutes. However, Congress has the right to eliminate an agency or regulations that are inconsistent with legislative objectives. The judiciary also has the authority to overrule actions of an agency when such actions are unconstitutional. The authority of the judiciary to overrule and invalidate law is not exercised lightly or frequently. The courts generally defer to the Congress unless there is a clear constitutional violation.

Examine the following situations and determine which source of law would most appropriately deal with each situation:

(a) The growing computer industry needs laws that will govern private transmission of information from one computer location to another.
(b) A person charged with bigamy claims that the first marriage was annulled and therefore was not valid according to statute at the time of the second marriage.
(c) A group of citizens wants everyone who sells, serves, or gives away alcohol to be responsible for the costs of injuries caused by intoxicated persons.
(d) Laws are needed that determine the liability of the space program for passengers who are killed or injured on space shuttles.

CHAPTER SUMMARY

This chapter has introduced you to the origins and development of the American legal system. The system began as a singular governmental structure under the Articles of Confederation, which were found to be ineffective and were replaced by the Constitution and the Bill of Rights. Under the Constitution, the government comprises three separate but interrelated branches designed to provide effective government of, by, and for the people: the judiciary, the executive branch, and the legislature (Congress). The Bill of Rights and subsequent constitutional amendments serve as the framework for the protection of individual rights and establish boundaries between areas subject to state and federal law.

The method of law followed in the United States is actually a combination of three theories. The naturalist theory believes that people know the difference between right and wrong and should be held accountable for any wrong conduct that results in injuries to another party. The positivist theory is represented by the principle that the supreme authority of a jurisdiction is the final decision in legal matters. Appeals may be made to the highest authority, but beyond this, decisions are not subject to challenge or question. The sociological theory tempers American law by providing for changes in the

law when they are in the best interest of society as a whole.

The three branches of government are the three sources of law: the legislature (statutes), the executive branch (administrative actions from administrative agencies created by Congress but overseen by the executive branch on a day-to-day basis), and the judiciary (judicial opinions). The legislative body issues broadly written laws that must be adhered to by all persons. Administrative agencies give definition to and enforce statutory law. Judicial law interprets statutory law for specific individual circumstances.

In all law—but most apparent in judicial law—are the balances that enable the American system to function so efficiently. Under the traditional balance, government strives to maintain maximum personal freedom while protecting the interests of society as a whole. The modern balance aims toward following existing legal standards to provide stability to the government and give clear guidance to citizens while responding with flexibility to changes in societal standards.

One constant is that the Constitution is the supreme law of the land. Ordinarily, statutes have priority over judicial opinions and administrative law. However, if the judiciary finds a statute or administrative law to be unconstitutional, it has the right to invalidate the statute or administrative law and to rule on the case based on judicial precedent or other applicable statutory or administrative law. No law, under any circumstance, can be enforced if it is in conflict with the Constitution. If society demands such a law be held valid, the Constitution must be amended.

The following chapters give much attention to the various branches of government and should be fully understood before proceeding to subsequent chapters that refer to the sources commonly responsible for establishing legal standards in particular subjects of law. Further, it is helpful in a more practical sense to understand where law originates as well as the law's place in the hierarchy. Such understanding enables one in a real-life situation to assess much more clearly one's position with regard to the law.

REVIEW QUESTIONS

1. What was the structure of the U.S. government under the Articles of Confederation?
2. What are the political theories that influenced the structure of the U.S. government?
3. How does the U.S. Constitution guarantee that power will not fall into the hands of one person?
4. Explain how each political theory appears in present-day government.
5. The flexibility and stability elements of the modern balance express what goals of the judiciary?
6. The individual elements and the elements of the people as a whole of the traditional balance represent what goals of the judiciary?

7. Explain the difference between stare decisis and precedent.
8. Give two characteristics of each type of legal standard: statute; case; regulation. (An example of a characteristic would be the source of the legal standard.)
9. What is the only situation in which judicial decision is more powerful than a statute?
10. Why does the executive branch have the power to create administrative law through administrative agencies?

CHAPTER TERMS

Administrative Law	Naturalist Theory	Stare Decisis
Judicial Law	Positivist Theory	Statutory Law
Legal Standard	Precedent	Traditional Balance
Modern Balance	Sociological Theory	

NOTES

1. William Statsky, *Legal Thesaurus/Dictionary* (St. Paul: West, 1982).
2. Id.
3. Statsky, *Legal Thesaurus/Dictionary.*
4. Statsky, *Legal Thesaurus/Dictionary.*
5. *Gonzalez v. Automatic Emp. Credit Union,* 419 U.S. 90, 95 S.Ct. 289, 42 L.Ed.2d 249 (1974).
6. *Schware v. Board of Bar Examiners,* 353 U.S. 232, 77 S.Ct. 752, 1 L.Ed.2d 796 (1957).

CHAPTER 2

The Courts

CHAPTER OBJECTIVES

After reading this chapter, you should be able to

- *Discuss the characteristics unique to judicial law.*

- *Explain the two-fold purpose of judicial law.*

- *Discuss the process of legal analysis.*

- *Apply the process of case analysis to a judicial opinion.*

- *Describe the structure of the federal court system.*

- *Describe the role of each primary level of federal courts.*

- *Describe the present-day function of the U.S. Supreme Court.*

- *Describe the two general types of state court structures.*

- *Discuss the types of cases generally considered by the U.S. Supreme Court.*

As explained in Chapter 1, American law comes from one of three sources: legislative, judicial, or executive/administrative. This chapter focuses on the law established by the judicial branch of government, giving consideration to the manner in which the federal and state court systems are structured as well as how they function with each other. In addition, the chapter addresses the method of analyzing past judicial law for present and future application.

THE PURPOSE AND EFFECT OF JUDICIAL LAW

Characteristics of Judicial Law

All elements of the legal system are equally necessary. The executive branch monitors the conduct of Congress and, through executive supervision of administrative agencies, establishes regulations for specific industries and specialized groups. Congress, through legislation, sets down statutory law that guides the conduct of all the people. The judiciary reviews the acts of Congress and the executive branch but, more importantly, serves as a forum for the people. Because every situation is different in some respect, judges are expected to have the knowledge and objectivity to examine individual situations and determine the legal standards that should apply and how. Everyone can have access to the governmental system through the judicial branch, which is designed to provide fairness and enforcement of rights of all persons.

The only avenue by which people can seek individual resolution of personal legal issues is the judicial branch. The court is the only forum in which a person can present information supporting a legal position and obtain court approval and enforced legal action. Legislatures enact laws to govern all people in a variety of circumstances. The executive branch, through administrative law, further defines and enforces legislative law. But the judiciary considers the situations of individuals on a case-by-case basis and attempts to apply the most appropriate law and reach the result that is most fair under the Constitution. In this way, the courts are the most responsive branch of government to the individual. The judicial branch is the only governmental authority with the power to create law for an individual situation when none exists. The legislative and executive branches are more indirect reflections of the needs of society as a whole. However, these branches are also necessary to establish legal standards that the people can, in most cases, follow without the need for judicial intervention.

Clarification of the Law

By necessity, statutes are written in general terms that apply to everyone. As a result, it is unclear many times whether a statute encompasses a very specific situation. This is where the assistance of the judiciary becomes essential. Judges are expected to have sufficient knowledge and training to evaluate statutes and determine whether they apply to a specific situation. In the event a judge finds a statute inapplicable, another statute or legal principle from a prior case can be applied. In doing so, the judge is performing one of the primary functions of the judiciary: to clarify the law as it applies to specific circumstances.

These interpretations of statutory or administrative law occur anytime a statute or administrative regulation or decision is an issue in a case. If, for example, someone challenges a speeding ticket, the government must prove that the statute of maximum miles per hour was violated. The judge must review the statute and the facts of the case. The judge must then determine whether under the facts the law applies and whether the law was violated. This is one example of a judicial interpretation of a statute.

 APPLICATION 2.1

A federal statute exists that permits law enforcement to seize property used in the manufacture of controlled substances. Joel Martinelli is a pharmacist who has operated a reputable pharmacy for the past fifteen years. However, he and two employees were arrested recently for the illegal manufacture and sale of steroids. Law enforcement agents seized all pharmaceutical equipment and inventory in Martinelli's pharmacy. Martinelli has challenged this action in court on the premise that the equipment and inventory in his store were not used to manufacture the drugs. Rather, he contends that his pharmacy was only the location where the steroids were dispensed and that he neither was involved in nor had knowledge of the activity. Further, if the property is allowed to be seized, he will be forced out of his legitimate business before he has had a trial on the criminal charges. Martinelli claims the government control over the pharmacy after the raid violates his constitutional right to due process (fair treatment) before seizure of property. The issue facing the judge is whether the ordinary tools of Martinelli's trade are also related to illegal activity and whether the law enforcement agents should be allowed to seize the property, thus penalizing Martinelli before he is convicted.

Points for Discussion
1. What factors do you think the judge should consider when deciding whether to apply the statute to this situation?
2. What could be a reasonable alternative to seizing the property before trial?

As the preceding application illustrates, most cases have much more complicated facts than the broad language of a statute addresses. There seem always to be specific questions that are not clearly answered by the statute and to which the judge must at this point establish answers. This is done by looking to the purpose of the statute and the intent of the legislature in passing the statute. Judges also look at how past similar cases were treated in the courts. Although no two cases are exactly alike, a judge may apply the same ruling in cases that have striking similarities. Such similarities may be in the facts of the case, in the legal issues involved, or in both. Finally, judges are required to draw on their knowledge and experience to establish what is considered to be a logical and fair interpretation of the statute.

In cases when no applicable statute exists, a judge is required to establish the law. This may be done by looking to case law (the precedents of past similar cases) and applying the principle of stare decisis. In the situation when no prior judicial precedent exists whatsoever, a judge must create one. This is known as common law, a term that has carried over from medieval times when judges created law for the common man. Technically, common law is defined as a newly established legal principle, whereas case law is the application of stare decisis (carryforward of a prior legal principle). In actual practice, the terms *common law* and *case law* have come to be used interchangeably. The basic concept is that the terms represent judicially created law. In some instances, such law may be a specific interpretation and definition of a statute, whereas in other cases, it refers to the creation or continuation of a legal principle where no statutory language applied. Still another case might call for the creation of a legal standard when no applicable law exists. (Recall the example of the automobile in Chapter 1.)

Case law significantly benefits the general public. Individuals can look at existing case law in relation to their own situations. By comparing established precedents, persons involved in lawsuits can often predict with some certainty the likely outcome of their case. In so doing, through a process known as legal analysis, they can make intelligent decisions about whether to pursue, settle, or dismiss a dispute. It is also a very useful method to determine the best course of action for avoiding a dispute. (Legal analysis is discussed in more detail later in the chapter.)

Assignment 2.1

Examine the following situations. Evaluate and determine which situation represents a court's application of statute, creation of common law, or application of stare decisis. Give reasons for your answers.

1. A judge decides for the first time ever that a landlord does not have the right to enter an apartment without prior notice to the tenant.
2. A judge decides that a doctor who leaves a sponge in a patient's body after an operation has violated a legal right just as the courts have found a violation by persons who shoot other persons.
3. After finding no statutes that apply, a judge decides that owners of robots (similar to the owners of vicious dogs) should be held responsible for the actions of the robot that injure innocent persons.
4. A judge determines that the defendant in a murder case was insane at the time of the murder and was not responsible for the crime according to the statutory definition of crime.
5. A judge decides that golf clubs swung by angry golfers are just as lethal as spears and that golfers can be charged with manslaughter if a club is hurled and accidentally kills a bystander.

6. The owner of a car who was not involved in drug dealing allowed a friend to use the car. The owner knew the friend frequented social clubs where illegal drugs were used and sold. The friend allowed another person to drive the car, and that person used the car during an illegal drug transaction. The court held that the owner knew of the use of the car by persons involved with drugs and that under the statute, the car was therefore subject to seizure. This application of the statute 21 U.S.C. Sec. 881 was upheld even though the owner of the car was in no way involved in illegal activity.

7. A person is invited onto one's property and is subsequently injured when she steps on a rotten board and falls through the porch. The court found that the landowner must warn the visitor of all dangers. However, if someone enters the property without invitation, the landowner is required only to warn of dangers that might be considered a trap. This was a holding in a prior similar case and was reiterated by the court in this case. The effect is to reestablish the legal principle and expand it to another situation that is similar but not identical.

8. A man dug a hole behind his store for the construction of a cellar. During the night, the store caught fire. A neighbor coming to help fell into the hole and was injured. The court held that the neighbor was not an invited guest and thus the landowner had no duty to warn the neighbor of the dangerous hole. This ruling was issued even though there was not a legal standard or precedent on which to base the ruling.

Protection of the Law

A second function of the judiciary is to protect and uphold law that is consistent with the Constitution. To provide such protection, the judiciary has the duty to impose legal liability when legal principles are violated. For example, when one person crashes into another person's car, the court would require the driver at fault to accept responsibility and pay for the damage to the innocent driver's vehicle and any other related damages. In a criminal situation, the police may arrest individuals who allegedly commit crimes, but it is up to the judge to determine whether allegations of such violations are true and to see that violators are penalized or make restitution for their actions or both. Essentially, when one person injures the rights, person, or property of another, the court must determine whether the law has been violated and what an appropriate compensation or penalty for the injury would be.

APPLICATION 2.2

A tourist takes a chartered trip. The tourist's luggage is stolen by a baggage handler employed by the tour company. The tourist sues the charter company. The company states that it gave all customers a written disclaimer of liability. The court must answer the following questions:

1. Is the charter company responsible for the acts of its employee?
2. Does the charter company have a legal right to deny liability to its customers?
3. Did the charter company act or fail to act in a way that caused or contributed to the theft of the tourist's property?
4. Did any action or nonaction by the charter company constitute a violation of an existing legal principle?
5. Did any action or nonaction by the tourist contribute to the loss of her property?
6. If the charter company is legally at fault, what should be done to remedy the situation?

To answer these questions the court must first look to cases and statutes that address the situation. The court must then determine the result that would be indicated when the legal principles of those cases and statutes are applied to the present situation. The court would then decide on a verdict.

THE STRUCTURE OF THE JUDICIAL SYSTEM

Federal Court

A court that is part of the U.S. court system that has limited authority and hears only cases involving the U.S. government, federal laws, or appropriate cases of diversity of citizenship.

State Court

A court that is a part of the judicial branch in the state in which it is located. Typically, state courts hear cases involving state law.

Trial Court

A court that has authority to hear the evidence of the parties and render a verdict.

Originally, the U.S. Constitution provided for a single **federal court.** Congress was also given the authority to create new courts as needed.[1] Similarly, each state was responsible for establishing **state courts** to address the needs of its population. In the 200 plus years since the U.S. Supreme Court was created, literally thousands of state and federal courts have been added to the judicial systems to handle the ever-increasing number of legal claims of both individuals and government.

Trial Versus Appellate Courts

The present federal and state court systems consist of two basic types of courts: trial and appellate. The **trial court** is the court in which the case is presented to the judge or jury. In the trial court, each party follows certain required procedures to prepare the evidence for a fair and complete presentation. The judge and, in many cases, a jury hear the evidence to support the claims of both sides of the dispute. A verdict is then given declaring whether the defendant is at fault for violation of a legal standard.

A court that hears trials is known as a court of original jurisdiction.[2] If a party thinks the trial court verdict is the result of failure to properly follow the legal requirements for the proceedings, that party may choose to appeal the verdict. When a case is brought on appeal, the judges of an **appellate court** will review part or all of the trial court's proceedings. An appellate court has authority superior to that of a trial court and has the power to change the trial court's verdict. Often, appellate courts consist of several judges who review cases as a panel. By utilizing multiple reviewers, there is less chance that mistakes will be made in the review of an application of law to a particular case. This type of judicial authority is known as appellate jurisdiction.[3] Quite often, panels of three judges will review a particular case. However, in very important cases, the entire group of appellate judges may review a case collectively. In such a situation, the decision the judges render is considered to be *en banc.*[4]

An important distinction between trial and appellate courts is the actual purpose of each court. It is the duty of the trial court to determine the applicable law, hear the evidence, and render a verdict, whereas it is the duty of the appellate court to only review what took place in the trial court and determine whether the law was correctly applied to the evidence presented. Appellate courts generally do not hear new evidence such as testimony of witnesses. Nor do appellate courts issue new verdicts. Rather, they affirm (approve) or reverse (reject) the trial (lower) court verdict. If the appellate court reverses the decision of the trial court, it also generally issues instructions as to the next stage of the proceedings, such as to order a new trial. Regardless of whether the court is part of a state system or the federal system, the distinction between trial and appellate court is essentially the same. More information regarding the actual proceedings in trial and appellate courts can be found in the chapters that discuss civil and criminal procedure.

The Federal Court System

The federal court system started with a single court, now known as the U.S. Supreme Court. Over time, Congress added several courts to the federal judicial branch. Currently, the federal court system comprises three levels (see Figure 2.1), each of which functions totally independent of state court systems, just as each state judicial branch functions independent of the other states.

An easy way to distinguish a federal court from a state court is by the court's name. All federal courts will have the words *United States* or *U.S.* in the title. No state court may include this language as part of its name. Of the three levels of federal courts, the trial courts—where the vast majority of federal cases originate—are known as the U.S. District Courts. Generally, the U.S. District Courts are used as trial courts. However, in limited circumstances, a federal case can be initially heard by an administrative hearing officer with the executive branch and appealed to the U.S. District Court. In such an instance, the U.S. District Court takes on appellate authority rather than its usual original jurisdiction. Also, there are very specific types of cases that may be initially filed for trial at the appellate level and bypass the U.S. District Court altogether. This is not a common occurrence, however. Typically, the appellate level is reserved for parties who wish to challenge the decision of the U.S. District Court. Such an

Appellate Court
A court that reviews the actions of a trial court and determines whether an error has been committed that requires corrective action.

FIGURE 2.1

The Three Tiers
of the Federal
Court System

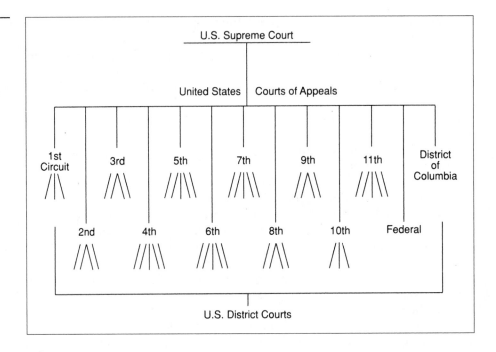

appeal is made to the next level, which is the U.S. Court of Appeals. Following such an appeal, a party who is still dissatisfied with the result of the case may seek appellate review by the U.S. Supreme Court.

The U.S. District Courts

Perhaps the busiest courts within the federal court system are the trial courts, known as the U.S. District Courts. Currently, there are over ninety such courts. Congress has increased the number of these courts when warranted by the number of cases filed and tried in the federal system. When the burden becomes too heavy for one court, Congress creates an additional court to handle part of the load.

The various U.S. District Courts are separated by geographical boundaries. Legal disputes over federal law that occur or have connections to the court within the court's physical boundaries are subject to the authority of the U.S. District Court. For example, if an individual violated a federal law in Montana, the U.S. District Court for the District of Montana would try the case.

For convenience and to facilitate understanding by the population, state lines have been used as district boundary lines. However, there is no connection between state court authority and federal court authority because of the setting of such boundaries. Courts simply use the same imaginary line to separate themselves from other courts. State and federal courts remain distinct even though a state court or U.S. District Court authority does not exceed the geographical boundaries of the state in which the court is located.

Some states with substantial population and litigation have more than one U.S. District Court divided by county lines (for convenience) within the state. For example, the state of Illinois has three U.S. District Courts: the Northern District, the Central District, and the Southern District. A district that covers a wide geographical area may be subdivided into divisions, which operate as branches of a district court, with buildings in each division as a means of making the court more accessible to the citizens.

The U.S. Courts of Appeals

A party to a lawsuit who is dissatisfied with a U.S. District Court decision may appeal to the U.S. Court of Appeals designated to hear cases appealed from the particular U.S. District Court where the case originated.[5] For example, someone who wanted to appeal a case from a U.S. District Court of Iowa would file the appeal with the 8th U.S. Circuit Court of Appeals. By requiring the appeals from each U.S. District Court to go to a specific U.S. Court of Appeals, parties are prevented from shopping for the appellate court that appears most favorable to their point of view. This system of pairing specific trial courts with a particular appellate court allows the appellate courts to create legal standards to be consistently followed by the designated U.S. District Courts subject to the appellate court's authority.

The U.S. Courts of Appeals in the federal court system are intermediate level appellate courts. Review at this level resolves cases that would otherwise be appealed to the U.S. Supreme Court, thus lessening the burden on the high court. U.S. Courts of Appeals were originally established to make appellate review faster, easier, and more accessible to parties in litigation. Over the years, as the number of cases filed has increased, so has the activity of these courts, which today are an essential element of the federal court structure.

Because of the tremendous number of cases filed and appealed in the federal court system, there are multiple U.S. Courts of Appeals, known as Circuit Courts. Specifically, there are currently a total of thirteen courts of appeal: eleven courts that are located across the country and identified by number (e.g., 1st U.S. Circuit Court of Appeals); the U.S. Circuit Court of Appeals for the District of Columbia, which hears cases originating in the U.S. District Court for the District of Columbia; and the U.S. Federal Court of Appeals, which hears cases from special federal courts such as the U.S. Court of Claims and the U.S. Court of International Trade.

The U.S. Courts of Appeals are the courts most responsible for establishing legal standards. These courts publish many more decisions than the U.S. District Courts or the U.S. Supreme Court. And while the U.S. Supreme Court opinions control in any situation, the limited number of opinions limits the amount of legal standards established by the high court. Thus, when one is looking for precedent on a federal issue, a likely source would be the published opinions of the U.S. Courts of Appeals. Further, since these courts are superior authorities to the U.S. District Courts, a precedent from such an appellate court would be more persuasive than one from a trial court.

Like the U.S. District Court, the physical limits of authority of each U.S. Court of Appeals are defined by geographical boundaries. For the sake of convenience rather than any connection with the states, the eleven circuits are divided by the boundary lines of several states. These boundaries delineate the area of authority of a particular Circuit Court of Appeals over the U.S. District Courts contained within the area. For example, the U.S. 5th Circuit Court of Appeals has authority over all appeals from U.S. District Courts located within Texas, Louisiana, and Mississippi. Similarly, the 8th circuit governs U.S. District Courts located in North Dakota, South Dakota, Nebraska, Minnesota, Iowa, Missouri, and Arkansas.

Each Circuit Court of Appeals is responsible for handling the appeals coming from the federal courts within the geographical boundaries of the circuit. These boundaries are determined by Congress and are altered periodically to adjust the flow of cases more equitably. As with the U.S. District Courts, when the burden of cases becomes too heavy for a U.S. Circuit Court of Appeals, Congress has the authority to create a new court or redefine the boundaries of the circuit.

Figure 2.2 indicates the boundaries of the U.S. Circuit Courts of Appeals and the U.S. District Courts.

No U.S. Court of Appeals has authority over any other. Each court functions independently and is accountable only to the U.S. Supreme Court. Frequently, different U.S. Courts of Appeals decide the same issue differently. When this occurs, the Supreme Court may accept one or more of these cases and decide what exactly the legal standard shall be. This eliminates any inconsistency that may arise among the rulings of the various circuits.

The U.S. Supreme Court

The U.S. Supreme Court is the final authority on all matters of federal jurisdiction in the American legal system.[6] It has the authority to review actions of Congress, the president, and the state governments. However, this authority is not limitless. Our legal system is based on the Constitution, and if the Court wants to take any action superior to one of the other branches of government, it must do so on constitutional grounds. In other words, the Court cannot overrule Congress or the president unless the legislative or executive branch has in some way violated or exceeded the authority granted to the branch by the Constitution.

The primary function of the Supreme Court is one of review. The Supreme Court reviews cases from the federal courts and, in some instances, from the highest state courts that have constitutional issues or that include the government as a party.[7]

The Supreme Court has limited original jurisdiction.[8] Cases involving original jurisdiction are not appealed but rather are filed in court for the very first time at the level of the U.S. Supreme Court. Original jurisdiction is limited to only the types of situations listed in Article III of the Constitution.[9]

FIGURE 2.2 U.S. Circuit Courts of Appeals and U.S. District Courts

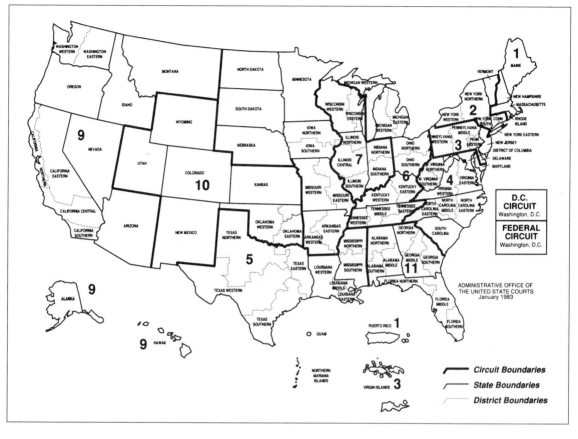

The U.S. Supreme Court has two common methods of obtaining review.[10] The first is by right. Certain types of cases are automatically entitled to review by the Supreme Court if the party so desires. The Court will review the case as long as the procedural rules for filing the appeal are complied with.

The second and more common method is known as certiorari (sir-shore-are-ee), which describes the authority of the Court to accept a number of cases for review where there is no right but where it would serve the interests of justice to have the Court make a final and ultimate determination of a legal standard. Well over 1,000 petitions for certiorari are filed with the Supreme Court each year. However, since the Court can consider only a limited number within its term, it often selects those cases that contain major issues that have been decided differently in various courts and require a final decision to settle the matter permanently.

Another significant factor in the determination of whether to grant certiorari of cases is when the decision offered for review involves constitutional rights. An ultimate goal of the Court is to ensure that the Constitution will be applied fairly for all persons. When the Court declines to accept a petition for certiorari, the practical effect is that it accepts and indirectly affirms the decision of the U.S. Court of Appeals. Finally, a U.S. Court of Appeals may "certify a question," in which case the appeals court may specifically request that the Supreme Court resolve a pertinent issue on which the various U.S. Courts of Appeals are divided.

Special Federal Courts

Although the vast majority of cases are brought to and decided through the U.S. District Courts and the U.S. Courts of Appeals, other federal courts are set up for the express purpose of handling specific types of cases. Specified types of claims made against the U.S. government must be filed with the Court of Claims. Claims involving federal taxation are tried in the U.S. Tax Court. The Court of International Trade hears disputes involving international trade agreements.

THE STATE COURT SYSTEM

Totally independent of the federal courts are the state court systems for each of the fifty states. Each state government has legislative, executive, and judicial branches, which in many ways parallel the federal government. Every state has a judicial system to provide a forum for the resolution of disputes among persons and entities within the state. Such disputes must involve acts or occurrences that are controlled by state rather than federal law. The law may be case law or state legislative law. Federal courts and state courts are independent of and not subject to the authority of one another. (The exception is that all courts of the nation are subject to the U.S. Supreme Court.) No state court is bound by the authority of a court from a different state. Nor is a court obligated to follow the rulings of an equivalent court. Like the U.S. Courts of Appeals, state courts have equal authority. If a state court system has an intermediate appellate level made up of several courts, the opinions of these courts would not be binding on one another. Rather, only the lower trial courts within the purview of authority of the particular appellate court would be bound.

The states utilize two basic judicial structures: three-tiered and two-tiered systems. The three-tiered system is comparable to that of the federal system. The three tiers are made up of a court of last resort (the highest court of the state), an intermediate appellate court level, and a trial court level. Heavily populated states may have several appellate courts similar to the numerous U.S. Circuit Courts of Appeals in the federal system. The trial courts include courts for civil and criminal trials, matters of domestic relations disputes, probate, juvenile, small claims, magistrates, and justices of the peace.

Approximately half the states employ the three-tiered system. The other states use a two-tiered system consisting of only one appellate (supreme) court and the various trial courts. However, because of the increase in litigation, more states are considering the three-tiered system. In the two-tiered system, appeals from the trial court are taken directly to the high court of the state, placing the total burden on a single group of judges. In the three-tiered system, appeals are first taken to the intermediate appellate court in the same manner as applied in the federal system. A party who wants further review may then appeal to the highest court of the state. However, most appeals end after the first review, as the likelihood of a reversal declines dramatically with each appeal.

The terms *District Court* and *Circuit Court* are employed in some states in the same way as in the federal system. Other states reverse these titles. The Circuit Court is the trial court, and the District Court is the appellate court. Some states use other names entirely to describe their courts. Persons not trained in the structure of the legal system can be misled as to the importance of a judicial opinion by attaching more weight to the decision than is warranted simply because of the name of the court that rendered the opinion. What matters is that each state has a trial court level and an appellate court level and the decisions carry lesser weight in descending order from the highest appellate level to the lowest trial court.

Since the trial courts of the states handle more cases than any other level of state or federal court in the American legal system, they must be organized to process the multitude of cases filed each year. Most often, state courts will divide the time of the various judges by the type of case filed. For example, certain judges will devote their attention to domestic relations (divorce, custody, support, adoption, etc.), while other judges will hear only criminal cases. These various divisions all operate together to create the trial court level. In addition, the trial courts within a particular state (usually at least one per county) are divided into geographical regions, usually bounded by county borders. Each court is responsible for the legal rights of persons and the legal issues arising from occurrences within the borders of the court's authority. By having a court within each county, the people are guaranteed reasonable access to the courts.

Figure 2.3 is a diagram of a three-tiered state court system. (A two-tiered system would eliminate the intermediate level of appellate courts.)

LEGAL ANALYSIS

Legal analysis is the process of learning from the past and acting accordingly. It is the cornerstone of the American judicial system. Legal professionals, judges, lawyers, and paralegals all utilize the process in their daily work. Legal analysis allows the judge to resolve a dispute consistent with the modern balance and allows the lawyer to advise the client as to the appropriate course of conduct based on past experiences of similarly situated persons. It enables the paralegal to know what information will be necessary to interview a client and prepare legal documents (see Chapter 15 for more information on roles of legal professionals).

Case analysis is the specific method of legal analysis of past judicial opinions and their impact on a current situation. The similarities and differences between the past cases and the current situation give insight with regard to

Legal Analysis
The process of examining precedent in detail in order to predict its effect on future similar circumstances.

FIGURE 2.3

Three-tiered State
Court System

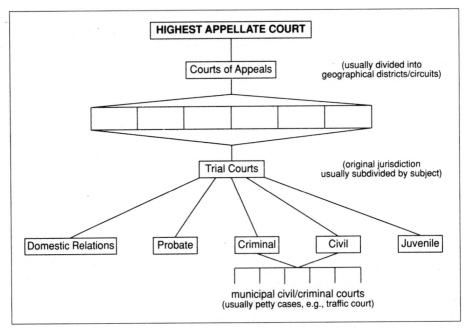

A two-tier court system is the same as the system pictured above, but with the intermediate level court of appeals deleted.

whether the outcome should be similar in the present case. Because case analysis is used so extensively, an organized system for publishing and arranging the cases is necessary so that cases on specific topics or from particular courts can be easily accessed.

Published cases are predominantly appellate for quite practical reasons. First, since trial courts are generally the lowest level of judicial authority, a trial court opinion does not have to be followed by a judge in a subsequent case. Appellate court opinions, on the other hand, must be followed by those trial courts that are subordinate to the authority of the appellate court that issued the opinion. Also, appellate decisions are usually rendered by a panel of appellate judges whose collective wisdom is respected by the legal community. Such opinions are infrequently overturned by higher appellate courts and thus provide a stable basis for comparison of the state legal standard to a present situation. A second reason for the limited number of published trial court opinions is cost effectiveness. Literally hundreds of thousands of trials take place annually in this country. It would not be reasonable to publish all of the opinions supporting the outcome of these cases when they are of such limited authority.

Judicial opinions are published in what are known as reports and reporters. New volumes of these books are continuously published and contain the judicial opinions as they are handed down by the courts.

The usefulness of published cases is immeasurable. By having access to opinions the courts have issued in the past, the parties can often determine with great accuracy the outcome of future disputes. Judges look to published cases to determine the appropriate legal standards and the manner in which the standards should be applied. The attorneys for the parties to a dispute also examine the cases as an indicator of their chances of winning the lawsuit. In addition, it is not uncommon for parties or their lawyers to examine the cases before taking any action whatsoever. Such examination often will guide the conduct of an individual or business.

Judicial opinions (cases) may at first appear to be long and drawn out with many difficult terms and references that seem to make no sense. However, with some training and a lot of practice, reading and analyzing a case can become second nature. Throughout the remainder of this text, many cases are provided that relate directly to the subject of the chapter. Although these cases have been edited somewhat to facilitate their reading, all of the elements of the judicial opinion are represented. The student is urged to thoroughly examine these cases for two reasons. First, the cases provide a practical application of the subject matter of the text which can make understanding the subject easier. Second, reading these cases can help students to develop a useful skill no matter what their future professional goals may be. Since all aspects of our society are influenced by the law, the ability to read and comprehend the law can prove to be invaluable.

The initial step in analyzing the meaning of a case is to know the elements of a judicial opinion. Note first that various methods are available for analyzing a case. Additionally, note that the elements are sometimes broken down differently and given different titles. Do not be discouraged or confused by this. No matter what the titles or number of elements a person assigns to a case analysis, the analysis contains the same basic information. The information is just packaged differently. Below is one method of analyzing a case. The analysis can be renamed or reorganized in any fashion but will still be made up of the same elements.

Virtually everyone who performs case analysis consistently uses the term *case briefing*. The legal profession employs many types of briefs. The term *case brief* describes a synopsis of a judicial opinion. A common purpose of a case brief is to facilitate a determination of the effects of a previously issued judicial opinion on a current situation. To accurately make such a determination, one must examine each aspect of the case and decide whether the case is sufficiently similar to the present situation to create a likelihood that the same legal standards would be applied in the same way today.

The following paragraphs describe the elements of a case. While judicial opinions may be lengthy, the case brief is usually not, since a brief's purpose is to identify only those points that were pivotal in the decision and consequently would be considered in a similar case. Therefore, when analyzing a case, no matter what element is being examined, one should focus only on those statements that directly affected the final decision.

The Facts

Since case law is the application of a prior judicial determination to a similar situation, the first step in preparing a case brief is to identify the key facts. In many situations, such identification will control whether the legal principles of a previous case would be applicable to another situation.

A case brief contains two types of facts: occurrence facts and legal facts. Occurrence facts are those things that happened between the parties to create a dispute and ultimately produced a lawsuit. An example is the circumstances of a shooting that led to a criminal prosecution and trial for the murder. Legal facts are those things that occurred during the lawsuit that led the case to an appellate court. An example is found in a decision by the judge to exclude certain evidence at trial; the party who had offered the evidence lost the case and brought it to an appellate court to determine whether the evidence should have been allowed.

Cases will often include a great deal of background information, which is helpful but not a pivotal part of the decision. Those facts that did not play a part in the outcome of the case should generally be disregarded in a case brief. For example, most cases will indicate the date and often the time of an occurrence. While this helps to set the scene, usually this information is not vital. An exception might be the date in a contract case or the time of day of an accident case if visibility was an important factor. But in most situations, such information is not relevant to the legal effect of the decision. Its only value is to explain more thoroughly the nature of the dispute and the issues involved. Consequently, only information that is absolutely necessary to understand the dispute, verdict, and reasons for appeal should be included in a case brief.

The Issue

Once the important facts have been determined, the reader should proceed to determine the issue of the case. It is important to note that the issue in most judicial opinions is not the guilt or innocence of a party in the suit. Rather, the issue in the vast majority of lawsuits is whether the correct legal standards were applied and whether they were applied properly in the trial court. Consequently, the determination of guilt or innocence is relevant only with respect to why or how the verdict was achieved. The goal of case analysis is to identify the legal standards that were applied and how they were applied so that the case might be compared to other situations. Therefore, the reader should not be unduly concerned with who won or lost in the previous case other than as a legal fact and an indicator of who would win under an application of the same legal standards under similar facts. When identifying the issue, one should focus on what the appellate court actually considered when it examined the trial court's selection and application of legal standards. The issue is identified by determining what question or questions the court answered in its opinion. One method to assist the inexperienced person to identify the issue in a judicial opinion is to complete the following statement: The appellant (party who appeals the verdict) alleges the trial court abused its discretion (authority) when it _____ .

The Law

The third step in case analysis is to determine the authority upon which the court's decision was based. Since judges always search for guidance from existing legal standards, if there are no such standards, the judge looks to the beliefs of society and the fundamentals of right and wrong as viewed by society. Often the latter are determined by looking to the opinions of legal scholars and other noted authorities on a subject. In any event, the decision in a case will be based on some existing statement of law or wisdom. The court uses such a statement as authority and applies it to the occurrence and legal facts of the case to determine the answer to the issue before the court.

Most often the court will use an established legal standard as authority. However, sometimes the judge applies an opinion of a scholar, but this is private opinion and not law. However, by incorporating such opinion into the judicial opinion, the private opinion becomes the legal standard in that court. Consequently, the use of the term *law* describes the authority adopted and applied by a judge as the guiding legal standard in deciding a case.

In a case brief, one should indicate the source of the "law" (legal principle) used to determine a case. Just as importantly, the actual principle should be stated. It is not helpful to know one without the other. When analyzing the effects of a case, it is necessary to know not only the source but also the content of the legal standard. When identifying the law for use in a case brief, the student should seek out those principles that address the issue at hand. The following excerpt from a judicial opinion that responds to the issue in that opinion is an example of legal authority:

> *Issue:* Can a person be convicted of assisting in a robbery when there is evidence that the person's life was threatened in order to coerce assistance?

> *Law:* "When a party is forced, under threat of serious harm, to perform an illegal act, then that party cannot be held accountable for committing a criminal act." *People of the State of Maine v. Jezbera,* 402 A.2d 777 (Maine Sup. Ct. 1980).

The quoted material is the legal standard. The information that follows is the source. Specifically given is the name of the case, the volume number, the name of the reporter series where the opinion is published, and the page number where the case begins. The information in parentheses indicates the court that decided the case and the year of the opinion.

If you looked up *Atlantic Reports,* 2d Series, at a library, located volume 402, and opened it to page 777, you would see the case of *Maine v. Jezbera.* You would also find information indicating that this opinion was handed down by the Supreme Court of Maine in 1980.

The Rule

Judicial opinions do not merely state the law (both principle and its source) and then follow with a blanket statement of the case's winner. Rather, the court will give some explanation regarding why or how the legal standard applies to the facts and issue of the case. In a case brief, such information is essential. It is impossible to predict the effects of a case without understanding the reasoning of the court in the judicial opinion. Unless this information is included in the case analysis (brief), one could not determine whether the same legal standards would apply in the present situation to the present facts and issue.

Once the facts, issue, law, and rule have been determined, the case brief can be used to compare the case with other situations of similar facts and issue. Similarities and differences should be identified. One should then determine whether the similarities are strong enough to create a likelihood that the same legal standards would be applied in the same way in the other situation. This can be done in large part by examining the rule of the case. One must ask just how and why the previous court applied the particular legal standard to the case. If the case is briefed for purposes of comparison to another situation, the next issue to explore is the likelihood that the law would be applied in the same way under the facts and issue of the other situation.

What follows are two judicial opinions. A case brief has been provided after the first opinion.

  CASE ──◆

NIBLO v. PARR MFG., INC.

445 N.W.2d 351 (Iowa 1989).

SCHULTZ, Justice.

In this retaliatory discharge case, employee Rose Marie Niblo recovered damages for loss of wages and emotional distress. The employer, Parr Manufacturing, Inc., challenges the allowance of damages for emotional distress arising out of this tort. If such damages are recoverable, it urges that the distress must be severe. Parr also claims plaintiff failed to present sufficient evidence to establish a claim for wrongful discharge. We affirm.

Plaintiff began her employment with defendant in June 1985. She worked with plastisol, a chemical which is used to cohere the parts of fuel filters. In late 1985, she noticed that she was developing a skin condition on her face. She was referred to a dermatologist who diagnosed her skin condition as work related. Following conversations with her supervisor and the president of the corporation, she was terminated from her employment.

Plaintiff brought this action for wrongful discharge, alleging she was discharged from her employment in violation of public policy. The trial

court instructed the jury that plaintiff had the burden of proving that she was fired because she wanted to file, or threatened to file, a worker's compensation claim. The jury returned a verdict of $12,000 for plaintiff.

I. Sufficiency of Evidence. At the close of plaintiff's evidence, defendant moved for a directed verdict based on the sufficiency of plaintiff's evidence to establish a claim for wrongful discharge. This claim was renewed in a motion for judgment notwithstanding the verdict. In each instance the trial court denied the motion. Defendant claims the trial court erred by these rulings.

It is undisputed that plaintiff's employment was at-will and that there was no definite term or contract governing the terms of her employment. Our general rule is that an employee at-will can ordinarily be fired at anytime by an employer. Abrisz v. Pulley Freight Lines, Inc., 270 N.W.2d 454, 455 (Iowa 1978). We recognized in Abrisz that under proper circumstances we would recognize a common law claim for wrongful discharge from employment when such employment is terminated for reasons contrary to public policy. Id.

More recently, we adopted this public policy exception and applied it in a case where the discharge allegedly was due to the filing of a worker's compensation claim. Springer v. Weeks & Leo Co., 429 N.W.2d 558, 560–61 (Iowa 1988). We described the cause of action as "tortious interference with the contract of hire." Id. at 560. We stated:

We deem this to be clear expression that it is the public policy of this state that employee's right to seek the compensation which is granted by law for work-related injuries should not be interfered with regardless of the terms of the contract of hire. To permit the type of retaliatory discharge which has been alleged in this case to go without a remedy would fly in the face of this policy.

Id. at 560–61.

On appeal defendant does not challenge our holding in Springer nor the trial court's instruction detailing the required proof of discharge based on plaintiff's desire or threat to file a compensation claim. Defendant limits its claim to the sufficiency of the evidence on this element. Specifically, defendant urges that there is not sufficient evidence that plaintiff was going to file a worker's compensation claim for the question to go to the jury. Defendant correctly asserts that plaintiff never testified that she wanted to or intended to file a worker's compensation claim, nor has she done so. Defendant maintains the evidence merely shows that its management and plaintiff had a dispute concerning the payment of her doctor bills.

When considering the propriety of a motion for directed verdict, the court views the evidence in the light most favorable to the party against whom the motion was made. Iowa R.App.P. 14(f)(2). Direct and circumstantial evidence are equally probative. Iowa R.App.P. 14(f)(16). If reasonable minds might draw different inferences from the facts, whether they are in dispute or contradicted, a jury question is engendered. Iowa R.App.P. 14(f)(17).

By applying these principles, a jury could have inferred from the evidence that plaintiff's discharge resulted from something more than a dispute over doctor bills. Plaintiff contacted her supervisor about going to a doctor. The supervisor ignored her first inquiry and responded to her second request by stating that he did not care what she did, but that defendant was not going to pay for her to go to a doctor. After plaintiff went to a dermatologist, she told the president of the defendant company of her visit and of the doctor's opinion that her skin condition was work related.

After a follow-up visit with the doctor, plaintiff was informed that she had a severe case of chloracne, needed goggles, protective cream and continued treatment, the president became irate. He told plaintiff that he was not going to pay workmen's compensation or unemployment benefits and that he did not think that her skin problem was his fault, or "factory related." He said that he was not going to pay to have plaintiff's face worked on at all. At the conclusion of this outburst, he fired plaintiff.

The issue of whether plaintiff threatened to file a compensation claim was for the jury. Plaintiff need not personally testify of her threat or intent. She supplied this evidence by testimony setting out the president's statements concerning compensation. A jury could deduce from this evidence that the plaintiff was discharged because she was threatening to file a claim for these benefits. The trial court did not abuse its discretion in denying a motion for a new trial based on the sufficiency of the evidence . . . Affirmed

Case Question
In addition to retaliation for filing a workers' compensation claim, what other bases for termination from employment would be improper?

Case Brief
What follows is a sample case brief of the preceding judicial opinion (edited version). Note how the significant information is extracted from the complete opinion and then organized into the essential components.

Niblo v. Parr Mfg., Inc., 445 N.W.2d 351 (Iowa 1989)

Facts: Plaintiff Niblo was employed by Defendant Parr. Her employment involved exposure to chemicals. She subsequently developed a skin condition that was diagnosed as work related. She reported the condition to her employer. She was subsequently terminated. Plaintiff brought a suit for wrongful discharge alleging she was fired for potentially exercising her right to benefits pursuant to a Worker's Compensation claim. She was awarded $12,000 in a jury trial. Defendant appealed claiming that there was insufficient evidence of plaintiff's possible worker's compensation claim to result in a finding of wrongful discharge.

Issue: Did the trial court err when it failed to direct a verdict in defendant's favor on the basis of insufficient evidence to create a question of fact regarding retaliatory discharge.

Law: *Springer v. Weeks & Leo Co.*, 429 N.W.2d 558 (Iowa 1988). Exceptions to the right of an employer to fire at-will employees include termination based on an employee's worker's compensation claim.

Rule: Plaintiff presented sufficient evidence of conversations with her employer regarding her medical condition and that it was work related to give a jury sufficient reason to believe plaintiff's subsequent termination was related to the potential claim. In accordance with Springer v. Weeks & Leo Co., supra, there was sufficient evidence to support a finding against defendant. Therefore, the court was proper in refusing to direct a verdict for defendant.

 CASE

DeBOER v. SCHMIDT

442 Mich. 648, 502 N.W.2d 649(1997).

LEVIN, Justice.

Opinion
Per Curiam.

These two related cases arise out of a child custody dispute involving the competing claims of the child's natural parents (Cara and Daniel Schmidt) and the third-party custodians with whom the child now lives (Roberta and Jan DeBoer).

While we will deal at length with the various arguments marshalled in support of their claims, we sum up our analysis of the competing arguments by reference to the words of the United States Supreme Court: "No one would seriously dispute that a deeply loving and interdependent relationship with an adult and a child in his or her care may exist even in the absence of blood relationship." Smith v. Organization of Foster Families, 431 U.S. 816, 843-844, 97 S.Ct. 2094, 2109-2110, 53 L.Ed.2d 14 (1977). But there are limits to such claims.

. . . The DeBoers acquired temporary custody of this child, with whom they had no prior relationship, through the power of the state and must be taken to have known that their right to continue custody was contingent on the completion of the Iowa adoption. Within nine days of assuming physical custody and less than one month after the child's birth, the DeBoers learned of Cara Schmidt's claim that the waiver of rights procured by the attorney acting on behalf of the DeBoers was unlawful because she had not been afforded the seventy-two hour waiting period required by Iowa law. Within two months of the child's birth, the DeBoers learned of Daniel Schmidt's claim of paternity when on March 27, 1991, he filed a petition to intervene in the DeBoers' adoption proceeding.

> Iowa Code Ann. 600A.4(2)(d). There is no dispute that a lawyer representing the DeBoers went to her hospital room and obtained the mother's signature on the consent form forty hours after the child was born.

The State of Iowa has not arbitrarily interfered "in a family-like association freely entered." Rather, the Iowa courts have proceeded with the adoption action initiated by the DeBoers, and at the conclusion of that litigation ruled that there would be no adoption, preventing the creation of the family unit that was the objective of the adoption petition.

In Docket No. 96366, we affirm the judgment of the Court of Appeals for two independent reasons. First, the Uniform Child Custody Jurisdiction Act (UCCJA) and the federal Parental Kidnapping Prevention Act (PKPA) deprive the Michigan courts of jurisdiction over this custody dispute and require the enforcement of the orders of the Iowa courts directing that the Schmidts have custody of the child. Second, the DeBoers lack standing to bring this custody action under our decision in Bowie v. Arder, 441 Mich. 23, 490 N.W.2d 568 (1992).

Docket No. 96366 began as an action by the DeBoers seeking an order rejecting or modifying the orders of the Iowa courts that directed that Daniel Schmidt have custody of the child. The Court of Appeals reversed the Washtenaw Circuit Court's denial of Schmidt's motion for summary judgment. The court concluded that the circuit court lacked jurisdiction under the Uniform Child Custody Jurisdiction Act, and that the Iowa judgment awarding custody to the child's father must be enforced. The Court of Appeals also ruled that under our decision in Bowie v. Arder, 441 Mich. 23, 490 N.W.2d 568 (1992), the DeBoers lacked standing to bring the action. We granted the DeBoers' application for leave to appeal.

In Docket Nos. 96441, 96531, and 96532 we vacate the orders of the Washtenaw Circuit Court and direct that the action be dismissed for failure to state a claim upon which relief may be granted. While a child has a constitutionally protected interest in family life, that interest is not independent of its parents' in the absence of a showing that the parents are unfit. In this case, in the Iowa litigation the DeBoers were unable to prove that the child's father would not be a fit parent, and no claim has been made that her mother is unfit.

I

The facts are set out at length in the opinion of the Court of Appeals. Briefly, on February 8, 1991, Cara Clausen gave birth to a baby girl in Iowa. Proceedings in Iowa have established that defendant Daniel Schmidt is the child's father. On February 10, 1991, Clausen signed a release of custody form, relinquishing her parental rights to the child. Clausen, who was unmarried at the time of the birth, had named Scott Seefeldt as the father. On February 14, 1991, he executed a release of custody form.

She and Daniel Schmidt married in April 1992.

On February 25, 1991, petitioners Roberta and Jan DeBoer, who are Michigan residents,

filed a petition for adoption of the child in juvenile court in Iowa. A hearing was held the same day, at which the parental rights of Cara Clausen and Seefeldt were terminated, and petitioners were granted custody of the child during the pendency of the proceeding. The DeBoers returned to Michigan with the child, and she has lived with them in Michigan continuously since then.

However, the prospective adoption never took place. On March 6, 1991, nine days after the filing of the adoption petition, Cara Clausen filed a motion in the Iowa Juvenile Court to revoke her release of custody. In an affidavit accompanying the request, Clausen stated that she had lied when she named Seefeldt as the father of the child, and that the child's father actually was Daniel Schmidt. Schmidt filed an affidavit of paternity on March 12, 1991, and on March 27, 1991, he filed a petition in the Iowa district court, seeking to intervene in the adoption proceeding initiated by the DeBoers.

On November 4, 1991, the district court in Iowa conducted a bench trial on the issues of paternity, termination of parental rights, and adoption. On December 27, 1991, the district court found that Schmidt established by a preponderance of the evidence that he was the biological father of the child; that the DeBoers failed to establish by clear and convincing evidence that Schmidt had abandoned the child or that his parental rights should be terminated; and that a best interests of the child analysis did not become appropriate unless abandonment was established. On the basis of these findings, the court concluded that the termination proceeding was void with respect to Schmidt, and that the DeBoers' petition to adopt the child must be denied. Those decisions have been affirmed by the Iowa appellate courts.

See In re BGC, 496 N.W.2d 239 (Iowa, 1992).

On remand from the Iowa Supreme Court, the district court ordered the DeBoers to appear on December 3, 1992, with the child. The DeBoers did not appear at the hearing; instead, their Iowa attorney informed the court that the DeBoers had received actual notice of the hearing but had decided not to appear. In an order entered on December 3, 1992, the district court terminated the DeBoers' rights as temporary guardians and custodians of the child.

B

[3] The DeBoers argue that the Iowa judgment should not be enforced because the Iowa courts did not conduct a hearing into the best interests of the child in making the custody decision. They maintain that this undercuts the Iowa decision in two respects. First, they say this means that the Iowa decision was not in conformity with the UCCJA, and therefore not entitled to enforcement under that statute. Second, they believe that the Iowa proceeding was repugnant to Michigan public policy.

The DeBoers also include arguments to the effect that even under Iowa law, a best interests hearing was required, citing several cases, Halstead v. Halstead, 259 Iowa 526, 144 N.W.2d 861 (1966); Painter v. Bannister, 258 Iowa 1390, 140 N.W.2d 152 (1966), and statutes, Iowa Code Ann. §§ 600.1, 600.13(1)(c) (Adoption Code); § 600A.1 (termination of parental rights); § 600B.40 (Paternity Act). The Iowa courts relied on the constitutionally protected opportunity interest of a biological father in Schmidt's circumstance to conclude that termination was not in the best interest of the child unless unfitness was shown, and found, as fact, that the DeBoers had not shown unfitness. We have not had occasion to construe our adoption statute, M.C.L. § 710.39(1); M.S.A. § 27.3178(555.39)(1), in light of Lehr v. Robertson, 463 U.S. 248, 103 S.Ct. 2985, 77 L.Ed.2d 614 (1983). We cannot say, however, that if the constitution requires such construction, it would be against our public policy to do so.

We reject the contention that the decision of the Iowa courts not to conduct a best interests of the child hearing in the circumstances of this case justifies the refusal to enforce the Iowa judgments.

V

The Court of Appeals also concluded that the DeBoers lacked standing to claim custody of the child. The Court said:

"We hold that the DeBoers lacked standing to bring this action in Washtenaw Circuit Court. The Iowa district court order of December 3, 1992, implemented the decision of the Iowa Supreme Court and stripped the DeBoers of any legal claim to custody of [the child]. The grant of temporary custody was rescinded. At that time, the DeBoers became third parties with respect to [the child], and no longer had a basis on which to claim a substantive right to custody. Bowie, supra, 441 Mich. at 43-45, 49, 490 N.W.2d 568, states that neither the Child Custody Act nor 'any other authority' gives a third party who does not possess a substantive right to custody or is not a guardian, standing to create a custody dispute. A right to legal custody cannot be based on the fact that a child resides or has resided with the third party. We take the reference in Bowie, supra at 45, 490 N.W.2d 568, to 'any other authority' to include the UCCJA.

M.C.L. § 722.21 et seq.; M.S.A. § 25.312(1) et seq.

"The DeBoers' argument that Bowie, supra, does not apply to this case is without merit. As noted, the pronouncement in Bowie, supra, regarding the standing of third parties to create custody disputes is expressly not limited to actions brought under the Child Custody Act. The Iowa Supreme Court decision, implemented by the Iowa district court's order of December 3, 1992, dismissed the DeBoers' petition to adopt [the child] and rescinded their status as temporary guardians and custodians. The DeBoers had no further legal rights to [the child]. The DeBoers initiated a custody dispute in this state. Pursuant to Bowie, supra, they had no standing to do so. To disavow Bowie in this case would give an advantage to third parties in interstate custody disputes not enjoyed by third parties in intrastate disputes.

"The DeBoers' reliance on In re Danke, 169 Mich.App. 453; 426 N.W.2d 740 (1988), and In re Weldon, 397 Mich. 225, 244 N.W.2d 827 (1976) (cases in which third parties with no legal right to custody were granted standing to bring a custody action), is misplaced. Both cases were decided before Bowie, supra. The Bowie Court specifically stated that Weldon, supra, was overruled, and that a third party could not gain standing simply by filing a complaint and asserting that a change in custody would be in the best interests of the child. Bowie, supra [441 Mich.] at 48-49 [490 N.W.2d 568]"

The United States Supreme Court cases on which the DeBoers rely do not establish that they have a federal constitutional right to seek custody of the child. None involved disputes between a natural parent or parents on one side and nonparents on the other. While some of those cases place limits on the rights of natural parents, particularly unwed fathers, they involve litigation pitting one natural parent against the other, in which, almost of necessity, one natural parent must be denied rights that otherwise would have been protected. Sometimes a nonparent in a sense "prevails" in such actions, but that has been in the context of adoption by a stepfather who is married to the child's natural mother or legitimization of the status of the natural mother's husband, who is not the biological father.

Lehr v. Robertson, supra; Quilloin v. Walcott, supra.

Several of the cases talk about an unwed father's rights as being dependent on the development of a relationship with the child. We read those decisions as providing the justification for denying the unwed father's rights, rather than as establishing that nonparent custodians obtain such rights merely by having custody. Further, as the Iowa district court noted after reviewing these United States Supreme Court cases:

"It is therefore now clearly established that an unwed father who has not had a custodial relationship with a child nevertheless has a constitutionally protected interest in establishing that relationship."

And, as the Iowa Supreme Court concluded:

"We agree with the district court that abandonment was not established by clear and convincing evidence. In fact, virtually all of the evidence regarding Daniel's intent regarding this baby suggests just the opposite: Daniel did everything he could reasonably do to assert his parental rights, beginning even before he actually knew that he was the father."

Michigan courts in similar circumstances have noted that prompt action by the father to assert parental rights, combined with the father's being prevented from developing a relationship with the child by actions of the courts or the custodians, are factors that excuse or mitigate the failure to establish such a relationship. See, e.g., In re Baby Boy Barlow, 404 Mich. 216, 237-238, 273 N.W.2d 35 (1978); In re Robert P., 36 Mich.App. 497, 500, 194 N.W.2d 18 (1971).

In the Iowa proceedings, a challenge to Daniel Schmidt's fitness was vigorously prosecuted by the DeBoers, and they failed to prove that he was unfit. That determination is no longer challenged.

In Docket No. 96366, we affirm the judgment of the Court of Appeals, and in Docket Nos. 96441, 96531, and 96532, we remand the case to the Washtenaw Circuit Court with directions that the action be dismissed for failure to state claims upon which relief may be granted. The clerk is directed to issue the judgment orders forthwith. Pursuant to MCR 7.317(C)(3), the filing of a motion for rehearing will not stay enforcement of the judgments.

We direct the Washtenaw Circuit Court to enter an order enforcing the custody orders entered by the Iowa courts. In consultation with counsel for the Schmidts and the DeBoers, the circuit court shall promptly establish a plan for the transfer of custody, with the parties directed to cooperate in the transfer with the goal of easing the child's transition into the Schmidt home. The circuit court shall monitor and enforce the transfer process, employing all necessary resources of the court, and shall notify the clerk of this Court 21 days following the release of this opinion of the arrangements for transfer of custody. The actual transfer shall take place within 10 days thereafter.

To a perhaps unprecedented degree among the matters that reach this Court, these cases have been litigated through fervent emotional appeals, with counsel and the adult parties pleading that their only interests are to do what is best for the child, who is herself blameless for this protracted litigation and the grief that it has caused. However, the clearly applicable legal principles require that the Iowa judgment be enforced and that the child be placed in the custody of her natural parents. It is now time for the adults to move beyond saying that their only concern is the welfare of the child and to put those words into action by assuring that the transfer of custody is accomplished promptly with minimum disruption of the life of the child.

Like the Iowa Supreme Court, we echo the sentiments of the Iowa district judge: "[T]he Court is under no illusion that this tragic case is other than an unbelievably traumatic

event. . . . While cognizant of the heartache which this decision will ultimately cause, this Court is presented with no other option than that dictated by the law in this state. Purely equitable principles cannot be substituted for well established principles of law."

Case Question
Why did the Michigan Court *not* have authority to rule on the Iowa Court's order of custody?

Assignment 2.2

> Prepare a case brief for *DeBoer v. Schmidt.*

 CASE

QUILL v. VACCO
(2nd Cir. 1996).

MINER, Circuit Judge.

Plaintiffs-appellants Timothy E. Quill, Samuel C. Klagsbrun and Howard A. Grossman appeal from a summary judgment entered in the United States District Court for the Southern District of New York (Griesa, Ch. J.) dismissing their 42 U.S.C. § 1983 action against defendants-appellees. The action was brought by plaintiffs-appellants, all of whom are physicians, to declare unconstitutional in part two New York statutes penalizing assistance in suicide. The physicians contend that each statute is invalid to the extent that it prohibits them from acceding to the requests of terminally-ill, mentally competent patients for help in hastening death. In granting summary judgment in favor of defendants-appellees, the district court considered and rejected challenges to the statutes predicated upon the Due Process and Equal Protection Clauses of the Fourteenth Amendment to the United States Constitution. Quill v. Koppell, 870 F.Supp. 78 (S.D.N.Y.1994). We reverse in part, holding that physicians who are willing to do so may prescribe drugs to be self-administered by mentally competent patients who seek to end

their lives during the final stages of a terminal illness.

Background
The action giving rise to this appeal was commenced by a complaint filed on July 20, 1994. The plaintiffs named in that complaint were the three physicians who are the appellants here and three individuals then in the final stages of terminal illness: Jane Doe (who chose to conceal her actual identity), George A. Kingsley and William A. Barth. The sole defendant named in that complaint was G. Oliver Koppell, then the Attorney General of the State of New York. He has been succeeded as Attorney General by Dennis C. Vacco, who has been substituted for him as an appellee on this appeal. According to the complaint, Jane Doe was a 76-year-old retired physical education instructor who was dying of thyroid cancer; Mr. Kingsley was a 48-year-old publishing executive suffering from AIDS; and Mr. Barth was a 28-year-old former fashion editor under treatment for AIDS. Each of these plaintiffs alleged that she or he had been advised and understood that she or he was in the terminal stage of a terminal illness and that there was no chance of recovery. Each sought to hasten death "in a certain and humane manner" and for that purpose sought "necessary medical assistance in

the form of medications prescribed by [her or his] physician to be self-administered."

The physician plaintiffs alleged that they encountered, in the course of their medical practices, "mentally competent, terminally ill patients who request assistance in the voluntary self-termination of life." Many of these patients apparently "experience chronic, intractable pain and/or intolerable suffering" and seek to hasten their deaths for those reasons. Mr. Barth was one of the patients who sought the assistance of Dr. Grossman. Each of the physician plaintiffs has alleged that "[u]nder certain circumstances it would be consistent with the standards of [his] medical practice" to assist in hastening death by prescribing drugs for patients to self-administer for that purpose. The physicians alleged that they were unable to exercise their best professional judgment to prescribe the requested drugs, and the other plaintiffs alleged that they were unable to receive the requested drugs, because of the prohibitions contained in sections 125.15(3) and 120.30 of the New York Penal Law, all plaintiffs being residents of New York.

Section 125.15 of the New York Penal Law provides in pertinent part:

A person is guilty of manslaughter in the second degree when:

. . .

3. He intentionally . . . aids another person to commit suicide.

A violation of this provision is classified as a class C felony. Id.

Section 120.30 of the New York Penal Law provides:

A person is guilty of promoting a suicide attempt when he intentionally . . . aids another person to attempt suicide.

A violation of this provision is classified as a class E felony. Id.

Count I of the complaint included an allegation that "[t]he Fourteenth Amendment guarantees the liberty of mentally competent, terminally ill adults with no chance of recovery to make decisions about the end of their lives." It also included an allegation that

[t]he Fourteenth Amendment guarantees the liberty of physicians to practice medicine consistent with their best professional judgment, including using their skills and powers to facilitate the exercise of the decision of competent, terminally ill adults to hasten inevitable death by prescribing suitable medications for the patient to self-administer for that purpose.

Count II of the complaint included an allegation that

[t]he relevant portions of . . . the New York Penal Law deny the patient-plaintiffs and the patients of the physician-plaintiffs the equal protection of the law by denying them the right to choose to hasten inevitable death, while terminally ill persons whose treatment includes life support are able to exercise this choice with necessary medical assistance by directing termination of such treatment.

In their prayer for relief the plaintiffs requested judgment declaring the New York statutes complained of constitutionally invalid and therefore in violation of 42 U.S.C. § 1983 "as applied to physicians who assist mentally competent, terminally ill adults who choose to hasten inevitable death." Plaintiffs also sought an order permanently enjoining defendants from enforcing the statutes and an award of attorney's fees.

By order to show cause filed on September 16, 1994, the plaintiffs moved for a preliminary injunction to enjoin then-Attorney General Koppell "and all persons acting in concert and participation with him from enforcing New York Penal Law sections 125.15(3) and 120.30 against physicians who prescribe medications which mentally competent, terminally ill patients may use to hasten their impending deaths." A declaration by each of the plaintiffs was submitted in support of the application, although Jane Doe had died prior to the filing of the order to show cause. Plaintiffs Kingsley and Barth were then in the advanced stages of AIDS and therefore sought an immediate determination by the district court.

In her declaration, Jane Doe stated:
I have a large cancerous tumor which is wrapped around the right carotid artery in my

neck and is collapsing my esophagus and invading my voice box. The tumor has significantly reduced my ability to swallow and prevents me from eating anything but very thin liquids in extremely small amounts. The cancer has metastasized to my plural [sic] cavity and it is painful to yawn or cough. . . . In early July 1994 I had the [feeding] tube implanted and have suffered serious problems as a result. . . . I take a variety of medications to manage the pain. . . . It is not possible for me to reduce my pain to an acceptable level of comfort and to retain an alert state. . . . At this time, it is clear to me, based on the advice of my doctors, that I am in the terminal phase of this disease. . . . At the point at which I can no longer endure the pain and suffering associated with my cancer, I want to have drugs available for the purpose of hastening my death in a humane and certain manner. I want to be able to discuss freely with my treating physician my intention of hastening my death through the consumption of drugs prescribed for that purpose.

Mr. Kingsley subscribed to a declaration that included the following:

At this time I have almost no immune system function. . . . My first major illness associated with AIDS was cryptosporidiosis, a parasitic infection which caused me severe fevers and diarrhea and associated pain, suffering and exhaustion. . . . I also suffer from cytomegalovirus ("CMV") retinitis, an AIDS-related virus which attacks the retina and causes blindness. To date I have become almost completely blind in my left eye. I am at risk of losing my sight altogether from this condition. . . . I also suffer from toxoplasmosis, a parasitic infection which has caused lesions to develop on my brain. . . . I . . . take daily infusions of cytovene for the . . . retinitis condition. This medication, administered for an hour through a Hickman tube which is connected to an artery in my chest, prevents me from ever taking showers and makes simple routine functions burdensome. In addition, I inject my leg daily with neupogen to combat the deficient white cell count in my blood. The daily injection of this medication is extremely painful. . . . At this point it is clear to me, based

on the advice of my doctors, that I am in the terminal phase of [AIDS]. . . . It is my desire that my physician prescribe suitable drugs for me to consume for the purpose of hastening my death when and if my suffering becomes intolerable.

In his declaration, Mr. Barth stated:
In May 1992, I developed a Kaposi's sarcoma skin lesion. This was my first major illness associated with AIDS. I underwent radiation and chemotherapy to treat this cancer. . . . In September 1993, I was diagnosed with cytomegalovirus ("CMV") in my stomach and colon which caused severe diarrhea, fevers and wasting. . . . In February 1994, I was diagnosed with microsporidiosis, a parasitic infection for which there is effectively no treatment. . . . At approximately the same time, I contracted AIDS-related pneumonia. The pneumonia's infusion therapy treatment was so extremely toxic that I vomited with each infusion. . . . In March 1994, I was diagnosed with cryptosporidiosis, a parasitic infection which has caused severe diarrhea, sometimes producing 20 stools a day, extreme abdominal pain, nausea and additional significant wasting. I have begun to lose bowel control. . . . For each of these conditions I have undergone a variety of medical treatments, each of which has had significant adverse side effects. . . . While I have tolerated some [nightly intravenous] feedings, I am unwilling to accept this for an extended period of time . . . I understand that there are no cures. . . . I can no longer endure the pain and suffering . . . and I want to have drugs available for the purpose of hastening my death.

A second amended complaint was filed on October 20, 1994. The parties, allegations and prayer for relief were the same as those contained in the first amended complaint, except that Robert M. Morgenthau, District Attorney of New York County, was added as a defendant in his official capacity. Both Dr. Grossman and Dr. Klagsbrun practice medicine in New York City, and Mr. Morgenthau is responsible for the prosecution of crimes occurring in New York County. The physician plaintiffs each filed second supplemental declarations on November 28, 1994, in support of the motion for a preliminary injunction. Each stated that he was currently treating mentally competent, terminally-ill patients who desired to hasten their deaths by self-administering drugs to be provided by the physicians "if and when medically and psychiatrically appropriate." These patients, according to the physicians, understood "their condition, diagnosis, and prognosis and wish[ed] to avoid prolonged suffering by hastening their deaths if and when their suffering [became] intolerable." None of the three terminally-ill plaintiffs named in the original complaint survived to the date of the district court's decision.

Turning to the equal protection issue, the district court identified a reasonable and rational basis for the distinction drawn by New York law between the refusal of treatment at the hands of physicians and physician assisted suicide:

> [I]t is hardly unreasonable or irrational for the State to recognize a difference between allowing nature to take its course, even in the most severe situations, and intentionally using an artificial death-producing device. The State has obvious legitimate interests in preserving life, and in protecting vulnerable persons. The State has the further right to determine how these crucial interests are to be treated when the issue is posed as to whether a physician can assist a patient in committing suicide.

Id. at 84-85. Accordingly, the court held "that plaintiffs have not shown a violation of the Equal Protection Clause of the Fourteenth Amendment." Id. at 85.

Discussion
I. Justiciability

As they did in the district court, the state defendants contend on appeal that this action does not present a justiciable case or controversy. We reject this contention.

In Babbitt v. United Farm Workers Nat'l Union, 442 U.S. 289, 99 S.Ct. 2301, 60 L.Ed.2d 895 (1979), the Supreme Court was faced with a constitutional challenge to an Arizona farm labor statute. The Court stated that, when contesting the constitutionality of a state criminal statute, it is not necessary that the plaintiff first expose himself to actual prosecution. Id. at 298, 99 S.Ct. at 2308–09.

Rather,

> [w]hen the plaintiff has alleged an intention to engage in a course of conduct arguably affected with a constitutional interest, but proscribed by a statute, and there exists a credible threat of prosecution thereunder, he "should not be required to await and undergo a criminal prosecution as the sole means of seeking relief."

Id. (quoting Doe v. Bolton, 410 U.S. 179, 188, 93 S.Ct. 739, 745, 35 L.Ed.2d 201 (1973)). The Court in Doe held that plaintiff physicians had presented a justiciable controversy despite the fact that none had been threatened with prosecution. 410 U.S. at 188, 93 S.Ct. at 745–46. The law that the physicians challenged was a criminal statute that directly criminalized the physician's participation in abortion. Accordingly, a sufficiently concrete controversy was presented.

[1] The same principles lead to the conclusion that there is a case or controversy at issue here. Dr. Quill has had a criminal proceeding instituted against him in the past, and the state nowhere disclaims an intent to repeat a prosecution in the event of further assisted suicides. The other two physician plaintiffs also face the threat of criminal prosecution. Like the physicians in Doe, they "should not be required to await and undergo a criminal prosecution as the sole means of seeking relief." Finally, under Doe, the physicians may raise the rights of their terminally-ill patients. See id.

II. Substantive Due Process
Plaintiffs argue for a right to assisted suicide as a fundamental liberty under the substantive component of the Due Process Clause of the Fourteenth Amendment. This Clause assures the citizenry that any deprivation of life, liberty or property by a state will be attended by appropriate legal processes. However,

> despite the language of the Due Process Clause[ ] of the . . . Fourteenth Amendment[ ], which appears to focus only on the processes by which life, liberty, or property is taken, the cases are legion in which th[at] Clause [ ] ha[s] been interpreted to have substantive content, subsuming rights that to a great extent are immune from . . . state regulation or proscription. Among such cases are those

recognizing rights that have little or no textual support in the constitutional language.

Bowers v. Hardwick, 478 U.S. 186, 191, 106 S.Ct. 2841, 2844, 92 L.Ed.2d 140 (1986).

[2][3][4][5] Rights that have no textual support in the language of the Constitution but qualify for heightened judicial protection include fundamental liberties so "implicit in the concept of ordered liberty" that "neither liberty nor justice would exist if they were sacrificed." Palko v. Connecticut, 302 U.S. 319, 325–26, 58 S.Ct. 149, 152, 82 L.Ed. 288 (1937). Fundamental liberties also have been described as those that are "deeply rooted in this Nation's history and tradition." Moore v. City of East Cleveland, 431 U.S. 494, 503, 97 S.Ct. 1932, 1938, 52 L.Ed.2d 531 (1977); see also Griswold v. Connecticut, 381 U.S. 479, 506, 85 S.Ct. 1678, 1693–94, 14 L.Ed.2d 510 (1965) (White, J., concurring). It is well settled that the state must not infringe fundamental liberty interests unless the infringement is narrowly tailored to serve a compelling state interest. Reno v. Flores, 507 U.S. 292, 301–03, 113 S.Ct. 1439, 1447, 123 L.Ed.2d 1 (1993). The list of rights the Supreme Court has actually or impliedly identified as fundamental, and therefore qualified for heightened judicial protection, include the fundamental guarantees of the Bill of Rights as well as the following: freedom of association; the right to participate in the electoral process and to vote; the right to travel interstate; the right to fairness in the criminal process; the right to procedural fairness in regard to claims for governmental deprivations of life, liberty or property; and the right to privacy. 2 Ronald D. Rotunda & John E. Nowak, Treatise on Constitutional Law § 15.7, at 434–36 (2d ed.1992). The right of privacy has been held to encompass personal decisions relating to marriage, procreation, family relationships, child rearing and education, contraception and abortion. See Carey v. Population Servs. Int'l, 431 U.S. 678, 684–85, 97 S.Ct. 2010, 2015–16, 52 L.Ed.2d 675 (1977). While the Constitution does not, of course, include any explicit mention of the right of privacy, this right has been recognized as encompassed by the Fourteenth Amendment's Due Process Clause. Id. at 684, 97 S.Ct. at 2015–16. Nevertheless, the Supreme Court has been reluctant to further

expand this particular list of federal rights, and it would be most speculative for a lower court to do so. See Rotunda & Nowak, Treatise on Constitutional Law, supra, § 15.7, at 433–37.

In any event, the Supreme Court has drawn a line, albeit a shaky one, on the expansion of fundamental rights that are without support in the text of the Constitution. In Bowers, the Supreme Court framed the issue as "whether the Federal Constitution confers a fundamental right upon homosexuals to engage in sodomy and hence invalidates the laws of the many States that still make such conduct illegal and have done so for a very long time." 478 U.S. at 190, 106 S.Ct. at 2843. Holding that there was no fundamental right to engage in consensual sodomy, the Court noted that the statutes proscribing such conduct had "ancient roots." Id. at 192, 106 S.Ct. at 2844–45. The Court noted that sodomy was a common law criminal offense, forbidden by the laws of the original 13 states when they ratified the Bill of Rights, and that 25 states and the District of Columbia still penalize sodomy performed in private by consenting adults. Id. at 192–93, 106 S.Ct. at 2844–46.

As in Bowers, the statutes plaintiffs seek to declare unconstitutional here cannot be said to infringe upon any fundamental right or liberty. As in Bowers, the right contended for here cannot be considered so implicit in our understanding of ordered liberty that neither justice nor liberty would exist if it were sacrificed. Nor can it be said that the right to assisted suicide claimed by plaintiffs is deeply rooted in the nation's traditions and history. Indeed, the very opposite is true.

In rejecting the due process–fundamental rights argument of the plaintiffs, we are mindful of the admonition of the Supreme Court:

> Nor are we inclined to take a more expansive view of our authority to discover new fundamental rights imbedded in the Due Process Clause. The Court is most vulnerable and comes nearest to illegitimacy when it deals with judge-made constitutional law having little or no cognizable roots in the language or design of the Constitution.

Bowers, 478 U.S. at 194, 106 S.Ct. at 2846. The right to assisted suicide finds no cognizable basis in the Constitution's language or design, even in the very limited cases of those competent persons who, in the final stages of terminal illness, seek the right to hasten death. We therefore decline the plaintiffs' invitation to identify a new fundamental right, in the absence of a clear direction from the Court whose precedents we are bound to follow.

The right to refuse medical treatment long has been recognized in New York. In 1914 Judge Cardozo wrote that, under New York law, "[e]very human being of adult years and sound mind has a right to determine what shall be done with his own body." Schloendorff v. Society of New York Hosp., 211 N.Y. 125, 129, 105 N.E. 92 (1914). In 1981, the New York Court of Appeals held that this right extended to the withdrawal of life-support systems. In re Eichner (decided with In re Storar), 52 N.Y.2d 363, 438 N.Y.S.2d 266, 420 N.E.2d 64, cert. denied, 454 U.S. 858, 102 S.Ct. 309, 70 L.Ed.2d 153 (1981). The Eichner case involved a terminally-ill, 83-year-old patient whose guardian ultimately was authorized to withdraw the patient's respirator. The Court of Appeals determined that the guardian had proved by clear and convincing evidence that the patient, prior to becoming incompetent due to illness, had consistently expressed his view that life should not be prolonged if there was no hope of recovery. Id. at 379–80, 438 N.Y.S.2d 266, 420 N.E.2d 64. In Storar, the companion case to Eichner, the Court of Appeals determined that a profoundly retarded, terminally-ill patient was incapable of making a decision to terminate blood transfusions. There, the patient was incapable of making a reasoned decision, having never been competent at any time in his life. Id. at 380, 438 N.Y.S.2d 266, 420 N.E.2d 64. In both these cases, the New York Court of Appeals recognized the right of a competent, terminally-ill patient to hasten his death upon proper proof of his desire to do so.

The Court of Appeals revisited the issue in Rivers v. Katz, 67 N.Y.2d 485, 504 N.Y.S.2d 74, 495 N.E.2d 337 (1986) (establishing the right of mentally incompetent persons to refuse certain drugs). In that case, the Court recognized the right to bring on death by refusing medical treatment not only as a "fundamental common-law right" but also as "coextensive with [a] patient's liberty interest protected by the due process clause of our State Constitution." Id. at 493, 504 N.Y.S.2d 74, 495 N.E.2d 337. The following language was included in the opinion:

In our system of a free government, where notions of individual autonomy and free choice are cherished, it is the individual who must have the final say in respect to decisions regarding his medical treatment in order to insure that the greatest possible protection is accorded his autonomy and freedom from unwanted interference with the furtherance of his own desires.

Id.

After these cases were decided, the New York legislature placed its imprimatur upon the right of competent citizens to hasten death by refusing medical treatment and by directing physicians to remove life-support systems already in place. In 1987, the legislature enacted Article 29-B of the New York Public Health Law, entitled "Orders Not to Resuscitate." N.Y. Pub. Health Law §§ 2960–79 (McKinney 1993). The Article provides that an "adult with capacity" may direct the issuance of an order not to resuscitate. § 2964. "Order not to resuscitate" is defined as "an order not to attempt cardiopulmonary resuscitation in the event a patient suffers cardiac or respiratory arrest." § 2961(17). "Cardiopulmonary resuscitation" is defined as "measures . . . to restore cardiac function or to support ventilation in the event of a cardiac or respiratory arrest." § 2961(4). An elaborate statutory scheme is in place, and it provides, among other things, for surrogate decision making, § 2965, revocation of consent, § 2969, physician review, § 2970, dispute mediation, § 2972, and judicial review, § 2973.

In 1990, the New York legislature enacted Article 29-C of the Public Health Law, entitled "Health Care Agents and Proxies." N.Y. Pub. Health Law §§ 2980–94 (McKinney 1993). This statute allows for a person to sign a health care proxy, § 2981, for the purpose of appointing an agent with "authority to make any and all health care decisions on the principal's behalf that the principal could make." § 2982(1). These decisions include those relating to the administration of artificial nutrition and hydration, provided the wishes of the principal are known to the agent. § 2982(2). The agent's decision is made "[a]fter consultation with a licensed physician, registered nurse, licensed clinical psychologist or certified social worker." Id. Accordingly, a patient has the right to hasten death by empowering an agent to require a physician to withdraw life-support systems. The proxy statute also presents a detailed scheme, with provisions for a determination that the principal lacks capacity to make health care decisions, for such a determination to be made only by the attending physician in consultation with another physician "[f]or a decision to withdraw or withhold life-sustaining treatment," § 2983, for provider's obligations, § 2984, for revocation, § 2985, and for special proceedings, § 2992, among other matters.

The concept that a competent person may order the removal of life-support systems found Supreme Court approval in Cruzan v. Director, Missouri Dep't of Health, 497 U.S. 261, 110 S.Ct. 2841, 111 L.Ed.2d 224 (1990). There the Court upheld a determination of the Missouri Supreme Court that required proof by clear and convincing evidence of a patient's desire for the withdrawal of life-sustaining equipment. The patient in that case, Nancy Cruzan, was in a persistent vegetative state as the result of injuries sustained in an automobile accident. Her parents sought court approval in the State of Missouri to terminate the artificial nutrition and hydration with which she was supplied at the state hospital where she was confined. The hospital employees refused to withdraw the life-support systems, without which Cruzan would suffer certain death. The trial court authorized the withdrawal after finding that Cruzan had expressed some years before to a housemate friend some thoughts that suggested she would not wish to live on a life-support system. The trial court also found that one in Cruzan's condition had a fundamental right to refuse death-prolonging procedures.

The Missouri Supreme Court, in reversing the trial court, refused to find a broad right of privacy in the state constitution that would support a right to refuse treatment. Moreover, that court doubted that such a right existed under the United States Constitution. It did identify a state policy in the Missouri Living Will Statute favoring the preservation of life and concluded that, in the absence of compliance with the statute's formalities or clear and convincing evidence of the patient's choice, no person could order the withdrawal of medical life-support services.

In affirming the Missouri Supreme Court, the United States Supreme Court stated: "The principle that a competent person has a constitutionally protected liberty interest in refusing unwanted medical treatment may be inferred from our prior decisions." Id. at 278, 110 S.Ct. at 2851. The Court noted that the inquiry is not ended by the identification of a liberty interest, because there also must be a balancing of the state interests and the individual's liberty interests before there can be a determination that constitutional rights have been violated. Id. at 279, 110 S.Ct. at 2851-52. The Court all but made that determination in the course of the following analysis:

> Petitioners insist that under the general holdings of our cases, the forced administration of life-sustaining medical treatment, and even of artificially-delivered food and water essential to life, would implicate a competent person's liberty interest. Although we think the logic of the cases discussed above would embrace such a liberty interest, the dramatic consequences involved in refusal of such treatment would inform the inquiry as to whether the deprivation of that interest is constitutionally permissible. But for purposes of this case, we assume that the United States Constitution would grant a competent person a constitutionally protected right to refuse lifesaving hydration and nutrition.

Id.

The Court went on to find that Missouri allowed a surrogate to "act for the patient in electing to have hydration and nutrition withdrawn in such a way as to cause death," subject to "a procedural safeguard to assure that the action of the surrogate conforms as best it may to the wishes expressed by the patient while competent." Id. at 280, 110 S.Ct. at 2852. The Court then held that the procedural safeguard or requirement imposed by Missouri—the heightened evidentiary requirement that the incompetent's wishes be proved by clear and convincing evidence—was not forbidden by the United States Constitution. Id. at 280–82, 110 S.Ct. at 2852–53.

In view of the foregoing, it seems clear that New York does not treat similarly circumstanced persons alike: those in the final stages of terminal illness who are on life-support systems are allowed to hasten their deaths by directing the removal of such systems; but those who are similarly situated, except for the previous attachment of life-sustaining equipment, are not allowed to hasten death by self-administering prescribed drugs. The district judge has identified "a difference between allowing nature to take its course, even in the most severe situations, and intentionally using an artificial death-producing device." Quill, 870 F.Supp. at 84. But Justice Scalia, for one, has remarked upon "the irrelevance of the action-inaction distinction," noting that "the cause of death in both cases is the suicide's conscious decision to 'pu[t] an end to his own existence.' " Cruzan, 497 U.S. at 296–297, 110 S.Ct. at 2861.

Indeed, there is nothing "natural" about causing death by means other than the original illness or its complications. The withdrawal of nutrition brings on death by starvation, the withdrawal of hydration brings on death by dehydration, and the withdrawal of ventilation brings about respiratory failure. By ordering the discontinuance of these artificial life-sustaining processes or refusing to accept them in the first place, a patient hastens his death by means that are not natural in any sense. It certainly cannot be said that the death that immediately ensues is the natural result of the progression of the disease or condition from which the patient suffers.

Moreover, the writing of a prescription to hasten death, after consultation with a patient, involves a far less active role for the physician than is required in bringing about death through asphyxiation, starvation and/or dehydration. Withdrawal of life support requires physicians or those acting at their direction physically to remove equipment and, often, to administer palliative drugs which may themselves contribute to death. The ending of life by these means is nothing more nor less than assisted suicide. It simply cannot be said that those mentally competent, terminally-ill persons who seek to hasten death but whose treatment does not include life support are treated equally.

A finding of unequal treatment does not, of course, end the inquiry, unless it is determined that the inequality is not rationally related to some legitimate state interest. The burden is upon the plaintiffs to demonstrate irrationality. See Kadrmas, 487 U.S. at 463, 108 S.Ct. at 2490. At oral argument and in its brief, the state's contention has been that its principal interest is in preserving the life of all its citizens at all times and under all conditions. But what interest can the state possibly have in requiring the prolongation of a life that is all but ended? Surely, the state's interest lessens as the potential for life diminishes. See In re Quinlan, 70 N.J. 10, 41, 355 A.2d 647, cert. denied, 429 U.S. 922, 97 S.Ct. 319, 50 L.Ed.2d 289 (1976). And what business is it of the state to require the continuation of agony when the result is imminent and inevitable? What concern prompts the state to interfere with a mentally competent patient's "right to define [his] own concept of existence, of meaning, of the universe, and of the mystery of human life," Planned Parenthood v. Casey, 505 U.S. 833, 851, 112 S.Ct. 2791, 2807, 120 L.Ed.2d 674 (1992), when the patient seeks to have drugs prescribed to end life during the final stages of a terminal illness? The greatly reduced interest of the state in preserving life compels the answer to these questions: "None."

The New York statutes prohibiting assisted suicide, which are similar to the Washington statute, do not serve any of the state interests noted, in view of the statutory and common law schemes allowing suicide through the withdrawal of life-sustaining treatment. Physicians do not fulfill the role of "killer" by prescribing drugs to hasten death any more than they do by disconnecting life-support systems. Likewise, "psychological pressure" can be applied just as much upon the elderly and infirm to consent to withdrawal of life-sustaining equipment as to take drugs to hasten death. There is no clear indication that there has been any problem in regard to the former, and there should be none as to the latter. In any event, the state of New York may establish rules and procedures to assure that all choices are free of such pressures. With respect to the protection of minorities, the poor and the non-mentally handicapped, it suffices to say that these classes of persons are entitled to treatment equal to that afforded to all those who now may hasten death by means of life-support withdrawal. In point of fact, these persons themselves are entitled to hasten death by requesting such withdrawal and should be free to do so by requesting appropriate medication to terminate life during the final stages of terminal illness.

As to the interest in avoiding abuse similar to that occurring in the Netherlands, it seems clear that some physicians there practice nonvoluntary euthanasia, although it is not legal to do so. When Death Is Sought, supra, at 133–34. The plaintiffs here do not argue for euthanasia at all but for assisted suicide for terminally-ill, mentally competent patients, who would self-administer the lethal drugs. It is difficult to see how the relief the plaintiffs seek would lead to the abuses found in the Netherlands. Moreover, note should be taken of the fact that the Royal Dutch Medical Association recently adopted new guidelines for those physicians who choose to accede to the wishes of patients to hasten death. Under the new guidelines, patients must self-administer drugs whenever possible, and physicians must obtain a second opinion from another physician who has no relationship with the requesting physician or his patient. Marlise Simons, Dutch Doctors to Tighten Rules on Mercy Killings, N.Y. Times, Sept. 11, 1995, at A3.

There are those who use the terms "assisted suicide" and "euthanasia" interchangeably. See Patricia A. Unz, Note, Euthanasia: A Constitutionally Protected Peaceful Death, 37 N.Y.L. Sch. L.Rev. 439, 439 n. 8 (1992). While

euthanasia is derived from the Greek words meaning "good death," id. at 441, it seems clear that most states, including New York, make a distinction between the two acts. See When Death Is Sought, supra, at 63. In euthanasia, one causes the death of another by direct and intentional acts. Id. Accordingly, euthanasia falls within the definition of murder in New York. See N.Y. Penal Law § 125.25(1) (McKinney 1987).

Finally, it seems clear that most physicians would agree on the definition of "terminally ill," at least for the purpose of the relief that plaintiffs seek. The plaintiffs seek to hasten death only where a patient is in the "final stages" of "terminal illness," and it seems even more certain that physicians would agree on when this condition occurs. Physicians are accustomed to advising patients and their families in this regard and frequently do so when decisions are to be made regarding the furnishing or withdrawal of life-support systems. Again, New York may define that stage of illness with greater particularity, require the opinion of more than one physician or impose any other obligation upon patients and physicians who collaborate in hastening death.

For example, the state might take steps to assure the competence of prescribing physicians by imposing education and training qualifications, . . .

Case Question
Why is assisted suicide *not* constitutionally protected?

Assignment 2.3

Prepare a case brief for *Quill v. Vacco*.

ETHICAL NOTE

While much discussion is given to the question of legal ethics of lawyers and their staffs, the courts are also bound by ethical principles. Judges must abide by the same type of conduct as other legal professionals regarding such issues as confidentiality, conflict of interest, and competence. In particular, the jurist has the burden of absolute objectivity.

Everyone has beliefs and value systems that guide his or her daily conduct both personally and professionally. However, judges are frequently presented with authority over the rights of individuals in emotionally charged issues. Judges have an ethical obligation to apply the law and not their personal opinion to each case.

Question

Assume that a state law requires parental or judicial permission for a minor to obtain an abortion. You are a judge with a strong opinion on abortion. How should you handle a case when a 16-year-old girl comes to you for judicial approval and her parents vehemently oppose abortion?

CHAPTER SUMMARY

This chapter has explored the judicial branch of the American legal system. The judicial system has several unique characteristics. The judicial branch of government deals with specific cases on an individual and direct basis. It has the authority to overrule an act of the legislature or the executive branch if the act violates the Constitution. When a dispute arises and no statutory law exists, the judicial branch has power to create law and provide an immediate resolution to the dispute.

The judicial system is set up to clarify and protect the law. The courts must determine whether a broadly written statute or existing precedent applies to an individual circumstance. The courts also have the duty to uphold the U.S. Constitution and to see that the other branches of state and federal government honor the Constitution.

Because state and federal governments operate independently, each has its own judicial system to interpret and apply law. As long as the states establish and apply only law that is consistent with the Constitution of the United States, they are free to enact and enforce any law that is necessary for an orderly society.

The federal judicial system is made up of three tiers. The U.S. District Courts, where cases are generally filed and trials are held, occupy the lowest tier. The next level is made up of the U.S. Courts of Appeals, which determine whether any error was committed by the U.S. District Court (trial court) in its determination of the dispute. Finally, the U.S. Supreme Court issues the final statement on disputes that claim that the Constitution has been violated. The states follow a similar type of structure, with approximately half incorporating the three-tiered system and the remaining half incorporating a two-tiered system by combining the functions of the court of appeals and the supreme court.

Many appellate (and some trial) judicial opinions are published for future reference. They contain certain information that allows an adequate comparison between the opinion and a case presently before a court. This information includes relevant facts, the actual issue in the dispute, the authority used to determine the dispute, and the manner in which the authority was applied.

Chapter 3 examines the legislative system in some detail. Chapter 4 addresses the functions of the executive branch. It is important to keep in mind that each branch of government has an effect on the law in a distinct way that complements the other two branches.

REVIEW QUESTIONS

1. List three characteristics that are present only in judicial law.
2. What are the two primary functions of judicial law?
3. Describe the three types of case law.
4. How is a trial court different from an appellate court?
5. Describe the federal court system.
6. Discuss the relationship among the various U.S. Courts of Appeals.
7. Describe the two types of state court structures.
8. Define legal analysis.
9. Define the various elements of a judicial opinion.
10. Explain the process and benefit of case analysis.

CHAPTER TERMS

Appellate Court
Federal Court

Legal Analysis
State Court

Trial Court

NOTES

1. *Black's Law Dictionary* (St. Paul: West, 1979).
2. Opinion of the Justices, 280 Ala. 653, 197 So.2d 456 (1967).
3. William Statsky, *Legal Thesaurus/Dictionary* (St. Paul: West, 1982).
4. Id.
5. *Black's Law Dictionary.*
6. 28 U.S.C. Rules of the Supreme Court, Rule 9.
7. Id.
8. Id., at Rule 10.
9. 28 U.S.C. Rules of Appellate Procedure, Rule 1,3.
10. Id., at Rules 3 and 4.

CHAPTER 3

Legislation

CHAPTER OBJECTIVES

After reading this chapter, you should be able to

- *Distinguish statutory law from judicial law.*

- *Describe the method of election of members to both houses of Congress.*

- *Describe the process of legislation.*

- *Discuss the effect of the presidential veto power on legislation.*

- *Discuss the publication process of new legislation.*

- *Describe the role of the lobbyist.*

- *Describe the role of the judiciary with respect to statutory law.*

THE LEGISLATIVE BRANCH

A primary source of U.S. law is legislation enacted by the federal legislative branch known as the Congress. (Since the legislative process at the state level is generally similar to the federal process, this chapter focuses on legislation by the U.S. Congress.) Although the judicial and executive branches make significant contributions to law in the American legal system, often they are responding to actions already taken by the legislature. A primary responsibility of the judicial branch is to interpret and apply the laws. According to the Constitution, the executive branch has the general task to faithfully execute the Constitution and the laws passed by Congress.

The authority of Congress is stated with specificity in Article I of the Constitution. Congress has the power to raise, through taxation, revenues that are used to support governmental functions. Congress also has the authority to determine the manner in which these revenues are to be spent. Another major power of Congress—and the subject of much legislation—is the authority to regulate commerce. This authority generally extends to all aspects of production, sale, and transfer of interstate commerce. Any commerce that is totally contained within a state and any other subject not addressed in the Constitution are the exclusive subject of state law. Congress also has the authority to raise and support armies and to declare and support wars.

Perhaps the most significant power of the Congress is the authority to establish such law as is necessary and proper to achieve congressional objectives. This broad authority vests in Congress the power to pass virtually any legislation that (1) is constitutional, (2) will facilitate the orderly operation of the government, and (3) will protect the constitutional rights of the citizens in such matters as health, safety, welfare, and personal freedoms. Congress has allowed for the creation of administrative agencies (see Chapter 4) to assist in the delivery of legal rights of the people.

The legislative branch at the federal level is a bicameral system (a two-part body), as provided for in Article I of the Constitution. The House of Representatives consists of persons elected based on the population in geographical districts. This component of the legislature guarantees that all people are represented whether they live in a heavily populated area or a small, rural district. The Senate comprises two senators from each state elected by the voters of the state. The body of the Senate guarantees that all states are represented equally regardless of size, population, or economical strength.

Representative

A person elected to the House of Representatives, which is designed to ensure equal representation of all citizens.

The members of the House of Representatives are elected every two years. A **representative** must be at least 25 years old, have been a U.S. citizen for at least seven years, and reside in the state that he or she is representing. The number of representatives for each state is based on the decennial census of the population. Invariably, with each census, as population moves and increases, the number of representatives for each state varies. However, the Constitution guarantees that there be at least one representative for each state.

The members of the Senate are elected to six-year terms. The elections of **senators** from the various states are staggered so that every two years one third of the seats in the Senate come up for election. A U.S. senator must be at least 30 years old, a citizen of the United States for nine years, and a resident of the state he or she is elected to represent.

The Senate and the House of Representatives function on a separate but related basis. To avoid duplicity of work, there are joint committees comprising members from both houses who work together to draft laws that will meet approval by the entire Congress. Although many laws proceed individually through the houses for passage or defeat, to enact law, approval is required by a majority of both houses.

Senator

A person elected to the Senate, which is designed to ensure equal representation of all states.

Assignment 3.1

Answer the following questions by referring to the U.S. Constitution in Appendix A. Indicate the section of the Constitution in which you find the answer.

1. Can legislative law be passed by the executive or judicial branch as well as by Congress?
2. Under what circumstances can a member of Congress be arrested while Congress is in session?
3. Who is the president of the Senate?
4. What is the length of term of a member of the House of Representatives?
5. How many votes does each member of the Senate have?
6. Has Congress ever been prevented from limiting immigration into the United States?
7. When can the president of the Senate vote on an issue?
8. If a member of the House of Representatives dies in office, how is the position filled until the next election?
9. What is required to expel a member of Congress?
10. Who in government has the actual authority to declare war?

THE PURPOSE OF LEGISLATION

In general, legislation serves three purposes, and the particular purpose a statute serves strongly influences the statute's content and scope. A primary purpose of the American democratic system of government is to provide laws that will protect society from what is unsafe for or unacceptable to the majority of citizens. Generally, statutes serve to protect the citizens as a whole from unnecessary physical, social, and financial dangers. Law as a protective measure began with the original ten amendments to the Constitution, known as the Bill of Rights. From the very start, specific laws were established to protect the people from unnecessary governmental influence or intrusion into their private lives. The Bill of Rights ensures people the right to live freely and to comment and produce change when laws are established or enforced unfairly. Unfortunately, it was some time before all races as well as women were identified as persons who were entitled to these basic rights. Also with the passage of time came additional constitutional amendments and statutes designed to provide protection from dangers that would interfere with other fundamental personal rights.

The protection of fundamental rights as put forth in the amendments to the Constitution is not the only way legislation protects the public. Many other laws serve another type of protective purpose. Any statute that sets out the type of conduct required of individuals protects the public from improper conduct by others. For example, something as simple as the statutes that govern motor vehicles serves an invaluable protective purpose. Without such laws, persons could drive as they pleased, and untold injuries and deaths could occur.

Many different types of laws serve a protective purpose. Laws that make it an offense to manufacture, sell, or distribute illegal drugs attempt to protect our society from an influence that can produce physical, financial, and social harm. Laws that ensure compensation to workers who are injured on the job protect such workers from being left physically disabled without funds to pay for adequate medical care. These statutes protect citizens not only from invasion of personal rights but also from injury to personal property.

Laws that serve as a protective measure come in a variety of forms and address many subjects that affect the order and members of society. There is, however, a common thread in all laws that serve a protective purpose. Protective laws are designed to set forth what people are entitled to expect as citizens of this country. Protective laws do exactly what their name implies: they protect what are considered to be the rights of the people to a safe and reasonable environment in which to live and work.

Legislative laws (statutes) can also serve a remedial purpose. A remedial statute has been defined as one that "provides a remedy or a means to enforce a right; a statute designed to correct an existing law or to redress an existing grievance."[1] As this definition indicates, remedial statutes are designed to cure something that has already gone wrong or caused injury. Occasionally, a remedial statute is one that supersedes a previous statute that was unfair or poorly drafted and resulted in injury or invasion of personal rights or property interests. One example of an extremely important remedial law is the Thirteenth Amendment, which states in part:

> AMENDMENT XIII, Section 1. Neither slavery nor involuntary servitude, except as a punishment for crime whereof the party shall have been duly convicted, shall exist within the United States, or any place subject to their jurisdiction.

With the ratification of this amendment to the Constitution, all previous decisions of courts and state and federal legislatures that permitted slavery were overruled. The amendment was the method of correcting laws that the majority of the people believed were wrong, unfair, and injurious to a large element of our society.

Another example of remedial legislation is the repeal of prohibition. Congress initially believed that the majority of the people wanted to be protected from the negative results associated with alcohol. With the Eighteenth Amendment, intoxicating liquor was outlawed. However, it became apparent in a very short time that this was not the opinion of the majority. Consequently, prohibition was repealed, and the sale of intoxicating liquor was legalized again by passage of the Twenty-first Amendment.

Remedial law is not always in the form of a constitutional amendment. More often, remedial laws are federal or state laws that are used to adjust law to the needs of the society. (They would fall under the heading of sociological theory, discussed in Chapter 1.) Familiar examples of such statutes are state workers' compensation laws. Every state has enacted laws that provide that an employer will be responsible for costs associated with the injuries of an employee if the injuries occur while the employee is performing duties of employment. Before these laws, many people injured on the job lost their income at the time of the injury. They could not pay their medical bills, and some were forced into poverty. Employees were left with no alternative but to file a formal lawsuit against their employers. Some verdicts were significant enough to put the employer out of business altogether. Those employers who remained in business were rarely willing to allow the employee to return to work after suit was filed.

The burden on individuals and the economy was increasingly great. The response was to pass workers' compensation laws in every state. Under workers' compensation laws, the employee's medical bills are covered. In addition, if disputes arise between the employee and the employer (and/or the employer's insurance company) as to how much money is necessary to compensate the employee for the injury, the law contains a legislative provision for a hearing process. The employee's medical bills can be paid, the employee is entitled to a living allowance while off work, the courts rarely become involved, and usually the employee can return to the job after recovery. With the advent of these laws, many employers took out insurance to cover the costs of medical and financial assistance to injured employees.

Workers' compensation laws are examples of both protective and remedial statutes. On the one hand, a statute may set out the rights that citizens are entitled to enjoy. At the same time, a statute may correct a situation that was dealt with ineffectively by the legal system or change a law that is considered unfair by the majority.

A third purpose that legislation serves is to ensure that protective and remedial statutes are available and applied to all citizens in the same way.[2] Such laws are known as procedural laws. Subsequent chapters on civil and criminal procedure discuss the need and actual application of procedural laws. For now, we will deal with procedural laws only in terms of the purpose they serve.

If it were not for procedural laws, citizens would have no effective way of enforcing the rights to which they are entitled. Procedural laws give specific directions on everything from how to initiate a lawsuit to how a trial is to be conducted. They even explain how to get a bill introduced to the legislature for consideration as law. Occasionally, people complain that the procedural laws are too numerous and that the legal system is more concerned with procedures than with resolving issues. In reality, our legal system guarantees all citizens the right to be heard. Consequently, hundreds of thousands of lawsuits are filed every year. All people in the nation have the right to submit their disputes to state and federal legislators, judges, and members of the executive branches of government. Given the size of their task, the procedural laws are extremely efficient.

Procedural laws are not designed solely to deal with great numbers of people. Rather, their true purpose is to ensure that everyone can enjoy the same basic rights in the legal system. All persons are entitled to have their case heard by a judicial officer. All are entitled to voice their opinion to elected delegates in Congress. All persons affected by law are entitled to dispute that law. The procedural laws make it possible for the orderly expression of rights to occur in a fair setting and provide for fair treatment to all parties in a dispute. Without procedural laws, there would be no clear, consistent, and fair method of seeking assistance from or input to the legal system.

Assignment 3.2

> Examine the statutory language in Figure 3.1 and determine whether the purpose of each statute is protective, procedural, or remedial.

THE LEGISLATIVE PROCESS

Each state has a somewhat different method of enacting statutes. With the exception of a few procedural details, the basic legislative process has remained the same in the federal government since 1787, when the U.S. Constitution was enacted. Article I, Section 7, of the Constitution is quite specific regarding this (see Appendix A).

Bills

Bill

Proposed law presented to the legislature for consideration.

When a proposed law is introduced to the legislature, it is called a **bill.** The Constitution requires that revenue-raising bills be initially introduced in the House of Representatives. Other bills may be initiated in either house of Congress. A bill is sponsored by a legislator who introduces it. When a bill is formally proposed as legislation, it is registered and assigned a number. Often, the bill is also known by the name of the legislators who introduce it, for example, the Graham Rudman Act. Officially, however, the statute is referenced in publications by its assigned number. As the bill progresses through the legislative

FIGURE 3.1 Statutory Excerpts

INDIANA RULES OF TRIAL PROCEDURE
II. COMMENCEMENT OF ACTION; SERVICE OF PROCESS, PLEADINGS, MOTIONS AND ORDERS
TRIAL RULE 4. PROCESS

(A) JURISDICTION Over Parties or Persons—In General. The court acquires JURISDICTION over a party or person who under these RULES commences or joins in the action, is served with summons or enters an appearance, or who is subjected to the power of the court under any other law.

(B) Preparation of Summons and Praecipe. Contemporaneously with the filing of the complaint or equivalent pleading, the person seeking SERVICE or his attorney shall promptly prepare and furnish to the clerk as many copies of the complaint and summons as are necessary. The clerk shall examine, date, sign, and affix his seal to the summons and thereupon issue and deliver the papers to the appropriate person for SERVICE. Affidavits, requests, and any other information relating to the summons and its SERVICE as required or permitted by these RULES shall be included in a praecipe attached to or entered upon the summons. Such praecipe shall be deemed to be a part of the summons for purposes of these RULES. Separate or additional summons shall, as provided by these RULES, be issued by the clerk at any time upon proper request of the person seeking SERVICE or his attorney.

(C) Form of Summons. The summons shall contain:

(1) The name and address of the person on whom the SERVICE is to be effected;

(2) The name of the court and the cause number assigned to the case;

(3) The title of the case as shown by the complaint, but, if there are multiple parties, the title may be shortened to include only the first named plaintiff and defendant with an appropriate indication that there are additional parties;

(4) The name, address, and telephone number of the attorney for the person seeking SERVICE;

(5) The time within which these RULES require the person being served to respond, and a clear statement that in case of his failure to do so, judgment by default may be rendered against him for the relief demanded in the complaint.

The summons may also contain any additional information which will facilitate proper SERVICE.

(D) Designation of Manner of SERVICE. The person seeking SERVICE or his attorney may designate the manner of SERVICE upon the summons. If not so designated, the clerk shall cause SERVICE to be made by mail or other public means provided the mailing address of the person to be served is indicated in the summons or can be determined. If a mailing address is not furnished or cannot be determined or if SERVICE by mail or other public means is returned without acceptance, the complaint and summons shall promptly be delivered to the sheriff or his deputy who, unless otherwise directed, shall serve the summons.

(E) Summons and Complaint Served Together—Exceptions. The summons and complaint shall be served together unless otherwise ordered by the court. When SERVICE of summons is made by publication, the complaint shall not be published. When JURISDICTION over a party is dependent upon SERVICE of PROCESS by publication or by his appearance, summons and complaint shall be deemed to have been served at the end of the day of last required publication in the case of SERVICE by publication, and at the time of appearance in JURISDICTION acquired by appearance. Whenever the summons and complaint are not served or published together, the summons shall contain the full, unabbreviated title of the case.

ARKANSAS CODE

15-4-502. Articles of incorporation—Contents.:

(a) The articles of incorporation shall state:

(1) The name of the corporation, which name shall include the name of the city, town, or county and the words "industrial development," and the word "corporation," "incorporated," "inc.," or "company." The name shall be such as to distinguish it from any other corporation organized and existing under the laws of this state;

(2) The purpose for which the corporation is formed;

(3) The names and addresses of the incorporators who shall serve as directors and manage the affairs of the corporation until its first annual meeting of members or until their successors are elected and qualified;

(4) The number of directors, not less than three (3), to be elected at the annual meetings of members;

(5) The address of its principal office and the name and address of its agent upon whom process may be served;

(6) The period of duration of the corporation, which may be perpetual;

(7) The terms and conditions upon which persons shall be admitted to membership in the corporation, but if expressly so stated, the determination of such matters may be reserved to the directors by the bylaws;

(8) Any provisions, not inconsistent with law, which the incorporators may choose to insert for the regulation of the business and the conduct of the affairs of the corporation.

(b) It shall not be necessary to set forth in the articles of incorporation any of the corporate powers enumerated in this act.

process, it carries the same number for identification until it is either voted into law or defeated.

Once a bill has been introduced, it is assigned to the appropriate committee of legislators for consideration of its contents and its potential ramifications as law. Congress has created a number of such continuing committees to study the need for legislation and proposed laws in specific areas of government, commerce, and other appropriate legislative subjects. At times, the bill will be revised while in committee with necessary additions or deletions to make it a complete and effective statute. After committee hearings, the bill is presented to the originating body of Congress (House of Representatives or Senate) for a vote by the legislators. The bill must pass by a majority vote before it can be sent to the corresponding body for consideration. Prior to a vote, the bill is discussed and debated by Congress. At this time, changes may be made in the language of the bill. Often such changes are necessary to gain the approval of a sufficient number of legislators to pass the bill.

If a bill succeeds by a majority vote in the body of Congress where it began, it moves on to the corresponding body. For example, if a bill is introduced in the House of Representatives and passes by a majority vote, the final version is then submitted to the Senate. If the bill passes by a majority in the corresponding body of Congress, it is forwarded to the president for approval or disapproval.

Veto

Presidential power to invalidate a law passed by a majority of Congress (two-thirds majority of each house is needed to override a veto).

At this point, the **veto** power of the president is exercised. The veto is a key element in the system of checks and balances. As mentioned in Chapter 1, each branch of government has a method to influence the other branches. Such a mechanism is designed to prevent one branch from obtaining too much power or acting in a way inconsistent with the Constitution. According to Article I of the U.S. Constitution, each bill that has received a majority vote in both houses of Congress shall be presented to the president. After the president receives a bill, under the Constitution, the bill must be acted upon within ten days (excluding Sundays).[3] If nothing is done during this time, the bill automatically becomes law. If the president signs the bill, the bill becomes law on the date indicated by Congress. If the president returns the bill with objections to the house where it originated, the bill is vetoed (rejected). Once a bill has been vetoed, a second vote can be taken. If each body of Congress approves the bill by at least a two-thirds majority (rather than by a simple majority), the bill becomes law regardless of the presidential veto. Figure 3.2 is a diagram of the legislative process.

In actuality, this method is quite effective. Congress passes those laws that the members believe to be the will of the people. If the president considers this belief to be misguided, the executive branch has the power to force Congress to reconsider the bill. However, if a significant majority of senators and representatives hold the position that the public contends the bill should become law, the veto can be overridden.

Sometimes a number of bills that address several aspects of one subject will be introduced to Congress as a package for legislation on that subject. Such a package of bills is known as an act. Other laws may be introduced individually or as additions or amendments to laws of an act that has been passed in a pre-

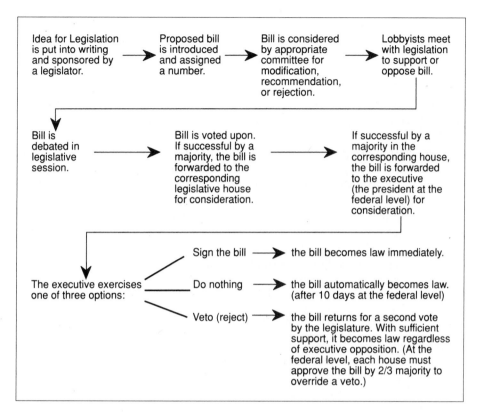

FIGURE 3.2

Typical Steps in
the Legislative
Process

vious session of Congress. Another type of bill has the sole purpose of repeal-
ing an existing law. Nevertheless, even this type of bill is assigned a number and,
if passed, is published in place of the law it reverses.

Constitutional Amendments

The process of passing a constitutional amendment is substantially similar to the
process of passing a bill. Because the Constitution is the ultimate law of the land,
an amendment must pass both houses by a two-thirds majority rather than the
typical simple majority. The amendment must then be approved by three-fourths
of the state legislatures before it is ratified and becomes part of the Constitution.
By placing such stringent requirements on constitutional amendments, it is extremely difficult to pass law that is not representative of the will of the people.

Lobbying

Throughout the legislative process, **lobbyists** make numerous contacts with the
legislators. Lobbyists are individuals who represent groups of citizens or industries
that have a special interest in certain bills. If a proposed bill is going to substantially
affect certain interests, groups often hire persons to lobby with the legislators to attempt to persuade them to vote in a particular way on the bill. The term originates

Lobbyist

Individual hired to
meet with legislators
regarding proposed
laws.

from the early days of our government when such persons would actually wait in the lobby of the buildings of Congress to speak with legislators.

Critics of lobbyists say that a few people unduly influence legislators who are supposed to represent the majority of the people. Proponents argue, however, that lobbyists in fact represent those people who stand to be directly affected by the legislation and that lobbying is a practical and effective method by which citizens' groups and industry can voice their opinions to legislators.

Lobbyists are generally very well educated in the subject of the legislation and the legislation's potential effects on the private sector. The lobbyist can often give insight to legislators about the strengths and weaknesses of proposed legislation. In turn, the legislators receive information with which to amend a bill and make a final decision on whether to support it. Without lobbyists, it would be up to legislators and their support staffs to research and learn about the subject of every bill introduced to Congress. Besides attending sessions of Congress and committee meetings and communicating with their home-state voters, legislators would find it virtually impossible to make informed decisions on all bills presented for a vote.

Public Hearings and Sessions

Another method of information gathering by Congress is through attending frequent public hearings at which citizens may appear and voice their opinions and concerns about contemplated or pending actions by Congress. Public hearings enable Congress to hear firsthand the voice of the people it was elected to represent. Although it would not be feasible to allow all interested persons to speak out on every item of proposed legislation, public hearings and direct contact between constituents and their legislators are effective tools to convey the general opinion of the public.

Session Law

Law passed during a particular session of Congress.

Congress meets several months of each year to consider proposed laws. These meetings are called sessions. Each annual session is numbered consecutively (e.g., 85th Congress). After a full session of Congress has been concluded, all laws passed during the session take on the collective name of **session law.**[4] Session laws are published in the *Statutes at Large*. Each session law is assigned a public law number, which represents the session of Congress in which the law was passed and the chronological order of the law in relation to other laws passed during the same session. For example, Public Law 92-397 would be the 397th law proposed during the 92nd session of Congress. Each session law is identified by its public law number until it can be incorporated into the publication of all statutes (organized by subject) currently in effect. This process of incorporating the public law into the existing law code is known as **codification.**

Codification

Process of incorporating newly passed legislation into the existing law code.

Publication of Legislation

All federal laws currently in effect are published in a multivolume set. Because laws are constantly being added, deleted, or modified, it is difficult to keep them organized in a single permanent set of books. Usually these collections of existing laws are known as Revised Statutes or Codes. The U.S. (federal) laws are officially published in the United States Code (commonly referred to as U.S.C.).

The U.S.C. is located in multiple-bound volumes, and the method by which the volumes are organized enables the statutes to remain current in light of constant change. First, all laws are divided by basic subject. For example, virtually all laws pertaining to banking institutions are located in one section in the statutes, known as a title (e.g., "Banking"). (This is similar to chapters in the text you are now reading. Each chapter deals with a different subject and bears a name that indicates the subject addressed in that part of the text.) Second, all subjects are arranged in alphabetical order. Third, each law within a title (subject) is assigned a section number, allowing for future revision of the organization of the laws. If one law exists and is later amended, the amendment is assigned the same number as the previous law. For example, Title 21, Section 1316, can be amended and the new language of Section 1316 printed where the prior language previously appeared. If an additional law is passed on a general subject (title) and that particular law is new to the subject, it is assigned a new section number that is not assigned to any other law on the subject. For example, assume Section 1316 is the last law to appear in Title 21. If a new law is passed, it might be assigned Section 1317. Consequently, the subject of law will lead one to the correct title (grouping of laws on a particular topic). Each title contains a table of contents listing specific sections (laws) of the title and descriptive headings for each section. The statutes also have an extensive subject index, making them even more accessible.

As stated previously, the U.S.Code takes up numerous volumes. It would be impractical to publish an entirely new set after every session of Congress to incorporate information from laws that are newly passed, amended, or repealed. For this reason, supplements are used between publications of the bound volumes. After each session of Congress, the session laws are codified (given their permanent title and section numbers) and published in supplemental volumes to the Code. Usually, these volumes are paperback books located within the back cover (called pocket parts) or next to the hardbound volume where the codified law will eventually appear. Supplements are published annually to incorporate changes from the most recent session of Congress and all past sessions that have occurred since the last bound publication. If an existing law cannot be found in the bound Code, it is probably located in the corresponding supplement. Periodically, newly bound editions are published that incorporate all prior supplements, and the process of supplementation starts over.

With regard to publication of federal statutes, and in many states, two types of publications are commonly used. The first, just discussed, is the Code. The second is known as an annotated statute. Such collections are no different in terms of the included text of the statutes, supplements, and organization by subject and number. However, an annotated statute has an added feature. Following the text of each statute are annotations—very brief (usually one-sentence) descriptions of judicial opinions that interpret the particular statute. For the person doing legal research, annotated statutes are especially helpful. Annotated statutes not only give the language of the law but also provide information about any attempts by the judiciary to apply the law. Because statutes are necessarily broad, judicial interpretations often give insight as to the true purpose of the statute.

LEGISLATION AND JUDICIAL REVIEW

Many times, parties will disagree with a court on one of two common issues relating to statutory interpretation. The first issue is whether a statute should even be applied to the particular situation. The second is how the statute should be applied to the specific circumstances of the case. Since the court system acts as an interpreter of the law, it is up to the court to make these determinations based on legal analysis. Statutes must therefore be analyzed in terms of their effect on a situation in much the same way case law is analyzed. There is, however, a striking difference. Statutes are broadly written and generally do not include discussions of exact case scenarios. Consequently, the process of legal analysis of a statute must be somewhat modified. When examining a statute, one should first break it down into each element that must be satisfied for the statute to apply. Second, one needs to compare each element to the facts of the particular case. If all elements are substantially met, the likelihood is very strong that the statute would be considered applicable. This method of legal analysis differs in that there are no specific case facts to compare. However, the analysis still requires a close comparison of the statute and current situation as well as a deduction as to the likely outcome of the situation if the statute is applied.

 APPLICATION 3.1

Jonah reported to the emergency room late one evening. He claimed that he injured his back at work. He received medical care for his injuries and was absent from work for some time. Jonah's employer refused to pay Jonah's medical bills based on a claim that Jonah's injury did not occur on the job. The employer also recently fired Jonah from his job based on a long history of problems at work. A judge must decide whether Jonah's injury more likely than not occurred on the job. If the judge decides the injury was job related, the workers' compensation laws would apply. If the laws do apply, the judge must then determine whether workers' compensation laws apply to the situation regarding Jonah's termination. In most states, an injured employee may not be fired for claiming workers' compensation but may be fired for other acceptable reasons. Thus, the judge must determine how to apply the law to these specific circumstances based on whether the firing was the result of the compensation claim or poor performance as an employee.

Point for Discussion
Why shouldn't an employer be allowed to fire employees who claim injury and ultimately drive up the cost of the employer's workers' compensation insurance?

Assignment 3.3

> Examine the statute in Figure 3.3 and break it down into elements that must be satisfied.

Assignment 3.4

> Determine whether the statute in Figure 3.3 should apply to the following situation. Explain your answer.
>
> SITUATION: Rita was employed by Acme Company. She had been reprimanded several times for violation of various company policies. Other employees filed written requests not to have to work with her. On October 9, Rita was injured on the job (three days before her annual performance evaluation). On October 12, she was terminated. Rita claims retaliatory discharge based on her injury and pending workers' compensation claim.

In most situations, the job of the court regarding legislation is limited to deciding which laws are relevant to the facts and how the laws apply to a particular situation. On occasion, however, the courts are called upon to protect constitutional guarantees from violation by a statute.

Legislatures do not intentionally violate the Constitution when they pass laws. Sometimes it is not apparent until a law is actually put into effect that the law violates the constitutional rights of a citizen. If a citizen's rights are violated and the citizen brings a claim to the courts, the court has the authority to overrule the statute in favor of protecting the person's constitutional guarantees. This is the only circumstance under which a court can invalidate action of the legislature. The U.S. Supreme Court has this authority over the Congress, as does the high court of each state over the state's legislative body. Such overruling rarely occurs, but when it does occur, the law is rendered ineffective and is no longer applied to the citizen.

A final role of the courts with respect to the legislature is a quasi-advisory role. From time to time, the courts will indirectly express an opinion through the language of case law as to what the law should be. However, it is not within the court's authority to write laws that will apply as legislation to all of the people. The courts can rule only on situations before them involving particular citizens. But because of its continuous personal contact with the citizens, the court is often in a position to assess the needs of the individual. Therefore, the courts will periodically issue opinions on specific cases that include messages to Congress. The courts can thus act as a bridge between the people and the legislators without exceeding their authority or purpose.

FIGURE 3.3

Florida Statute
Workers' Comp
Law Regarding
Retaliatory
Discharge

WEST'S FLORIDA STATUTES ANNOTATED
TITLE XXXI. LABOR
CHAPTER 440. WORKERS' COMPENSATION
440.205. Coercion of employees
    No employer shall discharge, threaten to discharge, intimidate, or coerce any employee by reason of such employee's valid claim for compensation or attempt to claim compensation under the Workers' Compensation Law.

ETHICAL NOTE

Legislators are particularly concerned with ethical issues. Because an elected official is required to represent the interests of the people, it is important that legislators avoid the appearance of improper influence by private interests. Extensive ethical rules are imposed on all legislators and their staffs. In addition, there are ethical committees, the function of which is to review any alleged violations of ethical rules by legislators. A pronouncement by a committee that a legislator has violated ethical rules can result in irreparable damage to the legislator's political career.

While in the past, some legislators openly disregarded the rules of ethics, that trend has largely reversed. With the advent of mass media, a legislator's constituents are informed almost immediately of any alleged improprieties. Consequently, the responsibility to act ethically and loyally to the office held is greater than ever.

Question

Can you list three instances in recent memory when legislators were charged with ethical violations?

CHAPTER SUMMARY

As with every branch of government, the legislative branch has a specific and necessary purpose. However, like the other branches, the legislature cannot function effectively without the influence of the other branches and the people. With the assistance of these branches, the legislature is able to enact laws that reflect the opinion of the majority regarding what our society should be.

The lawmaking authority of the Congress includes the power to tax, raise and support armies, declare and support war, regulate in-

terstate commerce, and enact laws that are necessary and proper to carry out its powers and objectives.

The legislature is able to adjust to changing times while keeping in sight those basic guarantees of the Constitution. When the legislature fails in this effort, the judiciary has the authority to act on a statute to prevent violation of a citizen's constitutional guarantees. Such adaptability helps to serve the various purposes of legislation, such as indicating what will be considered unacceptable conduct, protecting citizens from injury or damage to property, and providing remedies for those citizens when injury or damage does occur. Further, because of the enormous complexity of the legal system and the number of litigants, procedural laws are designed to process claims as efficiently as possible.

A primary reason for the tremendous adaptability of legislation lies in the method in which legislation is created. Citizens elect delegates (senators and representatives), who propose laws (bills) that, when approved by the majority of the delegates, become law. The citizens are thus represented, and laws can be enacted as necessary with little procedural difficulty.

Safeguards exist against the enactment of laws that are not in the best interest of the people or that violate the Constitution. An important safeguard is the president's veto power. Before a vetoed bill can become law, the bill requires approval by a much higher percentage of Congress than initially required. Presumably, this reflects a desire by a significant majority of the people to enact the law. The judicial branch has limited power to override statutory law. This exception to the general rule of superiority of statutory over judicial law takes place when the judiciary determines the statutory law to be in violation of the Constitution.

REVIEW QUESTIONS

1. Define and give an example of protective, remedial, and procedural law.
2. What are the minimum qualifications for election to the House and the Senate?
3. Why is the Congress made up of two houses, and how are the houses different?
4. Describe each step of legislation.
5. How can the president influence legislative law?
6. How can the courts influence legislative law?
7. What is the role of a lobbyist?
8. Define the following terms:
   session law
   statutory code
   annotated code
9. What is the function of a legislative committee?
10. How many legislators in each house need to support a bill before and after a veto in order to pass the bill?

CHAPTER TERMS

Bill	Representative	Session Law
Codification	Senator	Veto
Lobbyist		

NOTES

1. William Statsky, *Legal Thesaurus/Dictionary* (St. Paul: West, 1982).
2. *Litsinger Sign Co. v. American Sign Co.* 11 Ohio St. 2dl, 227 N.E.2d 609 (1967).
3. Article I, U.S. Constitution.
4. Statsky, *Legal Thesaurus/Dictionary.*

CHAPTER 4

The Executive Branch and Administrative Authority

CHAPTER OBJECTIVES

After reading this chapter you should be able to

- *Describe how the members of the electoral college are selected.*

- *Describe the process of the electoral college and discuss the effect of the Twelfth Amendment on the process.*

- *List the duties of the president.*

- *Describe the delegation doctrine.*

- *Identify the steps in the creation of an administrative agency.*

- *Discuss the function and purpose of an administrative agency.*

- *Identify the requirements of an administrative agency when proposing and issuing a new regulation.*

- *Describe the considerations of a court in the review of an administrative agency action.*

- *Discuss the purpose and nature of the Administrative Procedure Act.*

THE EXECUTIVE BRANCH

Article II of the U.S. Constitution establishes the executive branch as a fundamental element in our system of government. Consequently, the executive branch plays an important role in our legal system. Section I of Article II specifies the manner in which the president and vice president shall be elected and the term of office of the president and the vice president. Section I also contains provisions in case a president does not complete a term, specifies who may run for president, and describes the timing and method of elections. Sections 2 and 3 address the authority and responsibilities of the president. Section 4 of Article II lists the offenses for which a president, vice president, or other officer of the U.S. government can be removed from office. Review the text of Article II, Section I.*

Changes in the Electoral Process

In 1804, Section 1 of Article II was amended by passage of the Twelfth Amendment, which slightly altered the process of the electoral ballot and election of the president by the House of Representatives in the event no majority was achieved by the electoral college. Perhaps the most significant change was the method of selection of the vice president. Under the original Constitution, the person having the greatest number of votes in the House of Representatives (assuming no majority was reached in the electorate) would assume the position of president. Following this, the person with the greatest number of votes in the electoral college (other than the person elected president) would be the vice president. If there was no one person with a majority, the Senate would elect a vice president in a manner similar to the election of the president.

An obvious difficulty with the original process was that the person with the second greatest number of votes in the electorate would automatically become vice president. This person could very likely have been the president's strongest political opponent, which would make administration of government very difficult, given the opposing views of the two. By having both the president and the vice president go through a second election process (in the event no majority was reached in the electoral college), such a result could be avoided. With the 1804 amendment, the result of a failed majority in the electoral college would be two elections. The House of Representatives would elect the president. However, rather than an automatic appointment of vice president, that person would be elected by the Senate. While the possibility still exists for election of officials with contradictory views, at least some thought could be given to the most positive combination of personalities.

Powers and Authority of the President

Sections 2 and 3 of Article II describe the powers and obligations of the office of the president. Each of these sections of Article II is still influential in the daily

*Note irregularities in spelling, grammar, and punctuation are reflective of the original form of the Constitution.

Article II, Section 1

Section 1. The executive Power shall be vested in a President of the United States of America. He shall hold his Office during the Term of four Years, and, together with the Vice-President, chosen for the same Term, be elected, as follows

Each State shall appoint, in such Manner as the Legislature thereof may direct, a Number of Electors, equal to the whole Number of Senators and Representatives to which the State may be entitled in the Congress: but no Senator or Representative, or Person holding an Office of Trust or Profit under the United States, shall be appointed an Elector.

[The Electors shall meet in their respective States, and vote by Ballot for two Persons, of whom one at least shall not be an Inhabitant of the same State with themselves. And they shall make a List of all the Persons voted for, and of the Number of Votes for each; which List they shall sign and certify, and transmit sealed to the Seat of the Government of the United States, directed to the President of the Senate [who] shall, in the Presence of the Senate and House of Representatives, open all the Certificates, and the Votes shall then be counted. The Person having the greatest Number of Votes shall be the President, if such Number be a Majority of the whole Number of Electors appointed; and if there be more than one who have such Majority, and have an equal Number of Votes, then the House of Representatives shall immediately chuse by Ballot one of them for President; and if no Person have a Majority, then from the five highest on the List the said House shall in like Manner chuse the President. But in chusing the President, the Votes shall be taken by States, the Representation from each State having one Vote; A quorum for this Purpose shall consist of a Member or Members from two-thirds of the States, and a Majority of all the States shall be necessary to a Choice. In every Case, after the Choice of the President, the Person having the greater Number of Votes of the Electors shall be the Vice President. But if there should remain two or more who have equal Votes, the Senate shall chuse from them by Ballot the Vice-President.]

The Congress may determine the Time of chusing the Electors, and the Day on which they shall give their Votes; which Day shall be the same throughout the United States.

No person except a natural born Citizen, or a Citizen of the United States, at the time of the Adoption of this Constitution, shall be eligible to the Office of President; neither shall any Person be eligible to that Office who shall not have attained to the Age of thirty-five Years, and been fourteen Years a Resident within the United States.

In Case of the Removal of the President from Office, or of his Death, Resignation, or Inability to discharge the Powers and Duties of the said Office, the same shall devolve on the Vice President, and the Congress may by Law provide for the Case of Removal, Death, Resignation or Inability, both of the President and Vice President, declaring what Officer shall then act as President, and such Officer shall act accordingly, until the Disability be removed, or a President shall be elected.

The President shall, at stated Times, receive for his Services, a Compensation, which shall neither be encreased nor diminished during the Period for which he shall have been elected, and he shall not receive within that Period any other Emolument from the United States, or any of them.

Before he enter on the Execution of his Office, he shall take the following Oath or Affirmation: — "I do solemnly swear (or affirm) that I will faithfully execute the Office of President of the United States, and will to the best of my Ability, preserve, protect and defend the Constitution of the United States."

operation of government. Frequently, questions arise regarding the proper use of power by the branches of government and the effectiveness of the system as detailed in the Constitution. A closer look at these two sections may be helpful at this point.

The powers described in these sections indicate that the president has the basic authority to negotiate treaties, appoint judges and other government officers, convene the Congress, grant pardons or reprieves, appoint ambassadors and heads of departments (the Cabinet), and command the armed forces. Specifically, the president exercises great latitude in establishing, maintaining, or ending foreign relations with other countries. On occasion, this authority covers military actions as well. Under current statutes, however, the president must

Article II, Sections 2 & 3

Section 2. The President shall be Commander in Chief of the Army and Navy of the United States, and of the Militia of the several States, when called into the actual Service of the United States; he may require the Opinion in writing, of the principal Officer in each of the executive Departments, upon any subject relating to the Duties of their respective Offices, and he shall have Power to Grant Reprieves and Pardons for Offenses against the United States, except in Cases of Impeachment.

He shall have Power, by and with the Advice and Consent of the Senate, to make Treaties, provided two-thirds of the Senators present concur; and he shall nominate, and by and with the Advice and Consent of the Senate, shall appoint Ambassadors, other public Ministers and Consuls, Judges of the supreme Court, and all other Officers of the United States, whose Appointments are not herein otherwise provided for, and which shall be established by Law; but the Congress may by Law vest the Appointment of such inferior Officers, as they think proper, in the President alone, in the Courts of Law, or in the Heads of Departments.

The President shall have Power to fill up all Vacancies that may happen during the Recess of the Senate, by granting Commissions which shall expire at the End of their next Session.

Section 3. He shall from time to time give to the Congress Information of the State of the Union, and recommend to their Consideration such Measures as he shall judge necessary and expedient; he may, on extraordinary Occasions, convene both Houses, or either of them, and in Case of Disagreement between them, with Respect to the Time of Adjournment, he may adjourn them to such Time as he shall think proper; he shall receive Ambassadors and other public Ministers; he shall take Care that the Laws be faithfully executed, and shall Commission all the Officers of the United States.

---

report to the Congress on military actions, since the power to declare war is vested in the Congress under the Constitution.

In addition, the president is vested with the enforcement power over the laws. Consequently, federal law enforcement organizations are overseen by the executive branch. The president also appoints the attorney general, who serves as counsel for the executive branch on matters of enforcement.

The bulk of the powers of the president derives from one small portion of one sentence near the end of Article II, Section 3: ". . . he shall take Care that the Laws be faithfully executed. . . ." This statement has been expanded to create the executive authority to oversee administrative law, one of the principal sources of law in the United States.

The president cannot create administrative law directly but is responsible for supervising the activities of federal administrative agencies. A similar process occurs at the state level between the state executive branch (office of the governor) and the state administrative agencies. The creation and operation of an administrative agency are discussed in the following sections.

Assignment 4.1

Create a chart that details the two methods of presidential and vice presidential elections before and after the 1804 amendment.

ADMINISTRATIVE AGENCIES

Role of the Administrative Agency

An **administrative agency** has a unique and constantly growing place in the role of government in American society. The population of the country is so large, the geographical area so great and varied, and the system of government so complex that it is essential to have government officials who can respond to the specific needs of the many facets of society. When Congress passes a law, the law must be written broadly enough to encompass all situations it is designed to address. However, that same law must be specific enough to allow people to know whether their actions are in compliance with or in violation of the law. Hence the need for the administrative agency, whose basic role is to act as liaison between the Congress and the people. The administrative agency explains what Congress means in particular statutory language, clarifies and defines terms, and ultimately, under the supervision of the executive branch, enforces the law. (See Figure 4.1 for a partial list of administrative agencies and their acronyms.)

Administrative Agency
Government office created by the legislature and overseen by the executive branch. The purpose of such agencies is to apply certain specified laws created by the legislature.

The responsibility of the president to carry out and enforce the laws passed by Congress is immense. With the assistance of administrative agencies, individuals can have personal access to government. Congress first passes laws that enable the creation of an administrative agency and then passes additional statutes that must be enforced. The president staffs and oversees the administrative agency as it clarifies, defines, and enforces the statutes passed by Congress. Many of these agencies are controlled by the fourteen departments of the executive branch (for example, the Department of Justice controls the FBI and the Treasury Department controls the IRS), although some federal agencies are not part of a specific department. The heads of the executive departments serve as members of the president's Cabinet (for example, the secretary of defense and the attorney general).

Although the day-to-day operation of an administrative agency is largely within the control of the executive branch, an agency is ultimately created by the Congress. Article I, Section 8, paragraph 18, of the Constitution provides as follows:

> The Congress shall have power . . . To make all Laws which shall be necessary and proper for carrying into Execution the foregoing Powers, and all other Powers vested by this Constitution in the Government of the United States, or in any Department or Officer thereof.

From this statement, Congress has drawn its authority to make laws. This statement has also been interpreted to permit Congress to enact laws that allow government agencies to clarify the laws through regulations and administrative decisions. The president's power to appoint federal officers allows the executive branch to staff the agencies. The executive duty to see that the laws are faithfully executed vests in the president the authority to oversee the agencies as they enforce the laws passed by the Congress.

FIGURE 4.1

Common
Acronyms for
Federal Agencies

Note: The following is a partial list of existing federal agencies.
CIA—Central Intelligence Agency
CPSC—Consumer Products Safety Commission
DHHS—Department of Health and Human Services
DOD—Department of Defense
DOJ—Department of Justice
DOT—Department of Transportation
EEOC—Equal Employment Opportunity Commission
EPA—Environmental Protection Agency
FAA—Federal Aviation Administration
FBI—Federal Bureau of Investigation
FCC—Federal Communications Commission
FDA—Food and Drug Administration
FERC—Federal Energy Regulatory Commission
FRB—Federal Reserve Board
FTC—Federal Trade Commission
HUD—Department of Housing and Urban Development
ICC—Interstate Commerce Commission
INS—Immigration and Naturalization Service
IRS—Internal Revenue Service
NHTSA—National Highway and Traffic Safety Administration
NLRB—National Labor Relations Board
NRC—Nuclear Regulatory Commission
NSC—National Security Council
OSHA—Occupational Safety and Health Administration
SEC—Securities Exchange Commission
SSA—Social Security Administration
USDA—United States Department of Agriculture

Administrative agencies have been a part of the American legal system since the 1800s, since agencies can perform many legal functions that Congress, for practical reasons, cannot effectively accomplish. Administrative agencies offer several advantages, including the following:

1. They can deal with large groups of citizens or entire industries.
2. They have the ability to respond quickly to rapidly changing needs of industries or citizens.
3. Their staff members are more knowledgeable about the specifics of an industry or a group of citizens than the legislature or the judiciary.
4. They can provide consistent and fair standards for citizens and industries.

An example of an area in which an administrative agency has been particularly effective is Social Security, administered by the Social Security Administration. All working people in the United States pay into a Social Security fund, from which payments are made to persons who retire or become disabled. Given the number of persons who have worked in this country since the establishment of Social Security in 1935, the task of collecting and distributing the funds is incomprehensible. Such a task can be carried out most effectively by an administrative agency such as the Social Security Administration.

The Creation of an Administrative Agency

In many areas, an administrative agency is the most effective way to deal knowledgeably, efficiently, and equitably with many legal issues on an individual basis. The following paragraphs examine the basic process for creating an administrative agency in today's legal system. Be aware that many additional details must be dealt with in the actual agency creation process.

Before an agency comes into existence, Congress must pass a resolution saying that an agency is necessary to carry out the goals of certain legislation. Congress must determine that no more effective way to implement the goals exists and that the goals of the legislation need to be enforced. Congress then passes what is commonly referred to as an **enabling act**—a statute that expresses the goals of Congress on a particular subject of legislation.

An example is the enabling act that ultimately provided for the creation of the Environmental Protection Agency (EPA), which carries out and enforces legislation passed by Congress to protect, enhance, or correct problems in the environment. When the National Environmental Policy Act (NEPA) was passed as an enabling act in 1969, it was the first major environmental protection law enacted by Congress. Shortly thereafter, President Nixon issued an executive order in 1970 calling for the creation of an agency to carry out the goals of the NEPA. The executive order is a form of procedural law that implements the enabling act. Although executive orders have the weight of law, they are issued by presidents, or at their direction, and only affect administrative agencies or functions.

The acts that permit the creation of administrative agencies have been a great source of controversy for Congress over the years. In effect, by creating an administrative agency, Congress is relinquishing some of its lawmaking authority. Early on, the delegation of authority to make rules with the effect of law was strictly prohibited by the U.S. Supreme Court.[1] As time passed and the needs of the country grew, the Court relaxed its position somewhat to permit administrative agencies to play a larger role in the legislative process. Although they have never been allowed to "create law," agencies are permitted to create regulations to promote efficient, responsive, and effective government.

Enabling Act
Congressional enactment that creates the authority in the executive to organize and oversee an administrative agency by establishing specific legislative goals and objectives.

The delegation doctrine. Through cases that come before them, the courts have continued to monitor Congress and the executive branch very closely with respect to the creation and operation of administrative agencies. The chief concern of the courts with respect to the creation of administrative agencies is that the delegation doctrine not be violated. The **delegation doctrine** is based on the premise that Congress cannot be permitted to give away any of its actual lawmaking power.[2] Rather, Congress can only give up or delegate the authority to clarify and enforce laws passed. The delegation of the authority to clarify and enforce laws is permissible even if it means that the agency must enact additional law in the form of rules and regulations as needed to clarify or enforce the original laws of Congress. An agency to which Congress has delegated authority is not free to make original laws of

Delegation Doctrine
Principle that Congress may not assign its authority to create statutory law nor may any other government entity assume such authority.

its own. All agency law must serve the functions of clarification and enforcement.

Through its interpretations of the delegation doctrine, the Supreme Court has established several major criteria that must be followed in the creation and operation of any administrative agency. The authority delegated by Congress must not allow nonlegislative bodies to enact major laws. Therefore, the Court requires any act that enables the creation of an administrative agency to be clear in its purpose with definable limits.[3] In this way, an agency is prevented from enacting regulations in areas other than those it was created to administer.

If it appears from the language of the enabling act that Congress did not clearly state as its purpose an "intelligible principle to which the [agency must] . . . conform," the enabling act can be struck down as being unconstitutionally overboard.[4] The reasoning is that if a law is so broad that an agency is limitless in the extent of law that it can create, Congress has delegated its original lawmaking authority rather than the authority to clarify and enforce the laws. This violates the Constitution, which vests the authority to create statutes solely in the Congress.

A second major criterion of the delegation doctrine is that the agency's enforcement of the law must be accomplished fairly and openly.[5] If the enabling act and subsequent statutes enacted by Congress do not give some guidance to the president and the administrative agencies under the president's supervision in the manner of enforcing the law, the delegation doctrine has been violated. Under the Constitution, the people are entitled to know what the law is and how it will be enforced against persons who do not obey it. Since laws created by Congress must meet this standard, obviously any agency to which Congress gives the power to enforce the laws must also meet it. If an agency fails to create regulations that provide for the fair and open administration of laws, the president and the agency have not received proper guidance from Congress. Once again, the enabling act will be considered to be too vague or overboard and therefore inconsistent with the Constitution.[6]

Agency officers.   Finally, Article II of the Constitution states that the president should appoint government officers. With respect to agencies, officers are persons who will be responsible for the enforcement of the law. Agency staff members cannot be employed in any profession or industry that the agency oversees, since that would not constitute fair and unbiased administration of the law. Further, according to the Constitution, the laws are to be enforced by the government and not by the private sector. This particular situation came to the attention of the U.S. Supreme Court in 1936. In *Carter v. Carter Coal Company*,[7] many of the regulations for the coal industry were discovered to have been created by committees made up of persons employed at high levels in the industry. The Court found that this was an improper method of enforcing laws. The president may, however, ask persons who are experts in their field to leave private industry to come to work in the agency.

In summary, the passage of an enabling act and the creation of an agency must be done in a manner that at the very least meets the following criteria:

1. The goals of the statutes must be clear, and the statutes must have definable limits.
2. The methods the agency uses to enforce the statutes must be fair and open to all members of the public.
3. The enforcement of the statutes must be accomplished by officers of the government, not by persons with private interests.

Agencies Today

During the 1930s, the number of agencies increased dramatically. Agencies were part of the New Deal era, which sought to aid the country in its economic recovery from the Great Depression. Congress increased its use of administrative agencies and cooperated with the President in using them to deal quickly with the problems of the nation. Some people believed, however, that the agencies were not acting properly and within the bounds of their authority. In large part, the delegation doctrine was refined during and shortly after this time.

In the years that followed, the courts became more and more involved in reviewing the efforts of the executive branch to oversee agencies, and the delegation doctrine imposed more stringent requirements upon the manner in which agencies could be created and operated. Congress responded in 1946 with the **Administrative Procedure Act (APA),** which was to be used in addition to each agency's enabling act. The APA included the elements necessary to satisfy the requirements of the delegation doctrine. Since that time, the APA has been modified and improved on several occasions to ensure that agencies are in compliance with the criteria the courts have established under the delegation doctrine. Thus, the APA together with the enabling act provides for the creation of an agency as well as for the agency's fair and efficient operation.

Administrative Procedure Act (APA)
Congressional enactment applied to all federal administrative agencies that requires agencies to follow certain procedures in the issuance of administrative law.

The Operation of an Administrative Agency

Once an agency is staffed, its employees are responsible for organizing its administration and addressing the subject or industry that the statutes affect. An agency is permitted a virtual free rein in its methods of internal operations and management as long as it is well organized and efficient. Such organization and efficiency will vary among agencies. An agency such as the Federal Aviation Administration, which oversees public air travel, does not require the same type of staffing, organization, and procedures as the Internal Revenue Service, which administers the tax laws for both individuals and businesses.

The type of agency that is created influences not only the manner in which the agency is organized but also the agency's basic functions. Some of the more common responsibilities of agencies include enforcing federal statutes through prosecution; negotiating settlements of claims made against government entities; testing, inspecting, and monitoring industries; recalling, seizing, or suspending products or activities that violate federal laws; and advising the public of the legal effect of the law. These various functions are performed through information collection, investigation, issuance of regulations, and administrative hearings.

When an agency must collect information or conduct an investigation to meet the goals and purpose of its enabling act, it is permitted to obtain information from the public and industry. However, this information must be voluntary and obtained in a manner that does not infringe upon individuals' rights to privacy under the Constitution. In addition, individuals cannot be compelled to testify at agency hearings about any information that might result in criminal prosecution against them, just as they cannot be compelled to incriminate themselves before the judiciary or the legislature.

Authority of Administrative Agencies

Administrative Regulation

Form of administrative law, a regulation defines, clarifies, or enforces a statutory objective.

The most prominent function of administrative agencies is their authority to issue regulations. **Administrative regulations** must be required to achieve the goals of the enabling act or any other federal laws that the agency has the responsibility to enforce. Thus, all regulations must be derivative of legislation formerly enacted by Congress. If an agency holds a hearing and determines that a regulation has been violated, the agency may impose sanctions on the violator.

Assignment 4.2

Examine the administrative regulation in Figure 4.2, and break it down into its individual components.

Assignment 4.3

Determine whether the administrative regulation in Figure 4.2 applies to the following situation:
SITUATION: You attended a community college where you received student loans in 1985 and 1986. In 1987, you declared bankruptcy. However, the court would not discharge the student loan debt. In 1989, you resumed payment. You currently owe $800 from an original debt of $2,500. You want to resume your education at State U. Are you eligible for a student loan?

If an agency wishes to issue rules, it must follow a very specific procedure set forth in the APA. Additionally, some enabling acts dictate the precise steps an agency must take when establishing and publishing regulations that the public must abide by. These formal rule-making procedures often require public hearings, the opportunity for testimony, and other input from the public before any regulations are put into force. However, most agencies are also allowed to promulgate rules through an informal process governed by a series of detailed requirements set forth in the APA. Most agencies must adhere to the following

FIGURE 4.2 Regulation

CODE OF FEDERAL REGULATIONS
TITLE 34–EDUCATION

§ 682.201 Eligible borrowers.

(a) Student borrower. A student is eligible to receive a GSLP loan, and an independent undergraduate student or a graduate or professional student is eligible to receive a PLUS Program loan, if the student—

(1) Is enrolled or accepted for enrollment on at least a half-time basis at a participating school, and meets the requirements of paragraph (c) of this section;

(2) Provides his or her social security number;

(3) Authorizes the school in writing to pay directly to the lender that portion of any refund of school charges that is allocable to the loan, in accordance with 34 CFR Part 668;

(4) Meets the qualifications pertaining to citizenship and residency status, set forth in paragraph (d) of this section;

(5) Meets the qualifications concerning defaults and overpayments, set forth in paragraphs (e) and (f) of this section;

(6) Complies with the requirements pertaining to registration with the Selective Service, set forth in 34 CFR Part 668;

(7) Complies with the requirements for submission of a Statement of Educational Purpose, set forth in § 682.203; and

(8) In the case of an undergraduate student who seeks a GSLP loan for the cost of attendance at a school that participates in the Pell Grant Program, receives a preliminary or final determination from the school of the student's eligibility or ineligibility for a Pell Grant.

(b) Parent borrower. A parent is eligible to receive a PLUS Program loan if the parent—

(1) Is borrowing to pay for the educational costs of a dependent undergraduate student who meets all of the qualifications set forth in paragraphs (a) (1) through (6) of this section;

(2) Provides his or her social security number;

(3) Meets the qualifications pertaining to citizenship and residency status set forth in paragraph (d) of this section;

(4) Meets the qualifications concerning defaults and overpayments set forth in paragraphs (e) and (f) of this section; and

(5) Complies with the requirements for submission of a Statement of Educational Purpose set forth in § 682.203.

(c) Enrollment status. To be eligible as a student or a borrower under the GSLP or the PLUS Program, a student must—

(1) If currently enrolled, be maintaining satisfactory progress, as determined by the school;

(2) If enrolled or accepted for enrollment in a foreign school, be a national of the United States; and

(3) If enrolled in a flight school program at a vocational school or an institution of higher education, meet the additional requirements set forth in paragraph (g) of this section.

(d) Citizenship and residency status. Each borrower, and each student for whom a parent is borrowing, must be—

(1) A national of the United States;

(2) A permanent resident of the United States and must provide evidence from the Immigration and Naturalization Service of that status;

(3) In the United States for other than a temporary purpose and must provide evidence from the Immigration and Naturalization Service of intent to become a citizen or permanent resident;

(4) A permanent resident of the Trust Territory of the Pacific Islands or the Northern Mariana Islands; or

(5) A citizen of the Marshall Islands, the Federated States of Micronesia, or the Republic of Palau.

(e) Effect of default on eligibility. (1) Except as provided in paragraph (e)(2) of this section, a person is ineligible to be a borrower under the GSLP or PLUS Program if that person, or the student for whom a parent is borrowing, is in default on any loan made under any title IV student financial assistance program identified in 34 CFR Part 668. For loans made under the National Direct Student Loan Program, the term "default" is defined in 34 CFR Part 674.

(2) If a borrower, or student for whom a parent is borrowing, is in default, as set forth in paragraph (e)(1) of this section, the borrower may receive a GSLP or PLUS Program loan only if the person who is in default has made satisfactory arrangements with the holder of the loan to repay the defaulted loan.

(3) The school may rely on the borrower's or student's written statement that he or she is not in default, unless the school has information to the contrary.

(4) The Secretary does not consider either a loan that is discharged in bankruptcy or a defaulted loan that is paid-in-full after default to be in default for purposes of this section. . . .

procedures when passing rules that will have an impact upon the public, an industry, or a subject that the agency regulates:

1. The agency must give advance notice to the public of the basic terms of the rules it proposes to enact. At the federal level, this must be done in the *Federal Register,* a daily publication that includes information about the actions of federal administrative agencies.
2. The agency must give the public the opportunity to participate in the agency decision by submitting comments, ideas, and suggestions regarding the proposed rules.
3. After consideration of the public comment, the agency must issue, with the final rule, a general statement of the ". . . basis and purpose of the administrative agency."[8]

After all the requirements of the APA have been satisfied, the agency issues its formal regulations and publishes them first in the *Federal Register* and then in the **Code of Federal Regulations (CFR),** where all existing regulations are located. Each agency is assigned a title similar to a title in the Code. Each regulation is assigned a specific section number and is placed with the other regulations of that agency under its proper title. Like the Code, an index of the regulations within a title is included.

The APA requires agencies to review their regulations periodically to evaluate their effectiveness and necessity.[9] In addition, the APA gives citizens certain rights with respect to agencies. Citizens have the right of access to agency information that pertains to the public and a right to information the agency has about them personally. Business entities or individuals who believe that a regulation has an unfair and adverse effect may have their complaint heard by the agency. If they do not receive satisfaction, they may have the right to have the issue heard by a judge in the judicial branch of the government.

Frequently, citizens who challenge the authority of an agency to promulgate rules or to use a particular method to enforce an agency regulation are required to exhaust their remedies. This means that before they can turn to the courts, they must first pursue all opportunities to have the issue resolved by dealing directly with the agency. This may involve formal claims, hearings, or appeals at various levels of the agency structure. Exceptions to this requirement of **exhaustion of remedies** occur in very limited circumstances. For example, an individual may turn to the courts first when it is apparent that there is little or no chance that the matter can be resolved by the agency or if time is an important factor and irreparable damage will be done if the citizen must wait to file a claim in the judicial system. As a general rule, however, a citizen must exhaust any possible remedies at the agency level before bringing the issue before the courts.

If the judicial system does become involved in a dispute between a citizen and an agency, it will consider several factors. First, the court must determine whether the agency's authority was clearly defined and whether the agency's action exceeded the limits of the agency's authority under the delegation doctrine. Second, the agency must have followed proper statutory procedures

Code of Federal Regulations (CFR)

Publication that contains all current administrative regulations.

Exhaustion of Remedies

The requirement that anyone having a dispute with an administrative agency must first follow all available procedures to resolve the dispute within the agency before taking the issue before the judiciary.

according to the enabling act, the APA, and any other relevant statutes. Finally, the court must consider whether the agency's action was conducted fairly and openly and whether it violates any constitutional rights of the citizen. If all of these requirements are satisfied in the agency's favor, the court will not disturb the action of the agency.

Chapter 1 pointed out that a court will not invalidate laws or substitute its judgment for that of the Congress unless the Constitution has been violated. This is also true with agency law, which, although administered and enforced through the executive branch, is ultimately an extension of the Congress and is entitled to the same protection.

Earlier in this chapter, much attention was given to the role of the executive branch and its supervision of administrative agencies. Although this role is not always obvious in agency proceedings, the president has a great responsibility and considerable influence with respect to administrative agencies. The president is responsible for keeping the agency appropriately staffed. The president also has influence over the approval of the agency budget and may exercise authority over the agency through the issuance of an executive order. Such orders specify the manner in which the president wants laws to be executed.

Assignment 4.4

Which of the following would be more appropriate subjects for law enacted solely by legislature?

(a) Licensure provisions for ham radio operators.
(b) The requirements shelters for the homeless must meet to be eligible for state funds.
(c) The method by which trials are conducted.
(d) The type of safety equipment employers must provide to workers who use heavy machinery.
(e) The creation and administration of retirement plans for state employees.

Assignment 4.5

Which of the items in Assignment 4.4 would be more appropriate for supplemental law from an administrative agency?

Assignment 4.6

Create a flow chart that tracks a concept of law to creation of a regulation used to define the concept.

ETHICAL NOTE

As the primary elected official in government, the president takes an oath of loyalty to the people of the nation. As the leader of the United States of America, the president is the role model for ethical behavior by all other elected officials. It is the obligation of the president to enforce the laws of the nation fairly and without preference or prejudice.

As representatives of government, agency officials also are obliged to put personal issues aside and to administer the law fairly and equally. In fact, the very objective of the Human Rights Commission is to see that all persons are afforded equal legal rights and are not treated disparately because of a nonrelevant factor such as race, sex, age, or disability. The very theme of equitable treatment by government as an ethical foundation can be traced to the Declaration of Independence, which sets forth the principle that "all men are created equal."

Question

Why do you believe that the above-mentioned factors (race, sex, age, disability) are specifically legislatively protected from being used as a basis of discrimination?

CHAPTER SUMMARY

The executive branch has many important functions, such as foreign relations, negotiation of treaties, supervision of the armed forces, and appointment of ambassadors and heads of governmental units. One of the most important functions, and one that has a direct and immediate effect on the citizenry, is to see that the laws are faithfully executed. From this comes the power to oversee administrative agencies and to ensure that the goals of Congress are carried out.

The government operates more effectively with the use of administrative agencies. Because administrative agencies are heavily influenced by all branches of government, limits are placed on the opportunities for abuse of agency power by agency staff or by the executive or legislative branches. In addition, judicially imposed limitations on the areas that are subject to agency regulation also limit the potential for abuse.

An administrative agency can be created only by a legislative enactment. Agency authority is limited to the clarification and enforcement of statutory law. The agency is staffed and overseen by the chief executive (president or governor). In the event the executive fails to properly oversee the agency or the legislative body gives the agency too much authority, the courts have the power to invalidate agency actions.

REVIEW QUESTIONS

1. What is the electoral college?
2. How are members of the electoral college chosen?
3. What is the criterion to be a member of the electoral college?
4. How is the president chosen in the event there is no majority in the electoral college?
5. What effect did the Twelfth Amendment have on Article II of the Constitution?
6. What is an enabling act?

7. Describe the delegation doctrine.
8. What function does the Administrative Procedure Act serve, and who is subject to the act's rules?

9. Why are administrative agencies created?
10. What role does the executive branch play in the creation of an administrative agency?

CHAPTER TERMS

Administrative Agency	Code of Federal Regulations	Exhaustion of Remedies
Administrative Procedure Act	Delegation Doctrine	
Administrative Regulation	Enabling Act	

NOTES

1. *Buttfield v. Stranahan,* 192 U.S. 470, 24 S.Ct. 349, 48 L.Ed. 525 (1904).
2. Id.
3. *J. W. Hampton, Jr., & Co. v. United States,* 276 U.S. 394, 48 S.Ct. 348, 72 L.Ed. 624 (1928).
4. Id.
5. 5 U.S.C.A. § 551 et seq.
6. *Schware v. Board of Bar Examiners,* 353 U.S. 232, 77 S.Ct. 752, IL.Ed.2d 796 (1957).
7. 298 U.S. 238, 56 S.Ct. 855, 80 L.Ed.1160 (1936).
8. 5 U.S.C.A. § 551–§ 1305.
9. 5 U.S.C.A. § 551 et seq.

CHAPTER 5

Substantive and Procedural Issues

CHAPTER OBJECTIVES

After reading this chapter, you should be able to

- *Distinguish substantive and procedural law.*

- *Explain the difference in procedure between a jury trial and a bench trial.*

- *Discuss the function and application of an appellate court.*

- *Explain the purpose and method of applicability of the rules of evidence.*

- *List and describe each stage of a trial.*

- *Identify the difference between a Motion for Judgment NOV and a Motion for New Trial.*

- *Explain the purpose of exceptions to hearsay evidence.*

- *List the two functions of substantive law.*

SUBSTANTIVE AND PROCEDURAL ISSUES

The body of law that has developed in this country can be organized in count-less ways. Each method of organization provides a way of distinguishing one area of law from another. First, all law can be defined as substantive or proce-dural. In addition, law can be divided into criminal and civil law (of which con-tract law and tort law are types). The purpose of this chapter is to clarify the differences between substantive and procedural law and to provide an under-standing of the procedural aspects of civil law. Criminal procedure is addressed in Chapter 13. Later chapters will also examine various kinds of civil and crim-inal substantive as well as procedural law.

Criminal Versus Civil Law

Civil Law

Law that governs the private rights of individuals, legal entities, and government.

Before going any further, it might be helpful to more fully clarify the difference between civil and criminal law. **Civil law** governs the issues that arise between parties over private rights. Thus, a citizen who sues another for an invasion of personal rights has grounds for a civil case. An example of a civil case is an in-dividual suing the government for invasion of private rights. Another is the gov-ernment suing an individual for damage to public property, such as a stop sign. Still another example is a suit by one citizen against another for property dam-age or physical injury caused by an automobile accident. A civil case is brought by the injured party for damage to his or her personal rights, person, or prop-erty. The injured party seeks some sort of compensation (usually monetary) for the injury or damage to the person or property.

A criminal case is a suit that is brought by the government for violation or injury to public rights. Even though a crime may be perpetrated against a sin-gle victim, the public as a whole demands safety and certain conduct by all per-sons. An individual who violates these demands against anyone violates the rights of the public as a whole. The government enforces the rights of the pub-lic through prosecution based on criminal law, which ranges from parking vio-lations to murder. Criminal law includes all laws designed by the legislature to maintain order and safety in our society. It carries a penalty of a fine, impris-onment, or community service, paid to the government rather than to a par-ticular victim. A court may also order restitution (compensation) to the victim. With the exception of an order of restitution, generally any claim for damages by a victim who may have been injured by a crime must be resolved in a civil suit against the alleged criminal brought by the injured party.

Compensatory Damages

An award of money payable to the injured party for the reasonable cost of the injuries.

In a civil case, the penalties are quite different. For example, there is no im-prisonment. Secondly, any judgment that awards money is payable to the indi-vidual whose rights were invaded and injured. The award of money should be sufficient to compensate the injured party for the reasonable cost of the injuries, thus the term **compensatory damages.** Additionally, in cases where money cannot adequately compensate but some action could, the guilty party may be ordered to act or refrain from acting in a certain way. This is called injunctive relief and, more particularly, specific performance. This type of relief is quite limited. Some jurisdictions also permit the recovery of punitive damages (also known as exemplary damages), which are additional monies that the defendant is ordered to pay as a form of punishment. The reasoning behind punitive damages is that some actions are so grossly improper that the defendant should be punished in a way that will serve as an example to others who might contemplate the same wrongful conduct.

In civil cases, procedural law takes effect when citizens bring a dispute to the legal system. In criminal law, the law enforcement agencies and prosecutors who are part of the legal system initiate a claim against a citizen. Therefore, criminal procedural law begins at the time the law enforcement personnel anticipate that they will bring a dispute into the legal system. This is addressed at great length in Chapter 13. The remainder of the discussion in this chapter is confined to issues of civil law.

 APPLICATION 5.1

Irene was driving on a local highway when suddenly, an oncoming car swerved into her lane and collided with her car. Irene was severely injured and died a few days later. The driver of the other car was charged criminally with motor vehicle homicide under state drunken-driving laws. Irene's husband sued on behalf of Irene's estate and for his own loss due to the death of his wife.

Two trials were held. One was a criminal prosecution. The government charged the driver criminally for violation of drunken-driving laws that prohibit drunken driving and add penalties if a death ensues from the violation. The other trial was a civil trial on behalf of Irene's estate for her pain and suffering and ultimate death. Also claimed in the second trial was a claim for the loss of Irene's life and the impact on her husband. In the criminal case, any penalty would be paid or served to the government for injury to public good. The civil case, if won, would result in a monetary award to Irene's estate (ultimately to be received by Irene's creditors and heirs) for Irene's injuries and death and to Irene's husband for his losses.

Point for Discussion
Why would it be improper to determine the criminal and civil issues of a case in a single trial?

Assignment 5.1

Which of the following examples are likely to be part of a criminal action, and which would more likely be part of a civil action:

(a) Speeding ticket.
(b) Defendant is ordered to spend forty hours volunteering at a roadside cleanup project.

(c) Defendant borrows plaintiff's car and consequently wrecks it in a one-car accident.

(d) Defendant is ordered to move the fence on his property back three feet after a property dispute with plaintiff.

(e) Parking violation.

(f) Plaintiff's car was damaged while parked in defendant's parking garage.

(g) As a result of a divorce, defendant is required to pay plaintiff's attorney's fees.

(h) Defendant is charged by the state with motor vehicle homicide of an individual as a result of drunken driving.

(i) Defendant is sued by the family of an individual killed as the result of drunken driving.

(j) Defendant is ordered by the court to pay the cost of repairs for vandalism and to spend forty-eight hours in jail.

SUBSTANTIVE VERSUS PROCEDURAL LAW

For hundreds of years, substantive and procedural law have coexisted. Without procedural law, substantive law could never be created. Without substantive law, there would be no need for procedural law. It remains more clear than ever that in today's complex society, substantive law and procedural law play equally important roles in our legal system.

Substantive Law

Substantive Law
The law that creates and resolves the issue between the parties. Legal standards that guide conduct and that are applied to determine whether or not conduct was legally appropriate.

Substantive law creates, defines, and regulates rights, as opposed to adjective, procedural, or remedial law, which provides a method of enforcing rights.[1] It is exactly what its name implies: the body, essence, and substance that guides the conduct of citizens. It encompasses principles of right and wrong as well as the principle that wrong will result in penalty. It includes the rights and duties of citizens, and it provides the basis to resolve issues involving those rights. Every citizen has the right to live and enjoy his or her own property free from intrusion by other citizens. All members of a populous society are obligated to respect and to not interfere with the rights of others. Substantive law establishes the extent of this right and obligation to which all persons are subject.

When a person engages in conduct that has an adverse effect on another individual, an injury may occur. An innocent injured party who wants to be compensated for the damage caused by the injury may request assistance from the legal system on the basis that the injuring party acted wrongfully. Such wrongful conduct gives rise to the dispute between the two parties. The court will examine the situation to determine whether the conduct of the party alleged to be at fault was indeed wrongful by society's standards. If it was, the party will be judged and will be penalized. If it was not, the party will be judged innocent. In either situation, the court resolves the issue based on what society has determined to be right and wrong conduct between individuals and entities.

 APPLICATION 5.2

The issue arises: Jane is driving her car down the street when she notices that a local department store is having a giant sale. She quickly stops to turn into the store's parking lot. Suddenly, her car is hit from behind by another car. Jane's vehicle is badly damaged. She brings suit against Tom, the driver of the other car. Jane claims that Tom was driving carelessly and that his careless (wrongful) conduct caused damage to her vehicle. Tom claims he was driving carefully but could not avoid the collision when Jane slammed on the brakes of her car.

The issue is resolved: The court will hear the evidence of both Jane and Tom in this case. If it determines that Tom was driving carelessly and could have avoided the accident, Tom will be judged liable and will have to pay for the damage to Jane's car. If the court decides that even careful driving by Tom could not have prevented the accident, Tom will be found not to be liable. In either situation, the court will apply what society has determined to be a standard (requirement) of careful conduct. The conduct of the parties is measured against this minimum level of careful conduct. If the conduct of a party does not meet this standard, the party is guilty. If the conduct of the party does meet the standard, the party is considered not liable. Thus, the existing legal standards of rightful and wrongful conduct are used to resolve the issue between parties who are in dispute.

Point for Discussion
What occurs when no substantive law is applicable to a situation but two parties appear in court claiming conflicting rights?

Procedural Law

Procedural law prescribes a method of enforcing rights or of obtaining redress for the invasion of rights.[2] The basic function of civil procedural law is to facilitate the movement of a lawsuit through the legal system. Procedural laws are created to ensure that each party will be afforded fair and impartial treatment. Further, procedural law has its goal that judges and juries will receive only evidence that will allow them to make a fair and impartial decision.

Civil procedure can be likened to a large piece of machinery that assembles a product. It does not feel or possess opinions. The function of procedural law is to assemble all of the pieces into a complete product. The parties to the suit provide the pieces to the product at appropriate times and in the appropriate

Procedural Law
Law used to guide parties fairly and efficiently through the legal system.

manner. The completed product delivered from the machine is the decision that resolves the dispute. This decision is based on the pieces of information (substantive law and facts of the case) that have been fed into the machine and assembled.

In the lawsuit previously discussed, Jane and Tom became involved in litigation. The principles of law that were applied in their case to determine who should prevail, based on the most reasonable explanation of the facts, is substantive law. Procedural law also plays a part in the litigation and includes the following:

1. The time limit for bringing a lawsuit.
2. The manner in which the lawsuit is begun (e.g., by filing a complaint or petition).
3. The proper way to inform the defendant that a lawsuit has been filed.
4. The types of information that each party must release to the other party.
5. The procedure at trial.
6. The evidence that can be introduced at trial.
7. The method for appealing the decision if the losing party feels the decision was unfair.

The Common Ground

On occasion, substantive rights are affected by procedural law. Most often, when there is a conflict of law (different legal standards apply in different states) or when more than one jurisdiction has contact with the dispute there is the potential for procedural law to affect the outcome of the suit rather than substantive law. Such a case could arise when the parties bring their action in federal court based on diversity of citizenship (discussed in Chapter 6). Another situation might involve a dispute based on a series of events that occurred in different jurisdictions and ultimately resulted in an injury.

In different jurisdictions, procedural law and conflicting substantive law may be dealt with differently. The general rule is that a court should attempt to apply its own procedural rules regardless of which substantive law applies.[3] The courts, including the U.S. Supreme Court, have continued to address issues of this nature for quite some time with no final decision.

The issue of conflicting procedural and substantive standards from varying jurisdictions arises when more than one jurisdiction (area within a court's authority) could serve as the forum for a lawsuit. The party bringing the action will no doubt select the jurisdiction whose laws most favor the claim. An example is a choice between two states based on the statute-of-limitations laws. The statute of limitations is a procedural law in a jurisdiction that indicates the maximum amount of time in which a lawsuit can be commenced. For example, in some states, a personal injury claim must be brought within three years. In other states, the limit is one year. Thus, if a plaintiff in one of these states with a personal injury claim decides to file a suit two years after the injury, the suit could be brought only in a state with a three-year statute of limitations. In a jurisdiction with a one-year statute of limitations, the suit would be barred after one year had passed. Because the circumstances that produce a lawsuit sometimes occur in more than one jurisdiction, there is more than one place where suit could be brought. This particular issue is dealt with in greater detail in Chapter 6.

The conflict of the statute of limitations gave rise to the establishment of the outcome determinative test by the U.S. Supreme Court.[4] The test was originally created to be used by federal courts faced with a case based on state laws where more than one state is connected with the case or where either state law or federal law could be applied. Under this test, the court examines what would happen under each law. The goal is that the outcome should be the same whether the case is heard in federal court or state court (under state law). If the outcome of the suit would be different solely because of federal procedural rules (such as a statute of limitations that differs from the state statute of limitations), the state procedure rule should be applied. The idea is to discourage persons from filing a case in a particular court just because they could win in that court when they could not win in another. Courts encourage parties to select a court because it is the best equipped to hear their claim, not because it is the best strategically.

The most recent opinion of the U.S. Supreme Court on this issue has been a combination of the general rule and the outcome determinative test.[5] The Supreme Court held that a court should apply its own procedural rules. However, when the laws of the various jurisdictions involved are so different that it is clear that the plaintiff was shopping for the court with the most favorable laws and not for the most appropriate location for the case, the outcome determinative test should be applied.

Assignment 5.2

Determine which of the following situations are substantive and which are procedural issues:

1. Jake and Laura are involved in a divorce. Laura is asking that Jake be sentenced to time in jail because of his numerous violations of an earlier child support order. Jake alleges that he has paid Laura in cash but has no records of the payments.
2. Joyce sues Mishael for injuries received in an automobile accident. Mishael maintains that Joyce filed suit in the wrong court entirely.
3. Maxwell and Franco are brothers. Maxwell is sued, but he claims that the summons in the suit was given to Franco. Therefore, Maxwell maintains that since he never properly received the summons, he should not have to answer the suit against him.
4. Margo and Clay are involved in a breach of contract dispute. Margo alleges that Clay was obligated by the contract to paint her house yellow. In fact, Clay painted the house purple.

THE CREATION AND APPLICATION OF CIVIL PROCEDURE

Creating Laws of Procedure

Laws of procedure, sometimes referred to as rules, are created by the authority of the legislature. Procedural law applies to all people and is created to facilitate an organized court system and to protect the constitutional guarantees to citizens. Because the laws deal with the mechanics of the court system, judges are often better equipped than the legislature to create fair and reasonable rules that provide for an efficient court system. Therefore, in many jurisdictions, the legislatures vest the courts with authority to create such laws. At the very least, the courts have input into what the procedural laws should be.

Even though they are created with the assistance of the judicial branch, procedural laws are adopted by the legislature as statutes. Thus, they can often be found in the published statutes along with the other enactments of the legislature. Although procedural rules are not published with the opinions of the judges on individual cases, interpretations of the rules often appear in judicial opinions.

Types of Procedural Law

For the sake of convenience, procedural law has been divided into several categories. A person researching the law has a much easier time finding the particular laws or rules that apply to a given case if the law is organized according to subject. Most often, a jurisdiction will divide its procedural law into the following categories:

1. Rules of civil procedure
2. Rules of criminal procedure
3. Rules of evidence
4. Rules of appellate procedure

In addition to having the power to create rules that are enacted into law for an entire jurisdiction, courts generally have the power to create local rules, which apply only to the court that creates them and to no other court. An example would be a county rules court. Although the procedural laws of a state apply to all of the state courts including county courts, each county court may enact its own local rules as well. Local rules are designed to supplement the state laws of procedure.[6]

 APPLICATION 5.3

The state legislature enacts a rule of procedure that requires that all petitions for dissolution of marriage be filed in the court of the county where the petitioner is domiciled. This is an example of a rule of procedure that applies to the entire jurisdiction (the entire state). The county court of

Weir County, enacts a local rule that requires petitions for divorce to be filed only on Mondays with the Clerk of the Court, Domestic Relations Division. This local rule is created by the county court and would apply in no other county in the state.

Points for Discussion
1. Why are local rules necessary?
2. Wouldn't it be easier to have completely uniform rules for an entire jurisdiction?

RULES OF CIVIL PROCEDURE

The rules of civil procedure include the laws that dictate how a suit will be filed, all pretrial matters, trial proceedings (with the possible exception of rules of evidence), and posttrial issues until the case is concluded or an appeal is initiated. Most state rules of civil procedure follow or are similar to a standard model. It should be noted, however, that each state has the right to create its own procedural rules that are followed and enforced in the state courts and that may vary from the standard rules followed in most jurisdictions.

Pretrial Proceedings

Rules of civil procedure first become relevant at the time a lawsuit is begun. Indeed, the first rule of the Federal Rules of Civil Procedure states: "A civil suit is commenced by the filing of an action."[7]

Complaint. An action (lawsuit) is filed by the plaintiff, who presents the **complaint,** or petition (document alleging what the defendant did that was legally wrong), with appropriate filing fees (costs of processing the documents), to the clerk of the court. The complaint is organized into what are usually single statements that are numbered and referred to as paragraphs. Each statement is either a statement of the existing law or a statement of a fact that the plaintiff alleges has occurred. When read in its entirety, the complaint should state which laws have allegedly been breached and which facts state how the law was allegedly broken. Additionally, the complaint will indicate what compensation is necessary to satisfy the plaintiff's injuries. (See Figure 5.1.)

Complaint

Also known as a petition. The document that apprises the court and the defendant of the nature of the cause of action by plaintiff.

Summons. Once the lawsuit has been filed, the wheels of the judicial system begin to turn. A summons (formal legal notice of suit) is issued to the defendant in the lawsuit, and is usually accompanied by a copy of the complaint. The method of giving notice of the suit is also prescribed by procedural law. A

FIGURE 5.1   Complaint

In the District Court
45th Judicial District
State of Tucammawa

Buzzy Jamison,
Plaintiff
vs.
Malcolm Smythe,
Defendant.

COMPLAINT

Comes now the Plaintiff Buzzy Jamison, by his attorneys Marjoram, Coburn, and McEachern, and for his cause of action against Defendant Malcolm Smythe, complains as follows:

1. On or about March the 17th, 1990, Tucammawa state highway 7098, ran in an east-west direction through Langdon County, State of Tucammawa.
2. On the aforementioned date, at approximately 3:00 a.m., Defendant Malcolm Smythe was operating a motor vehicle in a westerly direction along said highway in the vicinity of highway mile-marker 31.
3. At the aforementioned place and time, Defendant Malcolm Smythe caused his vehicle to cross the median separating east- and westbound traffic, and did then and there enter the eastbound lanes.
4. Immediately following the entry of Malcolm Smythe's westbound vehicle into the eastbound lane, said vehicle collided with the vehicle operated by Plaintiff, in an easterly direction.
5. Said collision was the direct and proximate result of one or more of the following negligent acts or omissions of Defendant Malcolm Smythe:
   a) Driving while under the influence of alcohol and/or other drugs.
   b) Driving too fast for conditions.
   c) Failure to keep a proper lookout.
   d) Failure to properly maintain his vehicle in properly marked lanes.
   e) Westbound entry into lanes limited to eastbound traffic.
6. Said collision was with such force that Plaintiff's vehicle was severely damaged.
7. Said collision further caused serious and permanent injuries to the Plaintiff which include but are not limited to the following:
   a) Injuries to the Plaintiff's head, face, and neck.
   b) Injuries to the Plaintiff's right arm.
   c) Injuries to the Plaintiff's left leg.
   d) Injuries to the Plaintiff's back.
   e) Injuries to the Plaintiff's skeletal, muscle, and nervous system.
8. Said injuries to the Plaintiff have caused great physical and emotional suffering, loss of wages, and medical expenses incurred in an attempt to be cured of said injuries. Said injuries have further caused permanent disability and disfigurement to Plaintiff, and will result in additional future lost wages, and expenses in an attempt to be cured of said injuries.
   WHEREFORE, the Plaintiff prays that the Court will find the Defendant to be guilty of negligence, and further that the court will grant damages and costs to the Plaintiff as compensation for the above said injuries.

Buzzy Jamison
Attorneys Marjoram, Coburn, & McEachern
7719 Hamilton
Sequoia, Tucammawa 00000

summons indicates how long a party has to respond to the claims of the complaint. Methods of service include personal delivery to the defendant or a suitable representative and publication of the information in a newspaper where the defendant lives or is believed to live. Some states allow other methods, and as technology of communication expands, so most likely will methods of service. If the defendant does not respond to the complaint within the allowed time period, the court will accept everything alleged in the complaint as true and grant a decision in favor of the plaintiff. This is known as default judgment.

Response. A defendant may respond to the complaint in a number of ways. Responsive pleadings have different names in different states. However, the basic methods of responding to a complaint are the same. One method is through an answer, in which the defendant responds to each item specifically alleged in the complaint. Commonly, the defendant will respond by admitting, denying, or pleading the inability to admit or deny based on lack of information. This latter claim is given in response to an allegation that is vague or cannot be answered with an admission or denial unless more information is provided by the plaintiff. Claiming a lack of knowledge is generally treated as a denial to protect the defendant from having to admit to or deny claims about which too little is known at the time. If an answer is filed, the parties move into pretrial proceedings (see Figure 5.2).

Another response to a complaint might be a Motion for a Bill of Particulars, a claim by the defendant that the complaint as it is stated cannot be answered. A Motion for a Bill of Particulars requests the court to order the plaintiff to clarify one or more allegations of the complaint by explaining or adding information. If the motion is granted, the plaintiff will be required to provide the defendant with additional information. If the motion is denied, the defendant will be ordered to answer the complaint as it stands. (More information regarding motions is presented below.)

If the complaint is deficient in some way, a Motion to Dismiss (in some states, a similar document is known as a demurrer) may be filed. This simply states that the complaint either does not contain facts that warrant any type of lawsuit or that the complaint is improperly stated according to procedural rules. If granted, this type of motion can result in permanent dismissal of the lawsuit or dismissal without prejudice (this is the same as granted with leave to amend), which means that the plaintiff can correct the errors. Often, if this is done within a specified period of time, the suit does not even need to be refiled.

It is also important to note that the failure to properly serve the summons or complaint on the dismissal on the defendant can result in an action being dismissed. For example, if the summons and complaint was not served on the defendant, or an appropriate representative, or was served at an inappropriate place or time, the defendant could file a motion to dismiss. Each jurisdiction has its own procedural rules concerning the service of process that need to be followed closely.

Whether a motion is granted with or without prejudice depends upon the reason for the motion. If the reason is that there is no basis for a lawsuit, the

FIGURE 5.2

Answer

In the District Court
45th Judicial District
State of Tucammawa

Buzzy Jamison,
Plaintiff
vs.
Malcolm Smythe,
Defendant.

ANSWER

Comes now the Defendant Malcolm Smythe, by his attorneys Cochran, Eastwood, and McQueen, and with respect to the allegations of the Plaintiff's Complaint answers as follows:

1. Admitted.
2. Admitted.
3. Admitted.
4. Admitted.
5. Denied.
6. Denied.
7. Denied.
8. Denied.

AFFIRMATIVE DEFENSE

Defendant further states as an affirmative Defense that he was forced into the eastbound lane as the result of a hazard in the westbound lane; and that Plaintiff, seeing the Defendant approach, failed to take any evasive action whatsoever to avoid the collision. The Plaintiff is guilty of gross negligence in failing to take steps to avoid the collision, and as a result should not be permitted to recover against the Defendant.

Malcolm Smythe
Attorneys Cochran, Eastwood, and McQueen
Success Building, Suite 1
1700 Pennsylvania Ave.
Sequoia, Tucammawa 00000

suit may be dismissed with prejudice unless the plaintiff can demonstrate to the court that additional facts could be added to the complaint that would create the foundation for a lawsuit. If the motion is denied and the complaint is found to be proper, the defendant is ordered to file an answer to the complaint.

Discovery. During the period after a suit is filed and prior to trial or settlement, procedural rules guide the parties in their preparations for the ultimate conclusion of the dispute. The most significant event during this time is known as **discovery.** At this stage, the parties exchange information under strict guidelines and close supervision of the courts. A primary goal of discovery is to foster the fair exchange of information to enable the parties to clearly evaluate their positions.[8] Often, discovery will result in settlement of the case once the parties become aware of all the information pertinent to the case, since the parties may not have been aware of certain facts that would influence the outcome of the case in a trial. Discovery can be considered "show and tell" where both parties present their evidence. This practice encourages the objective assessment of the strengths and weaknesses of each side, thereby

Discovery

Court-supervised exchange of evidence and other relevant information between parties to a lawsuit.

FIGURE 5.3
Interrogatories

In the District Court
45th Judicial District
State of Tucammawa

Buzzy Jamison,
Plaintiff
vs.
Malcolm Smythe,
Defendant.

INTERROGATORIES

Comes now the Plaintiff Buzzy Jamison by his attorneys Marjoram, Coburn, and McEachern and with respect to the above-named case submit the following interrogatories pursuant to Court Rule 606. Pursuant to said rule, the interrogatories below are to be answered in writing and under oath within 28 days of the date submitted.

1. With respect to the Defendant please state:
   a) All names by which the Defendant has been known.
   b) All addresses at which the Defendant has claimed residence since 1970.
   c) The names and current address of any current or former spouse.
   d) The address, of Defendant's current employment, position held, and current wage rate.
   e) The Defendant's social security number.
2. State the whereabouts of the Defendant between the hours of 3:00 p.m. March 16, 1990, and 3:00 a.m. March 17, 1990.
3. With respect to the time and dates listed in interrogatory number 2, state the name and address of each person, business, or other entity which provided alcohol or other drugs, by gift or sale, to the Defendant.
4. State all prescription medications and the prescribing physician's name and address for all drugs the Defendant was taking March 16–17, 1990.

Buzzy Jamison
Attorneys Marjoram, Coburn, & McEachern
7719 Hamilton
Sequoia, Tucammawa 00000

Submitted to Defendant by placing the above-stated interrogatories, postage paid, in the United States Mail, on the 31st day of April 1991.

encouraging settlement. The parties may utilize several different methods of discovery.

Interrogatories. Frequently, the first step in discovery is the submission of interrogatories—written questions submitted to the opposing party in the case (see Figure 5.3). The party who receives the questions must answer them under oath and in writing. A party may object to answering questions that are irrelevant or immaterial, invade the attorney-client privilege, or violate some other procedural rule. When an objection is raised, the judge will determine whether the party must answer the questions. Many jurisdictions limit the number of interrogatories that may be sent to the opposition.

Request for production. Often interrogatories are accompanied by another means of discovery—the request for production of documents (see Figure 5.4). This is a written request to produce documents or copies of documents.

FIGURE 5.4

Request for
Production

Comes now the Defendant, in the above-captioned action, and pursuant to applicable rules of civil procedure, requests that the plaintiff produce for examination, testing, sampling or copying by the defendant or agents of the defendant the following items:

1. All photographs, recordings, reports, records, documents, videotapes, notes, memoranda, accounts, books, papers, and other recorded, written, photographic or transcribed information that represent, are pertinent or related to in any manner, the allegations of the plaintiff against the defendant. The only exception to such request are the working papers and/or notes of plaintiff's attorney which would be characterized as work product of said attorney.

Marvin Henry, atty.
Winter, Somers and Snow, P.C.
Suite 260 Park Place
Canoga, State 000000

FIGURE 5.5

Notice of
Deposition

Pursuant to the rules of civil procedure applicable to this proceeding, the oral deposition of Defendant shall be taken before a notary public on December 12, 1994, commencing at 1:00 p.m. and continuing thereafter until such time as completed. The aforementioned deposition will be conducted at place of business of the Defendant, 401 East 1st St., Knobbe, IK 030303.

Marvin Henry, atty.
Winter, Somers and Snow, P.C.
Suite 260 Park Place
Canoga, State 000000

Because many of the functions of our society are dependent upon written records, it is often very helpful to review documents for insight into what actually occurred. These requests are also subject to objection based on a claim that the answers contain privileged or irrelevant information, and a judge may rule whether or not they must be complied with. Privileged information is information that was conveyed within the context of a confidential relationship, such as the attorney-client, doctor-patient, or clergy-parishioner relationship. Irrelevant information is information that is not probative or likely to produce evidence that is probative of the facts in the case.

Deposition. One method of discovery—the deposition—applies not only to the parties in the lawsuit but also to all persons with relevant information about it. In a deposition, the attorneys ask a party or witness in the suit to respond to extensive questions about his or her knowledge of the case. Usually, depositions are taken in person and in the presence of the attorneys for each party. The entire proceeding is taken down by a stenographer who is also a notary public and asks the person deposed to swear to tell the truth (see Figure 5.5).

More often, depositions are taken on videotape. In another type of deposition, the party requesting the deposition sends written questions and the deposee is asked to answer the questions under oath and to provide a notarized statement that the responses are true and accurate to the best of his or her knowledge.

Comes now the Plaintiff, by and through her attorneys as requests that the Defendant admit the genuineness and truthfulness of content of the attached document for the purposes of the above-captioned action, and further to stipulate the admission of said document into evidence in the above-captioned action.

Marvin Henry, atty.
Winter, Somers and Snow, P.C.
Suite 260 Park Place
Canoga, State 000000

FIGURE 5.6

Request for Admission

If it is anticipated that the witness will not be present at trial, the deposition may be taken for evidentiary purposes. The procedure is basically the same, but in addition to the discovering party asking questions, the other attorneys may ask questions in the same manner as they would in a trial. Both direct examination and cross-examination are conducted. If objections are made, the questions are later presented to a judge. If it is determined that the witness should respond, the answers will be given and presented to the jury.

Physical evidence. In some cases, physical evidence is an integral part of the lawsuit. For example, if a person is injured by a tool or on private property, the condition of the tool or the property may become paramount in the lawsuit. When such physical evidence is owned or controlled by another party to the suit, the discovering party may file a request for inspection. This type of discovery allows a party to inspect, photograph, measure, and evaluate a particular item or place. If the party wants custody of an item or wants to subject the item to any procedures that might affect it, court approval may be required. Otherwise, in most cases, plaintiffs and defendants are entitled to reasonable inspection of items that may be produced as evidence in a trial.

Examination. A party may also request a physical or mental examination of an opposing party if such examination is relevant to the lawsuit. An example is a plaintiff who is claiming injuries as the result of alleged negligence by the defendant. In such a case, the defendant may very well be allowed to select a physician to examine the plaintiff and give an opinion as to the extent of the injuries. Another example is a custody battle by the parents of a child. If the child or one of the parents has a history of abnormal behavior, the court may allow a mental examination by a qualified specialist to determine whether the behavior has had an adverse effect on the child. However, the court may also enforce limits on the extent or nature of the examination.

Genuineness of documents. Finally, if a party discovers information from another party through discovery or through independent investigation and the information is so crucial that it could ruin the other party's case, a Motion to Admit Genuineness of Documents, or facts, may be filed. (In some jurisdictions, this is known as a Request for Admission—see Figure 5.6). Although this type of motion is not usually considered an official form of discovery, it is directly related to information discovered. It asks the party to review the facts or documents discovered and to either admit or deny the truthfulness of the content. If the truthfulness is admitted or verified, the party who filed the motion may seek an early end to the lawsuit with a Motion for Summary Judgment (the effect of which is discussed a little later). Usually, a Motion to Admit Genuineness of Documents or Facts is not submitted unless the evidence directly contradicts the core basis of the other party's case. Because most parties genuinely believe their case and have evidence to support it, these motions are not seen in the majority of lawsuits.

 CASE

OLIVERO v. PORTER HAYDEN COMPANY

241 N.J.SUPER. 381, 575 A.2d 50 (1990).

DEIGHAN, J. A. D.

Plaintiffs Ralph and Maria Oliviero filed an action against 19 suppliers, manufacturers and distributors of asbestos. The complaint alleged that Ralph Oliviero had contracted asbestosis from exposure to defendants' products while working as a materials technician at the American Cyanamid Company in Boundbrook between 1953 and 1982. Maria Oliviero sued per quod.

During discovery, plaintiffs answered a number of standard Middlesex County asbestos interrogatories, as well as several supplemental interrogatories. They also submitted a witness list containing the names of 118 witnesses. Among those named on this list, which was submitted ten days prior to trial, were Anthony Jannone, the purchasing agent for American Cyanamid and Samuel Jannone, a laborer.

Trial commenced on February 2, 1989. At this point, plaintiffs had settled with all of the defendants except the Porter Hayden Company (Porter Hayden), Eagle Picher Industries, Inc. (Eagle Picher) and Owens-Corning Fiberglass Corporation (Owens-Corning). Pursuant to a general order on asbestos litigation issued in 1982 by the Law Division in Middlesex County, Ozzard, Wharton Klein, Mauro, Savo & Hogan of Somerville was

designated as lead counsel; McCarter & English was designated as medical counsel.

On the fourth day of trial, plaintiffs' attorney called Anthony Jannone as a witness. Jannone testified about several asbestos products manufactured by Porter Hayden and Eagle Picher which had been present on American Cyanamid's premises during the term of Ralph Oliviero's employment. While defendants made several objections during the course of this testimony, they did not object to Jannone's appearance as a witness. On the next day, however, defendants moved for a mistrial on the grounds that Anthony Jannone had not been listed in plaintiffs' answers to interrogatories and had never been deposed. Counsel claimed that they had confused Anthony Jannone with Samuel Jannone, who had been listed in plaintiffs' answers to interrogatories and subsequently deposed. They argued that Anthony Jannone's testimony was severely prejudicial. Plaintiffs arguing that defendants had already heard his testimony and cross-examined him. The trial court denied this request. On appeal by plaintiffs, this court reversed and allowed Jannone to testify in the second trial. However, we instructed the Law Division to "assess reasonable costs, payable by plaintiffs' counsel to the Superior Court Clerk and not to be reimbursed by plaintiffs for the waste of publicly supported judicial resources occasioned by counsel's default and the resulting mistrial order." This court also noted that:

We view counsel's conduct as, at best, grossly negligent. We are advised defendants' counsel have moved for costs in the trial court. Our order shall not affect the outcome of their motion.

In a subsequent motion for attorneys' fees, defendants' lawyers certified the reasonable value of their services at $16,660 during the aborted first trial. Although the trial court granted their motion, it awarded only $2,400 per attorney, for a total of $9,600. In addition, it ordered plaintiffs' attorney to pay $2,346 in court costs. The court further ordered plaintiffs not to reimburse their attorney for these expenses. These decisions were formalized in orders dated March 10 and April 27, 1989.

I

Initially plaintiffs' attorneys argue that the trial court may not impose sanctions against a lawyer whose failure to comply with a discovery request causes a mistrial unless that lawyer acted in bad faith. They cite no authority to support this proposition. They submit that "this court should follow Federal Court interpretations of 28 U.S.C.A. s 1927, which authorizes sanctions against attorneys who 'unreasonably and vexaciously' complicate trial proceedings." We find that both of these proposals are clearly without merit. . . .

The discovery rules were designed to eliminate, as far as possible, concealment and surprise in the trial of law suits to the end that judgments rest upon real merits of the causes and not upon the skill and maneuvering of counsel. It necessarily follows, if such rules are to be effective, that the courts impose appropriate sanctions for violations thereof. Evtush v. Hudson Bus Transportation Co., 7 N.J. 167, 173, 81 A.2D 6 (1951).

Aside from specific rules, a court has inherent power to require a party to reimburse another litigant for its litigation expenses, including counsel fees. Vargas v. A. H. Bull Steamship Co., 25 N.J. 293, 296, 135 A.2D 857 (1957) ("Thus we find no error in conditioning the order of dismissal upon the payment of counsel fees. Allowance of fees under such circumstances is within the inherent power of the court; in effect, they are but reimbursement for expenses."); accord Busik v. Levine, 63 N.J. 351, 372, 307 A.2D 571 (1973); Crudup v. Marrero, 57 N.J. 353, 361, 273 A.2D 16 (1971); Trieste, Inc. II v. Gloucester Tp., 215

N.J.Super. 184, 188–189, 521 A.2D 864 (App.Div.1987) ("as a procedural sanction, [counsel fees are] within [the] broad constitutional power, and as such, they are within the statutory provision for costs").

Further, R. 4:23 (Failure to Make Discovery, Sanctions) specifically provides in several instances for expenses, "including attorney's fees" R. 4:23-1(c) (Motion for Order Compelling Discovery—Award of Expenses of Motion); R. 4:23-2 (Failure To Comply With Order); R. 4:23-4 (Failure of Party to Attend at Own Deposition or Comply With Demand or Respond to Requests for Inspection). Lastly, R. 1:2-4 (Sanctions: Failure to Appear; Motions and Briefs) provides: "(a) Failure to Appear. If without just excuse or because of failure to give reasonable attention to the matter, . . . an application is made for an adjournment, the court may order any one or more of the following: (a) the payment by the delinquent attorney . . . applying for the adjournment of costs, in such amount as the court shall fix, to the Clerk of the County in which the action is to be tried . . .; (b) the payment by the delinquent attorney . . . applying for the adjournment of reasonable expenses, including attorney's fees, to the aggrieved party. . . ."

It is perfectly clear from the foregoing that the trial court, aside from the mandate of this court, had more than ample authority to assess sanctions and counsel fees against plaintiff's attorneys for inconveniences and expenses incurred in attending an aborted three-day trial. Plaintiffs' attorneys were undeniably negligent in preparing the case and the defendants were substantially prejudiced by counsel's conduct. Anthony Jannone was the key witness for plaintiff and testified at the first trial that the defendants Porter Hayden and Eagle Picher had supplied a large portion of the asbestos products used by American Cyanamid during the period of Oliviero's employment. In view of the fact that defendants never had an opportunity to depose Anthony Jannone, the trial court had no choice but to declare a mistrial. In determining to grant counsel fees to defense counsel, Judge Reavey awarded only $2,400 each, for a total of $9,600. In so doing, she observed

Owens-Corning settled with plaintiffs prior to this litigation and waived its right to Judge Reavey's award of $2,400. For the purposes of this appeal, defendants' attorneys were therefore awarded only $7,200 in attorneys' fees.

. . . . [W]hile I appreciate the accuracy and the almost bare bones minimum application for each of those certifications appreciating the amount of effort and time and work that goes into preparation for a case of this kind, I can't award those kind of figures as far as costs of the litigation are concerned. I do think that I'm certainly authorized to, in fact, almost obligated to impose some compensation to each of these law firms for the time that they spent here that was truly a waste of time in light of the mistrial that had to be declared. . . . I find appropriate certainly the eight hour day that these trials do run figuring a little bit of time just to get to and from the courthouse. And I think $100 an hour is a reasonable compromise for their application despite the fact that I know that they're billing their clients more than that and everybody does. So again, I multiplied that out and it comes to $2,400.

II

Plaintiffs' attorneys also argue that the trial court abused its discretion by imposing costs in favor of the Superior Court for the three days of the first aborted trial. In our mandate to the trial court, we directed that "the Law Division will assess reasonable costs payable by plaintiff's counsel to the Superior Court Clerk . . . for the waste of publicly supported judicial resources occasioned by counsel's default and resulting in a mistrial." Plaintiffs' attorneys argue that the trial judge should have restricted her assessment of court costs to the statutory allowable tax costs and that actual costs are not expressly provided under the rules of court as required by R. 4:42-9(a)(7). They argue that costs over and above tax costs and costs of everyday running the court system is an expense that the State would have incurred in any event. We disagree.

As previously noted, if a party or counsel, "without just excuse" or for "failure to give reasonable attention to the matter" requires "an application . . . for an adjournment, the court may order . . . (a) the payment by the delinquent attorney . . . of costs, in such amount as the court shall fix, to the Clerk of the County in which the action is to be tried. . . ." R. 1:2-4(a).

In assessing $2,346 in court costs, Judge Reavey multiplied the three days which the first trial had taken by the estimated daily expense to the State. . . .

Affirmed.

Case Question

Should witnesses with vital information who are identified during a trial be excluded because they have not been named in the discovery?

Assignment 5.3

Assume you are involved in a lawsuit. The other side has access to the following information. Which type of discovery would best serve your goal of obtaining the information?

(a) The other party's employee was a witness to the incident.
(b) The other party has extensive documentation surrounding the incident.
(c) The other party knows of persons with relevant information.
(d) You believe the other party has been hospitalized numerous times for a neurotic hypochondria.
(e) You know that the other party has had multiple lawsuits against other persons on exactly the same facts and has claimed exactly the same injuries.

Motion practice. Throughout any lawsuit, the parties communicate with the court largely through motions. A **motion** is a request by an attorney whose party seeks assistance—or a ruling—from the court on a particular issue between the parties. Motions can result in something as serious as permanent dismissal of the lawsuit. The following discussion examines some of the more common motions in terms of what they request and the effect they have if granted. We have seen that motions can be used to request dismissal of suit when the complaint is deficient in some way. Motions also have many other uses through pretrial, trial, and even posttrial proceedings. Some of the more commonly sought motions are discussed here.

Motion

Formal request by a party to a lawsuit for court-ordered action/nonaction.

Motion to dismiss.   As stated earlier, this motion is used when a party believes that the facts of the case do not support a viable legal claim or that the complaint is improperly stated and does not conform to legal requirements as outlined by the rules of procedure (see Figure 5.7).

Motion to make more definite and certain.   Also called a Bill of Particulars, this document is filed by the defendant and asks that the plaintiff be required to provide more detailed information than that contained in the complaint (see Figure 5.8).

Motion to quash service of process.   This motion is filed when a plaintiff does not follow the rules of procedure for serving a summons and complaint on the defendant. If the rules are violated, the service is quashed, or rejected, and the plaintiff must attempt to serve the defendant properly.

Motion to inspect.   This motion is a discovery motion used to gain access to private property. If granted, the party is allowed to inspect the property as it pertains to evidence in the lawsuit. Examples include access to private property

---

Comes now the Defendant, Pauline McPaul, by and through her attorneys, Winter, Somers, and Snow, and moves the Court to enter an order dismissing the Complaint of Defendant. In support thereof, the Defendant states as follows:
1. On or about August 19, 1993, the Plaintiff instituted an action against the Defendant in the above-captioned court.
2. The Complaint of Plaintiff fails to state a cause of action upon which relief can be granted.
    Further, Plaintiff's allegations are legal conclusions and unsupported by any allegations of fact.
WHEREFORE, the Defendant prays that the Court enter an order dismissing the Plaintiff's complaint, awarding Defendant costs and such other and further relief as the Court deems necessary and proper.

Respectfully submitted,

Marvin Henry, atty.
Winter, Somers and Snow, P.C.
Suite 260 Park Place
Canoga, State 000000

FIGURE 5.7

Motion to Dismiss

FIGURE 5.8

Motion to Make
More Definite
and Certain

Comes now the Defendant, Pauline McPaul, by and through her attorneys, Winter, Somers, and Snow, and moves the Court to enter an order requiring Plaintiff to additional facts to support the allegations of his Complaint. In support thereof, the Defendant states as follows:

1. On October 31, 1993, Plaintiff instituted an action against the Defendant alleging breach of contract with respect to an agreement to which both Plaintiff and Defendant were parties.
2. That during the period 1990–1994, Plaintiff and Defendant had an ongoing business relationship, the product of which was no fewer than 70 separate contracts.
3. That Defendant is without information as to the specifics of the alleged breach and as a result is unable to frame a proper answer to the allegations of Plaintiff.

WHEREFORE, the Defendant prays that the Court will enter an order requiring the Plaintiff to more particularly describe the specifics of the facts supporting the allegations of Plaintiff's Complaint.

Respectfully submitted,

Marvin Henry, atty.
Winter, Somers and Snow, P.C.
Suite 260 Park Place
Canoga, State 000000

FIGURE 5.9

Motion to Inspect

Comes now the Plaintiff, Mortimer Vance, by and through his attorneys, Winter, Somers, and Snow, and moves the Court to enter an order permitting Plaintiff to inspect the premises under control of the Defendant. In support thereof, the Plaintiff states as follows:

1. On or about July 5, 1993, Plaintiff instituted an action in this Court against the Defendant alleging injury as the result of negligent conduct of Defendant.
2. Said allegations of neglect arose from an explosion that occurred on Defendant's property in which Plaintiff was seriously injured.
3. It is necessary for Plaintiff to inspect the aforementioned property of Defendant and site of Plaintiff's injuries for the proper preparation of Plaintiff's case.
4. Said inspection is appropriate pursuant to applicable rules of procedure.

WHEREFORE, the Plaintiff prays the Court will enter an order permitting Plaintiff to inspect the aforementioned property of Defendant upon reasonable notice and circumstances for the purposes of discovery in the above-captioned action.

Respectfully submitted,

Marvin Henry, atty.
Winter, Somers and Snow, P.C.
Suite 260 Park Place
Canoga, State 000000

that was the scene of an accident and inspection of an item, such as a weapon, that was involved in an injury (see Figure 5.9).

Motion for mental/physical exam. This motion is used when the mental or physical condition of a party or witness is relevant to the lawsuit. When granted, it allows the party to have the physician of choice examine the other party or witness and to give a report as to the person's mental or physical condition. An example would occur in a personal injury claim. The defendant

Comes now the Defendant, Pauline McPaul, by and through her attorneys, Winter, Somers, and Snow, and moves the Court to enter an order requiring the Plaintiff to submit to a physical exam upon reasonable notice by a physician of Defendant's choice. In support thereof, Defendant states as follows:

1. On or about August 31, 1993, Plaintiff instituted an action against the Defendant alleging negligence and consequent physical injury.
2. That pursuant to applicable rules of civil procedure, when Plaintiff places her physical condition in issue in litigation, the Defendant has the right to reasonable examination of Plaintiff's condition and medical records.
3. To date, Plaintiff has been unwilling to voluntarily undergo physical examination by a physician agent of the Defendant.
4. Said examination is essential to preparation of Defendant's defense to the allegations of the Plaintiff.

WHEREFORE, the Defendant prays that the Court enter an order requiring the Plaintiff, under reasonable notice and circumstances, to submit to a physical examination by a physician of Defendant's choosing and to order such other relief as the Court deems necessary and proper.

Respectfully submitted,

Marvin Henry, atty.
Winter, Somers and Snow, P.C.
Suite 260 Park Place
Canoga, State 000000

FIGURE 5.10

Motion for Physical Examination

might want to have his or her own doctor examine the plaintiff to render an opinion as to the extent of the plaintiff's injuries (see Figure 5.10).

Motion to compel.   During discovery, a party has certain time limits to respond to requests for information by the other party. When these time limits are not honored, the party expecting the information may request that the court order compliance immediately (see Figure 5.11).

Motion for sanctions.   This motion is used during discovery and at any other time during the proceedings when one party is of the opinion that the other party is willfully disregarding rules of procedure or orders of the court. The motion seeks punishment of the party at fault. If granted by the court, the penalty can range from being held in contempt of court to dismissal of the suit in the aggrieved party's favor.

Motion for summary judgment.   This is not a routinely filed motion. The basis of the motion is that the evidence is so overwhelmingly in favor of one party that no reasonable judge or jury could find in favor of the other party. Consequently, the party seeking the motion contends that there is no basis for a trial and the case should be determined without trial and in favor of the requesting party. The Motion for Summary Judgment is one of the most serious motions that can be filed in any lawsuit. It asks that the judge make a final decision on the issues of the suit without a trial. The decision is made

FIGURE 5.11

Motion to
Compel

Comes now the Plaintiff, Mortimer Vance, by and through his attorneys, Winter, Somers, and Snow, and moves the Court to enter an order compelling Defendant to respond to Plaintiff's discovery. In support thereof, Plaintiff states as follows:

1. On or about January 13, 1993, Plaintiff submitted interrogatories to Defendant in accordance with applicable rules of civil procedure.
2. Response from Defendant to said interrogatories was due on or about February 13, 1993.
3. Said date for response has passed, and Plaintiff has made further written requests to Defendant for compliance with this discovery. As of March 29, 1993, Defendant has failed to respond to the aforementioned interrogatories.
4. Defendant is in violation of the rules of discovery and is thwarting Plaintiff's attempts to proceed with this litigation.

WHEREFORE, the Plaintiff prays the Court to enter an order compelling the Defendant to respond to Plaintiff's interrogatories within 7 days and to order such other further and necessary relief as the Court deems proper.

Respectfully submitted,

Marvin Henry, atty.
Winter, Somers and Snow, P.C.
Suite 260 Park Place
Canoga, State 000000

---

solely on the basis of the evidence that exists at the time of the motion. The effect of such a motion is that the judge removes the case from the hands of the jury before it ever reaches them. Because our system of government places so much importance on the jury system, this is a very serious step for any judge to take.

When a Motion for Summary Judgment is sought, the judge must make a serious evaluation of the evidence. If the evidence is so strongly in favor of a party that a jury could only reasonably reach one decision and there is no substantial question left to be determined regarding the facts that occurred, a Motion for Summary Judgment may be granted. However, if there is any way that the jurors could reach a different conclusion as to whose version of the story is more probable, a Motion for Summary Judgment must be denied, and the case must be left to the trier of fact.[9]

Because the effect of a successful Motion for Summary Judgment is that there will be no trial in the case, such a motion must be filed before trial begins. Beyond that, when or if the motion is filed is up to the moving party. Usually, a Motion for Summary Judgment will not be filed unless there is evidence so strong that the opposing party's case is effectively defeated by the evidence. In most cases, each side has evidence that would tend to prove or disprove the case. Consequently, Motions for Summary Judgment are filed less often than other types of motions and are rarely granted (see Figure 5.12).

If a Motion for Summary Judgment by a defendant is granted, the case is dismissed with prejudice. This means that the lawsuit brought by the plaintiff will be dismissed and can never be brought again. No amendments to the complaint can be made, and the issue between the parties is permanently settled. If

Comes now the Defendant, Pauline McPaul, by and through her attorneys, Winter, Somers, and Snow, and moves the Court to enter an order of Summary Judgment in favor of Defendant and against Plaintiff. In support thereof, the Defendant states as follows:

1. On or about August 31, 1993, Plaintiff filed an Amended Complaint against Defendant alleging that the Defendant negligently caused Plaintiff's financial injury and ultimate bankruptcy as the result of a breach of contract. Defendant filed an answer denying the allegations of the Plaintiff.

2. The parties have subsequently engaged in discovery, and the information discovered indicates that no genuine issue of fact exists to support Plaintiff's allegations.

3. Attached in support of Defendant's motion is the affidavit of Plaintiff's former employee, Alexander Grant. Said affidavit states, inter alia, that as general manager of Plaintiff's business, Mr. Grant had full knowledge of Plaintiff's financial status at the time of the alleged breach of contract.

4. Affiant further states that at the time of the alleged breach of contract by Defendant, the Plaintiff was insolvent and consulting attorneys with respect to filing bankruptcy. Shortly following the alleged breach, Plaintiff did in fact file for bankruptcy.

5. Affiant avers that if called to testify, he would affirmatively state that Plaintiff suffered no financial injury by Defendant's breach and that said breach had no bearing on Plaintiff's subsequent bankruptcy.

WHEREFORE, the Defendant prays that the Court enter a finding that no genuine issue of facts exists with respect to Plaintiff's allegations of damage proximately caused by Defendant, and further that the Court enter an order of Summary Judgment in favor of the Defendant and against the Plaintiff and such other and necessary relief as the Court deems necessary and proper.

Respectfully submitted,

Marvin Henry, atty.
Winter, Somers and Snow, P.C.
Suite 260 Park Place
Canoga, State 000000

FIGURE 5.12

Motion for Summary Judgment

a Motion for Summary Judgment by a plaintiff is granted, the defendant is not entitled to a trial to present evidence in defense to the plaintiff's claims. If the plaintiff asked for a specific dollar amount of damages in the complaint, the defendant is automatically judged liable and must pay the plaintiff an appropriate amount. Sometimes the amount of damages specified in the complaint is appropriate, but other times a trial must be held to determine exactly how much the defendant should pay.

 CASE

BRECHER v. CUTLER

396 Pa.Super. 211, 578A.2d 481 (1990).

TAMILIA, Judge.

Appellants David Brecher and Janice Brecher, his wife, bring this appeal from the Order dated December 4, 1989, granting summary judgment to appellee Searle Pharmaceuticals, Inc. (now merged into and known as G. D. Searle & Co.), one of two defendants in the case. Appellants instituted this action on May 10, 1985 to recover damages for injuries allegedly sustained as a consequence of Mrs. Brecher's use of the Cu-7 copper contraceptive IUD, (Cu-7), manufactured by Searle. The basis of appellants' complaint was that Mrs. Brecher had been unable to become pregnant as a result of pelvic infection and adhesions caused by the Cu-7.

The facts which gave rise to this appeal may be summarized as follows from the Opinion of the trial court:

Mrs. Brecher had a Cu-7 inserted by her gynecologist, Dr. Cutler, on January 8, 1980, approximately three weeks after undergoing an abortion. She reported no problems with the Cu-7. On a follow-up visit, Dr. Cutler discovered that it had fallen out of position. It was removed and a second one inserted one week later. Mrs. Brecher wore that Cu-7 without problem until June, 1981. The Cu-7 was removed, not for any medical reason but because she had begun dating Mr. Brecher, who had had a vasectomy eight years earlier.

Plaintiffs were married to each other in June, 1982. As they desired to have children, Mr. Brecher underwent surgery to attempt a reversal of the vasectomy. His fertility was not restored, however, as reflected by a low sperm count and poor sperm motility.

In December, 1983, Mrs. Brecher began medical evaluation of her fertility by Dr. Ronald Traum. His evaluation revealed a problem with cervical mucus and an abnormal ovulatory pattern, neither of which were related to the Cu-7. In February, 1984 Mrs. Brecher underwent a laparoscopy which revealed a pelvic infection and adhesions surrounding her fallopian tubes, prohibiting pregnancy. The Brechers claim this was caused by the Cu-7. Dr. Traum informed the Brechers that surgery could lyse the adhesions but that, unless Mr. Brecher's sperm motility could be improved, he would not recommend it. Mrs. Brecher chose not [to] have the surgery.

Following the commencement of this suit and after the close of discovery, both Dr. Cutler and Searle moved for summary judgment as to liability. The undersigned granted this motion only as to Searle. Plaintiffs filed this timely appeal.

The basis of appellants' suit against Searle was, first, Searle failed to adequately warn Dr. Cutler of the hazards associated with the use of the Cu-7 or, in the alternative, their aggressive promotion of the contraceptive overrode the warnings, and second, Searle failed to warn Mrs. Brecher directly of the possible complications she could suffer from using the Cu-7. The trial court, following the "learned intermediary" doctrine, found Searle owed no duty to Mrs. Brecher and it had provided Dr. Cutler with both the physician's insert and the patient brochure as required by federal regulations, stating the appropriate warnings and precautions.

Appellants contend the court erred in granting summary judgment to Searle because the record indicates there is a genuine issue of material fact for the jury, as factfinder, to decide. They argue the court repeatedly refers to the lack of "evidence" and that the court, in essence, is admitting there is something to submit to a jury. They go on to say, "[i]t is not the function of the summary judgment to eliminate Appellant's right to try the case if it can show or argue successfully the negligence or culpability of the Appellee. Thus, it is conceivable that literature not yet produced because that is "evidence" will support Appellant's claim. . . ." (Brief of Appellants, p. 8.) For the reasons that follow, we disagree with appellants and affirm the Order granting summary judgment to appellee.

The pertinent sections of Pa.R.C.P. 1035, Motion for Summary Judgment, are as follows:

a. After the pleadings are closed, but within such time as not to delay trial, any party may move for summary judgment on the pleadings and any depositions, answers to interrogatories, admissions on file and supporting affidavits.

b. The adverse party, prior to the day of hearing, may serve opposing affidavits. The judgment sought shall be rendered if the pleadings, depositions, answers to interrogatories, and admissions on file, together with the affidavits, if any, show that there is no genuine issue as to any material fact and that the moving party is entitled to a judgment as a matter of law.

* * *

d. Supporting and opposing affidavits shall be made on personal knowledge, shall set forth such facts as would be admissible in evidence, and shall show affirmatively that the signer is competent to testify to the matters stated therein. . . . The court may permit affidavits to be supplemented or opposed by depositions, answers to interrogatories, or further affidavits. When a motion for summary judgment is made and supported as provided in this rule, an adverse party may not rest upon the mere allegations or denials of his pleading, but his response, by affidavits or as otherwise provided in this rule, must set forth specific facts showing that there is a genuine issue for trial. If he does not so respond, summary judgment, if appropriate, shall be entered against him.

While appellants are not required to present their entire case in opposing a motion for summary judgment, they cannot rest upon mere allegations in the pleadings but must present depositions, affidavits, or other acceptable documents which show there is a genuine issue of material fact to submit to the factfinder and the moving party is not entitled to judgment as a matter of law. "Bold unsupported assertions of conclusory accusations cannot create genuine issues of material fact." McCain v. Pennbank, 379 Pa.Super. 313, 318, 549 A.2D 1311, 1313–14 (1988).

We note initially that when reviewing an entry of summary judgment, an appellate court may disturb the order of the trial court only where there has been an error of law or a clear abuse of discretion. To uphold a summary judgment, there must not only be an absence of genuine factual issues, but also an entitlement to judgment as a matter of law. The trial court must examine the record in a light most favorable to the non-moving party and accept as true all well-pleaded facts in the non-moving party's pleadings.

Green v. K & K Insurance Co., 389 Pa.Super. 73, 74, 566 A.2D 622, 623 (1989) (citations omitted).

This is not the first time a plaintiff has argued that summary judgment was inappropriate because certain evidence could have been brought out at trial. In Roland v. Kravco, Inc., 355 Pa.Super. 493, 513 A.2D 1029 (1986), plaintiff fell in defendants' parking lot and commenced an action in trespass to recover for her injuries. Defendants filed motions for summary judgment claiming plaintiff did not set forth facts showing the parking lot was in a dangerous condition at the time of her fall. The trial court granted the motions and plaintiff appealed. This Court

reviewed the deposition of plaintiff which was the only evidence as to how the accident occurred. We agreed with the trial court that plaintiff failed to present facts showing there was a genuine issue for a jury to consider and defendants were not entitled to summary judgment as a matter of law.

The appellants contend that the court below erred in placing the burden of proof upon them to set forth facts showing that a genuine issue of material fact exists. However, as provided for in Pa.R.C.P. 1035(d) the non-moving party in his response to a properly supported motion for summary judgment must in the response "by affidavits or as otherwise provided in this rule, . . . set forth specific facts showing that there is a genuine issue for trial. If he does not so respond, summary judgment, if appropriate shall be entered against him." The appellant admitted that she did not see any ice or icy ridges on the parking lot surface, notwithstanding that she was looking at the ground at the time that she fell, and that she did not know what caused her to slip. Since by her own statements she did not observe any ice when she fell, she had the obligation to show by affidavit or otherwise that there were icy ridges or elevations which caused her to fall. On appeal, the appellant argues that she could produce two witnesses, a friend, Margaret Coyle, and Officer McNamara, who "could testify to the icy conditions of the parking lot within an hour of the appellant's fall." Nevertheless, the appellant did not disclose this information by way of affidavit, or otherwise, in response to the motion for summary judgment. As noted in Goodrich Amram, Procedural Rules Service, 2nd, s 1035(d):5, page 460: "The purpose of this amendment [Pa.R.C.P. 1035(d)] is to assure that the motion for summary judgment may 'pierce the pleading' and to require the opposing party to disclose the facts of his claim or defense." [Emphasis added in original.] Even if we assume that the undisclosed evidence might have affected the grant of summary judgment, the appellants chose not to disclose the basis for Mrs. Roland's claim with respect to the cause of her fall, and she did so at her own risk.

* * *

Rule 1035(d) requires the non-moving party to respond and set forth specific facts showing that there is a genuine issue for trial. Our rules of civil procedure are designed to eliminate the poker game aspect of litigation and compel the players to put their cards face up on the table before the trial begins. The appellant has done nothing to establish a genuine issue of material fact and accordingly summary judgment was properly entered.

Id. at 500-01, 513 A.2D at 1033-34 (footnote omitted).

In the instant case, the trial court found appellants failed to present facts to support their contention the learned intermediary doctrine does not apply and, therefore, Searle was entitled to summary judgment as a matter of law because the doctrine controls liability in cases such as this.

The foundation of the doctrine was propounded in Incollingo v. Ewing, 444 Pa. 263, 282 A.2D 206 (1971), where the Supreme Court dealt with the issue of the duty of drug manufacturers to warn of potentially dangerous side effects of their products and to whom the warning must be given. In reference to prescription drugs, the Court said, "[s]ince the drug was available only upon prescription of a duly licensed physician, the warning required is not to the general public or to the patient, but to the prescribing doctor." Id. at 285, 282 A.2D at 220.

This Court discussed the rationale of the rule from Incollingo in Leibowitz v. Ortho Pharmaceutical Corp., 224 Pa.Super. 418, 307 A.2D 449 (1973):

It is for the prescribing physician to use his own independent medical judgment, taking into account the data supplied to him from the drug manufacturer, other medical literature, and any other source available to him, and weighing that knowledge against the personal medical history of his patient, whether to prescribe a given drug.

Id. at 431, 307 A.2D at 457. Thus, the information supplied by the drug manufacturer is only one source a physician must consult and he is expected to make an independent medical judgment in determining whether a given drug is appropriate for a particular patient.

More recently, this Court was faced again with the question of who has the duty to warn the user of a prescription drug and whether the manufacturer may be liable.

It is clear that the manufacturer of a prescription drug known to be dangerous for its intended use, has "a duty to exercise reasonable care to inform those for whose use the article [was] supplied of the facts which make [the product] likely to be dangerous." Incollingo v. Ewing, supra, 444 Pa. at 285 n. 8, 282 A.2D at 220 n. 8. However, the warnings which are required to be given by the manufacturer must be directed to the physician, not the patient-consumer. This is so because it is the duty of the prescribing physician to be fully aware of (1) the characteristics of the drug he is prescribing, (2) the amount of the drug which can be safely administered, and (3) the different medications the patient is taking. It is also the duty of the prescribing physician to advise the patient of any dangers or side effects associated with the use of the drug as well as how and when to take the drug.

Makripodis v. Merrell-Dow Pharmaceuticals, Inc., 361 Pa.Super. 589, 596, 523 A.2D 374, 378 (1987).

The line of cases setting forth the learned intermediary doctrine make it clear that summary judgment in favor of Searle was appropriate, absent facts by appellants raising the question of whether Searle adequately warned Dr. Cutler. A manufacturer will be held liable only if he fails to exercise reasonable care to inform the one for whose use the product is supplied of the facts which make it likely to be dangerous. White v. Weiner, 386 Pa.Super. 111, 562 A.2D 378 (1989). Although all the cases cited herein concern prescription drugs, we hold that the law is equally controlling in cases such as this where a doctor prescribes a contraceptive. Therefore, appellants could not rely on unsupported allegations in response to Searle's motion for summary judgment but were required to introduce facts tending to show Searle failed to exercise reasonable care in informing Dr. Cutler of the dangers of the Cu-7.

The trial court found there was no dispute that Searle sent and Dr. Cutler received the physician's insert for each Cu-7 he prescribed for Mrs. Brecher. The pertinent language of the insert is as follows:

WARNINGS
Pelvic Infection: An increased risk of pelvic inflammatory disease associated with use of IUDs has been reported. While unconfirmed, this risk appears to be greatest for young women who are nulliparous and/or who have a multiplicity of sexual partners. Salpingitis can result in tubal damage and occlusion thereby threatening future fertility. Therefore is it

recommended that patients be taught to look for symptoms of pelvic inflammatory disease.

The decision to use an IUD in a particular case must be made by the physician and the patient with the consideration of a possible deleterious effect on future fertility. Pelvic infection may occur with a Cu-7 in situ and at times result in the development of tubo-ovarian abscesses or general peritonitis. The symptoms of pelvic infection include: new development of menstrual disorders (prolonged or heavy bleeding), abnormal vaginal discharge, abdominal or pelvic pain, dyspareunia, fever. The symptoms are especially significant if they occur following the first two or three cycles after insertion. Appropriate aerobic and anaerobic bacteriologic studies should be done and antibiotic therapy initiated promptly. If the infection does not show marked clinical improvement within 24 to 48 hours, the Cu-7 should be removed and the continuing treatment reassessed on the basis of the results of culture and sensivity [sic] tests.

ADVERSE REACTIONS
Pelvic infection including salpingitis with tubal damage or occlusion has been reported. This may result in future infertility.

Dr. Cutler stated he was aware of the possible side affects and that he did read Searle's insert and it was consistent with his understanding from other sources of the risks involved with the use of the Cu-7.

Indeed, Dr. Cutler remarked several times that he had a complete and independent awareness of the complications from which Plaintiff suffers, and he indicated that he chose this device based on his own professional judgment and Mrs. Brecher's preferences. (Deposition of Dr. Cutler, p. 62).

Although appellants argue the physician's insert was insufficient to warn of the risks of pelvic infection and infertility, the deposition testimony of Dr. Cutler compels us to find the warnings were adequate. Furthermore, appellants failed to factually support their assertion that the aggressive promotion of the Cu-7 nullified the warnings as to Dr. Culter, therefore, appellants' arguments against entry of summary judgment must fail.

Order affirmed.

Case Question
What disputed fact did plaintiffs allege the jury should decide?

Motion in limine. This motion is filed in an attempt to prevent certain evidence from being presented to a jury. It is based on the contention that certain evidence would interfere with an informed and fair decision by the jury. Usually, this motion is filed when there are graphic depictions of injuries or when information duplicates other evidence. It is granted only when the information would lead a jury to unfair conclusions and when there is other sufficient means of presenting evidence of the facts to the jury (see Figure 5.13).

Motion for directed verdict. Not to be confused with the summary judgment motion, this motion is filed after evidence has been presented to a jury (rather than before a trial has begun). However, similar to the summary judgment motion, the Motion for Directed Verdict asks that the judge make a determination that there is only one reasonable outcome to the suit and because of this, the jury should be told what its verdict will be (see Figure 5.14).

Motion for judgment notwithstanding the verdict (Non Obstante Verdicto). Also known as Judgment NOV, this request is made after the verdict has been delivered by the jury and a party contends that the jury misconstrued the

FIGURE 5.13

Motion in Limine

Comes now the Defendant, Pauline McPaul, by and through her attorneys, Winter, Somers, and Snow, and moves the Court to enter an order excluding certain evidence that Plaintiff has indicated it intends to submit in the trial of the above-captioned action. In support thereof, the Defendant states as follows:

1. This action involves allegations of personal injury to the Plaintiff as the result of claimed negligence of the Defendant.
2. Through discovery, Defendant has ascertained that Plaintiff intends to submit into evidence certain graphic photographs depicting Plaintiff's injuries.
3. Said photographs are immaterial in that they are not necessary to a fair and informed determination by the jury. Further, said photographs are of a nature that could inflame and prejudice the jury and prohibit the jury from making an objective finding.
4. Other suitable evidence of Plaintiff's injuries exist that would adequately and accurately depict the injuries for the jury's consideration.
5. Attached for the Court's consideration are copies of the aforementioned photographs and the alternative forms of evidence.

WHEREFORE, the Defendant prays that the Court enter an order excluding from evidence the aforementioned photographs and further that the Court order Plaintiff, Plaintiff's attorneys, witnesses, and all others from any direct or indirect reference to said photographs during the proceedings of the above-captioned action.

Respectfully submitted,

Marvin Henry, atty.
Winter, Somers and Snow, P.C.
Suite 260 Park Place
Canoga, State 000000

FIGURE 5.14

Motion for Directed Verdict

Comes now the Defendant, Pauline McPaul, by and through her attorneys, Winter, Somers, and Snow, and moves the Court to enter a Directed Verdict in favor of Defendant and against Plaintiff. In support thereof, the Defendant states as follows:

1. Plaintiff has concluded the presentation of her case in chief and in doing so has failed to present a prima facie case that would reasonably allow a jury to find in Plaintiff's favor based on a preponderance of the evidence.
2. "Where the plaintiff fails to present any significant evidence in support of the elements of the alleged cause of action, a directed verdict is appropriate." *Walston v. Dunham*, 111 E.W.2d 444 (CS App. 1987).

WHEREFORE, the Defendant prays that the Court will direct the jury in the above-captioned action to enter a verdict in favor of Defendant and against Plaintiff and such other relief as the Court deems necessary and proper.

Respectfully submitted,

Marvin Henry, atty.
Winter, Somers and Snow, P.C.
Suite 260 Park Place
Canoga, State 000000

evidence and reached a result that is in conflict with the totality of the evidence. If the motion is granted, the judge will substitute his or her own verdict for the verdict of the jury. Judges rarely grant this motion, however, because it usurps the jury's function to interpret the evidence.

Motion for new trial.   This motion is sought when a party contends that something occurred during the trial that prevented the legally correct result of the lawsuit. Errors can include the wrongful exclusion of certain evidence, improper testimony by a witness, or a procedural error by the judge. Actually, anything that a party can point to that had a significant impact on the case and that the party can convince the judge was irregular or inappropriate can serve as the basis for a Motion for New Trial.

It is important to note that motions such as those for summary judgment, directed verdict, and new trial are rarely granted. When they are, the judge removes the case from the hands of a jury and substitutes his or her own legal opinion for that of several peers of the parties in the suit. Most judges are not willing to take this responsibility without compelling reasons that the jury verdict is or would not be proper under the circumstances of the case.

Assignment 5.4

The following situations are appropriate for a motion. State the type of motion that would probably be filed for each situation.

1. Sarah is served with notice of a lawsuit. However, she is not the same person as described in the Complaint. In the suit, plaintiff claims only that Sarah's conduct in breaking a date hurt the plaintiff's feelings.
2. Jasper is the plaintiff in a lawsuit. Although Jasper's lawyer has called the opposition several times to request answers to interrogatories served six months ago, the defendant's counsel has yet to respond.
3. Corinne sued the Temple Insurance Agency for refusal to pay on an insurance policy against fire in her house (the house burned to the ground). The insurance agency has witnesses that Corinne confessed to torching her home. Also, Corinne has previously been convicted of arson.

Stages of Trial

Procedural rules help to guide the parties in assembling their evidence and presenting it at trial. Rules of evidence are examined in more detail later in the chapter. At this point, discussion will focus on the actual stages of the trial and the presentation of the evidence.

Voir dire.   The first stage of trial is generally the voir dire. During this stage, the jury that will hear the case is selected. In what is known as a bench trial, the trier of fact is the judge who hears the evidence and issues a decision. This is one option of the parties regarding the form of trial. In a bench trial, there is no jury and thus no need for the voir dire stage. If the case is to receive a jury trial, a fair and impartial jury must be selected.

Voir dire begins with a large pool of potential jurors who are brought into the courtroom. The attorneys for the parties—and sometimes the judge—ask each potential juror a number of questions, the goal of which is to determine whether a potential juror has any biases regarding the parties, attorneys, or circumstances of the case. If an attorney believes that a potential juror has a particular bias that would influence the decision in the case, the attorney has the right to challenge the juror's right to sit on the jury.

An attorney can exercise two types of challenges with regard to potential jurors: peremptory challenges and challenges for cause. Each party to a lawsuit may use a given amount of peremptory challenges, which vary in number from state to state. An attorney exercising a peremptory challenge does not have to give a reason to the court. A party has an absolute right to have the challenged juror removed from the jury. The only exception is if the removal is based on a person's status within a federally protected class, such as race.

In challenge for cause, an attorney asks that a juror be excused on the basis of a particular prejudice that was evident from the juror's answers to the questions previously asked. In challenge for cause, the opposing party can object to the challenge. Usually, the objection will state that the prospective juror did not exhibit a bias so strong that the juror could not fairly consider the case. The judge considers the challenge, any objections, and the statements of the juror and then renders a decision as to whether the juror will be excused.

When the required number of jurors has been reached, voir dire is ended. Traditionally, juries are composed of twelve persons and one or two alternates. Some states also have petit juries, usually juries of fewer people. Petit juries may be utilized in cases that are less serious but that still warrant the right to a trial by a jury of one's peers under state or federal law. Some states do not allow jury trials in very minor cases, such as traffic violations, where loss of liberty is not at stake.

 CASE

HUELSMANN v. BERKOWITZ

210 Ill.App. 3d 806,
154 Ill. Dec. 924,
568 N.E.2d 1373 (1991).

Justice **HOWERTON**
delivered the opinion
of the court.

We affirm the judgment entered on the verdict of a St. Clair County jury that found defendant liable for medical malpractice, awarding plaintiff $79,975.80 in actual damages, but we reverse the judgment for $15,000 in punitive damages.

We hold that the comments made during voir dire were not sufficient to cause the entire panel of veniremen to be discharged. . . .

Defendant, Dr. Wallace Berkowitz, performed a tonsillectomy on plaintiff, Florence Huelsmann.

After plaintiff returned home, she had several profuse bleeding spells.

During one middle-of-the-night spell, her husband called defendant.

According to plaintiff's husband, defendant advised plaintiff to gargle with hydrogen peroxide, but did not advise her to go directly to the hospital.

Defendant contradicted this, however, and testified that he told plaintiff's husband to take plaintiff to the hospital, and that defendant waited up two hours for the emergency room personnel to call him, but when no call came, he went back to sleep.

Defendant left on vacation the next day.

Several days later, plaintiff was taken to a hospital by her husband. A blood clot was removed from her throat and her throat was treated to prevent bleeding. She was given a shot to prevent shock and was transfused with two units of blood.

She returned home.

Again, she awoke, bleeding. This time, she went to a different hospital. She was admitted and a large ulcer was found where her tonsils once had been.

Treated, the ulcer healed and the bleeding stopped.

Post-bleeding, she was diagnosed as having a dysthymic disorder, a depression due to her profuse bleeding.

* * *

Defendant claims that he was denied a fair trial because of comments made by two veniremen, and because the circuit court failed to discharge the entire venire present when the comments were made.

There were two episodes of comments, and both criticized the caliber of medical care defendant had provided on other occasions.

Episode No. 1

"THE COURT: You know him as a patient of his?

JUROR: I was a patient of his.

THE COURT: You are or were?

JUROR: Sir?

THE COURT: You were?

JUROR: I was years ago.

THE COURT: What did he do for you?

JUROR: I had hemorrhaging of the nose, and I had changed doctors and had the problem corrected.

THE COURT: You say you changed doctors. You were not satisfied with his treatment?

JUROR: Right.

THE COURT: Okay. What did you feel the problem was, sir?

JUROR: I had—for no reason at all I'd start hemorrhaging and I had to go to the emergency room and they couldn't stop it. I finally had to have surgery.

THE COURT: All right. Well, let me ask you this, are you going to have a problem in this case?

JUROR: Well, I didn't have a happy experience on the first occasion, I finally had to have it taken care of with another doctor.

THE COURT: Well, the question is from personal experience with this doctor is it going to be so overwhelming that you just say, "Doc, I just don't think you did good?"

JUROR: I'd probably have trouble with that.

THE COURT: Okay. We'll excuse you. You can go back to the jury room, sir."

Episode No. 2

The second episode stands as proof that every now and again something can happen in trial that can make anyone bolt upright.

After the first episode everyone went back to their own business, the excused juror to the jury room, the court and counsel to the business of asking voir dire questions.

A panel member was being questioned. Down the box sat the others.

Suddenly, from down the box, a panel member who was not being questioned and never had been questioned, who simply had been sitting silently, announced:

"JUROR: I've been thinking, Dr. Berkowitz killed by brother."

The next words were spoken by the court.

"THE COURT: What is your name, sir?

JUROR: He was talking about Dr. Berkowitz, he let my brother die. I didn't know who it was—

THE COURT: You're Mr. who?

JUROR: Mr. (name deleted.)

THE COURT: We'll excuse you sir. You're juror number what?

JUROR: 22

THE COURT: We'll excuse you, sir.

JUROR: Sorry.

THE COURT: That's fine. Thank you."

Defendant concedes that the first episode alone would be insufficient to deprive him of a fair trial, but claims that the two incidents operating together were so prejudicial that they deprived him of a fair trial. He argues it was not enough to excuse these veniremen, and that no cautionary instruction ever could overcome the prejudice of these incidents to him, and therefore, the only remedy was to recuse the entire venire.

The circuit court has the discretion to determine whether jurors can weigh the evidence impartially, and that determination will not be set aside unless it is against the manifest weight of the evidence. Parson v. City of Chicago (1983), 117 Ill.App.3d 383, 72 Ill.Dec. 895, 453 N.E.2d 770.

In People v. Del Vecchio (1985), 105 Ill.2d 414, 429, 86 Ill.Dec. 461, 468, 475 N.E.2d 840, 847, veniremen heard another's personal opinion of the accused. Del Vecchio held that the jury had not been tainted. Taint would have resulted only if she who had expressed her preconceived opinion was allowed to remain on the jury.

The record does not establish that the panel members were prejudiced against the defendant, much less that prejudice was pandemic.

In this case, both the juror in episode number one and the juror in episode number two were discharged. The remaining veniremen each said they could be fair.

Trial judges, no less than trial lawyers, rely on instinct in assessing veniremen, their answers and whether they should serve as jurors. In this case, the trial judge had the opportunity to see and hear the veniremen. He concluded that the statements had not prejudiced them and was convinced that they could be fair and impartial. There is nothing in the record from which we can draw an inference that he was wrong. There is nothing in the record to show that he abused his discretion.

* * *

The judgment on the verdict for the plaintiff and against defendant, Wallace Berkowitz, M.D., assessing plaintiff's damages as being $79,975.80 is affirmed.

Case Question
Should someone who has been convicted of a crime be allowed to act as a juror in a criminal case?

Opening statements.   Following voir dire, the final jury is sworn in, and the proceedings begin. The first step in most trials is the opening statement. Usually, the party who has the burden of proof makes the first opening statement. The responding party has the option of making an opening statement at this time or of waiting until the presentation of his or her evidence. Opening statements are not to be argumentative. They are to serve as an opportunity for the attorneys to outline their evidence to the jury. Legal conclusions, arguments, and pleas for verdicts are inappropriate at this time. Opening statements are not evidence. Rather, they serve as an outline of the evidence to be presented.

Case in chief.   The case in chief is the stage of a trial during which the party with the burden of proof presents evidence to support its claim. The burden of proof previously mentioned refers to the party who must convince the jury of his or her case in order to win the suit. In a civil case, the burden of proof is generally on the plaintiff, who claims injury or damage due to the defendant's fault. The party with the burden usually presents evidence first. The standard burden of proof in most civil cases is to prove one's claim by a preponderance of the evidence. This means that the party with the burden must establish that the facts alleged in the complaint are more likely than not true. The party who does not have the burden of proof needs only to present enough evidence in opposition to prevent the burden (minimum level of evidence) from being met.

Consider the example discussed earlier in the chapter of the auto accident involving Jane and Tom. Assume the suit has commenced. Since Jane has brought the action against Tom, she is obligated to meet the burden of proof at trial. Jane claims that Tom was following too closely and caused the accident. Tom claims that Jane applied her brakes without warning to turn into a parking lot and that he could not avoid hitting her car. Jane must prove her case by a preponderance of the evidence. She must establish, with evidence, that her version of the case is more likely than not the way the accident actually occurred. In essence, the burden is on Jane to produce enough proof to convince the jury that her version is the most plausible.

Evidence for a case of this type might include photographs of the scene and the vehicles as well as expert opinions about skid marks on the road or other indicators of the speed and direction of the vehicles. The party with the burden of proof must meet an additional step known as presenting a prima facie case. Translated literally, prima facie means "on the face." In effect, a prima facie case is what the party with the burden must prove. The evidence brought at trial must be sufficient to establish each of the facts alleged in the complaint (the face of the claim) and to support the legal claims of the complaint. If there is not evidence to support each allegation of the complaint, a prima facie case has not been established.

If a prima facie case is not established, the claims of the complaint have not been proven. At this point, the party responding to the claims can make a Motion for a Directed Verdict, which requests the court to instruct the jury that there is no need to present a defense because the allegations of the complaint have not been proven. If the motion is granted, the judge directs the jury to render a verdict against the party with the burden of proof.

Most parties with the burden of proof attempt to establish a much stronger case than one that is merely prima facie. The evidence presented must withstand contradictory evidence presented by the defense and still prevail as the most likely explanation of the circumstances that created the dispute. Realistically, a prima facie case is usually not enough to win the case.

Defense.   After the party (usually the plaintiff) with the burden of proof has presented all of his or her evidence and made a prima facie case, that party will rest. At this point, the responding party—usually the defendant—will present his or her case. If the defense did not make an opening statement at the beginning of the trial, the opportunity to make one at this time is available. The opening statement is followed by the presentation of the defendant's evidence.

In the presentation of evidence, the defendant has no initial burden to meet. Rather, a burden occurs only if the plaintiff establishes a prima facie case. At this point, the burden shifts, and the defendant must present enough evidence in response to the plaintiff's evidence to create a question in the minds of the jury that the plaintiff's version is not the most likely version of the facts.

After the defendant has concluded the presentation of evidence, the plaintiff may request permission to reopen his or her case. This may be allowed when the plaintiff has evidence that will respond to some evidence introduced by the defendant. However, it is not permissible to present entirely new evidence that the plaintiff may have forgotten or otherwise failed to include in the original presentation of evidence. The plaintiff is permitted only to respond to the evidence of the defendant. The defendant may then be permitted to introduce rebuttal evidence.

Closing argument.   After both parties have concluded the presentation of evidence, the attorneys for the plaintiff and the defendant are allowed the opportunity to make closing arguments, also known as summations. In some jurisdictions, the defense presents its summation first and the plaintiff or prosecution gets the last word. In other jurisdictions, the plaintiff or prosecutor goes first and then gets a few moments of rebuttal to respond to the defendant's summation. At this stage, each attorney summarizes all of the evidence and attempts to persuade the jury of the most plausible explanation for the course of events that led to the lawsuit. Here the attorneys employ their advocacy skills and persuasive tactics to convince the jury in favor of their client.

Instructions and deliberation.   After the closing arguments, the judge will read instructions to the jury. These instructions explain the law that applies to the case as well as the burden of proof and indicate what the jury is to consider as evidence. The jury is then sequestered for deliberations; that is, the jurors are secluded from all outside influences while they reach a decision. Some courts will allow the jurors to take evidence such as documents and photographs into the jury room during their deliberation. In many jurisdictions, the verdict of the jury must be unanimous in favor of one party. If a jury needs more than one day to reach a verdict, the judge will determine whether the jurors can return home for the night or whether they must be sequestered, such as in a hotel, while they are not deliberating.

 APPLICATION 5.4

In 1992, a nationally publicized criminal trial was held in Indiana where world champion boxer Mike Tyson was charged in an incident involving a young woman. Because of the nature of the case and parties involved, the judge sequestered the jury in a local hotel. During the trial, the hotel caught fire, and the jurors had to be moved outside and eventually to another hotel. Many jurors came into contact with persons not associated with the trial. Some concern was expressed whether a mistrial should be declared and a new trial held with new jurors because the jurors had been unsequestered and exposed to the media for a time. The judge subsequently ruled that the jury was still impartial and trial could proceed.

Point for Discussion
What could have happened during this trial to affect juror impartiality?

Verdict. When the jury returns with a verdict, the verdict is read to the parties. If a party requests, the judge may poll the jury. When the jury is polled, the judge asks each juror whether the verdict represents his or her opinion in the case. This is used as a safeguard to assist the court in discovering situations where jurors have been coerced by other members of the jury to change their vote to reach a verdict. If the judge discovers that a juror does not actually support and believe in the verdict, the verdict is not unanimous. This would have the effect of a hung jury where the jurors return without a verdict. In a civil suit, when a jury cannot reach a decision that the plaintiff's case is more likely than not true, the burden of proof has not been met, and the defendant prevails.

Assignment 5.5

Examine the following statements and identify at what stage of trial each would occur:

1. "Ladies and gentlemen of the jury, it is our belief that the evidence you will see today will convince you by a preponderance that the defendant is not responsible for the death of the plaintiff as alleged."
2. "Mr. Smith, as a juror do you feel you could put aside your personal feelings about drunk drivers and consider the defendant as innocent until proven responsible for the accident in which the plaintiff was killed?"
3. "Ms. Johnson, isn't it true that you had been drinking yourself on the night you claimed to have witnessed the accident involving the defendant?"
4. "Your honor, it would appear from the total evidence presented by the plaintiff that the burden of proof has not been met, and at this time I would like to request a directed verdict."
5. "It is abundantly clear from the evidence that the plaintiff's death resulted not from the defendant's negligence but rather, from the plaintiff's own contributory negligence in driving at a speed too fast for conditions after working for a continuous eighteen hours at her job."

Rules of Evidence

The gathering and introduction of the various types of evidence are subject to many specific rules, but the rules of relevance and materiality apply to all evidence. Such rules are necessary to ensure that the evidence in any legal action is fair and proper. Evidence that is relevant and material and meets the requirements of more specific rules may be included in the trial and presented to the trier of fact.

Relevant Evidence

Evidence that tends to establish an essential fact in the dispute.

Relevant evidence.   **Relevant evidence** is that which tends to establish some basic element of the dispute.[10] Both sides in a lawsuit are allowed to introduce evidence that will tend to prove that their version of the story is true. For example, in the lawsuit involving Jane and Tom, evidence that Jane introduced that Tom has been fired from every job he ever held would not be relevant. Such evidence has nothing to do with the accident or the driving ability of either party. However, if Tom introduced evidence that Jane has been in six accidents in which her car was rear-ended under similar circumstances, the evidence might very well be relevant.

Material Evidence

Evidence necessary to a fair and informed decision by the trier of fact.

Material evidence.   **Material evidence** is that which is considered necessary to a fair and informed determination of the dispute.[11] The same information from twenty different witnesses may not be material. In most cases, a few of these witnesses could establish the facts just as well as twenty could. Additionally, evidence that may inform the court but is so extreme that it might prevent a jury from being fair could be considered immaterial. An example would be grotesque photographs of an injury. Although the jury needs to be informed about the extent of the injuries, often the jurors can be more fair if they consider medical reports rather than extremely graphic photographs. Often the basis for a Motion in Limine will be materiality.

Hearsay.   A rule of evidence that is employed in nearly every trial is that of hearsay. Entire volumes have been written about hearsay, defined as follows:

> An out-of-court statement offered to prove the truth of the matter asserted.

Hearsay follows the reasoning that everything said, written, or otherwise communicated in everyday life is not necessarily true. Therefore, such information should usually not be admitted as evidence in a trial where all other evidence is considered to be reliable and true. Hearsay evidence is testimony by a witness who repeats something that was communicated outside the trial by someone not under oath. Further, to be hearsay, the content of the communication must be offered as evidence of the truth. If it is offered only to show the ability to communicate, it would not be considered hearsay.

Because some statements are made under circumstances that are very reliable and promote only truthful communication, there are exceptions to the hearsay rule. Such information, which would otherwise be considered to be hearsay, is reliable enough in its truthfulness to warrant introduction as evidence in the trial. An example is a person's statement that is directly contrary to the person's own best interest, such as an admission of guilt. Ordinarily, individuals do not confess to acts for which they are not responsible. If there is evidence that a party or a witness made such a statement, the information may be admitted as an exception to hearsay.

When someone has an experience and makes an immediate statement about it, the statement may be considered an exception to hearsay. Statements made in circumstances where there was not time to formulate the best legal answer are highly reliable. Thus, spontaneous statements may be admitted.

Other exceptions include regularly maintained business records, statements made to physicians, and original documents. While there are many additional exceptions, it is important to remember that evidence of communication made out of court must have a high degree of reliability for truth before it will be admitted as an exception to hearsay.

 APPLICATION 5.5

A widow brings a lawsuit for the pain and suffering and subsequent death of her husband after a motorcycle accident allegedly caused by the defendant. The defendant denies causing the accident and further alleges that the man died instantly; thus, no pain or suffering was involved. If the widow introduces a statement made by her husband at the scene, such statement may be introduced to show the man was alive and did indeed suffer pain from his injuries. Whether the content of the statement will be admitted—if it was relevant to the suit—depends on whether it is hearsay evidence.

Point for Discussion
Why do you think the statement of the husband is
a. relevant or irrelevant
b. material or immaterial
c. hearsay, nonhearsay, or hearsay subject to an exception to the rule

---

Privilege.   Another important aspect of evidentiary law involves privilege. Generally, a person cannot be required to testify about confidential communications, including communications made in a physician-patient, attorney-client, clergy-parishioner, husband-wife, or any other relationship that the court determines should be protected. With respect to the husband-wife privilege, some exceptions have been made in recent years, especially in the area of criminal law. (This is addressed in Chapter 14.) Other exceptions to privilege occur when the party claiming the privilege has placed the very content of the communication in issue. For example, if a person is involved in a personal injury lawsuit, the privilege to withhold confidential medical records about the injury is waived.

Other evidence.   Numerous specific rules of evidence exist regarding such areas as opinion, habit, and personal background of a rape victim. Even when evidence is relevant, material, not hearsay, and not privileged, it may still be objected to on the basis of one of the more specific rules. Assembling and presenting admissible evidence is one of the most crucial elements of trial, if not the most crucial element. Consequently, anyone involved in litigation must be fully aware of the rules of evidence.

Rules of Appellate Procedure

Appellate procedure is largely governed by the appellate system in a jurisdiction. As discussed in Chapter 2, there are two types of appellate jurisdictional structures. One involves appeal directly to the highest court of the jurisdiction, whereas the other involves review by an intermediate court of appeals. If a jurisdiction involves an intermediate court of appeals, such as the federal judicial system's circuit courts of appeals, special rules must be created to guide a case through this level prior to reaching the highest court.

The appellate court generally reviews only what has occurred procedurally in the lower court. Such review may encompass what took place before, during or after the trial. Most often, appellate courts refuse to hear or consider any new evidence in a case. This does not mean that the court will only hear what was admitted at trial. Rather, it will hear all evidence that was offered, irrespective of whether the trial court admitted or refused the evidence. The appellate court will not hear evidence that was available but was not presented to the trial court.[12] Appellate court decisions are usually confined to the issue of whether an error was made in the trial court. Further, the error must be serious enough to warrant intervention by the appellate court. Consequently, an appellate court will not exchange its opinion of right or wrong or guilt or innocence for that of the trier of fact. It will only consider whether the opinion of the trier of fact was based upon a fair presentation of the case according to the requirements of substantive and procedural law.

 APPLICATION 5.6

Alfred was accused of murder. Several witnesses testified that Alfred acted in self-defense. Other witnesses testified that Alfred continued to attack the victim long after self-defense was no longer necessary. The trial court refused to admit a videotape of the incident that was offered by Alfred's attorney. Alfred was convicted of murder.

On appeal, Alfred alleged that had the jurors been allowed to watch the film, they would have reached the conclusion that the attack was in self-defense. The appellate court is not faced with the decision regarding Alfred's guilt or innocence. Rather, the only function of the court is to determine whether the tape was improperly excluded. In most jurisdictions, if an appellate court were to make the determination that the tape was improperly excluded, Alfred would not be entitled to a verdict of not guilty, but he would be entitled to a new trial.

Points for Discussion
1. Why wouldn't Albert be found not guilty?
2. Would Albert be guaranteed a verdict of not guilty after the new trial?

The appeals process is started by notice to the courts and all other parties from the appealing party (known as the appellant), who claims that something improper has taken place. The party who defends against the appeal and claims that the procedure has been proper is the appellee.

Once the courts and other parties have been given notice, several events must occur. The order and time for these events may vary from jurisdiction to jurisdiction. Generally, the appellant is responsible for having the trial court records of the case prepared and sent to the appellate court. These records enable the appellate court to review the entire history of the case, including the alleged error by the trial court. The records consist of all legal documents (commonly called pleadings and motions) filed with the court by the parties. Also included will be court orders in the case and transcribed statements of the parties, attorneys, witnesses, and the judge during court hearings.

In addition to submitting the court records, the appellant as well as the appellee may submit appellate briefs—detailed explanations of the case and the law applicable to the case of the particular party—to the reviewing court. The briefs set forth the facts of the case, the issues that arose in the lower court, and the result of the case. The briefs also suggest applicable law to the appellate court that supports the position of the party with respect to the issue. The appellate court's duty is to select the law that best applies to the situation.

In many appellate cases, the courts permit attorneys for the parties to present oral arguments of the briefs. At this stage, each attorney presents the brief and answers questions by the appellate court about the brief's content. The court may ask the attorneys to explain why they think a particular point of law is applicable to the present case. In addition, the attorneys may respond to the points raised in their adversary's brief.

The appellate court will consider the case and render a written opinion. The court may affirm (approve) the proceedings of the lower court, or it may reverse the lower court and remand the case to the trial court with an order for new or different proceedings to be conducted. Occasionally, the appellate court will hold that the lower court erred to the point that the proceedings should not even have been held. In such situations, the case is dismissed entirely.

Figure 5.15 shows the steps in a civil suit from occurrence of incident giving rise to a lawsuit to appeal and enforcement of judgment.

FIGURE 5.15   Steps in a Civil Suit

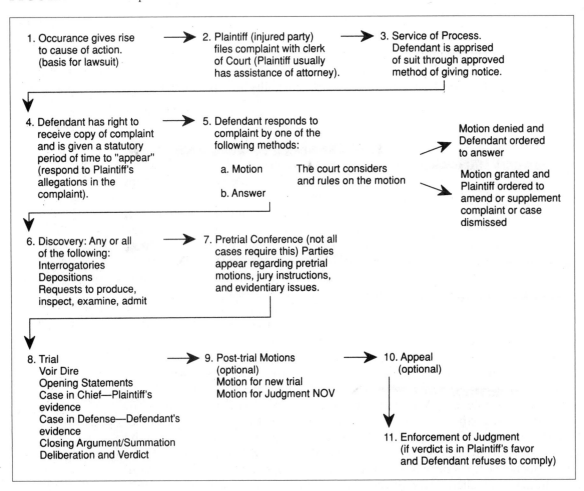

Assignment 5.6

Create a detailed chart that demonstrates each step of procedure from the time a lawsuit is filed through the appeal.

ETHICAL NOTE

Discussion frequently takes place about the ethical obligations of legal professionals. Individuals whose ethical duties do not attract much attention, however, are jurors. From the time an individual is selected for a pool of potential jurors, ethical requirements apply. Even potential jurors are asked to take an oath to consider and answer questions of the parties, counsel, and the court in an honest and forthright manner. The duty of a juror is a very serious one. The legal rights of total strangers have been entrusted to the juror on the premise that the juror will listen to the evidence objectively and apply only the law and not personal bias to the evidence when reaching a verdict.

Although a somewhat rare occurrence, it is not unheard of for a verdict to be reversed on appeal on the basis of discovered information that a juror considered information not presented as evidence or allowed personal bias to direct the verdict in a lawsuit. While courts are very reluctant to tamper with the sanctity of the jury process, it is necessary to monitor the process as any other aspect of the legal system for unethical conduct by those who are in such a position of trust.

Question

Can you think of a situation when a juror might act unethically?

CHAPTER SUMMARY

Procedural law is never constant. Every jurisdiction creates procedural law to conform to the needs of its particular judicial structure and its population. Then, as society changes, these needs change, and the rules must be altered. In spite of these constant changes, it would be impossible for a legal system as complex and as heavily used as the American legal system to function without some type of procedural standards. In reality, the procedural laws enable any citizen in this country to utilize the court system to obtain answers to legal questions and redress for legal wrongs.

The various types of procedural law address the various stages of litigation. Rules of civil procedure often deal with the pretrial phase of a lawsuit, including the important stage of discovery. Rules of evidence give the court and the parties direction as to what types of information would be appropriate for a jury to reach a fair and intelligent verdict. Rules of appellate procedure guide the parties through the appellate process to have a case properly reviewed by a higher court.

In any lawsuit, once the procedural concerns have been dealt with, the court is free to address the heart of the issue between the parties in dispute. The substantive law guides the judiciary in doing so. The facts are examined, the true issue is identified, and the law is applied to the circumstances to make the determination of which party should prevail. In fact, if more persons would look to these legal standards before taking action, the results would be apparent, and a great number of legal disputes could be avoided. But as long as people fail to inquire as to the law or disagree as to its meaning, disputes will continue, and procedural law will facilitate the application of substantive law in the determination of these disputes.

As a case proceeds through the steps of trial, a jury is selected through a process called voir dire. Next, the attorneys make opening statements, which describe the evidence they intend to present. The plaintiff presents evidence first in a stage known as the case in chief. The defense responds with evidence that weakens or contradicts the case of the plaintiff. After all the evidence has been introduced, the attorneys summarize the evidence presented in a light most favorable to their client. Following this, the jury is instructed on the law and deliberates until it reaches a verdict.

Throughout the entire litigation process, the attorneys communicate requests to the court in the form of motions. These formal requests seek everything from information about the evidence of the opposing party to dismissal of the case against the opposition or even a new trial entirely. The process of motion practice provides an efficient and effective method of resolving issues that arise during litigation and cannot be resolved by the parties.

REVIEW QUESTIONS

1. How does substantive law differ from procedural law? Give some examples.
2. Distinguish a jury trial from a bench trial.
3. What is a motion?
4. What is the function of an appellate court?
5. When are the rules of evidence applied in a lawsuit?
6. List and describe each stage of trial.
7. Distinguish a Motion for New Trial from a Motion for Judgment Notwithstanding the Verdict (Motion for Judgment NOV).
8. What is the difference between relevant and material evidence?
9. Why are there exceptions to the rule that hearsay evidence is inadmissible?
10. What are the two functions of substantive law?

CHAPTER TERMS

Civil Law	Discovery	Procedural Law
Compensatory Damages	Material Evidence	Relevant Evidence
Complaint	Motion	Substantive Law

NOTES

1. William Statsky, *Legal Thesaurus/Dictionary* (St. Paul: West, 1982).
2. Id.
3. *Erie R. Co. v. T Tompkins,* 304 U.S. 64, 58 S.Ct. 817, 82 L.Ed. 1188 (1938).
4. *Guaranty Trust Co. of N.Y. v. York,* 326 U.S. 99, 65 S.Ct. 1464, 89 L.Ed. 2079 (1945).
5. *Hanna v. Plumer,* 380 U.S. 460, 85 S.Ct. 1136, 14 L.Ed. 2d 8 (1965).
6. Federal Rules of Civil Procedure, Rule 1.
7. Id. at Rule 3.
8. *Stastny v. Tachovsky,* 178 Neb. 109, 132 N.W. 2d 317 (1964).
9. Federal Rules of Civil Procedure, Rule 56.
10. Federal Rules of Evidence, 28 U.S.C.A.
11. Id.
12. *In re Edinger's Estate,* 136 N.W.2d 114 (N.D. 1965).

CHAPTER 6

Jurisdiction

CHAPTER OBJECTIVES

After reading this chapter you should be able to

- *Distinguish in personam, in rem, and quasi in rem jurisdiction.*

- *Describe subject matter jurisdiction.*

- *Identify the conditions to establish federal jurisdiction.*

- *Discuss the circumstances of removal and remand of a case based on federal jurisdiction.*

- *List the possible domiciles of a corporation.*

- *Explain how the domicile of a corporation is determined.*

- *Discuss the doctrine of forum non conveniens.*

- *List the factors used to make a forum non conveniens determination.*

Jurisdiction plays a significant role in the American legal system. It is a necessary element of all lawsuits. Until a court has determined that it has proper jurisdiction, a case will not be allowed to proceed. In essence, jurisdiction is the authority of a court to pass judgment over a specific type of case and each party to the suit. The formal definition is as follows:

> "1. The power of a court to decide a matter in controversy. 2. The geographic area over which a particular court has authority."[1]

The first definition of jurisdiction can be quite complex. It is based on the principle that a court should not have authority to pass and enforce judgment or sentences over persons or issues with which the court has absolutely no connection. The court has the duty to uphold the rights of those within its boundaries and not to spend time interpreting cases that do not affect the citizens or property within those boundaries. Because the authority of the court is related to all of the parties to the lawsuit and all the incidents that ultimately produced the suit, the decision of exactly which court has jurisdiction can be a complicated process.

The judiciary and the legislatures have created various rules to help courts determine when they have authority over persons and issues associated with a particular lawsuit. Jurisdiction has been broken down into several categories, each of which represents subtypes of the general concept of court authority. Each type of jurisdiction addresses a particular aspect of the court's authority over a case.

TYPES OF JURISDICTION

Each category of jurisdiction pertains to a different aspect of the court's authority over a case. In any lawsuit, the court must have jurisdiction over the parties as well as over the dispute. This not only allows the court to determine who wins but also gives the court authority to enforce the verdict.

Subject Matter Jurisdiction

Subject Matter Jurisdiction
Authority of a court to determine the actual issue between the parties.

Subject matter jurisdiction is just what its name implies. It is the authority of a court over the actual dispute between the parties. This jurisdiction is concerned with the relationship of the court to the dispute.[2]

Persons cannot create this type of jurisdiction by an agreement as to which court will have authority to hear their case. Nor can this type of jurisdiction be created because a party fails to object if a case is improperly brought in a particular court. Rather, subject matter jurisdiction is an issue that each court must identify before any case proceeds.

APPLICATION 6.1

Carlos and Sharon are driving separate cars on a highway in Nevada when their cars collide. Carlos sues Sharon, claiming that she drove negligently and caused the accident. Sharon defends herself, claiming that it was Carlos' speeding that caused the accident. Carlos and Sharon are both citizens of the state of Nevada.

If Carlos were to bring suit against Sharon in Wyoming, the Wyoming courts would have no subject matter jurisdiction, since there is no connection whatsoever between the accident and the state of Wyoming. The citizens of that state could not possibly benefit from having the case decided there. Even if Sharon did not object—or perhaps even agreed to the suit in Wyoming, the court would still not have subject matter jurisdiction. The state of Wyoming would be burdened with another lawsuit and the costs of processing it through a trial. The citizens of Wyoming would be delayed in their own access to the courts. Subject matter jurisdiction would not exist. The court with subject matter jurisdiction would be Nevada, where the accident occurred and where the parties reside.

Points for Discussion
1. What if Sharon resided in Montana or Wyoming?
2. What would be the result if the accident had occurred in Wyoming? If the result is different, explain why.

The citizens of a jurisdiction as a whole must have some interest in a lawsuit before the court will have subject matter jurisdiction to hear the case. Stated another way, the laws of the jurisdiction must be promoted by the determination of the case. A primary obligation of the judiciary is to apply the laws of a jurisdiction for the benefit of the people. Therefore, applying laws of another jurisdiction, when not even one citizen would be affected, would be a misuse of the court's authority. To achieve subject matter jurisdiction, many states require that the circumstances giving rise to the dispute occur in the state or that the defendant reside in the state. This general rule has exceptions, and when determining the jurisdiction over a particular action, the appropriate state law should be consulted.

Assignment 6.1

Examine each of the following situations and determine which court(s) has subject matter jurisdiction. (At this point, assume there are no other rules regarding jurisdiction and no issue subject to federal jurisdiction.) Be prepared to explain your answer.

1. Susan is driving her car in Nevada. She lives in California. Arlene's car crosses the center line and strikes Susan's car. Arlene resides in California as well.

> 2. Mick buys a camcorder in Florida. The camcorder needs repair and Mick sends it to Ohio where the manufacturer loses the camcorder and refuses to replace it.

Original Jurisdiction

Authority of a court to determine the rights and obligations of the parties in a lawsuit (e.g., trial court).

In addition to the broad notion of subject matter jurisdiction, there is a more particular application. State and federal jurisdictions have several judges and, in fact, several courts to hear all of the cases. Chapter 2 discussed the many federal courts. In addition, the states have a court in each county, known as trial courts of general jurisdiction. These courts can hear at trial any type of case and parties over which they have authority. For matters of convenience and efficiency, many trial courts are divided into subclasses by the type of case or issue being addressed. Trial courts are also often called courts of **original jurisdiction.**

The following is an example of divisions within a trial court: one judge will hear criminal cases; another, domestic disputes; and yet another, major trials on contract and tort claims. The subject matter authority of the judges within each of these subdivided courts is limited by the type of case the judges are assigned to hear. Consequently, a judge assigned to the domestic relations court would not ordinarily have authority to hear a major breach of contract claim. This type of authority is based on the idea of organization of the courts, and is not considered a true form of jurisdiction.

APPLICATION 6.2

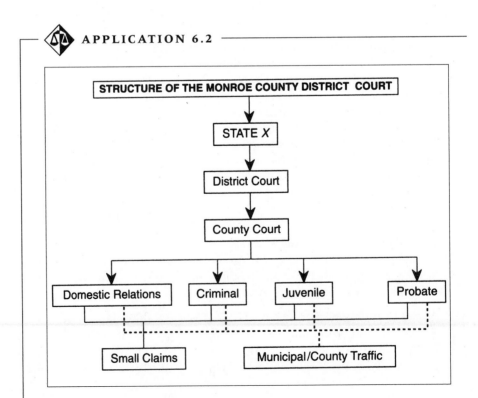

The following is an example of how a court structure, as diagrammed on the previous page, might function:

- District Court. Hears all major civil cases with a value assessed at greater than $20,000 and not otherwise assigned to a court by subject matter.
- County Court. Hears all civil cases with a value between $2,500.01 and $19,999.99 and not otherwise assigned to a court by subject matter.
- Domestic Relations. Hears all matters involving divorce, annulment, alimony (spousal maintenance), child support, child custody, and child visitation, regardless of the dollar value of the case.
- Criminal. Hears all matters involving criminal charges, with the exception of misdemeanor traffic charges and cases involving juveniles as defendants.
- Juvenile. Hears all cases in which juveniles are charged criminally.
- Probate. Hears all cases regarding the estate (property) of decedents, minors, and incompetents (persons legally determined to be incapable of managing their own affairs).
- Small Claims. Hears all civil cases of a value of $2,500.00 or less.
- Municipal/County Traffic. Hears all cases involving charges of traffic violations of the municipalities of the county, or county ordinances that are misdemeanor (penalty of less than one year incarceration or fine of less than $1,000) in nature.

Point for Discussion
Why would it be beneficial to have the same judge(s) hear all cases involving a particular area of law, such as domestic relations?

Occasionally, a dispute between two parties is not confined to a single issue. When several claims arise from the same occurrence, a court that has subject matter jurisdiction will also usually have **ancillary jurisdiction**—the authority to hear related claims that the court generally would not have the power to hear. Similar to this is **pendent jurisdiction**—the authority of a federal court presented with a federal claim to also hear claims based on state law that arise out of the same set of circumstances that produced the federal claim. Allowing courts to hear such matters prevents duplicity of trials.

Jurisdiction in Personam

Assume for the purposes of the following discussion that a suit has been filed in a court that has subject matter jurisdiction. The court has the authority to determine who will prevail in the lawsuit. However, the court must still have jurisdiction over the parties to enforce any judgment or ruling it might render in the lawsuit. The court can obtain such authority over the parties in any of three methods.

Ancillary Jurisdiction
Authority of a court over issues in a case that is subject to the court's authority on other grounds.

Pendent Jurisdiction
Authority of a federal court, presented with a federal claim, to also determine interrelated claims based on state law.

In Personam (Personal) Jurisdiction
Authority of a court to render and enforce rulings over a particular individual and the individual's property.

The first method of authority is **in personam jurisdiction**—the authority of the court over the person.[3] This type of authority gives the court the power to compel the person to appear in court and answer questions or claims of a party to the lawsuit. It also includes the power to seize all assets of the person or even to impose a jail sentence.

Domicile.   A court may obtain in personam jurisdiction over an individual in several ways. The most common is domicile—the place where one intends to make a permanent residence and has actual residence (even if periodic). A person is presumed to be subject to the authority of a court if that person lives in the geographical jurisdiction. The key to domicile is intent. Although a person may have residences in many states, the domicile is considered to be the primary residence. The domicile may be shown by examples of a strong connection to the jurisdiction, such as paying income taxes in a particular jurisdiction, registering to vote, obtaining a driver's license, or living in that residence more than any other place during the year. The greater the number of elements such as those mentioned, the more likely a certain jurisdiction will be considered one's domicile. A person can have only one domicile.

Consent.   The court may have authority over an individual who is not domiciled in a jurisdiction. Personal jurisdiction can be obtained by consent of the individual either voluntarily or by waiver. If a person agrees to be subjected to the authority of the court, the lawsuit may be filed with that court, assuming, of course, that subject matter jurisdiction exists. An example of this may be two persons who are separated and want to file for divorce. If the parties reside in different states, one may agree to be subject to the in personam authority of the state where the other resides and where the parties resided when living together. If a suit is filed against a person over whom the court has no personal jurisdiction and that party does not object at the onset of the lawsuit, the right to object is waived. When a person fails to object to a court's authority over him or her, it is presumed that the person agrees to the exercise of authority. Such authority is in personam jurisdiction by waiver.

Long-Arm Statute
Authority of a court to impose in personam jurisdiction over persons beyond the geographical boundaries of the court (allowed only in statutorily specified circumstances).

Long-arm statutes.   Finally, all states have what are known as **long-arm statutes,**[4] which refer to the authority of a court over someone because of his or her contacts within a state. Under these laws, the person need not live in the jurisdiction or consent to court authority. Rather, the person's acts are considered to be implied consent. The theory is that if a person accepts the benefits of a jurisdiction and that person subsequently injures a party within the jurisdiction, the courts of the jurisdiction have the right to impose responsibility for wrongdoing. Thus, the court has a "long arm" that will reach into other jurisdictions and draw the individual back.

The circumstances that trigger long-arm jurisdiction statutes vary from state to state. One circumstance used in many states is with regard to the operation of a motor vehicle. The reasoning is that if a person accepts the benefits of driving on a highway system within a jurisdiction, the person should also accept responsibility for any damage caused while driving. Another example involves persons who do business with parties in a jurisdiction. By accepting the financial benefits of doing business, the persons also must answer to injury claims as a result of doing business. Such claims may cover contract actions or any other type of injury that may occur. Each jurisdiction applies specific considerations to determine whether someone was actually "doing business" within the state (see Figure 6.1)

INDIANA RULES OF TRIAL PROCEDURE
II. COMMENCEMENT OF ACTION; SERVICE OF PROCESS, PLEADINGS, MOTIONS AND ORDERS

TRIAL RULE 4.4 SERVICE UPON PERSONS IN ACTIONS FOR ACTS DONE IN THIS STATE OR HAVING AN EFFECT IN THIS STATE

(A) Acts Serving as a Basis for JURISDICTION. Any person or organization that is a nonresident of this state, a resident of this state who has left the state, or a person whose residence is unknown, submits to the JURISDICTION of the courts of this state as to any action arising from the following acts committed by him or his agent.

(1) doing any business in this state;

(2) causing personal injury or property damage by an act or omission done within this state;

(3) causing personal injury or property damage in this state by an occurrence, act or omission done outside this state if he regularly does or solicits business or engages in any other persistent course of conduct, or derives substantial revenue or benefit from goods, materials, or SERVICES used, consumed, or rendered in this state;

(4) having supplied or contracted to supply SERVICES rendered or to be rendered or goods or materials furnished or to be furnished in this state;

(5) owning, using, or possessing any real property or an interest in real property within this state;

(6) contracting to insure or act as surety for or on behalf of any person, property or risk located within this state at the time the contract was made; or

(7) living in the marital relationship within the state notwithstanding subsequent departure from the state, as to all obligations for alimony, custody, child support, or property settlement, if the other party to the marital relationship continues to reside in the state.

(B) Manner of SERVICE. A person subject to the JURISDICTION of the courts of this state under this RULE may be served with summons:

(1) As provided by RULES 4.1 (SERVICE on individuals), 4.5 (SERVICE upon resident who cannot be found or served within the state), 4.6 (SERVICE upon organizations), 4.9 (in rem actions); or

(2) The person shall be deemed to have appointed the Secretary of State as his agent upon whom SERVICE of summons may be made as provided in RULE 4.10. . . .

FIGURE 6.1

Indiana Trial Rule 4.4(f)(1)

Assignment 6.2

For each of the following situations, state whether there would be in personam jurisdiction and, if so, whether it is because of domicile, consent, or long arm.

1. Midori, a California resident, was driving on a state highway in Utah when she knocked over a mile marker post with her car.

2. Max, a Pennsylvania resident, was sued by Agnes, a New York resident, in a Pennsylvania court.

3. John, a traveling salesman, routinely sold his goods in the state of Florida. Although John had no residence in Florida, he was sued there when a widget he had sold exploded and injured someone.

4. Mike and Blair entered a contract. Before the contract was completed, they became involved in a dispute over what the terms of the contract actually meant. Mike and Blair decided that a suit would be filed in Arizona, where Blair resided permanently, even though Mike's only residence was in New Mexico.
5. Marge sued Ken in Wisconsin. Marge's only home is in Illinois. Ken has a summer cabin on a lake in Illinois but lives primarily in Wisconsin. The suit is over a fight the two had in Wisconsin, when Ken struck Marge and injured her.

In Rem and Quasi in Rem Jurisdiction

In Rem Jurisdiction

Authority of a court over a specific item of property regardless of who claims the property or an interest in it.

Quasi In Rem Jurisdiction

Authority of a court over a person's interest in certain property.

In rem and **quasi in rem jurisdiction** refer to the authority of a court to affect property or a person's rights over property. A suit in rem is begun by naming the actual property as a defendant in the court of the state where the property is located. The party claiming ownership defends his or her rights over the property. In fact, if a suit is brought in rem, all persons who have an interest in the property must defend that interest. Because the authority is over the actual property, there is no need for personal jurisdiction over persons who claim it.

 APPLICATION 6.3

Sherry buys a vacation lot in sunny Texas and arranges for a contractor to build on the property. When she arrives at the property site, she finds that several other people have been sold the same lot. Sherry might sue the property in rem to have the rights of each person determined. If any of the owners are served with proper notice of the action and do not appear to defend their interest in the suit, they may lose their rights to the property.

Points for Discussion
1. What court(s) would probably have subject matter jurisdiction?
2. Why is in personam jurisdiction inappropriate for this situation?

The distinction between in rem and quasi in rem turns on the property owners who are affected. In an action in rem, all persons claiming ownership or some other type of interest in the property may be affected and therefore must defend their interest.[5] In an action based on quasi in rem, only the interests of the person or persons identified in the suit and who claim rights to the property are affected.[6]

Quasi in rem may be a way to obtain jurisdiction over the property interests of a person when in personam jurisdiction cannot be achieved. Assume a person is subject to the court's authority but cannot be located. Or, perhaps the person appears at trial and a judgment is rendered against the person, but the person seemingly has no assets in that state. In the first instance, the plaintiff can file an action on the basis of quasi in rem jurisdiction to attach any of the property of the missing person in the state where the property is located. In the latter situation, a suit that claims quasi in rem jurisdiction can be brought in any state where assets exist for the purpose of satisfying the judgment rendered in another jurisdiction.

In rem and quasi in rem actions are brought much less frequently than actions based on in personam jurisdiction. The primary reason is that if a suit is brought in personam and is won, virtually all of the assets of the defendant can be used to satisfy the judgment. In an action based on property, no matter how great a judgment, only the value of the property named or the degree of interest in the property can be used to satisfy the judgment. Therefore, if the injuries or rights one seeks to protect are greater than the value of the property, it is wiser to seek in personam jurisdiction.

 APPLICATION 6.4

Gary and Joe are co-owners of a boat valued at $125,000. The boat is docked in a marina on Lake Mead, in Nevada. Gary cannot be located. Nan has won a lawsuit against Gary, and the court awarded her $85,000. Rather than wait to locate Gary and try to obtain payment, Nan can sue the boat in rem or sue Gary quasi in rem for his interest in the boat. If Nan sues the boat in rem, Joe or anyone else who might claim an interest in the boat (e.g., a creditor) must appear in the suit and defend that interest or risk losing it. If Nan sues Gary quasi in rem, only Gary's degree of interest in the boat is at stake. If Gary owned one half of the boat, the most Nan could collect would be one half of the boat's value. The remaining half would belong to Joe.

Point for Discussion
Why wouldn't Nan want to try to collect from all of Gary's personal assets under in personam?

Assignment 6.3

Examine the following situations and determine whether each suit was brought in personam, in rem, or quasi in rem.

1. Partners Joy, Bob, and Bud were equal owners of a golf driving range. In his divorce settlement, Bob was ordered to pay $10,000 to his ex-wife Shirley. When Bob refused to pay, Shirley filed another suit to collect and was awarded the entire driving range.
2. Same situation as question 1, except Shirley is now equal partners with Joy and Bud.
3. Maxine sued Vince for damages he allegedly caused in a car accident. Maxine prevails and collects her judgment by seizing Vince's vacation cabin, boat, and gun collection.

FEDERAL JURISDICTION

As pointed out in Chapter 2, the federal and state court systems operate independently. Although similar in many respects, each system has its own substantive and procedural law, and each has its own system of appeals. The opportunity to present a case in a federal court is generally limited to those situations where (1) a federal law or the Constitution is involved, (2) the United States is a party, or (3) there is complete diversity of citizenship and a controversy valued in excess of $75,000. The following sections describe each of these situations.

As always, the federal court where the case is filed must have subject matter jurisdiction. If it does not, the case must be transferred to the federal court or the state court where such jurisdiction exists. If the suit is brought against a citizen of the United States, automatic in personam jurisdiction exists, since citizenship implies domicile in this country.

Subject matter jurisdiction in the federal courts can be established only in specific circumstances. The courts are careful to avoid unnecessary interference with the authority of state court systems and simultaneously burden federal courts with the time and expense of processing claims related to a state's own laws and citizens.

Federal Question

Federal Question
Authority of a federal court to hear a case on the basis of the Constitution and other federal law.

One type of federal jurisdiction is known as a **federal question,** which occurs when a primary issue in the dispute is based on federal law. Such law can include regulations of federal administrative agencies, federal laws, or elements of the Constitution or its amendments. For this type of jurisdiction to exist, the issue that arises out of federal law must be considered by the court to be a substantial issue in the case, for example, a claim that a police officer violated the civil rights of a minority citizen by using unnecessary force.

If it appears that a party has created a federal question by adding an issue of federal law to the suit when it was unnecessary or when it was not an inherent part of the claim, the court will not take the case.[7] The conspiring in such a tactic by a plaintiff and a defendant is referred to as collusion. As a result, no federal jurisdiction will exist. Similarly, a defendant cannot create a federal question in a countersuit—and thereby create federal jurisdiction by simply alleging application of a federal law in the answer to the plaintiff's lawsuit—unless the lawsuit is actually based on or affected by a federal law.

 APPLICATION 6.5

Farmer A and Farmer B are involved in a boundary dispute. Neither wants to have the case heard in the local court. Farmer A and the local judge have never gotten along. Farmer B is sponsored by a corporation, and local people (who would constitute the jury) have a strong dislike for big business. Farmer A and Farmer B decide that in addition to their filing the boundary dispute, Farmer A will claim that the applicable law in the case is unconstitutional. Such claim will create a federal question, the case can be heard in the U.S. District Court, and the local judge and jury will be avoided. If a court finds that there is no reasonable basis for the claim of unconstitutionality and that the two parties were in collusion, the case will be dismissed from the federal court.

Points for Discussion

If Farmer B doesn't agree to a claim of unconstitutionality:

1. Is there still collusion?
2. Is there still federal jurisdiction?

A pendent claim exists when there are separate issues based on federal and state law filed in the same lawsuit in federal court. In such a situation, the federal court has pendent jurisdiction. The federal court will usually not order that the case be split into two cases but rather may exercise pendent jurisdiction and hear the federal and state issues. When this is done, the federal court will follow principles of state law in determining the state issues and will apply federal law when determining the federal issues.

The case of pendent jurisdiction occurs frequently in federal courts. As legal disputes in our society become more and more complex and many issues must be decided, the likelihood increases that some of the issues will arise out of state law and others will arise from federal law. It would be far too expensive and time consuming for the parties and the courts to try all of the issues separately. Exercising pendent jurisdiction has become the solution to this problem. However, if the state and federal issues are totally distinct, the judge may order that the claims be severed and tried in separate courts.

Distinguished from pendent authority is **concurrent jurisdiction,** which occurs when more than one federal court or federal and state courts all have subject matter jurisdiction over a case. The case may have solely federal or state issues, but because of the domicile of the parties or the occurrence of several parts of the claim in different jurisdictions, more than one court finds itself with the authority to determine the issues. In such a situation, the case may be filed by the plaintiff in any court with subject matter jurisdiction. However, the case *may* be subject to transfer under forum non conveniens (see subsequent discussion).

Concurrent Jurisdiction
Situation in which more than one court has authority to hear a particular case.

The United States as a Party

An obvious type of federal jurisdiction exists when the United States has been named as a party to the suit. Since the federal courts are a branch of the federal government, when the U.S. government is sued, the suit must be filed in federal court. Such a suit might involve an employee, officer, or elected official of the federal government or a federal agency.

The U.S. government traditionally followed the English doctrine of sovereign immunity: the sovereign (the government entity) is immune from claims by the citizens; that is, the government may not be sued. The United States has made some exceptions to this rule. A handful of statutes have set forth specific instances in which the government may be liable for physical or financial injuries to a citizen. If a suit is brought against the United States, it must be done in accordance with these statutes.[8] Each requirement of the statutes must be met. Often this includes first making a claim to the appropriate administrative agency. If no satisfaction is received, a claim may then be filed in the courts. If there is no statutory provision for the type of claim an individual wishes to make, no suit can be filed against the United States.

Diversity of Citizenship

A much-used method of achieving federal jurisdiction is through diversity of citizenship. This basis for jurisdiction was developed because juries and judges in a state court system are drawn from that particular state. As a consequence, it is possible that a party to the suit who is from another state will not receive fair or adequate treatment. In today's mobile society, this possibility is less of a threat than two hundred years ago when there were great rivalries among the states. However, as a safeguard, the federal courts still accept cases of substantial value (more than $75,000) that involve parties from different states.

Diversity of citizenship means that all parties to the lawsuit must have citizenship in different states than an opposing party. Thus, all plaintiffs must reside in different states than all defendants. It is acceptable if the plaintiff resides in one state or several states; the same is true of defendants. But there can be no common state between any plaintiff and any defendant. Diversity among parties must be complete.

 APPLICATION 6.6

1. Jeff, the plaintiff, is domiciled in South Carolina, while Jack, the defendant, is domiciled in North Carolina. Thus, there is complete diversity of the state citizenship between the plaintiff and the defendant, and Jeff may sue Jack in federal court.
2. Jeff sues Jack and Molly in federal court. Jeff and Molly are domiciled in South Carolina, while Jack is domiciled in North Carolina. There would be no federal jurisdiction in this situation, because a plaintiff and one of the defendants are domiciled in the same state. Thus, diversity is not complete.

A simple method to determine whether diversity exists is to make a table with two columns. In one column, list the states of domicile of all the plaintiffs; in the second column, list the states of domicile of each defendant (see accompanying diagram). If any state appears in both columns, there is no diversity. Conversely, if no state appears in both columns, the first condition of diversity jurisdiction is satisfied. Like federal question jurisdiction, diversity cannot be created by collusion of the parties. Simply put, a party cannot represent domicile in a state different from the defendant for the purpose of creating jurisdiction. Domicile must be the intended permanent residence.

SITUATION 1		SITUATION 2	
PLAINTIFF	**DEFENDANT**	**PLAINTIFF**	**DEFENDANTS**
SC	NC	SC	SC
			NC

Points for Discussion

1. Regarding situation 1, assume Jeff has all relevant connections, including longest annual residence in North Carolina, except that he claims South Carolina as his domicile for purposes of paying federal income tax. Is the result different? Explain your answer.
2. Regarding situation 2, what if Jack and Molly were domiciled in South Carolina and Jeff was domiciled in North Carolina? Would the result be different?

A second aspect of citizenship diversity is required for federal jurisdiction to apply. The claim must allege damages of more than $75,000. It does not matter whether a single claim or several claims in the same suit exceed the minimum amount. It is necessary only that the claim be valued at more than $75,000. Generally, this is not a problem. However, if it is discovered that the claim could never be considered as reasonably worth $75,000, the federal court will dismiss the case. If a jury should return a verdict of less than $75,000, federal jurisdiction is not defeated. It must only be shown that the claim could reasonably have been considered as worth that much. Thus, it is important that a party claiming jurisdiction by diversity of citizenship be able to establish not only that the diversity is complete but also that the claim is reasonably worth more than $75,000.

Two exceptions exist to a claim of federal jurisdiction based on diversity of citizenship: domestic relations and probate cases. The law governing domestic relations (divorce, adoption, custody, support, alimony, and other related issues) is so specific from state to state that the federal courts will not become involved in these issues. The same applies to the law of probate, which includes distribution of estates of deceased persons and management of estates of minors and legally disabled adults. The federal government will not determine the rights of parties in these actions. The only exception is that after the case has been determined, if the requirements of diversity are met, the federal court may exercise jurisdiction to interpret or enforce the decrees of the state court.

Assignment 6.4

> Examine the following situations and determine whether federal juris-
> diction applies to each and, if so, what type.
>
> 1. Business A sues the Environmental Protection Agency. A claims that
>   new EPA regulations are designed not to protect the environment but
>   to eliminate the industry of A entirely.
> 2. X sues Y and P. X is domiciled in New Mexico but has a residence in
>   Missouri. Y is domiciled in Minnesota. P is domiciled in Missouri.
> 3. O sues the state police of Arizona, claiming he has been harassed by
>   the state police by repeated arrests, only to have the charges
>   immediately dismissed. O claims this violates his constitutional rights.
> 4. B sues D and F. B is domiciled in Virginia. D is domiciled in Oregon,
>   and F is domiciled in West Virginia.
> 5. M sues the State of Washington, claiming that the state income tax
>   violates the state constitution.

Removal and Remand

What happens when there is concurrent jurisdiction between the state and federal courts but the plaintiff brings the action in state court? Or, if there is no federal jurisdiction at the outset of the lawsuit but developments cause it to arise?
Examples include amendments of claims to add federal question issues and
change of domicile of a party, thereby creating diversity. The defendant is not
totally at the mercy of the plaintiff's choice of forum. When federal jurisdiction
exists or arises in a state court action, the defendant may seek to have the case
brought before the federal courts.

The Congress has passed the following law:

Title 28 United States Code Section 1441: Actions Removable Generally.
(a) Except as otherwise expressly provided by Act of Congress, any civil
action brought in a State court of which the district courts of the United
States have original jurisdiction, may be removed by the defendant or the
defendants, to the district court of the United States for the district and
division embracing the place where such action is pending.
(b) Any civil action of which the district courts have original jurisdiction
founded on a claim or right arising under the Constitution, treaties or laws
of the United States shall be removable without regard to the citizenship or
residence of the parties. Any other such action shall be removable only if
none of the parties in interest properly joined and served as defendants is a
citizen of the State in which such action is brought.
(c) Whenever a separate and independent claim or cause of action which
would be removable if sued upon alone, is joined with one or more

IN THE UNITED STATES DISTRICT COURT
DISTRICT OF MONTE VISTA

MATHIAS SNYDER,   ]
Plaintiff   ]
vs.   ]   Docket No. 94-321
                                       ]   Judge David Madde
BILL BOON,   ]
Defendant   ]

PETITION TO REMOVE

Comes now the Defendant, Bill Boon, by and through his attorneys, Smart, Steel, and Harper, and petitions this court to remove the above-captioned case from the state court where it is pending and to accept said case into this court for further proceedings. In support of his petition, the Defendant states as follows:

1. On or about June 1, 1993, the Plaintiff instituted an action against Defendant in the District Court of Diamond County, State A, which case is assigned state Docket number 93-1010.

2. Since the commencement of Plaintiff's action against Defendant, diversity of citizenship has occurred when Plaintiff's domicile changed on or about August 31, 1993, from State A to State B.

3. Plaintiff's complaint alleges damages due from Defendant in an amount in excess of $50,000.

4. The current circumstances of the pending case satisfy all requirements of diversity of citizenship, and consequently, this court is vested with the authority to remove said case pursuant to the Federal Rules of Civil Procedure.

WHEREFORE, Defendant prays that this court will grant said petition and cause the aforementioned case to be removed from the state court where it is currently pending and to be filed in this court for further proceedings.

Respectfully submitted,

Sam Harper
Attorney for Defendant Bill Boon
Smart, Steel, and Harper
1 Empire Drive
Union City, UN 11190

FIGURE 6.2

Petition to
Remove

otherwise nonremovable claims or causes of action, the entire case may be removed and the district court may determine all issues therein, or, in its discretion, may remand all matters not otherwise within its original jurisdiction.

Translated, the basic thrust of this statute is that if the federal court would also have jurisdiction to hear a case, the defendant can remove the case from the state and into federal court (see Figure 6.2). When this occurs, the case is actually transferred from the state to the federal system. The procedure for removal is quite specific:

a) A defendant has only thirty days from the date the defendant should be aware there is federal jurisdiction to file for removal. If federal jurisdiction exists from the outset, the suit must be filed within thirty days of the defendant being served with the suit. If something occurs during the suit that establishes federal jurisdiction, the defendant has thirty days from knowledge of that event to seek removal. An example of the latter would be if a party moved his or her domicile and there was diversity of citizenship.

b) To start the removal proceedings the defendant must file a Petition for Removal in the federal court. The Petition must be filed in the federal court whose geographical boundaries include the location of the state court. The Petition must state all of the facts of the case that indicate there is federal jurisdiction. The Petition must be verified. This means that the defendant must swear in writing that all of the information in the Petition is true and accurate. Also, all pleadings (legal documents) that have been filed in the case in state court must be attached to the Petition. A copy of the Petition must be sent to all parties.

c) In addition to the Petition, the defendant must file a bond with the federal court. This is a sort of insurance policy that the removal is properly based on actual federal jurisdiction over the case. A fee or promise of a fee is given to the court as bond. If the case remains in the federal court, then the defendant is entitled to have the bond returned. If it turns out that the case was removed improperly, then the defendant forfeits the amount of the bond to the court.

d) Once the Petition for Removal is filed, all proceedings in the state court stop. All future hearings, motions, and the trial will be conducted in the federal court. The state court loses authority over the case. Removal is automatic, and it cannot be prevented from happening by objections from the plaintiff.

A plaintiff who feels that a case was improperly removed may file a Motion to Remand—a motion filed with the federal court that asks the court to review the case and make a determination of whether federal jurisdiction actually exists (see Figure 6.3). If the court finds that it does not, the case will be remanded; that is, the case is sent back to the state court. The federal court will take no further action in a case after it is remanded. If a Motion to Remand fails, the case remains in the federal court.

Regardless of whether a case is filed in federal court by a plaintiff or removed by a defendant, the court will not entertain a case where federal jurisdiction is based on collusion. (Recall that collusion occurs when one or more of the parties to the lawsuit conspire to create the appearance of federal jurisdiction). For example, if a party changes domicile for the sole purpose of creating diversity of citizenship, such action is treated as an attempt to falsely allege the existence of federal jurisdiction, and the action will be remanded. Thus, the reason for federal jurisdiction must be a sincere and real part of the dispute.

FIGURE 6.3

Petition to Remand

IN THE UNITED STATES DISTRICT COURT
DISTRICT OF MONTE VISTA

MATHIAS SNYDER,　　　　]
Plaintiff　　　　　　　　　]
vs.　　　　　　　　　　　　]　　　　Docket No. 94-321
　　　　　　　　　　　　　　]　　　　Judge David Madden
BILL BOON,　　　　　　　　]
Defendant　　　　　　　　　]

PETITION TO REMAND

Comes now the Plaintiff, Mathias Snyder, by and through his attorneys, Hayford, Stanley, and Jackson and petitions this court to remand the above-captioned case to the state court where it was originally filed, for all further proceedings. In support of his petition, the Plaintiff states as follows:

1. On or about September 30, 1993, the Defendant filed a Petition to Remove the above-captioned case on the basis of diversity of citizenship and subject to the Federal Rules of Civil Procedure.

2. In said petition, the Defendant represented to this Court that the Plaintiff's domicile had changed to State B.

3. The Plaintiff has a temporary residence in State B for the purpose of attending State University during the months of August through May 1994.

4. At no time has the Plaintiff had the intent to adopt State B as his domicile and further has maintained all domiciliary ties with State A.

5. Defendant's petition is unfounded as both Plaintiff and Defendant continue to reside in State A. Therefore, diversity of citizenship does not exist between the parties to this action. WHEREFORE, the Plaintiff prays that his petition to Remand be granted and that the above-captioned action be permitted to resume proceedings in the District Court where it originated. Respectfully submitted,

Michael J. George
Attorney for Plaintiff Mathias Snyder
Firm of Hayford, Stanley, and Jackson
311 Lagoon Lane
Harristown, UN 11115

 CASE

DALAL v. ALLIANT TECHSYSTEMS INC.

934 P.2d 830
(Co. App. 1996).

TAUBMAN, Judge.

In this wrongful termination of employment action, plaintiff, Samir Dalal, appeals from the summary judgment entered against him and in favor of defendants, Alliant Techsystems, Inc., d/b/a Metrum Information Storage, and Honeywell, Inc. (collectively Alliant), on his claims of breach of implied contract and promissory estoppel. The dispositive issue in this appeal is whether these state law claims were properly barred under the doctrine of res judicata because Dalal failed in prior litigation to request that the federal court exercise its diversity jurisdiction over those claims. Because we agree with the trial court that the state law claims are barred by the doctrine of res judicata, we affirm.

Dalal was employed as a design engineer by Alliant for approximately eight years, until his employment was terminated in September 1990. After exhausting his administrative remedies, Dalal, in May 1992, filed an action against Alliant in the United States District Court for the District of Colorado alleging that he was unlawfully terminated on the basis of racial discrimination, in contravention of his rights under Title VII of the Civil Rights Act of 1964, 42 U.S.C. § 2000e-2, et seq. (1994) (Title VII). Dalal also alleged that his termination was unlawfully based upon his age, in violation of his rights under the Age Discrimination in Employment Act of 1967, 29 U.S.C. § 621, et seq. (1994) (ADEA). In addition, Dalal requested the court to exercise its pendent, or supplemental, jurisdiction over his state law claims for breach of implied contract and promissory estoppel. However, he did not assert jurisdiction based upon diversity of citizenship under 28 U.S.C. § 1322 (1994).

In an opinion issued June 7, 1993, the federal district court granted Alliant's motion for partial summary judgment on the Title VII claim and denied its motion with respect to the ADEA claim. Additionally, the federal district court dismissed Dalal's breach of contract and promissory estoppel claims without prejudice.

In so doing, the federal court declined to exercise supplemental jurisdiction over these claims pursuant to 28 U.S.C. § 1367 (c)(2) (1994), which permits a federal district court, in its discretion, to decline to exercise supplemental jurisdiction over state law claims if "the [state] claim substantially predominates over the claim or claims over which the district court has original jurisdiction." This statute was enacted by Congress in 1990 as a codification, in part, of federal courts' pendent jurisdiction as recognized in United Mine Workers v. Gibbs, 383 U.S. 715, 86 S.Ct. 1130, 16 L.Ed.2d 218 (1966). See 28 U.S.C.A. § 1367 (1993) (D. Siegel, Practice Commentary). Because Dalal had not alleged diversity jurisdiction as an additional basis for his claims, the federal district court did not address that issue.

Immediately after the federal court ruled, Dalal refiled his breach of contract and promissory estoppel claims in the state court. That court entered summary judgment against Dalal on April 18, 1995, on the basis of res judicata, determining that Dalal could have brought the state claims in federal district court under diversity jurisdiction. This appeal followed.

I. State Versus Federal Law

As a threshold matter, Dalal asserted that Colorado, rather than federal, law should govern

this dispute. However, inasmuch as both federal and state principles of res judicata, as pertinent here, are essentially the same, the outcome is not affected by whether we apply federal or state law. Compare City & County of Denver v. Block 173 Associates, 814 P.2d 824 (Colo. 1991) with Satsky v. Paramount Communications, Inc., 7 F.3d 1464 (10th Cir. 1993).

Thus, we analyze Dalal's res judicata contentions under both federal and state law.

II. Application of Res Judicata

Dalal contends that, because his state law claims were dismissed without prejudice in the federal litigation, he was free to reassert them in state court, and they were not barred by the doctrine of res judicata. Under the circumstances presented here, we disagree. Res judicata not only bars issues actually decided, but also any issues that might have been raised in the first proceeding but were not. Northern Natural Gas v. Grounds, 931 F.2d 678 (10th Cir. 1991). . . .

Under the same claim for relief or same cause of action test, a court must look to the injury for which relief is demanded, not the legal theory on which the person asserting the claim relies. Petromanagement Corp. V. Acme-Thomas Joint Venture, 835 F.2d 1329 (10th Cir. 1988). . . .

Whether Dalal was required to assert his state law claims in federal court under diversity jurisdiction is a question of first impression for our appellate courts.

If a plaintiff commences and actually litigates an action in federal court, but omits state law claims that could have been brought under pendent jurisdiction, his or her claim is extinguished upon adjudication and the plaintiff is barred from maintaining a second action on a different theory in state court. Shaoul v. Goodyear Tire & Rubber, Inc., 815 P.2d 953 (Colo.App.1990). The Supreme Court has, however, recognized that exercise of pendent jurisdiction is a matter of discretion. See City & County of Denver v. Block 173 Associates, supra.

Once it has been determined that the federal court has pendent jurisdiction over the state claims, a plaintiff may not, however, divide his or her claim based upon speculation that the federal court would decline to exercise such pendent jurisdiction. See Shaoul v. Goodyear Tire & Rubber, Inc., supra. Rather, the state claims should be brought in federal court, and in the event the federal court then declines to exercise pendent jurisdiction, the state claims should be dismissed without prejudice and left for resolution in state court. Indeed, any doubts concerning the federal court's execution of pendent jurisdiction should be resolved in favor of joinder. Shaoul v. Goodyear Tire & Rubber, Inc., supra.

If, however, a federal claim is dismissed on a motion for summary judgment, federal courts have consistently held that a sound exercise of discretion requires dismissal of the pendent state claims as well, without prejudice to the plaintiffs' right to litigate them in the proper state forum. City & County of Denver v. Block 173 Associates, supra.

Further, in Whalen v. United Air Lines, Inc., 851 P.2d 251 (Colo. App.1993), a division of this court held that after a trial in federal court, to avoid the preclusive effect of a federal judgment upon a state law claim arising from the same transaction, the burden was upon the plaintiff to demonstrate that the federal court would not have exercised pendent jurisdiction over those state claims. To do so, the plaintiff was required to present sufficient information to merit the conclusion that the first court would have declined to adjudicate the claims. This could have been done, the court indicated, for example, by requesting the federal court to accept pendent jurisdiction and to have that court rule on the matter.

Relying on these cases, Dalal contends that he needed only to assert his state law claims under supplemental jurisdiction, but was not required to bring such claims on the basis of diversity jurisdiction. We disagree.

Although Whalen held that the burden is upon the plaintiff to demonstrate that, if the federal court had jurisdiction, ti would not have exercised it over pendent state claims, its rationale also applies to the circumstances here to require that Dalal demonstrate that the federal court somehow would not have exercised its otherwise proper diversity jurisdiction over his state claims. This conclusion is based not only on the principle behind res judicata of avoiding claim splitting, but also upon the Whalen court's conclusion that: "A plaintiff must present sufficient information that the conclusion can be reached that the first court would have declined to adjudicate the claims." Whalen v. United Air Lines, Inc., supra, 851 P.2d at 253–54. Although

this conclusion was reached in the context of the plaintiff there attempting to establish pendent jurisdiction after trial, its rationale *834 applies equally here to Dalal being required to demonstrate diversity jurisdiction.

Further, two federal court of appeals decisions, which are directly on point, militate against Dalal's position.

In Shaver v. F.W. Woolworth Co., 840 F.2d 1361 (7th Cir.), cert. denied, 488 U.S. 856, 109 S.Ct. 145, 102 L.Ed.2d 117 (1988), a discharged employee sued in federal court for age discrimination, asserting federal question jurisdiction and joining pendent state claims. After the federal district court dismissed his ADEA claim, it declined to exercise pendent jurisdiction over the state claims and dismissed them. Shaver then refiled his state law claims in state court. Shaver realized that diversity jurisdiction existed in federal court, but made no effort to allege it as an alternative jurisdictional basis in order to pursue his state law breach of contract claims in the original federal action.

Shaver's state law action was subsequently removed to federal court. On appeal, the Seventh Circuit held that: "Because Shaver neglected to assert the existence of diversity jurisdiction in his prior action in order to pursue his breach of contract claims, both the strict test of and the policy behind the res judicata doctrine bar the present action." Shaver, supra, 840 P.2d at 1368.

Relying on Shaver, the First Circuit Court of Appeals held that: "When a plaintiff pleads a claim in federal court, he must, to avoid the onus of claim-splitting, bring all related state claims in the same lawsuit so long as any suitable basis for SUBJECT MATTER JURISDICTION exists." Kale v. Combined Insurance Co., 924 F.2d 1161, 1165 (1st Cir. 1991).

In Kale, as in Shaver, a second lawsuit was filed in state court and was removed to federal court. The Kale court noted that the outcome would have been the same even if the second lawsuit had not been removed to federal court. We agree that the fact the second lawsuits in Shaver and Kale were removed to federal court is of no legal significance.

Furthermore, we reject Dalal's contention that, because a dismissal without prejudice is not an adjudication upon the merits and thus does not have res judicata effect, res judicata should not apply under the circumstances.

Although res judicata does not generally apply when the judgment is a dismissal without prejudice, see Satsky v. Paramount Communications Inc., supra, here, it is not the dismissal without prejudice that has the res judicata effect. Rather, the determinative factor is that Dalal could have alleged diversity jurisdiction in his federal court action but deliberately chose not to do so.

Thus, as in Shaoul v. Goodyear Tire & Rubber, Inc., supra, if a plaintiff asserts all of his or her claims, including state law claims, in federal court, and the federal court declines to exercise supplemental jurisdiction, the plaintiff may refile those claims in state court. See 28 U.S.C. § 1367(d) (1994) (period of limitations for supplemental claim is tolled while claim is pending in federal court and for 30 days after it is dismissed unless state law provides for a longer tolling period). However, where a plaintiff has an alternative basis of federal jurisdiction, such as diversity jurisdiction, he or she must assert it in order to avoid the bar of res judicata.

Hence, Dalal does not dispute that he could have properly alleged diversity jurisdiction in his federal lawsuit. Thus, he could have asserted his breach of contract and promissory estoppel claims in federal court on the basis of diversity jurisdiction.

Accordingly, we hold that because Dalal neglected to assert diversity jurisdiction in his federal lawsuit in order to pursue his state law breach of contract and promissory estoppel claims, the doctrine of res judicata bars the present action.

The judgment of the district court is affirmed.

Case Question
What should have occurred in this case for the plaintiff to have avoided dismissal with prejudice?

OTHER JURISDICTIONAL CONSIDERATIONS

Corporations

As already discussed, the domicile of individuals is important for purposes of determining proper state jurisdiction, the existence of federal jurisdiction cases, and venue. Ordinarily, the law treats a corporation as a person (recall that a person can have only one domicile). This can create a particular problem when a corporation has a continuing business in several states. As a result, special rules have been developed to determine the domicile of a corporation.

The state in which a corporation has filed its articles of incorporation is presumed to be the corporation's domicile. A corporation that does regular business in a state other than where it was incorporated is required to register as a foreign corporation. In doing so, the corporation must appoint someone in that state who will accept notice on behalf of the corporation of lawsuits filed in the state courts. This person is known as the registered agent and may be someone in an office of the corporation or some other individual, so long as it is clearly designated who will accept legal documents. Many states designate or require their secretary of state to accept legal documents on behalf of any corporation registered to conduct business within the state.

For purposes of federal jurisdiction, a problem arises in determining diversity of citizenship. A corporation is not considered to be domiciled in every state where it does business. If this were so, it would be virtually impossible for large corporations to ever be subject to federal jurisdiction by way of diversity. In a determination of diversity, a corporation is considered to have dual citizenship, or domiciles. A corporation is considered to be domiciled in the state of incorporation as well as in the state where the corporation's central business is conducted. If the operations are diffuse, the court will apply the nerve center test, which examines the location of the administration of the corporation. An example is the corporate headquarters. Once the domiciles of a corporation have been identified, a determination can be made as to whether diversity exists with opposing parties.

 CASE

ALBERTS v. MACK TRUCKS, INC.

540 N.E.2d 1268
(Ind.App.1989).

GARRARD, Presiding Justice.

Delos K. Alberts (Alberts) appeals an order of the Jasper Circuit Court granting Mack Trucks, Inc.'s (Mack Trucks') and National Seating Company's (NSC's) motions to dismiss for lack of personal jurisdiction. We affirm in part and reverse in part.

Alberts alleges in his complaint that he was injured on May 14, 1985 while driving a Mack Truck and sitting in a seat manufactured by NSC. The incident occurred in Illinois when Alberts' truck hit a bump in the road which caused his seat to thrust him into the roof of his truck cab. Alberts is an Indiana resident employed at the Lafayette, Indiana terminal of the LCL Transit Company, a Wisconsin corporation.

In response to Alberts' complaint both Mack Trucks and NSC filed motions to dismiss pursuant to Indiana Rules of Procedure, Trial Rule 12(B)(2). An unrecorded hearing was held on these motions in the court's chambers. Prior to the filing of its motion, NSC mailed interrogatories to Alberts' counsel.

Alberts then filed a motion for leave to file amended complaint, which was granted. The motions to dismiss of Mack Trucks and NSC were also granted in the same order. Subsequently, Alberts filed a motion to set aside dismissal without prejudice. After a hearing, Alberts'

motion was denied by the court. Alberts next attempted to file a second verified amended complaint; however, this was not allowed by the trial court.

Thereafter, Alberts filed his motion to correct errors. Attached to the motion was the sworn affidavit of the attorney who represented Alberts at the hearing on his motion to dismiss.

Alberts' motion was denied. He now appeals raising . . . [the issue] for our review [of whether] the trial court erred in granting Mack Trucks' motion to dismiss.

Alberts . . . argues that the trial court abused its discretion in failing to find in personam jurisdiction over Mack Trucks. We agree.

His first contention, that the trial court erroneously overlooked arguments by counsel, we have already rejected.

Alberts secondly contends that the trial court misconstrued World-Wide Volkswagon v. Woodson (1980), 444 U.S. 286, 100 S.Ct. 559, 62 L.Ed.2d 490 when it found, based on that case, that Indiana did not have jurisdiction over Mack Trucks, Inc. Mack Trucks' brief alternatively argues that World-Wide Volkswagon supports the trial court's holding.

However, a discussion of World-Wide Volkswagon is premature. It is first necessary to consider the burden of proof in jurisdictional matters. In Indiana, jurisdiction is presumed and need not be alleged. TR 8(A). A party challenging jurisdiction must establish it by a preponderance of the evidence unless lack of jurisdiction is apparent on the fact of the complaint. Mid-States Aircraft Engines v. Mize

Co. (1984), Ind.App., 467 N.E.2d 1242, 1247. See also Town of Eaton v. Rickert (1968), 251 Ind. 219, 240 N.E.2d 821.

Mack Trucks argues that it should not be required to carry the burden of proof and cites Reames v. Dollar Savings Association (1988), Ind.App., 519 N.E.2d 175, 176 as support for its position. In Reames the first district did state that:

> The burden of proving the existence of personal jurisdiction is on the party claiming personal jurisdiction if challenged, as in this case by a motion to dismiss. Nu-Way Systems v. Belmont Marketing, Inc. (7th Cir.1980), 635 F.2d 617, 619, n. 2.

The cited footnote states:

> Nu-Way also argues that the district court committed reversible error by allocating to it the burden of proof on the personal jurisdiction question contrary to Trial Rule 8(C) of the Indiana Rules of Trial Procedure, which places the burden of proof on the moving party. However, despite ambivalent phraseology, the district judge did not actually shift the burden of proof. In essence he ruled that Nu-Way had failed to show 'a basis' for the exercise of in personam jurisdiction and had failed to contradict any of the facts in the record, which standing uncontradicted, were insufficient to establish the requisite 'minimum contacts' with Indiana as required by International Shoe Co. v. Washington, 326 U.S. 310, 66 S.Ct. 154, 90 L.Ed. 95. Any presumption of jurisdiction under Trial Rule 8(C) is of course rebuttable. Moreover, in another recent Indiana diversity case Chief Judge Steckler held the burden of proof to show personal jurisdiction based on the Indiana long-arm provision is on the plaintiff if challenged, as here, by a motion to dismiss. Oddi v. Mariner-Denver, Inc., 461 F.Supp. 306, 310 (S.D.Ind.1978).

Nu-Way Systems v. Belmont Marketing, Inc., supra. However, Oddi v. Mariner-Denver, Inc., supra, is a diversity action and therefore distinguishable from the present case. In that sense, federal courts are courts of limited jurisdiction whereas the court in the present case is a court of general jurisdiction. Oddi is not inconsistent with our Supreme Court's holding in Town of Eaton v. Rickert, supra, 240 N.E.2d at 824:

> In the case of a court of general jurisdiction, such as a circuit court of this state, the record need not affirmatively show such jurisdiction, although such a showing is necessary in a court of inferior or limited jurisdiction. The burden is on the party attacking jurisdiction to make a proper showing in a court of general jurisdiction.

Furthermore, Indiana law is consistent with Nu-Way because there the lower court ruled that Nu-Way had failed to show "a basis" for the exercise of in personam jurisdiction. Similarly, in Indiana, the party challenging jurisdiction does not have the burden of proof where the face of the complaint fails to reveal a basis for jurisdiction.

In the present case, Alberts alleges jurisdiction over Mack Trucks on the face of the complaint. The complaint alleges that "The Defendant, Mack Trucks, Inc., is a corporation doing business in the State of Indiana." Pursuant to Indiana's long arm statute, T.R. 4.4, "doing business in the State of Indiana" is a basis for the exercise of jurisdiction over Mack Truck by an Indiana court.

Therefore, it was Mack Trucks' initial burden to at least go forward with evidence to establish that Indiana courts did not have jurisdiction. Mack Trucks produced no evidence at the hearing on the motion to dismiss to carry this burden.

We recognize that there may be due process implications under World-Wide Volkswagon concerning where the ultimate burden of proving jurisdiction rests. However, in the present case that issue need not be reached because no evidence as to jurisdiction was presented by Mack Trucks (or by Alberts) at the hearing on its motion to dismiss. Since no evidence was presented, Mack Trucks did not meet its initial burden of going forward with the evidence. Therefore, the trial court erred in granting Mack Trucks' motion to dismiss.

Alberts next argues that the trial court erred in granting NSC's motion to dismiss. He first claims the trial court erred in finding that NSC did not waive jurisdiction by sending to Alberts' counsel interrogatories which sought to generate a defense on the merits. A party who is not otherwise subject to the personal jurisdiction of the court may, nevertheless, submit himself to the court's jurisdiction. State v. Omega Painting, Inc. (1984), Ind.App., 463 N.E.2D 287, 291. Alberts argues that by sending interrogatories to his counsel, Mack Trucks submitted itself to the Indiana court's jurisdiction. In Omega Painting, supra, 463 N.E.2D at 293, we held:

> While the State could have properly preserved the question of jurisdiction in its answer and then proceeded with a defense on the merits, by filing its interrogatories prior to the assertion of the defense, the State has waived the jurisdictional issue.

* * *

Alberts finally argues that the trial court erred in not allowing the plaintiff to file his verified second amended complaint as a matter of right after Mack Trucks' and NSC's motions to dismiss were granted. He argues that this was in error because TR 6(C)(2) allows a plaintiff to file a verified amended complaint as a matter of right. We disagree. TR 6 concerns the time limits for taking appropriate action. Subsection (C)(2) merely provides that if the court grants a Rule 12 motion and corrective action is allowed, it shall be taken within ten days. The pleading in question was Alberts' second amended complaint. Since the dismissal was granted pursuant to TR 12(B)(2), the automatic right to plead over where a TR 12(B)(6) motion is granted had no application. Pursuant to TR 15(A) Alberts was required to secure leave of court to again amend his complaint:

> (A) Amendments. A party may amend his pleading once as a matter of course at any time before a responsive pleading is served or, if the pleading is one to which no responsive pleading is permitted, and the action has not been placed upon the trial calendar, he may so amend it at any time within thirty [30] days after it is served. Otherwise a party may amend his pleading only by leave of court or by written consent of the adverse party; and leave shall be given when justice so requires. A party shall plead in response to the original pleading or within twenty [20] days after service of the amended pleading, whichever period may be the longer, unless the court otherwise orders. (emphasis added)

Since Alberts did not ask for leave to file his verified second amended complaint, the court did not err in denying Alberts' motion. Sekerez v. Gary Redevelopment Commission (1973), 157 Ind.App. 654, 301 N.E.2d 372.

Affirmed in part and Reversed in part.
STATON and BAKER, JJ., concur.

Case Question

Is a bus company that routinely travels through a state, without stopping, doing business in that state?

◆

Venue

If jurisdiction exists, all courts within a system, such as all federal district courts, have authority to hear a case. An additional requirement, however, is that the case must be brought in the proper venue—the specific court within a judicial system where a case is brought. Venue is the court where the case should be tried according to the law of procedure. Although each type of federal jurisdiction has its own rules regarding what constitutes proper venue, it can be safely said that proper venue will always have some relationship to the domicile of the parties or the subject of the lawsuit.

Typically, the proper venue is the court within whose geographical boundaries all defendants (and/or sometimes all plaintiffs) are domiciled or where the lawsuit arose. In state systems, the proper venue would be the trial court at the county level. In the federal system, it would be the particular district court within whose boundaries one of the jurisdictional elements exists.

Frequently, the media will feature a news story about a request for a change of venue in a much-publicized case. While the courts have the authority to hear cases over which there is proper jurisdiction and venue, they also have discretion to decline venue when a case could not be fairly heard. This discretion also extends to cases where there is concurrent jurisdiction with other courts and another court would be more suitable. The process of declining jurisdiction in such a case is known as forum non conveniens (discussed in the following section).

 APPLICATION 6.7

A resident of Tennessee is involved in a lawsuit with a resident of Oklahoma. Since diversity of citizenship exists, and assuming that the value of the case is in excess of $75,000, the case could be brought in federal court. Proper venue indicates which of the federal district courts has authority to hear the case. In this situation, if jurisdiction is based on diversity of citizenship, venue will be in the federal district court located in Tennessee or Oklahoma. There is also, however, state jurisdiction. Based on the state law and the type of case, one or both states could have jurisdiction. Within the states, the counties where the basis for the lawsuit arose or the county of domicile of the defendant (and possibly the plaintiff) will be the proper venue.

Points for Discussion
1. How is venue different from jurisdiction?
2. Why do so many different courts have jurisdiction in this situation?

Forum Non Conveniens

When more than one jurisdiction has authority to hear a case, the plaintiff is usually given the choice of where the lawsuit will be conducted. Literally translated, the term *forum non conveniens* means an "inconvenient forum" and refers to the situation in which a court, for all practical purposes, is nonconvenient when compared with other courts that also have jurisdiction to hear a case. In such a situation, the court has the discretion to use its own judgment and determine whether the case should be dismissed, with permission granted to the plaintiff to file suit in another jurisdiction.

The courts are hesitant to disturb the right of the plaintiff to choose the forum. However, if it appears that another court is in a much better position to decide the case, the first court may decline to exercise its jurisdiction based on forum non conveniens.

The issue of forum non conveniens is usually brought to the attention of the court by the defendant. The most common scenario is that a defendant believes that the plaintiff filed a suit in a particular jurisdiction for no other reason than to obtain the most favorable result. For example, such motions often appear in jurisdictions where jury verdicts are reported to be unusually high in certain types of cases. Whatever the plaintiff's reason for filing suit in a juris-diction, the court will not question it—that is, until a motion is made to the court based on forum non conveniens. When such a motion is filed, the court compares all courts with jurisdiction over the case.

The consideration of the court in such an issue is commonly referred to as an unequal balancing test.[9] The court presumes that the plaintiff's right to choose the forum will be honored unless the defendant shows that another court would be a far more appropriate place to have the trial. In making this determination, the court considers several factors:

1. The residence of the parties.
2. The location of the witnesses.
3. The location of the evidence.
4. The site of the occurrence (in cases where a judge wants a jury to see the site and where the site is accessible).
5. The docket of the two courts. (Where could the trial be held sooner?)
6. The interest of the citizens of the current jurisdiction in having the case heard. (Will the case help settle an issue of undecided law in the state?)
7. The state law to be applied.

If the balance of these facts strongly favors the defendant's suggested forum, it will be considered to outweigh the important right of the plaintiff to choose the forum. Although it occurs less frequently, the court may also invoke forum non conveniens on its own motion. In either situation, the same test is applied. If the test establishes a significantly more appropriate forum, the case will be dismissed in the original court, and the order of dismissal will indicate where the case should be filed.

ESTABLISHING JURISDICTION

To summarize, in establishing the appropriate jurisdiction, the court would ask the following questions:

1. Where did the actual basis for a lawsuit occur? What state? What county? What federal district?
2. Who are the plaintiffs?
3. Who are the defendants?
4. Are any of the parties corporations? If so, what is the state of incorporation? What is the nerve center of the corporation?
5. Does the suit involve federal law? If so, is the law subject to the authority of a special federal district court (e.g., U.S. District Court of Claims)?
6. Will any officer or branch of the U.S. government be named as a party?
7. Does any plaintiff share a common state of domicile with any party? If not, is the amount in controversy greater than $75,000?
8. Is property the basis for jurisdiction? If so, where is it located?
9. Does any one court have **exclusive jurisdiction?**

Exclusive Jurisdiction
Authority of a court to hear a case, which authority is superior to authority of all other courts.

10. What are the possible venues?
11. If there is concurrent jurisdiction, is there one court with significantly more contacts to the case than another?

 APPLICATION 6.8

An accident occurs between a truck and a family vehicle. The truck is owned by a corporation with businesses in Ohio and Pennsylvania. The truck driver is from Ohio. The corporation is incorporated in Delaware but is headquartered in Pennsylvania. The family members in the vehicle include a grandmother domiciled in New Jersey and a mother and daughter domiciled in Connecticut. The accident occurs in New York. The family sues the corporation.

Points for Discussion
1. Is there federal jurisidiction?
2. What states have jurisdiction? (Assume subject matter jurisdiction requires the incident or the residents of all defendants to be in the state of suit.)

ETHICAL NOTE

Jurisdictional issues are often raised in response to questions about the truthfulness of parties regarding domicile, place of injury, etc. The very doctrine that disallows collusion was developed in response to parties who conspired to circumvent the purpose of procedural laws. It is extremely important that parties to suit understand that their ethical obligations are not limited to telling the truth when on the stand but that these obligations commence with the very first representations to the court about matters as seemingly trivial as one's intended place of permanent residence. The procedural laws pertaining to jurisdiction are firmly embedded and well founded in the rationale of procedural law, and all those taking advantage of the benefits of the legal system are commensurately obligated to follow the system's standards.

Question

What might a person seek to gain by misrepresenting his or her domicile to obtain jurisdiction in a particular court?

CHAPTER SUMMARY

Jurisdiction truly opens the doors of the legal system to those persons who have need of the system's benefits. Jurisdiction should always be the first consideration of persons who consider seeking judicial review of an issue and of the court to whom the issue is brought. Parties should be aware that even though a court has jurisdiction, it may decline to hear the case at all. The ultimate function of the courts with respect to jurisdiction is to have the dispute between parties decided by the most appropriate law and in the appropriate court.

Jurisdiction must exist over the issue (subject matter) and the litigants (in personam) or their property or property interests (in rem,

quasi in rem). In federal courts, the jurisdiction must be based on either a federal law, the fact that the United States is a party to the suit, or diversity of citizenship and a controversy valued at more than $75,000. With regard to diversity, corporations may have residence in more than one state.

Clearly, no lawsuit can proceed until all jurisdictional questions have been addressed.

REVIEW QUESTIONS

1. How is subject matter jurisdiction different from in personam jurisdiction?
2. How is in rem different from quasi in rem jurisdiction?
3. What are the three bases for federal jurisdiction?
4. How is diversity of citizenship determined?
5. Distinguish removal from remand.
6. When is removal appropriate?
7. How is the domicile of a corporation determined?
8. What is the nerve center test?
9. Distinguish venue from jurisdiction.
10. What doctrine is applied when a court declines to exercise its authority over a case?

CHAPTER TERMS

Ancillary Jurisdiction
Concurrent Jurisdiction
Exclusive Jurisdiction
Federal Question

In Personam (Personal) Jurisdiction
In Rem Jurisdiction
Long-Arm Statute

Original Jurisdiction
Pendent Jurisdiction
Quasi In Rem Jurisdiction
Subject Matter Jurisdiction

NOTES

1. William Statsky, *Legal Thesaurus/Dictionary* (St. Paul: West, 1982).
2. *Lowry v. Semke,* 571 P.2d 858 (1977).
3. *Estate of Portnoy v. Cessna Aircraft Co.,* 603 F.Supp. 285 (S.D.Miss. 1985).
4. *Black's Law Dictionary,* 5th ed. (St. Paul: West, 1979).
5. *T.J.K. v. N.B.,* 237 So.2d 592 (Fla.App. 1970).
6. *Atlas Garage & Custom Builders Inc. v. Hurley,* 167 Conn. 248, 355 A.2d 286 (1974).
7. Federal Rules of Civil Procedure, 28 U.S.C.A.
8. Id.
9. 10 A.L.R. Fed. 352.

CHAPTER 7

The Law of Contracts

CHAPTER OBJECTIVES

After reading this chapter you should be able to

- *Identify the elements of a valid offer to contract.*

- *Differentiate between a unilateral and bilateral contract.*

- *Distinguish fraud in fact and fraud in the inducement.*

- *List the defenses to alleged breach of contract.*

- *Distinguish compensatory damages, liquidated damages, and specific performance.*

- *Explain the purpose of the statute of frauds.*

- *Discuss the application of assignment and delegation in a contract.*

- *Discuss the remedies available to one who has entered a contract with a mistaken understanding of the terms of the agreement.*

Contract law is based on the principle established in most societies that people should be secure in the knowledge that promises will be honored and are legally enforceable when made between persons in order to provide each party with some type of benefit. This principle has evolved and developed over the years into one of the most precise areas of the law. Because so many of the transactions among individuals involve some type of reliance on one another, contract law has pervaded virtually all aspects of society. Consequently, other areas of law are frequently affected by principles of contract law.

Since each situation is unique, the law of contracts is still changing even today. Rarely does anyone go through a day of his or her life without becoming involved in or receiving benefits from a **contract.** The food we eat is usually produced, shipped, bought, and sold through contractual agreements. The same applies to clothing. Even the utilities in our homes, such as heat, water, and cooling, are received through contractual agreements to provide and pay.

As technology grows and society changes, the potential for contractual agreements (and disputes) grows. This chapter discusses the basic and settled principles of contract law. Apart from slight variations or modifications in each of the states, these principles continue to be the accepted standards by which persons who enter contractual agreements should guide their conduct. Typically, when new situations arise, the essential principles of contract law are modified or adapted to reach a result that is fair and consistent with precedent whenever possible.

The leading authorities on contract law have defined a **contractual agreement** as follows:

> A promise or a set of promises for the breach of which the law provides a remedy, or the performance of which the law recognizes a duty.[1]

In essence, this means that if parties make a promise or promises to one another, those parties are obligated to perform (complete) the terms of the promise(s). Consequently, in the event a party fails to complete the obligations of a promise, the party who is injured by not receiving that to which he or she is entitled by the promise will have recourse in the courts against the party who broke the promise. For example, a person who borrows money from a bank promises to repay the money. If that person fails to repay the money, the bank can go to court and attempt to collect the money that is owed.

Contract

A legally binding agreement that obligates two or more parties to do something they were not already obligated to do or refrain from doing something to which they were legally entitled.

Contractual Agreement

A promise or set of promises for the breach of which the law provides a remedy and the performance of which the law recognizes a duty.

ELEMENTS OF A VALID CONTRACT

Every valid contract has certain characteristics. If any of them are absent, the enforceability of the agreement comes into question. Essentially, every contract must have parties who provide some act or benefit that the other party does not otherwise have the legal right to receive. Specifically, all contracts must involve (1) at least two parties, (2) parties who have legal capacity, (3) a manifestation of assent by all parties to the contract, and (4) consideration that supports an enforceable promise.[2] The following discussion addresses each of these elements in greater detail.

At Least Two Parties

A person cannot enter into a contractual agreement with him or herself. This issue has generally arisen in situations where a person who has a partial ownership interest in a business also attempts to make an agreement with the business to provide it with certain benefits. An example is a lawyer who is also a CPA who contracts with his or her own incorporated law firm to provide accounting services to the firm.

The rule traditionally has been that a person with an ownership interest in a business cannot contract to render services that are part of the primary purpose of the business. Generally, such services are deemed part of the responsibility of the owner. In recent times, however, exceptions to this rule have been made, especially when the services contracted for are not ordinary duties of an owner.[3] The preceding example would be such a case. Although the attorney/CPA would ordinarily be required to render the skills of an attorney, maintenance of accounting records for the firm probably would not be considered part of the duties of an attorney for the firm. Such services would not be within the ordinary expectations of the business toward any particular owner. Thus, the attorney very likely could contract as an individual to provide these services to the law firm as an entity. Consequently, two separate legal entities—the attorney/CPA as (1) an individual and as (2) a member of the total firm—are parties to the contract.

Typically, the contractual requirement of at least two parties is the most easily met when establishing the elements of a contract in a given circumstance. However, this remains a basic element of contract law.

Parties Who Have Legal Capacity

In contract law, legal capacity means that a person is an adult (based on the age defined by state statute) and has mental competence (which simply means that the person has not been declared by any court to be incapable of managing his or her own affairs). The law is relatively settled that only competent adults can be bound by the terms of contracts. An issue arises, then, when a party without **contractual capacity** enters into a contract.

Age. The age requirement is forthright. The parties to the contract must be of the age of majority according to the law of the state governing the contract at the time the agreement is entered. A simple determination of the beginning of the agreement and the date of birth of the parties is the only information necessary. However, a question may arise if there is a dispute as to the state whose law will govern the contract. This comes into question when the parties or the subject of the agreement involve more than one state. For example, an 18-year-old goes into State X where the age of majority is 18 and contracts to purchase a car. However, the state of domicile of the 18-year-old (State Y) considers the age of majority as 20. If the 18-year-old buyer defaults on the payments, does the law of State X or State Y control? If the applicable state law is that of X, there is an enforceable contract. However, if the law of

Contractual Capacity
The ability to enter into and be bound by a legal contract, which ability is not diminished by age of minority or adjudicated incompetence.

State Y is applied, there was no capacity and thus no valid contract between the parties.

Usually, to avoid such issues, a written contract will indicate by agreement the law of the state that will apply in the event of a contractual dispute. When there is no written agreement, the court will determine the law of the state to be applied. As you can see, this determination can substantially affect the suit. This is why most written contracts include an agreement as to the state law to be applied in the event of a dispute.

Mental capacity.   The issue of mental capacity is somewhat more complicated. Technically, lack of mental capacity only considers persons who have been legally adjudicated (by order of the court) to be without the ability to manage their own affairs. However, what of the case where someone is quite obviously insane? Generally, the law that only adjudicated incompetents lack capacity will be upheld.

Many people may appear to be outside the normal range of behavior. This does not mean they are without the ability to manage their own affairs. Many famous and wealthy individuals have been notorious for "odd" behavior. Yet, their behavior did not prevent them from amassing great fortunes. Conversely, some of the most notorious and vicious criminals of our time functioned in society relatively unnoticed for years. The law cannot be based on subjective individual perceptions of sane or insane behavior. Thus, anyone who has not been declared incompetent by a court is responsible for any contractual agreements to which he or she is a party regardless of his or her actual mental abilities.

Contracts with persons without capacity.   Traditionally, if a person with capacity entered a contract with a person without legal capacity, the person without capacity could choose whether or not to complete the terms of the contract. The other party to the contract was virtually at the mercy of the person without capacity. The party without capacity could disaffirm or withdraw from the contract at any time. It did not matter that the party with capacity had already performed all obligations under the contract. The minor or incapacitated person could accept the benefits of that performance without further obligation. The reasoning behind this was that because the party was legally incapable of being a party to a contract, a contract could not be enforced against the person.

The inherent unfairness of this situation caused the courts and some legislatures to set forth legal standards that would protect parties with capacity who entered in good faith into a contract with a minor or incapacitated person. This was done under the theory of restitution,[4] which is based on the principle of fairness. With respect to contracts, the theory basically states that if one person accepts or takes a benefit from another who was not obligated to provide that benefit, some sort of payment should be made.

In addition to enacting the law of contracts, many states have enacted statutes, and many courts have issued decisions that follow the theory of restitution. Such legal standards provide a remedy to those who have entered contractual agreements with parties who do not have capacity. However, these legal standards often limit the recovery from the minor or incapacitated person. Commonly, such limitations involve the amount of liability of the minor or incapacitated person. Such amount will be the reasonable value of the goods or services received rather than the amount contracted for. An example is a contract between a minor and a competent adult to purchase a car. Although the minor enters a contract to purchase a car for $8,000, if the minor fails to complete payment, the car owner may be able to recover only the actual value of the car under the theory of restitution. If a court determines that the car is worth only $4,000, that amount is all that could be recovered from the minor. Additionally, the law of several states regarding the liability of minors and incompetents is that restitution can be claimed only for items considered to be necessary to life, such as food and shelter.[5]

As a consequence of the law of contracts and the law of restitution, the person with capacity usually requires the minor or incompetent to have an additional party enter the contract in his or her behalf. For example, a competent adult might cosign a loan with a minor. Then, if the minor breaches the contract, the contract can be enforced against the adult who cosigned. (Note that competent persons may also be required to have a cosigner as a condition of the contract for other reasons, such as to guarantee good credit.)

Assignment 7.1

Identify which of the following parties could be bound by contract:

1. Marcel is 15 years old. His father is out of town and Marcel agreed to sell the family's tractor for $2,000 to a neighboring farmer. Marcel accepted the money and the neighbor took the tractor. Marcel did not know the tractor is an antique and worth much more.
2. Two weeks ago, Louise ordered a new vehicle with all of the options available. She agreed to pay in cash, the price asked by the dealer and signed the appropriate papers. Yesterday it was discovered that Louise suffers from a large brain tumor, which has impaired her thinking and reasoning significantly.
3. Cindy was out of town on a camping trip when her babysitter, Maxine, took Cindy's son into an orthodontist. The orthodontist recommended braces for the child (at a cost of $4,000) and Maxine agreed. The orthodontist placed braces on the child. Cindy refused to pay and is now being sued for the cost of the braces.
4. Ronnie is 21 years old and a severe diabetic. When his sugar level is low he often makes irrational decisions. On one such occasion, he signed the papers to finance a $10,000 stereo. Ronnie is unemployed and lives with his parents. The stereo store wants either Ronnie or his parents to comply with the agreement.

Manifestation of Assent by All Parties

In all contracts, each party to the agreement must signify acceptance of the terms in some way. This requirement to manifest or demonstrate a willingness to be bound by the contract is essential. Otherwise, it would be possible for persons to claim a contract existed where one party did not even have notice of a contract or the intention to enter one. The following discussion explores several issues relevant to the manifestation of assent: (1) the objective standard that must be met to prove there was assent, (2) circumstances that may affect the termination of whether there was assent, and (3) methods of creating a situation for assent to a contract by the parties.

Objective standard.   Whether or not someone has manifested assent to a contract is measured by an objective standard. There is a great difference between objectivity and subjectivity. When one is objective, no personal bias plays a role in one's perceptions. However, when one is subjective, personal bias greatly influences one's perceptions. For example, if you were named as a defendant in a lawsuit, you would probably have very strong feelings about your innocence. Your view of the lawsuit would be quite subjective. However, if I were to stop someone on the street and tell the person about the lawsuit, the person's perceptions would be objective if the person knew no one involved in the suit and was unfamiliar with the suit's details.

As discussed in Chapter 5, during the voir dire stage, the parties in a suit attempt to select jurors who have no personal experience or beliefs that would prevent an objective consideration of the evidence as it applies to the parties. Similarly, in contract law, as a fundamental part of determining whether all the elements of a contract were present, the judge and jury have the duty to determine whether there was mutual assent by all parties to the agreement.

The objective standard requires that a third person observing the transaction would perceive that the parties agreed to the terms of the contract and intended to be legally bound by those terms. The parties do not need to say or do any particular thing. Rather, only their conduct needs to indicate agreement to the terms of the contract.[6] The existence of subjective intent claimed or denied by a party is not relevant for the purposes of determining whether a contract existed. For example, the jury will not consider the claim of a party that the party's conduct, even though it may appear to indicate intent, wasn't what the party meant.

 APPLICATION 7.1

Fernando promises Antonio $15 if he doesn't speak for three hours. Antonio nods but does not say anything. He continues to remain silent for the next three hours. His nod and continued silence would indicate to an observer that Antonio had accepted the terms of the contract.

Point for Discussion
What if Fernando claims that he meant that Antonio would have to verbally agree before the contract would begin?

Circumstances.   The following are some of the situations that will *not* give rise to the creation of a valid and enforceable contract:

1.   Agreements made in jest or as jokes.
2.   Negotiations prior to the creation of an actual contract.
3.   Promises or indications of future gifts in exchange for another's promise or performance.
4.   Promises for what a person is already legally obligated to do.

Agreements made in jest.   With respect to the first situation, persons cannot be held to agreements that have been made in jest. If such agreements were enforced, everyone would have to be on guard against saying things in conversations that could later be construed as a contractual promise. An example is an individual who says in idle conversation that he or she would sell a second person a house for fifty cents. However, cases of this type are usually more realistic. Often a very real offer and acceptance will be made. However, one party will claim that the other party should have known that there was no real intent and that the discussion was just that and not the establishment of contractual terms.

A primary legal obstacle to enforcing contracts where there are circumstances indicating jest is the inability to prove that the party meant to be bound by the agreement. Normally, persons talking in jest have no real intent to form a contract. Therefore, when attempting to enforce a contract under such circumstances, it would be necessary to show that an objective observer would conclude that the parties actually intended to be bound by their statements or conduct regardless of the jovial manner of their discussion. In the preceding example, it would be necessary to show that the seller really intended to convey the house for only fifty cents. In nearly all cases, this would be quite difficult to prove. However, if someone at a party said to another guest, "I've always loved your house. If you ever wanted to sell it, I'd pay you $100,000—no questions asked." The guest responds, "It's yours for $100,000." If the buyer declined and attempted to avoid the purchase, the jury would have to determine whether, under the circumstances, there was real contractual intent.

Negotiations.   For much the same reason, negotiations do not constitute contractual agreements. During negotiation, there is no real intent to make a firm commitment. Rather, the intent of parties during negotiation is to explore whether the parties can meet on a common ground. If they cannot, no contract will have been entered, and both parties are left as they started. If this were not the case, little business would ever be accomplished, since parties who engaged in an initial discussion about a contract could later be bound by that discussion.

Future gifts or performance.   With respect to the third circumstance, it may at first seem illogical to refuse enforcement of contracts for future gifts. It is certainly possible to contract for a future performance of some act. It is also necessary in every contract that a person promise something he or she is not otherwise legally obligated to do. So why is it not legal to contract for a future gift? The answer is quite simple. In legal terms, a gift has the quality of something that one is never *required* to grant. In a contract, however, if something becomes the basis of a contractual agreement, it loses its gift quality and is required to be delivered. If not delivered, there are legal consequences. Consequently, it is a contradiction in terms to promise a gift (something one is not required to do) as part of a contract, where performance of the "gift" becomes a legal obligation.

Legal obligation. Another situation of interest occurs when someone contracts to do what is already legally required. The basis of any contractual agreement must be voluntary acts by the parties. If persons promised what they were already legally obligated to do, the receiving party would not be getting anything to which he or she was not already entitled. Therefore, there would be no basis for a mutual agreement. For example, Bridget and Larry enter into a contractual agreement. Under the terms of the agreement, Bridget promises to buy Larry a new car if Larry will promise not to drive above the speed limit. Under current laws, Larry already has the obligation to drive at or below the speed limit. Therefore, Bridget is receiving nothing that she would not receive in the absence of her promise. Consequently, there is no basis to support her promise in the agreement.

Elements of assent. Before there can be assent to a contract, the parties must have come to some meeting of the minds about the terms of the contract. Frequently, an offer to enter a contract does not occur until after various types of negotiation have taken place. When one party has actually made an offer, the other party can accept or reject the offer for as long as it is in effect. The following discussion examines the stages of offer and acceptance and some particular situations that affect these stages.

Offer. The terms *offer* and *acceptance* are commonly employed in reference to the assent by each party. The party who creates the opportunity to be bound by a contract (as opposed to negotiation) is the offeror. The party who accepts the offer is the offeree. The acceptance is the last step in the formation of a valid contract, assuming the subject of the contract constitutes appropriate consideration. (Acceptance is discussed more specifically a little later in this section.) An integral part of any offer and acceptance to contract is consideration. Simply stated, consideration is the value each party gives in exchange for the benefit he or she expects to receive. Consideration is examined later in the chapter in greater detail, not only as an element of assent but also as a necessary and integral part of any contract.

Bilateral Contract

An agreement between two or more persons in which each party promises to deliver a performance in exchange for the performance of the other.

An offer can be made to enter a bilateral contract or a unilateral contract. If the offeror makes a promise and by that promise induces the offeree to make a return promise, a **bilateral contract** has been created.[7] Each party gives a promise in exchange for the other party's promise. Completion of what is promised by each party will complete the contract. An example is the promise of a car salesperson to give title to a car to a customer who promises to make monthly payments for twenty-four months. At this point, the two parties have entered into the contract. The purchaser must make the payments, and the salesperson must deliver title to the vehicle. When these steps are accomplished, the contract and the obligations of the parties have been satisfied, and the agreement has reached its logical end.

A **unilateral contract** is created when a promise is made in exchange for actual performance (without first making a promise of that performance).[8] Using a scenario similar to the previous example, a unilateral contract would occur if the following took place: A car salesperson promises to give title to a car to a customer in exchange for payment of $5,000 (the promise). The customer gives the salesperson $5,000 (the performance). The salesperson gives title to the car to the customer (completion of the promise). At this point, all terms of the contract have been satisfied.

Unilateral Contract
A contractual agreement in which one party makes a promise to perform upon the actual performance of another.

When negotiations precede the contract, it is sometimes difficult to distinguish the offeror from the offeree. Usually, both parties will suggest terms for the contract. When negotiations take place, the point at which they cease to be mere negotiations—the point at which one party makes an offer that can become the basis for a contract—must be determined. Identifying when negotiations end as well as the identity of the offeror and the offeree is necessary to separate the terms of the contract from the terms of the negotiations. Only the terms of the contract will be enforceable. In the law of contracts, the following definition of an offer has been developed for use in making the determination of when the offer is made and by whom:

> . . . [the] manifestation of willingness to enter a bargain, so made as to justify another person in understanding that his assent to that bargain is invited and will conclude it.[9]

The question to be asked is, would a reasonable objective observer perceive the actions of a person to be those of one who is creating the opportunity for a second person to enter into a contractual relationship by doing nothing more than accepting the terms that are already clearly set forth by the first person? If so, the last person to have offered terms during the negotiations would be the offeror. The offeror is the person who identifies all significant terms of the actual contract and then promises or performs. All that needs to follow is the assent by promise or performance of the second person, who is the offeree. Additionally, the time for acceptance by the offeree must be reasonably ascertainable.[10]

Advertisements. Much of the general public shares the belief that all advertisements are offers to enter contractual agreements for the sale of goods or services. Conversely, much of the legal community believes that such advertisements do not create an offer, because certain terms of the agreement are lacking. In reality, both are partially correct and partially incorrect. Whether or not an advertisement is an offer must be judged on an individual basis.

As a consequence of the requirements of identity of the offeror, time for acceptance, and clearly defined consideration, most advertisements do not contain sufficient specificity to constitute an offer. Rather, they are an invitation to a buyer to make an offer after selecting specific goods or services. If, however, an advertisement indicates a particular good or service whose value can be reasonably ascertained by one who sees or hears the advertisement, the time for the contract to be accepted is clear, and the offeree is clearly identified (e.g., the first ten customers), the advertisement may be treated as an offer, and offerees have the opportunity to accept it and form a contract.

 APPLICATION 7.2 ———————————

The following newspaper advertisements illustrate the differences between nonoffers and offers:

Nonoffer: "All shoes on sale! Available to the public at one low price of $19.99 while supplies last."

Offer: "All genuine snakeskin shoes on sale! Available to first twenty customers, Saturday March 18, at one low price of $19.99 per pair. One pair per customer."

Point for Discussion

What is the significant difference between the two examples?

Indefinite promises. Similar to the advertisement is the indefinite promise. Even if all the terms necessary to a contract are technically present, an indefinite promise is not an offer and cannot lead to a valid and enforceable contract. A promise is indefinite if the benefit offered by the promise (the consideration) is vague or incapable of having its value reasonably determined.[11] For example, the promise by a cat breeder of simply "a cat" in exchange for $400 would probably not be a contract. However, if the breeder promises a registered kitten from a litter of Burmese cats, the value of such a kitten is much more easily discovered than a vague description such as "a cat." If the vague language in contracts were enforceable, persons could take advantage of others who had different expectations. Much of the determination of whether a promise is indefinite is based on the circumstances and whether the other party could, in fact, identify with specificity the value of the consideration to be received.

Auctions. When identifying the offeror and offeree in an auction, the key term is *reserve*. In an auction, all elements of the offer are usually present. The item is specific, it can be inspected and valued, and the time for acceptance is set (while the item is being bid upon). The only thing that will affect the identity of the party who makes the offer is a sale with or without reserve. If an auction is conducted with reserve, the auctioneer can reserve in advance the right to refuse a bid prior to the final sale of the particular item. In effect, this makes the auctioneer an offeree with the right to refuse an offer (bid). Therefore, until an auctioneer announces whether a bid will be accepted, the contract is not formed. In an auction without reserve, the auctioneer is an offeror upon calling for bids (acceptance) of the promise of any amount on an item. When a bid is received, the contract is established.[12] As noted earlier, the amount of the bid (promise to pay) is not a matter of legal concern.

Illusory promises.   An illusory promise is one in which the promisor retains the ability to negate the promise,[13] for example, "I may sell you my house if you promise to pay me $50,000." In reality, the owner of the house has promised nothing at all. Therefore, the person promising to pay $50,000 is receiving no consideration for that promise. There is nothing real to induce the promise.

Termination of the offer.   Until acceptance occurs, the offeror has the opportunity to retract the offer at any time. The only exception to this is when the offeree has purchased an option—a type of contract in and of itself. Generally, an offeror and offeree will enter into an agreement where the offeree has the exclusive right to accept the offer during a specific period of time. The offeree gives consideration of some type in exchange for the offeror's consideration of promising not to accept an offer from another offeree or cancel the offer during the specified time. Otherwise, the offeror may withdraw the offer at any time prior to acceptance. However, if the offer is for a unilateral contract and the offeree begins performance, the law will imply an option contract that prevents the offeror from revoking the offer during the performance by the offeree.[14]

 APPLICATION 7.3

Saul and Dorothy are considering the purchase of the home they now rent. Saul and Dorothy pay the landlord $1,000 for an option contract to purchase the property. In exchange for the payment of $1,000, the landlord promises not to sell the property to anyone but Saul and Dorothy during a certain period of time.

Point for Discussion
What happens to the $1,000 if Saul and Dorothy elect not to purchase the property?

Implied option contract.   Cindy contracts with Kelley to paint her house. Cindy promises to pay Kelley $500 after the house has been painted. Kelley accepts the offer by starting to paint Cindy's house. Two weeks later, when Kelley is approximately halfway finished, Cindy says she has changed her mind; she does not want the house painted and will not pay Kelley. Ordinarily, performance must be complete to accept a contract. However, in situations such as this, the law will imply an option on Kelley's part. Thus, the offer must remain open until Kelley has had the opportunity to complete the performance.

In addition to cancellation by the offeror, an offer may terminate prior to acceptance in other ways. An offer that is open for a specified time and is not accepted during that time will cease to be an offer. If no time is specified, the law will imply a reasonable time for that type of offer. If the offeree rejects the offer, the offer is no longer effective; to contract, a new offer must be made. A counteroffer by an offeree is considered a rejection of the offeror's offer and is treated as a new and different offer, thereby making the initial offeree the offeror. Finally, if the offeror or the offeree should die or lose legal capacity prior to acceptance, the offer will be terminated automatically.[15]

Acceptance.   The ultimate step in creating any contract is an acceptance of the terms by the offeree. What constitutes an acceptance is at least in part dictated by the type of contract. In a bilateral contract (a promise for a promise), before the contract becomes binding, the offeree must give a promise in exchange and as consideration for the offeror's promise. At that point, both parties are obligated to fulfill their promises according to their terms.

To solidify a unilateral contract, the offeree must begin performance in response to the offeror's promise. The contract is not actually accepted until the offeree has substantially performed what was asked by the offeror. At that time, however, the offeror cannot withdraw the offer that induced the offeree to perform and is obligated to allow the offeree to finish the job. This prevents an offeror from accepting the benefits of a performance and withdrawing the offer before the performance is complete. If the offeree completes the task, the offeror must provide the promised consideration. When an offeree does not complete performance of a unilateral contract, the offeror may have to pay partial consideration for the work done if the offeree substantially performed.

The offeree must have knowledge of an offer. Acceptance cannot be the result of coincidence. If by chance or for some other reason the offeree promises or performs what the offeror seeks, there will be no contract. For a contract to exist, the offeree must be induced by the offeror's promise to give a specific promise or performance in exchange. Similarly, the consideration for each party must be something the party would not otherwise be entitled to receive. If it is not, consideration would not act as an inducement to enter the contract.

As a general rule, but subject to the following exception (discussed under "Methods of acceptance"), an offeree cannot alter, delete, or add terms to the contract when accepting. The contract must be accepted or rejected "as is." If such changes were allowed, there would really be no offer at all. In bilateral contracts (where acceptance is by making a promise), the altered or additional terms would actually be nothing more than another offer or additional negotiations of what the offeree's promise should be. More importantly, in unilateral contracts (where acceptance is by performance), allowing changes in the terms could cause the offeror to receive something very different from what he or she sought. The offeror might not want the different type of consideration. Thus, performance by the offeree would no longer be of consideration that would encourage the offeror to honor the original promise.[16] An example of the latter situation would be if someone offered to pay $15,000 for the immediate delivery of an Arabian horse. In response, an offeree ships a Shetland pony. The offeror should not be bound in this situation, because a Shetland pony was not what the offeror contracted to receive.

The exceptions to this general rule are commercial transactions between persons engaged in the sale of goods. Merchants are governed by the laws of the state designed especially for commercial transactions and commercial contractual agreements. The Uniform Commercial Code (commonly referred to as the U.C.C.) is a series of laws regarding commercial transactions that have been adopted, at least in part, by all the states. The U.C.C. governs the various practices of sales and financing by commercial businesses with one another and the general public. A variety of other subjects, such as banking and bulk transfers, are included in the code. Each subject is addressed in a separate article, similar in organization to a book chapter. Article 2 of the Uniform Commercial Code sets forth provisions for commercial transactions involving the public sale of goods by merchants. Under Article 2, it is permissible for an offeree to include additional or varied terms when accepting a written contract. However, if the offer in the contract states that such changes must be expressly approved by the original offeror, no acceptance is valid, and no contract exists until the offeror has approved of the offeree's added or varied terms.[17] Article 2 also has provisions that guide the conduct of parties who are involved in a contract and the breach of that contract occurs or is imminent. (Breach of contract pertaining to financing agreements is discussed near the end of the chapter.)

Methods of acceptance.   Generally, acceptance is effective at the time it is tendered. The exception, of course, occurs in a unilateral contract. Acceptance by the tender of performance is sufficient to create an option to continue until the performance and, consequently, the acceptance are complete. If the offer is made to a specific individual or type of individual (e.g., the first ten customers), no one else may respond. If it is made to the general public, all who become aware of the offer are offerees and have the right to accept the contract.

In face-to-face confrontations, usually, little doubt exists as to when an acceptance becomes effective. At the moment an objective observer would perceive the offeree as tendering an acceptance of the contract terms, the contract would take effect. Often the situation is much different, however, and acceptance is communicated through a medium other than a face-to-face meeting.

A common situation occurs when an offeree accepts the terms of an offer by mail or telegraph. As a general rule, in such cases, the acceptance is effective when posted. However, it is necessary for the offeree to do everything that is required to ensure delivery. For an offer accepted by mail, the proper address must be included, the postage prepaid, and the acceptance deposited in a valid postal receptacle or post office. In the case of telegrams, the communication must be delivered to the telegraph office and paid for in advance. In the case of unilateral contracts, the offeror must have a reasonable basis to discover that performance has begun.[18]

At any time prior to acceptance, the offeror may revoke the offer. If this is done by mail, the offeror's revocation will generally be considered valid when received by the offeree. If an offeree mails an acceptance at approximately the same time an offeror sends a revocation, the court can use the mail carrier's date stamp to ascertain whether acceptance or revocation occurred first. If the rule was that acceptance was effective upon receipt, it would be up to the parties to convince the court when actual receipt occurred. In addition, in the case of unilateral contracts, if acceptance by performance begins and a communication is sent to inform the offeror of this, it would be unfair to require the offeree to

perform at his or her own risk until such time as the acceptance reached the offeror. After all, in local transactions, the start of performance binds the offeror,
and the rule should be no different for long-distance transactions.

An exception to the rules regarding acceptance conveyed by mail or telegraph is the reasonableness of mail or telegraph as a means of communication.
If the circumstances indicate that another method of acceptance, such as personal delivery or face-to-face acceptance, would be more reasonable, the court
may find that it was improper to accept by mail, and it will be ineffective to create
a contract.

Assignment 7.2

Which of the following situations describe an offer and acceptance sufficient to create a valid contract? If no contract exists, explain why.

1. Tomás promises Andy that he will take Andy's place on a blind date
   in exchange for $50.
2. A local dress shop advertises three "original dresses" for $100 per
   dress to the first three buyers on Saturday, June 12. On that date,
   Mariana comes into the store, says "I accept the offer for all three
   dresses," and hands the owner $300.
3. A local dress shop advertises three "original dresses by the designer
   Elaine" for $100 per dress to the first three buyers on Saturday, June
   12. On that date, Mariana comes into the store, says "I accept the
   offer for all three dresses," and hands the owner $300.
4. Paul tells Abigail, "I may give you $50 if you promise to buy me a
   fabulous birthday present."
5. Colleen verbally agrees to give Joe one year of piano lessons in
   exchange for Joe taking her to the prom as his date.
6. Susan agrees to pay $5,000 to Mark, a government official, for top
   secret information regarding government contracts that have not yet
   been awarded to private companies (several of whom employ Susan).

Consideration That Supports an Enforceable Promise

As stated earlier, to constitute an offer to contract, all material terms must be
present. One of these terms is consideration—the benefit received by a party in
exchange for the party's promise or performance. Essentially, consideration is
the element that induces a person to enter a contract.[19] The person promises or
does something he or she is not obligated to do in exchange for a promise or
performance he or she is not otherwise entitled to receive.

The value of the consideration for the specific contract must be determinable.
This is merely to ensure that a party is getting something of value in exchange
for the promise or performance. Essentially, such determination is required to
prevent deception of innocent parties. The courts will not recognize a contract
where the description of the consideration is vague or where the consideration's
value is incapable of being measured. The courts are not usually concerned with

the amount of value of a consideration or whether one party benefits more than another. That is a matter left for the parties to negotiate. The law does require, however, that a party to a contract be able to reasonably determine the value, quantity, and quality of the consideration to be received. This allows the party to make an informed decision of whether or not to enter the contract.

For consideration to be legally enforceable, it must be something that the law will recognize as a proper basis for a contract. Generally, this means that the consideration cannot be something that would be illegal or that would force the party to engage in illegal conduct. If, for example, one party promised another party $50 in exchange for stealing a typewriter, there would not be a valid contract. Because one party's consideration is an illegal act, the fourth element necessary to establish a contract (consideration that supports a legally enforceable promise) is not met.

In addition, the consideration must be something that is genuine. It does not matter that one party's consideration is seemingly inadequate when compared with the other party's offered consideration. The law does not concern itself with the adequacy of consideration.[20] The only exception to this would be if the consideration was represented as the real article and was actually a fake. If the consideration is a promise that turns out to be a sham in an attempt to deceive another party, it may not be treated as valid consideration, and the contract will not be enforced.

 APPLICATION 7.4

A salesman approaches a potential customer about investing in a diamond mine. In exchange for the customer's contribution of $10,000, the salesman promises that the customer will be given a controlling interest in a currently producing diamond mine. The customer agrees and gives the salesman $5,000. Before paying the balance, the customer decides to investigate and finds that the diamond mine is nothing but a swamp. Because the salesman's promise was a sham, the customer cannot be forced under contract law to continue her obligation and pay the remaining $5,000.

Point for Discussion
Can the customer recover the original $5,000 in investment?

 C A S E

GRANDE v. BEHLING

1997 WL 219758
(Conn. Super. 1977).

GAFFNEY, Judge.

The plaintiff sues to recover unpaid principal, interest and collectible fees and costs due on a promissory note given to him by the defendant on December 31, 1985. The defendant is a practicing attorney specializing in pension planning and law related thereto. The plaintiff is his former father-in-law.

During 1982 and 1983 the defendant offered to the plaintiff the opportunity to participate in a limited partnership investment in certain Texas real estate. The first of three investments proved to be financially successful, and the plaintiff reaped a significant profit. The remaining two investments, because of a downslide in the Texas economy, were unrewarding, and the plaintiff stood to lose all that he had contributed and more. [FN1]

The plaintiff, who was subsisting with his wife on retirement income, complained to the defendant about his losses on the investments and future exposure. It was at this point in 1985 that the defendant, in part at the urging of his then-wife and to appease his father-in-law, paid to the latter the sum of $5000 and executed and provided to him the promissory note on which he, the plaintiff, now sues. Curiously, the note is in the principal amount of $20,000, which amount together with the $5000 payment is four times the amount of the plaintiff's failed investment. Strangely as well, the note was given to the plaintiff at a time when the defendant urges the court to conclude that the investment was by then a failure, with no expectation that circumstances would change for the better.

The note provides for eight annual payments of $2500 each together with interest, the first payment being due in 1986 and the last on December 31, 1993. The defendant paid the first two installments, the second payment being accompanied by a signed cover letter, dated July 29, 1988 (Pl.Exh. 5). That date was more than two and one-half years after purchase of the plaintiff's investment interest and delivery of the promissory note to him. The letter and three prior letters from the defendant (Pl.Exhs. 2, 3, 4) confirmed the sale and acquisition of the plaintiff's share in the limited partnership.

In 1989, when contacted by the plaintiff, the defendant informed him that the investment was worthless and he (the defendant) was in no position to make any further payment on the note. None was made.

During much of this period the plaintiff and his wife saw their daughter, the defendant, and the couple's children socially on almost a weekly basis. This relationship continued until sometime in 1992

when the defendant's wife sued for a dissolution of their marriage. It is noteworthy that the marriage was dissolved in 1995, the year the instant action was brought, after a bitter and fully contested hearing. The dissolution court's decision and rulings on postjudgment motions which were adverse to the defendant's ex-wife have only served to enhance the bitterness which exists, the plaintiff describing under oath his dislike of the defendant and similar, but more intensive, negative feelings held by the plaintiff's wife and daughter.

The plaintiff and the defendant saw each other only occasionally from 1992 to 1994. At no time during the entire period from May 1989 to August 1995 did the plaintiff ever speak to the defendant about the promissory note and the plaintiff's wish to be paid the balance owing. By letter, dated August 15, 1995, (Def.Exh. 1), plaintiff's attorney made formal demand of the defendant for full payment of the amount claimed to be due.

The plaintiff's complaint is in one count and sets forth an action in contract for recovery on terms of the promissory note. Hartford Federal Savings & Loan Assn. v. Green, 36 Conn.Supp. 506, 513, 412 A.2d 709 (1979). The defendant's answer admits execution of the note, that two installment payments were made, that the plaintiff made demand for the balance due, and that no further payments have been made. It is the defendant's position, despite the foregoing, that no sum is due and owing. He asserts lack of consideration, laches, and set-off by way of special defenses [FN2] and, additionally, seeks to bar recovery by application of the doctrine of equitable estoppel.

I

It is axiomatic that a contract, to be enforceable, must be supported by consideration. "The doctrine of consideration is fundamental in the law of contracts, the general rule being that in the absence of consideration an executory promise is unenforceable." State National Bank v. Dick, 164 Conn. 523, 529, 325 A.2d 235 (1973). When, however, in a contractual context a benefit accrues to a promisor or a detriment to the recipient promisee, the contract is supported by consideration. Finlay v. Swirsky, 103 Conn. 624, 631, 131 A. 420 (1925).

Generous though the defendant may have been in the amount he committed himself to pay, the court is not persuaded that his motive was eleemosynary. Payment of the amounts due during the first two years of the term along with the defendant's repeated acknowledgment in writing of acquisition of the plaintiff's investment interest, all in the wake of financial rewards and success attained in an earlier, similar-type investment, persuades the court of the defendant's belief that at least a potential benefit had been obtained.

The court finds that the parties by word and deed manifested their mutual assent to the exchange, thereby forming the contract; Ubysz v. DiPietro, 185 Conn. 47, 51, 440 A.2d 830 (1981); which contract, drawn by the defendant, was, at the time of inception, supported by valuable consideration. Gruber v. Klein, 102 Conn. 34, 36, 127 A. 907 (1925).

II

In order to prevail on his defense of laches, the defendant must establish two elements. "First, there must have been a delay that was inexcusable, and, second, that delay must have prejudiced the defendant. Kurzatkowski v. Kurzatkowski, 142 Conn. 680, 685, 116 A.2d 906 (1955)." Giordano v. Giordano, 39 Conn.App. 183, 213, 664 A.2d 1136 (1995). Whatever support the evidence may lend toward establishing the required elements, the doctrine is inapplicable in the instant context, it being purely an equitable one which is not to be imputed to one such as the plaintiff, who has brought an action at law within the statutory period. A. Sangivanni & Sons v. F.M. Floryan & Co., 158 Conn. 467, 474, 262 A.2d 159 (1969); Giordano v. Giordano, supra, 214.

The defense of laches is inapposite and does not diminish the plaintiff's claim.

III

The doctrine of equitable estoppel, although, as its name suggests, of equitable origin, has equal application to remedies available in courts of law. Boyce v. Allstate Ins. Co., 236 Conn. 375, 384, 673 A.2d 77 (1996). "Its office is . . . to show what equity and good conscience require, under the particular circumstances of the case . . . Lebowitz v. McPike, 157 Conn. 235, 243, 253 A.2d 1 (1968)." Boyce v. Allstate Ins. Co., supra.

"[T]here are two essential ELEMENTS which must be established in order to find an estoppel: one party must do or say something that is intended or calculated to induce another into believing in the existence of certain facts and to act upon that belief, and the other party must actually change his position or do some act to his injury which he would otherwise not have done." John F. Epina Realty, Inc. v. Space Realty, Inc., 194 Conn. 71, 85, 480 A.2d 499 (1984); Middletown Commercial Associates Ltd. PARTNERSHIP v. Middletown, 42 Conn.App. 426, 442, 680 A.2d 1350 (1996).

The evidence does not establish the essential elements above described. There is no evidence that the plaintiff did or said anything deliberately to mislead the defendant or justify a belief that the former was willing to forgive and forget. What makes the plaintiff's conduct questionable is his silence and inaction for a long period of time leading the defendant to an erroneous interpretation thereof. It is quite likely that the plaintiff, when he took action, was at that time influenced by other incentives. Nonetheless, there is no evidence that the defendant changed his position or was caused to do anything other than what he would have been expected to do in any event; i.e., apply the unspent monies toward the payment of family necessities.

The court finds that equitable estoppel is not a valid defense to the relief which is sought.

IV

The plaintiff asks the court to enter judgment of $15,000 damages, representing the unpaid principal of the 1985 promissory note. Additionally, the plaintiff asks for an assessment of damages in the amount of $16,387.34. That sum represents simple interest of 12 percent per annum on unpaid principal for a period somewhat in excess of nine years. Further, the plaintiff asks for an award of attorneys fees in accordance with provisions of the note.

It is generally accepted that language of a contract is "construed most strongly against the party whose language it is and for whose benefit it was inserted." Sturman v. Socha, 191 Conn. 1, 9, 463 A.2d 527 (1983). That the defendant-drafter is himself a practicing attorney adds compelling force to the principle. Bridge-Mile Shoe

Corporation v. Liggett Drug Co., 142 Conn. 313, 318–19, 113 A.2d 863 (1955). In construing the contract, however, it is not just the language of the contract which should be examined, but it is also important to consider the situation of the parties and circumstances connected with the transaction. Foley v. Huntington Co., 42 Conn.App. 712, 730, 682 A.2d 1026 (1996). In other words, the court should "consider not only the language used in the contract but also the circumstances surrounding the making of the contract, the motives of the parties and the purposes which they sought to accomplish." Harvey v. Daddona, 29 Conn.App. 369, 375, 615 A.2d 177 (1992). And in so doing the court presumes that the parties did not intend to create an absurd result, or one that is inequitable. Waesche v. Redevelopment Agency, 155 Conn. 44, 51, 229 A.2d 352 (1967); New England Savings Bank v. FTN Properties Ltd. Partnership, 32 Conn.App. 143–45, 628 A.2d 30 (1993).

As noted above, the plaintiff and the defendant were related by marriage. Their relationship was in all respects favorable both before and after delivery of the 1985 note. Even following the plaintiff's verbal demand for payment in May 1989 the relationship remained friendly and cordial, the parties interacting, as above described, on an almost weekly basis until at least 1992. The evidence discloses no reason why the parties might have anticipated in 1985 the antagonism that later developed.

The amount of the note, if paid, would have provided the plaintiff with a 400 percent return on his investment. Notwithstanding the generous profit that was promised, it is absurd to conclude that the defendant expected to be burdened with 12 percent interest payments for an extended period. The arrangement reached was an amicable one, made by parties who enjoyed a good relationship, and was intended to relieve the plaintiff of the risk assumed in making the investment. The circumstances do not support a conclusion that the defendant contemplated a long period of time to complete payment. Likewise, there is nothing in the evidence which would have precluded a reasonable assumption by the defendant that the plaintiff-promisee, after more than six years of silence and inaction, had abandoned any effort at collection.

Interest that is expressly reserved in a contract is recoverable as a matter of right; 45 Am.Jur.2d, Interest and Usury, Sec. 35; and its allowance is not dependent on exercise of the court's discretion. Cf. Bertozzi v. McCarthy, 164 Conn. 463, 467, 323 A.2d 553 (1973). The court construes the significant interest amount claimed, an amount which exceeds unpaid principal, as a claim for contractual damages stemming from post-maturity payment delay.

The law is clear, whether it be in a contract or tort context, that a party entitled to a damages award has a duty to make a reasonable effort to mitigate damages. Ann Howard's Apricots Restaurant, Inc. v. CHRO, 237 Conn. 209, 229, 676 A.2d 844 (1996). In this regard the court finds that the defendant has sustained his burden of proof. Ann Howard's Apricots Restaurant, Inc. v. CHRO, supra; Newington v. General Sanitation Service Co., 196 Conn. 81, 86, 491 A.2d 363 (1985).

The court finds that the defendant, in response to the plaintiff's demand, unequivocally notified the plaintiff in May 1989 that no further payments would be made on the note. At that point it was incumbent on the plaintiff "to exercise reasonable conduct to minimize the damages occasioned by the defendant's breach." West Haven Sound Development Corporation v. West Haven, 201 Conn. 305, 332, 514 A.2d 734 (1986). Instead, the plaintiff did nothing and said nothing for six years and now asks that the court reward him for his inertia with a bloated award of interest damages. Reason, not to mention equitable considerations, militates against such an award. What this court will do, as it should do, is "measure damages as though [the plaintiff] had acted reasonably." Id.

The court finds that the plaintiff, had he expended reasonable efforts at collection, should have effected a mutually agreeable compromise of his claim or obtained judgment thereon, either result within a period of two years of maturity date.

V

In accordance with this opinion, judgment may enter in favor of the plaintiff to recover of the defendant damages of $18,600, which amount includes interest at 12 percent per annum for two years, plus costs. Further, an order may enter for reasonable attorneys fees which the court finds to be $3500.

It is so ordered.

The plaintiff had advanced $6,250 as his share of the investments and was liable additionally for interest charges and land development expenses incurred by the partnership.

A limitation of action defense initially raised was abandoned by the defendant after trial.

The amount affords the defendant a set-off of $5000 against principal. The plaintiff does not dispute the defendant's entitlement to the credit.

Case Question
What is required for consideration to exist?

THIRD-PARTY INVOLVEMENT IN CONTRACTS

Sometimes parties will enter a contract with the intent to benefit persons who are not directly involved in the contract. Such an agreement is known as a third-party contract, and the person entitled to the contractual benefits is known as a **third-party beneficiary.** Another situation occurs when a party enters into a contract and later turns his or her contractual interest over to a third party. This latter occurrence is called assignment and delegation. Specific rules govern the rights and duties of all concerned in such situations.

Third-Party Beneficiary
One who, as the result of gift or collateral agreement, is entitled to the contractual performance owed another.

Third-Party Contracts

Three types of third-party contracts exist. The third parties in these types of contracts are known as donee beneficiaries, creditor beneficiaries, and incidental beneficiaries. The donee beneficiary receives benefit from the contract as a gift from one of the promisors. The creditor beneficiary receives benefit from one promisor as satisfaction of an existing debt from the other promisor. The incidental beneficiary is not intended by the parties to benefit directly from the contract but receives the benefit as a side effect of the contract.

The various beneficiaries are distinguished in terms of their rights in satisfaction of the contract. A donee or creditor beneficiary can enforce the contract against the party obligated to provide the benefit. The creditor beneficiary can enforce the contract against the party who owes the benefit or against the party who has contracted to provide it.[21]

 APPLICATION 7.5

Donee beneficiary.   Susan and Patrice enter into a contract. Susan promises to pay Patrice $50. Patrice promises to clean Beverly's (Susan's mother) house. Beverly is a donee beneficiary. Susan is the donor (party making the gift); Patrice is the obligor (party required to satisfy the gift).

Creditor beneficiary.   Matthew and Keith enter a contract. Matthew promises to clean Keith's swimming pool for three months. Keith promises to pay Local Community College, Matthew's tuition, which Matthew owes for the current semester. Local Community College is a creditor beneficiary.

Incidental beneficiary.   Lily contracts to purchase a car from Johnny's Junkers. Part of the agreement is that Johnny will put new tires on the car from J. C. Montgomery Tire Company. J. C. Montgomery is an incidental beneficiary.

Point for Discussion
What are the significant differences between the types of beneficiaries?

The incidental beneficiary has no rights against either party to the contract, because there was never any intent to make the contract for the purpose of benefiting this party. If the contract can be satisfied without involvement of the particular beneficiary, the parties are not obligated in any way to make compensation for failure to provide the benefit. In the preceding application, if Johnny can provide tires from another source that is acceptable to Lily, J. C. Montgomery will have no rights to force Johnny to purchase the tires from the company.

Similarly, in the preceding application, Beverly could not force Susan to ensure that Patrice satisfied the contract. It was purely gratuitous, and there are no contractual rights to gifts from the donor. However, Beverly or Susan would have the right to compel Patrice to satisfy the contract and provide the benefit (gift) to Beverly as long as Susan had met her obligations under the contract.

Assignment and Delegation

Assignment or delegation takes place when one or more parties to a contract assign rights or delegate duties under the contract to a third party. Generally, assignment or delegation is acceptable unless (1) the parties have stipulated in the contract that it is not permissible or (2) the assignment or delegation would significantly alter the duty or rights of the other party to the contract.[22]

In assignment, a party assigns the rights or benefits he or she is entitled to receive under the terms of the contract. The party to the contract is the assignor; the party receiving these rights is the assignee. If there is a complete assignment, the assignee steps into the shoes of the assignor and can enforce the contract against the remaining party to the contract. In a partial assignment, the enforcement would come from the assignor.

The following is an example of an impermissible assignment: Pak has purchased and paid for a three-year maintenance agreement for his typewriter with a local office supply business. After one year, Pak closes his business and assigns his rights to maintenance of his typewriter to another business with two typewriters. This would significantly increase the obligations of the remaining party to the contract (the office supply store), and the assignment would probably not be considered valid.

To delegate one's duties under a contract, the person accepting the duties (delegatee) must be able to provide an equivalent performance. In addition, the party delegating the duties (delegator) remains responsible under the contract until the duties are performed satisfactorily by the delegate.[23]

The following is an example of delegation: Pak owns a fleet of taxi cabs. He has an agreement with a local service station for routine maintenance and major repairs at a specified rate. The owner of the station in turn delegates the duties of maintenance and repair to the local high school shop class. If the class does not perform the repairs satisfactorily, the station owner, in addition to the high school class, may be held responsible.

 CASE

LITTLE ROCK WASTEWATER UTILITY v. LARRY MOYER TRUCKING, INC.

321 Ark. 303, 902 S.W.2d 760 (1995).

DUDLEY, Justice.

Road widening project subcontractor brought action against sewer utility, alleging it was third-party beneficiary of sewer line relocation agreement between Highway and Transportation Department and utility, and contending that it suffered damages as result of delays caused by utility's failure to perform relocation agreement satisfactorily. The Circuit Court, Pulaski County, John Ward, J., entered judgment for subcontractor. Utility appealed, and subcontrators cross-appealed. The Supreme Court, Dudley, J., held that: (1) whether subcontractor was third-party beneficiary of sewer line with location agreement was question for jury; (2) the fact that subcontractor was not prime contractor did not preclude subcontractor from being third-party beneficiary of sewer line relocation agreement; (3) "no damage" provision in specifications for project that applied to construction contract between project prime contractor and Department did not preclude subcontractor from recovering against utility; (4) substantial evidence supported jury's award of damages; (5) proof of anticipated profit damages suffered by subcontractor was not impermissibly speculative, and (6) it would remand action to trial court for consideration of whether to award attorney fees to subcontractor.

The Arkansas State Highway Commission decided that Baseline Road in Pulaski County should be widened from two lanes to five lanes, and it knew that appellant, Little Rock Wastewater Utility, owned sewer lines that were located where the construction

would take place. In anticipation of the earthwork and construction involved in widening the road, the Commission, acting through the Arkansas Highway and Transportation Department, entered into a contract with the Little Rock Wastewater Utility to relocate Utility's sewer lines. In this agreement, dated August 12, 1988, and styled "The Relocation Agreement," Utility was to relocate its facilities when notified to do so by the Department. Upon notice, it was to act with diligence, begin the relocation work within thirty days, complete the work within 150 days thereafter "in a manner as will result in no avoidable interference or delay in the construction work," and adjust the sewer facilities as required by the construction work. After the contract was executed, Utility was given notice and started its work. By the spring of 1991, Utility had completed most of its relocation work. On March 5, 1991, the Department entered into a separate contract with Southern Pavers, Inc. to widen the roadway and surface the road. That same day, Southern Pavers, the prime contractor, entered into a subcontract with Larry Moyer Trucking, Inc. to clear and grub for widening the road and to install drainage and related facilities. The subcontractor, appellee Moyer Trucking, started its work.

In the performance of its subcontract with Southern Pavers, Moyer Trucking experienced delays. It contends the delays were caused by Utility's failure to perform its contract with the Department and that it suffered damages as a result of these delays. Moyer Trucking filed this suit in which it alleged it was a third-party beneficiary of the Relocation Agreement and it suffered damages as a result of Utility's failure to perform that agreement satisfactorily. Upon trial, a jury returned a $62,563.49 verdict in Moyer Trucking's favor. Utility appeals, and Moyer Trucking cross-appeals. We affirm on direct appeal and reverse and remand on cross-appeal.

Utility's first point on direct appeal is that there is no legal basis for Moyer Trucking's claim that it was a third-party beneficiary of the relocation contract between the Department and Utility. The presumption is that parties contract only for themselves, and a contract will not be construed as having been made for the benefit of third parties unless it clearly appears that such was the intention of the parties. Howell v. Worth James Constr. Co., 259 Ark. 627, 535 S.W.2d 826 (1976). However, a contract is actionable by a third party where there is substantial evidence of a clear intention to benefit that third party. Id. at 629, 535 S.W.2d at 828. It is not necessary that the person be named in the contract, and if he is otherwise sufficiently described or designated, he may be one of a class of persons if the class is sufficiently described or designated. Id. at 630, 535 S.W.2d at 829.

We held that a provision in the contract by which the subdivision retained forty percent of the contract price as a bond for the trenching contractor evidenced its intent to be a surety for it and that the utility contractor was an intended beneficiary. Id. at 630, 535 S.W.2d at 829.

Both Utility and Moyer Trucking agree that Howell is the leading case on third-party beneficiary contracts in this State, but each that ends the case supports its argument in this appeal. In *Howell,* the appellee contractor, Worth James Construction Co., constructed water lines for the appellant subdivision, Tall Timber Development Corp, *Id.* at 638, 585 S.W.2d at 827. Appellant subdivision contracted separately with co-appellant, Howell, for co-appellant to do trenching. *Id.* Howell damaged the water lines during trenching, and the appellee utility contractor, Worth James, sued for damages based upon a provision in the contract between the subdivision, and the trenching contractor. *Id.,* 535 S.W.2d at 827–28. The appellant subdivision argued that the contract sued upon was for the benefit of the subdivision and the trenching contractor only. *Id.* at 629, 535 S.W.2d at 828. We held that a provision in the contract by which the subdivision retained forty percent of the contract price as a bond for the trenching contractor evidenced its intent to be a surety for it and that the utility contractor was an intended beneficiary. *Id.* at 630, 535 S.W.2d at 820.

In the case at bar, Utility argues that, since there was no retainage provision in the relocation contract, this case does not come within the ambit of Howell. The argument is not persuasive. It is not necessary that there be a retainage provision in order for there

to be third-party beneficiary of a contract. Other factors may demonstrate that a third party was in the class of persons intended to be a beneficiary of the contract.

Here, the language of the Relocation Agreement shows that the relocation work to be performed by Utility was to be practically completed before the earthwork and surfacing contract would be let by the Department.

Larry Moyer, the president of appellee Moyer Trucking, testified that, when making Moyer Trucking's bid for the subcontract, he relied on the fact that Utility essentially had completed its work and would coordinate the remaining work with the Department while construction on the roadway was in progress. Randy McNulty, president of Southern Pavers, testified that he relied on this fact when he made the primary bid and that he bid less because the relocation of the utilities would be almost complete, there would be less interference, and it would cost less to complete the construction job. Billy Morgan, superintendent for Southern Pavers, testified that he understood that the utility moving had been done before the job was started, but, as it turned out, the moving had not been done, and the work done by Moyer Trucking was significantly impaired.

In determining whether Moyer Trucking was in the class to be benefitted by the contract, the reasoning underlying cases from other jurisdictions is helpful. In Moore Constr. Co. v. Clarksville Dep't of Elec., 707 S.W.2d 1 (Tenn. App. 1985), the Tennessee Court of Appeals considered the question of whether a contractor can be an intended beneficiary of a construction contract between an owner and another prime contractor for work being performed as part of the same construction project. Id. at 10. It held that unless the construction contracts involved clearly provide otherwise, prime contractors on construction projects involving multiple prime contractors will be considered to be intended or third-party beneficiaries of the contracts between the project's owner and other prime contractors. Id. The Tennessee court relied in part on a New Jersey case, Broadway Maintenance Corp. v. Rutgers, 90 N.J. 253, 447 A.2d 906 (1982), in which the New Jersey Supreme Court said that when parties conceived that the prime contractors would benefit from the performance of their fellow contractors, when the project could not have been finished without each contractor meeting its respective obligations, and when the obligations of others induced each contractor to undertake its job at the agreed price, the contractors could recover from each other as third-party beneficiaries of the contracts between them and the owner. Rutgers, 447 A.2d at 910.

Here, Utility agreed to move the sewer lines so they would not interfere with the construction work that the Department was to later undertake. Then the Department contracted with Southern Pavers, which in turn subcontracted with Moyer Trucking to do the construction work. Thus, the trial court correctly refused to grant a directed verdict in favor of Utility and correctly allowed the third-party beneficiary issue to be submitted to the jury.

In its final argument Utility contends that the trial court erred in charging the jury about the measure of damages because (1) there was no competent evidence to support giving the instruction and (2) the instruction incorrectly stated the elements of damage. We have already reviewed the evidence, and there is no need to repeat it in addressing this point of appeal. In addition to questioning the sufficiency of that evidence, Utility argues that the damages were speculative.

When a party seeks to recover anticipated profits under a contract, he must present a reasonably complete set of figures to the jury and should not leave the jury to speculate as to whether there could have been any profits. Lost profits must be proven by evidence showing that it was reasonably certain the profits would have been made had the other party carried out its contract. Such proof is speculative when based upon such factors as projected sales when there are too many variables to make an accurate projection. See Sumlin v. Woodson, 211 Ark. 214, 199 S.W.2d 936 (1947). In Kennedy Bros. Constr. Co., we upheld an award of profits when the appellee lost a bid from the U.S. Army Corps of Engineers because of a faulty surety bond. Kennedy Bros., 282 Ark. at 546, 670 S.W.2d at 799. The figures presented to the jury were based upon the cost of the job if it had been completed within the contract time. The work was not done because the bid was lost; therefore, expert testimony was used to estimate the figures, and we held the damages were reasonably accurate. Id. at 547, 670 S.W.2d at 800. The loss of profit in the case at bar was based upon work already completed, and this figure was accurate enough to be submitted to a jury.

In Utility's last part of this argument, it argues, without any citation of authority and actually without any real argument, that the instruction incorrectly stated the elements of damage. We have often said that assignments of error unsupported by convincing argument or authority will not be considered on appeal, unless it is apparent without further research that they are well taken. Mikel v. Hubbard, 317 Ark. 125, 876 S.W.2d 558 (1994).

Case Question
What is the role of each member of a third-party contract?

PROBLEMS IN CREATING OR ENFORCING THE CONTRACT

Terms of the Contract

On occasion, both parties intend to enter, and believe they have entered, into a valid contractual agreement, but as they begin to fulfill their contractual obligations, it becomes apparent that they have understood and agreed to different terms. When this situation occurs, the law has developed methods of determining whose expectations will be enforced.

Generally, in the case of an innocent mistake, the court will examine each side of the contract and make a determination as to what a reasonable person would perceive the terms to be under the circumstances (use of objective standard to determine intent). If it appears that a reasonable person would have understood what the offeror intended, the offeree will be bound by the offeror's original terms.

Similarly, if it is apparent that the offeror should have understood the intentions of the offeree and the terms that supported the offeree's consideration, the offeror will be bound by the offeree's interpretation of the terms of the contract.

In making this interpretation of the terms of the contract, the court will apply the plain meaning rule.[24] Simply stated, this means that in most cases the court will assume that the offeror or offeree should have used ordinary meanings and definitions when interpreting the terms of the contract. The court will, however, deviate from this rule when terms of art (terms of technical terminology or terms used in a particular trade) are used. If all parties to the contract are members of the profession or trade that utilizes this type of terminology, the common meaning of the term by members of the profession or trade will be used to determine what the offeror and offeree should have interpreted the term to mean.[25]

Assignment 7.3

> Which of the following items would be valid and enforceable consideration?
>
> 1. Spouse A promises to not use illegal drugs in exchange for custody of the children in a divorce proceeding with Spouse B.
> 2. Spouse A promises not to move out of state for ten years in exchange for custody of the children in a divorce proceeding with Spouse B.

Unconscionable Contracts

There are two basic types of unconscionable contracts. The first is the classic unconscionable contract, in which the innocent party had no real bargaining power or opportunity to decline. This is often based on a lack of knowledge of the true terms of the contract. The innocent party is given the terms of the contract without an opportunity to discover their real meaning and extent, for example, an unqualified person who went to the sight of a natural disaster, such as a hurricane, and took contracts for home repairs for elderly persons at exorbitant rates. The homeowners are in need of immediate shelter and have little choice but to pay the price regardless of how high it may be. Effectively, the homeowners are in an untenable position. They have nowhere to go and no shelter if they do not seize the opportunity. They do so only to find that the work is unsatisfactory and greatly overpriced. In such cases, the contract may be considered unconscionable.

Another type of unconscionable contract is known as an adhesion contract, which is induced by duress. The innocent party enters the contract under the threat of some type of force.[26] The threat may include physical injury, financial injury, injury to reputation, or anything else that might cause significant harm to the innocent party. A perfect example is a promise to pay money in exchange for a promise not to publish information that would be very damaging to a person's reputation. If a court finds that in reality a reasonable person would have no choice but to agree to the terms of the contract as a means of protecting himself or herself, the contract will be unconscionable because it is an adhesion contract.

Unconscionability is extremely difficult to prove for several reasons. First, the courts are reluctant to judge a party's real motivation for entering a contract. Second, there is a presumption that every party should investigate the terms of a contract before agreeing to it. Finally, if the terms are for an illegal purpose, the party has the option of calling the appropriate law enforcement agencies rather than succumbing to the other party's demands. Nevertheless, occasions do occur in which a party believes there is no alternative but to enter into a contract that is unconscionable. In such instances, the court will declare the contract to be invalid.

Fraud in Contracts

Fraud is an action that can be brought in a variety of situations, one of which is contract. Specifically, two types of actions for fraud can be brought to invalidate a contract: fraud in fact and fraud in the inducement. They occur under different circumstances and, if proven, have different results.

Fraud in fact occurs when one party tricks another into signing a contract by leading the other party to believe the contract is something entirely different,[27] for example, asking for a party's signature on a receipt for merchandise when, in fact, the "receipt" not only acknowledges receipt of that merchandise but also includes a purchase contract for additional merchandise.

Fraud is difficult to prove because parties generally have a duty to examine a document before affixing their signature. However, if it can be shown that the terms were not obvious or were added later, or that some other circumstance existed that prevented the party from ascertaining that he or she was actually signing a contract, the court may find fraud in fact.

When fraud in fact is proven, the result is recision; that is, the contract is treated as if it never existed. The court will take necessary steps to restore the parties to the condition they were in prior to the contract. For example, if an innocent party has incurred obligations because of the contract, the party responsible for the fraud may be forced to pay or to do whatever is necessary to satisfy or eliminate these obligations.

The elements of fraud in the inducement are as follows:

1. A misrepresentation of a present or past fact that is false must exist.
2. The party making the misrepresentation must know that what he or she is presenting is false and, further, must intend for it to operate as an inducement to another to enter a contractual agreement.
3. The innocent party must be reasonable both in the belief that the representation is true and in the reliance on the term as an inducement to enter the contract.
4. The misrepresentation must be a material element of the contract.[28]
5. The innocent party must suffer measurable damages as a result of its reasonable reliance on the misrepresentation.

Fraud in the inducement generally occurs when one party intentionally misrepresents the amount or quality of the consideration the opposing party is to receive under the contract. For example, a party takes reasonable steps to determine the value of the consideration he or she will receive in exchange for the promise or performance and relies on the value of the consideration in making the decision to enter the contract. In reality, the consideration is worth considerably less, and fraud in the inducement has occurred.

A real estate agent undertakes to sell a certain property to a young couple buying their first home. The agent encourages the couple to have the home appraised and even offers the names of qualified individuals. The couple has the home appraised, and the appraiser confirms the value of the home as originally stated by the real estate agent. In reality, the agent paid the appraiser to confirm a value that is actually much higher than what the home is worth. The couple purchases the home, only to discover that the insurance company will insure it for only half the purchase price. Assuming there have been no changes in the market or other influences on home values, this may be circumstances for an action for fraud in the inducement.

Point for Discussion

What if the agent did not conspire with the appraiser but did have knowledge about a major defect in the sewer system that was not apparent to the appraiser or the purchasers?

When an action for fraud in the inducement succeeds, a court will allow a party to disaffirm the contract. This means that each party walks away from the contract. An attempt may be made to achieve fairness based on the true value of the consideration, but the parties will not be restored to their original condition.

Statute of Frauds

Statute of Frauds

Statutory law that specifies what contracts must be in writing before they will be enforced.

While all states recognize oral and written contracts, it has long been established that certain types of contracts must be in writing before they are considered valid and enforceable. The concept of a **statute of frauds** originated in England. Historically, the courts established certain very important matters of agreement that should be in writing to minimize doubt or difficulty in completing the agreement. Today, this theory has been followed in each state with the enactment of a similar statute that states what types of contracts must be in writing before a court will enforce them. Generally, these are substantial contracts whose terms should be clearly stated to minimize the opportunity for mistake or misinterpretation.[29] There are some variations from state to state, but most jurisdictions require the following types of contracts to be written before they become effective:

1. A promise by the executor or administrator of an estate to answer personally for the debts or obligations of the deceased.
2. A promise by one party to answer for the debts or obligations of another.
3. A promise given in exchange for a promise of marriage.
4. A promise to sell, transfer, or convey an interest in land (this may include ownership, possession, control, or any other interest).

5. A promise for the sale of goods by a merchant in which the price exceeds $500.
6. An agreement that, by its terms, cannot be completed within one year.

If a contract is not required to be written and is, in fact, oral, the existence of a contract will be judged objectively by what the conduct of the parties would indicate they meant the terms of the agreement to be. If, however, the contract falls within one of the situations covered by the state statute of frauds, it must be in writing before a court will even recognize that a contract exists.

Assignment 7.4

In the following situations, determine whether the contract should be in writing to be enforceable:

1. Maya and Ella agree to split the money equally from a bank robbery in which Maya plans to demand (and receive) $10,000 and Ella agrees to drive the getaway car.
2. George promises to pay Sam $5,000 to marry George's daughter Maggie.
3. Jesse and Kenneth agree that Jesse will give Kenneth haircuts for one year in exchange for a one-time fee of $150.
4. Olivia is the 23-year-old daughter of Martin. Olivia is being threatened with a lawsuit to collect on a debt she owes a local department store. Martin phones the department store and offers to pay the amount of the debt plus an extra $100 if the store will refrain from suing Olivia. The store agrees.
5. Beau offers to sublet the house Jack is renting for the amount of the regular rent plus $25 per month. Jack agrees.

DEFENSES TO AN ALLEGATION OF BREACH OF CONTRACT

When an action for breach of contract is brought, several defenses are available that may prevent a judgment against the defendant. Many were discussed previously as defects or irregularities in the steps of creating a contract. The following paragraphs discuss these and other defenses in the context of defenses.

Some of the more common defenses include the following:

1. Absence of one or more essential elements to create a contract.
2. Unconscionable contract.
3. Fraud.
4. Statute of frauds.
5. Accord and satisfaction.
6. Justifiable breach.
7. Impossibility/impracticability.
8. Frustration of purpose/terminated duty.

A party may allege one, several, or all of the defenses alternatively. Thus, while a jury may not find sufficient evidence to support one defense, it might be persuaded that another applies, and the plaintiff's case will fail.

One defense is known commonly as accord and satisfaction. Under this defense, the defendant claims to have performed by completing a new and different performance on which the parties agree in place of the original consideration. The "accord" amends the original agreement by substituting a new performance for the original, and the "satisfaction" is the fulfillment of the original contract by the substituted performance. Thus, the defendant would claim to have satisfied the contract by painting the plaintiff's house instead of fixing the plaintiff's car, as promised in the original contract. If the defendant fails to complete the satisfaction, however, the plaintiff can sue on either of the defendant's promises.

A second type of defense is a justified breach of contract. When one party breaches a contract, the second party is excused from the completion of performance. The reasoning is that the second party did not receive the consideration that originally induced his or her own promise or performance. Therefore, if consideration fails, there is no basis for requiring the contractual agreement to continue.

In addition, some circumstances force involuntary breach of contract. When this occurs, the party who fails to perform as required by the contract will not be held liable. Most commonly, such situations are referred to as impossibility or impracticability of performance and include situations where the contract cannot be completed through no fault of the parties.[30]

 APPLICATION 7.7

Chiyoko contracts with Timothy to paint her house. She promises to pay Timothy $400 per week for two weeks in exchange for Timothy's performance of painting the house completely within two weeks. After one week of painting, Chiyoko pays Timothy $400 on Friday. On Saturday, Chiyoko's house catches fire, and although a badly burned shell is left standing, the house is considered a total loss. Timothy discontinues his painting. Chiyoko sues Timothy for breach. The likely result is that Timothy would not be found guilty of breach, because his continued performance was rendered impossible or at the very least impracticable by the fire. Timothy would also probably be entitled to retain the $400 already paid as a fair exchange for the portion of the performance he actually did complete.

Point for Discussion
What if the house hadn't been destroyed but the smoke damage was so severe it took Timothy an additional month to finish the job?

Similar to the impossibility or impracticability rule are the defenses of frustration of performance and terminated duty. Frustration of performance occurs when, through no action by the parties, the purpose of the contract is destroyed. Consequently, the duty to perform ends.[31] For example, a distributor contracts to sell liquor to a grocery store. If the legislature passes a law prohibiting the sale of liquor, the distributor is frustrated in performance of his or her obligations under the contract. When this occurs, the duty to perform is terminated, and there can be no action for breach of contract.

REMEDIES FOR BREACH OF CONTRACT

As the preceding examples illustrate, numerous defenses can be offered against the charge of breach of contract. However, it is up to the trier of fact to determine whether these defenses warrant a finding in favor of the defendant. When the finding is that a breach did occur and is not justified in any way, the plaintiff will be entitled to some type of remedy for the damage incurred as a result of the breach.

Breach of contract has three common remedies: compensatory damages, liquidated damages, and specific performance. Each is distinct and applies only in particular situations of breach.

The most common remedy is compensatory damages to a plaintiff who has suffered from a breach of contract. The purpose of compensatory damages is to award a sufficient amount of money to place the plaintiff in the same position he or she would be in if the contract had been fulfilled. In this way, the plaintiff is compensated for any loss or injury. Even if the injury or loss did not actually involve money, the purpose of the remedy is to enable the plaintiff to repair the damage.

Parties use a liquidated damage clause when they know that a court will have difficulty estimating actual damages in the event of breach. In a true liquidated damage clause, the parties will arrive at a fair compensation to be paid by a party in the event that party breaches the agreement. This clause will then be included in the terms of the contract. (See Figure 7.1.)

Liquidated damages are an alternative to compensatory damages. The court has the duty to determine whether a breach occurred and, if so, whether the liquidated damage clause of the contract was, in fact, for liquidated damages or merely a prestated penalty for breach. If the court finds that the clause is a penalty, the clause will not be enforced. The courts do not generally impose penalties set by the parties. Rather, the court will determine whether a penalty is appropriate in addition to the compensatory damages. The reasoning behind the refusal to enforce penalty clauses is quite simple. In some situations, a party does not have a defense to the breach but, for unforeseen reasons, must cease performance under the contract. Many times there are circumstances in which a party had no prior intent to breach but finds it necessary to do so. In such instances, it would not be fair to allow parties to penalize one another in excess of what would be reasonable compensation for the breach. The courts prefer to retain authority to determine appropriate circumstances for penalizing persons who breach a contract.

In the event that the seller fails to tender the property in satisfactory condition pursuant to the terms of this agreement, on the date heretofore agreed upon, the seller shall be in default of the terms of this agreement and shall pay to the buyer as liquidated damages the amount of $200 per day for each day the seller remains in default. Said liquidated damages shall serve as reasonable compensation for costs incurred as the direct and proximate result of seller's default. Provided, if seller should remain in default of this agreement for a period greater than 60 days, the buyer shall have the option of retaining liquidated damages for said period and further buyer may elect to be released from all obligations and liability associated with this agreement. In the latter event, the seller shall be similarly released from all further obligations to buyer with respect to this agreement.

FIGURE 7.1
Liquidated Damage Clause

In a very limited number of circumstances, a court will award specific performance in cases of breach. When specific performance is awarded, the party who has breached is ordered to continue performance under the contract to the best of his or her ability. Cases in equity are based on the principle that money is an insufficient remedy and fairness warrants the imposition of performance. The key to obtaining compelled performance is that the performance is so unique that the only way it can be satisfied is through the actual performance. In contract law, this equitable remedy is called specific performance. Before the court will award specific performance, the plaintiff must show that he or she has fully satisfied all obligations under the contract and that he or she has clean hands (meaning that the plaintiff has not acted in such a way as to cause the breach by the defendant, such as frustration or lack of cooperation). Another common requirement, known as "laches," is that the plaintiff must not have waited so long to raise the claim that the defendant is impaired in the ability to render performance.

 APPLICATION 7.8

Compare the following situations:

1. In October, Mrs. Sanchez contracts with a well-known artist to paint portraits of her three children as a Christmas present to Mr. Sanchez. The artist agrees to the contract but in November informs Mrs. Sanchez that he will not be completing the project because he is moving to another part of the country. Because an artist's talent is unique, money would be inadequate to compensate Mrs. Sanchez for the loss of the artist's expertise. In this situation, a court may very well award specific performance and order the artist to complete the portraits.

2. In October, Mrs. Sanchez contracts with an artist to paint portraits of her three children as a Christmas present to Mr. Sanchez. The artist agrees to the contract but in November informs Mrs. Sanchez that the portraits cannot be completed because Mrs. Sanchez has refused on numerous occasions to schedule sittings for the portraits. Although an artist's talent is unique, and money would be inadequate to compensate Mrs. Sanchez for the loss of the artist's expertise, in this situation, a court would probably not award specific performance and order the artist to complete the portraits, because Mrs. Sanchez would be seeking the specific performance with "unclean hands." The breach is directly related to Mrs. Sanchez' frustration of the artist's attempts to satisfy the contract.

Point for Discussion
What is the problem with an order of specific performance of a unique talent such as that described in the application?

ETHICAL NOTE

An obligation underlying all contractual agreements is the duty to act ethically. This includes fair dealing and honesty. As seen in the preceding discussion, dishonesty regarding the terms of the contract, misrepresentations as to the consideration, and taking unfair advantage of the vulnerabilities of the other party can all result in legal action against the wrongdoer. Consequently, anyone who is engaged in a contractual agreement has made an unspoken additional commitment to act in a manner that would be considered by an objective observer to be ethical. This is not to say that one contracting must put the interests of the co-contractor above one's own interests. Rather, the duty is to act in such a way that the co-contractor is not the victim of unfair advantage or dishonesty.

Questions

If you were selling your car and you knew that the tires (which are obviously worn) do not handle well in snow, do you have an ethical obligation to tell this to all prospective buyers? What if, instead, the defect were a loose electrical connection that had caught fire in the past but is not readily noticeable?

CHAPTER SUMMARY

The law of contracts is complex and contains many intricacies not addressed here. It is also an area of law that continues to change and adapt to new situations. Therefore, it is important to remember that in addition to the basic principles set forth here, there are many, many variations of these themes that should be explored when confronted with a contractual dispute. The best approach is always to prepare a contract with the fullest expectation that it will be litigated someday. By using this approach, many of the grounds for dispute can be prevented through clear and appropriate language and good faith compliance by the parties.

When preparing or interpreting a contract, one should be mindful that there must be two or more parties, legal capacity, assent, and consideration. Each of these elements is determined by objectively looking at the situation surrounding the creation of the contract. Further, the terms of the contract, such as time of performance, price, quantity, and identity of the offeror and offeree, must be definite. Many contracts must be in writing before a court will enforce them. Enforcement may also be denied on the basis of irregularities in the circumstances surrounding the contract such as mistake, fraud, illusory promises, frustration of purpose, or unconscionable terms. Persons with a third-party relationship to a contract, such as beneficiaries, assignees, or delegatees, may also have certain rights or obligations with respect to the contract that must always be addressed.

Finally, the remedies for a broken or breached contract include money damages, recision, reformation, and, in limited cases, specific performance. The appropriateness of each of these remedies depends entirely upon the nature of the contract and the circumstances under which the contract was created. Therefore, when evaluating or creating a contract, be particularly aware of the situation that surrounds it.

REVIEW QUESTIONS

1. Define the elements of a valid contract.
2. What information must be included to create a valid offer to contract?
3. Explain the difference between a unilateral and bilateral contract.
4. Distinguish fraud in fact and fraud in the inducement.
5. Define the defenses to alleged breach of contract.
6. Explain the difference between compensatory damages, liquidated damages, and specific performance.
7. What are third-party beneficiaries?
8. What is the statute of frauds?
9. When is assignment or delegation permitted?
10. What remedies are available to mistake in common understanding of the terms of the contract by the contract's parties?

CHAPTER TERMS

Bilateral Contract
Contract
Contractual Agreement

Contractual Capacity
Statute of Frauds
Third-Party Beneficiary

Unilateral Contract

NOTES

1. William Statsky, *Legal Thesaurus/Dictionary* (St. Paul: West, 1982).
2. 17 Am.Jur.2d., Contracts, Section 10.
3. Id., Section 15.
4. Restatement (Second) of Contracts, Section 12.
5. Id.; Childres and Spritz, Status in the Law of Contracts, 47 *New York Law Review* 1 (April 1972).
6. *Kilroe v. Troast,* 117 N.H. 598, 376 A.2d 131 (1977).
7. 1 Williston on Contracts 3d ed., Section 13.
8. *Flemington National Bank & Trust Co. (N.A.) v. Domler Leasing Corp.* 65 A.D.2d 29, 410 N.Y.S.2d 75 (1978).
9. Restatement (Second) of Contracts, Section 24.
10. 17 Am.Jur.2d, Contracts, Section 31.
11. *European-American Banking Corp. v. Chock Full O' Nuts Corp.,* 109 Misc.2d 615, 442 N.Y.S.2d 715 (1981).
12. 7A C.J.S., Auctions and Auctioneers, Section 11.
13. *Schmidt v. Foster,* 380 P.2d 124 (Wyo. 1963).
14. *Mobil Oil Corp. v. Wroten,* 303 A.2d 698, aff'd 315 A.2d 728 (Del. 1973).
15. *Taylor v. Roberts,* 307 F.2d 776 (10th Cir. 1962).
16. *Honolulu Rapid Transit Co. v. Paschoal,* 51 Hawaii 19, 449 P.2d 123 (1968).
17. 17 C.J.S., Contracts, Section 43.
18. *Reserve Insurance Co. v. Duckett,* 249 Md. 108, 238 A.2d 536 (1968).
19. *Clausen & Sons Inc. v. Theo. Hamm Brewing Co.,* 395 F.2d 388 (8th Cir. 1968).
20. *Wavetek Indiana, Inc. v. K. H. Gatewood Steel Co., Inc.,* 458 N.E.2d 265 (Ind. App. 1984).
21. Id.
22. Restatement (Second) of Contracts, Section 302, et seq.
23. Id.
24. 17A C.J.S., Contracts, Section 586.
25. *Damora v. Christ-Janer,* 184 Conn. 109, 441 A.2d 61 (1981).
26. *Mitchell v. Aetna Casualty & Surety Co.,* 579 F.2d 342 (5th Cir. 1978).
27. *Christian v. Christian,* 42 N.Y.2d 63, 396 N.Y.S.2d 817, 365 N.E.2d 849 (1977).
28. See note 21. Sections 151, 152.
29. Id.
30. 17 Am.Jur.2d. Contracts, Section 400, et seq.
31. Id.

CHAPTER 8

Property Law

CHAPTER OBJECTIVES

After reading this chapter, you should be able to

- *Explain the concept of undivided interest.*

- *Distinguish tenancy in common, joint tenancy, and tenancy by the entirety.*

- *List the elements of adverse possession.*

- *Discuss the remedies to retrieve wrongfully taken or held personal property.*

- *Distinguish habitability and quiet enjoyment.*

- *Explain the concept of constructive eviction.*

- *Discuss the basic obligations of landlord and tenant.*

The law of property in this country stems in large part from the common law principles of English property law. During the Middle Ages, the English court system created general rules for the possession, transfer, and disposition of property upon death of the owner. While many of these principles continue in the American legal system, in some ways, the states altered, modified, and, in some cases, even abolished certain rules over time to develop the statutory and common law of property in our country today. These legal changes have been the result of an effort to adapt to the changes that have occurred in society and in the types of land interests in this country that did not exist in feudal England. This chapter defines and examines the current law of property, including personal property, real property, and associated interests.

Before discussing the types of property and the rights related to the purchase, conveyance (transfer), ownership, possession, or alteration of property, let's clarify the legal definition of the term *property,* which generally means the right to possess or control.[1] This meaning is different from the everyday language used to interpret property as an actual physical thing, such as a parcel of land. Consequently, in legal terms, when discussing an interest in property, the focus is on the type of right to possess, control, or own the item in question rather than on the item itself. This chapter is organized by type of area subject to property law, and within those areas, the rights associated with them are discussed.

REAL PROPERTY

Real Property

Land or anything permanently affixed to land and no longer movable.

Real property is land or that which is attached to the land in such a way that it is permanent, fixed, and immovable.[2] The law of real property governs all that is part of the land naturally or as a result of being artificially incorporated into the land in a permanent way. Real property includes houses, buildings, and other structures that are affixed to the property by some permanent means. An example of something that would not ordinarily be considered real property is a mobile home that has not been permanently affixed to the ground. This type of structure is considered movable and falls into the category of personal property (discussed at the end of the chapter).

The following sections discuss the types of interest or rights to real property. These interests and rights can be affected by ownership, inheritance, marital status, and terms of possession. The right to control or own property can be obtained in a number of ways, and as they are explored, it should become clear that property law is one of the most well developed areas of law in our country.

Freehold Estates

Freehold Estate

An interest in real property that involves certain rights of ownership.

Traditionally, **freehold estate** has been the term used to describe ownership and interests in land.[3] This is to be distinguished from non-freehold estates, such as lease or rental agreements (discussed later in the chapter). Freehold estates involve the rights of a property owner and the conditions or limitations that might be imposed on that ownership. Several types of freehold estates exist, including single ownership, ownership by two or more persons, and certain rights of uninterfered possession without actual ownership.

Fee simple. **Fee simple** is the most common type of ownership in America.[4] Under English common law, when a man obtained property in fee simple, it meant that the man owned the property for the duration of his lifetime.[5] In other words, the man possessed a life estate (discussed next). At the end of the owner's life, the property automatically reverted back to the original owner.

To own property outright on a permanent basis, the property had to be owned in fee simple absolute, which required special language in the document used to transfer the property (deed) that prevented the property from reverting to the original owner. In the United States today, fee simple has an interpretation of fee simple absolute. All transfers of ownership of property are by fee simple unless otherwise stated. Such transfers are considered to be a sale of total and absolute rights over the property. In most jurisdictions, a limited term of possession/ownership must be granted by express language in the transferring document.

Life estates. A **life estate** gives the holder the right to totally control the property for the holder's lifetime without interference. Such an estate includes the right to do all things an owner in fee simple could do, with one exception. The property cannot be disposed of (sold or given away) or treated in such a way as to ruin it for its usual purpose[6] (known as wasting). An example of wasting property would be one who had a life estate in farmland and put toxic chemicals on the land that prevented the land from being used in the future as farmland. If a life estate holder is found to be wasting the property, the life estate can be legally terminated. When the life estate ends by legal termination of the estate or death of the holder, ownership goes to the party who originally owned the property or to the person designated by the original owner to receive the property.

A life estate is considered to be a type of freehold estate in and of itself, even though it does not contain the basic element of transferability. A person with a life estate cannot transfer *ownership* to someone else, but can transfer part or all of his or her *interest* in the property, if allowed by the grantor. This means that a life tenant could lease the property during the course of his or her lifetime, but such a lease would expire when the life tenant died. Thus, with the exception of limitations on transferability and the condition of not wasting the property, the life estate holder has all the rights otherwise associated with ownership. One common situation of creation of a life estate occurs when a spouse leaves a life estate in solely owned real property to the surviving spouse. When the surviving spouse dies, the estate passes completely and automatically to an heir named in the will of the spouse who originally owned the property.

Fee Simple

In American law, this involves absolute ownership of real property.

Life Estate

The right to possess and use real property for the duration of one's life with limited ownership rights.

APPLICATION 8.1

Martine Booker owns a large greenhouse and wholesale flower business. She has employed the same caretaker to maintain and live on the grounds for more than forty years. In her will, Martine leaves a life estate to the caretaker. Martine dictates that upon the caretaker's death, the land and greenhouse will pass to Martine's grandson, who plans to take over the business. The caretaker has a life estate. Only in the event the caretaker took steps to destroy the greenhouse would the grandson have possible legal grounds to terminate the caretaker's life estate and accelerate the grandson's own possession of the property.

Point for Discussion
What rights does the grandson have during the caretaker's life estate?

Other estates. Various other types of conveyances in fee (transfers of property interest) exist. Conveyances subject to reversion require that under certain conditions, the property revert back to its original owner. The effect of such estates is similar to the old definition of fee simple but occurred under different circumstances. An example is one who is buying land by paying rent along with a payment toward ownership each month. The agreement might provide that if the lessor/buyer died before the property was paid for, all interests in the property would revert to the original owner.

Defeasible fees are those that end ownership upon the happening of a certain event, at which time the property would pass to another named person. While the various fee estates had great influence historically in property rights, today they rarely become an issue. Land is owned predominantly in fee simple or fee simple subject to a life estate.

The remainder interest is one type of interest that has survived the changes in property law. It is an interest that is created automatically upon the end of another. Giving one's surviving spouse a life estate is one type of remainder interest. Unless the remainder interest is indicated on the document used to transfer title (e.g., the deed), a conveyance of property ownership is presumed to be in fee simple absolute, with total control and ownership vested in the receiving party.

Today, the law is much more equal to spouses in the distribution of property than in old English law. Under original property law, women could not own property. Even property inheritances were passed on to the woman's spouse and male children. Currently, there is no distinction between men and women on the issue of property ownership and inheritance. In the event that a spouse does not provide adequately for the surviving spouse by will, a statutory provision for what is commonly known as a **forced** (or elected) **share**[7] permits a surviving spouse to claim or elect a certain percentage of the property (real and personal) of the deceased. This claim is superior to all other heirs and prevails even if it decreases the amount received by persons designated in a will. One can generally totally disinherit children or anyone else by will except for a

Forced Share
The legal right of a surviving spouse to receive a certain percentage of the estate of a deceased spouse, superior to the terms of a will or other rights of inheritance of heirs.

spouse. The law makes no distinction whether the surviving spouse is husband or wife. The interest received is in fee simple (rather than a life estate), and surviving children are not necessary for the interest to be received. (The rights of surviving spouses are discussed in greater detail in Chapter 11.)

Assignment 8.1

Identify the various parties in each of the following situations as examples of fee simple, life estate, remainder interest, wasting.

1. The life estate holder wants to purchase fee simple. When the owner refuses, the life estate holder burns down the house.
2. A life estate holder is declared mentally incompetent and placed in an Alzheimer's unit of a nursing home. The other person on the deed takes full possession.
3. A woman buys a home from her grandmother, but does not receive possession until the grandmother turns 90 years old. The grandmother is 72 years now.
4. Same as question 3 except that the grandmother dies in a hang gliding accident at age 73.

Types of Ownership between Multiple Parties

Today it is common for more than one party to hold the title to (own) real property. The relationships of these persons and reasons for multiple ownership vary. As a result, certain types of ownership have evolved that govern the rights of these various multiple ownership arrangements. Such arrangements may be for business or personal reasons. The different types of multiple ownership of property clarify such issues as what portion of the property is possessed by each person, who has the right to sell or dispose of the property, and what should happen in the event one of the owners dies. The most commonly employed types of multiple ownership are tenancy in common, joint tenancy, and tenancy by the entirety.

Tenancy in common.   Unless otherwise stated in the purchase agreement, the type of tenancy of multiple owners is presumed to be **tenancy in common.** With this type of ownership, each owner has an undivided interest in the property,[8] meaning that each owner has an equal share in every part of the property. The undivided interest guarantees that no one owner has a better portion of the property. Each owner has a balanced interest in both the positive and negative aspects of the property as a whole. The percentage of undivided interest is equal to the percentage of ownership. For example, if one tenant owns 50 percent of the property and two remaining partners each own 25 percent of the property, the first partner is entitled to a one-half undivided interest in all the property and the other partners are each entitled to an undivided 25 percent share in the total property.

Tenancy in Common
A form of multiple ownership of property whereby each tenant (owner) shares with the other(s) an undivided interest in the property.

APPLICATION 8.2

Two brothers purchase property as tenants in common for the purpose of building several retail stores. Each brother possesses a one-half undivided interest in the property. That is, each owns one half of every foot of every acre of the land. The land is not arbitrarily divided so that the north half belongs to one and the south half belongs to another. If this were allowed, endless disputes would take place as to who received the better share of the property. Under the undivided interest theory, all parties share equally in the best and the worst aspects of the property.

Points for Discussion
1. What if four tenants in common own a single parcel of land?
2. What is the interest of each?

In addition to their undivided interest, tenants in common may do all things with their interest as if they owned the property entirely. The only limitation is that they cannot act in such a way as to interfere with the rights of the other tenants in common. A tenant in common cannot make use of the property in a way that is inconsistent with the other tenants, nor can the tenant waste the property. A tenant who does either of these things with any part of the property is doing it with a portion of the property controlled by the other tenants.

When tenants in common (or other types of multiple ownership tenants) cannot agree on the rights and use of the property, a legal action for partition may be brought by one or more of the tenants. In a partition action, the court divides the land into individual portions and creates an individually owned portion of land for each of the parties. The effect of this is to equitably extinguish the tenancy in common and create two or more fee simple tenancies. Another possible result in such a situation would be for a tenant to buy the interest of another tenant and thus convert the tenancy in common to a single tenancy in fee simple.

 APPLICATION 8.3

In Application 8.2, two tenants plan to erect several retail stores. Assume that the parking for the stores is limited. The intent of the parties is to lease all but one of the stores and share profits. One tenant intends to operate one of the stores. The other tenant decides to bring in bunge jumping equipment and sell jumps. The area needed for the equipment effectively deletes the retail parking area. Because customers do not have access to the stores, the use of one tenant is detrimentally affected by the use of the property by the other tenant.

Point for Discussion
If this situation resulted in partition, how do you think the matter should be resolved?

When one tenant in common voluntarily sells or conveys his or her interest in the property, the new owner becomes a tenant in common with the other tenants in common. Similarly, when one tenant in common dies, the heirs of the estate become tenants in common with the other tenants in common. Tenants in common have no rights of survivorship. The exception to this rule is when the property is owned by members of a partnership, in which case, when a tenant in common dies, the ownership of that tenant goes to the tenant's heirs rather than to the surviving co-tenant(s).

In a tenancy in common, the individual's ownership interest can be conveyed during that person's lifetime, but no more than the tenancy in common interest can be transferred. In other words, one cannot convey a type of tenancy not possessed. Since the rights are those of tenancy in common, that is all that can be transferred. This will become clearer as the other types of tenancy are explored.

Joint tenancy. Joint tenancy must be specified in the instrument transferring the property (the deed). It is generally accepted that **joint tenancy** includes the **right of survivorship**,[9] that is, when one joint tenant dies, the remaining joint tenants automatically take ownership of the property. The heirs of the deceased owner have no claim or inheritance.

The right of survivorship, simply stated, means that when a party to joint tenancy dies, the interest automatically vests by operation of law in the other tenant or tenants. In this way, the joint tenancy among *surviving* tenants is preserved. However, technically, a new joint tenancy is created when each surviving tenant simultaneously receives an undivided right of possession from the deceased party. The previous rights of the parties remain the same, and there is usually no requirement to formally create a new joint tenancy through a new deed.

The right of survivorship restricts a party's interest from flowing naturally to the descendants. Because of this, it is necessary for a party involved in a joint tenancy to formally agree from the outset that there is the intent to create such an interest. In this way, the heirs are protected from losing an interest in property when it was not the desire of the deceased to do so.

For joint tenancy to exist, the joint tenants must establish four common points of ownership, called unities:

1. Each tenant must have received his or her interest in the property at the same moment (unity of time).
2. The interest for each must come from the same source, namely, the previous owner (unity of title).
3. Each tenant must have identical rights regarding the property, such as an equal share (unity of interest).
4. Each party must have an undivided interest in the land itself (unity of possession).

Thus, the only way to have a joint tenancy is when the multiple owners agree to it with the intent of right of survivorship among themselves and they purchase the entire property at the same time, from the same owner, in equal

Joint Tenancy
A form of multiple property ownership whereby the property owners have fee simple and share four unities and each owner shares in the right of survivorship.

Right of Survivorship
A characteristic associated with multiple property ownership in which the ownership interest transfers automatically to surviving co-owners upon death of an owner rather than passing by will or intestate succession.

shares, and with an undivided right of possession. If all of the preceding occur and a state statute does not indicate otherwise, the parties also receive the right of survivorship. In some states, the statute requires that the intent for a right of survivorship be specified in the conveying instrument (usually the deed). If no such statute exists, the right is usually presumed from the words *joint tenancy* in the deed.

It should be recognized that a joint tenancy exists only so long as the four unities exist. When one party conveys his or her interest in the property to an outsider, only the remaining original joint tenants remain as joint tenants. The new owner is a tenant in common. The important effect of this is that the new tenant does not have a right of survivorship should one of the original joint tenants die.[10] Consequently, if any party conveys any right to title or interest or possession in the property, the joint tenancy as to that party is destroyed. Any conveyance to another would violate the unity of time and title, because the new recipient would obtain an interest at a different time and from a different source than the other owners. Joint tenancy is also severed when a party conveys his or her interest to other members of the original joint tenancy.

 APPLICATION 8.4

Burt, Jill, Jeff, and Nina are joint tenants. Burt comes into financial difficulty and decides to sell his interest in the property. He conveys his interest to Petra. The result is as follows:

Previously: Burt, Jill, Jeff, and Nina owned the property as joint tenants.

Now: Jill, Jeff, and Nina are joint tenants with one another. Petra is a tenant in common with Jill, Jeff, and Nina.

Effect: Under the old situation, if any joint tenant dies, the other three split the interest of the deceased. Under the new situation, if Petra dies, his interest passes to his heirs. If Jill, Jeff, or Nina dies, the interest of the deceased is split between the remaining joint tenants but not with Petra.

Point for Discussion
How would the tenancy be affected if all of the tenants were originally tenants in common?

The basic rights of joint tenants are similar to those of tenancy in common. The joint tenant can use and possess the property in any way that does not waste the property or interfere with the rights of the other joint tenants. However, a joint tenant cannot successfully devise (give) his or her interest to heirs in a will. Such conveyance would take place after the owner's death, which would violate the right of survivorship. Therefore, a bequest in a will does not sever the joint tenancy and will not be honored if a right of survivorship exists in the joint tenancy. When the right of survivorship does exist, it occurs by operation of law; that is, it is automatic upon the death of a joint tenant as a matter of law, and the wishes of the tenant expressed in a will are not considered. Consequently, if a joint tenant wants to sever the joint tenancy, such severing must be done prior to death by legal conveyance of one or more of the unity interests to another.

 CASE

BRADFORD v. DUMOND

675 A.2d. 957 (1996).

WATHEN, Chief Justice.

Defendant Danny G. Dumond appeals from a judgment of the Superior Court (Cumberland County, Brodrick, J.) in an action to partition real estate. The court granted plaintiff Laura H. Bradford one-half of the two parcels of real estate owned in common by the parties. The court adjusted the final division to reflect mortgage payments made by defendant and acts of conversion committed by defendant. On appeal defendant argues that (1) the court erred in ruling that the parties owned equal shares of both parcels of real estate, (2) the court erred in finding defendant liable for conversion of plaintiff's personal property, (3) the court erred in assessing damages for conversion, and (4) the court abused its discretion in limiting defense counsel's cross-examination of plaintiff on the issue of damages. Because the court erred with respect to one parcel of real estate, we vacate in part.

The facts presented at trial may be summarized as follows: The parties started dating in 1983. In August 1984, plaintiff moved in with defendant in a rented camp in Standish. Plaintiff and defendant talked about getting married and started planning their future, including purchasing property together. Plaintiff began to work without pay at a steel yard owned and operated by defendant. Plaintiff and defendant commingled their funds extensively and paid their personal and household expenses primarily with funds from the business.

In August of 1986, the couple purchased a house and a parcel of land abutting the steel yard. ("The Scarborough Property"). The deed conveyed the property to both defendant and plaintiff as joint tenants. The down payment of $35,000 was provided by defendant. The taxes, mortgage payments and insurance payments for the property were paid with funds from his business. Plaintiff performed all of the maintenance and upkeep on the property, including landscaping, while working full-time at the steel yard without pay.

In the spring of 1987, plaintiff began to receive $150 per week for her services at the steel yard. Plaintiff testified that this amount did not accurately represent the value of her services and in fact the funds were deposited in a joint account and used to pay joint expenses.

In January 1983, the couple purchased a camp and a lot of land in Standish. The deed conveyed the property to the parties as tenants in common. Plaintiff provided $8,000 for the down payment. Defendant provided between $30,000 and $40,000 for the remainder of the down payment and closing costs.

Subsequent payments for taxes, mortgage, and insurance were paid from the steel yard account. Plaintiff performed all of the maintenance and upkeep on this property as well while continuing to work at the steel yard.

> The trial testimony on this figure was conflicting, and the trial court did not make a specific finding on this amount.

Problems developed in the relationship and plaintiff moved out permanently in January 1990. She packed a few belongings and drove her Ford Bronco (which she claimed was a gift from defendant, although it was registered in the name of his business) to Maryland to stay with relatives. A week later, plaintiff reported that the Bronco had been stolen; it was later located in defendant's possession. When plaintiff moved back to Maine and inquired about retrieving the rest of her personal property and items the couple jointly owned, defendant threatened to harm her physically if she returned to either property.

After 1990, defendant retained exclusive possession of the two properties and collected rent from a tenant on the Standish property. He has paid all taxes, insurance, and mortgage payments since that time. In addition, he has paid off the outstanding mortgages on both properties.

Plaintiff commenced this action seeking division of the real estate and damages for conversion of her personal property. After a nonjury trial, the Superior Court ruled in favor of plaintiff on all claims. The court found plaintiff's version of the events more credible than defendant's and concluded that the parties had agreed and intended to be joint owners of both parcels.

The court then considered each party's contribution in order to fairly and equitably partition the real estate. The court declined to consider defendant's initial contributions towards the purchase of either property, as the court considered both properties to be held in JOINT TENANCY. Although it found that defendant paid all mortgage, tax, and insurance payments, the court offset defendant's contribution with plaintiff's undercompensated services for the business, her services in maintaining both properties, and the fact that defendant enjoyed sole possession of the properties for the period after the breakup and collected rental income which was not shared with plaintiff. Finding the properties equal in value, the court granted the Standish property to defendant and the Scarborough property to plaintiff. The court granted defendant a lien on the Scarborough property for the amount of $58,066, representing defendant's prepayment of plaintiff's half of the outstanding mortgages. This lien was reduced by $17,295, representing the value of the personal property that the court found had been wrongfully converted by defendant. From this judgment, defendant appeals.

I. Initial Contributions Towards Purchase of Jointly Owned Properties.

The issue of a proper accounting for the down payment made by defendant in purchasing each parcel of real estate is confused by the parties' failure to differentiate between a JOINT TENANCY and a tenancy in common.

The pleadings, the pretrial memoranda, and the exhibits accurately reflect that the Scarborough property was held in a JOINT TENANCY and the Standish property was held in a tenancy in common. Throughout the trial, however, the parties used the loose phrase "joint ownership." As a result, in its judgment the court treated both parcels as though they were held in JOINT TENANCY and, despite the parties' differing views on the treatment of defendant's initial contribution, the court was never disabused of its mistaken belief. Although the trial judge is not to be faulted, the error is obvious and the judgment is tainted by the parties' failure to distinguish between the two forms of joint ownership.

In general, joint tenants own equal undivided shares even though their initial contributions may have been unequal. That result is a consequence of the right of ownership that attaches to a JOINT TENANCY. Tenants in common, on the other hand, are presumed to own equal shares, but this presumption may be overcome by evidence, such as evidence of unequal initial contributions, establishing an intention to have unequal shares. Thus it is evident that the court erred in failing to consider defendant's initial contribution to the Standish property, held as a tenancy in common. Because this results in the necessity for vacating only a part of the judgment, we proceed to consider the remaining issues.

In addition, defendant argues the court erroneously refused to consider the initial payments he made in purchasing the Scarborough property. Even though this property was held in JOINT TENANCY, defendant argues that Boulette v. Boulette, 627 A.2d 1017 (Me.1993), cited by the trial court, is inapplicable because that case dealt with the creation of a JOINT TENANCY after the acquisition of the property. Defendant argues that where, as here, the purchase money for the property was extended simultaneously with the creation of the JOINT TENANCY, the joint tenant who extended the purchase money should be credited that amount on partition.

Defendant's argument is contrary to the very purpose of JOINT TENANCY. In Boulette, we stated:

[A]s joint tenants, the parties initially held an undivided one-half interest in the property. The division of property held in JOINT TENANCY should take into account all equities growing out of that relationship. Contributions of the parties to the property prior to the JOINT TENANCY, however, are not equities growing out of the JOINT TENANCY relationship. To allow the consideration of contributions preceding the JOINT TENANCY would defeat joint ownership.

Boulette v. Boulette, 627 A.2d 1017, 1018 (Me.1993). See also Lalime v. Lalime, 629 A.2d 59 (Me.1993) (where husband deeded his own property to himself and his wife in JOINT TENANCY, the rules of ownership unique to JOINT TENANCY would apply regardless of husband's assertion that the transfer was solely for the purpose of securing a loan and was not intended as a 'true' JOINT TENANCY).

Although it is true that in Boulette we did not specifically deal with a simultaneous contribution and creation of a JOINT TENANCY, this issue has been settled in Maine for over half a century. In Greenberg v. Greenberg, 141 Me. 320, 323–24, 43 A.2d 841, 842 (Me.1945), we held that the joint tenants owned an equal, undivided share of the property, even when one joint tenant supplied 100% of the purchase price and simultaneously had the land deeded to himself and another as joint tenants.

II. Co-tenant's Contributions Towards the Properties. Defendant next argues that the court erred in finding that, after purchase, both parties had contributed equally to the properties. Specifically, defendant argues that plaintiff's performance of housekeeping and maintenance duties should not be considered as a contribution. Defendant also argues that the court erred in finding that plaintiff was undercompensated for the services she provided at the steel yard.

The court's findings as to the value of each parties' contributions are findings of fact. "Findings of fact shall not be set aside unless clearly erroneous, and due regard shall be given to the opportunity of the trial court to judge the credibility of the witnesses." M.R.Civ.P. 52(a) (1995). We will not disturb the court's determination of the monetary value of plaintiff's services, as it is supported by competent evidence in the record. The record also supports the finding that plaintiff's maintenance of the properties was in furtherance of the parties' agreement concerning both properties.

Judgment vacated in part. Remanded for further proceedings consistent with the opinion herein.

All concurring.

Case Question
What must occur differently in the creation of a tenancy in common as opposed to a joint tenancy?

Tenancy by the entirety.   The last and least common type of tenancy is **tenancy by the entirety,** held by husband and wife. Many states no longer recognize this tenancy as different from joint tenancy, and those that do, often require it to be specified in the deed. This type of tenancy includes the presence of the four unities. In addition, the unity of person (that the tenants be husband and wife) is necessary. Tenancy by the entirety also has the right of survivorship: when one spouse dies, the other receives the property as the sole owner in fee simple.

Tenancy by the entirety cannot be conveyed, because of the unity of person requirement. Any conveyance by one spouse would result in a tenancy in common between the remaining spouse and new purchaser. The interest of a tenant by the entirety also cannot be conveyed by a will to another person. Nor is the interest of one of the tenants subject to claims of nonjoint creditors. By operation of law, when one spouse dies and there is a tenancy by the entirety, the surviving spouse automatically receives the entire share of the property. Thus, because the property has already been transferred, there is nothing to pass under the terms of the will.

Tenancy by the Entirety
A form of multiple ownership of property between spouses that includes the characteristics of joint tenancy, including the right of survivorship.

Assignment 8.2

> In the following situation, indicate (a) what type of tenancy exists, (b) whether the tenancy changes, (c) when a change occurs, if one does, and (d) what is the resulting tenancy.
>
> 1. Suelin, Karl, and Dinah form an equal partnership, and together they buy a parcel of property from Charles. They are going to use the property as an agricultural investment and hire someone to farm it. They agree that if one of them should die, the others should receive the deceased partner's interest so that the partnership can continue. Karl, however, puts in his will that upon his death, his dear daughter Camille will inherit his share.
> 2. José and his brother Juan purchase a parcel of land. They grow Christmas trees on it until José becomes too ill to continue his share of the work. José then sells his interest in the land to Ricardo.
> 3. Tori and Marty are married. They want to share everything completely and equally. Consequently, they buy a lot from Michael upon which to build their dream house. During the construction, Tori and Marty divorce each other. They agree, however, to remain owners of the property until the market improves and they can sell the house.
> 4. On January 1, four brothers purchase a piece of property as a group from their sister. Each brother agrees that the property will be used as a place to build an ice cream stand and that each will work an equal amount and receive an equal share of profits. Subsequently, the youngest brother joins the Army and sells his interest to a neighbor.

Air and Subsurface Rights

Since the early days of property principles in common law, it has been held that the ownership of property extends below the property to the center of the earth and above the property to the top of the sky.[11] With respect to moving waters, when a nonnavigable stream flows on property, the owner possesses the bed of the stream but not the water flowing on it, because that water is not a permanent part of the land. Navigable streams are part of the public domain, and ownership of property adjacent to them generally extends to the shore.[12]

As population and technology have grown, these concepts have been altered slightly, but remarkably, the basic principle still holds true. While an owner possesses all of the property to the very heights, the public necessity of flight cannot be abridged, and it overrides the right to control the entire sky above one's property. Similarly, while an owner is entitled to control a stream bed on the property, the course of the bed cannot be changed so as to substantially alter the flow of water across another's property, since such change could flood the land or deprive the owners of the use of the water.

The owner has the right, consistent with these rights above and below the land, to sell or lease these portions of property (except that which is controlled for public use). For example, the owner of a condominium on the twelfth floor of a high rise actually owns the air space occupied by that condominium. However, the owner is not entitled to alter the construction of the air space because—as with moving land or water—such change would invade another's right over his or her own property. Similarly, one who owns the land can sell the rights to property below the land's surface, for example, sell mineral rights to another and allow the person to set up a drill to obtain oil or other deposits from beneath the land.

Incorporeal Interests

In the law of property, the term *incorporeal interests* describes rights or privileges associated with ownership of real property. One such right that is highly protected is the right of quiet enjoyment. It is presumed that the right to possess real property automatically includes the right to such possession and use free from interference by others. When someone invades another's property, he or she is, in effect, invading the right of quiet enjoyment. A corresponding area of incorporeal interests deals with the law of easements—rights of nonowners to affect the use of the owner's real property. Essentially, this area of law permits the holder of the easement a limited right of interference with the property otherwise protected by the right of quiet enjoyment. The law of easements is fairly complex and is only briefly introduced here.

Easements.   An easement is a right of one other than the owner to affect the property owned by another. In simpler terms, it is a limited legal right to invade the right of possession and quiet enjoyment of a property owner.[13] The property that is affected is sometimes referred to as the servient tenement (it serves someone other than its owner). The party with the right to affect use of someone else's property is known as the dominant tenement (it dominates the servient owner). An easement is not a right to possess part or all of the servient tenement. Rather, it is the limited right to use or control the use of the servient tenement. If an easement is *in gross,* the dominant tenement is the right of a specific person or group to use the servient tenement and this right cannot usually be transferred (although some commercial or business easements in gross are transferrable). If an easement is *appurtenant,* the dominant tenement is a specific parcel of land whose owner has the right to use the servient tenement, and this right passes to each new owner of the dominant parcel.

An easement is an interest associated with real property and is therefore subject to the statute of frauds, which, as noted in Chapter 7, requires that certain legal transactions be in writing before a court will enforce them. Among them is the transfer of any interest in real property. If real property or an easement affecting it is conveyed, conveyance must be done in writing to be effective. Therefore, the voluntary creation or continuation of an easement must be in writing before a court will enforce it.

An easement can be created in several ways. Two common methods are easement by necessity and easement by conveyance. An easement of necessity (implication by circumstances) can be created when no other reasonable alternative exists to satisfy the rights of others. Because all property is adjacent to other property, it is somewhat common for the use of one's property to interfere with another's. An easement created by necessity may be without the consent of the owner but, unless agreed to by the owner, must be recognized by a court before it can be enforced. Easement by conveyance occurs when a party voluntarily grants an easement affecting his or her property. Often this is an easement in gross and done in exchange for compensation of some type, such as the right to drill for oil on another's land. Finally, an easement can be created by prescription when a landowner acquiesces to someone else's use of his or her land without permission for a certain period of time. A prescriptive easement is similar to adverse possession, which is discussed later in the chapter.

Easements are classified in two ways. The first is known as an affirmative easement, which occurs when the party holding the dominant tenement has the right to enter onto the servient tenement for a particular purpose.[14] This could be having the right to cross the land of another party to reach your own property when no other reasonable means of reaching it exists.

 APPLICATION 8.5

Gary Swedlund purchases property on Lake Warsaw. Joan Breslin owns the property between the highway and Gary's lakefront lot. The only reasonable means of reaching Gary's property is to cross Joan's. Consequently, a court would be likely to grant Gary an easement of necessity, giving Gary the right to cross a specified portion of Joan's property to reach his own.

Point for Discussion
Why do you think that the owner's right of quiet enjoyment is not considered superior to a nonowner's right of access across private land?

The other type of easement is known as a negative easement—the right to prevent certain uses of property by the owner of the servient tenement because these uses would adversely affect the rights of the dominant tenement.[15]

 APPLICATION 8.6

A utility company has a negative easement over a homeowner's property. The homeowner is precluded from placement of any buildings on the portion of the property that would cover utility lines because the utility company must have access to the underground utility lines when necessary for the public benefit.

Point for Discussion
Why doesn't the utility company have to buy the portion of property from the homeowner?

Assignment 8.3

With respect to the following situations identify (a) the servient and dominant tenement and (b) whether the easement is affirmative or negative.

1. Landowner X has property that is bordered on the west by a major waterway and is bordered on the north, east, and south by the property of Landowner M. Landowner X uses a roadway across M's property to reach his own.
2. Jules has the right to come onto Anne's property and mine for gold.
3. Ichiro has the right to electricity in his house even though the lines would have to cross his neighbor's farmland.

Buyers' and Sellers' Rights

Persons who have not previously been involved in the sale of real property are not aware of the many issues that must be addressed before such a sale is completed. The sale generally includes not only the buyer and the seller but also a broker, a mortgagor, a financier, and an attorney, as well as others who play a necessary role in completing the transaction.

Documents associated with the sale of property include the following:

1. Purchase agreement (seller agrees not to sell to another; buyer pays earnest money as a deposit) (see Figure 8.1).
2. Mortgage or financing agreement (agreement between buyer and party financing the sale for repayment).
3. Deed (used to record the transfer of title).
4. Required government forms (used to make necessary records of property transfers within a state).
5. Required inspections (often required by government and also customary for parties to produce certificates of inspection of the property, such as a termite certificate, and to ensure the property is structurally sound).
6. Escrow agreement (written agreement between buyer and seller as to who—usually an independent party—will hold the earnest money deposit during the completion of the transaction).
7. Buyer and seller agreements (often called contract for deed, used when the seller finances the sale and turns over the deed to the property when the buyer has completed payment).
8. Title policy (an insurance policy from a title company that guarantees that it has searched the chain of title to the property, that no other claims to the property are superior to the prospective buyer, and that the seller has the right to convey the title).

Although it is generally true that conveyances of title to real property must be in writing under the statute of frauds, an exception is recognized in some jurisdictions. Under the doctrine of part performance, if a substantial portion of the purchase price has been paid and actual possession of the property has been

FIGURE 8.1 Purchase Agreement

THIS IS A BINDING CONTRACT, IF NOT UNDERSTOOD
SEEK COMPETENT LEGAL ADVICE.

The undersigned BUYERS agree to purchase and the undersigned OWNERS agree to sell the real estate and all improvements located at _____

Upon the following terms:

$_____ shall be Earnest Money evidenced by personal check to be deposited upon acceptance of this offer as deposit on the purchase price. Said Earnest Money shall be deposited in escrow in an interest-bearing account at _____ Bank and shall not be subject to withdrawal prior to closing unless this Contract should become null and void and for failure of one or more of the conditions of sale set forth in this Agreement. Upon closing, said Earnest Money shall be paid directly to OWNERS. In the event this contract fails due to any fault, neglect, or intentional breach by BUYERS, said _____ Earnest Money and all interest accrued thereon shall be paid directly to OWNERS. In the event this contract fails due to any fault, neglect, or intentional breach by OWNERS, said Earnest Money and all interest accrued thereon shall be paid directly to BUYERS.

$_____ Balance due on the specified date of closing, upon delivery of Warranty Deed conveying merchantable title free and clear of liens and encumbrances except easements, restrictions, and covenants of record, and which have been made known to BUYERS.

$_____ :Purchase Price.

This sale is contingent upon BUYERS obtaining a home mortgage at a fixed rate of _____ % plus one point or less, for a term of no less than 3 years amortized over 30 years. Loan to be applied for within 10 days and approved within 30 days. Appraisal to be equal to or greater than the purchase price. BUYERS and OWNERS agree to pay in equal shares costs of closing, including but not limited to title insurance and recording fees. Closing to be on May 30, 1994.

Upon acceptance of the terms by OWNERS, the Earnest Money shall be applied as part payment on the purchase price but shall be held in escrow prior to closing as stated above. If this offer is rejected by the OWNERS, or if title to said premises is not merchantable or cannot be made so within sixty (60) days after written notice is delivered to OWNERS stating the defects, or if no effort is made to make the said property merchantable by OWNERS, this contract shall be null and void and all earnest money shall be refunded to BUYERS who shall have no further claim against the OWNERS. If this sale is not consumated within 30 days of the closing date stated above, time being of the essence, because of neglect or failure on the part of the BUYERS to comply with the terms and conditions herein agreed to, then all Earnest Money shall be forfeited and this Contract shall be of no further binding effect. But such forfeiture shall not release BUYERS from any liability for the fulfillment of this Contract of sale if OWNERS shall, within 30 days after BUYERS have defaulted, give BUYERS written notice by certified mail of their intention to sue.

The property is to be conveyed by good and sufficient Warranty Deed and insured Title Policy, in an amount equal to the purchase price, showing merchantable title free and clear of all liens and encumbrances except easements, or restrictions of record, or those which the purchaser agrees to assume as part of the purchase price as herein set forth. OWNERS shall pay all costs and expenses necessary to convey title in fee simple.

OWNERS shall maintain fire and extended coverage insurance on the premises until the date of closing. In the event the premises shall be destroyed or damaged prior to closing, BUYERS shall have the option to accept the insurance settlement and complete the transaction or to declare this Contract void, and thereupon all deposits made hereunder shall be refunded to the BUYERS. BUYERS shall make said election within seven (7) days after receipt of written notice of the injury to the property.

Real estate taxes, utilities, and sewer charges due, if any, shall be prorated as of the date of closing or the date of possession, whichever is later, taxes to be prorated on the last known tax bill which buyers agree to assume and pay accordingly.

BUYERS have personally inspected the property and are accepting it in its present condition, with the exception of any contingencies listed. OWNERS agree to maintain the heating, sewer, plumbing, and electrical systems and any built-in appliances and equipment in normal working order and to maintain the grounds and to deliver the property in the same condition as at the time of inspection by BUYERS.

OWNERS hereby warrant that prior to the execution of this instrument, neither they nor their agent has received any notice issued by any city, village, or other governmental authority, of a dwelling code violation upon the premises herein described.

FIGURE 8.1   (Continued)

It is understood and agreed that only the personal property listed below is included in the sale: all built-in appliances, water softener, all ceiling fans, computerized temperature monitor and sensors, custom-made draperies, 2 garage door openers with remote controls, retractable clothesline.

OWNERS agree that any personal property left upon the premises after delivery of possession has been abandoned by OWNERS and becomes the property of BUYERS. OWNERS agree to leave premises in a clean condition, free of all litter and debris.

In the event OWNERS shall remove any personal property included in this Contract, or any improvements, OWNER(s) shall pay BUYERS in an amount equal to the replacement or repair cost of the item or items so removed or damaged.

OWNERS agree to vacate the premises prior to closing and shall pay a rent from the date of closing the sum of $_____ per month in advance for each month or portion thereof OWNERS remain in possession of the premises.

OWNERS to provide a termite certificate showing no active infestation.

This agreement shall be binding upon the parties hereto, their heirs, executors, administrators, and assigns.

This sale is subject to the terms and conditions set forth in this agreement.

We, the BUYERS, hereby agree to purchase the above-described property on the terms above and agree to pay the price of $176,000 for said property.

Dated:_____

Buyer: _____

Buyer: _____

We, the OWNERS, hereby approve the above sales agreement and agree to sell the above described real estate for $ _____

Dated:_____

Accepted by Owner _____

Accepted by Owner _____

Dated:_____

Accepted by Buyer _____

Accepted by Buyer _____

---

turned over, the transaction will be enforced.[16] The court infers from the actions of the parties that the parties intended the conveyance of the property, and the court will require the parties to complete the transaction. The courts are divided on this issue, and in many states, a written agreement is required to enforce completion of a real property transaction.

Even when a written agreement exists, the problem often arises as to responsiblity for the property during the completion of the purchase requirements. The numerous documents associated with the purchase of property are not prepared overnight. Often, a sale of property takes two to six months to complete. During this time, what happens if the property is partially or totally destroyed? What if the property is discovered to have a claim on it? What if the seller wastes the property? These are all issues that have arisen in the past.

While there is some variation among the courts, general principles have been established. Generally, if something occurs during a pending sale that partially or totally destroys the property through no fault of the seller, the liability for the loss is on the buyer.[17] An example is a house that is destroyed by fire and the house is the only real asset of the property. The seller may require the buyer to complete the sale. If the property is only partially destroyed and repair is feasible, the seller is given a reasonable amount of time to adequately repair, and the buyer may be held to the purchase agreement. Because the buyer bears some risk of loss, the buyer may also insure the property to the extent of the risk, even though title has not yet passed.

A minority of jurisdictions place on the seller the cost of loss due to a casualty. However, the most common occurrence is that the purchase agreement will specify who bears the risk of loss. If it is the buyer, the buyer has a valid interest that can be insured even though title to the land has not yet been formally passed.

If some defect or irregularity in the title is discovered, the seller is given a reasonable amount of time to cure the defect and is generally allowed to use part of the purchase price to do so.[18] If, for example, there is a government lien on the property for back taxes, the seller would be allowed a reasonable amount of time to raise the money to satisfy the tax debt or would be allowed to accept the purchase price and pay the debt before conveying title. Ordinarily, the purchase price and title are conveyed simultaneously.

All sellers are under a general duty to care for the property and prevent it from waste during the time necessary to complete the sale. In the sale of real property with dwellings on it, a seller is also under a duty to convey the property in habitable condition (generally interpreted to mean safe for occupancy and having access to utilities).

Not all duties, however, are on the seller. The courts do apply the theory of "caveat emptor"—"let the buyer beware."[19] Under this theory, a purchaser of property has the limited duty to reasonably investigate and discover defects in the property. Failure to do so can result in the court's refusal to rescind the purchase agreement or require the owner to repair the defect. If, for example, a buyer notices an air-conditioning unit outside the house, he or she should not assume that the unit works properly. Questions regarding the working order and age of all appliances and portions of the house that might require replacement or repair should be asked. Then, if the seller makes representations that turn out to be false, the buyer may have recourse in actions for breach of an express warranty or fraud.[20] Any of the generally accepted duties of buyer and seller can be altered by agreement.

Adverse Possession

Not all real property is obtained by purchase or gift. The law has created a method by which a party can gain good title to land simply by using the land. The theory of adverse possession is recognized as a means of obtaining title to property without consent or voluntary transfer by the owner when certain conditions are met. The reasoning behind adverse possession is that the government encourages the productive use of land, and if the owner does not productively use the land and does not protect the right to possess owned property, the law will recognize ownership in one who will.

While every state has a statute setting the requirements, the following elements are usually needed to prove title by adverse possession:[21]

- open and notorious possession
- continuous possession
- exclusive possession
- adequate duration of possession

Open possession requires that the person seeking title by adverse possession actually possess the property. This does not mean that the person must spend the days walking the boundaries. However, the adverse possessor must act in such a way that others, including an alert property owner, would perceive such actions as those of one exercising control over the entire property. An example is farming a large acreage or building a permanent home on the property.

Continuous possession is designed to prevent transients and squatters from claiming title to the property. The law does not propose to vest title in anyone who wants the property. Rather, it gives title to persons who show an ongoing concern for the property. Therefore, it is necessary to exercise control or possession of the property in a way that is perceived as continuous. Abandonment for a significant time will prevent this element from being proven.

Exclusive possession is necessary to show that the person claiming title by adverse possession acted in a way to exclude others from possessing the property. Until all the elements are sufficiently met, this does not apply to the original owner. The true owner of the property who becomes aware of someone else possessing the property can retrieve it. However, after the statutory period, the adverse possessor does have the right to exclude others from the property, for example, by erecting No Trespassing signs.

The final element requires the adverse possessor to do all of the preceding for a specified period of time. Statutes vary on the length of time, but generally, the provision requires possession for a period of five to twenty years. The reasoning is that possession should be for a period of time that not only demonstrates a continuing intent to utilize the land but also gives the true owner every opportunity to reclaim his or her property.

Many states as well as the federal government do not permit claims of adverse possession over their land. Those that do allow such claims do so only in specified areas. For example, national parks are not subject to claims of adverse possession. Preservation of these large areas of protected wilderness takes precedence over any needs or rights of private individuals.

Adverse possession can be established even though a series of different persons actually possessed the property during the specified period of time. When this occurs, it is called tacking and is allowed only under certain circumstances. When a statute permits tacking, it usually requires succeeding owners to be descendants/heirs, a spouse, or someone who was voluntarily granted possession during the life of the first adverse possessor.[22]

The law gives every chance to the original owner to retain the rights of title to the property. However, when there is a total failure to utilize property for a significant period of time and there is a party who would make beneficial use of the property, adverse possession takes effect.

CASE ───

STOKES v. KUMMER

85 Wash. App. 682,
936 P.2d 4 (1997).

SCHULTHEIS, Judge.

The court denied Duane Stokes, Sandra Baker, Terry Johnson and B. G. Knight's claim for ejectment and quieted title to three parcels of land used by brothers Terril Kummer, Arlan Kummer and Kevin Kummer for dry land wheat farming, based on their adverse possession of the fields for more than 10 years. The court also granted the brothers a 75-foot easement across Mr. Stokes's and Ms. Baker's property, for access between two of the fields. On appeal, Mr. Stokes, Ms. Baker and Mr. Knight contend the Kummers' use of field 2 was permissive at its inception, negating the element of hostility required to demonstrate adverse possession. Mr. Johnson contends the Kummers conceded his superior title in 1982 by not contesting an easement he granted to others and did not prove adverse possession for a sufficient period thereafter. All of the appellants contend biennial cropping of agricultural land is insufficient use to establish title by adverse possession. We affirm.

The property at issue in this case is in a fairly desolate part of Kittitas County, accessible only by a gravel county road. The region is rocky and arid, covered mostly with sagebrush and tumbleweeds. There are pockets or hummocks of soil, however, that are suitable for dry land wheat farming. Aerial photographs show the three fields at issue have been cultivated since at least 1954. Sometime during or before October 1971 the quarter section where these fields are located, the northeast one-quarter of Section 33, Township 17 North, Range 18 East, Willamette Meridian, and the quarter section immediately west, the northwest one-quarter of Section 33, Township 17 North, Range 18 East, Willamette Meridian, were divided into tracts of roughly 20 acres each. The platted subdivision, known as the Valley View Ranch tracts, was not recorded. Nor was it surveyed, permanently staked or fenced. The appellants each own a Valley View Ranch tract underlying the

three wheat fields that the Kummer brothers have been farming since 1976. See the field survey map attached as an appendix.

It is unclear from the record when Lawrence Hall began growing winter wheat in the area, but in 1953 he leased from Agnes C. Meagher "all that certain crop land owned by [her] and lying within a certain fenced area" in the northeast one-quarter of Section 33 to grow wheat. The lease was for four years, from October 1, 1953, to October 1, 1957. Mary Hall married Lawrence Hall in 1956, and in 1957 moved to the old homestead house on his property south of Umptanum Road and west of Durr Road. Mrs. Hall said that when she moved out to the property, Mr. Hall was farming the same fields across the road (Umptanum Road) that the Kummer brothers later farmed. Mr. Hall originally farmed some of the property north of the road for Estil Wright under a crop share agreement, but later bought that property.

On January 28, 1976, the Kummer brothers bought out the Halls. They acquired title to 2,540 acres, including that part of the northeast one-quarter of Section 33 lying south and east of Umptanum Road, and most of the northwest one-quarter of Section 34, which borders the Valley View Ranch tracts on the east. Mr. Hall drove them around the various fields on the property and also gave the Kummers a 1954 aerial photograph of the area. It shows numerous wheat fields, which are irregularly spaced and shaped due to uneven topography and soil.

In March 1976 the Kummers moved onto the property and began farming the same areas Mr. Hall had farmed, including the three fields just north of Umptanum Road. There were no fences, posts or other markers suggesting the northeast one-quarter of Section 33 had been divided into parcels. The Kummers have continuously harvested wheat from all their fields every other year, beginning in 1976—except one year in the early 1980s when they participated in a federal program and ended up harvesting in an odd year, 1981. During crop years they reseed the fields if necessary early in the season, spray later for weeds, harvest the wheat with a combine, and, when soil moisture permits, plow the stubble under in the fall. During the intervening fallow years, they plow, cultivate, fertilize and seed the fields. Every year the Kummers post the perimeters of their wheat fields against trespassing and hunting, and they regularly tell people to get off the land during hunting season.

Meanwhile, S & S Enterprises, Inc., was selling Valley View Ranch tracts. Duane Stokes acquired tract 40 in August 1988 by quitclaim deed from his parents, who had bought it in approximately 1972. When Mr. Stokes first visited the property in fall 1973, he observed most of it was sagebrush, but there was evidence the northern part had been farmed. It looked substantially the same when he next visited in fall 1980—he saw wheat stubble on the northern end. When he last visited in fall 1991 it looked the same, "like somebody had plowed the field."

Sandra Baker (nee Burchfield) acquired tract 41 in June 1973 by deed from S & S Enterprises, after her brother assigned her his interest under a 1971 purchase contract. She first visited the property shortly after she acquired it and was thoroughly unimpressed. It was dry, arid and rocky, covered with sagebrush and tumbleweeds. She visited the property again in the early 1980s, twice in one year, but she only looked at the tract from the road. She did not walk the property and could not see the northern part of it. She did the same thing once more later in the 1980s. Every visit was during winter. Until the lawsuit, she had never seen the north end of the property where the wheat fields extend onto it.

B.G. Knight acquired tract 36 in the 1970s from Melvin and Emma Orness, who deeded the tract to him in January 1980 in fulfillment of his contract with them and their 1971 purchase contract. He saw only a picture of the property when he bought it and it was apparent from the picture that it had been farmed. He learned about the Valley View Ranch tracts from Alex Varunok, a close friend and fellow Boeing employee, who had bought tracts 34 and 35.

In 1978 Mr. Varunok approached the Kummer brothers and told them they were farming on property north of Umptanum Road that did not belong to them. He showed them a deed and a map. After some discussion and correspondence between Terril Kummer and Mr. Varunok, they reached a lease agreement. On May 7, 1978, Mr. Varunok signed a handwritten "farm lease/share agreement," apparently drafted by him, in which Kevin Kummer agrees to farm tracts 35 and 36, belonging to Mr. Knight and Mr. Varunok, and to provide 25 percent of the gross proceeds of the 1978 and 1979 crops and thereafter 33 1/3 percent. Mr. Knight signed on May 8 and Kevin Kummer signed on May 17 at the request of his brother Terril. Terril Kummer then returned the signed lease agreement to Mr. Varunok with a note advising him that they normally harvest wheat every other year, so the next crop after 1978 would likely be 1980.

On November 20, 1978, Terril Kummer sent Mr. Varunok a note and a check for $1,035. In August 1979 Terril Kummer sent Mr. Varunok a letter and newspaper article explaining they had had serious crop damage from grasshoppers. On November 1, 1981, Terril Kummer sent Mr. Varunok a note and a check for $1,810.90. In June 1983 the Kummers bought tracts 34 and 35 from Mr. Varunok. They continued farming field 2 as they always had, believing they now owned the tracts underlying it.

Mr. Knight received his share of the 1978 and 1981 lease payments from Mr. Varunok. He never met or talked with any of the Kummer brothers. Though he did not receive any payments after 1981, he did not ask Mr. Varunok about it. When Mr. Knight visited his property in winter 1982 or 1983, he noticed it had obviously been farmed in wheat because there was wheat stubble on part of it and sagebrush on part. Mr. Knight visited his property probably once more in the 1980s and again in about 1991, both times in the winter. He said he assumed somebody would send him money if the Kummers farmed his property, and since he was not receiving any money, he concluded they must not be farming it. Mr. Knight did not try to contact the Kummers until approximately 1991 or 1992, when he learned from a Realtor that his property was being farmed. At that time, he was unable to locate a telephone number for the Kummer brothers and did not pursue the matter further.

Finally, Mr. Johnson acquired tract 39 in December 1990 by quitclaim deed from his parents, who had bought it in September 1975 from the original purchasers, Derwin and Avis Lisk. Mr. Johnson first saw the property in 1975 just before the Lisks transferred it to his parents, and at that time, part of it was a wheat field, early fallow or stubble. Tract 39 is divided roughly into western and eastern halves by a road that provides access from Umptanum Road to the north. The road was not shown on the unrecorded plat map, but it was there when the Johnsons bought the tract and Milo England had been using it to get to his property ever since he bought his acreage in summer 1976.

Mr. England remembered the fields on either side of the road had been farmed when he moved there, and that the Kummers had farmed both fields since 1976. In fact, they crossed the road to get from one field to the other and when they did not raise their tractor attachments high enough they disturbed the already rough road surface. In October 1982 Mr. England contacted the Johnsons, after determining from county records that they owned tract 39, and asked if they knew their property was being farmed. They apparently did not. Terry Johnson visited the property and ascertained it was being farmed by the Kummers. He met with Mr. England and Earl and Lorna Lyon, who also used the road to get to their property, and on behalf of his parents gave them a recorded, handwritten easement to use the road.

Mr. Johnson also met with at least two of the Kummer brothers. He advised them he was giving the Englands and the Lyons an easement and discussed the Kummers' farming of his property. According to Mr. Johnson, he insisted the Kummers sign a written lease with him and agree to pay something for the crops they had taken in previous years, or he would not give them permission to continue farming. No agreement was reached, but the Kummers continued farming as they always had. Mr. Johnson returned in January or February 1987, and once again in winter 1990. Both times the property was just as it was when he first saw it in 1975. He did not contact Mr. England or the Kummers after October 1982.

The tract owners, all of whom live west of the Cascade Mountains, joined in this ejectment suit. The Kummers were served on January 12, 1994, and the summons and complaint were filed on March 18. They answered, and counterclaimed to quiet title in themselves under the doctrine of adverse possession. After a two-day bench trial in February 1995, the court quieted title to the three wheat fields in the Kummers and granted them a 75-foot easement across tracts 40 and 41 for access between fields 1 and 2. The tract owners appeal.

Adverse Possession

In order to establish a claim of adverse possession, there must be possession that is (1) open and notorious, (2) actual and uninterrupted, (3) exclusive, and (4) hostile, all for a period of 10 years. ITT Rayonier, Inc. v. Bell, 112 Wash.2d 754, 757, 774 P.2d 6 (1989); RCW 4.16.020. Because the presumption of possession is in the holder of legal title, the party claiming adverse possession has the burden of establishing each element. ITT Rayonier, 112 Wash.2d at 757, 774 P.2d 6. Adverse possession is a mixed question of law and fact. Whether essential facts exist is for the trier of fact; but whether the facts, as found, constitute adverse possession is for the court to determine as a matter of law.

Field 2

Tract owners Mr. Stokes, Mr. Knight and Ms. Baker contend the Kummers farmed field 2, covering much of the Knight tract and a small portion of the Baker and Stokes tracts, after they received permission to do so under the May 1978 lease agreement. They assert permissive use is not hostile and does not commence the running of the prescriptive period. They argue the permissive use of this wheat field could not ripen into a prescriptive right unless the Kummers made a distinct and positive assertion of a right hostile to the owners.

As the Kummers point out, and the court found, Mr. Stokes and Ms. Baker were not privy to the lease and could not gain any benefit from it. The Kummers established they adversely possessed those parts of tracts 40 (Stokes) and 41 (Baker) that they and their predecessor Mr. Hall had farmed continuously from the 1950s into the 1990s, including the prescriptive easement granted by the court.

With respect to Mr. Knight, use of his property was not permissive at its inception, though it may have been from mid-1978 to mid-1983. The lease does not make it clear that Mr. Knight was the Kummers' landlord for any specific property, or that he owned one of the tracts outright. The court found the statutory period began running at the latest in June 1983, when the Kummers bought tracts 34 and 35 from Mr. Varunok.

The tract owners assign error to the finding that the Kummers thought they were buying the 40 acres covered by the Varunok and Knight lease. The finding is supported by the evidence, although it is not necessary for a determination of adverse possession since it is irrelevant whether they appropriated the land knowingly or by mistake. Chaplin, 100 Wash.2d at 860, 676 P.2d 431.

As the court pointed out in its memorandum decision, the assertion that the Kummers never repudiated the lease is without merit. Apart from questions whether it was ever valid or whether it terminated with Mr. Varunok's sale of his tracts, the sale itself signaled a significant change in the parties' relationship. Mr. Varunok had handled all aspects of the lease arrangement, including paying Mr. Knight his share; Mr. Knight had never even spoken with any of the Kummer brothers. When Mr. Varunok advised Mr. Knight he was selling out, Mr. Knight was put on notice he would have to make different arrangements regarding the lease, which, as previously noted, did not specify his interest in any event. He did nothing. That fall, when he did not receive a lease payment, he again did nothing. He did nothing until this suit was commenced in January 1994 by service on the Kummers, and by then it was too late.

Possession is hostile when one holds property as his own, whether under mistaken belief or willfully. Here, after they bought the two tracts upon which they thought their wheat field was located, the Kummers no longer made lease payments because they held the property as their own. They continued to farm it openly and they kept the proceeds from the crops. The Kummers' actions were of such open, notorious and hostile character that Mr. Knight would have known they were farming his land, had he looked or inquired.

Fields 1 and 3

Mr. Johnson contends the Kummers did not prove adverse possession for the requisite 10 years. First, he argues they did not establish tacking because Mr. Hall farmed the property under a 1953 lease and Mrs. Hall recalled he farmed some property north of Umptanum Road under a verbal agreement with another landowner. There was no evidence that Mr. Hall's occupancy was anything other than permissive; thus, if there was adverse possession it could not have begun before 1976.

The evidence establishes Mr. Hall farmed both fields from 1957 to 1976, but it does not establish

he did so under a lease or with other permission. The property descriptions in the 1953 lease and Mrs. Hall's deposition testimony are too vague to determine what property was covered. The evidence also does not establish Mr. Hall possessed the property adversely, except that the Johnsons never gave anyone permission to farm tract 39. Under these circumstances, the earliest the prescriptive period could begin was September 1975, when the Johnsons acquired their interest.

Second, Mr. Johnson argues the Kummers deferred to and acknowledged the superior title of Mr. Johnson to the tract 39 wheat fields in October 1982 when they permitted him to grant and record an easement to Mr. England and the Lyons.

From 1976 when they acquired their property from the Halls, the Kummers' use of fields 1 and 3 was open, notorious and hostile. By at least October 1982, Mr. Johnson had actual notice they were farming his land. He confronted them and told them he owned the property, wanted payment for crops already harvested, and would not allow them to continue farming his land unless they executed a written lease. Had the Kummers stopped farming, Mr. Johnson's actions would have interrupted their possession and restarted the prescriptive period. But they did not. They continued farming the fields just as if they owned them, not in a manner indicating recognition of or subordination to Mr. Johnson.

Mr. Johnson's grant of the easement was nothing more than permission for the Englands and the Lyons to use an existing road to access their properties. That did not interfere with or interrupt the Kummers' use of the fields on either side of the road. The Kummers' possession of the fields was (1) exclusive, (2) actual and uninterrupted, (3) open and notorious, and (4) hostile. Because he failed to effectively assert his own ownership over the fields (as opposed to the road) for more than 10 years after acquiring actual knowledge of the Kummers' adverse possession, Mr. Johnson lost his title.

Finally, the tract owners contend adverse possession cannot occur by cultivation of open farm land for crops harvested on a biennial basis when the land lies fallow in the intervening years.

The contention is completely without merit. The use and occupancy of the property need only be of the character that a true owner would assert in view of its nature and location. Chaplin, 100 Wash.2d at 863, 676 P.2d 431. That requirement is easily met by the Kummers' dry land farming of these fields in precisely the same manner they farm the rest of their acreage in the area. Ample evidence, including the aerial maps and the testimony of some of these tract owners, demonstrates just how visible is the Kummers' use of the property. As the surveyor put it, when asked if he had any difficulty discerning the difference between the fields and the surrounding property: "It's either field or sagebrush."

The decision of the superior court is affirmed.
SWEENEY, C.J., and BROWN, J., concur.

Case Question
What is meant by the term "quiet title," and why is it used in adverse possession proceedings?

Assignment 8.4

> SITUATION: Steve owns property on which he has a quick shop. He erects a large, lighted sign next to the driveway on land that actually belongs to the adjoining property owner, a fundamentalist church. The owner does not object because Steve often advertises "Church Specials" for persons who attend services at the church. After twenty years Steve dies and his son moves into town and converts the shop into a nude dancing establishment, which he advertises on the sign. The church demands the sign be removed.

Rights and Duties of Ownership

As stated previously, ownership of property generally includes the right of possession and control free from interference of third parties. Often called the right of quiet enjoyment, this right protects the right of one to do with one's own property as one pleases. Although this right is strongly protected by the law, certain obligations accompany it.

Public or private nuisance. The first obligation is not to use one's property in such a way that it becomes a public or private nuisance to surrounding areas. A private nuisance is a use that has a direct adverse effect on specific persons,[23] such as unreasonable noise or noxious fumes emitted from the property or any continuing conduct that is harmful or poses a danger in some way to certain persons in the area. If this conduct continues, these persons have a right of action for private nuisance. They can sue in equity to have the conduct cease, and they can sue at law for damages as a result of the nuisance.

A public nuisance is one that generally has a continuing adverse effect on the public good, welfare, or safety.[24] Conduct, even though it is entirely done on one's own property, can be considered a public nuisance if its effects extend beyond the property. An example is a manufacturing plant that pollutes a waterway or emits noxious fumes over a broad area. If such harmful conduct becomes a continuing problem, public authorities may bring an action for public nuisance at equity to stop the conduct and at law to seek compensation for damages already incurred. Generally, a private party cannot bring an action for public nuisance unless the party's injury is different from that to the general public.

Condition of property.   Basic obligations also exist regarding the condition of one's property for persons entering it. This includes trespassers, licensees, and invitees. Some states treat licensees as invitees. In other states, the obligations toward each are different. However, all are owed some degree of protection from harm even if trespassing on the property.

Trespassers.   A trespasser is one who enters onto another's property without consent of any kind by the owner. The law does not offer any special protections to persons who violate the right of quiet enjoyment belonging to a landowner. However, the landowner does owe a duty to keep the property free from unreasonable dangers that a trespasser could not be expected to discover. There is no general duty to warn or take action to protect. Rather, there is only the duty to correct conditions that would cause injury or to give notice of these conditions.[25] (The owner's rights against a trespasser are discussed in Chapter 12.)

Licensees.   Licensees are persons who enter with the permission of the landowner but are not associated with the landowner's business. For example, a person hunting on property with permission free of charge and a person attending a party are common types of licensees. In states that distinguish between licensees and invitees, the obligation of a landowner toward these persons may be slightly greater than that owed trespassers. With respect to licensees, a landowner owes a general duty to warn of dangers present on the property. The reasoning is that because they are there by consent or invitation, the landowner owes a greater duty to see to their safety. This duty is somewhat broader than the duty toward trespassers and requires additional action on the part of the landowner.[26]

Invitees.   The invitee is invited (expressly or impliedly) to the property of the owner for business purposes—for the purpose of obtaining benefit for a business or for reasons of employment. Consequently, shopkeepers and landowners have a duty to actively inspect their premises to protect their invitees from harm.[27] For example, a grocery store owner has a duty to clean up a spill in one of the aisles and to restore the aisle to a safe condition in a reasonable time. An owner who does not could be held liable for injuries to anyone who steps on the area, slips and falls, and is injured.

While the privilege of quiet enjoyment is protected, the law recognizes that there are those who would abuse the privilege, and there are always occasions of persons entering on the property of others for various reasons. Consequently, the imposing of these basic duties on the landowner places the landowner under minimal obligation in return for virtually unlimited use of the property.

Condominiums

A somewhat specialized area of law is that regarding condominiums. The concept of owning property that has both freehold and non-freehold interests is not new. Records dating to medieval Europe indicate that this type of land interest existed even then. It was not unusual at that time for a person to purchase a room, apartment, or floor of a building. The owner of the building would maintain any hallways or surrounding yard. This type of ownership occurred primarily in crowded cities, where land and entire buildings were too expensive for the majority of the population. For many reasons, including the lack of established principles setting forth responsibilities of the parties to such an arrangement, this type of property ownership saw a decline. In recent times, however, with the problem of crowded cities, fast-paced lifestyles, and rising costs of purchasing and building homes, the concept of condominiums has dramatically increased in popularity, especially in the United States.

A condominium is a freehold interest. It is an absolute ownership in the property described. The property is real in that it is inextricably attached to the land. However, it may be located far above the actual soil and has specific dimensions without traditional air and subsurface rights. A condominium, however, has some non-freehold characteristics as well. Condominium ownership usually involves collateral obligations to abide by certain rules regarding the use of the property, payment of fees for maintenance of surrounding areas, and restrictions on the sale of the property. Consequently, condominiums are a hybrid of landlord/tenant (non-freehold) estates (discussed in the following section) and ownership in fee (freehold) estates.

The owners of adjoining condominiums are considered to be owners by tenancy in common over the air and subsurface rights. They are owners in fee simple over their own particular building or portion of a building. Because of this individual/multiple ownership between persons who do not have common interests and are usually strangers, all fifty states have enacted laws to govern the establishment and running of condominium complexes.[28]

Usually, a condominium complex is established by developers who create a document known as a declaration to dedicate its use to that type of ownership. A plan created to provide for the ongoing needs of the complex allows for a committee to make decisions regarding upkeep of the property, collection of fees from the owners for standard maintenance, and enforcement of any restrictions regarding purchase or sale of the property.

While it is permissible to impose restrictions on owners regarding the sale and purchase of their condominiums, these restrictions cannot be unconstitutional or even unreasonable. The law has been clear that restrictions based on race, religion, sex, or nationality are not permitted.[29] Furthermore, a restriction that is so enforced that it effectively prevents the owner of disposing of the property may be considered unreasonable.

 APPLICATION 8.7

The board of directors of a condominium complex, under a restriction, has the right to approve a prospective buyer. If the members refuse all applicants for unsound reasons, the restriction would be considered unreasonable, and the court would probably not enforce it.

Point for Discussion
Why are some restrictions enforced and others not?

Because the owners of the individual units are tenants in common over the air and subsurface rights and common areas, their obligations are equal as landowners. Therefore, if a trespasser, licensee, or invitee is injured on a common area through negligence, the owners are equally liable for the injuries. Consequently, the courts do allow some restrictions so that owners can ensure that they will become tenants in common with reasonable persons.

Non-Freehold Estates

In addition to interests associated with freehold estates of ownership, numerous non-freehold estate interests are present in American property law. **Non-freehold estates** are those that include specific rights to possess property, control it, and even exclude the true owner. However, these estates generally are by agreement, are for a fixed time, and do not include any rights of ownership. One who possesses a non-freehold estate cannot convey ownership. Nor does the party in possession have the right to waste the property, and the possessor must return the property to the true owner at the agreed time or upon proper eviction proceedings. Most often, this relationship between owner and possessor is that of landlord and tenant and is governed in part by property law and in part by contract law.

Non-Freehold Estate
An interest in real property that is limited in duration and involves the right of possession but not ownership.

Non-freehold estates are commonly called leaseholds. The parties are generally referred to as landlord and tenant. Leaseholds may or may not be in writing, depending upon the specific nature of the agreement. Generally, agreements that will extend beyond one year must be in writing under state law according to a statute of frauds, because the agreement involves real property. Basic elements should be present for an oral or written leasehold agreement to be valid. Each party must have contractual capacity; that is, each party must have reached the age of majority and be considered legally competent. A clear agreement to give and accept possession of the property upon specified terms must exist. A description of the property must be included that adequately describes the exact premises of which the tenant will have possession.[30]

The terms of the agreement should be clearly understood. If the agreement contains an option to renew and the option is not formally exercised but the tenant remains in possession beyond the original term, the leasehold becomes one at will. This and other types of leaseholds and tenancies are discussed subsequently. It is important, however, to first understand the rights and obligations of a landlord and tenant.

Rights and obligations of landlord and tenant. The landlord and tenant each have basic rights and obligations associated with non-freehold property interests (see Figure 8.2). The landlord has the duty to turn over the property free from latent (not reasonably discoverable) defects or dangers and to ensure that the property is habitable.[31] Although the definition of habitability varies from state to state, it is presumed to be that which is absolutely necessary to make a premises one on which persons can reasonably be expected to

FIGURE 8.2   Landlord and Tenant Law

Excerpts from VERMONT STATUTES ANNOTATED
TITLE NINE. COMMERCE AND TRADE
PART 7. LANDLORD AND TENANT
CHAPTER 137. RESIDENTIAL RENTAL AGREEMENTS

§ 4455. Tenant obligations; payment of rent

(a) Rent is payable without demand or notice at the time and place agreed upon by the parties.

(b) An increase in rent shall take effect on the first day of the rental period following no less than 60 days' actual notice to the tenant.

§ 4456. Tenant obligations; use and maintenance of dwelling unit

(a) The tenant shall not create or contribute to the noncompliance of the dwelling unit with applicable provisions of building, housing and health regulations.

(b) The tenant shall conduct himself or herself and require other persons on the premises with the tenant's consent to conduct themselves in a manner that will not disturb other tenants' peaceful enjoyment of the premises.

(c) The tenant shall not deliberately or negligently destroy, deface, damage or remove any part of the premises or its fixtures, mechanical systems or furnishings or deliberately or negligently permit any person to do so.

(d) Unless inconsistent with a written rental agreement or otherwise provided by law, a tenant may terminate a tenancy by actual notice given to the landlord at least one rental payment period prior to the termination date specified in the notice.

(e) If a tenant acts in violation of this section, the landlord is entitled to recover damages, costs and reasonable attorney's fees, and the violation shall be grounds for termination under section 4467(b) of this title.

§ 4457. Landlord obligations; habitability

(a) Warranty of habitability. In any residential rental agreement, the landlord shall be deemed to covenant and warrant to deliver over and maintain, throughout the period of the tenancy, premises that are safe, clean and fit for human habitation and which comply with the requirements of applicable building, housing and health regulations.

(b) Waiver. No rental agreement shall contain any provision by which the tenant waives the protections of the implied warranty of habitability. Any such waiver shall be deemed contrary to public policy and shall be unenforceable and void.

(c) Heat and water. As part of the implied warranty of habitability, the landlord shall ensure that the dwelling unit has heating facilities which are capable of safely providing a reasonable amount of heat. Every landlord who provides heat as part of the rental agreement shall at all times supply a reasonable amount of heat to the dwelling unit. The landlord shall provide an adequate amount of water to each dwelling unit properly connected with hot and cold water lines. The hot water lines shall be connected with supplied water-heating facilities which are capable of heating sufficient water to permit an adequate amount to be drawn. This subsection shall not apply to a dwelling unit intended and rented for summer occupancy or as a hunting camp.

---

live. Typically, habitable property has access to electricity, hot water, shelter from the elements, and, in some states, heat. If the landlord fails to provide these things or fails to continue them during the term of the agreement, the warranty of habitability is violated and the landlord is presumed to have breached the terms of the lease agreement.

 APPLICATION 8.8

1. Carla rents a house from David. David decides to raise the rent without notice (in violation of state law). Carla doesn't have the extra money. David has the water to the house turned off. David has also violated the warranty of habitability and, consequently, has breached the lease agreement.

The landlord has the right to enter the premises only to make reasonable repairs and to prevent waste of the property. The landlord must generally give notice and enter the property at reasonable times except in an emergency. The failure of a landlord to respect the tenant's right of possession is a violation of the lease agreement.

2. Mr. Romine is landlord to college student Malina. Frequently, Malina comes home to find that Mr. Romine has been in her apartment and has gone through her personal property. Mr. Romine contends that he is suspicious of Malina's activities and is protecting his property from being used as a place where illegal drugs are kept and sold. Mr. Romine is violating Malina's right to possession and, consequently, the lease agreement.

3. Mr. Romine is also landlord to college student Suzanne. It is not uncommon for Suzanne to find that Mr. Romine has entered her apartment in her absence. However, Mr. Romine contends that he enters Suzanne's apartment only when he smells gas near the windows. He has gone in only to turn off the gas stove, which Suzanne frequently forgets to turn off. Mr. Romine has every right to enter the property for this purpose and is not in violation of the lease agreement when he does so.

Points for Discussion
1. Why can't David take steps to increase rent on his own property?
2. What would be a reasonable alternative to entering Malina's apartment?
3. Why isn't the unpermitted entry into Suzanne's apartment a violation of the lease agreement?

In contrast, the tenant is responsible to prevent waste from occurring on the property, to discover patent (reasonably obvious) defects or dangers, and to make ordinary repairs.[32] If a significant patent defect exists or occurs, the tenant is obligated to notify the landlord and to give the landlord a reasonable opportunity to repair it. If the defect does not affect habitability, such as a clogged sink, the tenant is generally responsible for the repair, and in many states, any costs of having the sink cleared would be the responsibility of the tenant.

The tenant is bound by the terms of the agreement and is expected to pay the rent and to give reasonable notice when vacating the property, commonly referred to as quitting the property. The tenant has the right to quiet enjoyment.

If either party substantially fails to meet his or her responsibilities, such failure may be treated as a breach, and the innocent party has the right to terminate the agreement. A landlord's failure to meet the required obligations is termed *constructive eviction.*[33] In other words, the tenant is left in a position where he or she has no reasonable choice but to vacate the premises.

222   Chapter 8

The landlord does not necessarily have to *intentionally* fail to meet his or her legal responsibilities. In cases where the property is so damaged by fire or otherwise damaged that it becomes uninhabitable, the tenant is constructively evicted. Many times, the lease agreement will allow the landlord a reasonable time to repair the premises before the lease agreement will be terminated. It is important to carefully read the lease (as all legal documents should be read!) to determine just what the obligations of the parties are with respect to damage to the property and continuation of the agreement. If the lease is effectively terminated by a constructive eviction, the question of whether or not the tenant is able to recover any advance deposits depends on the terms of the agreement between the parties and whether the damage was the fault of the tenant.

Regardless of who initially breached the agreement, many states impose on both parties a duty to mitigate any damage caused by the premature end of the landlord-tenant relationship. *Mitigation of damages* is the term used when one is required to lessen or minimize the damage when possible. This prevents persons from adding to their damages to increase the amount of monetary recovery in a lawsuit. In the event the property is significantly damaged, the landlord is often required to make every reasonable effort to repair the premises and restore habitability. Further, if a tenant vacates or abandons the property, the landlord must make reasonable attempts to rent the property. The landlord cannot merely let the property stand empty and seek to collect the balance of the rent from the tenant.

The tenant also is responsible for mitigating damages. A tenant who is forced to move on grounds of constructive eviction must make reasonable efforts to minimize the cost of the move and damage to any personal property before recovering compensation from the landlord. The tenant who played a role in creating the condition that forced the constructive eviction probably has no recourse against the landlord.

 CASE

ESTATE OF VASQUEZ v. HEPNER

564 N.W.2d. 426 (1997).

ANDREASEN, Justice.

Daniel Vazquez died as a result of INJURIES sustained in a fire in the duplex where he was living. The fire started as a result of faulty wiring located in the ceiling space between the first and second floors. Vazquez's estate sued the landlords, alleging they violated the implied warranty of habitability and Iowa Code section 562A.15 (1993) by not making a reasonable inspection of

the premises. The district court held that the landlords were not liable for the defects because they had no knowledge or reason to know about the wiring problems. We affirm.

I. Background Facts and Proceedings.
The following facts were stipulated to the district court. In 1992, Daniel Vazquez orally leased the upstairs apartment in a duplex owned by Donald and Betty Hepner. The Hepners had purchased the duplex, located in Davenport, Iowa, in 1986, and it was approximately 100 years old.

On November 23, 1992, a fire broke out in the duplex. Daniel died as a result of INJURIES he received during the fire. The investigation revealed that the fire started in the ceiling space between the floor level of the second floor and the ceiling of the first floor. The downstairs apartment was vacant at the time. The fire was caused by an electrical fault that occurred as a result of faulty splicing of Romex type wiring with older knob and tube wiring that led to a porch light. The faulty splicing had been done before the Hepners purchased the building and was concealed between the first and second floors.

The Hepners had no knowledge of the existence of the wiring problem, they never performed any repair work near the origin of the fire, and they never hired an electrician to inspect the wiring in the duplex. Further, Daniel never notified the Hepners of any electrical problems in the duplex.

On November 21, 1994, Leonardo Vazquez, as administrator of Daniel's estate, filed a wrongful death petition against the Hepners, alleging common law negligence claims and a violation of the implied warranty of habitability. Before trial, both parties entered into an agreement, asking the district court to accept their stipulations of fact and decide three issues of law. The three issues were:

1. Whether the common law implied warranty of habitability or Iowa Code section 562A.15 creates liability for an electrical defect or wiring defect in a rental premises when the landlord did not know and had no reason to know of the electrical defect or wiring defect.
2. Whether Defendants breached any duty arising from Iowa Code section 562A.15 or from a warranty of habitability under the facts of this case.
3. Whether a breach of any alleged duty as above stated allows for the recovery of personal INJURY damages.

In the agreement, the parties stipulated that the estate's damages were $95,000. The parties also agreed the court could consider the facts and opinions contained in depositions and previously disclosed reports of the parties and the parties' answers to discovery.

By agreement, the court entered judgment for the Hepners on Vazquez's common law negligence claims. Vazquez was permitted to amend the petition to include claims based on both the implied warranty of habitability and negligent breach of duties imposed by statute and ordinance.

The case was submitted to the court by stipulated facts on January 8, 1996. On April 3, the district court filed its decision. It addressed only the first of the three issues, ruling in favor of the Hepners. The court held that the Hepners were not liable for electrical or wiring defects that they had no knowledge of or reason to know about. Without any duty, the court stated there could be no breach of that duty or damages arising from the breach. The court further stated:

To determine the first issue of law presented to the Court by the parties in favor of the Plaintiff would require this Court to determine that landlords are strictly liable for any defect in electrical facilities of which they have no knowledge or any reason to know about. The imposition of such a legal duty is best left to statutory or legislative action, not to courts.

The district court entered judgment in favor of the Hepners. Vazquez filed timely notice of appeal. On appeal, Vazquez claims the duties of a landlord to maintain electrical wiring, based on the implied warranty of habitability and Iowa Code section 562A.15, require a landlord to make inspections on a reasonable basis.

II. Scope of Review.
Our scope of review is for the correction of errors at law. Iowa R.App.P. 4; Paul v. Luigi's, Inc., 557 N.W.2d 895, 897 (Iowa 1997). We are bound by the district court's findings of fact if they are supported by substantial evidence. Iowa R.App.P. 14(f)(1); Paul, 557 N.W.2d at 897. When reviewing evidence for its substantiality, we view it in the light most favorable to upholding the district court's judgment. Paul, 557 N.W.2d at 897.

III. Dismissal of Claims Based on Doctrine of Res Judicata.
We first address the Hepners' argument that all of Vazquez's claims in the amended petition must be dismissed because of the doctrine of res judicata. They argue that each count in the amended petition is based on common law negligence, and the district court already entered judgment on those claims by accepting the parties' stipulations and agreement. This contention is without merit.

Even though the first three counts of Vazquez's amended petition do not cite Iowa

Code section 562A.15, they clearly recite its statutory language. A petition is not required to recite the Iowa statute being relied upon. Iowa R.Civ.P. 94. Further, the judgment entered on the negligence claims does not affect Vazquez's claim involving the implied warranty of habitability. Negligence and the implied warranty of habitability are two different causes of action with distinct elements.

IV. Violation of Implied Warranty of Habitability.
Vazquez claims the district court erred in finding that the Hepners did not violate the implied warranty of habitability. We disagree.

An implied warranty of habitability exists in all oral or written leases of a dwelling, which includes houses, condominiums, and apartments. Mease v. Fox, 200 N.W.2d 791, 796 (Iowa 1972). Under this warranty, the landlord impliedly warrants at the outset of the lease that there are no LATENT DEFECTS in facilities and utilities vital to the use of the premises for residential purposes and that these essential features shall remain during the entire term in such condition to maintain the habitability of the dwelling. Further, the implied warranty . . . in the lease situation is a representation there neither is nor shall be during the term a violation of applicable housing law, ordinance or regulation which shall render the premises unsafe, or unsanitary and unfit for living therein.

The breach must be of such substantial nature that the premises are unsafe or unsanitary, and thus unfit for habitation. If the implied warranty of habitability is breached, the tenant is entitled to basic contract remedies, including damages, reformation, and rescission. Id. Damages are measured by "the difference between the fair rental value of the premises if they had been as warranted and the fair rental value of the premises as they were during occupancy by the tenant in the unsafe or unsanitary condition." Id. at 797. A tenant may also recover incidental and consequential damages proven. Roeder v. Nolan, 321 N.W.2d 1, 5 (Iowa 1982).

There can be no violation of the implied warranty of habitability without a LATENT DEFECT or a material violation of a housing code. A LATENT DEFECT is a "hidden or concealed defect." Black's Law Dictionary 794 (5th ed. 1979). Further, a LANDLORD is only liable for INJURIES resulting from a hidden or LATENT DEFECT if the LANDLORD knew or should have known of the defect. Knapp v. Simmons, 345 N.W.2d 118, 122 (Iowa 1984).

In all other instances, the TENANT must notify the LANDLORD of the defect or the need for repair. See Mease, 200 N.W.2d at 797. In other words, a LANDLORD is not strictly liable for all defects that result in INJURIES to TENANTS.

Even if a LANDLORD has no actual knowledge of a defect, the LANDLORD may have a duty to discover LATENT DEFECTS. In describing this duty, one court stated:

The LANDLORD'S obligation is only to do what is reasonable under the circumstances. The LANDLORD need not take extraordinary measures or make unreasonable expenditures of time and money in trying to discover hazards unless the circumstances so warrant. When there is a potential serious danger, which is foreseeable, a LANDLORD should anticipate the danger and conduct a reasonable inspection before passing possession to the TENANT. However, if no such inspection is warranted, the LANDLORD has no such obligation.

Resolution Trust Corp. v. Rossmoor Corp., 34 Cal.App.4th 93, 40 Ca.Rptr.2d 328, 333 (1995).

Here, neither the Hepners nor Vazquez had knowledge of the wiring problem. Both parties stipulated to that fact in their agreement. Therefore, we must determine whether the Hepners should have known of the defect. In arguing they should have been aware of the problem, Vazquez claims the implied warranty of habitability requires a landlord to make electrical inspections on a reasonable basis.

We agree with the district court's conclusion that the Hepners were not obligated to make an electrical inspection because they had no reason to know of the wiring defect. Because the porch light, which was connected to the defective wire, was working properly, there were no indications of any wiring problems. Without any foreseeable potential of danger, there was no duty to inspect. The implied warranty of habitability does not explicitly require a LANDLORD to inspect all wiring in a structure before leasing it to a

TENANT. It simply requires a LANDLORD to keep the premises safe, sanitary, and fit for habitation. See Mease, 200 N.W.2d at 796. As the district court stated, "the habitability of a dwelling unit is not destroyed by defective wiring [that] is unknown and unknowable to both the LANDLORD and the TENANT."

A landlord is not required to take extreme measures and expend significant amounts of time and money trying to discover hazards that may not even exist. Further, in this case, Vazquez's expert testified that even if the Hepners had hired a licensed electrician to make an inspection, there is no guarantee that the electrician would have discovered the faulty splicing, thus preventing the fire. The Hepners did all that was required by the implied warranty.

V. Duty of Landlord Under Iowa Code Section 562A.15.

Vazquez also claims that the Hepners, in failing to inspect the electrical wiring, violated certain provisions of Iowa Code section 562A.15. We disagree.

Iowa Code section 562A.15 provides in relevant part:

1.   The LANDLORD shall:

a. Comply with the requirements of applicable building and housing codes materially affecting health and safety.
b. Make all repairs and do whatever is necessary to put and keep the premises in a fit and habitable condition.

* * *

d. Maintain in good and safe working order and condition all electrical . . . facilities. . . .

Iowa Code s 562A.15. If the LANDLORD fails to comply with section 562A.15, and it materially affects health and safety, the TENANT may commence an action under Iowa Code section 562A.21.

The district court was correct in finding no violation of Iowa Code section 562A.15(1)(a), which requires a landlord to comply with applicable building and housing codes. There is no evidence that the Hepners violated the Davenport Uniform Housing Code. To the contrary, the premises passed inspection by the City of Davenport in 1988.

We also agree with the court that the Hepners did not violate Iowa Code section 562A.15(1)(b), which requires a LANDLORD to make repairs and keep the premises in a fit and habitable condition, or section 562A.15(1)(d), which requires a LANDLORD to maintain all electrical facilities in good and safe working order. As is the case with the implied warranty of habitability, the statute does not explicitly require a LANDLORD to inspect all wiring before leasing the premises to a TENANT. Inspections are not always required to satisfy Iowa Code section 562A.15. As with the common law duty of LANDLORDS under Mease, the key factor in determining a LANDLORD'S liability under section 562A.15 is whether the LANDLORD knew or should have known of the defect. The statute is not intended to hold LANDLORDS strictly liable for any defect that causes INJURY to a TENANT.

Here, it would have been unreasonable to require the Hepners to tear up their walls and ceilings to inspect the wiring. Because the Hepners did not have actual knowledge of any wiring problems, and the defect was not foreseeable, the Hepners had no obligation to hire an electrician to inspect the premises. The statute was satisfied because the premises appeared to be in good and safe working order.

VI. Conclusion.
The district court did not err in concluding that neither the implied warranty of habitability nor Iowa Code section 562A.15 imposes liability for electrical defects when the landlord did not know and had no reason to know of the defect. Therefore, we affirm the decision of the district court.
    AFFIRMED.

Case Question
What is the difference between a latent and patent defect?

Assignment 8.5

For each of the following situations, identify the circumstances that represent the terms listed (terms may be used more than once):

- mitigate
- habitability
- ordinary repairs
- latent defect
- patent defect
- constructive eviction

Situation 1.   Brad is walking along the front porch of his second-floor apartment to the stairs leading to the ground level. Two of the boards give way, and Brad falls through the porch to the ground. Brad's landlord refuses to repair the property, saying such repairs are Brad's responsibility.

Situation 2.   Liz signed a lease for an apartment being built as part of a new complex. She signed the lease based on seeing a model apartment. On February 1, Liz picked up the keys to the new apartment at the realtor's office. The next morning, she arrived with her belongings. The only running water in the apartment was in the bathroom. Several electrical outlets were unfinished, with raw wires hanging out of the wall. The back door was completely blocked by construction debris. The kitchen countertops were missing entirely. Liz refused to move in and demanded that the landlord immediately return her 500-dollar deposit and the two months' rent she had paid in advance. The landlord refused. Further, the landlord made no attempts to rent the apartment between February 1 and May 1, when Liz brought the landlord to court to recover the money.

Types of leasehold. The type of leasehold is determined by the length of the lease, which will dictate whether the lease must be in writing under the statute of frauds. Generally, leases that extend beyond the period of one year and those that contain the option to purchase the leased property are required to be in writing. Shorter and less restrictive leases may be based on an oral agreement. However, it is always best to have the agreement in writing and signed by the parties to avoid future disputes as to the exact original terms of the agreement. (Figure 8.3 is a sample lease.)

Month-to-month tenancy. Also called periodic tenancies, month-to-month tenancies are the least restrictive. The agreement between the parties is effective for one month. Unless otherwise stated, the month is presumed to begin on the first day and end on the last day of the calendar month following the date of the agreement. This type of lease automatically renews each month thereafter until

FIGURE 8.3
Sample Lease

RESIDENCE LIFE
CONTRACT

NAME_____   SOCIAL SECURITY NUMBER _____
HOME (mailing) ADDRESS: _____   DATE OF BIRTH_____
_____   STATUS:
_____   1st year _____ 2nd year _____
HOME TELEPHONE NUMBER_____   3rd year _____ 4th year _____
PARENT'S NAMES: FATHER _____   MOTHER _____

Resident hall occupancy shall be subject to all rules and regulations of the College, includ-ing those stated in the Student Handbook. A copy of the Student Handbook is available from the Student Services Office.

GENERAL REGULATIONS

The same obedience to the laws of the land and the conduct rules of the College expected of students generally is also expected of students as residence hall residents, visitors or guests. Therefore, acts contrary to federal, state or local laws constitute violations of residence hall rules. Recognition of the personal and property rights of others is expected of residence hall oc-cupants, visitors and guests. Interference with the rights of other occupants to the use of their rooms for study or sleep constitutes violation of residence hall rules. Room-to-room canvassing and unauthorized defacing or permanently altering residence hall facilities is prohibited. Only these electrical devices may be used: coffee pots, self-contained popcorn poppers, hair dryers and electric blankets. See Handbook for further information on residence hall regulations.

Date _____   _____
                                    Signature of Student

                                    _____
                                    Dean of Students

one of the parties chooses to terminate it by giving the other party reasonable notice. The states have statutes indicating what reasonable notice is. In most cases, it is the equivalent of a one-month term and would therefore be one month. Generally, notice must be given on or before the first day of a term.

 APPLICATION 8.9

Assume an agreement automatically renews on the first day of each month. The tenant must give notice to quit on or before the first day of the term. If the tenant gives notice on or shortly before the first of March, he or she can end the tenancy on the 31st of March. If however, the tenant gives no-tice on the 15th day of March, the tenancy will not end on March 31, and the tenant's responsibilities will continue until the 30th day of April.

Point for Discussion
What do you think is the purpose of required notice to terminate?

Year-to-year tenancy.   The law is basically the same for agreements to lease on a year-to-year basis. Such agreements that will extend for more than one year are required to be in writing under the statute of frauds. This type of lease may renew each year unless otherwise stated, or it may require formal renewal, depending upon the terms of the agreement by the parties. The reasonable time to end a year-to-year lease is often specified in a state statute or in the agreement between the parties. A common number is three or six months. Many states have laws that limit the length of extended leases. Usually this is not a problem for landlords and tenants, because the limitation is often 100 years.

A tenant who remains in possession of the property beyond the agreed term without exercising an option to do so or without automatic renewal has no legal right to remain on the premises. Such persons are considered tenants at sufferance and can be evicted without notice. However, state statutes generally prescribe the procedure for eviction. The law does not permit "self help." In other words, a person cannot be physically, forcibly removed from the premises by the property owner. The eviction must go through a court, and often, when physical eviction is ordered, it is overseen by law enforcement officers. (See *Flickinger v. Mark IV Apartments Association*, 315 N.W.2D 794 at the end of the chapter.)

Tenancy at will.   An additional type of tenant is a tenant at will—one who enters or remains on the property with no certain terms of agreement. Consent of the owner is sufficient. Tenancy at will continues indefinitely and has no fixed term on which it will end. The amount of notice to end such a tenancy is usually set by statute. Often reasonable notice is considered to be one month. This type of tenancy and tenancy at sufferance are the least desirable for the tenant because he or she may be required to vacate with very little or no notice.

Assignment 8.6

Examine the following lease provision and answer the questions following it:

Lease Term: The initial term shall be for a period of 12 months commencing on the 1st day of August, 1993, and ending on the 31st day of July, 1994. This lease may be terminated by either party giving written notice to the other at least thirty (30) days prior to the expiration of the original or any renewal term thereof. Failure to give such notice shall constitute an automatic renewal of this lease for an additional term at the same rental and for the same term of 12 months.

1. What type of leasehold (tenancy) exists?
2. On or before what date should notice be given to renew or vacate?
3. If the term is renewed, what is the first date, assuming proper notice is given, that the second term can be ended?

Fixtures

Fixtures are articles of personal property that have become attached to real property; they do not include houses and buildings. Fixtures are actually considered to be part of the real property because they have none of the characteristics of personal property, such as being ordinarily movable. Fixtures are those items that are affixed to the real property in such a way that they cannot be easily moved but are capable of being moved. Common examples of fixtures are items that have been physically incorporated into the structure but are removable, such as lighting and bathroom fixtures. Typically, fixtures are conveyed when the property is conveyed.

Fixture
An item of personal property that has been affixed to real property for a specific purpose and in a semipermanent manner.

Disputes have arisen in the past as to what is and is not a fixture when the buyer and seller both want the personal property that is claimed to be a fixture. Generally, to determine whether something is a fixture, four things are considered: (1) intent, (2) mode of annexation, (3) adaptation, and (4) damage that will result if the object is removed (significant damage to the building indicates a fixture). Intent means the original intent of the party who attached the personal property to the real property.[34] If intent was to make the item a permanent attachment, the law would tend to consider the property to be a fixture. The mode of annexation is the actual method of attaching the fixture to the real property. Personal property that was attached in such a way that it cannot be removed without altering or damaging the real property has taken on the characteristic of a fixture. Finally, adaptation involves the function of the personal property. If the property has become attached in a way that it serves to benefit the real property in some functional way, it would be considered a fixture. The function need not be necessary, but it must directly enhance or benefit the property in some way other than its mere presence.

A special type of fixture is known as a trade fixture—an item of personal property attached to the real property for the purpose of benefiting the particular trade or business of the party who is responsible for attachment of the fixture.[35] For example, a man opening a dry-cleaning business would buy or lease property and install very specialized equipment. When he terminates ownership or possession, the presumption would be that the equipment he installed is a trade fixture and would not be conveyed with the real property. Often, it is necessary to attach such items to the real property for practical purposes. In this example, however, because the equipment is necessary for the owner's livelihood, the owner is allowed to remove it when leaving the property. The owner of trade fixtures, however, has a duty to restore the real property substantially to the condition it was in before the trade fixtures were installed.

Assignment 8.7

Identify the following as a fixture, trade fixture, or personal property:

1. An ice cream machine in an ice cream shop.
2. A bookcase built into an open closet by a lease tenant.
3. A Tiffany light fixture that screws onto an ordinary ceiling light socket.

> 4. A refrigerator that is recessed into an opening in the kitchen wall. (Attachment consists of pushing the appliance into the opening and plugging it in.)
> 5. A built-in dishwasher that a tenant installs in his apartment.
> 6. Five built-in convection ovens that a tenant with a catering business installs in his apartment.
> 7. Carpet that a tenant has professionally laid over hardwood floors in his apartment.
> 8. An aluminum utility shed that a property owner places in a concrete footing in his backyard (the owner subsequently sells the real property).

PERSONAL PROPERTY

Personal Property

Movable items that are not land or items permanently affixed to land. Personal property includes tangible (physical) and intangible items, such as rights of ownership in property held by others (e.g., bank accounts or ownership in legal entities such as stock). It does not include the rights to bring legal action against others, commonly known as a chose in action.

Personal property includes money, goods, and movable, tangible items.[36] Legally, personal property can be sold, lent, given, lost, stolen, abandoned, or altered. Personal property does not include land or, generally, items permanently attached to land (such as permanent buildings) (known as real property). Nor does it ordinarily include personal rights to certain intangible interests, such as the right to bring an action at law or equity (commonly called a chose in action). For example, if a person's car was damaged in an accident, the person could not sell the right to sue the person who caused the damage. Examples of intangible items that are considered to be personal property are patents and goodwill of a business, which are rights that are indirectly associated with movables.

Bailment

Bailment takes place when one party having possession of personal property (the bailor) temporarily delivers possession of the property to another party (the bailee). The delivery is made for a specific purpose and/or as part of a contract, with the understanding that the property will be cared for and returned to the original party upon demand.[37]

Specifically, the elements of a bailment are as follows:

1. Personal property
2. Transferred by a party with the right to possession
3. To a second party for a specific purpose and/or as part of the terms of a contract
4. That the property will be protected and
5. That the original party has the right to reclaim the property.
6. In some cases, an additional element requires compensation in return for some act pertaining to the property.

States often have statutes that address bailment. Examples are safe deposit boxes and vehicle parking services (garages or valet parking). In the absence of statutes, general principles of common law principles of bailment apply.

Types of bailment. Bailments generally fall into one of two categories. The type of bailment depends on the rights and duties of the bailee.

Gratuitous bailment.   Gratuitous bailment occurs when one party is benefited by the bailment without obligation or benefit to the other.[38] An example of sole benefit of bailor is free storage of winter clothing by a dry cleaners. Allowing the use of one's property by another without expecting compensation, such as lending a lawnmower, is an example of bailment that benefits only the bailee. In either situation, the bailee (party receiving the property) has the duty to exercise ordinary care to protect the bailed property. Ordinary care includes reasonable precautions under the circumstances.

Mutual benefit bailment.   A bailment for hire or compensation (payment of some type) is the most frequent kind of bailment. Such bailment encompasses all occurrences of a temporary nature where one party promises to pay some sort of compensation in return for a second party's safekeeping of personal property that belongs to the first party. In turn, the receiving party will return the property upon demand or at a time provided for by contract in exchange for the compensation.[39] Additional terms of the bailment may require the performance of some duty other than safekeeping of the property. Often, bailments include the duty to clean or repair property for compensation. An example is giving one's watch to a jeweler for repair. The jeweler is responsible for the care as well as the repair of the watch in exchange for compensation by the owner.

Whether or not property has been bailed is based upon the giving party's demonstrated intent to divide the rights of possession and ownership.[40] For example, leaving a vehicle in someone else's care is not considered a bailment unless the keys are turned over, since without keys to a vehicle, the receiving party cannot exercise the control over the car associated with the right of possession. If the car is parked but the owner retains the keys, the relationship is one of a lease or license dependent upon the terms and duration. The owner leases or has a license to use the space in which to park the car but retains possession of the car at all times through the car's keys. In bailment, the owner retains the title and right to ownership of the property but temporarily gives up the right to exercise possession.

When faced with a decision of whether a bailment exists and, if so, what type of bailment exists, a court will examine the relationship of the parties and determine the reasonable expectations under the circumstances. For example, if the court finds, based on the circumstances, that the two parties are close friends and often exchange property with each other, it is likely the court will find the reasonable expectation to be a gratuitous bailment, with no duty beyond ordinary care and no requirement of compensation.

Generally, the duty of a bailee is only to possess and protect the bailment from damage unless other conditions are specified by an agreement between the parties. Such an agreement can be inferred from the circumstances, and in cases of a bailment for mutual benefit, the duty to care for the bailed property is greater than in a gratuitous bailment. For example, taking a coat to a dry cleaners implies that the bailor wants the coat cleaned and that the bailee will clean it in addition to holding it in safekeeping for the bailor. A compensated bailor is expected to take greater steps than mere ordinary care to protect the property. The compensation is, at least in part, for the ensured well-being of the property.

Assignment 8.8

> Does a bailment exist in the following situations? If so, what type of bailment is it? Explain your answer.
>
> 1. Miles takes several personal items to an auction and turns them over to the auctioneer to put up for sale.
> 2. Carol leaves her pearls with the local jeweler and asks that he restring them.
> 3. Jorge goes to a large shopping center and leaves his car in the attached parking garage while he shops.
> 4. Renee borrows Beth's car to go to the grocery store.
> 5. As a favor, Lisa volunteers to keep Dorothy's dog while Dorothy is out of town.
> 6. Tony works in a crowded downtown area. He leaves his car each day with a parking attendant, who parks the car in a lot and then returns the car to Tony at the end of the day.
> 7. Lawrence takes his new suit to the tailor and requests that he make alterations to it.
> 8. Deniece attends a college where she pays a fee each semester for the use of a locker. While in possession of the locker, she is the only one with a key to open it.
> 9. Natalia takes the keys to her neighbor's house and watches the house while the neighbors are on vacation.

Lost and Mislaid Property

Lost property is property that is separated from its owner involuntarily and accidentally,[41] whereas mislaid property is property that is intentionally left in a place and later forgotten.[42] Most states have statutes as well as common law principles that govern the rights and obligations of the finder of lost or mislaid property. Regarding the statutory law, some jurisdictions treat the finder of lost or mislaid property as a constructive bailee for benefit of bailor.[43] In such cases, it is implied that the finder is holding the property for its true owner. The bailee has a duty to care for the property until it is recovered and, depending on the statute, may or may not have the right to receive compensation for costs of the care of the property. If a statute permits recovery of compensation, the duties will be those of a bailee for hire, which are somewhat greater than those of a gratuitous bailee.

Other jurisdictions do not consider lost or mislaid property to be a bailment. In such states, the finder has the right to claim possession and ownership. In the case of lost property, claims to the property may be made by the finder wherever the property is found.[44] In contrast, mislaid property belongs to the owner of the premises where it is located (this party is not always the finder of the property,[45] since the mislaid property was intentionally left on the premises belonging to the owner). The exception to this is the concept of treasure trove.[46] When an item or items of great monetary value are found, they may be claimed by the finder regardless of whether they were lost or mislaid. For treasure trove to apply, the item must usually be cash or its equivalent, e.g., coins, gold, or bullion. In any event, a person who finds personal property having value should always consult the law of his or her jurisdiction to determine his or her rights and obligations with respect to the property.

Abandoned Property

If property has been abandoned, it must be shown that the owner gave up possession with the intent to give up dominion, control, and title to the property.[47] If so, the finder can take over possession and be declared its owner so long as the intent to dominate, control, and exercise title is continuously shown. For example, one cannot come across an item such as a piece of jewelry on the beach and ignore it and later try to claim ownership as the first finder with rights superior to another who also found it and identified it as valuable. It must be apparent to others that one intends to make the property one's own.

Confused Property

An additional aspect of property whose ownership is unclear deals with items that become confused with other similar items. An example is money. If several persons put their money in the same place and a party alleges that a certain portion of a sum of money is actually that person's property alone and that party is responsible for its becoming confused with the other money, the burden of proof is on the party claiming right to a specific portion to establish what amount of money actually belongs to that party. In cases where the items become confused and the proof cannot be established as to particular rights, the value of the confused items is shared equally by those who can establish that they are entitled to any share.[48]

Actions to Recover Property or Its Value

Many legal disputes over property arise when there is disagreement over the rights of possession or ownership. In cases dealing with persons who claim to have somehow lost possession of their property, there are several legal alternatives to regain the property. Of course, if the property was stolen, criminal laws apply. If a contract existed between the original and subsequent possessor regarding the property, an action for breach of contract may exist. In addition, other civil actions provide methods to regain wrongfully obtained property, or at least its value.

Conversion. Conversion is the basis for an action when one party receives possession of the property of another and wrongfully holds the property.[49] This can occur in one of two ways. In the first instance, a party may seize control of property without permission. In the second, and more common, instance, a party may refuse to return property that was previously bailed.

In the case of a bailment that becomes a conversion, there may also be a cause of action for the tort of negligence or for breach of contract if either element can be proven. (A further discussion of negligence and breach of contract is presented in Chapters 12 and 7, respectively.) The owner is also permitted to allege a lawsuit based on conversion that requires only that it be shown that there is wrongful possession of the property by another and the intent of that other party is to exercise control and to exclude the owner from rightful possession and ownership of the property. If the owner proves conversion, the property may be recovered, or if the property has been altered or disposed of, its value may be recovered. If the property is returned, the owner may also recover the fair market value of the use of the property during the time he or she was deprived of it. In many cases where conversion is applicable, there may also be a criminal action available to punish the party responsible for taking the property.

Trespass to chattels (personal property).   This type of action for return of property occurs when a party substantially interferes with another's possession or ownership of property. The primary difference between conversion and trespass to chattels is that in trespass to chattels, there is no need to show intent of the second party to exercise control of the property. It is only necessary to show that the second party dispossessed the first party of his or her property permanently or for a substantial period of time.[50]

As in the action for conversion, the party claiming trespass can claim the fair market value of the property. If the property was ultimately returned, a claim can still be made for the fair market value of its use during the period the true owner was denied access to the property.

Replevin.   Some jurisdictions still provide for the common law action of replevin, developed in England and still a recognized cause of action in many states. The purpose of an action in replevin is to regain possession of the actual property that was wrongfully taken, and not its value. This is actually a type of equity action and is based on a claim that money damages are insufficient to remedy the wrong.[51]

To bring an action for replevin, it is necessary to prove the following:

1. Plaintiff has right to immediate possession, providing plaintiff and defendant do not both have right to immediate possession.
2. Property in issue must be personal property.
3. Property must be unlawfully possessed and detained by defendant at the time the action is commenced. (The defendant need not have unlawfully taken the property.)

 APPLICATION 8.10

Otis owns a prize-winning champion bloodline hound. Emily is hired to groom the hound and refuses to return it.

a. If Emily intends to make herself the owner of the hound and benefit from that ownership, Otis would have an action for conversion against her.
b. If Emily deliberately allows the hound to run away, Otis would have an action for trespass to chattels.
c. If the hound was a longtime family pet and mere money could not replace its worth to Otis and his family, Otis could have an action for

replevin on the theory that money cannot adequately compensate the loss.

Point for Discussion
What type of legal relationship originally existed between Otis and Emily?

 CASE

FLICKINGER v. MARK IV APARTMENTS ASSOCIATION

315 N.W.2d 794
(Iowa 1982).

SCHULTZ, Justice.

Defendant, Mark IV Apartments Association, appeals and plaintiff, Barbara A. Flickinger, cross-appeals from the judgment of the trial court in a replevin action, which was tried to the court. We find no error and affirm the trial court.

On September 4, 1976, Flickinger was delinquent on her rental obligation to Mark IV. She returned to her apartment at approximately 9:00 p.m. but was unable to gain entrance because Mark IV had installed a new lock. Mark IV had previously utilized such a "lock-out" as a means of collecting rent from Flickinger. On this occasion, however, Flickinger did not contact Mark IV with respect to either access to the apartment or payment of the overdue rent. She left Iowa City and within a few days was arrested in Hardin County, where she was incarcerated until November 10, 1976.

Flickinger's parents, Pennsylvania residents, came to Iowa and took custody of her children. Before returning to Pennsylvania, the parents apprised Mark IV of Flickinger's situation and were allowed to remove the children's clothing and toys from the apartment. Mark IV then moved the contents of Flickinger's apartment to a locked storage facility. When she was released from jail, Flickinger made no attempt to contact Mark IV to recover her property.

In January 1977, at which time Flickinger resided in Eldora, Iowa, Mark IV obtained a default judgment against her in the Johnson District Small Claims Court in the amount of $500 for the delinquent rent. Subsequently, Flickinger moved to Pennsylvania to be with her children and parents. Telephonic and written communications followed.

During a telephone conversation in August 1977, Mark IV advised Flickinger that her property had been stored and that she could settle the default judgment for $200. On January 20, 1978, Flickinger's attorney, a staff member of Hawkeye Legal Services Society, informed her that Mark IV wanted her property removed by February 15. On February 16 Mark IV gave Flickinger written notice to remove her possessions by March 13 or to give it written permission to dispose of the property. Flickinger responded by requesting that the property be allowed to remain in storage until May, and Mark IV assented. Flickinger then sent Mark IV three checks for $20 each, to be applied toward the settlement for the delinquent rent. Flickinger did not remove her furniture in May, however, and in September Mark IV notified Flickinger that if she did not remove her property it would be given to Goodwill Industries.

The evidence concerning the disposition of Flickinger's property is conflicting. Flickinger testified that she returned to Iowa City in the fall of 1978 and removed items of her property from the storage facility on three occasions. However, there was evidence by Mark IV that Flickinger removed property on a fourth occasion and told an employee of Mark IV to dispose of the remaining items. Flickinger testified that she received some, but not all, of her property. She stated that during her last telephone conversation with Mark IV she was informed that her remaining property was in the process of being disposed of and would not be there when she came to claim it. A representative of Mark IV testified that Flickinger had removed all of her property, however.

Flickinger introduced into evidence a schedule of the items of personal property she allegedly did not recover from Mark IV. The trial court found as a matter of fact that all of the items on the schedule, with the exception of baby clothes, had been wrongfully detained by Mark IV. The court ordered Mark IV to return the property to Flickinger or, if it were unable to do so, to pay her damages of $2471, the value assigned to the property by the court.

Mark IV contends that (1) the record does not support the trial court's finding that it wrongfully detained Flickinger's property, and (2) the trial court erred in refusing to award it storage charges for the period of time it had possession of the property. . . .

General Principles.
Replevin is an action to recover specific personal property that has been wrongfully taken or wrongfully detained, with an incidental right to damages caused by reason of such detention. See generally 66 Am.Jur.2d Replevin § 2 (1973); 77 C.J.S. Replevin § 1 (1952). In Iowa the action is statutory, ch. 643, The Code; it combines the features of the common-law actions of replevin and detinue, Dvorak v. Avery, 208 Iowa 509, 510, 225 N.W. 947, 947 (1929). The pleading requirements are contained in section 643.1, The Code. The petition must state, inter alia: facts showing the plaintiff's right to possession of the property; that the property was neither taken pursuant to court order or judgment nor attachment or execution, or, if so, that it was exempt from seizure by such process; and the alleged cause of the detention of the property. § 643.1(3)–(5), The Code.

[1] The gist of a replevin action is enforcement of the plaintiff's right to immediate possession of the property wrongfully taken or

detained. Iowa Truck Center, Inc. v. Davis, 204 N.W.2d 630, 631 (Iowa 1973); Marx Truck Line, Inc. v. Fredricksen, 260 Iowa 540, 546, 150 N.W.2d 102, 105 (1967); Ritchie v. Hilmer, 251 Iowa 1002, 1004, 103 N.W.2d 858, 859 (1960); Harrow v. Ryan, 31 Iowa 156, 158 (1870); Gimble v. Ackley, 12 Iowa 27, 30 (1861). A wrongful taking need not be by forcible dispossession; any unlawful interference with, or assertion of control over, the property is sufficient. 77 C.J.S. Replevin § 53. A wrongful detention occurs when the defendant wrongfully withholds or retains possession of the property sought to be recovered. 66 Am.Jur.2d Replevin § 24.

Replevin is an action at law. § 643.2, The Code. When the action is tried to the court, its findings of fact have the force of a jury verdict and are binding on appeal if supported by substantial evidence in the record; review is upon assigned errors of law. Ritchie, 251 Iowa at 1004, 103 N.W.2d at 859; Glenn v. Keedy, 248 Iowa 216, 219, 80 N.W.2d 509, 511 (1957).

II. Wrongful detention.
The trial court found that Mark IV, without legal process, locked Flickinger out of her apartment and wrongfully detained her personal property that furnished the apartment. The court, however, also found that Mark IV was amenable to allowing Flickinger to recover her property and did not at any time deny her the opportunity to remove the property. Mark IV contends that the court seems to have found a wrongful taking rather than a wrongful detention. It concedes that the "lock-out" constituted a wrongful taking, since it thereby obtained control over Flickinger's property. However, it claims that, unless followed by a wrongful detention, a wrongful taking will not sustain an action in replevin.

[2] Mark IV's assertion that the fact that Flickinger was at all times free to recover her property changed the nature of its possession from wrongful to rightful is without merit. Once there has been a wrongful taking or detention, possession does not become rightful until some form of redelivery occurs. Wrongful possession of property does not become rightful merely by

agreeing to allow recovery by the party entitled to possession.

[3][4] When the plaintiff in a replevin action satisfies the burden of proving a wrongful taking of property, the burden shifts to the defendant to show that he or she no longer has possession; if the defendant fails to do so, it is presumed that possession continues. Waterhouse v. Black, 87 Iowa 317, 322, 54 N.W. 342, 344 (1893); 29 Am.Jur.2d Evidence § 239 (1967); 66 Am.Jur.2d Replevin § 99; 77 C.J.S. Replevin § 173. Although Mark IV maintained that Flickinger had recovered all of her property, the trial court's finding of facts reveal that it believed Flickinger's contradictory evidence. Since Mark IV failed to satisfy its burden to show that it no longer had possession, the trial court was entitled to presume that its wrongful possession continued. See Waterhouse, 87 Iowa at 322, 54 N.W. at 344.

Since Mark IV did not have rightful possession of Flickinger's property, we find no merit in its contention that it was entitled to storage charges.

III. Damages for loss of use.
In Universal C.I.T. Credit Corp. v. Jones, 227 N.W.2d 473, 478 (Iowa 1975), this court summarized the law of damages in a replevin action as follows:

(1) The injured party may demand the return of his property plus damages for its wrongful detention.

(2) He may seek judgment for the money value of the property, treating the conversion as complete either at the time it was taken or at the time of trial.

(3) If the former, he may have interest on the value as determined by the trier of fact from the date of the seizure until the date of judgment and nothing more. The judgment itself, of course, bears interest thereafter.

(4) If he elects under (2) above to rely on a conversion as of the time of trial, he may have the money value of the property as of that date, plus damages for loss of use from the time it was seized until the time of trial.

Flickinger maintains that since she elected to treat the conversion as occurring at the time of trial she is entitled to loss-of-use damages from the time of the lock-out until the time of trial.

We have thoroughly considered all of the parties' contentions, whether or not expressly addressed in this opinion, and find no reversible error.

Accordingly, we affirm the judgment of the trial court.

AFFIRMED.

Case Question
Why shouldn't the landlord have the right to hold property in lieu of rent?

Assignment 8.9

Create a factual setting that is an example of each of the following:

(a) gratuitous bailment
(b) lost property
(c) mislaid property
(d) confused property
(e) property subject to an action for conversion
(f) property subject to an action for trespass to chattels
(g) property subject to an action for replevin

ETHICAL NOTE

Pervasive throughout property law are ethical principles. Because most property agreements are contractual in nature, the same ethical concepts of honesty and fair dealing apply to property transactions as to other types of contracts. In addition, some aspects of property lease or ownership involve long-term relationships between the interested parties. As a result, the parties have an ongoing duty to consider the legal and ethical expectations of the other when taking action with respect to the property. A landlord should make defects in rental property known to a tenant. Additionally, the landlord has the obligation not only legally but also as a matter of business ethics to keep the property habitable. One who sells property to another makes certain representations about the condition of the property. Failure to do this in an honest manner not only can have legal implications but also reflects on the seller's ethical standards and may, in fact, affect future transactions. Ethics in property—and in all activities, for that matter—not only involve moral standards of the individual but also have a direct effect on professional interactions in society.

Question

If a property seller knows of a significant defect in property but the buyer does not ask about it, does the property seller (owner) have an *ethical* (not necessarily legal) obligation to tell the buyer about the defect?

CHAPTER SUMMARY

Property law is a very complex area and is still changing today. It is important to remember that principles of property law may vary somewhat from state to state. Consequently, it is necessary to examine the laws of a particular state before evaluating the rights or obligations with respect to personal or real property. This chapter has discussed basic principles as they have developed until now. However, as changes continue to occur, it is necessary to keep abreast of modifications of the law of property.

A final note to remember in all property transactions is that each of the areas discussed in the text, when relevant, should be thoroughly addressed in clear and written terms in any document that represents the property interests of owners and others with an interest or rights in the property. Most legal disputes occur as the result of misunderstandings at the time of the transactions. Such misunderstandings can

be avoided through prudent consideration of all pertinent issues by each party.

The basic tenets of property law are that real property involves all land and items so attached to the land that they are immovable. Personal property are those movable items in which ownership can be readily transferred and actual possession exchanged. Fixtures are those items of personal property that have been affixed to real property in such a way that they cannot be removed without damage to the real property.

Interests in personal property can be affected by bailment or by losing, mislaying, or abandoning the property by the owner. Nonowners can obtain the property by sale, conversion, or trespass or by finding it. Real property interests can be affected by sale, inheritance, devise, easements, trespass, or adverse possession. The remedy for one whose property or interest in it has been altered depends upon the type of property and the manner in which the property was affected. In some cases, the original owner may actually lose his or her interest in the property if care is not taken to protect it.

REVIEW QUESTIONS

1. What is the right of survivorship, and when is it considered part of an ownership interest?
2. How may one obtain ownership of property without a voluntary transfer by the current owner? Name the term and its elements.
3. What is tenancy in common?
4. What type of interest does a single purchaser of real property receive in American law?
5. Distinguish replevin, conversion, and trespass to chattels.
6. What is an easement, and who are the dominant and servient tenements?
7. If personal property is left in a known place, with a known person, and with the intent to retrieve the property, what has occurred?
8. Define and distinguish habitability and quiet enjoyment.
9. Define constructive eviction.
10. State and define the implied warranty given by every landlord to every tenant.

CHAPTER TERMS

Fee Simple

Fixture

Forced Share

Freehold Estate

Joint Tenancy

Life Estate

Non-Freehold Estate

Personal Property

Real Property

Right of Survivorship

Tenancy in Common

Tenancy by the Entirety

NOTES

1. Statsky, *Legal Thesaurus/Dictionary* (St. Paul: West, 1982).
2. Id.
3. Boyer, *Survey of the Law of Property*, 3rd ed. (St. Paul: West, 1981), p. 12.
4. Id.
5. Id.
6. Id.
7. Id.
8. *Wagman v. Carmel*, 601 F.Supp 1012, 1015 (E.D.Pa. 1985).
9. *Bouska v. Bouska*, 159 Kan. 276, 153 P.2d 923 (1944).
10. *Daniel v. Wright*, 352 F.Supp. 1, 3 (D.D.C. 1972).
11. 63 Am.Jur.2d, Property.
12. *Sneed v. Weber*, 307 S.W.2d 681, 690 (Mo.App. 1958).
13. Powell & Rohan, *Powell on Property*: Matthew Bender (1968); Restatement of the Law of Property Sec. 404, American Law Institute.
14. *Putnam v. Dickinson*, 142 N.W.2d 111, 124 (N.D. 1966).
15. *Huggins v. Castle Estates, Inc.* 36 N.Y.2d 427, 369 N.Y.S. 2d 80, 330 N.E.2d 48, 51 (1975).
16. 40 Annot., 27 A.L.R. 2d 444.
17. Annot., 36 A.L.R.4th 544.
18. 8 American Jurisprudence Sec. 2, Bailments.
19. Ch. 12, Torts, Infra.
20. Annot. A.L.R. 3d 1294.
21. See note 18, page 239.
22. *Carpenter v. Coles*, 75 Minn. 9, 77 N.W. 424 (1898); *Thomas v. Mrkonich*, 247 Minn. 481, 78 N.W.2d 386 (1956).

23. See note 34, Sec. 1014[2] Annot. 96 A.L.R.3d Sec. 1014[2].
24. See note 23, Sec. 865.6[4][c][ii][B].
25. Id.
26. *Thacker v. J.C. Penney Co.,* 254 F.2d 672, 676 (8th Cir. 1958).
27. Id.
28. *Paul v. Traders & General Ins. Co.,* 127 So.2d 801, 802, (La.App. 1961).
29. See note 23, Sec. 633.33.
30. Id.; 42 U.S.C.A. § 2000a et seq.
31. Rose, *Landlord & Tenants:* (Transactions Books, 1973), p. 14.
32. Id., pp. 38–41.
33. Id.
34. Annot. 96 A.L.R.3d 1155.
35. See note 16, page 512.
36. Id.
37. *Ralston Steel Car Co. v. Ralston,* 112 Ohio St. 306, 147 N.E. 513 (1925).
38. See note 18.
39. Id. See note 18.
40. Id.
41. *United States Fire Ins. Co. v. Paramount Fur Services, Inc.,* 168 Ohio St. 431, 156 N.E.2d 121 (1959).
42. *Favorite v. Miller,* 176 Conn. 310, 407 A.2d 974 (1978).
43. *Paset v. Old Orchard Bank & Trust Co.,* 62 Ill.APp.3d 534, 19 Ill.Dec. 389, 393, 378, N.E.2d 1264, 1268 (1978).
44. 8 American Jurisprudence, Sec. 62, Bailments.
45. See note 8.
46. See note 8.
47. *Schley v. Couch,* 155 Tex. 195, 284 S.W.d 2d 333, 335 (1955).
48. See note 7.
49. Annot., 39 A.L.R. 553.
50. 63 American Jurisprudence Sec. 14, Property.
51. *Ready-Mix Concrete Co. v. Rape,* 98 Ga.App. 503, 106 S.E.2d 429, 435 (1958).

CHAPTER 9

Torts

CHAPTER OBJECTIVES

After reading this chapter, you should be able to

- *Distinguish negligence from intentional torts.*
- *Distinguish negligence from strict liability.*
- *Explain the applicability of respondeat superior in tort cases.*
- *List the defenses to claims of negligence.*
- *Discuss the applicability of the doctrine of last clear chance.*

- *List the types of action for defamation.*
- *List the elements of negligence.*
- *List the requirements for application of res ipsa loquiter.*
- *Distinguish the torts of assault and battery.*

Tort law encompasses a wide range of subjects, including most subjects of law not directly related to contract principles (see Chapter 7) or criminal law (see Chapter 12). An exploration of some of these subjects may be the best way to explain or define the place of torts in the American legal system.

WHAT IS A TORT?

Legal authorities have been unable to agree on a single definition of a tort, although most would accept the following:

> A civil (as opposed to criminal) wrong (other than a breach of contract) that has caused harm to person or property.[1]

This definition cannot begin to encompass everything that constitutes the law of torts in this country. Fittingly, it concentrates on what is not a tort.

By definition tort law involves only civil matters, including disputes between individual citizens and businesses or governments (state or federal) over private or proprietary rights. In other words, the parties in a tort case are involved in a dispute over rights of an individual's person or property or the property of the government. Tort law does not include criminal matters (matters in which the government acts against a party charged with a crime that injures the public good and, in many cases, specific citizens). Criminal law encompasses cases ranging from speeding in a vehicle to murder in the first degree. Tort claims that involve the government are actions regarding the value of property owned by the government or actions involving disputes between government officials and private citizens over private rights, for example, a car accident involving a government official driving a government vehicle and a private citizen driving his or her private vehicle. Dependent upon fault for the accident, one party might sue the other for personal injuries and property damage to the vehicle. This particular action would not encompass any criminal charges that might arise from the accident. Such charges would be dealt with in a separate criminal case.

A tort does not include breach of contract. Although contract actions are included in the definition of civil law, the elements of a lawsuit in tort are different from the elements of a case in contract. Contract actions occur when two or more parties voluntarily enter into a legal relationship with certain rights and obligations and subsequently a dispute arises as to the nature or extent of those rights or obligations. In contrast, a tort arises when a party infringes on the rights of another person (or government) when there was no permission or agreement to do so and causes harm as a result of that infringement. This does not mean, however, that the parties were never involved in a relationship. Rather, it means that the action (tort) committed by one party was without permission or approval of the other party irrespective of the parties' relationship.

The formal definition of a tort indicates that some harm must occur. This is an important element of the definition. No matter how seriously one party may infringe upon the rights of another party, unless there is a verifiable harm that requires some form of compensation to repair it, there is no action in tort.

The individual circumstances of a situation have a great influence on the viability of a lawsuit. In an attempt to provide a better understanding of tort law and the role circumstances play in it, the following sections explore the development of tort law and some specific types of torts that are commonly litigated in this country.

THE DEVELOPMENT OF TORT LAW

Like much of the law in the majority of U.S. jurisdictions, the American concept of tort law began in England. During the Middle Ages, the royal government instituted what came to be known as forms of action.[2] These forms were similar to modern laws that state the types of lawsuits that can and cannot be brought by a citizen. When someone had a grievance against another, the injured party was required to file a complaint stating the facts and, specifically, which form of action (law) allowed him or her to bring the lawsuit. The forms were very limited and vague as to the types of conduct allowed as the basis for a lawsuit. Thus, it was often difficult to know whether one had a successful legal claim against another.

Trespass and Trespass on the Case

Two of the most commonly employed forms of action were trespass and trespass on the case.[3] To avoid confusion, it is important to note that during the Middle Ages the word *trespass* meant "wrong" rather than its current meaning of intrusion into another's property. The difference between trespass and trespass on the case was at first quite simple. A lawsuit based on trespass meant that the alleged guilty party had acted in such a way that the party bringing the lawsuit was directly injured because of the wrongful conduct. Trespass on the case, on the other hand, was appropriate when the injury was indirect. Consider the following scenarios:

1. A farmer is building a new fence for his pasture. He takes the old fence posts and throws them alongside the adjacent road. Just as he throws a large post, a horse and rider round the bend and are struck and injured by the post.
2. A farmer is building a new fence for his pasture. He takes the old fence posts and throws them alongside the adjacent road. Some of the posts actually land in the road. That night as a neighbor is returning home in the dark, he trips over a fence post and lands unconscious in the ditch by the road.

Scenario 1 illustrates an action of trespass, while scenario 2 is an action of trespass on the case. The difference is that the injury in the second example did not result directly from the farmer's throwing the post. Rather, the injury occurred as an indirect result. The direct result of the farmer's action was the post landing in the road, and as a further (or indirect) result of that, the neighbor was injured.

Through the years, lawsuits were filed on this type of basis in both England and America. It became increasingly difficult, however, to distinguish between trespass and trespass on the case. In addition, insufficient attention was being paid to whether or not the act was intentional. In response, the courts and law-making authorities attempted to define the terms, but the confusion continued.

Liability of Parties

In the early 1800s, several things happened that led to the development of tort law as it exists in the United States today. At that time, the law in effect made certain persons dealing with the public liable (responsible) for injuries caused by them.[4] For example, doctors and smiths (metal workers) were automatically considered to be liable as a matter of contract with their customers. Others, such as innkeepers and carriers (stagecoaches and the like), were liable by legislative statutes for failure to provide adequately for the safety of their customers. As the populations of urban areas increased, carriage accidents among private citizens rose dramatically, as did injuries from employment as the industrial revolution got under way. These developments led the American courts in the 1820s to accept the action of negligence as a basis for liability.[5] Negligence applied to all persons, including parties not previously included by contract or law, in disputes over injuries received as the result of a person's failure to act carefully in the interest of others.

Shortly after the emergence of negligence as a legal concept, the courts began to develop and refine related bases for liability, such as the actions for intentional torts and, later, strict liability. Hand in hand with these came the creation of legal defenses for conduct that would otherwise be considered improper.

Increase in Tort Claims

In recent years, the term *litigation explosion* has become commonplace. With the increase in technology, industry, and population, the number of lawsuits has increased dramatically. While property and contract suits are prevalent, much of the focus of law has been on the increasingly large number of tort claims filed each year. A primary reason for the attention given to these claims are the effects of such claims on the economy as a whole. Many actions in tort are defended by insurance companies that insure the defendant, for example, automobile insurance that covers claims that the insured person caused damage with the insured automobile. Claims of professional liability, premises liability (home or business owners), etc., all contribute to the suits in which the cost of defending a lawsuit is borne by the insurance company. The chain reaction is that as costs for the insurance company increase, costs of insurance premiums go up. As these increases are passed on in costs to consumers they contribute to overall inflation.

In response to this "explosion," many legislatures have adopted laws that place restrictions on the amounts that can be awarded in certain types of tort claims and sometimes even on the circumstances under which certain tort claims can be filed. With the increased amount of litigation in tort law has come a refinement of many tort concepts into well-established doctrines. Although many of these doctrines are examined later in the chapter, keep in mind that as society changes and evolves, so does its law.

TERMINOLOGY IN TORTS

It is helpful at this point to examine certain essential terms frequently encountered in the law of torts. The following list, though not exhaustive, provides an initial explanation of some of the more commonly employed terminology in torts.

- *Negligence.* The term **negligence** is the basis for those causes of action among parties who claim (1) that a legal duty was owed by another; (2) that by failing to engage in reasonable conduct (of a standard that would prevent the harm), that duty was violated or breached; and (3) that as a proximate (reasonable) result of that breach, the complaining party was significantly injured. Specifically, the elements that must be proven by facts introduced to the court to sustain a cause of action in negligence are (1) duty, (2) the standard of care, (3) breach of the standard, and (4) damage proximately caused by the breach.

- *Reasonable conduct.* Throughout the law of negligence, conduct of the alleged wrongdoer is measured against the standard of reasonableness (what would have been proper). Most often, the actions or omissions of a party accused of negligence are measured against what the conduct of a reasonable person would have been. The conduct of a reasonable person varies with the circumstances of each case. However, this person is always presumed to be one who would act with care and attention to all details that affect the situation. **Reasonable conduct** requires the actor to evaluate the surroundings, all benefits, and all risks and to respond in the most careful manner. This measurement of the reasonableness of the alleged liable person does not usually take into account the mental state of the actor. It does, however, take into account the intelligence, age, experience, and physical conditions over which the actor has no control.

- *Foreseeability.* In negligence, one cannot be held responsible for an injury caused as a result of one's conduct unless the risk of that injury was apparent (foreseeable). Foreseeability is determined by a finding of whether the risk of harm was known to the actor by constructive knowledge. This finding is generally based on what the actor knew or, by reasonable examination of the situation, should have known. Foreseeability plays a key role in determining what the reasonable standard of care should have been. A person must be able to foresee an occurrence before he or she can be held responsible for it.

Negligence
An act or failure to act toward another when (1) a duty was owed to the other person; (2) the act or failure to act was less than a reasonable person would have done under the circumstances; (3) the act or failure to act was the direct cause of injury to the other person; and (4) the injury resulted in measurable financial, physical, or emotional damage to the other person.

Reasonable Conduct
That action or nonaction that is appropriate under the circumstances when all risks and benefits are taken into account.

Proximate Cause
The direct cause that is sufficient to produce a result. There can be no other intervening force that occurs independently and prior to the result that is also sufficient to produce the result.

Intentional Tort
An act that the actor knows or should know, with substantial certainty, will cause harm to another.

Strict Liability
Liability without fault. Applied in situations where the intention or neglect of the party is immaterial. The mere performance of the act will result in liability.

- *Proximate cause.* The necessary relationship between a breach of a duty and claimed damage in a negligence action is **proximate cause.** To sustain an action for negligence, the injured party must prove that the injuries occurred as a consequence of the breach of the duty by the actor both as a matter of fact and as a matter of law.
- *Intentional tort.* This category of torts differs from negligence in several respects. The primary distinguishing factor is the element of intent. In an **intentional tort,** it is necessary for the actor to have the intent to engage in conduct that will, with near certainty, produce a result that invades the rights of or injures another. It is necessary not that the intent be to invade or injure but that the actor know or should know that the action will in all probability produce such an invasion or injury.
- *Strict liability.* A narrower (but steadily growing) area of tort law in the United States is **strict liability.** It is not concerned with fault or intent to cause injury. Rather, it is applied in situations where the actor derives some benefit from an activity that is extremely dangerous to other parties who have no control over the situation. The reasoning behind strict liability is that one who benefits from such a dangerous activity should shoulder the responsibility for injuries to innocent persons or property caused by it regardless of how carefully the actor conducts the activity.

Throughout the remainder of the chapter, additional peripheral terms will be introduced that play an important role in the various aspects of tort law. It is important to note that although these terms have general meanings accepted by most, some states have employed variations of these definitions when developing their own tort law.

NEGLIGENCE

In an action for negligence, the injured party must plead, and ultimately prove at trial, facts of an occurrence showing that each of the necessary elements existed. Only after such proof will the defendant (the party who is alleged to be at fault) be required to compensate the plaintiff for the injuries. The following elements[6] must be proven:

1. The actor (defendant) owed a *duty* to the injured party (plaintiff) to refrain from conduct that would cause injury.
2. By failing to exercise a care of a reasonable *standard,* the actor *breached* his or her duty.
3. The breach of the duty *proximately caused* an *injury* to the plaintiff.
4. The plaintiff's injuries are significant enough to warrant *compensation* from the actor.

The Concept of Duty

The first element that must be proven in any negligence action is that of duty. Specifically, the injured party (plaintiff) must demonstrate that the actor (defendant) owed a duty of acting with care for the plaintiff's safety or well-being.

It is commonly accepted that all persons have a general duty not to act negligently and thereby harm others around them. This general duty also includes the responsibility to act carefully for one's own safety under the circumstances. It should be noted that there are occasions when the duty is to act rather than to refrain from acting. Therefore, failing to act—an omission—can also be a violation of a person's duty. An example of such an omission is a situation where danger to another is within a person's control and the person fails to exercise that control even though he or she has the opportunity to do so.

 APPLICATION 9.1

Albert was driving while eating food from a fast-food restaurant. While pouring ketchup on his french fries, he swerved into the oncoming lane, forcing another car off the road.

Michelle was mopping floors in an office building. She generally displayed a Wet Floor sign, but on this occasion forgot to place the sign up in an area she had just mopped.

Point for Discussion
What was the duty owed in each of the preceding situations?

Range of Possible Injury

To prove the element of duty in a negligence action, several things must be shown. The first is that the defendant owed a duty to the plaintiff who was injured. It is not necessary to show that the defendant owed a duty to this particular individual. Rather, it must be shown that the defendant knew or should have known that others within a certain range (which included the plaintiff) could be affected by his or her actions.

Two primary schools of thought exist as to the area this range should include. One theory is often called the Zone of Danger,[7] which refers to the area that the defendant should reasonably expect or foresee his or her actions to affect. Consequently, no duty is owed, and no negligence can be shown for injuries that occur beyond the Zone of Danger. This means that usually there can be no recovery for injuries that are the result of remote or bizarre chain reaction events. Whether something is remote or not is generally determined by whether the defendant's conduct proximately caused the plaintiff's injuries. (Proximate cause is addressed in greater detail later.)

The second theory is the World-at-Large Approach,[8] which takes into account a much wider range. It requires the defendant to foresee more remote possibilities of harm to persons not in the immediate area and of injuries not as readily foreseeable to occur from his or her conduct. The defendant is expected to identify all persons in the surroundings who could reasonably be subjected to danger of injury as the result of the defendant's actions. The extent of this range also turns on a question of whether the conduct proximately caused the injury, but it allows a more indirect chain of events to be included as to what composes proximate cause.

Degree of Duty

Once it has been shown that the plaintiff was within the area that the defendant should have expected to be affected by his or her conduct, it is necessary to establish the degree of duty that is relative to the degree of risk of injury. The defendant's actions will expose the plaintiff to certain risks in the range where risk exists. The defendant is responsible for those risks that foreseeably could cause significant harm. What this means is that when a party engages in conduct that may affect others in the surrounding area, that actor must act carefully so as not to allow that conduct to injure those persons in ways that can be reasonably foreseen. Thus, the lower the risk of significant injury, the less the degree of duty owed to others to protect them. An example is the floor of a grocery store. Although the store would have a duty to keep its floor reasonably clean from spills and debris, it would not be required to post a guard in each aisle to warn customers of recently mopped areas. A cautionary sign would be sufficient.

In some instances, a specific duty is imposed by statute or common law. The legislature and judiciary have identified particular situations as those in which a duty is always warranted. An example is traffic laws. With the establishment of these laws came the duty to obey the laws for the safety of others as well as oneself.

The Standard of Care

Once it has been established that a duty existed between the defendant and the plaintiff, it must then be established that the defendant violated the duty. This is accomplished by first establishing the appropriate standard of care to which the defendant should have adhered.

The usual test applied in negligence actions is whether the defendant, under all the circumstances, exercised ordinary (reasonable) care.[9] Whether the defendant acted with ordinary care or not is determined by measuring his or her conduct against what the reasonable person would have done in a similar situation. On the one hand, no two situations are alike, and each must be judged in light of its own unique circumstances. On the other hand, there are generally enough similarities to other commonly encountered situations that a determination can be made of what a reasonable person would have done.

It is important to note that the reasonable person in each case is presumed to have the same characteristics of age, intelligence, experience, and physical ability (or disability) as the defendant.[10] Also to be considered are (1) the underlying reason or necessity of the defendant's conduct (was it an act of great social value, such as saving a life?), (2) the surrounding physical environment, (3) any activities that were taking place, and (4) the types of people in the area (was it an area, for example, where disabled children were playing?).[11]

The particular mental ability or disability of the defendant is generally not considered.[12] The mental ability of an intoxicated defendant is no doubt impaired, but intoxication is a voluntary condition, and liability for one's actions cannot be escaped through this method. In addition, one cannot possibly identify degrees of mental ability in all those possible negligent persons who surround him or her and then take appropriate measures of protection. Consequently, most courts have determined that the actor is in the best position to determine what is and is not safe conduct given his or her mental ability. Keep in mind that the courts can moderate this rule by considering the age, experience, intelligence, and physical condition of the defendant, which may affect the mental ability consideration. An example is a defendant who is mentally retarded. In some cases, retardation so affects a person's intelligence that mental ability to evaluate circumstances is impaired. Conversely, someone certified or serving in the capacity of a specialist or an expert in some field (like a brain surgeon or bankruptcy lawyer) can be held to a higher standard of care than the average member of his or her respective profession.

After determining who the reasonable person is in a situation, the court must determine how the reasonable person would have acted. This is done while keeping in mind that the reasonable person takes into account all details of the surroundings, appreciates all foreseeable risks, and acts in the most prudent and careful manner. Once this is determined, the standard of care is established.

It should be pointed out that in some cases, standards other than ordinary care are applied. Two other standards sometimes applied are extraordinary (great) care and slight care. The standard of extraordinary care is usually applied in situations identified by the lawmaking authorities where the plaintiff is not capable of protecting himself or herself from the defendant's actions.[13] An example is common carriers such as buses, trains, and airplanes. Many jurisdictions require common carriers such as these to act with extraordinary care for the safety of their passengers who have virtually entrusted their lives to the carrier.

Slight care is the most basic of all duties to take even the most minimal action to prevent injuries to those in the surrounding area.[14] When this most basic and minimal duty is violated, many jurisdictions permit an action in addition or as an alternative to one for negligence. If there is a standard of ordinary care in place, the plaintiff may also be permitted to sue for punitive damages for the failure to exercise even slight care. Punitive damages are used in some jurisdictions in addition to compensatory damages. Punitives—or exemplary damages, as they are sometimes called—punish the defendant and are designed to deter others from such gross carelessness. Circumstances that impose only a duty of slight care include situations such as the duty of a landowner to trespassers. Although there is not a duty to obey a standard of ordinary care to persons invading another person's property, neither can a person willingly expose others to substantial risks of danger.

Proximate Cause

Regardless of the *degree* of duty (standard of care), a duty must be shown in each case of negligence. The plaintiff must also establish that the defendant in some respect breached or failed to meet the standard of care that accompanied the duty to the plaintiff. Following this, the plaintiff has the further burden of establishing a legally recognized causal link between the breach and the plaintiff's injury.

Proximate cause is a major element of any negligence action. The plaintiff must demonstrate that the defendant's conduct proximately caused the plaintiff's injuries.[15] The issue is decided in two parts. First, it must be shown that the injuries were the result of the conduct as a matter of factual occurrence (known as cause in fact). Second, it must be shown that the injuries were caused by the conduct as a matter of law (commonly called the legal cause).

Prosser, a well-known and respected authority on tort law, has said that proximate cause is the "reasonable connection between the act or omission of the defendant and the damage which the plaintiff has suffered. . . . Legal responsibility must be limited to those causes which are so closely connected with the result and of such significance that the law is justified in imposing liability."[16]

In the test of proximate cause, the cause in fact is generally the simplest factor to establish. The plaintiff needs only to trace a chain of events, short or long, that leads directly from the defendant's conduct to the plaintiff's injuries. This is influenced somewhat by the extent of the duty of the defendant, as discussed earlier. In simple situations, where there are no intervening forces or remote circumstances, cause in fact and legal cause may be established by the same evidence.

Tests for determining proximate cause. Two tests are commonly employed when deciding whether there has been proximate cause. Both are used in determining cause in fact. The first is often called the But For test.[17] Simply put, the question is asked, "But for the defendant's actions, would the plaintiff's injuries still have occurred?" This test is rarely applied, because a multitude of variables can contribute to the severity of an injury. Thus, the But For test is not appropriate for many situations.

The decline in the application of the But For test has been matched by the increasing use of Substantial Factor analysis,[18] which examines whether or not the defendant's conduct was a substantial factor in producing the plaintiff's injury.[19] If it was, irrespective of other factors that may have contributed, cause in fact has been established. Overall, substantial factor analysis seems to be a fairer method of determining cause in fact than the But For test.

 APPLICATION 9.2

Theresa is bicycling on a city street. She is listening intently to her radio and does not notice that she is approaching an intersection. As she enters the intersection, a car coming from another direction does not stop at a red light and proceeds directly toward Theresa. At the last moment, Theresa sees the car and swerves. In attempting to avoid the car, she rides her bike into a pedestrian.

Under the But For test, the pedestrian might not have a cause of action against Theresa for her careless biking. The accident might very well have happened anyway because of the negligence of the automobile driver. Applying substantial factor analysis, however, would result in a much stronger case against Theresa. Theresa's failure to acknowledge the intersection and its potential dangers was very likely a significant contributing factor to the accident.

Point for Discussion
Which test would provide a fairer result in this situation, and why?

Proving proximate cause.　When proximate cause becomes an issue, it can be the most disputed point in the case. Proximate cause is heavily influenced by the extent of the duty imposed by the court: the larger the area to which a defendant owes a duty, the greater the chance of a remote occurrence causing an injury to someone within that area. Consequently, such situations present a greater likelihood for an issue of proximate cause.

Sometimes an injury occurs and the cause is not easily foreseeable. In such a situation, proximate cause is not easily proven. Proximate cause is more than a chain of events from the act to the injury. It is a chain of events in which the actor should have reasonably foreseen the likelihood of injury. Proximate cause can be established in fairly remote situations, even when other forces come into play in producing the injury. However, when these remote situations are so removed that the occurrence is bizarre or is what is known as a freak accident, proximate cause will be difficult to establish. Similarly, when an intervening force capable of producing the injury independently occurs between the moment of conduct by the defendant and the moment of injury, the proximate cause is very difficult to prove in terms of the original defendant. Again, the courts often apply the But For test or Substantial Factor analysis to determine legal cause.

 APPLICATION 9.3

A collision occurs between vehicles A and B. The driver of car A begins walking along the highway to find help. As he is walking, a passing truck driver offers him a ride. While the driver of car A is in the truck, the truck driver has a heart attack and dies at the wheel. The truck crashes into a hillside, and the driver of car A is seriously injured. Although the driver of car B may have been negligent in the original collision, he most likely is not the proximate cause of the physical injuries to the driver of car A in the truck accident. Although the heart attack of the truck driver was a bizarre event, in and of itself, it was primarily responsible for the injuries to the driver of car A. This is true even though, as a matter of cause in fact, driver A's presence in the truck was substantially due to the collision with driver B.

Point for Discussion
Would there be legal causation if driver B (instead of a passing truck driver) was taking driver A for help and B suffered the heart attack?

Damage

A key element in any action for negligence is that of damage. The plaintiff must prove that he or she suffered some type of compensable injury, that is, that something happened to the plaintiff or the plaintiff's property as the proximate result of the defendant's breach of the standard of care that warrants compensation by the defendant to the plaintiff. For example, the fact that the plaintiff was delayed by the defendant's actions in and of itself is probably not sufficient. However, if the defendant's negligent conduct is the cause of a delay to the plaintiff that causes the plaintiff to suffer monetary loss (e.g., miss a flight for an important business trip), the defendant may be required to compensate the plaintiff.

Damage comes in many forms—monetary, physical, or mental/emotional. It may affect the person or the person's property. However, in a negligence action, it must be significant enough under the circumstances to warrant a monetary award as compensation.

 C A S E

**JORDAN v.
ATLANTA
REPLEX CORPORATION**

1997 WL 575875
(228 Ga.App. 670, 492 S.E.2d 536).

ELDRIDGE, Judge.

On January 8, 1995, Willie Jordan, the plaintiff and appellant, went with her family to the defendant's ice skating rink to skate. When plaintiff arrived, the rink was in use for a hockey practice which was running late, and plaintiff had to wait to skate. No one was allowed on the ice to skate until the hockey team finished their practice; at that time, the public, including the plaintiff, was allowed on the ice. Plaintiff had never ice skated prior to that day. Plaintiff began skating as soon as the ice rink was opened to the

public shortly after 6:45 p.m. Plaintiff's injury occurred around 7:30 p.m., after plaintiff had been skating about 30 minutes.

While skating, plaintiff felt her foot jerk, causing her to fall. Plaintiff described the fall as her toe catching and being grabbed and twisted around.

Aaron Jordan and William Pelham looked for the cause of plaintiff's fall and found a hole in the ice about two or three feet from her. The hole was grayish-white, ragged edges, two or three inches in diameter, about an inch in depth, and had a jagged ice skate mark coming out of the hole, which was filled with mushy ice and water; the hole had slush built-up around the edges as if someone had skated into the hole, knocking slush out. Ice was stuck in the front tip of plaintiff's skate. Unless someone was looking for the hole in the ice, it was not readily observable. Aaron Jordan stated his opinion that, based on the size of the hole, position of the hole and the plaintiff, and the ice in the toe of her left skate, plaintiff had tripped in the hole.

At the time of plaintiff's injury, Mr. Salim Barday was working at the ice rink as assistant manager. After plaintiff's fall, he inspected the ice in the area of the fall and did not find any hole in the ice. However, Mr. Jordan testified that he showed the hole to a skate monitor, who then covered the hole with a warning cone.

The plaintiff's family testified that the general condition of the ice surface was poor, in that there were a number of tiny little holes or divots in the surface and slushy areas. After the plaintiff was removed from the ice, the ice then was resurfaced.

Mr. Barday and Mr. Robinson testified that the ice rink surface is resurfaced just before each new skating session. The ice surface is about five to five and one half inches of frozen sand with about two to two and one half inches of ice on top. A skate guard or ice monitor continuously looks for holes or rink defects. Prior to resurfacing the ice, the surface is inspected by walking the rink and any "snow," i.e., shaved ice on the rink surface, is removed by running the Zamboni over it; if any big holes in the ice are found, then the hole is packed with snow. A hole an inch deep and two inches across is considered a small hole and can be easily repaired with a snow packing. A hole more than an inch deep would be very unusual. To resurface, the surface is shaved, watered, and allowed to freeze. To resurface and inspect takes only about ten minutes. The normal resurfacing schedule is after about 20 minutes for public or hockey sessions, in the middle of a session, and every 40 minutes for figure skating. A resurfaced ice rink allows skaters to glide better and is safer.

Mr. Barday does not recall if the rink was resurfaced between the hockey session and the public session, which would have been the normal thing to do. However, if the hockey practice ran late, then the ice is inspected only, and if the surface is deemed satisfactory, then the resurfacing is delayed. Mr. Barday does not remember inspecting the ice immediately prior to plaintiff's fall. An employee of the defendant told the family immediately after the fall that the ice rink had not been inspected or resurfaced after the hockey practice, because the practice had run late. Such inspection could have been done by the ice monitor after the rink had been cleared of the hockey team, which inspection would take five minutes to do. There are two ice monitors on the ice at all times who control conduct and look for debris and holes.

Ms. Stacy Kingry was the employee of the defendant who filled out an accident report for plaintiff based upon what the plaintiff and plaintiff's family told her. She never saw the hole in the ice or looked for it and was not told by any other employee that there was a hole.

Mr. Charles Robinson worked as the assistant manager of the Mountain Ice Chalet at Stone Mountain Memorial Association Park, which qualified him as an expert witness by experience on the operation and maintenance of an ice rink. He was working for the defendant as manager at the time of plaintiff's injury. According to Mr. Robinson, it is common and standard practice to inspect and resurface the ice after a hockey practice and prior to public admission. The reason to resurface the ice is to make the surface smooth and safe for skating. A rink should be resurfaced after a hockey practice and every hour to maintain a smooth surface.

At the time when plaintiff fell, the ice rink was crowded with between 200 and 300 skaters. Plaintiff was not looking at the ice in front of her while she skated and never saw the hole in the ice, because she could not skate while looking down, and with the number of skaters on the ice, she had to lookout for other skaters.

Plaintiff sued defendant for injuries caused by the fall. Defendant answered and filed a MOTION for SUMMARY JUDGMENT. The trial court granted summary judgment. Plaintiff filed a timely notice of appeal.

Plaintiff's enumeration of error is that the trial court erred in granting summary judgment. We agree.

Under Lau's Corp. v. Haskins, 261 Ga. 491, 450 S.E.2d 474 (1991), on MOTION for SUMMARY JUDGMENT must, the trial court must give the plaintiff the benefit of all reasonable, favorable inferences, and the burden to produce evidence does not shift to the plaintiff unless or until the defendant pierces the allegations of plaintiff's complaint by producing evidence that either shows that the facts alleged are not true, i.e., negates such essential elements, or shows that the plaintiff can produce no evidence to demonstrate the existence of such essential elements. OCGA s 9-11-56(e). "Summary judgment is appropriate when the court, viewing all the evidence and drawing reasonable inferences in a light most favorable to the non-movant, concludes that the evidence does not create a triable issue as to each essential element of the case." Jenkins v. Bi-Lo, 223 Ga.App. 735, 479 S.E.2d 14 (1996).

(a) This is a negligent maintenance case, because this case involves the alleged failure of the defendant to properly maintain its ice rink's surface in a condition that is safe and free of holes in the ice. "Because the defendant [deferred resurfacing the ice] or authorized the [failure to resurface the ice, it] is presumed to have knowledge of [the ice surface's condition]. See American Nat. Bank of Brunswick v. Howard, 117 Ga.App. 834, 161 S.E.2d 838 (1968). In this type of case, the plaintiff [made] out a cause of action by showing an act or omission on the part of the defendant which was the proximate cause of [her] injury, and when the defendant raised an affirmative defense and made out the elements of the prima facie defense, the plaintiff showed that [she] could not have avoided [such negligence] . . . through the exercise of ordinary care. See Hogg v. First Nat. Bank [of West Point], 82 Ga.App. 861, 62 S.E.2d 634 (1950). The weight of authority in cases where the plaintiff slips and falls, allegedly due to the defendant's negligence by maintaining a [dangerous ice surface], is that proof of nothing more than the occurrence of the fall is insufficient to establish the proprietor's negligence. . . . What the law requires is not warranty of the safety of everybody from everything, but such diligence toward making the [ice rink] safe as a good business man is in such matters accustomed to use. Thus the plaintiff must, at a minimum, show that the defendant was negligent either in the materials [it] used in treating the [ice rink] or in the [failure to resurface the rink]. . . . Defendant introduced testimony of [the assistant manager] who had examined the [ice rink surface some time] after plaintiff's fall and who found [no hole in the ice] nor any other defect in the [ice]. Defendant also introduced evidence that the [ice rink] had been [resurfaced prior to the hockey practice at 4:50 p.m.] prior to plaintiff's fall and had been trafficked [from 5:00

until 7:30 p.m.] by other [skaters]. Defendant's evidence was sufficient to pierce the pleadings of the plaintiff and to shift the burden to her to produce issuable evidence or suffer judgment. See Meade v. Heimanson, 239 Ga. 177, 236 S.E.2d 357 (1977)." Alterman Foods v. Ligon, 246 Ga. 620, 624-625, 272 S.E.2d 327 (1980).

While both Mr. Barday and Mr. Robinson testified that it was normal to inspect and resurface the ice for safety reasons between the hockey practice and the public session, they had no knowledge of whether or not it had been done on January 8th between the sessions at 6:45 p.m. They testified that the ice surface needed to be resurfaced about every 20 to 40 minutes, but if the hockey session ran late, then the resurfacing would be deferred until later, after a standard inspection had been made for holes. They had no knowledge of whether or not such inspection had, in fact been made, and none of the skating monitors testified. In his deposition, Mr. Barday testified that he could not recall whether or not the ice rink had been resurfaced between 5:30 and 6:45 p.m. If the last resurfacing of the ice was done at 5:30 and the fall occurred at 7:30 p.m., then the delay in resurfacing exceeded the time period set by the defendant by 80 to 100 minutes.

However, in his affidavit, Mr. Robinson, who was not at the rink at the time of the fall testified that "Mr. Barday and Stacey Kingry indicated to me that they believed the ice had in fact been resurfaced prior to the free skate." (Emphasis supplied.) Such statements are hearsay and lay opinions without a factual predicate, which required the trial judge to disregard this testimony on summary judgment. OCGA s 24-9-65; O'Kelley v. State, 175 Ga.App. 503, 507(3), 333 S.E.2d 838 (1985).

Mr. Barday testified both by affidavit and by his deposition that, upon inspection, he could not find the hole that plaintiff allegedly tripped in. Since the plaintiff, herself, did not know why she fell and never saw the hole, then this shifted the burden of producing evidence to the plaintiff.

If the plaintiff did not know the cause of her fall and could not present evidence to create a material issue of fact as to the cause of her fall and demonstrate that such cause was the consequence of a breach of duty of the owner/occupier, then the grant of summary judgment to the defendant would be appropriate. See Alterman Foods v. Ligon, supra at 624, 272 S.E.2d 327.

Plaintiff met her burden of producing evidence that created material issues of fact for the jury to decide. See OCGA s 9-11-56(e). First, the testimony of plaintiff's witnesses described her prone position on the ice as being three feet beyond a three inch wide hole, one inch deep, in the ice; skate marks that went through the hole; slush that had been knocked out of the hole and around the edge; and ice found in the left toe of plaintiff's ice skate, which was consistent with catching the skate in the hole. Mr. Jordon, a lay witness, after stating the foundational facts upon which his opinion was based, stated his opinion that the plaintiff had tripped on the hole. Plaintiff's testimony that something seemed to grab her left leg as she was skating and caused her body to twist around so that she fell on her back is consistent with catching the toe of the skate in the hole. These facts created a jury question as to the existence of the defect, a hole in the ice, and causation of the injury. Second, the testimony of plaintiff's family as to the existence of the hole in the ice created a conflict of material fact with Mr. Barday's testimony that he could not find a hole. Third, the plaintiff's family testified that there had been no resurfacing of the ice from the time of their arrival after 6:00 and their being allowed on the ice after 6:45 p.m., and that the condition of the ice at that time was poor. This evidence created material issues of fact as to defendant's lack of proper maintenance and the proximate cause of plaintiff's fall.

Finally, testimony as to the defendant's usual, normal, or customary practice regarding inspection and resurfacing is not evidence that such maintenance actually occurred on January 8th. Such evidence was a form of opinion testimony as to what possibly occurred. Absent testimony that the delay in resurfacing was, in fact, preceded by an inspection of the ice for holes by the ice monitors, such evidence is merely an inference of fact based upon custom and practice. Such favorable inference cannot be made for the defendant as all inferences drawn must be favorable to the plaintiff, as the non-movant. The reasonable inference, therefore, would be that no inspection was made, based on the existence of the hole and other defects in the ice.

The trial judge erred in granting summary judgment on the basis that plaintiff failed to produce evidence creating a material issue of fact as to breach of defendant's duty and causation of plaintiff's fall. The trial judge cannot make findings of fact on a MOTION for SUMMARY JUDGMENT by picking and choosing which evidence he will believe and by deciding that there is no evidence showing causation, when there is contrary evidence in the record; the jury must make a determination of weight and credibility as to disputed facts, as well as to opinion evidence. There was evidence creating jury issues as to breach of duty and causation. Union Camp Corp. v. Daley, 188 Ga.App. 756, 758, 374 S.E.2d 329 (1988).

(b) Since review of summary judgment is de novo, then we must determine whether defendant is entitled to summary judgment for any affirmative defense asserted, even though the trial court did not grant the motion on such basis. The defendant has the burden of proof of an affirmative defense at trial as well as on summary judgment. To prevail on summary judgment, the defendant must prove each and every essential element of such defense before the burden to produce evidence shifts to the plaintiff. See Continental Research Corp. v. Reeves, 204 Ga.App. 120, 127, 419 S.E.2d 48 (1992).

(b) (1) Contributory negligence.

Under the evidence presented by the plaintiff, the hole was white or grayish-white and looked much like the ice. Prior to the slush being knocked out, the hole was filled with slush and water so that it may be reasonably inferred that there was no depression in the ice which would indicate the presence of a hole beneath the slush. Both of these facts and reasonable inferences made thereon indicate that the hole was not readily discoverable; the witnesses found the hole only after searching for it. Following plaintiff's fall, the hole was discoverable, because the slush had been knocked up on the sides of the hole when plaintiff had skated across it. The hole was so difficult to discover that Mr. Barday, the assistant manager, never found it, even after the area was pointed out to him. Furthermore, the ice rink was crowded with between 200 and 300 people; skating faster than a walk made observing the ice ahead difficult to do, particularly with that number of people on the ice. The presence or absence of the hole is a jury question, because there exists a conflict in the evidence between the evidence of the plaintiff and the evidence of the defendant, which can not be decided by either this Court or the trial court as was done by the trial court and which creates a material issue of fact for jury determination, because the trier of fact must decide the weight and credibility to give to the evidence to determine whether or not a hole existed in the ice. There are several reasonable inferences that may be drawn from the testimony of Mr. Barday: (1) that there was no hole; (2) that he did not make a thorough search to discover the presence of the hole; or (3) that the ice monitor who placed the cone over the hole came back and repaired the hole by filling it with shaved ice to repair the hole prior to resurfacing the ice before Mr. Barday made his search. The trial court and this court on de novo review must make the inference most favorable to the plaintiff. Lau's Corp., supra at 491, 405 S.E.2d 474, which would require the denial of the MOTION for SUMMARY JUDGMENT.

The defendant presented no evidence that plaintiff failed to exercise ordinary care for her own safety, so that she could have avoided the hole; the hole was camouflaged by slush and by its color. Leonardson v. Ga. Power Co., 210 Ga.App. 574, 576, 436 S.E.2d 690 (1993). For plaintiff to be held to be contributorily negligent, plaintiff must have had an opportunity to avoid the result of the defendant's negligence, which means plaintiff knew or should have known of the danger and failed to avoid it when given the opportunity to avoid. Nelson & Budd, Inc. v.

Brunson, 173 Ga. App. 856, 857(3), 328 S.E.2d 746 (1985). There has been no evidence which shows that plaintiff knew of or could have reasonably discovered the hole, or that she had the opportunity to avoid it; therefore, summary judgment on this basis would have been error.

(b) (2) Assumption of the risk.

As a first time ice skater, plaintiff may be inferred to have been aware of at least two dangers from the common experience of a reasonably prudent person: (1) the slipperiness of the ice surface; and (2) danger of collision with other skaters. There was no evidence in the record that a first time skater should have known that the ice skating surface of the rink, if not timely resurfaced, would contain cracks, holes, pits, or defects in the surface or that a first time user would know to look for such defects and appreciate subjectively the danger of such defects. The record shows that she had no actual or subjective knowledge of the danger of tripping on holes in the ice. Absent evidence establishing plaintiff's actual and subjective knowledge of the danger, appreciation of the danger, and a conscious decision to take the known risk of injury, the affirmative defense of assumption of the risk has not been established. Vaughn v. Pleasent, 266 Ga. 862, 864(1), 471 S.E.2d 866 (1996). Thus, summary judgment could not be granted on this affirmative defense.

Judgment reversed.

Case Question

What is the material issue of fact in this case?

Res Ipsa Loquitur

"The thing speaks for itself" is the traditional translation of the Latin term *res ipsa loquitur.*[20] This doctrine has been applied for many years in cases of negligence involving very special circumstances. A plaintiff may claim the doctrine to ease the burden of proof in a case of negligence only when he or she can prove that (1) the occurrence was of a type that would not happen without negligence, (2) the instrument producing the injury during the occurrence was exclusively in the control of the defendant, and (3) the plaintiff did not contribute to the injury.[21]

Res ipsa loquitur is used in cases where the evidence that would disclose how the defendant was negligent is not available to the plaintiff. Such cases arise where the plaintiff or his or her witnesses have no opportunity to determine precisely which conduct produced the injury. To prevent unwarranted claims of negligence, however, the plaintiff must prove the three elements noted previously.

Although the doctrine of res ipsa loquitur is limited in its application, in appropriate cases, the plaintiff can use it to prove negligence where a cause of action might not otherwise be available for the simple reason that the plaintiff does not have access to information in the defendant's control or because there were no witnesses to the injury. It should be realized, however, that with broadening rules of discovery of information by parties, the doctrine is declining steadily.

 APPLICATION 9.4

Jennifer purchases a jar of jelly. Inside the cap is a plastic seal over the top of the jar. Jennifer breaks the seal and uses the jelly to make a sandwich. As she bites into the sandwich, she immediately feels a sharp pain in her mouth. Upon examination, she finds that the jelly contains ground glass. She brings a lawsuit against the manufacturer of the jelly on the basis of res ipsa loquitur. Jennifer has no access to evidence or witnesses concerning the actual cause of negligence. In an ordinary case, she could not prove the defendant's negligence was the cause of her injuries. Under an application of res ipsa loquitur, she need only prove that the injury would not ordinarily occur without negligence, that the instrument causing injury (the jar of jelly) was in the exclusive control of the defendant, and that she did not contribute to the cause of her injuries.

Point for Discussion
Would the case be treated any differently if there had been no protective seal on the product?

 CASE

HOLZHAUER v. SAKS & CO.

346 MD 328, 697 A.2d 89 (1997).

CHASANOW, Judge.

The United States District Court for the District of Maryland has certified the following three questions to this Court pursuant to the Maryland Uniform Certification of Questions of Law Act,

Maryland Code (1974, 1995 Repl.Vol., 1996 Supp.), Courts & Judicial Proceedings Article, ss 12-601 through 12-613, and Maryland Rule 8-305.

1. Do Appellant's allegations with respect to negligence amount to a waiver of RES IPSA LOQUITUR, as in Dover Elevator Co. v. Swann, 334 Md. 231, 638 A.2d 762 (1994)?
2. If not, does the doctrine of RES IPSA LOQUITUR apply under the facts thus far alleged in the instant case?

3. If the doctrine of RES IPSA LOQUITUR does apply, is there any reason, including the views expressed by the Court of Appeals in Dover, why the facts of this case require a different approach than that in Beach v. Woodward & Lothrop, Inc., 18 Md.App. 645, 308 A.2d 439 (1973) (Where the escalator "stop[ped] and start[ed] up with a jerk")?

We answer the first two questions in the negative. Our decision regarding question number two renders question number three moot.

The facts of the case are not disputed. On February 24, 1994, Appellant, Eugene Holzhauer, was shopping in the Saks Fifth Avenue department store in Owings Mills Mall. Appellant injured his right shoulder when the escalator upon which he was riding, with his hand on the railing, came to a sudden stop, causing him to stumble down ten to twelve steps in a twisting motion. Appellant filed suit in the United States District Court for the District of Maryland against Saks & Co., the owner of the escalator, and Montgomery Elevator Company, the organization hired to service and maintain the escalator (collectively "Appellees"). Appellant alleged that Appellees were negligent in:

> The suit was originally instituted in the Circuit Court for Baltimore County, but it was removed to the United States District Court for the District of Maryland based on the parties' diversity of citizenship. 28 U.S.C. s 1441.

a. "[M]aintain[ing] as a part of such escalator and the operating mechanism thereof, old, loose, worn, frayed, and antiquated parts, apparatus and equipment;

b. [F]ail[ing] to install in such escalator as a part of the operating mechanism thereof, a proper device to prevent said escalator from suddenly stopping when in use . . . ;

c. [P]ermitt[ing] such escalator and the working parts thereof to be and remain in a condition of disrepair for an unreasonable length of time;

d. [F]ail[ing] to inspect such escalator in a proper manner and at proper intervals;

e. [F]ail[ing] to warn plaintiff of the dangers connected with the escalator and to provide to plaintiff any protection from such dangers."

Appellant alleged, additionally, that Montgomery Elevator Company "negligently installed and maintained the escalator and failed to properly maintain, inspect and repair the escalator."

The following additional information was revealed during discovery. The parties do not know what caused the escalator to stop on February 24, 1994. The escalator had been inspected by the Maryland Department of Licensing and Regulation, Division of Labor and Industry Safety Inspection Unit in June of 1993. The escalator had not malfunctioned between the time of the inspection and the time of Appellant's injury, and it has not malfunctioned since Appellant's injury. On the day of the incident, the escalator remained stopped until a store employee restarted it with a key, at which time the escalator immediately began to run properly. Upon restarting, the escalator made no unusual movements or noises, and it did not require any repairs. Montgomery Elevator Company, in fact, was not informed of the events that occurred on February 24 until this suit was instituted.

The escalator was turned on and off daily, using a key, at the opening and closing of business by Saks & Co.'s Building Engineer or by a member of its Security Department. Any individual can also cause the escalator to stop by pushing one of the emergency stop buttons located at the top and bottom of the escalator, respectively. Once stopped, the escalator will not run again until it is started with a key.

Appellant has offered no additional evidence to support the allegations of negligence in his complaint, and it appears that he does not intend to offer expert testimony in the field of escalator maintenance, operations, or repair. The only expert witness listed on Appellant's Designation of Expert Witnesses is Dr. Steven Friedman, a medical doctor. Furthermore, in his Response to [Saks & Co's] Motion for Summary Judgment, Appellant states that "[he] is not offering any direct evidence or expert testimony, other than evidence of the event itself. He is not attempting to prove how or why the escalator stopped suddenly, only that it did."

Appellees filed Motions for Summary Judgment at the close of discovery, arguing that Appellant failed to produce evidence sufficient to sustain his burden of proof at trial. The Honorable Frank A. Kaufman initially granted the Appellees' Motions for Summary Judgment in a one sentence memorandum stating: "For reasons which this Court will shortly set forth in a more detailed document, to be filed in this case, this Court will enter summary judgment for defendants." When Judge Kaufman began to write the opinion in support of his ruling, however, he concluded that he could not continue without the answers to the three questions certified to this Court. Judge Kaufman has denied Appellees' Motions for Summary Judgment, and he will reconsider them once this Court has announced its decision.

The United States District Court seems to suggest by its phrasing of question number one that Dover Elevator Co. v. Swann, 334 Md. 231, 638 A.2d 762 (1994), stands for the proposition that the pleading of specific acts of negligence will preclude a plaintiff from relying on the doctrine of RES IPSA LOQUITUR. This is not so. Dover did not concern the mere pleading of acts of negligence; rather it dealt with a plaintiff's attempt to establish specific grounds of negligence at trial. We held, in that case, that one of the reasons why the plaintiff was prohibited from relying on res ipsa was because he proffered direct evidence of negligence at trial. Dover, 334 Md. at 237, 638 A.2d at 765 ("[N]umerous Maryland cases have explained that a plaintiff's 'attempt to establish specific grounds of alleged negligence precludes recourse to the doctrine of RES IPSA LOQUITUR.' ") (quoting Smith v. Bernfeld, 226 Md. 400, 409, 174 A.2d 53, 57 (1961)).

In Dover, David Swann was injured when he entered an elevator car, the floor of which was approximately one foot below the floor outside of the elevator. 334 Md. at 234, 638 A.2d at 764. He sued three defendants, one of which was Dover, the company that manufactured, installed, and maintained the elevator at issue. Id. Swann alleged in his Complaint that the defendants negligently designed, manufactured, installed, and maintained the elevator. Dover, 334 Md. at 234-35, 638 A.2d at 764. These pleadings, however, were not the reason that Swann was precluded from relying on res ipsa. Rather than ask the jury to draw an inference of defendant's negligence

from the mere fact that the elevator misleveled, Swann had an engineer/elevator consultant testify at trial that the elevator misleveled because the elevator's contacts were "burned" and that Dover was negligent in, inter alia, cleaning rather than replacing the burned contacts. Dover, 334 Md. at 244, 638 A.2d at 769.

We held that, under the circumstances, "the doctrine of RES IPSA LOQUITUR was inapplicable to the evidence before the jury. . . ." Dover, 334 Md. at 262, 638 A.2d at 777. The purpose of res ipsa, we explained, is to afford a plaintiff the opportunity to present a prima facie case when direct evidence of the cause of an accident is not available or is available solely to the defendant. Dover, 334 Md. at 237, 638 A.2d at 765. Direct evidence of the specific cause of his injuries was available to Swann, however, and he proffered that direct evidence to the jury in the form of an expert opinion. Thus, one of the reasons we held res ipsa to be inapplicable was because the expert "purport[ed] to furnish a sufficiently complete explanation of the specific causes of [the elevator's] misleveling, which . . . preclude[d] plaintiff's reliance on RES IPSA LOQUITUR." Dover, 334 Md. at 239, 638 A.2d at 766.

Unlike the petitioner in Dover, Appellant in the present case has not had the chance to proffer direct evidence as to the specific cause of his injuries. Thus far, he has only pleaded specific acts of negligence. This Court discussed the impact that pleading specific acts of negligence has on a claim of RES IPSA LOQUITUR in Joffre v. Canada Dry Ginger Ale, Inc., 222 Md. 1, 158 A.2d 631 (1960). In that case, a woman in a delicatessen was cut in the leg by a piece of glass when a Canada Dry soda bottle shattered. Joffre, 222 Md. at 3, 158 A.2d at 632. Appellant sued the Canada Dry bottler and the delicatessen. Id. Appellant alleged that the bottler was negligent in "placing on the market . . . a product designed for purchase in the original package without making that package safe against reasonably-to-be-anticipated variations in temperature and hazards of handling, and that the bottle was defective or the pressure within it excessive." Id. She alleged that the delicatessen "was negligent in failing to so locate and guard the bottle as to prevent injury to customers, knowing it might explode." Id. The judge directed a verdict for both defendants at the close of the plaintiff's evidence, and Appellant argued on appeal that summary judgment was improper and that she was entitled to submit her claim to the jury under the theory of RES IPSA LOQUITUR. Id. The delicatessen argued that Appellant was precluded from relying on that theory because she had pleaded specific acts of negligence. Joffre, 222 Md. at 3-4, 158 A.2d at 632.

This Court stated that the delicatessen's argument had previously been rejected in Maryland. Id. (citing State for Use of Parr v. Board of County Com'rs of Prince George's County, 207 Md. 91, 103-04, 113 A.2d 397, 402-03 (1955)). We explained that " '[t]he doctrine RES IPSA LOQUITUR is not a rule of pleading. It relates to burden of proof and sufficiency of evidence.' " Joffre, 222 Md. at 6, 158 A.2d at 634 whether a party will be precluded from relying on the doctrine of RES IPSA LOQUITUR turns upon the evidence produced by the party and whether that evidence satisfies the three essential components of RES IPSA LOQUITUR; whether specific allegations of negligence have been pleaded is of no moment. We answer the first certified question in the negative.

Appellant cannot satisfy the three essential components of RES IPSA LOQUITUR, however, and, for that reason, he may not rely on the doctrine in the present case. Three elements must be proven in order to create an inference of negligence on the part of a defendant: (1) a casualty of a kind that does not ordinarily occur absent negligence, (2) that was caused by an instrumentality exclusively in the defendant's control, and (3) that was not caused by an act or omission of the plaintiff. Dover, 334 Md. at 236-37, 638 A.2d at 765. Appellant cannot satisfy the first two criteria.

In order to rely on RES IPSA LOQUITUR, Appellant must first prove that the accident would not have occurred in the absence of Appellees' negligence.

"[T]he doctrine of RES IPSA LOQUITUR is applicable only when the facts and surrounding circumstances tend to show that the injury was the result of some condition or act which ordinarily does not happen if those who have the control or management thereof exercise proper

care. It does not apply where it can be said from ordinary experience that the accident might have happened without the fault of the defendant."

Greeley v. Baltimore Transit Co., 180 Md. 10, 12-13, 22 A.2d 460, 461 (1941). Appellant cannot satisfy this requirement because the evidence and inferences fairly deducible from the evidence indicate that, in addition to the possibility that Appellees were negligent, there is an equally likely explanation for the escalator's abrupt stop.

For safety reasons, the escalator in question was equipped with two emergency stop buttons, located at the top and bottom of the escalator, respectively. When either button is pushed, if the escalator is functioning as intended, the escalator will stop. The buttons are safety devices designed to stop the escalator quickly should a hand, foot, or article of clothing become caught; thus, ready accessibility to the buttons is only sensible. We cannot say that the escalator would not stop in the absence of Appellees' negligence because the escalator would also stop whenever any person pushed one of the emergency stop buttons.

The record is silent as to whether anyone did, in fact, push one of the stop buttons, but this is of little concern. The facts need not show that a stop button definitely was pushed to preclude reliance on res ipsa; they need only show that something other than Appellees' negligence was just as likely to cause the escalator to stop. The fact that the escalator had never malfunctioned before the day in question, and has not malfunctioned since, makes it equally likely, if not slightly more likely, that the escalator did not malfunction on the day in question but, rather, that it stopped because somebody intentionally or unintentionally pushed an emergency stop button.

Appellant also cannot rely on RES IPSA LOQUITUR in the present case because he cannot satisfy the second essential component of the doctrine, that the injury-causing instrumentality be in the exclusive control of the defendant.

"The element of control has an important bearing as negativing the hypothesis of an intervening cause beyond the defendant's control, and also as tending to show affirmatively that the cause was one within the power of the defendant to prevent by the exercise of care. Thus it has been held that the inference is not permissible where . . . the opportunity for interference by others weakens the probability that the injury is attributable to the defendant's act or omission." (Citations omitted).

Lee v. Housing Auth. of Baltimore, 203 Md. 453, 462, 101 A.2d 832, 836 (1954). This Court has often held res ipsa to be inapplicable when the opportunity for third-party interference prevented a finding that the defendant maintained exclusive control of the injury-causing instrumentality. See, e.g., Joffre, 222 Md. at 8-10, 158 A.2d at 635-36 (holding defendant's control not exclusive where customers had access to soda bottles for approximately two months before one bottle inexplicably shattered); Williams v. McCrory's Stores Corp., 203 Md. 598, 604-05, 102 A.2d 253, 256 (1954) (holding defendant's control not exclusive where thousands of customers had access to revolving stools every week).

In the present case, we must necessarily conclude that Appellant is unable to satisfy the second essential component of res ipsa. Hundreds of Saks & Co.'s customers have unlimited access to the emergency stop buttons each day. If the escalator's two emergency stop buttons are readily accessible to all persons in the vicinity and any customer can cause the escalator to stop simply by pressing one of the buttons, then it is impossible to establish that the escalator was in Appellee's exclusive control.

In Trigg v. J.C. Penney Company, 307 F.Supp. 1092 (D.N.M.1969), the United States District Court for the District of New Mexico held res ipsa inapplicable to facts very similar to those in the present case. In that case, the plaintiff was injured when the escalator upon which he was riding, in a department store, stopped suddenly. Trigg, 307 F.Supp. at 1092. The escalator was equipped with emergency stop buttons. Trigg, 307 F.Supp. at 1093. Although there was no evidence that anyone had pushed the button on the day that the plaintiff was injured, the court concluded that the "plaintiffs failed to prove . . . two crucial elements of the doctrine of RES IPSA LOQUITUR. There is no showing that the instrumentality was within the exclusive control of the defendant. Anyone could push one of [the emergency stop buttons] causing the escalator to stop. This conclusion necessarily leads the court to find that the second element has also not been proved. If anyone could stop the escalator by pressing the button, either

intentionally or unintentionally, the accident is not one that ordinarily would not have happened in the absence of negligence on the part of the defendant."

Id.

There is yet a third reason that res ipsa is inapplicable to the case sub judice. We have, for many years, held that res ipsa is only applicable when "the circumstances attendant upon an accident are themselves of such a character as to justify a jury in inferring negligence as the cause of that accident." Benedick v. Potts, 88 Md. 52, 55, 40 A. 1067, 1068 (1898). This is the case when "the common knowledge of jurors [is] sufficient to support an inference or finding of negligence on the part of " a defendant. Meda v. Brown, 318 Md. 418, 428, 569 A.2d 202, 207 (1990); any person who regularly uses stairs knows that they rarely collapse beneath one's feet. See Blankenship v. Wagner, 261 Md. 37, 273 A.2d 412 (1971). The plaintiffs were permitted to rely on res ipsa because lay jurors possess the background knowledge necessary to decide whether these events ordinarily occur in the absence of someone's negligence. See also Strasburger v. Vogel, 103 Md. 85, 63 A. 202 (1906) (explaining that res ipsa would be proper where brick from defendant's chimney fell onto the head of an infant on the sidewalk below if defendant had not presented evidence of an intervening cause).

In some cases, however, "because of the complexity of the subject matter, expert testimony is required to establish negligence and causation." Meda, 318 Md. at 428, 569 A.2d at 207. For example, Orkin, supra, addressed the applicability of res ipsa in a medical malpractice case. In that case, the plaintiff sustained an injury to her median, ulnar, and radial nerves on her right side during surgery to repair a perforated ulcer. The plaintiff was under general anesthesia while her surgery was being performed, and she "could not 'ascribe a particular negligent act to any defendant.' " Orkin, 318 Md. at 432, 569 A.2d at 209. She proffered proof that her injury was one that usually does not occur absent negligence through the testimony of a neurologist.

The trial court granted summary judgment in favor of the defendants, and the plaintiff appealed, arguing that she should have been permitted to present her case to a jury under the theory of RES IPSA LOQUITUR.

Although this Court held that the trial court erred in granting the defendants' motion for summary judgment, and, therefore, remanded the case to the circuit court, we explained that the plaintiff should not be permitted to rely on RES IPSA LOQUITUR on remand. We stated that a case involving complex issues of fact, for which expert testimony is required, is not a proper case for RES IPSA LOQUITUR.

"This is not an 'obvious injury' case. Resolution of the issues of negligence and causation involved in a case of this kind necessarily requires knowledge of complicated matters, including human anatomy, medical science, operative procedures, areas of patient responsibility, and standards of care. Complex issues of the type generated by a case of this kind should not be resolved by laymen without expert assistance. RES IPSA LOQUITUR does not apply under these circumstances. Meda v. Brown, [318 Md. 418, 569 A.2d 202]."

We quoted this language with approval in Dover, where we held RES IPSA LOQUITUR to be inapplicable in a case involving the misleveling of an elevator, in part, because the common knowledge of jurors was insufficient to support an inference that the misleveling was caused by the defendant's negligence. Dover, 334 Md. at 254, 256, 638 A.2d at 773-74. An elevator "may experience problems absent anyone's negligence," and, thus, we explained that "[w]ithout [an expert's] opinion that the misleveling was [most likely] caused by negligence, an inference that this elevator did not mislevel or experience other problems absent someone's negligence may be unjustified." Dover, 334 Md. at 255, 638 A.2d at 774.

" 'Mechanical, electrical, and electronic devices fail or malfunction routinely—some more routinely than others. A speck of dust, a change in temperature, misuse, an accidental unforeseen trauma—many things can cause these devices to malfunction. To allow an inference that the malfunction is due to someone's negligence when the precise cause cannot be satisfactorily established appears . . . to be unwarranted.' "

Dover, 334 Md. at 255, 638 A.2d at 774. Thus, in cases concerning the malfunction of complex machinery, an expert is required to testify that the malfunction is of a sort that would not occur absent some negligence.

When an expert raises an inference of a defendant's negligence, however, a plaintiff must necessarily be precluded from relying on RES IPSA LOQUITUR. "If expert testimony is used to raise an inference that the accident could not happen had there been no negligence, then it is the expert witness, not an application of the traditional RES IPSA LOQUITUR doctrine, that raises the inference." Dover, 334 Md. at 254, 638 A.2d at 773. In such a case, the jury is not asked or permitted to draw an inference unaided by expert testimony. Meda, 318 Md. at 425, 428, 569 A.2d at 205, 207. Instead, the jury's function is to decide whether the expert's inference that a defendant was negligent is credible.

In the present case, Appellant has declined to present expert testimony. In doing so he has, perhaps, "confused the question of whether an inference may be drawn by an expert with that of whether an inference may be drawn by a layman." Meda, 318 Md. at 428, 569 A.2d at 206. It is not the presence of expert testimony that, if presented, would prevent a jury in the present case from drawing an inference of Appellees' negligence, rather, it is the complex and technical issue presented by the facts of this case. Like the elevator in Dover, an escalator is a complex machine. Leaving aside the presence of any emergency stop buttons, whether an escalator is likely to stop abruptly in the absence of someone's negligence is a question that laymen cannot answer based on common knowledge. The answer requires knowledge of "complicated matters" such as mechanics, electricity, circuits, engineering, and metallurgy. RES IPSA LOQUITUR does not apply under these circumstances.

For all of the foregoing reasons, we answer the second certified question in the negative. We are called upon to answer the third certified question only if the doctrine of RES IPSA LOQUITUR applies to the present case. We have stated that the doctrine does not apply.

In sum, we answer the first certified question in the negative; the allegations in Appellant's Complaint with respect to negligence do not amount to a waiver of RES IPSA LOQUITUR. We also answer the second certified question in the negative; res ipsa does not apply to the facts of the instant case because Appellant cannot prove that the event would not occur in the absence of

Appellees' negligence. In addition, Appellant cannot prove that the escalator was in Appellees' exclusive control. Finally, because of the complex and technical nature of the issue presented in this case, lay jurors would not be permitted to draw an inference of negligence without the aid of expert testimony, negating the very definition of RES IPSA LOQUITUR.

Case Question
What are the factual elements of res ipsa loquitur in this case?

Assignment 9.1

In each of the following fact situations, identify which facts would support a claim of negligence by determining the following:

- Who owes the duty?
- To whom is the duty owed?
- What is the duty?
- How is the duty breached?
- How does the breach cause injury in fact and in law?
- What is the damage?

1. Karen takes a group of neighborhood kids on a trip to the zoo. In the petting barn one of the children is bitten by a goat and loses a finger. Karen was getting ice cream at a concession stand and not present at the time of the accident. The zoo employee in charge of monitoring the petting barn was in the bathroom and no other employees were in the vicinity.
2. Ariel raises and trains pit bulls used as guard/attack dogs for businesses in high crime areas. While mowing her yard, she leaves the gate open. A 19-year-old neighbor comes into the yard and is immediately attacked and mauled by the dogs.

STRICT LIABILITY

Strict liability is a much narrower area of tort law, but it is also one of the fastest growing areas of civil law. Traditionally, strict liability was applied in cases of extremely dangerous activities. This area of law grew out of the law of negligence, to be used in special circumstances. Specifically, strict liability was developed for use in cases of persons who obtained some personal or financial benefit from an activity that could not be made safe and from which the innocent public could not protect itself. Originally, strict liability was applied in cases where a person dealt with dangerous animals or was involved in other activities that could greatly injure members of the public who were in no position to protect themselves, for example, persons who used explosives, such as construction or demolition crews.

Fault, carelessness, or intent is not an issue in actions for strict liability, since no matter how carefully an activity might be conducted or an animal might be guarded, it is a near certainty that if the danger escapes into a public area, innocent bystanders will be harmed. It is further reasoned that the persons in control of the activity or animal benefit from it and it is only reasonable that they should bear the costs of harm.

More recently, strict liability has been the primary basis of litigation against manufacturers of products. Consumers (users) of products have no means of knowing how the product was designed and what aspects of it could cause injury. The manufacturer who designed the product, however, is well aware of the product's defects or dangerous aspects, and if the defect is not corrected or if a proper warning of the dangers is not given, the manufacturer has placed in commerce a dangerous instrument that is likely to injure innocent persons. This is a basis for liability of the manufacturer who ultimately benefits most from the sale of such products.

 CASE

IRVINE v. RARE FELINE BREEDING CENTER INC.

1997 WL 564203 (685 N.E.2d 120).

JUDITH S. PROFFITT, Judge

CHEZEM
Appellant-Plaintiff, Scott Irvine ("Irvine"), appeals an order denying his motion for partial summary judgment. We affirm.

Issues
The parties raise various issues which we restate as:

I. Whether STRICT LIABILITY is the law in Indiana WILD animal cases;
II. Whether any exceptions or defenses to STRICT LIABILITY should be recognized; and,
III. Whether a genuine issue of material fact exists regarding either Irvine's status or any available defenses.

Facts and Procedural History
For the past thirty years, Mosella Schaffer ("Schaffer") has lived on a fifty acre farm in Hamilton County, Indiana where she has raised and maintained exotic ANIMALS. These ANIMALS have included zebras, llamas, camels, kangaroos, and, beginning in 1970, Siberian tigers. Although her original intent was to breed and sell the ANIMALS, she soon found it difficult to part with many of them.

In 1993, Scott Bullington ("Bullington") was renting a room in the garage area of Schaffer's house. Aware of his friend Irvine's interest in WILD ANIMALS, Bullington informed Irvine of Schaffer's farm and the ANIMALS she kept there. Irvine, then in his late twenties, began to stop by and see the ANIMALS as per Schaffer's open invitation. Over the next two years, Irvine visited Schaffer's farm several dozen times. During these visits, people would occasionally pet the tigers through a fence.

On the afternoon of December 2, 1995, Irvine arrived at Schaffer's home to see Bullington. The two men drank alcohol and watched television until early evening when Bullington announced that he had to leave to attend his employer's Christmas party. Because Irvine had consumed a substantial amount of alcohol, Bullington told Irvine he could stay over night on the couch. Some time after Bullington had left, Irvine exited Bullington's apartment, walked to the front of Schaffer's property and visited with the llamas and zebras. As he was doing so, Schaffer drove up, stopped her car, had a brief, friendly conversation with Irvine, and went into her house.

Around 8:00 p.m., Irvine decided to visit the tigers before going to sleep. Thus, he went through Schaffer's garage, proceeded through the utility room, continued through the sun room, and ended up in the back yard. Irvine then approached the wire caging, as he and others had done in the past, placed a couple fingers inside the enclosure, and attempted to pet a male tiger. As he was scratching the male tiger, a female tiger made some commotion, which caused Irvine to look away from the male tiger. At that moment, the male tiger pulled Irvine's arm through the two inch by six inch opening of the wire fence.

Upon hearing Irvine's shouts, Schaffer came out of her house, banged an object against the fence, and freed Irvine. Schaffer immediately drove Irvine to the hospital. Schaffer was treated and admitted to the hospital. Later, he was transferred to another hospital, and underwent six surgeries during a thirteen day hospital stay. Further surgeries are indicated though Irvine is uninsured.

On May 30, 1996, Irvine filed a complaint against Schaffer containing four counts: negligence, STRICT LIABILITY, nuisance, and punitives. On September 6, 1996, Irvine filed his motion for partial summary judgment on the basis that incurred risk and assumption of risk are not valid defenses to a STRICT LIABILITY WILD animal claim, on the basis that assumption of risk is not available in a non-contract case, and on the basis that the defense of open and obvious is not available in an animal liability case. Schaffer filed a response on January 14, 1997. Irvine filed a reply on January 21, 1997. The trial court denied Irvine's motion for summary judgment on the STRICT LIABILITY count, denied summary judgment on the issue of assumption of risk, and granted summary judgment on the issue of open and obvious. The trial court granted Irvine's petition to certify three issues for interlocutory appeal: 1) whether incurred risk or other defenses are available in a STRICT LIABILITY animal case; 2) whether Irvine was an invitee as a matter of law; and 3) whether the defense of assumption of risk is available in a noncontractual case. We accepted jurisdiction of the interlocutory appeal.

Discussion and Decision
Irvine first argues that Indiana has historically adhered to strict tort liability in WILD animal cases. He further argues that when the Indiana

Comparative Fault Act (Ind.Code s 34-4-33-1 et seq., the "Act") was adopted, it did not change the law in WILD animal cases. Moreover, he claims that no exceptions to STRICT LIABILITY in WILD animal cases have ever been applied in Indiana. He also argues that even if his status is somehow relevant, he was clearly an invitee. Thus, he asserts that the trial court should not have denied his summary judgment on the STRICT LIABILITY issue. In contrast, Schaffer argues that Indiana has not adopted, and should not adopt, STRICT LIABILITY animal cases. . . .

Upon review of the grant or denial of a summary judgment motion, we apply the same legal judgment is appropriate only when there are no genuine issues of material fact and the moving party is entitled to judgment as a matter of law. Ind.Trial Rule 56(C); North Snow Bay, Inc. v. Hamilton, 657 N.E.2d 420, 422 (IND.CT.APP.1995). On review, we may not search the entire record to support the judgment, but may only consider that which had been specifically designated to the trial court. Id. The party appealing the trial court's grant or denial of summary judgment has the burden of persuading this court that the trial court's decision was erroneous. Id.

I. Liability in a WILD Animal Case
We first address whether STRICT LIABILITY is the common law rule for WILD animal cases in Indiana. The parties have not cited and we have not found a case specifically applying STRICT LIABILITY to a true WILD animal case in Indiana. However, the basic rule has been frequently stated in various contexts. Holt v. Myers, 93 N.E. 31 (Ind.Ct.App.1910)(mentioning WILD animal STRICT LIABILITY rule although case dealt with vicious dog). Accordingly, we have little difficulty concluding that Indiana's common law recognized the STRICT LIABILITY rule for WILD animal cases—despite the fact that previously, Indiana courts have not had the opportunity to apply the rule.

We next address the issue of whether the adoption of the Act changed the common law rule of STRICT LIABILITY in WILD animal cases. "We presume the legislature does not intend by the enactment of a statute to make any change in the common law beyond what it declares, either in express terms or by unmistakable implication." An abrogation of the common law will be implied

(1) where a statute is enacted which undertakes to cover the entire subject treated and was clearly designed as a substitute for the common law; or, (2) where the two laws are so repugnant that both in reason may not stand. Id. "As a statute in derogation of the existing common law, the Act must be strictly construed." Indianapolis Power & Light Co. v. Brad Snodgrass, Inc., 578 N.E.2d 669, 673 (Ind.1991).

The Act, enacted in 1983 and effective in 1985, "governs any action based on fault [.]" Ind.Code s 34-4-33-1. STRICT LIABILITY, by definition, is liability without fault. Thus, the Act would seem to be inapplicable to a STRICT LIABILITY action. The legislative history lends further support for this conclusion. The original version of Ind.Code s 34-4-33-2 provided that "Fault," for purposes of the Act, "include[d] any act or omission that [was] negligent, willful, wanton, reckless, or intentional toward the person or property of others, or that subject[ed] a person to strict tort liability, but [did] not include an intentional act. The term also include[d] breach of warranty, unreasonable assumption of risk not constituting an enforceable express consent, incurred risk, misuse of a product for which the defendant otherwise would be liable, and unreasonable failure to avoid injury or to mitigate damages." (Emphasis added).

By the time of its effective date, that same section had been changed to its current form: " '[f]ault' includes any act or omission that is negligent, willful, wanton, reckless, or intentional toward the person or property of others. The term also includes unreasonable assumption of risk not constituting an enforceable express consent, incurred risk, and unreasonable failure to avoid injury or to mitigate damages." Ind.Code s 34-4-33-2. The current form includes no reference to STRICT LIABILITY. Narrowly construing the Act, we conclude that it does not explicitly apply to a STRICT LIABILITY claim. See Templin v. Fobes, 617 N.E.2d 541, 544 n. 1 (Ind.1993) (products liability case in which our Supreme Court noted, "practical problems arise, at least in part, because of the operation of Indiana's Comparative Fault Act, which would apply in Templins' negligence claims against Fobes but not in the Templins' STRICT LIABILITY claim against Rockwood.").

II. Exceptions or Defenses

Having concluded that the Act has not changed common law STRICT LIABILITY in WILD animal cases, we next address Irvine's contention that no exceptions to STRICT LIABILITY in WILD animal cases have ever been applied in this state. While we agree with Irvine's contention, this fact is of no surprise in view of the lack of any true WILD animal cases in Indiana. As this is an issue of first impression, we look to the reason behind the STRICT LIABILITY WILD animal rule and consult other sources as necessary.

We have previously set out the rationale for imposing STRICT LIABILITY against owners for injuries caused by an attack by a naturally ferocious or DANGEROUS animal. See Hardin v. Christy, 462 N.E.2d 256, 259, 262 (Ind.Ct.App.1984). STRICT LIABILITY is appropriately placed:

upon those who, even with proper care, expose the community to the risk of a very DANGEROUS thing. . . . The kind of "DANGEROUS animal" that will subject the keeper to STRICT LIABILITY . . . must pose some kind of an abnormal risk to the particular community where the animal is kept; hence, the keeper is engaged in an activity that subjects those in the vicinity, including those who come onto his property, to an abnormal risk . . . The possessor of a WILD animal is strictly liable for physical harm done to the person of another . . . if that harm results from a DANGEROUS propensity that is characteristic of WILD ANIMALS of that class. Thus, STRICT LIABILITY has been imposed on keepers of lions and tigers, bears, elephants, wolves, monkeys, and other similar ANIMALS. No member of such a species, however domesticated, can ever be regarded as safe, and liability does not rest upon any experience with the particular animal.

Although having done so in an asbestos case and using slightly different terms, Judge Posner concisely set out the rationale for the WILD animal STRICT LIABILITY rule using the following hypothetical:

[k]eeping a tiger in one's backyard would be an example of an abnormally hazardous activity. The hazard is such, relative to the value of the activity, that we desire not just that the owner take all due care that the tiger not escape, but that he consider seriously the possibility of getting rid of the tiger altogether; and we give him an incentive to

consider this course of action by declining to make the exercise of due care a defense to a suit based on an injury caused by the tiger—in other words, by making him strictly liable for any such injury.

G.J. Leasing Co. v. Union Electric Co., 54 F.3d 379, 386 (7th CIR.1995).

With the rationale for the rule in mind, we analyze whether any exceptions or defenses to the STRICT LIABILITY WILD animal rule are appropriate. Like the sources previously cited, the Restatement provides:

(1) A possessor of a WILD animal is subject to liability to another for harm done by the animal to the other, his person, land or chattels, although the possessor has exercised the utmost care to confine the animal, or otherwise prevent it from doing harm.

(2) This liability is limited to harm that results from a DANGEROUS propensity that is characteristic of WILD ANIMALS of the particular class, or of which the possessor knows or has reason to know.

Restatement (Second) of Torts s 507 (1977). However, because the general rule in s 507 is "subject to a number of exceptions and qualifications, which are too numerous to state in a single Section," s 507 should be read together with s 508, s 510, s 511, s 512, s 515, and s 517. Restatement, supra cmt. a, s 507. Thus, we look to those other sections to help flesh out the Restatement's rule.

Section 510(a) provides: "The possessor of a WILD animal . . . is subject to STRICT LIABILITY for the resulting harm, although it would not have occurred but for the unexpectable . . . innocent, negligent or reckless conduct of a third person." However, "[a] possessor of land is not subject to STRICT LIABILITY to one who intentionally or negligently trespasses upon the land, for harm done to him by a WILD animal . . . that the possessor keeps on the land, even though the trespasser has no reason to know that the animal is kept there." Restatement, supra s 511. Invitees and licensees are dealt with in s 513, which states: "The possessor of a WILD animal . . . who keeps it upon land in his possession, is subject to STRICT LIABILITY to persons coming upon the land in the exercise of a privilege whether derived from his consent to their entry or otherwise." Yet, if the invitee or licensee

"knows that the DANGEROUS animal is permitted to run at large or has escaped from control they may be barred from recovery if they choose to act upon the possessor's consent or to exercise any other privilege and thus expose themselves to the risk of being harmed by the animal. (See s 515)." Restatement, supra, cmt. a, s 513.

Section 515(2), in turn, provides: "The plaintiff's contributory negligence in knowingly and unreasonably subjecting himself to the risk that a WILD animal . . . will do harm to his person . . . is a defense to the STRICT LIABILITY." Comment c. to s 515(2) explains:

Although one harmed by a WILD . . . animal that has escaped from control of its possessor or harborer is not barred from recovery because he has not exercised ordinary care to observe the presence of the animal or to escape from its attack, he is barred if he intentionally and unreasonably subjects himself to the risk of harm by the animal. Thus one who without any necessity for so doing that is commensurate with the risk involved knowingly puts himself in reach of an animal that is effectively chained or otherwise confined cannot recover against the possessor or harborer of the animal. So, too, although a licensee or an invitee upon land of another upon which he knows that WILD . . . ANIMALS are kept under the possessor's control does not take the risk that they will escape and harm him, he does nonetheless take the risk of harm by the ANIMALS that he knows are roaming at large, so that he will to a reasonable certainty encounter them if he avails himself of the invitation or permission held out to him by the possessor of the land. (Emphasis added).

Comment d. to s 515(2) states: "This kind of contributory negligence, which consists of voluntarily and unreasonably encountering a known danger, is frequently called either contributory negligence or assumption of risk, or both."

Section 515(3) provides: "The plaintiff's assumption of the risk of harm from the animal is a defense to the STRICT LIABILITY." The comment to s 515(3) states that "one employed as a lion tamer in a circus may be barred from recovery by his assumption of the risk when he is clawed by a lion. In the same manner, one who voluntarily teases and provokes a chained bear, or goes within reach of a vicious dog, is barred from recovery if he does so with knowledge of the danger." (Emphases added).

As indicated by the extensive quotations above, the Restatement clearly recognizes exceptions or defenses to WILD animal STRICT LIABILITY. Prosser and Keeton also agree that defenses are available to a STRICT LIABILITY WILD animal claim. "[C]ontributory negligence by way of knowingly and unreasonably subjecting oneself to a risk of harm from an abnormally DANGEROUS animal will constitute a defense" to a STRICT LIABILITY claim. Prosser and Keeton, supra s 79, at 565. "Thus, a plaintiff who voluntarily and unreasonably comes within reach of an animal which he knows to be DANGEROUS, . . . has no cause of action when it attacks him." Id. at 566.

Because we agree with the rationale of the exceptions and/or defenses set out in the Restatement, and because we find it to be in keeping with Indiana's recent policy regarding allocation of fault, we adopt the Restatement's approach in WILD animal cases.

B. Defenses
In adopting the Restatement's view that incurred risk/assumed risk may be a defense to a STRICT LIABILITY WILD animal claim, we must next examine whether genuine issues of material fact exist regarding a defense in Irvine's case. Incurred risk requires a mental state of venturousness and a conscious, deliberate and intentional embarkation upon the course of conduct with knowledge of the circumstances. Perdue Farms, Inc. v. Pryor, —

N.E.2d -, 63S01-9509-CV-172, (Ind. July 22, 1997), slip op. at 7. In other contexts, we have stated that the defense of incurred risk is generally a question of fact, and the party asserting it bears the burden of proving it by a preponderance of evidence. Schooley v. Ingersoll Rand Inc., 631 N.E.2d 932, 939 (Ind.Ct.App.1994).

Here, the parties designated conflicting evidence regarding whether Irvine knowingly and unreasonably put himself within reach of a WILD animal that was effectively chained or otherwise confined. There was evidence that around the time of the accident, Irvine had been volunteering at the Indianapolis Zoo and had been told not to have contact with tigers. Moreover, there was evidence that Irvine was aware of a prior incident wherein the tiger which injured him grabbed another man's thumb. However, there was other evidence tending to indicate that Schaffer and others had petted the tiger safely in the past. Also, there was evidence that Irvine may have been rather intoxicated on the night in question. In view of the conflicting evidence and inferences, summary judgment was properly denied on the issue of whether a defense was appropriate in this case.

Affirmed.

Case Question
Why is strict liability allegedly applicable in this case as opposed to a case of gross negligence?

INTENTIONAL TORTS

A second major category of torts is a tort where the primary element is intent. This is an action where the defendant has manifested an intent to bring about a particular result and, as a consequence, the plaintiff was injured. It must be shown that the defendant acted voluntarily, even with the knowledge that the act would almost certainly bring about the injury. In some instances, the injury itself is the desired result, but it need not be to constitute an intentional tort. It must only be shown that the defendant knew or should have known with substantial certainty that his or her action would bring about the injury.[22]

Intentional tort differs from the concept of degree of duty in negligence, because in an intentional tort, the risk is so great it can be counted upon to produce the injury. If the actor commits the action anyway, such action constitutes an intentional tort against the injured party. A major distinction between gross negligence and intentional tort is that in an intentional tort, mere knowledge and appreciation of a danger are insufficient. As stated, there must be evidence of voluntary conduct in light of the knowledge and appreciation of the danger. In addition, the risk of harm must be a near certainty rather than a likelihood.

Several types of intentional torts provide a basis for liability. Some of the more common types are discussed here to demonstrate the basis for the more commonly litigated actions. (Figure 9.1 lists the elements of these and other torts.)

Assault

Assault is commonly considered to be a physical attack of some sort, but in tort law, its meaning is quite different. To prove an act of assault, it must be shown that the actor engaged in physical conduct, that may or may not have been accompanied by words, that placed the plaintiff in apprehension of immediate and harmful contact.[23] By definition, the tort of assault involves no physical contact, only the threat of such contact. A plaintiff cannot claim assault when the threatening act consisted only of words. Nor is an assault committed when a threat is made for some future point in time. The basis for an assault action is that the threat of immediate physical harm produces such fear, and/or a reaction, that it actually injures the plaintiff. For example, if I threaten to beat you up at the park the next time I see you there, no assault has occurred, because you have no realistic fear. You can avoid the attack by avoiding the park. However, if I am in the park with you and tell you that I am going to beat you up, your response may be such fear of an imminent harmful contact that the fear causes injury (e.g., heart attack), and consequently, an assault has occurred.

Battery

The tort of battery is perhaps the most litigated intentional tort, because it includes all unpermitted physical contact that results in harm. Battery encompasses physical attacks, medical treatment without consent, and every other conceivable act that results in physical contact between two parties as long as (1) there is the intent to make physical contact; (2) there is no consent to such contact; (3) the contact occurs to the person or to anything that is so closely attached that it is considered part of the person, e.g., clothing; and (4) the contact results in injury to the person.[24]

Battery encompasses much more than a physical fight between two persons. In fact, in recent years, battery has been the basis for medical malpractice claims, including such actions as leaving foreign objects (sponges or instruments) in a patient's body or performing a procedure to which the patient had not previously consented.

The Emergency Rule is an exception or defense to actions for battery.[25] The rule states that unpermitted physical contact (including medical treatment) may be allowed if a medical or other emergency exists that prevents the person from making a decision as to whether or not to permit the contact. For example, if an unconscious patient suffers heart failure during an operation, doctors are permitted to perform additional measures to save the patient's life even though the patient never consented to such procedures.

FIGURE 9.1   Torts and Related Causes of Action*: The Elements

The Cause of Action	Its Elements
1. Abuse of Process	i. Use of civil or criminal proceedings ii. Improper or ulterior purpose iii. Actual damage
2. Alienation of Affections	i. Intent to diminish the marital relationship between spouses ii. Affirmative conduct iii. Affections between spouses are in fact alienated iv. Causation of the alienation

3. Assault (Civil)	i. Act
	ii. Intent either
	  a. to cause a harmful or offensive contact or
	  b. to cause an apprehension of a harmful or offensive contact
	iii. Apprehension of an imminent harmful or offensive contact to the plaintiff's own person
	iv. Causation of the apprehension

4. Battery (Civil)	i. Act ii. Intent to cause harmful or offensive contact iii. Harmful or offensive contact with the plaintiff's person iv. Causation of the harmful or offensive contact
5. Civil Rights Violation	i. A person acting under color of law ii. Deprives a citizen of federal constitutional or federal statutory rights
6. Conversion	i. Personal property (chattel) ii. Plaintiff is in possession of the chattel or is entitled to immediate possession iii. Intent to exercise dominion or control over the chattel iv. Serious interference with plaintiffs' possession v. Causation of the serious interference
7. Criminal Conversation	Defendant has sexual relations with the plaintiffs' spouse (adultery)

8. Deceit	i. a. Statement of past or present fact or
	  b. Concealment of past or present fact or
	  c. Nondisclosure of past or present fact when there is a duty to disclose or
	  d. A statement of opinion (only some opinions qualify)
	ii. The statement is false
	iii. Scienter (intent to mislead) (some states say negligence in misleading is enough)
	iv. Intent to have the plaintiffs rely on the statement or a reason to believe the plaintiff will rely
	v. Causation in fact (actual reliance)
	vi. Justifiable reliance
	vii. Actual damages

Defamation (two torts)
9. Libel
	i. Defamatory statement by the defendant (written)
	ii. Of and concerning the plaintiff
	iii. Publication of the statement
	iv. Damages:
	  a. In some states, special damages never have to be proven in any libel case
	  b. In other states, only libel on its face does not require special damages. In these states, libel per quod requires special damages
	v. Causation

*With the exception of negligence and strict liability torts, the causes of action identified here constitute intentional torts.
Statsky Torts: Personal Injury Litigation p2–6 1991.

FIGURE 9.1   (Continued)

The Cause of Action	Its Elements
10. Slander	i. Defamatory statement by the defendant (spoken)
	ii. Of and concerning the plaintiff
	iii. Publication of the statement
	iv. Damages:
	a. Special damages are not required if the slander is slander per se
	b. Special damages must be proven if the slander is not slander per se
	v. Causation
11. Disparagement	i. False statement of fact
	ii. Disparaging the plaintiff's business or property
	iii. Publication of the statement
	iv. Intent
	v. Special damages
	vi. Causation
12. Enticement of a Child or Abduction of a Child	i. Intent to interfere with a parent's custody over his or her child
	ii. Affirmative conduct by defendant:
	a. to abduct or force child from the parent's custody or
	b. to entice or encourage the child to leave the parent or
	c. to harbor the child and encourage him/her to stay away from the parent's custody
	iii. The child leaves the custody of the parent
	iv. Defendant caused child to leave or to stay away
13. Enticement of Spouse	i. Intent to diminish the marital relationship between the spouses
	ii. Affirmative conduct by the defendant:
	a. to entice or encourage the spouse to leave the plaintiff's home or
	b. to harbor the spouse and encourage him/her to stay away from the plaintiff's home
	iii. The spouse leaves the plaintiff's home
	iv. Causation
14. False Imprisonment	i. An act that completely confines the plaintiff within fixed boundaries set by the defendant
	ii. Intent to confine plaintiff or a third person
	iii. Causation of the confinement
	iv. Plaintiff either was conscious of the confinement or was harmed by it
15. Intentional Infliction of Emotional Distress	i. An act of extreme or outrageous conduct
	ii. Intent to cause severe emotional distress
	iii. Severe emotional distress is suffered
	iv. Causation of this distress
16. Interference with Contract Relations	i. An existing contract
	ii. Interference with the contract by defendants
	iii. Intent
	iv. Damages
	v. Causation
17. Interference with Prospective Advantage	i. Reasonable expectation of an economic advantage
	ii. Interference with this expectation
	iii. Intent
	iv. Damages
	v. Causation
Invasion of Privacy (four torts)	
18. Appropriation	i. The use of the plaintiff's name, likeness, or personality
	ii. For the benefit of the defendant

FIGURE 9.1 (Continued)

The Cause of Action	Its Elements
19. False Light	i. Publicity ii. Placing the plaintiff in a false light iii. Highly offensive to a reasonable person
20. Intrusion	i. An act of intrusion into someone's private affairs or concerns ii. Highly offensive to a reasonable person
21. Public Disclosure of a Private Fact	i. Publicity ii. Concerning the private life of the plaintiff iii. Highly offensive to a reasonable person
22. Malicious Prosecution	i. Initiate or procure the initiation of legal proceedings ii. Without probable cause iii. With malice iv. The legal proceedings terminate in favor of the accused
23. Negligence	i. Duty ii. Breach of duty iii. Proximate cause iv. Damages
Nuisance	
24. Private Nuisance	An unreasonable interference with the use and enjoyment of land
25. Public Nuisance	An interference with a right that is common to the public
26. Prima Facie Tort	i. Infliction of harm ii. Intent to do harm (malice) iii. Special damages iv. Causation
27. Seduction	The defendant has sexual relations with the plaintiff's daughter with or without consent
28. Strict Liability for Harm Caused by Animals	Domestic Animals i. The owner had reason to know the animal has a specific propensity to harm others ii. Harm is caused by the animal by that specific propensity Wild Animals i. Keeping a wild animal ii. Causes damage
29. Strict Liability for Abnormally Dangerous Conditions or Activities	i. The existence of an abnormally dangerous condition or activity ii. Knowledge of the condition or activity iii. Damages iv. Causation
30. Strict Liability in Tort	i. Seller ii. A defective product that is unreasonably dangerous to person or property iii. User or consumer iv. Physical harm v. Causation
31. Trespass to Chattels	i. Personal property (chattel) ii. Plaintiff is in possession of the chattel or is entitled to immediate possession iii. Intent to dispossess or to intermeddle with the chattel iv. Dispossession, impairment, or deprivation of use for a substantial time v. Causation of element (iv)
32. Trespass to Land	i. An act ii. Intrusion on land iii. In possession of another

CASE

SUDUL v. CITY OF HAMTRAMCK

221 Mich.App. 455, 502
N.W.2d 478 (1997).

CORRIGAN, Judge.

Defendants were not accorded a fair trial because the error regarding assault and battery by gross negligence pervaded the jury instructions and rendered the other special verdicts unsound. We reverse and remand for further proceedings consistent with this opinion.

We specifically agree with the discussion in the dissent/concurrence regarding the nonexistence of a tort called "assault and battery by gross negligence." We especially also hold that an individual employee's intentional torts are not shielded by our governmental immunity statute, a proposition that too frequently is mired in confusion. Nonetheless, we disagree with the position taken in the dissent/concurrence on two grounds.

I. Effect of Defective Jury Instructions on Integrity of Special Verdicts

We part company with the position taken in the dissent/concurrence with respect to the scope of the reversal. While we accept the utility of special verdicts in saving sound portions of a verdict, we nonetheless vacate all the special verdicts in this case because the flaws in the jury instructions regarding assault and battery by gross negligence tainted the entire verdict.

Justice Otis Smith observed in Sahr v. Bierd, 354 Mich. 353, 365, 92 N.W.2d 467 (1958), quoting Sunderland, Verdicts, General and Special, 29 Yale LJ 253, 259 (1920):

"The special verdict compels detailed consideration. But above all it enables the public, the parties and the court to see what the jury really has done. The general verdict is either all wrong or all right, because it is an inseparable and inscrutable unit. A single error completely destroys it. But the special verdict enables errors to be localized so that the sound portions of the verdict may be saved and only the unsound portions be subject to redetermination through a new trial."

We cannot say that the special verdicts concerning excessive force, grossly negligent infliction of emotional distress, and the various derivative claims were unaffected by the instructional error. The instructional error was not harmless.

After being instructed incorrectly that defendants could be held responsible for assault and battery if they were grossly negligent, the jury retired to deliberate. Three hours later, the jurors posed several questions to the court. They first inquired whether excessive force constituted assault and battery. The court, with the agreement of counsel, replied that it did. The court's answer that excessive force was the same as assault and battery reinforced the original error that defendants could be liable for assault and battery by an act of gross negligence.

The court earlier had instructed the jury:

Gross negligence is defined in our state by statute, and it is defined as conduct so reckless as to demonstrate a substantial lack of concern for whether an injury results. The same statute states—grants immunity from tort liability to police officers performing their duty, provided that the police officers' actions are not grossly negligent. This means that the officers are not liable to plaintiffs for assault, battery or excessive force unless you find that their actions were grossly negligent.

The court then gave the correct definitions of assault and battery as set forth in SJI2d 115.01 and 115.02. The court further instructed the jury that the City of Hamtramck may be liable where if you find that the plaintiffs have been subjected to excessive force in plaintiff's arrest and excessive force was done pursuant to a governmental custom, policy, or practice.

The court also merged the concepts of gross negligence and assault and battery in its instructions regarding compensatory and future damages:

If you decide that the plaintiffs, Anthony and Bernard Sudul, are entitled to damages, it is your duty to determine the amount of money which reasonably, fairly, and adequately compensate[s] each of them for the elements of damage which you decide has resulted from the assault, battery and excessive force by the defendants' grossly negligent conduct and/or from the violation of plaintiffs' federal constitutional rights by each police officer or the city, taking into the account the nature and extent of the injury.

If you decide that the plaintiffs, Anthony and Bernard Sudul, are entitled to damages in the future, it is your duty to determine the amount of money which reasonably, fairly and adequately compensates each of them for each of the elements of damage in the future which you decide has resulted from the assault/battery and excessive force by the defendants' grossly negligent conduct and/or from the violation of plaintiffs' federal constitutional rights by each of the police officers or the city, taking into account the nature and extent of the injury.

The verdict form asked specifically whether the officers assaulted plaintiff Anthony Sudul by an act of gross negligence or battered plaintiff Anthony Sudul by an act of gross negligence. As noted, defendants specifically objected on the very ground on which they have here prevailed—that the tort of assault and battery by gross negligence does not exist.

It is critical to us that this misinstructed jury nevertheless returned verdicts of no cause of action for three of the five individual defendant police officers involved in Anthony Sudul's arrest. The jury found only Officers David Donnell and William Robinson, who pushed Sudul to the ground to handcuff him after he resisted arrest, liable with respect to the claims of grossly negligent assault and battery and excessive force.

We cannot conclude that the instructions as a whole, some correct and some incorrect, clearly apprised the jury of the governing law and protected defendants' rights. The court improperly defined assault and battery, then equated it with excessive force and gross negligence. Where a court gives conflicting instructions, one of which is erroneous, we generally presume that the jury followed the erroneous instruction. Kirby v. Larson, 400 Mich. 585, 606-607, 256 N.W.2d 400 (1977). Indeed, the jury's subsequent intelligent questions reflected its attempt to understand and follow the court's confusing instructions. The court's instructions permitted the jury to find liability without the requisite finding of intent for

assault and battery, then merged a charge of assault and battery with the definition of excessive force in response to the jury's explicit question regarding the nature of those torts.

The author of the dissent/concurrence would also recognize a novel tort of grossly negligent infliction of emotional distress, not recognized previously in any reported case. Our Supreme Court has yet to recognize formally the tort of intentional infliction of emotional distress. We doubt that the Supreme Court would recognize such grossly negligent emotional distress where the shocking and outrageous event that the child bystander witnessed may well have been nothing more than a lawful arrest involving the use of reasonable force. On this record, we have serious reservations regarding the correct application of law to facts. These defendants are as entitled as any litigant to deliberations by a jury that has been instructed correctly concerning the law. The instructional error is manifest, is not isolated, and is not harmless. In our view, failure to reverse all the verdicts affected by the defect is inconsistent with substantial justice. Id.

At various points during trial, both plaintiffs' counsel and the court erroneously stated that the officers could be held liable for their subjective "bad faith" in the use of excessive force, a standard repudiated nearly five years earlier in Graham v. Connor, 490 U.S. 386, 109 S.Ct. 1865, 104 L.Ed.2d 443 (1989). Instead, the excessive force claim should have been analyzed under an objective reasonableness standard. In our view, the trial court improperly collapsed the excessive force and the assault and battery claims, despite the fact that they involve distinct harms, Garner v. Michigan State Univ., 185 Mich.App. 750, 764, 462 N.W.2d 832 (1990), and failed in its duty to provide clear guidance with regard to the governing law. This result was manifestly unjust, regardless of whether defendant specifically objected.

Reversed and remanded for further proceedings consistent with this opinion. We do not retain jurisdiction.

Case Question

How does gross negligence vary from ordinary negligence?

False Imprisonment

False imprisonment occurs when a party (not necessarily a law enforcement agency) creates boundaries for another party, with the intent that the other party be confined within those boundaries. It requires also that the second party is aware of the confinement, does not consent to it, and perceives no reasonable means of escape.[26] False imprisonment has been the basis for lawsuits ranging from false arrests by law enforcement officers to kidnapping and unwarranted detention in stores by store security and personnel.

The boundaries in a false imprisonment action need not be actual walls. It is only necessary to show that through physical barriers, conduct, or words, the injured party reasonably believed his or her liberty was restricted.[27] There is also no requirement of actual damages. The loss of liberty is considered to be an injury in and of itself, although there are often other more tangible injuries as well.

It is important to understand that an action for false imprisonment cannot be brought if the defendant was exercising a privilege when detaining the plaintiff. For example, security officers and law enforcement agencies are given a wide latitude in detaining persons suspected of criminal activity. Even if the persons are innocent, public policy requires that investigation of reasonable suspicions be allowed. If the suspicions are wholly unfounded, however, or if the investigation or detention is for an unreasonable period of time, the privilege may not apply. This most often becomes an issue in cases when store security guards detain customers on suspicion of shoplifting. If the suspicion, the detainment, and treatment of the customer are reasonable, there would probably be no grounds for an action of false imprisonment.

Trespass

Trespass is the intentional invasion of property rights. It occurs whenever someone personally or through his or her property enters the land of another or permits such an invasion to continue when another takes control of the property.[28] An example of the latter occurs if you sell your house to someone but leave your car parked in the backyard. This is an invasion of the purchaser's right to the property.

It is not necessary that the actor have the intent to commit a trespass or even the knowledge that he or she is doing so. It is enough that the actor intends to commit the invasive act and, as a result of the commission of that act, a trespass occurs. Such a case often occurs when hunters are on publicly owned land and unknowingly enter onto private property. Even though they believe they are still on public land, they have violated a property interest. Violation of this right of landowners to quiet enjoyment free from intrusion is enough to bring an action for trespass. If the trespasser causes damage to persons or property, he or she is liable for that as well.

Fraud

The intentional tort of fraud is perhaps the most commonly claimed tort in business and financial dealings. Fraud is not easily proven, however, because the injured party must be able to show that he or she did not have the opportunity to detect any misdealing. The elements required to prove an action for fraud are numerous. It must be shown that (1) the defendant made a material (significant) representation to the plaintiff that was untrue, (2) the defendant knew the statement was untrue or that his or her failure to ascertain its truth was reckless, (3) some affirmative conduct by the defendant indicates the intent to have the plaintiff rely on the statement, and (4) the plaintiff reasonably relied on the statement and as a proximate result was injured by it.[29]

 APPLICATION 9.5

A used-car dealer sells a vehicle that has been repaired and put in running order only long enough to be sold. When asked specifically about the condition of various parts of the engine, the dealer states that the car is in excellent shape. An innocent consumer who relies on this statement to purchase the vehicle—which falls apart so that the consumer loses money—would very likely have an action for fraud.

Point for Discussion
Would a different result occur if the item being misrepresented was a wooden chair? Why or why not?

Defamation

Defamation is the combined name for two types of intentional torts: libel and slander. Libel is an action for injuries that occur as the result of a written communication to a third party.[30] Slander is the appropriate action when the injuries occur as the result of an oral communication.[31]

In both types of actions, it is necessary to show that the defendant actor made a communication to a third party about the plaintiff that caused other third persons to have a lowered opinion of the plaintiff or be discouraged from associating with him or her.[32] This communication must be made by the speaker with the intent that the receiving party perceive it as directed to himself or herself. For example, giving a written statement about someone to a secretary for the sole purpose of having it typed is not a communication of libel. Communicating the statement to the secretary with the intent that he or she believe it or giving the message to another party would constitute a communication of libel.

A different standard of defamation requirements exists with respect to public figures. Persons who place themselves in the public light are inviting comment or publicity under the constitutional rights of free speech. Nevertheless, there are limits to what can be said publicly about another. If it can be shown that a statement was made with actual malice (knowledge that the statement was false or reckless disregard for its truth or falsity), even a public figure can maintain an action for defamation.[33]

Some defenses are peculiar to actions based upon defamation. First, the truth is always a defense. If a truthful statement is made about another, no matter how damaging, no action for defamation can be brought. Another defense is known as privilege. Since certain communications are deemed to serve the public interest, someone's opinion may be exempt from an action for defamation. For example, an employer who fires an employee for suspected drug use is privileged with respect to reporting this information to government agencies, such as unemployment agencies. Generally, if a terminated employee seeks unemployment compensation, the employer will be asked the reasons for termination. The employer may not be able to prove the absolute truth of this statement about a former employee. If the suspicions were reasonable, however, the employer is permitted to give the information to government agencies who will keep it confidential. Privilege applies whenever public policy requires communication between the private sector and the government.

Emotional Distress

Emotional distress is often called the catchall tort. A plaintiff can plead it as a negligence action or as an intentional tort. Frequently, when it is difficult to prove the necessary elements of a specific intentional tort, emotional distress is used as the cause of action. It can also accompany an intentional tort as a separate and independent action.

Jurisdictions are divided on the issue of whether an actual physical contact must accompany the emotional injury. But to prove an action for intentional infliction of emotional distress, it must be shown that the actor intentionally engaged in conduct so outrageous that the actor knew or should have known that its likely result would be a mental or emotional disturbance to the plaintiff of such a magnitude that it could produce a resulting physical injury, for example, falsely or mistakenly informing a new mother that her baby was stillborn. Such a severe blow to one in an already weakened condition could likely have physical effects.

Emotional distress can also be brought as the basis of negligence. This generally occurs when the conduct was unquestionably unreasonable, but proving the intent (under the definition of an intentional tort) of the actor is difficult. This type of action is based on conduct so extremely reckless that it is considered unreasonable.

Some jurisdictions also acknowledge a separate action for negligent infliction of emotional distress. The requirements are those of an action in negligence with a damage requirement of emotional distress as previously defined.

Damages Awarded for Intentional Torts

Many of the intentional torts discussed here may also be the basis for a separate criminal prosecution. However, the action for an intentional tort is a dispute that is purely between the private parties, and no imprisonment or fines are imposed. If proven, however, because of the element of intent, civil actions for intentional torts often result in more severe money judgments than in cases of negligence based on careless conduct. In addition, when a jurisdiction permits, punitive damages are often awarded to the plaintiff in addition to the ordinary compensatory damages. This occurs because the courts want to send a message that conduct that intentionally results in harm to another will be dealt with severely.

Assignment 9.2

Examine the following situations and indicate whether an intentional tort was committed and, if so, what type of intentional tort occurred:

(a) An irate customer takes a swing at a store clerk but misses when the clerk jumps aside.

(b) A priceless antique is found to be missing during a party. The host gathers all of the guests together and locks them in his windowless basement until the culprit confesses.

(c) In a near collision, one driver yells at the other, "Get out of your car so I can punch you in the nose!"

(d) A hunter crosses a boundary line into private property but does not damage the property.

(e) At a local business luncheon, one store owner publicly accuses another of selling stolen goods.

(f) In the hallway at school, one student puts his foot in the path of another, who trips over it and falls.

(g) A man is falsely told that his wife has been killed. He is so grief stricken that he suffers a heart attack.

(h) A real estate agent sells an avid fishing fan who lives in Connecticut a "lakefront lot" as a vacation home on a dude ranch in Arizona based on pictures of the property. The real estate agent knows but does not disclose that the photographs were taken many years ago and the lake is now completely dry.

(i) In a private meeting between two athletes, one professional athlete accuses the other of cheating in competitions.

(j) A bystander is shot when a gunman fires a gun toward a crowd.

PRODUCT LIABILITY

Product liability is not a specific body of tort law such as negligence, strict liability, or intentional torts. Rather, it describes a subject of a tort action that may be based on any one of the major tort theories. The common denominator is that the action involves a product that has been placed in commerce. The number of variety of commercial products has grown to such proportions that an entire area of law has been developed to establish precedent for disputes that arise out of the sale and use of products. Each year, several million injuries result from use of manufactured products. It is not surprising that the number of lawsuits in this area has grown accordingly.

Causes of Action

Some of the legal standards that have been established include causes of action in products cases and standards of care. For example, the commonly encountered causes of action in product liability cases include the following:

- Breach of express warranty
- Breach of implied warranty of fitness for a particular purpose
- Breach of implied warranty of merchantability
- Negligence
- Deceit
- Strict liability

It is apparent that many of the causes of action resemble ordinary tort actions. In reality, product liability actions are derived from basic tort law. However, to accommodate the unique position of the consumer/injured party and manufacturer, certain modifications have been made. Also note that res ipsa loquitur is commonly employed in product liability cases, since quite often the plaintiff has no opportunity to discover the exact action of the defendant that produced the danger in the product.

Specific legal standards regarding the standard of care in product liability cases include the idea that a manufacturer is presumed to be an expert on the product and therefore must manufacture the product with the same care as someone with extensive knowledge about the product and its potential dangers. A manufacturer who does not have such knowledge or does not utilize it to make reasonably sure that the product is safe can be held accountable for injuries caused by the product.

Defenses

Defenses in product liability cases are similar to those found in other areas of negligence. Additionally, a manufacturer may also claim as a defense extreme misuse of the product. It is established that manufacturers must foresee a certain degree of misuse of a product. However, if the consumer significantly modifies the product or uses it in a manner that the manufacturer could not have been reasonably expected to foresee, the manufacturer will not be held liable for any injuries.

 APPLICATION 9.6

Christopher purchases a power drill. The box the drill is packaged in clearly states, "Light duty wood drill. Read all instructions before operating." Christopher does not read the instruction book, which clearly states that the drill is not intended for use on metal. He proceeds to attempt to drill through the side of a safe that he has lost the combination to. The safe wall is one inch thick. During the drilling, the motor burns out, and Christopher is seriously injured by an electrical shock.

Point for Discussion
What is the significance of Christopher's failure to read the instructions?

Statute of Limitations

One area of difficulty in product liability law involves the statute of limitations. Typically, the statute of limitations begins to run at the time the plaintiff knows or should know he or she has a cause of action. This was found to create a problem in the area of product liability because many times, the injury did not occur until many years after the product was manufactured. Consequently, the defendant manufacturer was at a tremendous disadvantage. Much of the evidence and many of the witnesses with knowledge about the product design and creation were no longer available. In response, many state legislatures enacted what are known as statutes of repose, which place an absolute limit from the time of manufacture in which an action can be brought. For example, in a state with a statute of repose of fifteen years, no product liability action can be brought more than fifteen years after the manufacture of the product or when the statute of limitations runs out, whichever is first.

The unique characteristics of commercial products that are distributed (often in mass quantities) and that remain in use for many years have necessitated the development of special rules of law. With these precedents, manufacturers and consumers alike have a better awareness of their rights with respect to the sale, purchase, and use of products.

EMPLOYMENT AND TORTS

Tort law has had a significant influence in the area of employment. It concerns not only the actions by or against third parties but also the relationship between the employer and the employee. All states have certain statutes and case law governing the employment relationship and indicating when actions for tort based upon it are permitted. Certain exceptions to these statutes also give rise to actions in tort.

Third Parties

Under a long-established rule of law in this country commonly known as "respondeat superior,"[34] a superior may be held responsible for injuries caused by his or her employee. Generally, an injured third party has the right to elect to sue the employer if the third party can demonstrate that the employee was a regular employee and not an independent contractor (someone who works on a per-job basis, such as a plumber who goes to someone's office to repair a leaky faucet) and that the injury was caused by the employee while acting within the scope of his or her employment. Simply stated, the latter means that the employee is acting subject to the ultimate supervision of the employer. The employee does not need to be engaged in a regular job duty as long as he or she is engaged in a task that benefits the employer in some direct manner. Generally, employers are not responsible for occurrences while the employee is going to or from work. However, a different rule would apply if the employee were running an errand for the employer (even though it may not be a part of his or her regular duties to do so).

Ordinarily, employers will not be held responsible for intentional torts committed by an employee. An intentional tort requires that the actor knew or should have known with substantial certainty that the act would produce the injury. An employer cannot be held responsible for such intentional acts over which he or she has no control. If this were permitted, employees could escape responsibility for acts that the employer neither benefited from nor condoned. The exception to this rule takes place when the intentional tort is considered to be within the scope of the employee's duties. Security guards are a common example. Often, such personnel are required to restrain customers physically or compel them to leave the premises. In such a situation, the actions of the employee are presumed to be directed by the employer. Therefore, any injuries resulting from the guard's conduct could result in liability of the employer.

Statutes Governing the Employment Relationships That Affect Tort Actions

Workers' compensation.   Every state in the United States has a statute in effect for workers' compensation.[35] Although the details of these statutes vary from state to state, the principle is the same. The statutes were enacted to provide a basis for compensation to employees who are injured while working within the scope of employment. The benefits from such statutes are many.

First, the statutes provide fairly well defined limits of compensation for injuries, which gives employers the ability to pay compensation without being put out of business by huge money judgments from juries. Secondly, the compensation statutes are generally not concerned with fault or negligence. Thus, the employee does not have to prove a standard theory of tort against the employer. Finally, in a majority of states it is against public policy and illegal to fire an employee because a workers' compensation claim was filed.[36] Therefore, employees can seek compensation for their injuries and time lost from work without fear of losing their jobs for doing so. Ultimately, the statutes have greatly reduced the number and expense of lawsuits between employers and employees and have directly contributed to the flow of industry in this country.

Injuries not subject to workers' compensation laws.   Although all states have workers' compensation laws in effect, some injuries or, actually, causes of injury are exempt from these statutes. Such a case may occur when an employer willfully or deliberately places an employee in great danger and that danger results in injury to the employee. Such willful or deliberate misconduct is often an exception to workers' compensation laws, and the employee has the opportunity to file a civil action for damages against the employer.[37] Although this action imposes the requirement of proving the wrongful conduct, there is no limitation on the amount of damages that can be claimed.

Employer Liability Laws

Although each law has specific provisions, an employer liability law will generally permit a civil action by an employee against an employer for injuries received within the scope of employment. It must be shown, however, that both parties are subject to the statute and that the employer was somehow negligent.

Numerous states have such laws in effect. There are also several federal employer liability laws. The federal laws do not necessarily apply to federal employees. Rather, they are laws passed by the national government that apply to an entire industry that operates on an interstate basis. Actions arising under the federal laws may be litigated in federal courts, for example, the Jones Act,[38] United States Code Section 683, et seq., which applies to the shipping industry.

Originally, employer liability laws were enacted to provide protection to a class of workers who were engaged in a hazardous occupation where serious injuries or fatalities were frequent and where the workers were often at a disadvantage. The reasoning behind such laws was to provide protection to employees whose education and ability to seek other employment were often very limited. Further, the injuries that commonly occurred in the industry were so serious that the employees were often prevented from ever working again, and their families were left with no means of support. Consequently, the legislatures enacted statutes to ease the burden of proving civil suits against the employers. Although the statutes usually require the proof of negligence, they make such proof easier to establish.

Discriminatory Practices by Employers

Traditionally, the employer could expect liability under civil law or workers' compensation laws for injuries incurred by the employee while acting within the scope of employment. Most often these involved physical injuries received on the job. Recently, however, legislatures, regulating agencies, and the courts have been focusing more on those injuries that affect the psychosocial and economical aspects of employment. Employers are subject to certain minimum standards in the reasons used for hiring and terminating employees. Certain requirements must also be met in providing a suitable work environment.

During the latter part of the twentieth century, much evidence demonstrated that many employers would not hire or would treat individuals with certain characteristics differently from other employees. As a result, legislation and regulations were passed to protect various classes of people. These laws were designed to keep employers from discriminating against employees for possessing characteristics that had nothing to do with their ability to adequately perform the duties of employment. Such characteristics include gender, race, religion, and, in many cases, age. Similar restrictions apply for handicapped individuals. If an employer is found to treat an employee differently, refuse to hire, or use as a cause for termination one or more of the protected classes, the employer is subject to scrutiny under federal law. If it is determined that the employer violated the law by using improper reasons for hiring, termination, or discipline, then the employer may be subject to a variety of penalties.

Another area of employment law that continues to develop is the work environment. Just as federal agencies such as OSHA strive to protect the employee from physical dangers on the job, the branches of government are now focused on protecting the employee from unnecessary psychological and emotional dangers on the job as well. One such example is sexual harassment. If an employee can demonstrate that an employer participated or acquiesced in a course of conduct that subjected the employee to an environment that was reasonably perceived as hostile because of differential treatment based on the gender or sexual preference of the employee, the employee may have a basis for legal action against the employer. This places the responsibility on the employer to monitor the conduct of all employees and to maintain a workplace that encourages fair and professional treatment of each employee by the employer and coworkers alike.

TORT DEFENSES

In response to the many theories of liability in tort, defenses for conduct have been developed. These defenses are used to justify the defendant's actions or to expose the plaintiff's own part in the occurrence that produced the injury. Even today, these defenses are developing and changing. Although they vary slightly from jurisdiction to jurisdiction, the underlying principles are substantially the same.

Contributory and Comparative Negligence

Contributory negligence is a well-known defense in this country. At one time, it was highly popular but is now experiencing a decline in popularity. In the past, the courts applied this defense when a defendant could prove that the plaintiff contributed to his or her own injury by some form of negligent conduct. For example, in a car accident, while the defendant was driving under the influence of alcohol, the plaintiff may have been speeding on a dark and rainy night. The plaintiff was also acting negligently and contributed to the cause of the accident. When a court applies the defense of contributory negligence, the plaintiff cannot recover any damages from the defendant. The rationale for this defense is that one should not ultimately receive compensation for injuries caused by one's own wrongdoing.[39]

The defense of contributory negligence has declined in popularity for several reasons. As society has become increasingly complex, so have the causes of injuries. No longer are causes of injuries simply determined. In addition, a growing body of thought reasoned that although plaintiffs should not recover for their own misconduct, neither should defendants be relieved of liability for theirs. Accordingly, the theory of comparative negligence was developed. In **comparative negligence,** the degree of negligence of each party is assigned a percentage of the fault for the occurrence.[40] The jury arrives at such a calculation and reduces the judgment for the plaintiff by the percentage that the plaintiff contributed to his or her own injury.

Some jurisdictions apply pure comparative negligence where a plaintiff who the jury finds to be 99 percent at fault recovers only one percent of the damages. However, many jurisdictions apply modified comparative negligence, which prevents any recovery if a plaintiff was the significant cause of the injury, that is, was more than 50 percent at fault. In some states, a combination of contributory and comparative negligence applies. If a plaintiff is grossly negligent, contributory negligence will apply. Otherwise, comparative negligence will apply.[41]

Comparative negligence responds to negligence of the plaintiff without relieving the defendant of liability for his or her own misconduct. A steady trend by jurisdictions in this country has been to adopt the theory of comparative negligence in some form and abandon the traditional theory of contributory negligence.

Contributory Negligence
The doctrine that maintains a plaintiff who, in any way, contributes to his or her injury cannot recover from a negligent defendant.

Comparative Negligence
Degree of plaintiff's own negligent conduct that was responsible for plaintiff's injury.

Assumption of Risk

Assumption of Risk
Defense to negligence on the basis that the plaintiff knew of, appreciated, and voluntarily encountered the danger of defendant's conduct.

The defense of **assumption of risk** is also seeing some decline in response to the growth of comparative negligence. Traditionally, a defendant could prevent recovery by a plaintiff if the defendant could prove that the plaintiff was aware of the risk of danger, appreciated the seriousness of the risk, and voluntarily exposed himself or herself to the risk.[42] As with the application of comparative negligence, the recovery would not be barred but would be modified.

Many jurisdictions still accept assumption of risk as a defense to establish the degree to which the plaintiff was responsible for his or her own injury. An example of assumption of risk is a person attending a car race who sits at the edge of the racetrack. It is easily foreseeable that a car traveling at high speed could lose control and strike the onlooker. If the onlooker nevertheless remains in this position of danger, it may well be held that he or she assumed the risk of the danger.

Last Clear Chance

Last Clear Chance
Defense of plaintiff responding to defenses of allegedly negligent defendant, in which plaintiff claims defendant had the last opportunity to avoid plaintiff's injury irrespective of plaintiff's own negligence.

Another defense still widely used is the doctrine of **last clear chance** which, in reality, is a defense to a defense. When a defendant claims a defense such as contributory negligence that would bar recovery by a plaintiff, the plaintiff may respond with a claim of last clear chance. The doctrine states that even though a plaintiff contributed to endangering himself or herself, the defendant had the last clear opportunity to avoid the occurrence and prevent the plaintiff's injury but failed to do so.[43] An example is the preceding driving case. Even though the plaintiff was speeding in bad weather, if the defendant could have swerved at the last second and did not, the plaintiff could still recover for the defendant's failure to take advantage of the last clear chance to avoid the occurrence.

Intentional Tort Defenses

Defenses raised in response to claims of intentional tort include the charge that not all of the elements were satisfied as well as consent, privilege, immunity, and various procedural defenses.

Although the first defense—that not all elements were satisfied—may be raised as a defense in any type of tort action, it is very appropriate in an intentional tort case. By definition, the elements of intentional torts tend to be quite specific. Thus, it is usually much easier to establish the absence of a specific event than it is to establish that the defendant's conduct met the reasonable standard of care under the circumstances in a negligence action.

Similarly, the defenses of consent, privilege, immunity, and involuntary conduct are seen most often in intentional tort suits. The defense of consent consists of proof by the defendant that the plaintiff in fact consented to or agreed overtly or by implication to the defendant's action. For example, a plaintiff might sue a defendant for battery that allegedly occurred when the defendant physician operated on the plaintiff. The defendant could claim that the plaintiff, by subjecting himself to the surgery, consented to procedures that the defendant deemed appropriate during surgery.

The defense of privilege is quite different from that of consent. Whereas in consent, the focus is on the conduct of the plaintiff toward the defendant, in privilege, the view is taken that regardless of the plaintiff's agreement or protestations, the defendant had a special legal right to act. For example, a plaintiff attempts to collect unemployment and is denied because the defendant (plaintiff's former employer) informed the Labor Department that the plaintiff was fired for drug use on the job. The plaintiff cannot successfully sue the defendant for defamation, because the employer has a privileged relationship with the government. By protecting employers, the government has the benefit of full disclosure and can therefore deny benefits to someone who is guilty of criminal activity. A variety of situations exist in which a party has a privileged relationship, and any tortious activity resulting from that privileged relationship cannot be prosecuted by a plaintiff. Another common privilege is that of self-defense. Depending on the circumstances, a person has the right to use reasonable or necessary force to defend himself or herself, and can even use force to defend someone else if that person was entitled to use self-defense. Limited force can also be used to defend property, but not if it would result in a breach of the peace, and the privilege never extends to the use of deadly force to defend property.

Like privilege, immunity gives protection to otherwise guilty defendants. The most common example is that of sovereign immunity. Historically, no lawsuit could be brought against the government for the torts committed by government servants. This was inherently unfair. However, to totally lift this ban could result in enough lawsuits against the government to bankrupt it. Consequently, federal and state legislatures have enacted laws that allow suits against the government in limited circumstances and in accordance with strict procedural rules. In this way, the government is accountable for its torts but is not at risk of being victimized by a litigation explosion of its own.

Assignment 9.3

For each of the following tort defenses, create a factual tort situation that would give the defendant a successful defense. Identify the facts that support the necessary elements to succeed with the defense.

(a) Truth in a libel case
(b) Assumption of risk
(c) Last clear chance
(d) Intentional tort by an employee in a case based on respondeat superior
(e) Comparative negligence example of the defense of assumption of risk: A hitchhiker meets a group of young people at a roadside park. He observes them consuming large amounts of alcohol. He later accepts a ride from the group. The driver is drunk and causes an accident that injures the hitchhiker.

1. Observing consumption of alcohol = Hitchhiker knew or should have known this could impair one's driving. Further, he should have appreciated that impaired driving could result in an accident and injuries.
2. Accepting the ride in light of the above knowledge and appreciation = Voluntary encounter with known and appreciated danger.

DAMAGES IN TORT ACTIONS

In the successful tort action, the trier of fact is faced with the task of awarding damages. In all actions at law, damages are monetary. The amount depends on a myriad of factors as well as the law of the jurisdiction. Some legislatures have enacted law that precludes anything but strictly compensatory damages; others allow punitive damages, prejudgment interest, and attorney's fees. The purpose here is to distinguish the types of damage that are possible if permitted legally by law of the jurisdiction.

DAMAGE	PURPOSE
Compensatory	To compensate the plaintiff for injury.
Specials	Those items of compensatory damage that can be specifically calculated, e.g. medical bills.
Generals	Those items of compensatory damage that must be estimated as to monetary value, e.g., pain and suffering, loss of reputation.
Punitive (also known as exemplary damages)	To punish defendant and to deter defendant and others from future similar conduct.
Nominal	Allowed in other than negligence (in which actual damage is an element that must be proven) for commission of a tort by defendant but for which no actual loss by plaintiff is proven.

Typically, the award to the plaintiff will consist of compensatory damages. The types of damage that support an award of compensatory damage include property damage, physical injury, lost wages, and more abstract notions such as pain and suffering, shortened life expectancy, loss of consortium (elements of the marital relationship), and emotional distress. If proven, all are acceptable bases for compensation. In those jurisdictions where punitives are permitted, they may be awarded in especially egregious cases where the defendant's conduct was particularly reckless.

ETHICAL NOTE

The importance of ethics is obvious in such areas of law as contract, property, and business. At first glance, it is not so obvious in tort law. However, the requirement for ethical conduct is especially important in torts, since in these cases, juries are required to consider intangible factors such as pain, suffering, lost future wages, disability, and disfigurement. All of these factors contain built-in emotional triggers. For the unethical person, such cases provide an opportunity to manipulate and take advantage of a situation to the detriment of another. Early in the chapter, the litigation explosion was mentioned. In addition to this "explosion," a great deal of publicity has focused on some lawyers and plaintiffs who file frivolous claims in the hope of monetary gain. The response of many legislatures has been to enact statutes that penalize anyone found guilty of filing an unfounded claim. In turn, lawyers and their clients alike have been put on notice to carefully evaluate a situation before proceeding with a formal lawsuit.

Question

Assume you are a lawyer and a client comes to you with what appears to be an attempt to obtain money from a proposed defendant through an obviously unfounded claim of injury. What should you do?

CHAPTER SUMMARY

The law of torts is growing and changing on a day-to-day basis. The courts are constantly being presented with variations on the basic principles. Legislatures in every state are considering additional statutes that will affect tort law. As a result, it is a challenge to keep current on these changes and the way that they affect our lives both personally and professionally.

Some constants remain in tort law, especially the recognized areas of tort. Negligence is the appropriate claim when one party has a duty to act with a certain degree of care toward another party and that duty is breached. For a negligence claim to succeed, it must be shown that the breach was the legal and factual cause of an injury and that the injury is of a type and extent that is compensable.

When a party's conduct goes beyond mere disregard for potentially dangerous circumstances and involves actions that are nearly certain to result in significant injury to another, an intentional tort has been committed. Although

the knowledge of the actor may be more difficult to prove in such cases, when it is accomplished, the penalties are often more severe.

Finally, there are certain extremely dangerous situations in which no amount of care can prevent injury to innocent bystanders. In such instances, the party that produces the situation and benefits from it will be held responsible for the injuries. This is totally irrespective of whether that party knew of or took steps to avoid the injury. The cost of the benefit is responsibility for the injury as a matter of strict liability.

These principles have remained basically constant, although the manner and circumstances in which they are applied have changed. In addition, defenses to tort law continue to evolve and develop into principles that will produce the fairest result for all concerned. This is evidenced by the shift from the absolute defense of contributory negligence to the defense of comparative negligence, which apportions fault between the parties.

REVIEW QUESTIONS

1. How does negligence differ from an intentional tort?
2. When is an employer liable for the acts of an employee?
3. Under what circumstances is assumption of risk applied?
4. Which party claims last clear chance?
5. What are the types of defamation actions?
6. How have workers' compensation laws affected tort actions?
7. When can res ipsa loquitur be applied?
8. What types of claims involve strict liability?
9. How do the torts of assault and battery differ?
10. How does a claim of strict liability differ from a claim for negligence?

CHAPTER TERMS

Assumption of Risk	Intentional Tort	Proximate Cause
Comparative Negligence	Last Clear Chance	Reasonable Conduct
Contributory Negligence	Negligence	Strict Liability

NOTES

1. William Statsky, *Legal Thesaurus/Dictionary* (St. Paul: West, 1986).
2. Prosser, *Handbook on Torts* (St. Paul: West, 1971), Chapter 2, Section 7.
3. Id.
4. Id.
5. Id.
6. Id. at Chapter 5, Section 30.
7. *Palsgraf v. Long Island R. R. Co.*, 248 N.Y. 339, 162 N.E. 99 (N.Y. 1928).
8. Id., see dissent of Justice Andrews.
9. 65 C.J.S., Negligence, Section 10 (1955); (1987 supp.).
10. 65 C.J.S., Negligence, Section 11 (1955); (1987 supp.).
11. See note 9, supra.
12. See note 10, supra.
13. Id.
14. Id.
15. Id.
16. Prosser, *Handbook on Torts,* Chapter 7, Section 41.
17. Id.
18. Id.
19. William Statsky, *Torts: Personal Injury Litigation* (St. Paul: West, 1982), p. 364.
20. Id.
21. Annot., 23 A.L.R.3rd 1083.
22. Prosser, *Handbook on Torts,* Chapter 5, Section 31.
23. American Law Institute, Restatement of the Law on Torts II, Section 21(1), 1976.
24. Id., Section 13; *Mason v. Cohn,* 108 Misc.2d 674, 438 N.Y.S.2d 462 (1981).
25. Statsky, *Torts: Personal Injury Litigation,* p. 415.
26. See note 23, Section 35; *Cimino v. Rosen,* 193 Neb. 162, 225 N.W.2d 567 (1975).
27. Id.
28. See note 23, Section 217; *Guin v. City of Riviera Beach Fla.,* 388 So.2d 604 (Fla.App. 1980).
29. See note 23, Sections 525–552.
30. See note 23, Sections 558–559.
31. Id.
32. Id.
33. Id.; *New York Times v. Sullivan,* 376 U.S. 254, 84 S.Ct. 710, 11 L.Ed.2d 686 (1964).
34. See note 23, Section 46.
35. 81 Am.Jur., Workers' Compensation, Section 1; 315.
36. Annot., 32 A.L.R.4th 1221.
37. Annot., 96 A.L.R.3rd 1064.
38. See note 23, Section 463; Annot., 32 A.L.R.3rd 463.
39. Id.
40. Id.
41. See note 23, Section 479; *Ortego v. State Farm Mutual Auto Ins. Co.,* 295 So.2d 593 (La.App. 1974).
42. See note 23, Section 496; *Parr v. Hamnes,* 303 Minn. 333, 228 N.W.2d 234 (1975).
43. Prosser, *Handbook on Torts.*

CHAPTER 10

The Law of Business

CHAPTER OBJECTIVES

After reading this chapter, you should be able to

- *Discuss the role of agency in partnerships and corporations.*

- *Distinguish actual and apparent authority.*

- *Distinguish by characteristic the business forms of partnership, corporation, and sole proprietorship.*

- *List the determining factors for the existence of a partnership.*

- *Discuss limited partnerships' unique characteristics and describe the steps to create a corporation.*

- *Discuss a corporate promoter's role.*

- *Explain the rationale behind the doctrine of piercing the corporate veil.*

- *Describe the process of dissolution of a corporation.*

TABLE 10.1 Business Organizations	Characteristic	Sole Proprietorship	General Partnership	Limited Partnership	Corporation
	Number of Owners	1	2 +	2 +	1 +
	Life	Limited	Limited	Limited	Unlimited
	Liability	Unlimited personal	Unlimited personal	General—Unlimited personal Limited—Limited personal	Limited personal
	Control	Complete	Shared	General—Shared Limited—None of day-to-day	Limited to policy changes
	Income	All personal	All personal	All personal	Only dividends personal
	Legal Status	None	Very limited	Very limited	Separate entity

This chapter focuses on the major categories of business entities: sole proprietorships, general and limited partnerships, and corporations (see Table 10.1). In addition, the law of agency is discussed within the context of business organizations.

The way a business entity is organized will dictate who receives the income of the business, who is liable for debts or judgments against the business, and who in the business has the authority to make decisions regarding the operation of the business. In addition, the law of agency governs such issues as who is permitted to represent the business in dealings with other entities and the methods and procedures for such dealings.

This chapter contains references to certain model laws that have been adopted by all or a majority of the states. These laws, often known as uniform acts, are precisely what the name implies. They are designed for adoption by all the states so that every state will treat a particular business entity or transaction in substantially the same way. With interstate transactions becoming more and more frequent, these laws provide for fair and consistent treatment of business no matter where it is transacted. In the law of business, one of the most frequently employed uniform laws is the Uniform Commercial Code, or U.C.C.

The U.C.C. has been adopted, at least in part, by every state. It contains a series of laws that detail the legal rights and obligations of parties to formal business transactions. The adoption of this code has eliminated many of the inconsistencies in the way legal disputes over common transactions were dealt with in the various state courts.

AGENCY

An **agency** is formally defined as

> A relationship in which one person acts for another or represents another by the latter's authority.[1]

The person who gives authority to another to act in his or her behalf is the principal; the person who receives authority to act on behalf of another is the agent. An example of a typical agency relationship is a retail company and its sales force. As agents, these salespersons have the authority to act on behalf of the retail company (who is their principal) to sell the company's products.

 APPLICATION 10.1

Marcia is employed by Roberto as an administrative assistant in an interior design business. Part of Marcia's job duties include preparing and submitting bids to potential customers. Marcia is the agent, and Roberto is the principal. Marcia's actions are done on behalf and in place of Roberto's.

Point for Discussion
Assume Marcia and Roberto are partners. Would Marcia still be an agent. If so, for whom?

Creation of the Agency Relationship

Before an agency can be created, the principal must have the legal capacity to authorize such a relationship;[2] that is, the principal must have the ability to enter into a contract. Specifically, the principal must be over the age of majority in the jurisdiction (usually 18 or 21) and must be legally competent. A declaration of legal incompetence means that the court has found that a person is not capable of managing his or her own affairs. If the principal is a business entity such as a corporation or partnership, it should be organized in such a way that it is recognized as that type of business entity by the laws of the state.

Conversely, it is not necessary for an agent to have contractual authority.[3] Conceivably, a principal could appoint a minor or a person who has been declared legally incompetent to act as an agent. In agency, it is still possible for such a person to have authority to deal in the affairs of a principal. Most jurisdictions, however, do impose minimum levels of competence for an agent. Generally, lunatics or persons who are virtually totally deficient in mental ability will not be considered part of a valid principal-agent relationship.

Agency
When one party known as the agent acts on behalf of another party known as the principal. In a valid agency relationship, the agent can legally bind the principal.

APPLICATION 10.2

Karen, age 32, starts a retail basket business. She hires Anne and Barbara to go door to door soliciting orders for baskets. Anne is 16, and Barbara is 17. Both Anne and Barbara are agents of Karen and can contract on Karen's behalf. It is not necessary that Anne and Barbara have contractual capacity, because they are not parties to the contract. Rather, only Karen and the customer are the parties obligated by the contract and must therefore have contractual capacity.

Point for Discussion

What if Anne is mentally retarded? Can she still legally function as Karen's agent?

Assignment 10.1

Identify whether an agency relationship exists and if so, whether it is employment related.

1. After work, Joe and his boss go out for a drink. Joe goes to the bar to purchase the drinks with money given to him by his boss.
2. Just before leaving for lunch, Joe's boss tells Joe to pick up two cases of beer to provide to other workers at a surprise party for a retiring employee. Working hours are 9:00 to 5:00. The party begins at 4:00.
3. Laura is driving to work when she runs a red light and causes an accident.
4. Laura is driving to work but stops on the way to pick up her boss's dry cleaning as a favor. Laura runs a red light in front of the dry cleaners and causes an accident.
5. Laura is driving to work but stops on the way to pick up uniforms from a local dry cleaner. The uniforms are used by the staff members. Laura runs a red light in front of the dry cleaners and causes an accident.

Agent's Duties

The agent has several duties toward the principal. First is the duty of a fiduciary. The agent owes complete loyalty to the interests of the principal, including protecting those interests and any confidential communications regarding them.[4] If the agent acts on behalf of another or even on his or her own behalf in a way that is in conflict with the principal's interest, the agent has violated the fiduciary duty.

Second, every agent owes the principal a duty to act with reasonable care to protect the assets and interests of the principal. An agent who is in possession of property belonging to the principal must take reasonable steps to protect the property. An agent with confidential knowledge regarding the interests of the principal must act reasonably not to allow this information to be exploited. Failure to do either of these things would constitute a breach of the agent's duty of reasonable care.[5]

Finally, the agent owes the principal a certain degree of obedience. Within the principal-agent relationship, the principal can, to a reasonable extent, direct the actions of the agent in accomplishing the purpose of the agency.[6] For example, if the agency involves the sale of the principal's product, the principal may, to a reasonable extent, dictate the sales methods used by the agents. If an agent deviates substantially from the directions of the principal, the agent has breached the duty of obedience.

If an agent does breach one of the duties owed to a principal, several things may occur. First, the responsibility of the principal to be bound to third parties by the agent's acts may be affected. The principal may also have an action at law against the agent to recover any damage suffered as a result of the breach. If the agent was paid for the services rendered, the principal may sue for damages incurred directly as a result of the breach of one or more of the duties.

Whether an agent is paid for services rendered or performs the services as a gratuitous gesture, the principal may sue the agent in tort for the breach of reasonable care of property or the failure to make reasonable efforts to accomplish the purpose of the agency. Specifically, the principal could sue the agent for negligently or intentionally failing to perform the duties of an agent.

If the agent breaches the fiduciary duty and profits from dealing on his or her own behalf rather than on behalf of the principal, the principal may recover all of the profits accumulated through the agent's self-dealing. This is allowed to prevent agents from profiting at the expense of the principal.

Principal's Duties

Just as binding are the duties of the principal toward the agent. Unless the agent has agreed to act gratuitously, every principal owes an agent a duty of reasonable compensation for the services performed on behalf of the principal.[7] In addition, an agent is entitled to reimbursement by the principal for reasonable expenses incurred in achieving the objective of the agency.[8] This duty of reimbursement also extends to losses the agent may suffer while engaged in the agency relationship. Finally, a principal has the duty to cooperate in allowing the agent to complete his or her assigned tasks.

An exception to the duty of compensation and reimbursement occurs when the loss is incurred through the fault of the agent. For example, if an agent traveling on behalf of the principal's business is in an automobile accident, the principal could be held responsible for the agent's property loss, such as damage to the car, as well as for the agent's medical costs for treatment of injuries. If, however, the accident is caused by the agent's careless driving, the principal would have no liability for the agent's losses. (Note that this does not relieve the principal of liability for injuries caused to third persons by the agent's conduct. This is addressed in Chapter 9 under "Third Parties".)

If the principal fails or refuses to honor any of these duties, the agent is entitled to bring an action at law against the principal for breach of contract. In addition, the agent may be entitled to impose a possessory lien on property of the principal that the agent holds. For example, if an agent is in possession of property of the principal and the principal does not pay the agent due compensation for work performed, the agent often has the option of holding the property until the principal complies with the duty of compensation or reimbursement.

Types of Authority

Assuming that both parties have the requisite capacity and are aware of the duties of each, four general types of authority can be exercised: actual authority, apparent authority, inherent authority, and authority by ratification. They are distinguished by the kind of authority given to the agent and the manner in which it is given. Each is created in a different way and imposes different degrees of responsibility on the parties.

Actual authority.   For actual authority to exist, the element of consent must be present.[9] The principal and the agent must both speak or act in a way that manifests agreement to the relationship. In addition, the principal must have legal capacity. The agency is not required to serve a purpose that will benefit both the principal and the agent. It is entirely possible for an agency to exist in which the agent receives no consideration for representing the principal.

Usually, a written agreement regarding the agency relationship is not required. Words or actions of the two parties are enough to establish that an agency exists between them. Some states, however, have an exception to this, that is, if a purpose of the agency is to grant authority to the agent to enter into written contracts on behalf of the principal. In this situation, the agent must have written evidence of authority from the principal. This rule is known as the equal dignities rule.[10] If a contract must be in writing under the statute of frauds (the statute in each jurisdiction that states which contracts must be in writing to be valid), it is only logical that the grant of authority to enter into the contract on behalf of another should also be in writing.

An agency based on actual authority is created solely by the principal and agent through agreement and is not based on what a third party perceives as the relationship between the principal and the agent. Actual authority includes two subcategories that indicate the way in which the agency was created and, to some degree, the extent of the agent's authority.

Actual express authority.   Actual express authority occurs when the principal gives to the agent an overt verbal or written communication stating the nature of the authority.[11] The principal need not put specific limits on the authority, such as time or degree, although this is desirable. If no limits are placed on the agent and a question arises as to whether the agent exceeded the authority, the court will limit the authority to what would be usual and customary under the circumstances.[12]

An example of express authority is the relationship between the owner and the sales staff at an automobile dealership. The owner (principal) gives actual express authority to the sales personnel to negotiate for the sale of cars in the inventory of the business. The authority of the agents would not ordinarily extend to the point of giving the cars away or selling the property where the business is located.

Actual implied authority.   Actual implied authority takes effect when the principal acts in such a way that the agent reasonably believes that the authority to act for the principal has been granted.[13] In limited situations, implied authority can occur in conjunction with express authority. The agent who has express authority to accomplish certain objectives for the principal also has the principal's implied authority to do whatever is reasonably necessary to accomplish the objectives. For example, a housekeeper who is authorized to manage a household, clean the house, and prepare meals would generally also have implied authority to purchase necessary cleaning supplies and groceries on behalf of the principal.

It is also considered reasonable for an agent with express authority in a particular type of business to employ customs and methods generally used in that type of business. For example, a construction company (principal) gives express authority to an agent to submit bids for building contracts. If the customs or methods used in the bidding include negotiating first with subcontractors, it is implied that the agent has the authority to engage in such negotiations to be competitive and to obtain contracts for the principal.

A type of actual implied authority that is independent from actual express authority is called implied authority by acquiescence. It takes place when the principal has not given an agent the express authority to do certain acts on behalf of the principal.[14] Nevertheless, the agent does act, and the principal does not interfere or object and accepts any benefit that results from the agent's actions. When this type of conduct occurs, the agent is presumed to have implied authority to continue acting on behalf of the principal, and the principal will be bound by the acts of the agent that are consistent with previous actions agreed to or acquiesced to by the principal.

 APPLICATION 10.3

A dairy owner hires a clerk to serve ice cream at the counter in a dairy store. If the employee undertakes to start ordering inventory and continues this practice without objection or interference by the employer (principal), the employee (agent) will be considered to have the actual implied authority to order inventory for the ice cream counter. This is so even though the principal never told the clerk to order inventory as part of the job of serving at the counter.

Point for Discussion
Could the owner claim that he had told the clerk to stop ordering inventory and thereby avoid being bound by the contractual obligation to pay for it? (The ice cream melted, so there's no possibility of returning it.)

Actual authority (express or implied) can be terminated. The simplest means of terminating an agency is to make the termination part of the original agency agreement. When the agency is created, the principal states when it will end. Often this is based on a certain date or the happening of a specified event. For example, if the agent is hired to obtain a certain construction contract, the agency will end when the contract is awarded to a construction company.

More complicated are agencies that end because of unforeseen circumstances. If something occurs that effectively prevents the purpose of the agency from being accomplished, a court will often find that the agency terminated at that point. If the agent continues on after the occurrence, a court may hold the agent entirely responsible for any contracts or obligations incurred. Examples of circumstances that would automatically terminate an agency include the loss or destruction of items necessary to the purpose of the agency (a fire that destroys the equipment of the construction company); a drastic change in business conditions (the opening of a new highway that diverts all traffic away from the dairy); a change in relevant laws; potential bankruptcy of the principal or agent if it is relevant to the purpose of the agency; death of the principal or agent; total loss of capacity of the agent; loss of capacity by the principal; or, if the principal is a business entity, dissolution of the entity. In addition, if an agent takes action that is adverse to the principal or the principal's purpose in hiring the agent, the agency will automatically terminate. With respect to the last method, however, if a contract is involved, there may still be liability for breach of contract.

Apparent authority.   Apparent authority, also known as ostensible authority, is created through the acts of the principal and the perception of these acts by third parties.[15] Generally, a third party cannot conclude that an agency agreement exists based solely on the acts and assertions of the agent. The general rule regarding apparent authority is that if a principal acts in such a way that third parties would reasonably believe an agency relationship exists, the third parties can rely on and deal with the agent, and the principal will be bound by such dealings.[16]

First, assume an agent represents to a third party that he or she has the authority to act for the principal. If the principal knows of this and does not tell the third party differently, the third party is justified in believing the agent has the authority. Apparent authority can also be created if the principal acts in such a way or makes statements that would reasonably lead the third party to believe the agent has authority. In such a case, if the third party and the agent make an agreement, regardless of whether the agent in fact has authority, the principal will be bound to the terms of the agreement.

 APPLICATION 10.4

Jeff employs Emma to work in Jeff's shoe store. He takes Emma to several buyers marts, where he orders his stock of shoes for the upcoming season. Jeff introduces Emma as his assistant manager. A few months later, Emma arrives at a buyers mart alone and orders shoes to be delivered to Jeff's store. Based on the prior communication with Jeff, the wholesalers are reasonable in their belief that Emma has apparent authority to represent Jeff.

Point for Discussion
If Emma purchased inventory other than shoes—for example, dresses—at the buyers mart, would the wholesalers be reasonable in believing that Emma had apparent authority?

A principal can be held responsible for an agent whose authority has previously been terminated if the principal does not make the termination known to parties who previously did business with the agent. This is known as lingering apparent authority.[17] If the principal does not make such notification, third parties are reasonable in believing that the agency still exists. As a consequence, the principal will continue to be held responsible for the agent's actions. An exception to this rule is the death or incompetency of the principal, in which case, no notice need be given to third parties. The agent's authority automatically ceases, and the principal's estate will not be bound to any agreements entered into after the death or declaration of incompetence of the principal.

APPLICATION 10.5

Refer to Application 10.4. If Jeff had fired Emma two weeks earlier and Emma nevertheless went to the buyers mart and ordered several hundred pairs of shoes to be delivered to Jeff's store, Jeff could be held to the purchase agreement. This is, however, assuming Jeff took no steps to notify the wholesalers that Emma no longer had Jeff's authority.

Point for Discussion
Would Jeff be responsible under lingering apparent authority if Emma ordered five times the ordinary purchase of shoes by Jeff?

Inherent authority. In certain limited situations, a principal will be held responsible for the acts of an agent even though nothing has occurred to give the agent actual or apparent authority. This is called inherent authority, which is based on a balance of the interests of the principal and innocent third parties. Inherent authority is often imposed when an agent has actual or apparent authority to do one thing and does another.

Two circumstances in which the courts will impose inherent authority are respondeat superior and similar conduct. Under respondeat superior,[18] a principal is held liable for the acts of an employee even when the specific act complained of was not authorized. For example, a delivery truck driver crashes the truck into another vehicle. The employer (principal) authorized deliveries, not automobile accidents. Nevertheless, the principal is liable because the accident took place while the driver (agent) was performing an authorized act.

The theory of similar conduct is based on the concept that a principal should be held responsible for actions that are so similar to the authorized acts that third parties would not be expected to know the difference. Refer to the earlier example of a construction company that hires an agent to submit bids for building contracts. If the agent is represented to have authority to bid and then modifies the bid slightly, a third party would be justified in believing the agent had this type of authority. Consequently, if a principal wants to place precise limits on the authority of an agent, such limitations should be clearly conveyed to any third parties.

Ratification.   Ordinarily, if no agency relationship exists but someone represents agency authority to a third party, who then relies on the representation and deals with the agent, the principal will not be bound. However, if the principal becomes aware of the representation after the fact and agrees to it, agency by ratification exists. In essence, the principal agrees to the agency after the agent has already acted on behalf of the principal.[19] If the principal does not agree, no agency exists, and the principal is not bound by the acts of the agent.

This theory is distinct from the other possible theories of agency that may apply in similar situations, such as actual implied authority or respondeat superior if the agent's acts were similar or closely related to those for which authority had been granted. If the principal ratifies the actions of the agent, normally that ratification is retroactive. For example, if the purported agent enters into a contract on behalf of the purported principal, the contract will be in effect from the day it was entered, not the day the principal ratified it. If the contract is one that must be completed in a certain period of time, this may be quite significant.

An exception to the time element of ratification occurs when the principal did not have legal capacity at the time of the agent's actions. Thus, if the principal gains capacity (for example, reaches the age of majority) on or before the date of ratification, the agency and acts of the agent become effective as of the date of ratification.

A principal cannot ratify only part of the agent's actions. If the principal accepts any part of the agent's actions, all of the agent's actions must be accepted.[20] To do otherwise would be unfair to the third party, who is already in peril because of reliance on the agent who did not really have authority.

A final requirement of the entire agreement is knowledge of material facts. The principal must have access to knowledge of all facts that affect the transaction entered into by the agent before the principal ratifies them. To do otherwise would be to lead a principal blindly into an agreement that may not serve his or her best interest.

Respondeat Superior

The requirements for an action of respondeat superior based on an agency are generally the same as those based on employment. First it must be shown that there was a master-servant relationship,[21] that is, a relationship that had a clearly defined authority figure and a person to carry out the directions from the authority. This may be either an employer-employee or a principal-agent relationship. A partner in a partnership is an example of a principal-agent relationship that does not involve an employer and an employee. The partnership as a business entity has authority to give direction. The partners as individuals carry out these directions. Thus, the partnership would be the principal, and the partners would be the agents. Partners are not considered employees of the partnership, however.

The second requirement of respondeat superior is that the agent acts within the scope of the agency. Specifically, this means that the act of the agent who injured the third party must have been committed while the agent was engaged in performance of the purpose of the agency.[22] An example is an agent who is running an errand for a principal and causes an auto accident on the way. A third person who is injured in the accident could have an action against the principal as well as the agent because the agent was involved in carrying out the purpose of the agency at the time of the accident.

It is not relevant that the principal did not authorize the specific act of the agent that precipitated the injury to a third person. It is only necessary that the action be reasonably required for the completion of the agency and/or be of the same general nature as the conduct authorized. Thus, an agent who takes a slightly different route from that directed by the principal would still be considered to be acting within the scope of the agency.

An exception to a principal's responsibility for an agent under respondeat superior occurs when the agent deviates substantially from the instructions of the principal or when the agent is engaged in conduct that ultimately serves the agent rather than the principal.[23] In most jurisdictions, the doctrine does not apply to incidents that result from the agent's smoking while driving. For example, assume an agent who is a smoker is driving to a certain location for a principal. While handling, lighting, or disposing of a cigarette, the agent is inattentive to the road and causes an accident. The agent—not the principal—would be responsible for injuries to any third parties. Examples of deviation from the purpose include picking up hitchhikers, making personal stops, changing routes for personal purposes, and driving while intoxicated. Generally, any activity that substantially departs from the purpose of the agency and benefits the agent more than the principal will be considered sufficient to relieve the principal of liability.

An additional exception to a principal's liability for the acts of an agent is an intentional tort. A principal will not be responsible for injuries to third parties if the injuries were caused intentionally by the agent.[24] The reasoning behind this is that all persons should be responsible for their own intentional acts. A principal may be held responsible for intentional acts, however, if it is the general nature of the principal's business to engage in such acts and the agent's intentional acts further the purpose of the agency. A commonly used example is a bouncer in a bar. It is customary for bouncers to employ physical force against unruly patrons. Because this serves the purpose of the principal and is done with the principal's consent, the principal can be held liable for injuries caused by the agent.

Assignment 10.2

In each of the following situations, determine whether there is an agency relationship and, if so, whether it involves (a) actual express authority, (b) actual implied authority, (c) apparent authority, (d) inherent authority, or (e) authority by ratification. Explain your answers.

1. Juan and José are neighbors. Juan offers to take José's lawnmower to the repair shop in his truck. José agrees. Juan takes the mower and authorizes the shop to perform all necessary repairs.

2. Dee works for Lori. Her job is to place temporary employees for Lori's placement service. When Dee was hired, Lori sent announcements to all of her business customers stating that Dee would be the personnel placement officer for the placement service.
3. Lori (see situation 2) fires Dee but does not send out announcements of the firing as she did of the hiring.
4. Lori (see situation 2) fires Dee and sends out letters to all of her business customers advising them of this fact.
5. Dean and Margo are friends. Margo knows that Dean collects rare stamps. At an auction, Margo spots an extremely rare stamp and, unknown to Dean, successfully bids on it for him. Dean subsequently pays for the stamp and adds it to his collection.
6. Greg agrees to put up fencing around the perimeter of Shondra's yard. In doing so, Greg trims several bushes that extend across the property line into an adjacent yard.

 CASE

DRAKE v. MAID-RITE CO.

681 N.E.2d 734
(Ind.App. 1997).

GARRARD, Judge.

Shirley Drake ("Drake") appeals from a grant of summary judgment in favor of defendant Maid-Rite Company ("Maid-Rite") upon her claim that Maid-Rite failed to comply with Indiana Code s 23-2-2.5 et seq., commonly referred to as the Indiana Franchise Act. We affirm.

See Continental Basketball Assoc. Inc. v. Ellenstein Enterprises, 669 N.E.2d 134, 135 (IND.1996).

Facts and Procedural History
In the fall of 1989, Sam Sweeden ("Sweeden") entered into a license agreement with Maid-Rite, an Iowa corporation operating restaurants in Iowa and other states. Under the agreement, Sweeden was authorized to establish a Maid-Rite restaurant at the corner of Jefferson and Logan streets in Mishawaka, Indiana ("Store # 1"). In the first half of 1990, Maid-Rite and Sweeden entered a license agreement authorizing Sweeden to establish a second restaurant on Grape Road in Mishawaka

("Store # 2"). Record at 34-53. The agreement also authorized Sweeden to develop or resell additional franchises in the state of Indiana. Based on the possibility that he would develop additional franchises, Maid-Rite charged Sweeden a lesser than normal franchise fee. Additionally, the license agreement provided that Maid-Rite's approval was not required for Sweeden to sell Store # 2.

After operating Store # 2 for approximately five weeks, Sweeden advertised the store for sale in the newspaper as a Maid-Rite franchise. Drake responded to the advertisement and met with Sweeden. Sweeden did not provide Drake with any books or records relating to the restaurant's operation, but he did indicate that the restaurant generated $300 to $500 per day in gross receipts. Sweeden agreed to sell Store # 2 to Drake for $40,000, which included all equipment and the Maid-Rite franchise. On July 2, 1990, a purchase agreement was drafted on Maid-Rite letterhead and signed by Drake and Sweeden. On July 20, 1990, a bill of sale, which was signed by Drake and Sweeden, provided for monthly payments on the remaining $25,000 balance, payable to Sam Sweeden, over a period of sixty (60) months. Subsequently, Drake began operating the restaurant, but it did not produce the revenues which Sweeden had indicated. She did not receive assistance from Sweeden or Maid-Rite as Sweeden had represented. She contacted Maid-Rite for the first time in September 1990, after purchasing and operating Store # 2. Drake closed the restaurant in March 1991 and subsequently filed this action. She now appeals the trial court's grant of summary judgment in Maid-Rite's favor.

> Sweeden indicated in his deposition, however, that his daily receipts were in "the hundred and fifty to three, four hundred dollar area, depending on the day." Record at 272.

Issues

Of the issues Drake presents on appeal, we address only the following issue which we find dispositive.

Whether the trial court erred in finding that Sweeden's sale to Drake was not effected by or through Maid-Rite, and therefore that Maid-Rite had no duty to comply with the disclosure requirements of the Indiana Franchise Disclosure Act, Indiana Code s 23-2-2.5-1 et seq.

Standard of Review

"Summary judgment shall be granted by the trial court if the designated evidentiary matter shows that there is no genuine issue of material fact and that the moving party is entitled to judgment as a matter of law." Welch v. Scripto-Tokai Corp., 651 N.E.2d 810, 813 (Ind.Ct.App.1995), reh'g denied: Ind. Trial Rule 56(C). "On appeal from a trial court's grant of summary judgment, the appellant has the burden of proving that the trial court erred in determining that there were no genuine issues of material fact and that the moving party was entitled to judgment as a matter of law." Id. "Summary judgment shall not be reversed on the ground that there is a genuine issue of material fact unless the material fact and the relevant evidence had been specifically designated to the trial court." Id; Ind. Trial Rule 56(H). The rule does not require designation of the evidentiary materials in any particular manner; rather, it requires that the trial court be " 'apprised of the specific material upon which the parties rely in support of or in opposition to a motion for summary judgment. . . .' " Id. "Further, the designation of evidentiary materials shall occur at the time of the filing of the motion or the

response." Id; T.R. 56(C). The evidence designated to the trial court shall be viewed in a light most favorable to the nonmovant. Peele v. Gillespie, 658 N.E.2d 954, 957 (Ind.Ct.App.1995), reh'g denied, trans. denied.

Discussion and Decision

In Drake's complaint, she indicated that she was bringing her action "pursuant to I.C. 23-2-2.5-1 through 23-2-2.5-51. . . ." Record at 6. Drake contends that Maid-Rite violated Indiana Code s 23-2-2.5-1 et seq., the Franchise Disclosure Act, because it failed to provide her with the required disclosure so that she could make an intelligent, informed decision.

Drake argues that the trial court erred in awarding summary judgment because there was a genuine issue of material fact as to whether Sweeden was acting with actual authority or APPARENT AUTHORITY as Maid-Rite's agent. She contends that if Sweeden was Maid-Rite's agent, the sale of the franchise was "effected by or through a franchisor" as prescribed in Indiana Code s 23-2-2.5-4. She concludes that since the sale was "effected by or through a franchisor," Maid-Rite failed to provide a disclosure statement as required under Indiana Code s 23-2-2.5-9.

Indiana Code s 23-2-2.5-4 provides for an exemption from the section 9 disclosure statement requirement. This exemption provides:

The offer of sale of a franchise by a franchisee who is not an affiliate of the franchisor for his own account is exempt from section 9 if the offer or sale is not effected by or through a franchisor. A sale is not effected by or through a franchisor if a franchisor is entitled to approve or disapprove a different franchisee.

Ind.Code s 23-2-2.5-4 (emphasis added). In reviewing Drake's argument that the sale of the franchise was "effected by or through a franchisor," we examine her contention that Sweeden had actual or APPARENT AUTHORITY to act as an agent of Maid-Rite.

Both parties agree that actual authority is "created by written or spoken words or other conduct of the principal which, reasonably interpreted, causes the agent to believe that the principal desires him so to act on the principal's account." Appellant's Brief at 11-12 (quoting RESTATEMENT (SECOND) OF AGENCY s 26

(1958)). As Maid-Rite indicates in its brief, the focus of actual authority is the belief of the agent.

In the affidavit submitted by Maid-Rite, Sweeden stated that he sold the restaurant to Drake "for my own account," and that Maid-Rite "had no involvement whatsoever in the sale of the Grape Road restaurant to Ms. Shirley Drake." Record at 60. Additionally, Sweeden understood that he could transfer Store # 2 without Maid-Rite's approval, an understanding supported by the license agreement.

Drake argues that despite Sweeden's statements that he was acting for his own account, Sweeden was an agent because he was acting in furtherance of Maid-Rite's interest by helping Maid-Rite expand into Indiana by purchasing a franchise and reselling it. If we accept Drake's argument, franchisees who acquire a franchise and subsequently sell it are acting in the interest of and are therefore agents of the franchisor. Sweeden's franchise fee may have been reduced based on the possibility that he would develop further franchises for Maid-Rite in Indiana, but he paid at least a partial franchise fee, bought equipment, executed a lease for the physical facility, and operated the restaurant, albeit for a short period of time. Sweeden's ownership of the franchise, with all the accompanying risks of ownership, support his stated belief that he was selling the franchise for his own account. Additional support is found in Sweeden's agreement with Drake which provided that Drake would make monthly payments to Sweeden for the remaining $25,000 balance.

As Drake asserts, Sweeden had the right to develop or resell additional Maid-Rite franchises in Indiana. However, his transaction with Drake involved the sale of Store # 2, a restaurant that he owned and operated for his own account. Likewise, Sweeden's subsequent sale of the restaurant to Drake was for his own account. In our review of the designated materials, we find no genuine issue regarding the fact that Sweeden possessed no actual authority as an agent of Maid-Rite.

Drake also contends that Maid-Rite's approval of the sale placed Sweeden in a position of authority. We find it unnecessary to address the appellee's argument that a sale is not effected by or through the franchisor solely based on an approval clause. Maid-Rite's "approval" acted as nothing more than an acknowledgment of what the license agreement provided. Pursuant to the agreement, Maid-Rite's approval was not required for Sweeden to sell the franchise.

"APPARENT AUTHORITY is the authority that a third person reasonably believes an agent to possess because of some manifestation *738 from his principal." Pepkowski v. Life of Indiana Ins. Co., 535 N.E.2d 1164, 1166 (Ind.1989). "The necessary manifestation is one made by the principal to a third party, who in turn is instilled with a reasonable belief that another individual is an agent of the principal." Id. at 1166-67. "It is essential that there be some form of communication, direct or indirect, by the principal, which instills a reasonable belief in the mind of the third party. [Citation omitted]. Statements or manifestations made by the agent are not sufficient to create an apparent AGENCY relationship." Id. at 1167.

Drake contends that Maid-Rite placed Sweeden in a position to make representations to her upon which she could reasonably believe that she was buying a franchise through Maid-Rite. She supports her contention by noting that the advertisement was for the sale of a Maid-Rite franchise, the purchase agreement was on Maid-Rite stationery, and that Maid-Rite knew and approved of the sale to Drake. However, she offers no evidence of any communication or contact, direct or indirect, between herself and Maid-Rite prior to purchasing the restaurant from Sweeden. Drake indicated in a deposition that she made no attempts to gain information on Maid-Rite, and although she remembered receiving an address or contact name for Maid-Rite from Sweeden, she made no attempt to contact Maid-Rite prior to closing the purchase.

In her affidavit submitted in opposition to summary judgment, Drake indicated that her reference to Sweeden as Maid-Rite's agent was "based upon the testimony of Sam Sweeden in his deposition in the same action." Record at 168. Sweeden's deposition was taken subsequent to litigation and well after Drake purchased the restaurant. Drake does not refer us to any evidence in the record whereby she had any contact with anyone regarding the transaction other than Sweeden. In her deposition, Drake admits that she had no contact with Maid-Rite until September 1990, after she purchased the restaurant from Sweeden.

Although it may have been reasonable for her to conclude that Sweeden had some kind of authority to act on Maid-Rite's behalf, based on Sweeden's statements that Maid-Rite would support her efforts, Indiana law requires more. "Statements or manifestations made by the agent are not sufficient to create an apparent AGENCY relationship." Pepkowski, 535 N.E.2d at 1167. As we indicated in Nobles v. Cartwright, 659 N.E.2d 1064 (Ind.Ct.App.1995):

In the instant case, it is not illogical for Cartwright to have assumed that those making promises concerning confidentiality and/or continued employment would not do so unless they could effectuate the promises. Thus, one may begin to understand how Cartwright might have developed the impression that either Nobles, Moreau, or Hamilton, or perhaps all of them, had some kind of authority to act upon behalf of the Lottery Commission. Regardless, Indiana law requires that to establish an APPARENT AUTHORITY, it is essential that there be some form of communication, direct or indirect, by the principal which instills a reasonable belief of the agent's authority in the mind of the third party. [Citations omitted]. Statements, manifestations, or bald assertions made by the purported agent are, by themselves, insufficient to create an apparent Agency relationship. [Citations omitted].

Id. at 1080 (emphasis added).

Aside from Sweeden's statements, Drake alludes to Sweeden's use of Maid-Rite stationery for the purchase agreement and the Maid-Rite logo for the advertisement. However, use of franchise trademarks and commercial symbols are benefits that are typically gained by a franchisee who pays for the right to associate his business with the recognition of a franchise. Maid-Rite authorizing Sweeden, as a franchisee, to use Maid-Rite's letterhead and logo was not a sufficient act to clothe Sweeden with APPARENT AUTHORITY.

In Pepkowski v. Life of Indiana Inc. Co., 535 N.E.2d 1164 (Ind.1989), an insurance company permitted the purported agent to possess its application form and benefits booklet and accepted the plaintiff's application. Our supreme court found that "[t]hese acts are not a sufficient manifestation to clothe Wytrykus with APPARENT AUTHORITY to bind Life of Indiana and Quinet." Id. at 1167.

We also note that the definition of "franchise" provided in Indiana Code s 23-2-2.5-1(a)(2) means a contract by which "the operation of the franchisee's business . . . is substantially associated with the franchisor's trademark, service mark, trade name, logotype, advertising, or other commercial symbol designating the franchisor or its affiliate. . . ."

Drake fails to designate evidence, and we find none, which establishes some form of communication by Maid-Rite which instilled a reasonable belief in Drake's mind that Sweeden had the authority to act on Maid-Rite's behalf.

Based on the evidence specifically designated to the trial court, we find no genuine issue of material fact regarding the applicability of the Franchise Disclosure Act to the transaction between Sweeden and Drake. Sweeden did not possess actual or APPARENT AUTHORITY as an agent of Maid-Rite. Therefore, Sweeden's sale to Drake was "not effected by or through" Maid-Rite, and Maid-Rite did not violate the Franchise Disclosure Act. Accordingly, the trial court did not err in determining that Maid-Rite was entitled to judgment as a matter of law because it had no duty to comply with the disclosure requirements of the Franchise Disclosure Act in the transaction between Sweeden and Drake.

Affirmed.

HOFFMAN and RUCKER, JJ., concur.

END OF DOCUMENT

Case Question

Why was the presence of actual authority an issue in this case?

SOLE PROPRIETORSHIPS

The sole proprietorship is the simplest of all forms of business entity. The entire ownership of the business is vested in one individual. Consequently, it is unnecessary to have an agreement that indicates who has authority in the business, how profits and losses will be shared, or who is responsible for debts or judgments against the business. A sole proprietorship may employ any number of employees, but as long as the employees do not take part in ownership decisions or have the right or obligation to share in profits and losses, the business remains individually owned.

Sole proprietorships were once the most common form of business. Although they are still popular, many sole proprietorships are changing their legal status, usually to that of a corporation even if it is a corporation with only one shareholder. The reasons for this vary, but two reasons in particular are making the sole proprietorship less and less attractive to entrepreneurs. First, an individual operating a sole proprietorship must claim all profits of the business as personal income. A corporation, however, pays taxes on its own income, and the shareholders pay taxes only on the actual income they receive from the business. Often the tax liability for the individual is much less as a shareholder than as a sole proprietor. For example, if nearly all profits are reinvested in a corporation, the shareholders would not pay personal income tax on these profits. And if an individual has several sources of income, heavy profits from a sole proprietorship could increase personal income so that the owner is placed in a much higher tax bracket.

A second reason for the decline of sole proprietorships is judgment liability. When an outside party sues a sole proprietorship and wins, the judgment can be enforced against the individual owner, including all of the owner's personal assets. For example, if a person who is injured while in the shop of a sole proprietor sues and wins, the judgment can be collected from the business and from the personal assets of the individual owner, such as houses, cars, and bank accounts. Although businesses often have insurance and business assets, these may be insufficient to satisfy the judgment. Consequently, personal assets are pursued. In the case of corporations, the shareholders are vulnerable only to the amount of their previous investment in the business. With the increasing number of lawsuits against and among businesses, many sole proprietors are left with no choice but to incorporate in order to protect their own personal and real property.

PARTNERSHIPS

The Nature of Partnerships

Partnership

An agreement of two or more parties to engage in business or enterprise with profits and losses shared among all parties.

A **partnership** is defined as follows:

> A voluntary contract between two or more competent persons to place their resources or services, or both, in a business or enterprise, with the understanding that there shall be a proportional sharing of the profits and losses.[25]

Most often an issue in partnership is resolved through the law of contracts and agency. Over time, however, some rules specific to partnership law have been developed. In addition, the Uniform Partnership Act, a model law adopted by a majority of the states, outlines procedures for the creation, operation, and termination of a partnership. Because the Uniform Partnership Act has been adopted as law by a majority of the states, the principles discussed here are consistent with the Act's principles.

Characteristics of a Partnership

In a partnership, each partner is the agent of the partnership and represents the other partners. This authority allows one partner to legally bind the partnership and, ultimately, personal assets of the partners in contractual agreements. Generally, a partner's personal assets are not protected from being applied to pay debts of the business. The liability for debts of the partnership is joint and several among the partners.[26] If there is a determination that the partnership owes a debt that exceeds the worth of the partnership assets, any individual partner (as several individuals) or all partners (as joint individuals) together may be forced to pay the debt. An obligation does not have to be divided among the partners equally. Thus, a partner who is particularly wealthy has the greatest risk of being forced to pay partnership debts after the business assets have been applied. If, however, one partner is required to satisfy a large portion of the debt, the Act permits that partner to require the other partners to reimburse a share of the payment that was made. This, of course, assumes that the other partners have the financial ability to reimburse that share of debt. As you can see, a major concern before one enters a partnership is the personal financial stability of the other partners.

Generally, in a partnership, the partners share profits and losses equally. The exception would be if the partners had a written agreement that provided for a different distribution, such as 70/30, which could be the case if one partner had more invested in the business. The partnership is required to file tax returns for recordkeeping purposes only, since any actual taxes are paid personally by the partners based on the income they receive from the partnership. Similarly, if the partnership has an annual financial loss, the partners can claim their proportionate share of the loss against their total annual income on their personal returns in accordance with federal and state tax laws.

Each state has its own rules of procedure that indicate the manner in which a partnership is sued. Some states require that the name of the partnership as well as the names of the partners be included in the suit. Other states require only that one or the other be named.

Limited Partnerships

A special type of partnership, known as a **limited partnership,** can be used to protect the personal assets of a partner from liability and to provide other benefits with respect to investments and taxes. The Revised Uniform Limited Partnership Act, another model law adopted by a majority of the states as a statute, sets forth the specific rights, liabilities, and means of creating and dissolving a limited partnership. Generally, in a limited partnership, a limited

Limited Partnership

Partnership of two or more persons in which the limited partners can be held liable for partnership debts only to the extent of their investment and cannot take part in the general management and operation of the partnership business.

partner is held liable only for the amount of his or her investment or promised investment in the partnership.[27] In this sense, a limited partner is similar to a corporate shareholder. The cost to a limited partner, however, is the loss of all control or influence in the operation of the partnership.

A limited partner can have no input into the operation of the business of the partnership. A limited partner cannot work for the partnership. Finally, the limited partner's name cannot be used in the partnership name. If any of these rules are broken, a limited partner may be treated as a general partner and be subject to joint and several liability.[28] Because limited partners cannot contribute services to the partnership, as a practical necessity, the partnership must have general partners as well who operate the business of the partnership. Although these general partners manage the continuing business of the partnership, their personal assets are at risk as well.

The Relationship of Partners

Partners have a fiduciary obligation to each other. A fiduciary relationship is one in which there is a particular trust between the parties. In a partnership, each partner is trusted to place the interest of the partnership above personal interest. Therefore, any partner who makes a profit in a business venture of the type the partnership would ordinarily be involved in owes that profit to the partnership.

The partnership should decide in advance whether a partner is to be compensated for work done in the partnership. A partner is not entitled to payment for services rendered as an employee but is only entitled to a share of the profits or losses, as are the other partners. The exception to this is when a partner or partners are winding up the partnership business after the death of another partner. In that case, it is proper to provide reasonable compensation to the survivors for their services in closing the partnership accounts.

Partners are entitled to receive payment for monies they have expended in the ordinary business of the partnership.[29] Thus, it is not necessary to have partnership approval for payment of every expense. If the expense is one that would reasonably be incurred in the operation of the business, a partner generally has the right either to obligate the partnership for payment or to receive reimbursement if he or she makes payment personally on the partnership's behalf.

If a dispute arises among parties to a partnership, certain legal actions are permitted. Specifically, a partner may sue the partnership for an accounting of partnership assets and liabilities when one or more of the following instances[30] occur:

1. The partnership is winding up business.
2. A partner has been improperly excluded from activity in the partnership.
3. There is a reasonable basis to suspect a partner has made personal profit at the expense of the partnership.

Other than in these instances, a partner is generally not permitted to sue a partnership, because as an individual, the partner would be the plaintiff, but as a member of the partnership, he or she would be the defendant. The law does not permit persons to sue themselves, even in different capacities.

Partnership Property

Partnerships are generally allowed to own personal property or real property in the name of the partnership. Financing for such purchases, however, is still sometimes required to be in the names of the partners, because if it becomes necessary to sue the partners for repayment, the original loan documents clearly state who the partners were.

Although partners have individual rights to the partnership's income, they cannot claim an individual interest in the partnership's assets (such as vehicles or office supplies) unless otherwise agreed. Occasionally, a conflict arises regarding whether property belongs to the partnership or to a particular partner individually. When this happens, a court will look to the following[31] before making a finding as to true ownership:

1. Was the property acquired with partnership funds?
2. Has the partnership made use of the property?
3. Does the partnership have legal title to the property?
4. Is the property of a type that would be used in the business of the partnership?
5. Has the partnership taken any steps to maintain or improve the condition of the property?
6. Is the property recorded in the books of the partnership as an asset?

If the answers to these questions strongly indicate that the partnership was the rightful owner of the property, all partners will be held responsible for any obligations with respect to the property. Likewise, if the property should suddenly increase in value, the partners will be joint owners of the property for that purpose as well.

The Life of a Partnership

Creation.   A partnership is an entity that must be created by agreement of those who will be responsible for its existence. The agreement is covered by the law of contracts. An example is the contractual requirement of capacity. If a person without capacity attempts to enter a partnership agreement, the law would not recognize the person's role as partner, and the person would have no liability for partnership debts. Thus, it is in the best interest of potential partners to ascertain in advance the legal capacity of one another.

In some states, the statute of frauds does not require that a partnership contract be in writing. Oral agreements are permissible as long as the conduct of the parties is clear enough to permit inference of the agreement.

Recognition.   Several factors must be considered to determine whether a partnership actually exists and should be legally recognized as such. The following questions are most often considered:

1. Do the alleged partners have some type of joint title to real or personal property?
2. Do the alleged partners operate under a single name?

3. Do the alleged partners all share in the profits and losses of the business?
4. How much money and time does each alleged partner invest in the business?

Since none of these factors independently establishes a partnership, all of them are considered jointly. If it is determined that most of them indicate an agreement between the parties to act as a partnership, the likely result is that the law will recognize a partnership.[32]

A partnership may also be established under the principle of partnership by estoppel. This occurs when one party allows a second party to represent himself or herself as a partnership to outsiders. If the outsider relies on the representation, the original party may be held responsible for the acts of the second party. The first party is precluded from denying the existence of a partnership after allowing another to represent to outsiders that such a relationship, in fact, existed.[33]

Partnership Dealings with Third Parties

Generally, every partner in a partnership has authority to act as an agent of the partnership. The partnership entity acts as the principal. A general principle of partnership is that a partner has apparent authority.[34] A partner may transfer title to property held in the partnership name or obligate the partnership in business agreements or purchases that relate to the business of the partnership. If, however, the transaction is one that would not ordinarily be encountered in the business of the partnership, a partner must have actual authority from the partnership before he or she can make a binding agreement with third parties.

 APPLICATION 10.6

A partnership is created for the purpose of operating a retail store. General supplies and replenishment of inventory could normally be accomplished by any partner under the theory of apparent authority. However, a partner who attempted to purchase a new building for the partnership would have to have actual authority before the partnership could be bound by such an agreement.

Point for Discussion
Would there need to be actual authority to lease a new building if the building is to be used by the partnership?

In addition to having joint and several liability for contract obligations, a partnership may also be held responsible to third parties for wrongful acts of the partners or partnership employees. For example, if a partner or partnership employee negligently injures another while engaged in the business of the partnership, the partnership may be held liable for the injuries.[35]

The liability of partners in such a situation can be claimed in one of two ways. Some jurisdictions take the position that liability is joint and that every partner must be sued for the injuries. Many other jurisdictions have made the liability joint and several, which means that all the partners or an individual partner may be sued. As in contract situations, however, if an individual partner must satisfy the entire debt of the partnership, that partner may require the other partners to contribute toward reimbursement for payment of the judgment.[36]

 CASE

MEYER v. LOFGREN

949 S.W.2d 80
(Mo.App. 1997).

EDWIN H. SMITH,
Judge.

This is an appeal and cross-appeal from a judgment in a bench-tried case for an equitable accounting upon the dissolution of an *81 accounting partnership. The trial court found a partnership existed between Don Lofgren (Lofgren) and Joyce Meyer (Meyer), and that the dissolution of the partnership entitled Meyer to an equitable accounting and distribution of her partnership interest. Lofgren asserts two points on appeal. [FN1] He asserts that the trial court erred: 1) in finding the existence of a partnership; and 2) in failing to sustain his motion for a jury trial on the issue of whether a partnership existed between the parties. Meyer asserts two points on her cross-appeal. She asserts that the trial court erred in its accounting and distribution of her partnership interest by failing to include goodwill in its determination of the fair market value of the partnership assets at the time of dissolution; and 2) in apportioning the special master's fees.

Lofgren designated in his brief four points relied on. However, Points II and III, as he admitted in oral argument, are not claims of error, but responses to the two points Meyer raised on her cross-appeal.

We affirm in part and reverse in part.

Facts
Lofgren, appellant/cross-respondent, and Meyer, respondent/cross-appellant, had known each other for a number of years before they decided in May, 1990, to merge their C.P.A. practices. At trial, Meyer testified that she and Lofgren determined to form a partnership under the name Don K. Lofgren, C.P.A. The court found that the partnership officially began on May 25, 1990. Around that time, she and Lofgren circulated announcements indicating the formation of their practice, with Meyer designated as partner in charge of personal financial planning. Meyer testified at trial that Lofgren held her out to third parties as a partner, evidenced by the business cards they gave clients and his personal introductions.

Meyer was to contribute some equipment and client files, and Lofgren was to provide office space in addition to the use of his already existing practice. Meyer also made an initial capital contribution of $5,000 on May 24, 1990, followed by another loan and her personal guarantee to establish a line of credit for the partnership. Meyer testified that although the terms of their partnership were not reduced to writing, management of the partnership was to be shared, and profits and losses were to be divided proportionately based upon their individual gross billings for the year. She later testified that since Lofgren had refused to produce accounting records, she believed that their default agreement provided for equal partnership. Lofgren and Meyer agreed that beginning in August, 1990, she was to receive a $700 draw every other week.

In late 1990, the partnership was changed to a professional corporation, to be named Lofgren & Co., P.C. Although Meyer was listed as vice-president in the incorporation documents, she was not issued any shares in the corporation to reflect her partnership interest. A few months later, in April, 1991, the relationship between Meyer and Lofgren began to deteriorate. Meyer drafted a memorandum to Lofgren concerning her perception that he was preventing her from participating in the management of the firm, and she demanded access to the accounting records. She followed the memorandum with a letter on May 14, 1991, again demanding financial information about the partnership. In late May, 1991,Lofgren directed the bank to release Meyer from her personal guarantee, and he told her that he was recasting her capital contribution as a loan. On May 21 or 22, 1991, Lofgren told Meyer that she was fired and demanded she turn over her keys.

Meyer filed her amended petition for equitable relief and damages on May 29, 1991, naming Lofgren and Lofgren & Co., P.C., as co-defendants. The parties proceeded on Meyer's claims for a mandatory injunction, for an accounting, and for restitution and unjust enrichment. Hearings were held on December 27, 1991, February 21, 1992, and July 31, 1992. The court issued an order on August 17, 1992, which found the existence of a partnership, the need for an accounting and the appointment of a special master. The special master issued three reports. The trial court had two more hearings on January 23, 1995, and February 10, 1995. On September 11, 1995, the court issued its final judgment. Incorporating its August 17, *82 1992, order, the court found the partnership interests to be divided equally between Lofgren and Meyer. It held that Meyer should be returned her $5,000 capital contribution, as well as $38,708.97, which represented one-half of the value of the partnership at the time of dissolution. Finally, the court entered judgment in favor of the special master against Meyer and Lofgren, jointly and severally, in the amount of $13,500.00. Both Meyer and Lofgren appeal from the judgment.

Lofgren's Appeal
I. Existence of Partnership
In his first point, Lofgren claims that the trial court erred in finding the existence of a PARTNERSHIP between the parties. In support of his claim, he alleges that there was insufficient evidence from which to establish the necessary ELEMENTS of a PARTNERSHIP, specifically, the requisite element

that the parties agreed to share the profits and bear the losses of the accounting firm. We disagree.

A partnership is statutorily defined as "an association of two or more persons to carry on as co-owners of a business for profit. . . ." s 358.060.1.

All statutory references are to RSMo 1994, unless otherwise noted.

A partnership has been judicially defined as "a contract of two or more competent persons to place their money, effects, labor and skill, or some or all of them, in lawful commerce or business and to divide the profits and bear the loss in certain proportions." Stuart v. Overland Medical Center, 510 S.W.2d 494, 497 (Mo.App.1974). The partnership agreement need not be written but may be expressed orally or implied from the acts and conduct of the parties, Id. at 497, with the intent of the parties serving as the primary criterion for determining whether such a relationship exists.

The requisite intent to find a partnership is not the intent to form a partnership, but the intent to enter a relationship which in law constitutes a partnership. Schreibman v. Zanetti, 909 S.W.2d 692, 701 (Mo.App.1995) . . .

Section 358.070 provides rules for determining the existence of a partnership. This section provides in pertinent part:

(2) Joint tenancy, tenancy in common, tenancy by the entireties, joint property, common property, or part ownership does not of itself establish a partnership, whether such coowners do or do not share any profits made by the use of the property:

(3) The sharing of gross returns does not of itself establish a partnership, whether or not the persons sharing them have a joint or common right or interest in any property from which the returns are derived;

(4) The receipt by a person of a share of the profits of a business is prima facie evidence that he is a partner in the business, but no such inference shall be drawn if such profits were received in payment:

    (a) As a debt by installments or otherwise;
    (b) As wages of an employee or rent to a landlord;

* * *

(d) As interest on a loan, though the amount of payment vary with the profits of the business; . . .

Although not reduced to writing, Meyer testified that on May 12, 1990, she and Lofgren met and specifically agreed to form an accounting partnership. At the firm's expense and with the agreement of Lofgren, announcements were printed and sent out announcing the fact that Meyer had joined the accounting firm of Lofgren. The announcement indicated that she was the "partner in charge of personal financial planning." Meyer also had business cards printed which indicated she was a partner of the firm. She also testified that Lofgren referred to her as a partner when talking with third persons.

Meyer testified that they agreed to share profits and losses based on percentages determined by comparing their individual gross billings for the year to the total partnership gross billings for the year. She also testified she was to receive a $700 draw every other week against year-end profits. The firm never withheld any amounts for income taxes, social security, or unemployment on these draws. Other than her draws, Meyer never received any distribution from the firm or any accounting as to the firm's or her annual gross billings. Meyer testified that the parties' agreement provided for equal interest in the partnership profits in the event there was no year-end accounting.

Meyer also testified that they agreed the parties were to share in the hiring and firing of employees, citing specific examples of this subsequently occurring. She also testified that they agreed she was to make an unspecified capital contribution to the partnership, which she made on May 24, 1990, in the amount of $5,000. Meyer testified that during the subsequent incorporation of the firm, the firm sought a line of credit of $20,000 from the Midland Bank. In this regard, she and her husband were required to put up collateral and sign personal guarantees.

From the foregoing synopsis of Meyer's testimony, which the trial court was free to believe, it is apparent the trial court had sufficient evidence to find the existence of a PARTNERSHIP between Meyer and Lofgren. Although Lofgren argues the absence of proof as to the necessary ELEMENTS of a PARTNERSHIP and that the weight of the evidence is against the trial court's finding that a PARTNERSHIP existed, he does little other than to reargue the evidence and take issue with what evidence the trial court chose to believe. This is insufficient to cause a reversal under our standard of review.

In support of his claim that the evidence was insufficient to establish the requisite ELEMENTS for the creation of a PARTNERSHIP, specifically, that the parties had agreed to divide the profits and bear the losses of the accounting firm, Lofgren cites us to Brotherton v. Kissinger, 550 S.W.2d 904 (Mo.App.1977), . . . We find these cases to be factually distinguishable from the case at bar and unpersuasive. In finding that a PARTNERSHIP did not exist in Nesler, the court keyed on the testimony of the plaintiff and found that plaintiff was to receive a percentage of profits as compensation for work performed, and that there was no evidence from which it could be found that he was to acquire ownership in the business. Nesler, 703 S.W.2d at 525. The court also found that there was no evidence that the plaintiff was to share the losses of the firm. Id. In Brotherton, the court found that there was no PARTNERSHIP to dissolve because the creation of the PARTNERSHIP was contingent on the occurrence of a future event, which had not occurred. Thus, the court held the PARTNERSHIP was not a PARTNERSHIP in praesenti subject to dissolution, but a PARTNERSHIP in futuro. Brotherton, 550 S.W.2d at 908.

Point denied. . . .

Meyer's Cross-appeal
III. Failure to Include Goodwill in Fair Market Value
In Meyer's first point on her cross-appeal, she claims that the trial court erred in its valuation and award of her interest in the partnership, because the court's valuation and award did not take into account the value of the partnership's goodwill. We agree.

Section 358.310 of the Uniform Partnership Act, dealing with situations which result in the dissolution of partnerships, has been interpreted to include the unilateral expulsion of a partner, which is our situation here. Schoeller v. Schoeller, 465 S.W.2d 648, 654 (Mo.App.1971). Section 358.290 provides: "The 'dissolution' of a partnership is the change in the relation of the partners caused by any partner ceasing to be associated in the carrying on as distinguished from the winding up of the business." It is unclear how the change of the accounting firm from a partnership to a corporation prior to the partnership being dissolved by the expulsion of Meyer would affect the equitable accounting and the valuation of Meyer's interest in the partnership at the time of dissolution. The issue was not raised by either party at trial or on appeal. In any event, the change to the corporate form without issuing shares to Meyer to reflect her partnership interest was an act of expulsion which would dissolve the partnership, just as the subsequent "lockout" of Meyer was an act of expulsion.

Section 358.300 provides: "On dissolution the partnership is not terminated but continues until the winding up of partnership affairs is completed." Thus, under this section, although the partnership of the parties here was dissolved when Lofgren expelled Meyer from the accounting firm, the expulsion did not terminate the partnership, but it continued until the winding up of the partnership affairs. Schoeller, 465 S.W.2d at 654 . . .

In the case at bar, Meyer did not immediately seek to terminate and wind up the affairs of the firm upon her expulsion. According to Lofgren, no partnership ever existed. Consequently, the business of the accounting firm continued without a "winding up of the partnership affairs." Subsequently, Meyer did file suit asking, inter alia, for an accounting and a valuation and distribution of her interest in the firm, or in other words, sought to wind up the partnership affairs. The phrase "winding up of partnership affairs" "means the administration of the assets for the purpose of terminating the business and discharging the obligations of the partnership to its members. Smith v. Kennebeck, 502 S.W.2d 290, 293[1] (Mo.1973)."

Although Lofgren has denied the existence of a partnership from the time this lawsuit was commenced, he does not contest on appeal the fact that if a partnership is found to exist, Meyer is entitled to have an accounting and to receive her

interest in the partnership. *86 Regardless, under s 358.380, Meyer has a right to receive her net interest in the partnership upon the winding up of the partnership affairs. . . . Pursuant to s 358.420, Meyer could elect to either receive her interest in the partnership valued at the time of dissolution with interest thereon from the date of dissolution or receive the profits of the firm attributable to her interest in the partnership from the date of dissolution. . . . Meyer elected the former.

Where the partnership agreement does not specify the method of valuing a partner's interest in the partnership upon winding up of the partnership affairs, then under s 358.420, "fair market value" must be used to value the interest. Chapman v. Dunnegan, 665 S.W.2d 643, 649 (Mo.App.1984). Here, the partnership agreement makes no provision for the valuation of partnership interests upon the leaving of a partner. Thus, the trial court was obligated to use "fair market value" to determine Meyer's interest in the partnership to be distributed to her. In this determination, Meyer claims that the trial court was obligated to include an amount for "goodwill," . . .

In Smith, the court held that in determining the interest of a partner in a partnership post-dissolution, where the business was continued without a winding up of partnership affairs, the value of the interest would include asset appreciation and "goodwill." Id. at 293-94. We can find no contrary authority to Smith. And, because it is well settled that the "goodwill" of a professional practice, such as the accounting firm here, is considered property which is incident to the continuation of the practice, we find no reason to hold contrary to Smith. Thus, unless there was a "waiver" of goodwill, as contended by Lofgren, the trial court here was obligated to consider goodwill in its determination of Meyer's interest in the partnership.

Lofgren contends that the inclusion of goodwill in the calculation of Meyer's partnership interest was waived, citing a specific portion of the transcript. A review of this citation would seem to indicate that goodwill was waived. However, the transcript reveals at a later hearing, prior to the submission of the issue to the trial court, that Meyer expressly indicated to the trial court that she was seeking the inclusion of an amount for goodwill as part of the court's determination of fair market value. Under these circumstances, we find there was no waiver of goodwill by Meyer.

The special master included, as part of his accounting findings, valuations of goodwill for the partnership from the time of dissolution until the time of winding up of the partnership. However, the trial court was not requested to make specific findings of fact and did not make any as to goodwill. As a consequence, we cannot with any

certainty determine from the record if the trial court considered and included goodwill in the amount it determined to be Meyer's interest in the partnership. Thus, we are forced to reverse and remand for consideration and findings by the trial court on this issue.

Case Question

What facts supported or disputed the existence of a partnership in this case?

Termination or Dissolution

Any change in the partners of a partnership will result in the dissolution of that partnership.[37] Thus, when a partner dies, declares bankruptcy, sells his or her interest in the partnership, or withdraws, the partnership is dissolved. This does not mean that the partnership will cease to do business. The business of the partnership may be terminated or a new partnership begun. In addition, if the previously lawful business of the partnership becomes illegal, the partnership is dissolved and business must cease.

When a partnership is dissolved, third parties who have done business with the partnership are entitled to notice. This prevents partners from wrongfully representing apparent authority and binding the members of a dissolved partnership to third parties. All partners have the right to act as agents of the partnership and perform such duties as are required to conclude existing business obligations and concerns. However, a partner who has declared bankruptcy is no longer considered to be an active partner and cannot act on behalf of the partnership. The dissolving partnership is not allowed to engage in any new business, such as entering contracts or taking new orders.

Any partnership assets that remain after all creditors have been paid in full are distributed according to a specific procedure. First, any partner who has loaned money to the partnership, over and above investment in the partnership, will be repaid. Second, all partners are repaid the amount of their contribution or investment in the partnership. Any cash that still remains is distributed among the partners on a pro rata basis. If one partner contributed 50 percent and two other partners contributed 25 percent each of the capital for the partnership, the funds will be distributed in a 2:1:1 ratio. The first partner will receive 50 percent of the remaining funds, and the other two will each receive 25 percent of the funds.

More often, after paying the creditors, a partnership's assets are insufficient to repay all the partners for their investment. In such cases, the shortage is also distributed on a pro rata basis. To follow the preceding example, the 50 percent contributor would absorb 50 percent of the shortage, and the other two partners would each be responsible for 25 percent of the shortage.

Assignment 10.3

In each of the following situations, determine how much each partner would be entitled to in a dissolution/termination proceeding.

1. LaToya, Phylicia, and Dolores were partners. LaToya contributed $2,500 as investment in the partnership, Phylicia contributed $1,500, and Dolores contributed $1,000. The partnership is being dissolved, and after all creditors are paid, $30,000 remains in the partnership accounts.
2. Martin, Saul, and Derek were partners. Initially, Martin put $12,000 into the partnership, Saul contributed $18,000, and Derek put in $20,000. At the close of the partnership business and after all creditors are paid, a total of $30,000 remains in the partnership accounts.
3. Daniel, Joann, and Jacques, were partners. Each invested $10,000 in the partnership. In addition, Daniel loaned the partnership $10,000. After dissolution of the partnership and payment to all outside creditors, $13,000 remains in the partnership accounts.

CORPORATIONS

Corporation
Entity legally recognized as independent of its owners, known as shareholders. A corporation can sue or be sued in its own name regarding its own rights and liabilities.

Legal advantages make the **corporation** one of the most common forms of business. In addition, because a corporation is created purely by statute, the legislatures have been free to create different subtypes of corporations to suit the needs of different types of businesses. Nevertheless, most corporations share standard characteristics, many of which have been embodied in the Model Business Corporation Act (see Appendix B).

Corporate Characteristics

A legal person.   Under the law, a corporation is recognized as a person. It can be taxed and held responsible for its acts for the purposes of lawsuits. Generally, in the past, however, a corporation was not considered to be capable of committing crimes. When criminal conduct occurred, the individuals who actually committed the crime were held responsible.[38] This outlook has been changing. More and more statutes permit corporations and their agents to be convicted of criminal acts. Although a corporation cannot be imprisoned, it can be fined or dissolved as a penalty for illegal conduct. In addition, the acting individual can be held criminally responsible.

Life.   Generally, the life of a corporation goes on indefinitely as long as the requirements of the statutes that permitted its creation are met. The statutes that set forth the ways in which a corporation must be created often establish annual obligations that must be met for the corporation to continue to exist.

Often these obligations include such things as payment of an annual fee for continued registration with the state as a recognized corporation and annual reports describing the activities of the corporation during the preceding year.

Limited liability.   Perhaps the greatest advantage of a corporation is that individuals who invest in it have limited exposure for losses. Ordinarily, a person who invests in a corporation is called a shareholder. In return for the investment, a shareholder is given shares of stock in the corporation. The shares represent a percentage of ownership. The greater the investment, the greater the percentage of ownership. If the corporation does well, the shareholder's ownership becomes more valuable in terms of the price of the shares or the distribution of profits. If the corporation does badly or a large monetary judgment is rendered against it as the result of a lawsuit, the shareholders usually stand to lose only the amount of their original investment.[39] Thus, the corporation differs from most other types of business entities in which the owners are responsible for the entire judgment irrespective of whether it exceeds their investment.

 APPLICATION 10.7

Gary owns 35 percent of the stock in Heyward Company, which manufactures widgets. Because of a defect in manufacturing, several widgets cause serious injuries to consumers. Many lawsuits arise, and judgments against Heyward total 3.4 million dollars. The total assets of Heyward Company are 1.3 million dollars. Gary is a multimillionaire, but because of the limited liability of shareholders, he is not personally responsible (nor are any other shareholders) for the debts of the corporation.

Point for Discussion
What would Gary's responsibility be if Heyward were a partnership and Gary were a partner?

Ownership versus control.   A corporation may have many thousands of shareholders. Often the persons who are in a position to invest are not the persons who are best qualified to run the corporation. Therefore, for this and other practical reasons, another characteristic common only to corporations is that management of the business is separate from ownership. When a corporation is created, a board of directors is appointed that oversees the general operation of the corporation and the officers of the corporation who supervise day-to-day activities. This method of separating the management from ownership protects the interests of shareholders who do not wish to be involved in management. It is not necessary for members of the board of directors or the officers to have any ownership interest in the corporation.

Sale of ownership.   Unlike other types of businesses, ownership (represented by shares of stock) in a corporation can be freely transferred by sale or gift with virtually no effect on the corporation. This allows the investors the opportunity to profit from their investments, and because management and ownership are separated, the corporation can continue operating uninterrupted.

Articles of Incorporation
Document filed with the state at the time of incorporation that states the purpose of the corporation and defines the corporate structure.

Bylaws
Document of a corporation that details the methods of operation, such as officers and duties, chain of command, and general corporate procedures.

Limits on operation.   When a corporation is formed, the reasons for the corporation and other information are set forth in a document called the **articles of incorporation,** or charter. These documents generally contain the name and purpose of the corporation; the number of shares to be issued and their value per share to the corporation; the voting rights of shareholders; and provisions for the election, removal, or appointment of board members or officers. The basic rules of operation and the methods to be used in carrying out the corporate purpose and in governing the corporation are set forth in **bylaws.** These charter documents can generally be changed only with the consent of the shareholders. The officers and board of a corporation cannot depart from what is set forth in the bylaws and articles of incorporation in any substantial manner without prior approval.

Assignment 10.4

> Prepare a list of questions that should be asked to collect sufficient information to prepare articles of incorporation and bylaws.

Creating a Corporation

Promoter
One who is hired as a fiduciary to recruit investors in a proposed corporation.

Promoters.   For some businesses, a corporation is formed by **promoters**—persons who are often initial incorporators and shareholders. A promoters' primary duty is to obtain sufficient funding (capitalization) for the corporation and ensure that all the formalities required by the statute for incorporation are satisfied. In some jurisdictions, promoters are personally liable for the contracts they make on behalf of the corporation unless and until the corporation agrees to substitute itself for the promoter in the contract (known as a *novation*). If more than one promoter is involved in forming a corporation, each has a fiduciary duty to the other and cannot act in his or her own self-interest if it will harm the interests of the other promoters.

The promoters also have a fiduciary duty to the corporation and its shareholders.[40] They cannot use secret corporate information for their personal benefit or gain. If a promoter does use secret information for self-profit, the corporation and its shareholders can file suit to reclaim that profit. If, however, the promoter fully discloses the information to the corporation and the corporation or interested shareholders who would be affected approve, the promoter may use the information to obtain all possible profits.

APPLICATION 10.8

Assume a promoter who is forming a corporation (an art gallery) becomes aware of an opportunity to purchase a rare painting at a bargain price. As long as the promoter gives the shareholders notice of this opportunity and the shareholders either decline to make the purchase or give the promoter approval to make the purchase personally, the promoter may buy the painting and sell it for the highest available profit. However, if the promoter does not apprise the corporation of this opportunity and purchases the painting as a personal investment, the corporation can file suit to claim any profits from the investment.

Point for Discussion
Would the situation be any different if the promoter was planning to sell the painting to the gallery?

Statutory requirements. All states have some type of statutory law to govern the creation, operation, and dissolution of corporate entities. A majority of the states have enacted a uniform law known as the Model Business Corporation Act (see Appendix B), a series of laws that address all legal aspects of corporate existence. The Act includes provisions for everything from establishing a corporate name to the proper procedures for dissolution. By establishing the same basic statutory provisions in most states, the process of handling legal disputes over corporate statutes is much easier to accomplish. The following is an example of a provision of the Model Business Corporation Act (MBCA):

Sec. 32 **Quorum of Shareholders**

Unless otherwise provided in the articles of incorporation, a majority of the shares entitled to vote, represented in person or by proxy, shall constitute a quorum at a meeting of shareholders, but in no event shall a quorum consist of less than one-third of the shares entitled to vote at the meeting. If a quorum is present, the affirmative vote of the majority of the shares represented at the meeting and entitled to vote on the subject matter shall be the act of the shareholders, unless the vote of a greater number or voting by classes is required by this Act or the articles of incorporation or bylaws.

Assignment 10.5

You are the officer of a corporation. A number of important issues are on the agenda for the upcoming shareholders meeting. You are concerned that insufficient shareholders will vote to legally pass on any of the issues. Analyze the preceding statutory language. Break it down into the basic components and outline the exact requirements to bind the corporation on any of the issues voted upon at the meeting.

Some of the most important statutory requirements of the MBCA or any statutory law with respect to corporations are those that provide for the creation of a corporation. Typically, this is accomplished through a number of steps, including the drafting of certain documents. The articles of incorporation and bylaws must be drafted and signed by the incorporators. Necessary documents and fees must be submitted to the secretary of state or other designated person where the business is incorporated. When the incorporators have complied properly with these formalities, the secretary of state will grant a certificate of incorporation.

The mere drafting of these documents does not establish a corporation. All other statutory requirements of the particular state must be met for the corporation to be recognized by the state as a corporation doing business in that state. Until these requirements are met, the corporation will not be entitled to the benefits generally afforded to corporations, such as limited liability. But when an outside party makes a claim against an alleged corporation in court, the court may find that a corporation exists for the purposes of the dispute even though the state has not previously recognized it.

Each state also has statutes that explain the procedure for the formation of a professional corporation (sometimes referred to as a PC). The states use various names for this entity, but the concept is basically the same. A professional corporation allows a member or members of a certain profession such as law, medicine, dentistry, or accounting to form a business that has many of the legal advantages of a corporation.[41] These corporations often do not have actual shares of stock, and when they do, the shares are usually held entirely by the professional members.

Types of Corporate Status

A de jure corporation (corporation by law) is created by meeting each requirement of relevant statutes that provide for corporation formation and maintenance. These statutes usually require that incorporators have legal capacity and submit articles of incorporation and bylaws. When all of the provisions for incorporation have been satisfied, the state issues a certificate of incorporation that is generally valid as long as the corporation continues to satisfy the statutes.

 On occasion, incorporators attempt to satisfy the statutes but are not successful. In some cases, the law will recognize the organization as a de facto corporation (corporation by fact or actions). The shareholders of a business that is recognized as a de facto corporation are protected in liability the same as de jure corporation shareholders would be.

To establish a de facto corporation, there must be evidence that the incorporators made a good faith attempt to comply with the state laws regarding incorporation and continuance of corporations and that the business has been conducted as if it were a corporation. It must also be shown that the corporation was represented as such and not as another type of business entity and that outside persons dealt with the business as if it were a corporation.[42] When all such evidence exists, the court may recognize the entity as a de facto corporation and allow it to claim all of the privileges of a de jure corporation.

Another type of corporation is the close corporation. This form of business is just what the name indicates. Ownership is closed to the public.[43] The stock is held by a few persons and is not traded on a public market. Small businesses often form such corporations. A very popular form of close corporation is the S corporation. The name is derived from the similarly titled federal tax laws that grant this form of corporation special status. S corporations comply not only with state corporation statutes but also with state and federal tax laws. Ordinarily, a corporation is considered to be a person and pays taxes on its income as such. In addition, the shareholders must also pay personal tax on income received from the corporate ownership. In an S corporation, however, each shareholder claims a percentage of income or loss from the business as personal gain or loss. The percentage is determined by the percentage of ownership the shareholder has.[44] PC corporations are often also close corporations and in some cases are S corporations as well.

Finally, corporation by estoppel (preclusion from denial of corporate existence) comes into play in one of two ways. In the first, a person or persons hold a business out as a corporation to the public and deal with the public as a corporation but later attempt to deny that the corporation ever existed.[45] The second occurs when outsiders deal with a business as a corporation with knowledge that it is not a proper corporation. Then, when a dispute arises between the two, the outsiders attempt to deny that a corporation exists and claim that the owners should be personally liable.[46] In either instance, the courts will often treat the business as a corporation by estoppel and apply the law as if it were a real corporation. The rationale is that people should not be able to derive all of the benefits from acting as or dealing with a corporation while avoiding the obligations of one.

Piercing the Corporate Veil

A court will sometimes ignore the corporate structure of a de jure corporation and hold all or some of the shareholders, officers, and directors responsible for the acts of the corporation. Thus, the court ignores the wall of protection from exposure to liability that shareholders usually enjoy as owners of a corporation. This is called piercing the corporate veil and happens when a court finds that the members of a corporation have improperly used corporate status.

Generally, a corporation may be subject to piercing of the corporate veil in three instances: (1) when it is necessary to prevent fraud, (2) when there is inadequate capitalization, and (3) when the corporation refuses to recognize the formalities necessary to a de jure corporation.

Prevention of fraud.   In the case of the prevention of attempted fraud, the veil will be pierced only when it can be shown that a person or persons formed the corporation in a direct attempt to avoid legal obligations to creditors or others with legal rights. Usually, such debts were incurred through the corporation but the funds were used in ways to benefit the shareholders personally. This is not the same as protecting the shareholders from obligations incurred as the result of the ordinary business of the corporation. If the obligations were originally intended to benefit the business of the corporation or were the result of doing business of the corporation, the corporation will be responsible for the obligations, and the shareholders will continue to be protected.

Inadequate capitalization. In the case of inadequate capitalization, the point at which the corporate veil will be pierced is not as clear. Although it is true that shareholders are generally responsible only for the amount invested in the corporation, it is also true that the original corporate structure must provide for investment that is adequate to allow the corporate purpose to be achieved. For example, a family who wanted to form a corporation to operate a shoe store would have to invest enough money to purchase inventory, fixtures, and a place for the store to operate. In addition, a sufficient amount of the profits of an ongoing corporation must be reinvested to enable the corporation to continue until such time as the shareholders agree to dissolve it. If this is not done, the corporation is destined for failure, and the evidence indicates there was never a true intent to form a legal corporation for the purpose of doing legitimate business.[47]

Refusal to recognize corporate formalities.   Finally, the corporate status of a corporation that refuses to recognize corporate formalities will be ignored, and the shareholders will be held individually responsible as if they were partners in an ordinary business venture. One basis for piercing the corporate veil because of lack of corporate formality is to claim alter ego. Specifically, this means that the corporation has no true purpose of its own but is simply a tool of another organization. While a corporation may be properly created and actually engage in the business stated as its purpose, a close examination will reveal that the business is merely a front for another business. In determining whether a business is an alter ego corporation, a court may consider whether the business shares employees, funds, equipment, and any other element usually used exclusively by a business entity.

One type of alter ego corporation involves very small or close corporations, which generally consist of only a few shareholders, all of whom are often active in the business of the corporation. The problem arises when the shareholders begin to treat the property of the corporation as personal property. For example, the shareholders may use corporate funds to pay private debts, fail to keep separate corporate accounting records, or take or use corporate funds or property without following proper procedures. If the shareholders are engaging in such activities, a court is likely to find that the corporation has not had a true corporate existence.[48]

Another situation in which the alter ego theory may be applied involves parent and subsidiary corporations. It is entirely legal for one corporation to totally own and control another corporation. However, unless both corporations operate independently, comply separately with the legal corporate formalities, and represent themselves to the public as separate and distinct, the courts may consider them to be a single corporation, with one corporation acting as the alter ego of the other.[49] In that event, the parent or owning company, which usually has the greater assets, can be held liable for the debts of the subsidiary.

A situation that is encountered less frequently but is nevertheless a basis for the alter ego theory is that of joint ownership. If a shareholder has a major interest in more than one corporation and strongly influences the policies and actions of the various corporations so that they become mere common tools for the manipulation of the business of this shareholder, the corporations may be considered alter ego corporations and be held liable for the actions of one another.

Liability of parties. When a corporation, large or small, consistently engages in any such conduct, the court is likely to find that the intent of the parties was not to carry on the business as a corporation. In addition, if it is found that the conduct of the shareholders, officers, or directors has resulted in injustice to outside persons, the court may refuse to recognize the corporate status. This forces the shareholders to be individually responsible to injured outsiders for the damage that resulted from the injuries.

When the court does ignore the corporate structure and holds the shareholders liable, it does not necessarily follow that all shareholders will have to bear the losses of the business. If a corporation consists of many shareholders, only those who actively engaged in the wrongful conduct will be held responsible.[50] Innocent shareholders who did not take part in the management of the corporation will not ordinarily be held responsible for the acts of the persons in control.

Claims resulting in piercing of the veil. Certain types of claims most commonly result in piercing of the corporate veil. One type is tort claims, made by persons whose person or property has been injured by some negligent or intentional act of the corporation. Usually, such persons had no business dealings with the corporation. If the corporate veil could not be pierced, those who have been unjustly injured could be placed in a position of suing a corporation that is nothing more than a shell with no assets against which to file a claim. For example, assume that a person is involved in a car accident with a bus. Assume also that the bus company has no assets and does no business other than renting three old buses for charters. Assume further that the bus company carries no insurance on the buses. If it can be shown that the owners of the bus company acted in one of the ways previously discussed, it would be unfair to force the injured person to bear the total cost of the injuries while the owners continued to profit from the business of the bus company.

A second instance of piercing the corporate veil occurs in contract claims. In such situations, a party has business dealings with the corporation, only to find out later that the corporation was a sham. In most cases, the courts will find that the outsider had an opportunity to investigate the credibility of the corporation before doing business with it. If the situation did not lend itself to this, however, and would have appeared proper to reasonable persons, the corporate veil will be pierced. For example, if a seemingly credible advertisement appears in the media and persons respond to it only to find later that they have been swindled, the corporate veil might be pierced.

Assignment 10.6

Create a factual situation that would be appropriate for piercing the corporate veil of a corporation.

CASE

LEVINE v. ALPHA ANESTHESIA, INC.

145 Or.App. 549, 931
P.2d 812 (1997).

EDMONDS, Judge.

Plaintiff seeks to hold defendant Treibick, the sole shareholder, director and president of defendant corporation, personally liable for damages awarded to plaintiff following her successful action against another corporation for breach of her employment contract. Plaintiff appeals from a judgment entered after the trial court granted Treibick's motion for summary judgment. ORCP 47. We reverse. Defendant Alpha Anesthesia, Inc., was dismissed on appeal.

We review the record in the light most favorable to plaintiff. Treibick, an anesthesiologist, is the sole shareholder, director and president of two corporations. In 1985, he incorporated Alpha Anesthesia, Inc. (AAI), a Massachusetts corporation, for the purpose of managing the anesthesia departments of small hospitals in the eastern United States. As part of its business, AAI contracted with anesthesiologists and certified registered nurse anesthesiologists (CRNA) to provide services to the hospitals.

In 1989, AAI entered into a contract with Josephine Memorial Hospital (JMH) in Grants Pass to provide similar services. AAI also contracted with Dr. Genskow, an anesthesiologist, to provide services to JMH pursuant to its agreement with JMH. As a part of that agreement, Genskow agreed not to compete with AAI in Josephine County for 18 months in the event that his contract with AAI was terminated. In 1990, defendant incorporated Anesthesia Affiliates of Oregon, Inc., (AAO), in order to provide services to JMH and also in the hope that a local corporation would attract new business in the western United States. In December 1990, AAI assigned the AAI/JMH contract to AAO, but in 1991 JMH terminated the assigned contract.

The record does not disclose when in 1991 AAO's contract with JMH was terminated.

Also in 1991, Genskow sued AAI to resolve disputes regarding his contract with AAI and his ability to practice medicine at JMH. In part to settle that law suit, AAI and AAO entered into a contract with Genskow on September 9, 1992. That contract provided, in part:

"2.01 AAI and AAO shall assign, transfer and sell to Dr. Genskow, effective as of the Closing, their right and interest in the intangible assets of their business of arranging anesthesia coverage for [JMH], specifically consisting of their rights to engage persons to perform anesthesia services at [JMH] who previously had performed such services under arrangements with AAI or AAO and the benefit of any non-competition covenants such persons may have executed in favor of AAI or AAO. In consideration of said transfer and sale, Dr. Genskow shall pay AAI the amount of $25,000.

"2.02 AAI and AAO each agrees that, for a period of three (3) years following the Closing, it shall not, either directly or indirectly, establish, engage in, own, manage, operate, join, control, or finance or participate in the ownership, management, operation or control of, an anesthesia department or an anesthesia medical practice in Josephine County, Oregon. In consideration for these covenants not to compete, Dr. Genskow shall pay AAI the amount of $175,000."

In the agreement, Genskow also released AAI, AAO and their stockholders and officers from all claims arising from their previous relationship.

Plaintiff is a CRNA. In 1990, AAO contracted with plaintiff for her to provide CRNA services to JMH. In March 1991, plaintiff was injured while working and filed a workers' compensation claim against AAO. AAO and plaintiff settled the workers' compensation claim, and, in a document dated October 7, 1992, plaintiff released AAO from liability for that claim. AAO also terminated plaintiff's employment in May 1991.

Plaintiff sued AAO for breach of her employment contract in March 1993 and was awarded judgments for damages and attorney fees in 1994. AAO failed to satisfy the judgment. In this action, plaintiff seeks to hold Treibick personally liable for the 1994 judgments against AAO, alleging that as the sole shareholder, director and president of both AAI and AAO, he improperly caused the proceeds from the AAI/AAO/Genskow contract to be paid to

AAI in order to avoid payment of any obligations to plaintiff under AAO's contract with her.

Because there is no transcript of oral argument on the motion for summary judgment, our ability to determine what was argued below is limited to the parties' written memoranda submitted to the trial court. On appeal, plaintiff also seeks to "pierce the corporate veil" on the ground that AAO was undercapitalized at inception. Plaintiff failed to raise this issue to the trial court. Therefore, we will not consider that argument on appeal. Finney v. Bransom, 143 Or.App. 154, 159, 924 P.2d 319 (1996).

Pursuant to ORCP 47, Treibick moved for summary judgment. He argued that the $200,000 was paid by Genskow to AAI because AAO was no longer in business after the AAO/JMH contract had been terminated by JMH in 1991 and that there is no evidence that AAO conveyed anything of value to Genskow. Plaintiff responded:

"By defendant's own affidavit, there is evidence that defendant controls both corporations and that AAI, AAO and [defendant] shifted capital, liabilities, and receivables back and forth at the whim and pleasure of [defendant]. It is also apparent that the $200,000 receivable [from the AAI/AAO/Genskow contract] should belong to AAO. If that $200,000 was still a part of AAO's capital account, plaintiff's judgment would be satisfied." (Emphasis supplied.)

Summary judgment is appropriate only if there is not genuine issue as to any material fact and the moving party is entitled to judgment as a matter of law. ORCP 47 C; Jones v. General Motors Corp., 139 Or.App. 244, 911 P.2d 1243, rev. allowed 323 Or. 483, 918 P.2d 847 (1996). To preclude summary judgment, plaintiff must offer evidence that raises a genuine issue of material fact in support of her argument that Treibick is personally liable for AAO's corporate debt. A genuine issue of material fact exists if an objectively reasonable juror could find for plaintiff.

As a general rule, the corporate form will not be disregarded solely because all of the stock of the corporation is owned by one person who also exercises control of the corporation. Amfac Foods v. Int'l Systems, 294 Or. 94, 107, 654 P.2d 1092 (1982). To pierce the corporate veil for purposes of personal shareholder liability where actual control by the shareholder exists, improper conduct by the shareholder must be demonstrated. Also, a plaintiff must prove a relationship between the shareholder's misconduct and the plaintiff's injury. Id. at 111, 654 P.2d 1092.

In this case, it is uncontroverted that Treibick exercises actual control of both AAI and AAO. We turn first to the question of whether there is evidence in the summary judgment record that his conduct was improper. Even though AAO no longer has its contract with JMH, it was a party to the contract with Genskow. The AAI/AAO/Genskow contract refers to contract rights held by AAO to engage persons who had previously provided services to it and assigns those rights to Genskow. Also, AAO agrees in the contract not to compete with Genskow for a period of three years. Those are interests that are separate from the terminated contract with JMH. In exchange for those interests, AAO received no consideration. The fact that AAO conveyed interests of apparent value under the agreement gives rise to a reasonable inference that they have value. Based on this record, an objectively reasonable juror could find that the compensation due AAO for the interests that it conveyed to Genskow was funneled to AAI.

Also, there is evidence that workers' compensation claim settlement negotiations were conducted between March 1991, the date of plaintiff's injury, and October 7, 1992. Plaintiff's employment contract was breached within that same time period. AAO, by Treibick as president, signed the AAI/AAO/Genskow contract on September 9, 1992. An objectively reasonable jury could find that Treibick knew at that time that AAO had exposure under its contract with plaintiff and that he diverted monies owed to AAO under the Genskow contract to AAI in order to render AAO judgment-proof. Such a finding would satisfy the "improper conduct" element of the Amfac test and also establish the requisite relationship between the "improper conduct" and plaintiff's damage. We conclude that, because of those issues of fact, the trial court erred by granting summary judgment to Treibick.

Reversed and remanded.

Case Question
When is it appropriate to disregard the personal liability protection of corporate status?

Corporate Stock

As stated earlier, a person who invests in a corporation owns a percentage of the corporation. This ownership is evidenced by shares of stock. The articles of incorporation state specifically how many shares will be issued. The total number of shares represents the total ownership of the corporation. The corporation will also usually give the shares a stated value, or par value, that is, the amount the corporation considers the shares to be worth.

Normally, the greater the investment, the greater the number of shares one possesses; and the greater the number of shares, the greater the percentage of ownership or control. As the corporation's profitability increases, however, so does the public value of having an ownership interest. Therefore, in times of great earnings by the corporation, the shares increase in public value, and an investor may have to spend large amounts to obtain only a few shares. The investor hopes, of course, that the shares will increase even more in value so they can be sold to the next investor at a profit. The corporation continues to value the shares at the stated value.

Types of stock.   Corporations have different classes of stock. All corporations have common stock. Corporations may also choose to issue preferred stock, which is usually entitled to higher and more frequent dividends and thus may be more marketable.

Some corporations issue what is called cumulative preferred stock. This type of stock accumulates rights to dividends. In the event there is not enough money in one year to declare a dividend, the dividend right of the preferred stock is added to the next year. When a dividend is finally declared, the preferred shareholders are entitled to payment of back dividends before any dividend can be declared on common stock.

Stock rights.   Certain rights are acquired along with some types of stock. If, for example, a shareholder purchases voting stock, in addition to having ownership interest, the shareholder receives the right to cast one vote for each share of stock. Voting is usually done annually to elect new directors and to approve major changes, such as an amendment to the articles of incorporation.

Some shares also have certain provisions regarding dividends. When the board of directors determines that a corporation is profitable, it may declare a dividend after reinvesting a reasonable amount of the profits. When a dividend is declared, the money assigned to the dividend is split among the shareholders, based on the type and number of shares owned. Preferred stock usually has a higher value than common stock and is entitled to dividends first. If sufficient funds are left, a dividend for common stock may then be paid. Ordinarily, dividends are paid in cash, but some may be given in the form of additional stock or some product of the corporation.

Also to be considered are liquidation rights, the rights of shareholders to receive the value of assets of the corporation in the event of dissolution. Preferred shareholders may have the first right to receive these assets up to the value of their stock. Common shareholders are apportioned remaining assets toward their investment. Regardless of how much a shareholder may have paid for stock, only the par or stated value is paid. This is what the corporation originally indicated each share of preferred and common stock would be worth.

> Explain how the sale of corporate assets during a dissolution would be apportioned between preferred shareholders and common shareholders who each have liquidation rights.

Some corporations will sell stock with preemptive rights. This means that when a corporation decides to issue additional stock, the shareholders with preemptive rights are given an opportunity to purchase the shares of new stock based on their percentage of ownership before the shares are offered for sale to the public. Such rights are a sort of reward for investors who have previously contributed to the corporation. Additionally, they allow an investor to maintain the same percentage of ownership.

Stock subscriptions. A corporation may sell subscriptions to stock when it is formed or after its formation when approved by the directors. Generally, a stock subscription is an agreement between the corporation and a subscriber for the stock to purchase a certain number of shares at a certain price. A corporation that has not yet been formed accepts such agreements at the time of incorporation when shares are authorized and issued. Generally, persons who offer to purchase subscriptions do not have a contract with the corporation until the board of directors accepts the subscription; instead, the subscribers have an option that the board may accept or reject.[51]

If a corporation accepts a stock subscription and the subscriber defaults and does not pay for the stock, the corporation has all of the remedies that are available in the case of a breached contract, including an action against the subscriber for the value of the stock under the subscription agreement.[52]

Stock subscriptions are especially helpful to promising new corporations. The corporation receives adequate capitalization from the investors, and in return, the investors obtain the opportunity to purchase large amounts of stock at a price that is usually lower than the cost on the open market. Thus, if the prospects for a new corporation are hopeful, subscribers have an opportunity to buy more shares.

The securities and exchange commission. The courts have addressed issues such as improper profits and other illegal behavior by corporations, but significant issues with respect to the buying, selling, and trading of stock resulted in the creation of the Securities and Exchange Commission (SEC). Following the stock market crash of 1929, the Securities and Exchange Act of 1934 established the SEC to oversee the stock market system in the United States. The SEC administers laws of Congress and issues regulations with respect to major transactions of stock, corporate ownership, and management. The goal of the SEC is to see that corporations and major corporate shareholders do not take advantage of unwary minor shareholders or vulnerable corporations.

As mentioned earlier, a person who owns a controlling interest in a corporation has certain influence in corporate operations and opportunities. Under SEC rules, a shareholder who possesses 10 percent or more of the corporate stock is considered to have certain responsibilities.[53] The SEC further considers a 10 percent shareholder to owe a fiduciary duty to the corporation and its shareholders. Officers and directors have an even greater fiduciary duty to the shareholders.[54]

When a controlling shareholder sells the controlling interest in a corporation, the fiduciary duty requires that the stock not be transferred to someone who would injure the corporation. Therefore, before selling a controlling interest, the shareholder has the duty to investigate the interested purchaser. If this is not done, or if the interest is sold to someone the shareholder should know will injure the corporation to obtain personal gain (sometimes called "looting"), the shareholder may be personally liable for any damage to the corporation or other shareholders.[55]

In addition, a controlling shareholder, officer, or director who purchases controlling stock and sells that stock within a six-month period must disclose and return any profits to the corporation. This prevents the use of inside information for personal gain that will injure the corporation. The minority shareholders and the public are thus not at a disadvantage. It would be unfair to allow persons with access to information that may affect the value of the stock to avoid losses or to obtain huge profits while other shareholders or the public who lack the information lose or at least do not have the same opportunity to improve their investment. The key to legal stock transactions is disclosure. If major shareholders fully disclose their actions and adhere to the other requirements of the SEC, the corporation, its shareholders, and the public are protected.

The Corporate Existence

As stated earlier, the first board of directors of a corporation is responsible for complying with all of the statutory formalities, including preparation of the articles of incorporation and bylaws. Generally, the officers of the corporation will be responsible for daily management and administrative decisions, while long-range decisions about the policies of the corporation are made by the board.

Shareholders also have limited input into the operations of the corporation. They usually vote on major changes in the direction of the corporation and elect new board members when a term ends or a vacancy occurs. Shareholders also generally have the right to remove a director with or without reason. Examples of justifications for removal include mismanagement of the corporation or negligent risking of the shareholders' investments.

In smaller corporations, the officers, board of directors, and shareholders are often all the same people. In large corporations, however, many shareholders never even meet the board or the officers. Voting at annual meetings may be conducted by mail, and the shareholders make decisions on the basis of annual reports of the progress of the business and other printed materials provided by the corporation.

Shareholders who are dissatisfied with the job a particular director is doing may vote against the reelection of the director or vote to remove the director during a term of office. Each state has statutes that indicate when and how this may be accomplished. Each state's statutes also contain provisions that dictate the minimum number of meetings each corporation must have with shareholders annually. Statutes also provide for the type, timing, and method of notice that must be given to each shareholder before a meeting, and the procedure for voting by mail if a shareholder cannot attend a meeting.

Voting by Shareholders

Fixed rules exist with regard to which shareholders are entitled to vote on a corporate matter. Because stocks are continually sold and transferred on the stock market, a corporation's shareholders may change every day. Statutes specify a record date, the date by which one must own stock in a corporation prior to a shareholders' meeting to be eligible to vote on corporate changes. The board of directors then includes this time frame, or an even longer one, in the bylaws of the corporation when stating the amount of notice of a meeting that will be given to shareholders. Only persons whose names appear as shareholders in corporate records on the record date are entitled to vote at the annual meeting.[56]

If a shareholder cannot attend a meeting or does not vote by mail, the vote may be made by proxy, the written consent of one person to vote on behalf of another. It is also legal for a group of persons to request other shareholders to give their proxies so that votes can be accumulated on a certain issue. With respect to public corporations, this is strictly controlled by the SEC and must follow very specific guidelines. A proxy can be solicited only if the shareholders are given an accurate description of the matter to be voted on and are allowed to vote for or against the issue on appropriate proxy forms. This enables the persons soliciting the proxies to determine in advance how many votes they have secured in favor of a given issue. Statutes require that at least a majority of the issued shares be voted. An amendment to the articles of incorporation may require more than a mere majority. Generally, every share is entitled to at least one vote. However, the articles of incorporation may allow for the issuance of shares without the right to vote, such as some preferred shares.

In a corporation with a very large number of shareholders, persons owning only one or a few shares would not have the opportunity to have much influence over decisions, because other persons own a great many shares. Under the method of cumulative voting, each share is entitled to one vote, and when several different issues are to be decided, each shareholder will cast one vote for every share on every issue. For example, if three new directors are to be elected and a person owns one share, that person will cast three votes total (one share vote for each issue). If a shareholder has five shares and three issues are up for vote, the shareholder has the right to cast a total of fifteen votes (5×3). If cumulative voting is permitted, the shareholder can apportion the votes in any way he or she wants. Shareholders can also add their votes together to increase voting power.

Some states allow what are commonly called voting trusts and pooling agreements. In a voting trust, several shareholders give their proxies to one person who is known as the trustee, who votes on the issues. The advantage of a voting trust is that the weight of shares on a single issue is greater.[57] The disadvantage is that the trustee votes on all issues in the manner most advantageous to the group. This may not always be perceived as what is most advantageous to an individual.

A pooling agreement is somewhat similar to a voting trust. The goal here is to concentrate the votes on an issue. In a pooling agreement, the members of the pool agree that they each will vote in the way that the majority of the members of the pool indicate.[58] Generally, in a pooling agreement, a vote per share will be cast for or against each issue. Also, a written contract states what persons are involved in the agreement.

Indicate whether each of the following is an example of a voting trust, a pooling agreement, or cumulative voting:

(a) Many shareholders agree to put their total number of votes behind a single candidate in the election for several new directors.
(b) Many shareholders elect a few persons to decide how all their shares should be voted on all issues at an annual corporate meeting.

Rights of Shareholders

In most states, all shareholders, by virtue of their ownership interest in the corporation incorporated there, are entitled to certain rights in the corporation in addition to voting rights. Shareholders ordinarily have the right to inspect the corporate records upon reasonable notice and at a reasonable time.[59] Although shareholders do not ordinarily have input into the day-to-day management and operations of the corporation, they are entitled to observe them to some extent. The rationale is that they will be better informed about their investment and will be able to make intelligent decisions when voting on corporate issues or selling their stock. In addition, limited inspection is not seen as unnecessary interference with the business of the corporation. Historically, shareholders were given the right to inspect only if they could show a proper purpose. In response, most states have now enacted statutes that do away with the requirement of proper purpose.

The right to inspect corporate records is subject to limitation. Generally, inspection must be done during a time and subject to conditions set out in the corporate bylaws. This permits shareholders to inspect and also allows the corporation to avoid unreasonable interruptions of its operations. If a state statute permits such inspections and a corporation refuses or through its bylaws makes it virtually impossible to inspect, the corporation and the officers who refuse inspection may be subject to legal penalties in the event the shareholder sues the corporation. In addition, a shareholder has the alternative of bringing an action against the corporation.

In addition to having the right of inspection, shareholders have privileges that are specified in the articles of incorporation for the particular type of stock they own. As stated earlier, these privileges may be liquidation, voting, and dividends. Finally, shareholders have the right to sue persons involved with the corporation when they have mismanaged the corporation.

Corporate Actions

Two types of actions can be brought against persons who have a fiduciary relationship to the corporation. The first is a direct action by shareholders, generally, brought against officers of the corporation. If it becomes apparent that an officer has placed self-interest or the interest of a third party above the interest of the corporation in business dealings, the fiduciary duty has been breached. If this breach results in direct injury to the shareholders, such as the loss of their investment, the shareholders may maintain a direct suit against the officers.[60] It is only necessary for the shareholders who bring the suit to have been damaged and not for them to have been shareholders at the time of the wrongful conduct. If the shareholders are successful in such a suit, they may be awarded damages.

The second type of action is called a derivative action. This can be brought only by persons who were shareholders at the time of the wrongdoing and throughout the duration of the suit. Such shareholders act on behalf of the corporation against officers or others who owed a fiduciary duty to the corporation. It must be shown that the duty was breached and as a result the business of the corporation was damaged.[61] Any damages that are awarded are payable to the corporation.

Assignment 10.9

An inventor approaches a group of investors about financial backing for a new mechanical widget. The investors are interested in the project, but they do not want to expose all of their personal assets to creditors in the event the business venture should fail. Should they incorporate? Why or why not?

Assignment 10.10

Several unscrupulous business associates arrive in a small town posing as representatives of a corporation selling a new product. They take orders and receive advance cash payments from local retailers. When nothing is delivered, the retailers decide to sue the corporation. When they attempt to do so, they discover that the corporation never existed and thus there are no assets to make claims against. Can the associates be sued as a corporation? On what basis?

Dissolution of the Corporation

As stated at the outset of this discussion, the life of a corporation is created by statute. It ends in the same manner. As long as the corporation complies with statutory requirements, the secretary of state will continue to recognize the business as a corporate entity. A corporation may dissolve, however, on grounds that include failure to comply with legal requirements or the action of shareholders or creditors. It may also dissolve by voluntary assent of the board of directors and, when necessary, of the shareholders. Although each state has specific requirements for dissolution, the items discussed in the following paragraphs are generally common to all state statutes.

When a corporation decides to dissolve voluntarily, several things must be accomplished prior to the dissolution. Before a formal voluntary dissolution takes effect, the following[62] are generally required:

1. The shareholders consent to the dissolution.
2. Notice is given to creditors.
3. All assets are sold.
4. No suits are pending against the corporation.
5. Debts are paid, and the remaining cash is distributed to shareholders.

Although court proceedings are usually not required in a voluntary dissolution, the corporation is usually required by statute to file documents that indicate the intent to dissolve the corporation. With the exception of what is required for the sale of assets and payment of debts, the corporation must stop doing business. After all business is completed, articles of liquidation are filed with the secretary of state. If all requirements have been complied with, a certificate of dissolution is issued.[63]

Involuntary dissolution of a corporation may come about in one of several ways. Persons who have legal authority to request an involuntary dissolution in court are the attorney general of the state, shareholders, and creditors. When an outside party is attempting to force the cessation of business, the grounds for involuntary dissolution are limited and specific.

The attorney general of the state may bring an action to dissolve a corporation when the corporation fails to appoint a registered agent to accept service (delivery) of legal documents, when the corporation exceeds or abuses its authority as stated in the articles of incorporation, or when the corporation was created through fraud.[64] Frequently, statutes provide that the attorney general must file a complaint in the courts requesting an order of involuntary dissolution. The corporation may respond to the complaint, and the court will make a determination as to the validity of the allegations.

Shareholders are entitled to bring an action to dissolve the corporation when the conduct of the directors seriously threatens the shareholders' well-being. Examples of such activities include mismanagement, fraud, deadlock on corporate decisions, wasting of corporate assets, and illegal conduct. Generally, the courts will look to the actions of the directors and, in some cases, the controlling shareholders to determine whether the directors' conduct is likely to cause irreparable injury to the shareholders.[65]

Creditors are the most limited in their ability to cause the involuntary dissolution of a corporation. In most cases, this can be accomplished only when the creditor has an actual legal judgment against the corporation and the corporation is unable to pay the debt, or when the debt has not been declared by a court but the corporation admits the existence of the debt and its inability to pay.[66]

Bankruptcy

Every business venture is not a success. Neither is every personal financial situation. In some instances the debt to profit or income ratio becomes so extreme, the only reasonable alternative is to abandon the current endeavor. Bankruptcy laws have been developed over the years to provide a variety of options and protections to both debtors and creditors.

A common misconception is that when bankruptcy is declared, the creditors lose all hope of collection. In reality, the effect of bankruptcy in many respects can be a positive result. Several different forms of bankruptcy will be discussed in this section. The forms of bankruptcy depend on either the nature of the entity or the person seeking relief, and on the type of relief sought. However, a few characteristics are common to all forms.

Initially, when a petition is made to the bankruptcy courts, an immediate "stay" is granted. The stay prohibits further attempts at collection and effectively freezes the financial activity of the debtor. To ensure fairness, the debtor is required to list all creditors with the court and provide notice of the filing of the bankruptcy petition to those creditors. By doing so, not only is the debtor protected from further collection attempts, but the creditors are also protected because they are advised of the financial situation of the debtor and have the opportunity to discontinue further extensions of credit.

Generally, following the filing of a bankruptcy petition, a series of hearings are conducted to allow input by the debtor and creditors so that the court may make an informed finding regarding whether the bankruptcy petition filed is an appropriate form of relief for the debtor and creditors. Ultimately, an order is rendered by the court which details the rights of the debtor and creditors with respect to repayment or discharge of debts.

The two primary forms of bankruptcy are reorganization and liquidation. The first, reorganization, allows an entity or person protection from collection while a plan for repayment of all debts is developed and implemented. Sometimes, the amount and time of payment is different from that originally agreed upon by the debtor and creditor. However, the creditor does receive repayment of either the total debt or an accepted amount. The law also imposes limits as to how long repayment under the plan may take.

Liquidation is the absolute discharge of debt. In this type of bankruptcy, the assets of the debtor (subject to some exceptions) are liquidated or converted to cash. The court prioritizes the debts and begins the process of repayment. What are known as secured debts have the highest priority. Secured debts are those for which there is a written pledge of collateral such as a car or house. If the amount of liquidated assets is not sufficient to cover the total amount of debt, those at the bottom of the priority list are discharged, meaning that these creditors must accept that they will never receive payment for the amount owed and thus write it off as a bad debt. Just as certain assets cannot be seized and liquidated in a bankruptcy, there are also certain debts that cannot ordinarily be discharged. These are listed in the statutes and are only included in the discharged debts in extreme circumstances, and in some cases not at all.

When discussing the different types of bankruptcy, various references are made to the term *Chapter*. The term in this case refers to the chapter in the bankruptcy statutes that deals with the particular type of entity or person in bankruptcy or the specific type of relief sought. For example, Chapter 7 of the federal bankruptcy statutes is the chapter that provides for the liquidation of assets and discharge of debts. Chapter 13 provides for a reorganization plan by the individual and Chapter 11 provides for reorganization by most corporations and partnerships. Various other chapters provide for relief to farmers and highly regulated industries such as insurance companies.

When the individual or company wants to continue attempting repayment, there is a form of relief sometimes used by creditors known as involuntary bankruptcy. This type of bankruptcy occurs when a number of creditors of a single debtor cooperatively file a petition asking the court to declare a stay and impose bankruptcy. At first the question may arise, why would a creditor seek bankruptcy and possibly foreclose the chance of full repayment? The answer is quite simple: If the debtor shows an established pattern of accumulating debt beyond the value of assets, the creditors may want to put a halt to the increasing debt and thereby protect their chances of at least a partial repayment.

Bankruptcy has been a part of American law for more than a hundred years. The laws continue to evolve in an attempt to provide fairness to both creditors and debtors. Consequently, bankruptcy is an area of law that is subject to frequent changes and variations.

ETHICAL NOTE

Members of the business community are required to honor a code of proprietary behavior in addition to the required ethical behavior of all legal professionals. The core of any business is the relationship of the business with customers, whether they be other businesses or members of the general public. To maintain an ongoing customer relationship—or for that matter to encourage new customers—it is essential that a business follow certain practices that incorporate fairness and honesty. The failure to do so results in bad customer relations and often bad publicity.

While some transactions are open to scrutiny—thus making unethical conduct easy to detect—other activities are not so visible. Many times, such situations are dealt with through administrative agencies, such as the Securities and Exchange Commission (SEC), to protect an unwary public from unethical persons. However, the ultimate responsibility for enforcing ethics is within the business arena. Companies do not want to be known for unethical practices or be associated with companies committing such practices. Consequently, ethical behavior in the workplace is an increasing concern, not only at an academic level but also in the real world of work.

Question

If you are one of four partners in a business and have knowledge that the other three partners routinely engage in unethical conduct that could result in injury to an unwary customer, realistically, what are your options?

CHAPTER SUMMARY

This chapter has discussed the unique characteristics as well as the similarities of various types of businesses. Sole proprietorships involve a single owner, with all profits considered personal income of that owner. The life of the business is limited to the time in which the individual owner operates the sole proprietorship. Similarly, partnership profits are considered to be the personal income of the partners, and the life of the partnership is limited in much the same way as that of the sole proprietorship. The liability of a sole proprietorship and of a partnership is personal, subject, however, to the exception of limited partnerships. In exchange for liability limited to the extent of investment, the limited partner gives up the privilege of input in management decisions for the business. The corporation has unlimited life, regardless of any change in the owners. Liability is limited to the investment. Management decisions are made by the officers and directors, who may or may not be shareholders.

All of the forms of business typically involve the use of agency in which persons (agents) represent the fiduciary interests of other individuals or businesses (principals) for a specific purpose. Under the law of agency, the principal may be bound by the acts of the agent. Under the theory of respondeat superior, the principal may be held legally responsible for any actions by the agent that injure other parties, so long as the actions are within the scope of the agency relationship.

REVIEW QUESTIONS

1. What role does agency play in a partnership? In a corporation?
2. How does actual authority differ from apparent authority?
3. When is respondeat superior applicable? When is it inapplicable?
4. How does a partnership differ from a sole proprietorship?
5. How does a partnership differ from a corporation?
6. What elements are examined to determine whether a partnership exists?
7. What must be done to create a corporation?
8. When can the personal assets of shareholders in a corporation be reached by someone suing the corporation?
9. What is a promoter?
10. How is a corporation dissolved?

CHAPTER TERMS

Agency	Corporation	Promoter
Articles of Incorporation	Limited Partnership	
Bylaws	Partnership	

NOTES

1. William Statsky, *Legal Thesaurus/Dictionary* (St. Paul: West, 1982).
2. 3 Am.Jur.2d, Agency, Sections 9–16.
3. Id.
4. *Sim v. Edenborn*, 242 U.S. 131, 37 S.Ct. 36, 61 L.Ed. 199 (1916).
5. 3 Am.Jur.2d, Agency, Sections 222–224.
6. Id., Section 218.

7. *Consolidated Oil & Gas, Inc. v. Roberts,* 162 Colo. 149, 425 P.2d 282   .

8. *Lauderdale v. Peace Baptist Church,* 246 Ala. 178, 19 So.2d 538 (1944).

9. 3 Am.Jur.2d, Agency, Section 73.

10. *McGirr v. Gulf Oil Corp.,* 41 Cal.App.3d 246, 115 Cal.Rptr. 902 (2d. Dist. 1974).

11. *Elliott v. Mutual Life Insurance Co.,* 185 Okl. 289, 91 P.2d 746 (1939).

12. 3 Am.Jur.2d, Agency, Section 77.

13. *Bronson's Ex'r v. Chappell,* 79 U.S. (12 Wall.) 681, 20 L.Ed. 436 (1871).

14. 3 Am.Jur.2d, Agency, Section 75.

15. *Cavic v. Grand Bahama Dev. Co.,* 701 F.2d 879 (11th Cir. 1983).

16. Id.

17. *Pfliger v. Peavey Co.,* 310 N.W.2d 742 (N.D. 1981).

18. *Shafer v. Bull,* 233 Md. 68, 194 A.2d 788 (1963).

19. 3 Am.Jur.2d, Agency, Section 185.

20. Id., Section 280.

21. Id.

22. *Pacific Tel. & Tel. Co. v. White,* 104 F.2d 923 (9th Cir. 1939).

23. 3 Am.Jur.2d, Agency, Section 280.

24. *Friedman v. New York Telephone Co.,* 256 N.Y. 392, 176 N.E. 543 (1931).

25. Uniform Partnership Act.

26. Id., Section 15.

27. Uniform Limited Partnership Act, Section 7.

28. Id., Section 4, 5, 7.

29. Id., Section 18(b).

30. Id., Section 22.

31. *In re Belle Isle Farm,* 76 B.R. 85, 88 (Bkrtcy. Va. 1987).

32. Uniform Limited Partnership Act, Section 7.

33. Uniform Partnership Act, Section 16.

34. Id., Section 9.

35. Id., Section 13.

36. C.J.S., Partnership, Section 95.

37. Uniform Partnership Act, Section 29.

38. Model Business Corporation Act, Section 4.

39. Id., Section 25.

40. 18 Am.Jur.2d, Corporations, Section 104.

41. Model Business Corporation Act, Section 37.

42. *Lamkin v. Baldwin & Lamkin Mfg. Co.,* 72 Conn. 57, 43 A. 593 (1899).

43. Id., Section 36.

44. *Jefferson v. Holder,* 195 Ga. 346, 24 S.E.2d 187 (1943).

45. *Lettinga v. Agristor Credit Corp.,* 686 F.2d 442 (6th Cir. 1982).

46. *Fitzpatrick v. Rutter,* 160 Ill. 282, 43 N.E. 392 (1896).

47. 18 Am.Jur.2d., Corporations, Section 2804.

48. Id., Sections 45, 51.

49. Id., Section 49.

50. Id., Sections 55, 61.

51. Model Business Corporation Act, Section 17.

52. Id., Section 25.

53. Id.

54. Id.

55. Id., Section 48.

56. Id., Section 30.

57. Id., Section 34.

58. Id.

59. *Guthrie v. Harkness,* 199 U.S. 148, 26 S.Ct. 4, 50 L.Ed. 130 (1905).

60. 18 Am.Jur., Corporations, Sections 2245, 2246, 2249.

61. Id., Section 2260.

62. Id., Sections 82–93.

63. Id.

64. Id., Sections 94–98, 102.

65. Id.

66. Id.

CHAPTER 11

Estates and Probate

CHAPTER OBJECTIVES

After reading this chapter, you should be able to

- Distinguish per stirpes and per capita distribution.

- List the requirements for a valid will.

- List the grounds to contest a will.

- List the steps of probate.

- Describe the obligations of the personal representative.

- Discuss the rights of a surviving spouse.

- Distinguish testate from intestate distribution.

- Describe the process of dealing with the inheritance of one alleged to be responsible for a decedent's death.

- Discuss the requirements for a valid oral will.

The law of estates affects every facet of society. Of course, there are those persons who stand to inherit when another person dies. But just as importantly, virtually every entity with whom the deceased was in financial contact prior to death is affected. Popular misconceptions are that when someone dies, the person's possessions are immediately divided up among the surviving family. In reality, the process is much more complicated. The following discussion addresses such topics as the distribution of an estate when there is no will and when there is a valid will. The probate process is also explained. Although probate (administration of estates) is governed by state law, many of the procedures are similar in most states. This discussion is limited to those general procedures observed in most jurisdictions.

INTESTATE SUCCESSION

Intestate
Dying without a valid will.

When someone dies **intestate,** it means that the person died without leaving a known valid will. Often persons with substantial assets do not make provisions for the distribution of those assets after death. The obvious disadvantage to not leaving a valid will is that distribution by the state may not be at all what the deceased would have wished. Nevertheless, it is such a frequent occurrence that the states have designed several methods to distribute the assets of a deceased person. The manner in which this is done is called intestate succession (see Figure 11.1). Literally, this means that the state decides who will succeed to the assets of a person who dies without a valid will.

Per Capita Distribution
Distribution of an estate in equal shares, with each person representing one share.

One method that is now seldom applied in laws on distribution of estates is called **per capita distribution,** discussed here for purposes of comparison. Per capita is a rather simple method. The initial task is to identify all living relatives of the deceased. The assets of the deceased that remain after probate of the estate are divided equally among the number of survivors.[1] For example, assume that two children, one grandchild, three aunts, and four cousins were left as survivors of the deceased. The entire estate would be distributed into ten equal shares (the total number of survivors).

Per Stirpes Distribution
Distribution of an estate in equal shares to one level or class of persons. If a member of this level or class is deceased, his or her heirs divide the share.

The second method, and the one employed by the majority of states, is known as **per stirpes distribution.** Under this method, as with per capita, all surviving relatives are identified. However, entitlement to receive any of the estate and the percentage received depend upon the proximity of the relationship.[2] For example, if children of the deceased are living but no spouse survives, the children would be entitled to the entire estate, irrespective of the fact that many cousins and siblings of the deceased may still be living. This is because the children are direct descendants of the deceased. If, in the previous example for per capita distribution, the example were modified to leave no surviving descendants, the ascendants (aunts and possibly cousins) would receive portions of the estate. Another reason that a majority of states use per stirpes distribution is its equitable nature. In a per stirpes jurisdiction, members of a certain degree of relationship or generation will inherit equally, so that, for example, a grandchild would not inherit more than a child or other grandchild.

Assignment 11.1

Based on the statute in Figure 11.1, identify how your own estate would proceed by intestate succession.

FIGURE 11.1 Wisconsin Statutes Annotated Chapter 852— Intestate Succession

852.01. Basic rules for intestate succession

(1) Who are heirs. The net estate of a decedent which he has not disposed of by will, whether he dies without a will, or with a will which does not completely dispose of his estate, passes to his surviving heirs as follows:

(a) To the spouse:

1. If there are no surviving issue of the decedent, or if the surviving issue are all issue of the surviving spouse and the decedent, the entire estate.

2. If there are surviving issue one or more of whom are not issue of the surviving spouse, one-half of that portion of the decedent's net estate not disposed of by will consisting of decedent's property other than marital property and other than property described under 861.02(1).

(b) To the issue, the share of the estate not passing to the spouse under part (a), or the entire estate if there is no surviving spouse; if the issue are all in the same degree of kinship to the decedent they take equally, but if they are of unequal degree then those of more remote degrees take by representation.

(c) If there is no surviving spouse or issue, to the parents.

(d) If there is no surviving spouse, issue or parent, to the brothers and sisters and the issue of any deceased brother or sister by representation.

(e) If there is no surviving spouse, issue, parent or brother or sister, to the issue of brothers and sisters; if such issue are all in the same degree of kinship to the decedent they take equally, but if they are of unequal degree then those of more remote degrees take by representation.

(f) If there is no surviving spouse, issue, parent or issue of a parent, to the grandparents.

(g) If there is no surviving spouse, issue, parent, issue of a parent, or grandparent, to the intestate's next of kin in equal degree.

(2) Requirement that heir survive decedent for a certain time. If any person who would otherwise be an heir under sub. (1) dies within 72 hours of the time of death of the decedent, the net estate not disposed of by will passes under this section as if that person had predeceased the decedent. If the time of death of the decedent or of the person who would otherwise be an heir, or the times of death of both, cannot be determined, and it cannot be established that the person who would otherwise be an heir has survived the decedent by at least 72 hours, it is presumed that the person died within 72 hours of the decedent's death. In computing time for purposes of this subsection, local standard time at the place of death of the decedent is used.

(2m) Requirement that heir not have intentionally killed the deceased. (a) If any person who would otherwise be an heir under sub. (1) has unlawfully and intentionally killed the decedent, the net estate not disposed of by will passes as if the killer had predeceased the decedent.

(b) A final judgment of conviction of unlawful and intentional killing is conclusive for purposes of this subsection.

(bg) A final adjudication of delinquency on the basis of unlawfully and intentionally killing the decedent is conclusive for purposes of this subsection.

(br) In the absence of a conviction under par. (b) or an adjudication under par. (bg), the court, on the basis of clear and convincing evidence, may determine whether the killing was unlawful and intentional for purposes of this subsection.

(c) This subsection does not affect the rights of any person who, before rights under this subsection have been adjudicated, purchases for value and without notice from the killer property that the killer would have acquired except for this subsection; but the killer is liable for the amount of the proceeds. No insurance company, bank or other obligor paying according to the terms of its policy or obligation is liable because of this subsection unless before payment it has received at its home office or principal address written notice of a claim under this subsection.

(3) Escheat. If there are no heirs of the decedent under subs. (1) and (2), the net estate escheats to the state to be added to the capital of the school fund.

Each state that utilizes the per stirpes method has particular methods for determining exactly how the estate will be distributed. The common thread is that whether a person inherits depends upon the person's relationship to the deceased and how many other persons have the same relationship. Generally, the estate is distributed to descendants. If there are none, it is distributed to ascendants, such as parents, and across to siblings (brothers and sisters) and then to the descendents of the siblings. If there are no living relatives at these levels, it proceeds to ascendants such as aunts and uncles and their descendants (i.e., cousins). Depending on the limit set by the state statute, this may continue on for several degrees of family relation. The following are some of the more common rules employed based on the survivors.

If there are

(a) A surviving spouse and children all born to the surviving spouse and deceased: The spouse receives a lump sum of money and an additional percentage of the estate. The children receive the entire remaining percentage to be distributed equally.

(b) A surviving spouse and children, some or all of whom are not the children of the surviving spouse: Spouse and children receive one half of the estate each. If there is more than one child, the one half will be divided equally among the number of children.

(c) A surviving spouse, no children, surviving parents and/or siblings or children of siblings: Surviving spouse is entitled to a lump sum of cash and one half of the estate. Parents and siblings each take an equal share of the remaining one half of the estate. If a sibling is deceased but leaves children, the children each take an equal share of what would have been the sibling's share.

(d) Surviving parents, siblings, and children of siblings: The entire estate would be distributed on the same basis as indicated in (c).

As indicated, under per stirpes, the shares are divided based on categories of *living* relatives. Thus, if siblings are alive, the shares are divided among the number of living siblings, and the siblings' children are entitled only to split a deceased sibling's share. This is different from per capita, which gives no attention to the level of the relationship but rather distributes according to the number of relations.

 APPLICATION 11.1

Assume the deceased is survived by her parents, spouse, child, aunt, brother, and two children of a deceased sister. Under per capita distribution, the estate would be divided into eight equal shares. Under per stirpes distribution, the spouse takes a lump sum of cash according to state law and one half of the estate. The child takes the other half.

Assume now that there was no wife or child. Under per capita, the estate would be divided into six equal shares. Under per stirpes, the parents and the brother would each take one third. The final third would be divided among the children of the deceased sibling who would have inherited had she survived.

The per stirpes method does not search out relatives to an infinite degree to receive the estate. Rather most states have a maximum level of relationship, such as a fifth cousin, who can inherit the estate.[3] If there are no sufficiently close relatives left surviving, the estate of the deceased goes into what is called escheat, the process by which the assets are taken over by the state. The assets become the property of the state, and no individuals are entitled to inherit.[4]

What of persons who have a partial blood relationship or relationship created by law to the deceased? As previously indicated, a spouse is considered to be a blood relative for purposes of inheritance, even though the relationship is a legal one. But what is the status of adopted children? The relationship is recognized by law. Generally, when a parent adopts a child, for all purposes of intestate succession, the child is treated as a natural child of the parent.[5] The states are divided on the status of any remaining testamentary relationship between the adopted child and the biological parents. Many states permit the child to claim inheritance from the biological parents. Other states consider the bond severed at the time of adoption and do not permit such claims. However, most states do not permit the biological parent to inherit from the adopted child in the event the parent survives the child. Any permitted inheritance in such a situation would, of course, require knowledge of the identity of the parties involved.

Siblings of half-blood relationships share only one parent with the deceased. In most states, a half-blood sibling is entitled to inherit at least some portion of the estate.[6] These states vary from a percentage inheritance to a full entitlement, as a full blood brother or sister would receive.

If a child is born out of wedlock and subsequently makes a claim of inheritance against the father's estate, it is usually required that the father made some formal acknowledgement of the child during the father's lifetime.[7] This can be demonstrated by a legal finding of paternity or by actions of the father that would indicate the father believed the child to be his. However, with the advancement of scientific technology, it may very soon be the general rule that proof of paternity as evidence to claim inheritance can be produced after the death of the father.

A child who is born within ten months of the death of a parent can make a claim as a posthumous heir to the estate.[8] Otherwise, all persons claiming against the estate must be alive at the time of, and for a specified period of time after, the decedent's death.[9] Consider how this latter situation could create a question.

A husband and wife are killed in an accident. The wife had two children by a previous marriage. The husband had some distant relatives (but still close enough to inherit under per stirpes). If it can be proven that the wife outlived the husband by a sufficient period of time, the wife's estate would be entitled to the entire estate of the husband. Consequently, the wife's two children (from a former marriage) would be entitled to the entire estate of their mother. If the wife did not survive the husband for a requisite period of time, the children would inherit only their mother's estate and none of their stepfather's. Ultimately, the distant relatives of the husband would inherit his entire estate by per stirpes.

Another matter that affects both intestate succession and testate succession (distribution by will) arises when the deceased was murdered. Anyone who is found by the probate court to be responsible for the death of the decedent as the result of foul play cannot inherit.[10] Many states do not even require a criminal conviction. Rather, it need only be established in probate court that the person was accused and prosecuted for the murder. Some states have a hearing in the probate court to determine whether by probate standards a murder occurred (these standards are generally less stringent than what is required for a conviction of first-degree murder in a criminal prosecution).

Additionally, in some states, certain acts by a spouse prior to the death of the deceased may cause the spouse to lose rights of inheritance. Examples include adulterous conduct, abandonment for a long period of time, and other acts that indicate the spouse discarded the marital relationship. Further, a spouse who is divorced from the decedent cannot inherit by intestate succession.[11]

As this discussion has shown, intestate succession is a well-developed area of the law because of the numerous cases of death without a will. However, while the law prefers creation of a will, there are many rules that govern this process to ensure that the testator (deceased who left a will) created the will intentionally, without improper influences, and with a clear mind.

Assignment 11.2

> For each of the following groups of survivors, determine who would inherit and what percentage of the estate the heirs would be entitled to based on the rules previously discussed. (Assume half-blood siblings are entitled to one half of that entitled to a full-blood sibling.)
>
> 1. A surviving spouse and one parent.
> 2. One half-blood sibling, one full-blood sibling, one parent.
> 3. One child, one full-blood sibling, one parent.
> 4. One full-blood sibling, one parent, one spouse.
> 5. Seven half-blood siblings, one full-blood sibling, two parents.

TESTATE SUCCESSION

Requirements of a Valid Will

Before a will can be used as the instrument to distribute an estate, it must be declared a valid will. Contrary to what may be depicted in old movies, notes written on a slip of paper immediately prior to death rarely meet the requisites of a valid will. Every state has statutes that dictate the exact procedure for the preparation of a will. If the procedure is not followed or if any significant irregularities are present, the will may be declared invalid and the estate distributed by intestate succession.

A majority of states now require that a will be in writing. Although oral wills are permitted in some states, it generally must be shown that at the time of the oral will (1) the deceased believed death to be imminent and (2) the terms of the will were declared to witnesses who would not stand to inherit.[12] The rationale for upholding oral wills by states that still honor them is that such circumstances would lend credence to the terms of the testator's oral will and thus would be truly indicative of the deceased's intent.

APPLICATION 11.2

Felicia Williams, a wealthy widow, went on a boating trip with friends. During high winds, Felicia fell from the boat and struck her head on the bottom of the boat. She was pulled aboard and regained consciousness for about five minutes before her death. During that time, she indicated that she wanted her estate divided equally between the two friends who pulled her aboard after the accident. The only people on the boat were the two friends and their two very young children (who stood to ultimately inherit anything of their parents). Because the parents are interested parties (the persons designated to inherit), they could probably not validate the oral will. Because the children are so young, they also would probably be incompetent to testify and validate the will.

Point for Discussion
Assume the children were old enough to testify. Would they be able to validate the will?

Oral wills are an increasingly rare occurrence. Rather, the bulk of the statutes pertain to the requirements for a valid written will. It is required that a testator sign the will with knowledge that the instrument being signed is a declaration of intent for distribution of assets upon death. Thus, if it is established that someone was tricked into signing a document without knowledge that it was a will, the document will be invalid. If the testator knows the document is a will but because of some limitation is unable to sign it, the testator can direct another to affix the signature so long as it is accomplished in the presence of the testator.[13]

It is also required that the testator have capacity to issue the will. This does not mean that the testator must have legal capacity as required in contract law. Rather, it must only be shown that the testator understood the extent and value of the estate and the effect of a will, that is, giving the estate to specified others upon death.[14]

If it is established that the testator prepared the will under some mental impairment that would prevent a full comprehension of the will's effects, the testator may be considered to not have had the requisite capacity. Additionally, if the testator prepares the terms of the will under false information, undue influence, fraud, or some other factor that would impede the ability to exercise a voluntary testamentary document, the testator would be considered to have lacked capacity. Either circumstance will result in an invalid will, and the estate will be distributed by the law of intestate succession.

Witnesses are a necessary element to any valid will.[15] It is not required that they know the contents of what they are signing. Rather, the purpose of witnesses is to establish that the document was voluntarily signed by the testator. If the testator signs the document in the presence of the witnesses and the witnesses then affix their signatures, the requirement has been met. Witnesses generally do not have to sign in the presence of one another, so long as they each were present when the testator signed the document or acknowledged the testator's signature. Thus, witnesses could sign the document at a later point in time and the requirement of witnesses to the signature would still be met.

A significant issue that arises in many will contests is the intention of the actual terms of the will. Often, a will cannot be entirely stated on one page. Thus, when there are several pages, there is the opportunity for unscrupulous individuals to insert additional terms in the will. Therefore, any will of multiple pages should indicate on each page the page number and the total number of pages. This decreases the chances of alterations. Also, many courts prefer that the testator and witnesses initial each page of the will and affix their signature to the final page of the document.

Some wills mention other documents and incorporate the terms of those documents. This is done by reference to the document and by indicating the intent that the document become part of the will. An example is a parent who, as part of the will, wants to create a trust fund for a child. The will would make reference to the documents used to create a trust fund. This type of reference to other documents is incorporation by reference.[16] The documents to which the will makes reference are incorporated into the terms of the will as if they were actually a physical part of the will. To incorporate another document by reference, it is required by statute that the document already existed at the time the will was created and that it referred to the will within its contents. This prevents persons from creating the document to serve their own purposes after the will is executed and the testator is deceased.

A testator may also place conditions on bequests received under a will. The testator may indicate an intent to grant the bequest only if the person receiving the bequest performs certain conditions. If these conditions are not met, that portion of the will is considered ineffective, and the inheritance will not occur.[17]

It is permissible for a testator to disinherit anyone but a spouse.[18] Testators can direct almost without limitation who will receive under the will as well as very specific bequests of property or money. However, by state law, a spouse is entitled to a portion of the estate unless one of the circumstances of misconduct mentioned previously exists at the time of the testator's death.

Will Codicils and Will Revocation

Many times, a person continues to live for many years after the will has been executed. During such time, circumstances may take place that alter the intent of the person with respect to the person's estate after death. Such factors as death of other family members, divorce, birth, marriage, and changed financial status all influence testamentary intent. At some point, it may become necessary to alter the contents of one's will. This can be accomplished through a codicil or the execution of a new will and revocation of the old one. Which is more appropriate depends upon the extent and type of changes to be made.

A codicil is an addition to an existing will.[19] It is necessary that any codicil incorporate by reference the preexisting will. Otherwise, the codicil may be considered a complete and new will. All of the requirements necessary for a valid will are also required of a codicil because the terms in the codicil actually become part of the will for all legal purposes. When a codicil is executed and signed, the incorporation by reference serves as a sort of reaffirmation of the terms of the original will. As a result, the date of the will is considered to be that of the codicil.[20] This is important when several wills are presented to the court, because the most recent is presumed to be the valid will reflecting the final intent of the testator.

A codicil should not contradict the terms of a previous will. If this is necessary to accomplish the objective of the testator, an entirely new will should be prepared. Often codicils are included to make new provisions for bequests when a party who would have inherited dies before the testator. Also, codicils can be used to distribute assets acquired after the original will was executed.

Will revocation becomes necessary when the intent of the testator changes with respect to the distribution of assets upon death. Whenever a new will is executed, all prior wills are considered to be revoked and invalid, as they no longer reflect the intent of the testator.[21] Even if a testator does not execute a new will, the old will can still be revoked. If not revoked by a written document, it is often required that the testator take some steps to physically destroy or obliterate the existing will. It is not usually required that the will be totally destroyed. Rather, it need only be shown by the condition of the will and acts of the testator that destruction was intended.

In some instances, after revocation a testator will seek to have the prior will made valid again. This can occur in one of several ways. When a new will is executed, it can contain a statement that if it is declared invalid, the old will should be reinstated. This prevents automatic intestate succession if the new will is defective. Another method is for the testator to say and do acts in the presence of witnesses that clearly establish the intent that the former will be revived. A condition of this method is usually that the original will is still in existence. Assuming that a will is located and presented to the court for probate (the process of the distribution of the estate), parties still have the opportunity to challenge the contents of the will. This occurs during probate and can be based on several different grounds, as discussed in the next section, "Will Contests."

 APPLICATION 11.3

Eric Tan executed a will in 1966. He subsequently revoked his will with a new will in 1982 to include inheritance for his daughter Millie. Millie was killed in an accident in 1993. Eric phoned his lawyer to ask that the 1966 will be revived. The message was taken by the secretary, and the lawyer confirmed it with Eric by phone. On his way to the lawyer's office to sign a document to revive the former will, Eric was hit and killed by a crosstown bus. Because of the testimony of independent witnesses, it is likely that a court would revive the former will rather than allow the estate to proceed intestate.

Point for Discussion
Assume the lawyer is Eric's brother and is the primary heir under the 1966 will. However, if the estate proceeded by intestate succession, Eric's parents would receive one half of the estate. Would the result of reviving the will be altered?

CASE

BRITTIN v. BUCKMAN

279 Ill.App. 3d
512, 664 N.E.21d 687,
216 Il.Dec. 50 (1996).

Justice
GOLDENHERSH
delivered the opinion
of the court:

Respondent, Mary Ann Buckman, natural daughter of decedent, Stephen Glenn Brittin, and administrator of his estate, appeals from an order of the circuit court finding petitioners, Deborah J. Roeder, Linda Brittin, Denise Brittin, Stacie Brittin, and Laura Moore, the natural children of decedent's adopted son, William Eugene, to be decedent's legal HEIRS and reopening decedent's estate.

On appeal, respondent contends the trial court erred in finding petitioners, for purposes of INTESTATE succession, to be the legal HEIRS of decedent and in reopening decedent's estate. We affirm.

I

The facts are undisputed. The record reveals that when William Eugene was about three years of age, his mother, Estelle Willet, married the decedent, Stephen Glenn Brittin. From age three, Stephen and Estelle raised William as their son. The couple had one natural child, Mary Ann Buckman, respondent herein. Estelle Willet Brittin died on July 28, 1975. Shortly thereafter, on October 20, 1976, Stephen adopted William in an adult adoption proceeding in St. Clair County. William was 46 years old at the time of the adoption and had five children, petitioners herein. The adoption decree specifically provides that William was the child of Stephen Glenn Brittin "and for the purposes of inheritance and all other legal incidents and consequences, shall be the same as if said respondent had been born to Stephen Glenn Brittin and Estelle Willet Brittin (now deceased) in lawful wedlock." William died on May 17, 1979, predeceasing his adoptive father and leaving his five children as his descendants and HEIRS.

On February 8, 1993, Stephen died INTESTATE leaving Mary, his natural daughter, and petitioners, descendants of his adopted son, William, as his HEIRS. Decedent's INTESTATE estate was opened on March 10, 1993. The court found respondent to be the sole heir and appointed her administrator of the estate. The estate was closed on October 4, 1993, with the proceeds going to respondent. Petitioners were unaware that the administration of decedent's estate was underway without their participation until December 1993, when they learned that the estate had been closed.

On February 9, 1994, petitioners filed a petition to vacate the order of discharge and order finding heirship and to reopen the estate. Petitioners alleged in the petition that they are HEIRS of the decedent and are entitled to share in decedent's estate as the children of decedent's adopted son. After a hearing, the trial court entered its order finding petitioners legal HEIRS of decedent and reopening the estate. Respondent filed a motion to reconsider, which was denied on January 30, 1995. Respondent appeals.

II

Respondent contends that petitioners are not descendants of the decedent and may not take, by representation, their deceased father's share of the decedent's estate. Respondent acknowledges that pursuant to section 2–4(a) of the PROBATE Act (755 ILCS 5/2–4(a) (West 1992)), petitioners' father, as the adopted child of the decedent, is a descendant of his adoptive parent, and had he not predeceased decedent, he would be entitled to half of decedent's estate. However, defendant argues that the legislature, in using the term "adopted child" in section 2–4(a) of the PROBATE Act, intended to limit INTESTATE succession to the descendants of a child adopted as a minor. Respondent further asserts that the legislature did not intend to include as descendants of an "adopted child" children born to the adopted adult prior to that adult's adoption. According to respondent, because petitioners were already born at the time of decedent's adoption of their father, they are not the descendants of an "adopted child" and therefore cannot take by representation their deceased father's share of decedent's estate. We disagree.

The case before us is one of first impression and requires our consideration of the issue of whether the natural children of an adult adoptee are descendants of the adopting parent for purposes of inheritance. In considering this issue, we must consider whether the legislature, in enacting the statute granting an adopted child the status of a descendant of the adopting parent, intended to limit succession rights of the adoptee's children to the natural children of a child adopted as a minor and to exclude the natural children born to the adult adoptee prior to his adoption by the adopting parent.

The DISTRIBUTION of an INTESTATE real and personal estate of a decedent whose spouse is predeceased but who is survived by his descendants is governed by section 2–1(b) of the PROBATE Act, which provides:

"§ 2–1. Rules of descent and DISTRIBUTION. The INTESTATE real and personal estate of a resident decedent and the INTESTATE real estate in this State of a nonresident decedent, after all just claims against his estate are fully paid, descends and shall be distributed as follows:

(b) If there is no surviving spouse but a descendant of the decedent: the entire estate to the decedent's descendants PER STIRPES." 755 ILCS 5/2–1(b) (West 1992).

Where the decedent is survived by an adopted child, the adopted child may take a share of the INTESTATE estate as a legal heir of the decedent pursuant to section 2–4(a) of the PROBATE Act, which provides:

"§ 2–4. Adopted child and adopting parent. (a) An adopted child is a descendant of the adopting parent for purposes of inheritance from the adopting parent and from the lineal and collateral kindred of the adopting parent. For such purposes, an adopted child also is a descendant of both natural parents when the adopting parent is the spouse of a natural parent." 755 ILCS 5/2–4(a) (West 1992).

To determine the intent of the legislature, a court should first consider the statutory language, for its language best indicates the legislature's intent. Solich, 158 Ill.2d at 81, 196 Ill.Dec. at 657, 630 N.E.2d. "In applying plain and unambiguous language, it is not necessary for a court to search for any subtle or not readily apparent intention of the legislature." Di Foggio v. Retirement Board of the County Employees Annuity & Benefit Fund of Cook County, 156 Ill.2d 377, 383, 189 Ill.Dec. 753, 756, 620 N.E.2d 1070, 1073 (1993).

The Adoption Act (750 ILCS 50/1 et seq. (West 1992)) provides for the adoption of an adult as well as the adoption of minor children. Section 3 of the Adoption Act sets forth the conditions under which an adult may be adopted, stating:

"§ 3. Who may be adopted. A male or female adult [] may be adopted provided that such adult has resided in the home of the persons intending to adopt him at any time for more than 2 years continuously preceding the commencement of an adoption proceeding, or in the alternative that such persons are related to him within a degree set forth in the definition of a related child in Section 1 of this Act." 750 ILCS 50/3 (West 1992).

A careful review of the Adoption Act reveals no statutory distinction between an adopted adult and an adopted minor with respect to the nature of the legal relationship created between the adoptee and the adopting parent, namely, a parent–child relationship. The adoptee, regardless of his age upon adoption, attains the status of a natural child of the adopting parents. In re M.M., 156 Ill.2d 53. 62, 189 Ill.Dec. 1, 7, 619 N.E.2d 702, 708 (1993). Likewise, the Adoption Act makes no reference to the rights of an adopted child with regard to his ability to inherit from his adopting parents. Therefore, for the proper resolution of the issue before us, we must examine section 2–4(a) of the PROBATE Act.

Respondent maintains that section 2–4(a) of the PROBATE Act does not include adult adoptees because, had the legislature intended to include adopted adult children, it would have changed the word "child" to "person" so as to include all adopted persons. Respondent argues that the legislature has amended section 2–4(a) several times and has not made this change and, therefore, the legislature intended to limit inheritance to minor adopted children. We do not agree with this contention.

"Where the terms of a statute are not defined by the legislature, courts will assume that they were intended to have their ordinary and popularly understood meanings, unless doing so would defeat the perceived legislative intent."

People v. Hicks, 101 Ill.2d 366, 371, 78 Ill.Dec.
354, 357, 462 N.E.2d 473, 476 (1984). Further, in
determining the legislature's intent in using a
particular term, "a reference to the subject matter
and the context will ordinarily disclose the sense
in which the word is used." Bartholow v. Davies,
276 Ill. 505, 511, 114 N.E. 1017 (1916).

"There are two meanings which may be given to
the word 'child:' one an offspring or a descendant,
when a person is spoken of in relation to his parents:
another, a person of immature years. The word
'child,' when used with reference to the parents,
ordinarily has no reference to age, but to the
relation. When used without reference to the
parents, as indicating a particular individual, it
usually bears the meaning of a young person of
immature years." Bartholow, 276 Ill. at 511, 114
N.E. at 1019. (NOTE: Bartholow was decided prior to
statutory changes allowing the adoption of adults.)

Considering the subject matter and context in
which the word "child" is used in section 2–4(a),
the plain language of the statute indicates that the
legislature intended to use the word "child" in its
relational sense; referring to the parent–child
relationship between the adoptee and the adopting
parent. The word "child," as used here, cannot be
interpreted fairly as meaning a minor, in light of
section 3 of the Adoption Act which permits adult
adoptions. Moreover, there is nothing in section
2–4(a) indicating a distinction between the
adoptee's status as an adult or a minor at the time
of adoption with regard to the adoptee's
classification as a descendant of the adopting
parent. The only qualification set forth in the
statute is that the adoptee be legally adopted.
Nothing more is required. Accordingly, petitioner's
deceased father is an adopted child of the decedent
and, as such, obtained the right of succession as
decedent's legal heir.

III

Respondent next asserts that the children of an
adopted adult who were born before the adult's
adoption are not the legal HEIRS of the decedent
because they are not the children of an adopted
adult. Respondent argues, therefore, that
petitioners, as already-born children at the time of
their father's adoption, cannot take by
representation their predeceased father's share of
decedent's estate. This contention is not persuasive.

As discussed above, section 2–4(a) deems all
adopted children to be descendants of the
adopting parent. This provision places the adopted
child and the natural child in equivalent positions
with respect to the child's capacity to inherit from
an INTESTATE parent. Similarly, the act of
adoption itself accords the adoptee the status of a
natural child of the adopting parent. In re M.M.,
156 Ill.2d at 62, 189 Ill.Dec. at 7, 619 N.E.2d at
708. As with natural children, the children of the
adoptee, by virtue of the adoption, become the
grandchildren of the adopting parent, thereby
creating a grandparent–granchild relationship.

Because section 2–4(a) deems an adopted child
the descendant of the adopting parent, it logically
follows that, for purposes of inheritance, the
children of the adopted adult are also descendants
and can take as grandchildren of the decedent.
Accordingly, if the adopted child predeceases the
adopting parent, leaving children, as is the case
here, those children, as grandchildren of the
adopting parent, are entitled to represent their
deceased parent and to receive from the adopting
parent's estate the share to which the adopted
adult child would have been entitled to receive
had he survived the adopting parent. Annotation,
Adoption of Adult, 21 A.L.R.3d 1012. 1034–38,
§§ 14, 16 (1968); 2 Am.Jur.2d Adoption § 205, at
1132 (1994).

We believe this to be the correct reading of
section 2–4(a) since section 2–4(a) does not
impose any restrictions or conditions on the ability
of the natural children of a predeceased adopted
child to inherit from the estate of the adopting
parent. Nor does the provision either expressly or
impliedly state that the adopted child's children
must be born subsequent to the adoption in order
to be legal HEIRS of the adopting parent. Because
"the plain meaning of the language used by the
legislature is the safest guide in constructing any
[statute]," the court cannot inject provisions not
expressly included or fairly implied by the statute.
Munroe v. Brower Realty & Management Co., 206
Ill.App.3d 699, 706, 151 Ill.Dec. 761, 767, 565
N.E.2d 32, 38 (1990). Further, "the words of a
statute must be read in light of the purposes to be
served, and those words must be read to reach a
common-sense result." Munroe, 206 Ill.App.3d at
706, 151 Ill.Dec. at 767, 565 N.E.2d at 38. Our
reading of section 2–4(a) gives effect to the

legislative policy of according adopted children a status of inheritance equivalent to that of natural children. With this legislative purpose in mind, we can read section 2–4(a) in no other way but as including, as descendants of the decedent, the natural children of an adopted adult. Accordingly, we find that the trial court did not err in finding petitioners to be the legal HEIRS of the decedent. As such, petitioners are entitled to represent their deceased parent, the adopted child of the decedent, and to receive the adopted child's PER STIRPES share of decedent's estate.

For the foregoing reasons, the judgment of the circuit court of Madison County is affirmed.

Affirmed.

HOPKINS, P.J., and CHAPMAN, J., concur.

Case Question

What distinguishes an heir from a descendant?

Assignment 11.3

In the following situations, determine whether the will should be revoked, amended with a codicil, or left as is. Give reasons for your decision.

1. Husband whose first will does not mention his wife by name but provides for "my wife" is now married to a different woman.
2. Woman who bequeaths her antique car to her neighbor Bob sells the car.
3. Mother of four children provides specific bequests to each child, but one of the children subsequently predeceases the mother.
4. A man has a valid will but before his death inherits a large sum of money.

Will Contests

Most publicity regarding probate cases is centered around will contests, when a person challenges the validity of a will. The three common grounds for will contests are mistake, duress or improper influence, and fraud. Generally, one who contests a will has the burden of proof to establish by clear and convincing evidence (less than the standard of beyond a reasonable doubt but more than a mere preponderance of the evidence) that the will is not a valid testamentary instrument properly executed by the deceased.

When a will is challenged on the basis of mistake, the challenger must allege that the testator either did not know a final will was being signed or was not aware of all of the terms and the effects of what had been included in the will.[22] When mistake is proven as to any part of a will, most courts will declare the entire instrument invalid. The reasoning is sound: if it can be shown that the testator made a significant mistake with respect to one part of the will, who is to say that other mistakes were not made as well? When the entire will is declared invalid, the estate passes by intestate succession.

The second method used to challenge a will is that of duress or improper influence. The thrust of this type of challenge is that the testator did not execute the will independently and voluntarily. In most cases, it must be shown by the contestant that the testator was convinced that there was no real intent to execute the will. Rather, the testator was so impaired that the contents of the will reflect the desires of another and that the testator would not have executed the terms of the will but for the existence of improper influences.[23]

As stated before, it is the general rule that the person challenging the will has the burden of proving the duress or improper influence. There is, however, an exception to this rule. Whenever the will is drawn up or witnessed by someone who is a fiduciary (one who is in a position of personal trust to the testator) or who stands to receive under the will, many states will presume that there was undue influence.[24] Thus, a will should always be drawn and witnessed by disinterested parties. Otherwise, no matter how sincere the testator could have been, the burden is shifted against the parties alleging the will is valid. The presumption is that there was undue influence, and the will is considered ineffective unless it can be shown by clear and convincing evidence that there was no improper influence. Because attorneys are fiduciaries, they should avoid drafting or witnessing wills in which they are beneficiaries (although most states will make an exception if the will is for a close or immediate family member).

Persons who may not draft or witness a will without the presumption of improper influence are specified in the statutes of each state. Similarly, the burden of proof (amount of evidence) needed to show that the will was properly executed is also dictated by statute. The preceding are common rules, but variations may exist in some states. Consequently, before relying on these propositions, one should always consult existing statutes in the particular state of interest.

The final reason for challenging a will is an allegation of fraud. The contestant must prove several elements before a will is considered to be ineffective on the grounds of fraud. Specifically, it must be demonstrated that (1) an identifiable person made false statements to the testator, (2) such person did so with the intent of misleading the testator by the statements, (3) the testator was in fact misled and executed a will based on the false statements, and (4) the testator would not have executed the terms of the will in the absence of reliance on the false allegations.[25]

An example of fraud is the case whereby a child (presumably an adult child) convinces a parent that another child of the parent is dead. The parent then executes a will leaving the entire estate to the child who made the false allegations. If the parent would not have executed the same will with the knowledge that the second child was living and there is no reasonable basis of determining whether the parent would have executed the will, the will was created under circumstances of fraud.

 C A S E ───◆

COOK v. LOFTUS

414 N.E.2d 581 (1981).

RATLIFF, Judge.

Statement of the Case
Sandra K. Cook, as executrix of the last will and testament of Victor Chapelier and as devisee, appeals the judgment of the Floyd Superior Court which vacated the probate of the pretended will of Victor Chapelier dated December 22, 1976,

because of undue influence and admitted to probate the will of Victor Chapelier dated January 23, 1975.

Statement of the Facts
Victor and Agnes Chapelier were married in 1919 and lived their married life on West First Street in New Albany, Indiana. During their marriage, Victor and Agnes led a frugal life. Victor was a mechanic for a machine company in Louisville, Kentucky, and Agnes took in washing, sewing, and ironing. They were childless; however, Agnes

had six brothers and sisters and many nieces and nephews including the appellees.

On January 23, 1975, Victor and Agnes executed their wills. Each will contained the same or similar provisions. Victor left everything to Agnes unless she predeceased him, in which event the estate was to be devised and bequeathed to various individuals including the appellees. At the time of these wills, Victor and Agnes owned their home, another home on West First Street, and a farm . . .

Sandra Cook (Sandra) and her family lived next door to Victor and Agnes in a home which she rented from the Chapeliers. Sandra was Agnes' great niece. Agnes and Victor gave a parcel of land on their farm to Sandra and in late 1974 or early 1975, they also loaned $20,000 to Sandra for her to build a new home. Under the terms of the loan, Sandra was to pay $200 per month to the Chapeliers.

On May 2, 1976, Agnes Chapelier died. At that time Victor was in poor health. Dr. Streepy testified that as a result of the cerebral arteriosclerosis Victor would be lucid at times and confused and disoriented at other times. Various relatives stayed with Victor during the first two weeks after his wife's death. . . After approximately one month, Victor's furniture was sold, and Victor, Sandra, and her family moved into her new home on the farm. . . . Subsequent to Agnes' death, John Richards was given a Power of Attorney to take care of Victor's financial affairs. Richards continued to do so until September or October 1976, when he found discrepancies between his records and the bank balance. It was discovered that Victor had written checks and made withdrawals without telling Richards.

While Victor was living with Sandra, it was agreed that Sandra would not make payments on the $20,000 loan, and she discontinued these payments two months after Agnes' death. In the fall and winter of 1976, Sandra bought a new car and Jeep with Victor's funds. She explained that Victor gave her the money because her Volkswagen was too small and the road to their house was impassible in the winter.

On December 22, 1976, Victor made an appointment with an attorney to make a new will. Victor told the attorney what he wanted the terms of the will to be and returned a couple of days later to sign it. Sandra accompanied Victor to the attorney's office both times. On the second visit, she read the will to Victor, and he went into another room with two witnesses to sign it. This new will left his entire estate to Sandra. Victor took home both the 1975 and 1976 will and tore up the 1975 will before throwing it in the trash. He told Sandra that he was upset with his other relatives for trying to put him in a nursing home. Several parties testified that both Victor and Agnes had a severe aversion to living in a nursing home. Sandra admitted that she told Victor that others were going to put him in a nursing home; however, Geraldine Shirley, Jerry Shirley, and Jean Loftus testified that they did not know of anyone who planned to do so. . . .

Victor Chapelier died on February 2, 1978. The 1976 will was admitted into probate on February 6, 1978. The appellees, devisees or legatees under the 1975 will, filed a complaint to contest the 1976 will upon the grounds that it was unduly executed and that Victor Chapelier was of unsound mind at the date of its execution. The trial court found that the 1976 will was executed as a result of undue influence; that the 1975 will was not validly revoked; and that the 1975 will was valid. . . .

Before trial, the parties entered into a stipulation that the will of Victor Chapelier dated January 23, 1975, was validly executed; however, an issue remained whether Victor had the testamentary capacity. The trial court in its judgment found that Victor had the testamentary capacity, and Sandra contends the judgment of the trial court is contrary to law since it is not sustained by any evidence.

When a judgment is attacked as being contrary to law because of insufficient evidence, this court may neither consider the credibility of the witnesses nor weigh the evidence. We will look only to that evidence most favorable to the appellee. Cynthiana State Bank v. Murphy, (1949) 119 Ind.App. 685, 88 N.E.2d 252, trans. den. (1950). If there is any evidence of probative value to support the verdict on any grounds specified in the complaint, we must affirm the judgment. Noyer v. Ecker, (1954) 125 Ind.App. 63, 119 N.E.2d 902, trans. den. After a careful examination of the record in this case, we conclude that the evidence is sufficient to uphold the trial court's decision that Victor had the requisite testamentary capacity on January 23, 1975.

The record reflects that Dr. Jefferson Streepy testified that Victor suffered from cerebral arteriosclerosis from 1974. Victor's condition became worse as time passed, and by 1976, Victor was of unsound mind part of the time and sound mind the rest of the time. From this testimony, the trial court could infer that Victor Chapelier was of sound mind in 1975 since his condition prior to 1976 was less acute. However, this is not the only testimony which was contained in the record. Louise Payne, Victor's cousin, visited Victor and Agnes every two to three weeks and stated that every time she was around Victor his mind was all right; she never saw him when he was confused. Sandra also testified that Victor always knew what he was doing. It is clear that this testimony supports the trial court in finding Victor of sound mind in January 1975.

Sandra also contends that the 1975 will was revoked, and therefore, the appellees do not have standing. She argues that her testimony that Victor destroyed the 1975 will is the only evidence concerning whether the 1975 will was in force at Victor's death. Therefore, she alleges that the evidence is insufficient as a matter of law *586 to uphold the trial court's finding that the 1975 will was not validly revoked. We disagree.

It is true that physical destruction by the testator is sufficient to revoke a will if coupled with the intent to revoke. Ind.Code 29-1-5-6. However, the intention to revoke must be as clear and unequivocal as was the intention to devise and bequeath. Estate of Granger v. Gosport Cemetery Ass'n., (1954) 124 Ind.App. 686, 118 N.E.2d 386, trans. den. Whether the required intent to revoke

was present at the time of revocation is a question of fact. Cope v. Lynch, (1961) 132 Ind.App. 673, 176 N.E.2d 897, trans. den. (1962).

The trial court found that the 1976 will of Victor Chapelier was executed as a result of undue influence. It is clear from the testimony Victor was told by Sandra that the appellees wanted to put him in a nursing home; Victor had a severe aversion to being put into a nursing home; the 1976 will was executed and the 1975 will was destroyed on the same day with Sandra present; and Victor destroyed the 1975 will because he believed that appellees had tried to put him in a nursing home. We find that the evidence in the record is sufficient to uphold the trial court's finding of undue influence. The undue influence which caused the execution of the 1976 will to be invalid can also be viewed as causing the revocation of the 1975 will to be ineffective. 95 C.J.S. Wills § 285 (1957); 2 Bowe-Parker, Page on Wills § 21.27 (3d Ed. 1960). Therefore, we find that there is sufficient evidence to uphold the trial court's judgment. The 1975 will was validly executed and in existence at the time of Victor's death, and appellees have proved that they are interested parties.

Judgment affirmed.

NEAL, P.J., concurs.

YOUNG, P. J. (sitting by designation).

Case Question
What consitutes testamentary capacity?

PROBATE OF ESTATES

Probate
Process of paying creditors and distributing the estate of one who is deceased.

Testate
Dying with a valid will.

Probate is the term that describes the process of distributing the estate of a person who is deceased. Whether the person dies intestate or **testate**, the court determines what creditors are entitled to funds from the estate and what persons are entitled to receive a share of that which remains after debts of the estate are paid.

Originally, each state developed laws of probate. These laws established formal procedures for the handling of assets, evaluation and payment of persons claiming to be creditors of the deceased, and distribution of the remaining assets to heirs and persons named in wills. With the increasing mobility of our society, it is no longer unusual for a decedent's assets to be scattered throughout several states. Laws of property generally require that real property be governed by the law where it is located. However, the law of estates often requires the probate to take place in the jurisdiction where the decedent was domiciled at the time of death. In response to these and similar potential conflicts, the Uniform Probate Code was adopted. A majority of states have adopted the code, which establishes

Testate	Intestate	TABLE 11.1
1. Filing of petition* (to admit will and appointment of personal representative).	1. Filing of petition (to open estate and appointment of personal representative).	Typical Steps in Probate
2. Notification of heirs/beneficiaries.	2. Notification of heirs.	
3. Notice to creditors.	3. Notice to creditors.	
4. Inventory of estate.	4. Inventory of estate.	
5. Hearing on creditors' claims/payment of creditors.	5. Hearing on creditors' claims/payment of creditors.	
6. Final accounting of estate.	6. Final accounting of estate.	
7. Distribution of estate to beneficiaries in accordance w/terms of will.**	7. Distribution of estate in accordance w/laws of intestate succession.	
5. Hearing on creditors' claims/payment		

*Law varies by state regarding when a hearing on a will contest occurs.
**In some cases, bequests cannot be honored because the property did not exist in the estate or the property was sold or otherwise used to satisfy creditors or the spouse's statutory rights.

identical probate procedures and standards in each adopting state. In the past, it was possible that under differing state laws the rights of inheritance could vary dramatically. But with the Uniform Code, the inheritance rights are determined in the same manner irrespective of where the property of the estate is located.

Regardless of whether a state has adopted the Uniform Probate Code, the procedure for probating an estate follows some common basic steps (see Table 11.1). When an individual dies, state law often requires that all assets be frozen (businesses owned by the person may continue). All bank accounts, stocks, bonds, and other financial transactions in the name of the deceased must stop. These assets are frozen until such a time as the court has finally determined the status of the deceased's estate (assets and liabilities).

The first step in probate is to file with the court the appropriate documents, which generally include the original copy of the will and affidavits by the witnesses that they signed the will after witnessing the signature of the testator.[26] If there is no will, a petition is presented to the court for probate of an intestate estate.

Before going any further, challenges to the validity of the will are made and decided. Once determined, the court decides whether to probate the estate testate (with a will) or intestate (without a will) according to procedures of state law. For all practical purposes, the estates are probated in the same manner until such time as it becomes necessary to distribute the assets of the estate.

The next step in probate is to appoint someone to oversee the assets of the estate during probate. In many states, such persons are called administrators (in the case of an intestate estate) or executors (in testate cases). These persons are responsible to oversee the estate. They must inventory the assets, pay creditors (when approved by the court), and generally protect the estate until it is finally distributed. The administrator/executor is a fiduciary of the estate[27] and is under an obligation to care for the assets of the estate and not to convert them to personal use or waste them. Any breach of the duty as a fiduciary can result in criminal charges.

If the deceased is survived by a spouse or minor children, claims can be made for living allowances—sums of money that the spouse and/or children can use for daily living expenses until such time as the estate is probated.[28] Statutes give some direction and judges have discretion as to what is a suitable allowance based upon the size of the estate and the needs of the spouse and children.

In addition to allowances, certain property in which the deceased may have had an interest is exempt from probate.[29] Generally, such property includes the primary residence of the deceased (if the surviving spouses and/or minor children reside there), an automobile, apparel, home furnishings, and other personal items specified by statute. The idea is to protect the family from claims against the property by creditors. Again, these allowances are generally effective only when there is a surviving spouse or minor children, and state statutes list exactly what may be considered exempt from the estate of the deceased.

After an executor or administrator is appointed, inventory of the estate is completed, and allowances to the spouse and children are dealt with, it is necessary to process the claims of creditors. In modern times, it seldom occurs that a person dies totally free of obligations. Thus, each state has procedures for notifying creditors of the deceased person. Often such procedures include publication in the legal section of the classified ads of local papers and other methods designed to reasonably alert potential creditors of the pending probate of the deceased's estate.[30]

Creditors are generally given a specific amount of time to come forward with claims against the estate, often several months to provide every opportunity for claims. Creditors who seek to have obligations paid by the estate must file the appropriate forms with the court that document the amount and nature of the claim. If the administrator or executor challenges the validity of the claim, a hearing is needed to determine whether it should be paid by the estate in whole or in part.

After the deadline has passed for making claims, the court considers all requests by creditors. Arrangements are made for the payment of the claims from the assets of the estate. Occasionally, it is necessary to sell items of property to obtain enough money to pay all of the creditors. This is so even if the sale of assets depletes items that were bequeathed in a will.

Following the payment of creditors, in a testate estate, many states give the surviving spouse the option of accepting what he or she is entitled to under the will or claiming what is known as a **forced share.** This law grants an absolute minimum to a surviving spouse, generally, a significant portion of the estate. The only exception to such a case might be if the spouse had previously waived the right to claim a forced share by signing an antenuptial agreement (see Chapter 14).

Once all creditor claims and the claim by the spouse have been addressed, the court can proceed to distribute the estate. If there is a will, the estate will be distributed according to its terms so long as the assets bequeathed (granted in the will) are still in the estate. Each state has provisions that indicate how situations are to be dealt with when a bequeathed asset is no longer part of the estate (known as *ademption*) either because the testator disposed of it before death or because sale was necessary to satisfy the claims of creditors.

Most wills also have what is known as a residuary clause, which identifies a beneficiary to receive all remaining assets in the estate after bequests have been satisfied. This can cover a major portion of the estate if a person entitled to receive property died before the testator. Another possibility that could greatly increase the residuary clause is if additional assets were acquired after the execution of the will and no codicil was prepared to distribute them.

Forced (Elected) Share
Right of a spouse to receive a statutorily designated percentage of a deceased spouse's estate.

In the case of intestate estates, the common procedure is to reduce the assets to cash or appraise their value and distribute them according to the intestate method of distribution recognized by the state. As stated previously, this is generally going to be by per stirpes.

ETHICAL NOTE

As demonstrated in the discussion of will contests, ethics plays a significant role in probate law. A person's inheritance can be directly affected by the propriety of conduct exercised with respect to the testator. Probate courts are required to consider everything from an allegedly greedy family member or friend to cases of murder. Lawyers who prepare wills are under an obligation to take the necessary steps to eliminate doubts about the capacity of the testator, and personal representatives have the responsibility to care for and protect the inventory of the estate until it can be distributed. All of the preceding responsibilities inherently require ethical conduct, including both objectivity and fiduciary duty. The failure to undertake such conduct could result in a distribution of an estate that has no resemblance to the intent of the testator.

Question

If you are a paralegal and are asked to sign as a witness to a will of a client of your firm whom you have never met, what should you ask to ethically undertake the responsibility of witness?

CHAPTER SUMMARY

It is hoped that this chapter has produced a better understanding of some of the complexities of estate law. From the discussion in the chapter, it should be clear that the death of someone does not affect only the family, employers, and insurance companies. Banks and all persons or entities with whom the deceased had any financial dealings may also be drawn into the probate process. Consequently, in any aspect of business or industry, it is important to understand the legal consequences of a person's death.

When a person leaves a will, the document must have been properly written and under fair and reliable circumstances. When irregularities exist in a will or no will was left by the deceased, the law of intestate succession takes effect. While this does not always account for all of the wishes of the deceased, it does provide an equitable distribution of the property to the heirs who are presumed to be the most likely candidates for devise had the testator left a valid will. If one wants control over the distribution of the estate, the solution is quite simple. A proper will should be executed and kept current as changes occur in the estate or the people selected to inherit.

Regardless of whether a person dies testate or intestate, the probate courts serve the function of ensuring that the debts of the estate are paid and that the remaining assets of the estate are properly distributed. This is also accomplished with the assistance of an administrator in an intestate case and an executor in a testate estate. In either case, this party keeps the estate organized and intact until the final order of the probate court is issued to dissolve and close the estate.

REVIEW QUESTIONS

1. How is per stirpes different from per capita distribution?
2. What is required for a valid will?
3. On what grounds can a will be contested?
4. What are the major steps in probate of an estate?
5. Define the term *estate.*
6. What are the duties of an administrator or an executor?
7. Who can be disinherited in a will?
8. Who can inherit by intestate succession?
9. Who determines the inheritance of a person charged with murdering the testator?
10. Explain the common requirements of an oral will in states where such a will is permitted.

CHAPTER TERMS

Forced Share	Per Capita Distribution	Probate
Intestate	Per Stirpes Distribution	Testate

NOTES

1. *Martin v. Beatty,* 253 Iowa 1237, 115 N.W.2d 706 (1962).
2. Id.
3. *Richard Trust Co. v. Becvar,* 440 Ohio St.2d 219, 339 N.E.2d 830 (1975).
4. *United States v. Board of Com'rs of Public Schools of Baltimore City,* 432 F.Supp. 629 (D. Md. 1977).
5. 1a C.J.S., Adoption of Children, Sections 63–65.
6. 26A C.J.S., Descent and Distribution, Section 25.
7. 3 C.J.S., Bastards, Sections 24–29.
8. Id.
9. *Debus v. Cook,* 198 Ind. 675, 154 N.E. 484 (1926).
10. *Lofton v. Lofton,* 26 N.C. App. 203, 215 S.E.2d 861 (1975).
11. *McLendon v. McLendon,* 277 Ala. 323, 169 So.2d 767 (1964).
12. 79 Am.Jur.2d., Wills, Section 289.
13. Id., at Section 321.
14. *In re Bernatzki's Estate,* 204 Kan. 131, 460 P.2d 527 (1969).
15. 71 A.L.R.3d. 877.
16. *In re Erbach's Estate,* 41 Wis.2d 335, 164 N.W.2d 238 (1969).
17. *Wright v. Benttinen,* 352 Mass. 495, 226 N.E.2d 194 (1967).
18. *Solomon v. Dunlap,* 372 So.2d 218 (Fla.App. 1st Dist. 1979).
19. *Remon v. American Sec. & Trust Co.,* 110 U.S.App. D.C. 37, 288 F.2d 849 (1961).
20. *Estate of Krukenberg,* 77 Nev. 226, 361 P.2d 537 (1961).
21. *Crosby v. Alton Ochsner Medical Foundation,* 276 So.2d 661 (Miss. 1973).
22. 79 Am.Jur.2d, Wills, Sections 415–418.
23. 36 Am.Jr.2d, Proof of Facts, Section 109.
24. Id.
25. 92 A.L.R. 784.
26. 79 Am.Jur.2d, Wills, Section 407.
27. C.J.S. Wills, Section 1262.
28. Id.
29. Id., at Section 1311.
30. Id., at Section 1288.

CHAPTER 12

Criminal Law

CHAPTER OBJECTIVES

After reading this chapter, you should be able to

- *Distinguish actus reus and mens rea.*

- *Identify the parties to crime under common law principles.*

- *Identify the parties to crime under the Model Penal Code.*

- *Explain the distinction between theft and robbery.*

- *Define and distinguish the types of homicide.*

- *Discuss the concept of corporate criminal liability.*

- *Distinguish justifiable and excusable conduct.*

Criminal Law

Law created and enforced by the legislature for the health, welfare, safety, and general good of the public.

As discussed in Chapter 9, **criminal law** applies to those situations wherein public standards are violated and the public welfare is thus injured. Consequently, the government prosecutes on behalf of the people, and penalties (with the exception of restitution) are paid or served to the public. While many crimes result in injury to specific victims, such injuries are personal and are typically dealt with in civil actions, such as those for tort or breach of contract. In addition, the government may prosecute for violation of the criminal law.

In the United States today, criminal law is statutory; that is, the legislature determines what will be criminal conduct. All crimes must be stated as such by statute before the conduct described will be considered criminal. When presented with the prosecution of a defendant based on a criminal statute, the judiciary examines the particular situation to determine whether it falls within the definition of the crime specifically charged. The legislature cannot enact a statute making certain conduct criminal and provide for punishment of persons who performed the conduct before it was declared illegal.

The process of punishing someone for conduct that occurred before it was made illegal is known as an ex post facto law and is prohibited by Article I, Section 9, of the U.S. Constitution. In the United States, a primary element of all criminal laws is the concept of fair warning. Under the Constitution, this means that one must be capable of determining that conduct would be considered criminal before the fact. Allowing persons to perform some act and then making that act a criminal offense and prosecuting them for it would not be fair. This does not mean that persons must actually be aware of the criminality of their conduct but means only that they could have discovered it in advance and altered their course of action had they so chosen. Thus comes the saying, "Ignorance of the law is no excuse."[1] All persons are presumed to be responsible for ascertaining the rightfulness of their actions in advance. Generally, this is not a problem, because in everyday life, right and wrong are quite apparent to persons who act in accordance with the established societal standards.

The discussion that follows examines the basic principles of criminal law that exist today in the United States. Although criminal law encompasses offenses from the most minor traffic violation to capital murder, the focus will be on the elements of more serious crimes. Further, because a majority of the states have adopted the Model Penal Code as the basis of their criminal statutes, reference will be made to the Code when appropriate. States that have not adopted the Code rely on principles and definitions created in common law as the basis for criminal statutes. Accordingly, reference will be made to the basics of common law as well. States that are described as common law jurisdictions here are states that have established their statutes on the basis of common law principles developed and adopted by the courts. Jurisdictions identified as Model Penal Code states are those that follow the principles of the Code in their criminal law.

DEFINITIONS AND CATEGORIES OF CRIME

Categories of Crime

The two basic categories of crimes are felony and misdemeanor. A **felony** is any offense punishable by death or imprisonment exceeding one year. A **misdemeanor** is a crime punishable by fine or by detention of one year or less in a jail or an institution other than a penitentiary.[2] Many states have further divided felonies and misdemeanors into subclasses, usually, for the purpose of sentencing. For example, crimes that are considered Class 1 misdemeanors may carry a heavier penalty than crimes considered Class 2 misdemeanors. Once the classes are established, the various crimes are placed within a class. The definition of the criminal offense itself will indicate the elements necessary for conviction of the crime. The category and subclass will indicate to the court what sentence should be imposed.

In some cases, a mandatory sentence is required. This means that the judge has no discretion to impose or suspend a sentence. The statute prescribes exactly what the sentence must be. In the absence of a mandatory sentence, the judge is usually given a range of punishment. The judge is responsible for imposing a sentence within this range that will adequately punish the defendant for the crime committed. This range allows the judge to take the circumstances of each case into account.

Felony
Serious crime punishable by imprisonment in excess of one year or death.

Misdemeanor
Criminal offense punishable by a fine or imprisonment of less than one year.

Definition of Crime and the Elements of Criminal Conduct

Crime has been defined as follows:

> A positive or negative act or omission that violates the penal law of the state or federal government; any act done in violation of those duties for which an individual offender shall make satisfaction to the public.[3]

In more general terms, criminal conduct refers to acts that may be injurious not only to an individual but, more importantly, also to society. All persons in society should have the right to expect and enjoy certain basic privileges, including privacy, ownership of property, and physical safety. When one person invades the basic rights of another, the basic rights of society are also invaded. Therefore, criminal laws have been set up to punish and deter individuals from such actions.

Criminal law differs from civil law in several respects. Perhaps the most significant is that in criminal law, the government protects and upholds society's rights. In a civil case, *individuals* bring lawsuits to seek remedy for their personal injuries. In criminal law, the *government* prosecutes the offender to punish the person who caused the injuries. Thus, the purpose and goals of the two are distinct, although civil and criminal issues may arise from the same situation.

Actus Reus

Element of physical conduct necessary to commit a criminal act.

Mens Rea

Mental state required as an element to convict one of criminal conduct.

Included in all crimes are two basic elements: the physical conduct and the mental conduct of the perpetrator necessary for violation of a penal law. The physical conduct is called the **actus reus,** a Latin term meaning "the wrongful act."[4] All crimes require an actus reus, although in some circumstances, the wrongful conduct can be a failure to act. The mental conduct of the person is known as the **mens rea,** which means "a guilty mind or guilty purpose."[5] The state of mind element requires a certain degree of intent to commit the wrongful act or omission.

Actus reus.   Under the Model Penal Code, three steps are followed in establishing the actus reus.[6] First, it must be shown that actual conduct, either affirmative or by omission (failing to act when one should have acted), took place. If the criminal conduct is an omission, it must be shown that the accused was capable of acting and was obligated directly or indirectly by law to act. Secondly, if the definition of the particular crime requires a result from the criminal conduct, that result must occur to prove actus reus. For example, to charge a person with battery, the victim must have suffered some actual physical injury as the result of unpermitted physical contact. This would satisfy the requirements of prohibited conduct and a result that is necessary to prove an offense of physical battery. Finally, under some statutes, certain circumstances must exist for conduct to constitute a crime. For example, by definition, the crime of burglary involves an unlawful or unpermitted entrance onto one's property. Thus, this is a required circumstance. If someone entered the property with permission, burglary could not be established.

 APPLICATION 12.1

Act: While hunting, John raised a gun and pulled the trigger, which resulted in the shooting of his brother, who stood before him.

Omission: While hunting, John saw his brother cross his path. John did not, however, change the direction of his gun, and as a result, his brother was shot.

These preceding scenarios describe criminal acts. Although one was an overt act and the other a failure to act, both resulted in the commission of a crime that could have been prevented had John conducted himself differently. A person cannot be convicted of a crime based on physical conduct alone. It must also be proven that the perpetrator had the requisite mental state at the time of the crime (discussed next).

Point for Discussion

Why is physical conduct alone not sufficient for criminal conduct?

Common Law

General Intent: Driving above the speed limit.
Specific Intent: Deliberately running down a pedestrian.

Model Penal Code

Negligence:	Driving above the speed limit.
Recklessness:	Driving while intoxicated.
Knowledge:	Driving a car that you know has unsafe tires (pieces of tread frequently tear away at speeds over 50 mph).
Purpose:	Deliberately running down a pedestrian.

TABLE 12.1

Examples of Intent and Act under Common Law and under the Model Penal Code

Mens rea. The definition of each crime in the statutes requires a mens rea, which means "guilty purpose, wrongful purpose, criminal intent, guilty knowledge, willfulness."[7] Mens rea describes the state of mind or the degree of intent that the actor has toward accomplishing a criminal goal. Under common law, the two basic subtypes of mens rea are known as specific intent and general intent. More serious crimes often require specific intent on the part of the actor to produce the result of the crime, whereas general intent crimes require a basic awareness of the likely consequences of one's actions.[8] Under the Model Penal Code, the state of mind required for commission of a crime is based on degrees of knowledge that range from criminal negligence to recklessness to knowledge, with the most serious crimes requiring a criminal purpose. Table 12.1 shows examples of intent and act under common law and under the Model Penal Code.

In common law jurisdictions, the statute for a particular crime or group of crimes will generally indicate only whether the intent required is specific or general. Specific intent requires that the actor form the actual intent to achieve the result of the crime,[9] whereas general intent only requires knowledge of the likelihood of the result of the act.[10] Similarly, a Model Penal Code jurisdiction will indicate the degree of awareness in the language of the statute.[11] Statutes with a mens rea standard of criminal negligence require only that the actor knew or should have been aware of the probability that the action would produce a criminal result.[12] The standard of recklessness requires, in addition to a general awareness, that the actor demonstrate a disregard for the consequence of the action. Criminal knowledge requires an awareness that the conduct would undoubtedly produce a criminal result. Finally, criminal purpose requires premeditated intent to act in a manner consistent with criminal activity.

Criminal law follows a theory similar to tort law regarding transferred intent. In criminal law, although an individual may intend to injure or kill one person and, in fact, injures or kills an entirely different person, the intent is transferred to the person actually injured or killed. The intent and act were present. It need not be shown that the intent and act were meant for a particular person or object.

A few excepted crimes have no requirement of mens rea. Commission of such crimes can result in conviction irrespective of general or specific intent. These are known as crimes of strict liability. Strict liability crimes have none of the ordinary intent requirements. Under criminal statute that imposes strict liability, an individual can be prosecuted on the basis of the act irrespective of the presence of general or specific intent.

Strict liability laws are often established to protect the general good of society. Crimes of strict liability generally do not require a preconceived intent to do or not do a particular act.[13] Rather, they are usually applied when someone's preventive measures could greatly reduce social or public harm.

An example of a strict liability crime is a violation of the statutory duty of persons selling liquor to sell it only to persons over the age of 21. Such persons may not intend to break the law, but when they allow minors to be served liquor, they are endangering both the minors and the public at large. Simple monitoring of the persons served could totally prevent the harm that is presumed by law to result from the sale of liquor to minors. Therefore, if the duty to take preventive measures is minimal when compared to the social value of these measures, strict liability may be imposed. In other words, failure to take the preventive measures may result in conviction regardless of whether there was general or specific intent to cause the harm. Rather, the guilt is based on the failure to prevent the harm.

Assignment 12.1

For each of the following situations, indicate whether (1) the situation describes criminal intent, (2) the intent would be considered specific or general under common law standards, and (3) the intent would be considered purpose, knowledge, recklessness, or negligence under the Model Penal Code.

1. Richard went out with friends to several New Year's Eve parties. Although he had far too much to drink, he refused to allow any of his friends to drive him home. On the way home, he struck and killed two pedestrians.
2. After being dumped by her boyfriend, Patsy was distraught and decided to get even. She worked at the same establishment as her former boyfriend. She stole a large sum of money and placed it in the ex-boyfriend's briefcase. She then turned him in, and he was prosecuted. Eventually, Patsy was identified as the real thief.
3. Mark left his jacket at a friend's house. The friend went out of town, and Mark really wanted his jacket back. He broke a window and entered the house to retrieve his jacket.
4. Blair considers himself a law-abiding citizen. One day, he purchases some cough syrup. Upon arriving home, he discovers a crack in the bottle. He returns the syrup, but the pharmacy won't accept it without a receipt (which Blair has lost). Blair places the damaged bottle on the counter and picks up a new bottle and leaves the store. He is convicted for shoplifting.
5. Paul loves to hunt with a bow and arrow and knows this takes a lot of practice. Considering himself a marksman, he does not hesitate to practice on tin cans in a city park. Paul is aware that discharging deadly weapons is illegal in the city.

C A S E

COMMONWEALTH v. MILLER

1997 WL 14763
(455 Pa.Super. 534, 689 A.2d 238).

Indirect criminal contempt proceeding was brought based on alleged violation of protection from abuse (PFA) order. The Court of Common Pleas, Criminal Division, Centre County, No. 1996-601, Charles C. Brown, Jr., J., found defendant guilty of violating order by harassing and/or stalking victim. Defendant appealed. The Superior Court, No. 00435 Harrisburg 1996, Olszewski, J., held that: (1) defendant's benign explanations for being in same area as victim did not obviate finding that he possessed requisite criminal intent; (2) mens rea element of harassment of stalking could be shown without proof that defendant attempted to approach or harm victim; (3) victim's testimony allegedly showing lack of severe distress from encounters with defendant did not negate finding that defendant possessed requisite mens rea; (4) evidence supported indirect criminal contempt conviction; (5) defendant failed to state claim that PFA order impinged on constitutional right to travel; and (6) PFA order was not overbroad.

Judgment of sentence affirmed.

Beck, J., concurred in the result.

With respect to appellant's first issue, our standard of review is well settled. This Court must view the evidence and all reasonable inferences derived therefrom in the light most favorable to the Commonwealth, as verdict winner, and determine whether sufficient evidence was presented to prove each element of the crime beyond a reasonable doubt. See, e.g., Commonwealth v. Berkowitz, 537 Pa. 143, 147, 641 A.2d 1161, 1163 (1994); Commonwealth v. Smolko, 446 Pa.Super. 156, 162, 666 A.2d 672, 675 (1995).

Appellant maintains that, although he was in close proximity to Ms. McDonald four times within one afternoon, intent to harass, annoy, alarm, cause reasonable fear of bodily injury or substantial emotional distress cannot be inferred. This argument is purportedly supported by the fact that appellant offered innocuous explanations for his actions on the day in question, that there was no actual or attempted bodily harm caused and that the victim did not testify that she suffered severe emotional distress as a result of the altercations.

Addressing the initial averment, that appellant provided benign explanations for why he was in the same area as the victim on the date in question, we find that this in no way obviates a finding that appellant possessed the requisite criminal intent. Indeed, this proffer runs contrary to the very standard of review that this Court must utilize in assessing appellant's claim; for in finding that appellant acted with the necessary intent, the trial judge must have concluded that appellant's narration was baseless.

Next, appellant claims that the mens rea element was not proven because at no time was there actual physical harm or the threat thereof. This argument is ludicrous. An intent to place one in fear of bodily injury is but one mens rea that will sustain a conviction under § 2709(a) and (b). Alternatively, a conviction may be upheld upon a showing that the accused intended to harass, annoy, alarm or cause substantial emotional distress. Therefore, we find the fact that appellant did not attempt to approach or physically harm the victim to be of no consequence.

Finally, appellant claims that his lack of intent may be gleaned from the testimony of the victim that she had an "uneasy feeling" about the events in question. Even accepting as true that the victim's distress was not severe, we are unpersuaded that this precludes a finding that appellant's intent was to cause such a reaction.

We are aware of no caselaw which holds that the extent of a person's intent may be measured from the ultimate effect upon the victim. Furthermore, as previously stated, the intent to annoy, harass or alarm will also serve to sustain a conviction under § 2709.

In sum, our review of the evidence, viewed in the light most favorable to the Commonwealth, amply supports appellant's indirect criminal contempt conviction. Within the short time span of several hours, appellant came into contact with the victim five times. These encounters encompassed both residential and commercial environments, and continued even after the police made an initial contact with appellant. While the occasional encounter may possibly be explained as an innocent and random happenstance, the present facts do not support such a finding.

Appellant's second issue presents this Court with the opportunity to determine whether the PFA order issued against him was unconstitutionally overbroad and prohibitive of protected activities. Additionally, appellant maintains that the PFA order impinged upon his constitutionally protected right to travel.

We will first consider appellant's averment that the PFA order impinged upon his federal constitutional right to travel. After careful review of the applicable caselaw, we find that appellant has failed to properly state a claim for our Court to review.

The federal constitutional right to travel guarantees and protects the ability to migrate from one state to another and to receive the rights and benefits of the newly adopted state without obtrusive residency requirements. See, e.g., Shapiro v. Thompson, 394 U.S. 618, 89 S.Ct. 1322, 22 L.Ed.2d 600 (1969) (invalidating the denial of welfare benefits to residents who had not resided in a jurisdiction for at least one year); Memorial Hospital v. Maricopa County, 415 U.S. 250, 94 S.Ct. 1076, 39 L.Ed.2d 306 (1974) (invalidating the denial of non-emergency medical care to indigent persons who had not resided in a jurisdiction for at least one year.)

Instantly, appellant has alleged that the PFA order infringed upon his "constitutional right to travel within the Commonwealth of Pennsylvania." Appellant's brief at 18. Appellant has cited no caselaw, nor have we discovered any, which holds that there is a federal constitutional right to travel throughout Centre County, Pennsylvania. Moreover, appellant has not alleged that the PFA order in any manner impeded his right to interstate migration. We therefore decline to address appellant's claim that the provisions of the PFA order unconstitutionally denied his right to travel.

Next, we consider whether the PFA order was unconstitutionally overbroad in that it criminalized legitimate, protected activities. At the outset, we note that properly enacted statutes enjoy a strong presumption of constitutionality. See, e.g., Commonwealth v. Barud, 545 Pa. 297, 304, 681 A.2d 162, 165 (1996); Commonwealth v. Swinehart, 541 Pa. 500, 508, 664, A.2d 957, 961 (1995). Therefore, our standard of review is limited to a consideration of whether the legislation at issue is "clearly, palpably, and plainly in violation of the constitution." Swinehart, 541 Pa. at 508, 664 A.2d at 961.

When considering whether a statute is overbroad, and thus violative of due process guarantees, this Court must determine whether the challenged legislation gives a person fair notice of the type of activity that is prohibited. Barud, 545 Pa. at 304-05, 681 A.2d at 165. This encompasses an inquiry into the certainty and definitiveness of the statute in order to assess whether the average person would be able to identify forbidden conduct. Id.

Applying this test to the instant case, we find that neither the harassment nor the stalking provisions of the PFA order were unconstitutionally overbroad. The intent elements of both offenses, which appellant so vigorously challenged in the initial portion of his argument, obviate such a finding.

With respect to the harassment provisions of 18 Pa.C.S.A. § 2709(a), our Court held some time ago that the statute "requires the fact finder to infer a specific intent, and it specifies that the conduct must be of a nonlegitimate nature—conduct which is not constitutionally protected." Commonwealth v. Duncan, 239 Pa.Super. 539, 549, 363 A.2d 803, 808 (1976).

Similarly, in the recent case of Commonwealth v. Schierscher, 447 Pa.Super. 61, 668 A.2d 164 (1995), we had occasion to consider the constitutionality of the stalking portion of § 2709 when faced with an overbreadth challenge. Therein, we held that "[t]he Stalking statute is quite clear that engaging in repetitive conduct aimed at an individual evidencing an 'intent' to evoke 'substantial emotional distress' is prohibited conduct." Schierscher, 447 Pa.Super. at 78, 668 A.2d at 172.

We therefore hold that the PFA order assessed against appellant, which provided the underlying corpus for the indirect criminal contempt conviction, did not infringe upon appellant's constitutional right to due process.

Indeed, the PFA order does not even prohibit appellant from merely being in the victim's presence. The essential factor which appellant has omitted from his argument, and which controls the outcome of this issue, is that appellant must act with the requisite intent in order to fall within the parameters of the PFA order.

Case Question

What "intent" is required to establish harassment or stalking?

PARTIES TO CRIME

Usually, one thinks of a criminal as the person who actually committed the criminal act that caused injury or damage. Many times, however, persons act together to commit a crime. This may involve cooperation in the criminal act or assistance before or after the crime. In criminal law, one who assists in a crime can also be accused and convicted of criminal conduct. Since common law principles and the Model Penal Code are somewhat different on this point, they are discussed separately. The issue of cooperation in a joint enterprise, commonly referred to as conspiracy, is discussed later.

Under common law, there are four basic categories of participants in criminal conduct. Specific terms describe the various types of involvement by the principals—persons who are actually involved in the primary criminal conduct[14]—and the accessories—persons who aid the principals before or after the crime.[15] Common law defines two types of principals and two types of accessories.

Principal in the First Degree

The principal in the first degree is the party or parties who actually take part in a criminal act. It is necessary that they perform the actus reus and that they have adequate mens rea at the time they commit the crime. Under a variation of the definition, persons who can be charged as principals in the first degree include those who possess the mens rea but convince another to perform the actual physical conduct. This would include situations of coercion, threat, trickery or involve trained animals.

Principal in the Second Degree

Principals in the second degree are persons who actually assist in the physical commission of a crime or persons whose conduct enables the principal in the first degree to commit the crime. If the conduct of a party is required to complete the crime successfully, either at the moment of the crime or immediately before or after, that person would be considered a principal in the second degree, for example, someone who makes deliveries for a dealer of illegal drugs. The person does not obtain, sell, or perhaps even use the drugs, but by assisting in the delivery of the drugs, he or she is enabling the crime to be completed.

Accessory before the Fact

Accessories before the fact are those persons who enable or aid the principal to prepare for a crime. Their conduct may consist of providing the principal a place to plan or wait until the time has arrived for the actual commission of the crime. A very famous example involved the owners of a boarding house in Washington, D.C., who supposedly knew the assassination of President Abraham Lincoln was being planned. These persons were convicted and subsequently hanged for their participation in the assassination.

Accessory after the Fact

Persons who assist in a successful escape or concealment of criminal activity are accessories after the fact. This category includes anyone who is aware of the criminal activity and aids the principal in successfully avoiding prosecution. Conduct of this type ranges from giving the principal a place to hide to rendering medical care or misleading authorities about the principal or facts of the crime. Persons who are closely related to the principal are an exception to the rule. Under common law, it was considered detrimental to family unity to prosecute someone for aiding his or her spouse or children. Therefore, these persons could not be charged as accessories. This exception is still recognized in most states. Additionally, a person charged as a principal cannot also be charged as an accessory.

Usually, the division into principals and accessories applies to felonies. In the commission of misdemeanors, all who are involved are considered equally guilty. Common law also held that accessories could not be prosecuted, convicted, and sentenced unless the principal was convicted. Today, most of the jurisdictions that apply common law rather than the Model Penal Code no longer require the conviction of the principal prior to the conviction of the accessory.

Another present-day change in these jurisdictions is that principals in the first and second degree and accessories before the fact are generally all considered principals. Conduct that aids the preparations for a crime or enables a crime to be committed is considered as serious as the actual commission of the crime. Modern laws tend to grade the involvement of the principals and accessories as a way of determining the severity of punishment to be imposed. Thus, one who actually committed the crime may be graded more seriously than an assistant.

	Common Law	Model Penal Code	**TABLE 12.2**
Actus Reus	Physical conduct	Physical conduct or encouragement of physical conduct	Basic Concepts of Modern Common Law and Model Penal Code Jurisdictions
Mens Rea	General Intent Specific Intent	Negligence Recklessness Purpose	
Parties	Principal 1st degree Principal 2nd degree Accessory before fact Accessory after fact	Knowledge Principal Accessory Obstructing Governmental Operations	

Under Modern Common Law, these are also considered equal principals.

Parties to Crime under the Model Penal Code

The Model Penal Code recognizes principals, accessories, and persons who commit offenses of "obstructing governmental operations."[16] The Code defines "principals" as persons who actually possess the mens rea and who either commit the required actus reus or control the commission of the actus reus by such means as coercion, trickery, or manipulation. Accessories are persons who agree to aid or actually aid in the completion of the crime, including actual physical assistance or mere encouragement. Persons who commit offenses of obstructing governmental operations can be prosecuted for assisting in the escape of the principal or the accessory or the concealment of the crime.

Under the Model Penal Code, it is not necessary that the principal be convicted before the accessory or the person who has obstructed governmental operations. Instead, each is judged on his or her own criminal conduct, although the seriousness of the penalty may be adjusted to reflect the amount of criminal involvement of the individual. This is done in much the same way as the trend toward grading the severity of each person's involvement under modern common law.

The primary difference between modern common law jurisdictions and Model Penal Code jurisdictions lies in terminology. With a few adjustments, the basic concepts are the same, as Table 12.2 illustrates.

Assignment 12.2

In what category would the individuals in the following situations be placed under (1) common law, (2) modern common law, and (3) the Model Penal Code, or would there be no criminal liability?

1. Angie wrote James a letter telling him that his planned bank robbery was the bravest act she had ever heard of and that she would marry him after he completed it.

2. Kenneth and Jeff agreed to steal from a pharmacy owned by Jeff's father. Jeff was to make sure the doors were left unlocked, while Kenneth entered at night and stole the money and merchandise.
3. Susan's third cousin showed up at Susan's house with cuts and bruises. Unaware that these injuries were obtained while running from police officers, Susan cleaned and bandaged her cousin's wounds.
4. Kerry told his sister to take a package to a certain address. His sister did so without knowing the package contained a bomb.
5. Mike told the police that April had left town, when in reality he was allowing her to stay in his attic after she had escaped from jail.
6. Gerald created disguises for Rachel to wear when she mugged people. Gerald and Rachel would then share the profits from the muggings.

ELEMENTS OF SERIOUS CRIMES

The following discussion explains some of the basic elements that must be present before an individual can be convicted of some of the more common crimes in our society. In addition to submitting the required proof of criminal conduct by the accused, the legal system must follow the criminal procedures outlined in Chapter 13. The laws and procedures are designed to avoid conviction of innocent persons based on improper or unfair evidence of criminal conduct.

Inchoate Offenses

Some crimes are described as inchoate offenses,[17] crimes that occur prior to but facilitate or enable other crimes. Inchoate crimes include conspiracy to commit, attempts to commit, and solicitation to commit criminal acts. Each is addressed individually.

Conspiracy to commit criminal acts. The crime of conspiracy involves the cooperation of two or more people in planning and completing a crime as a joint undertaking.[18] Conspiracy in itself is a crime distinct from the additional criminal act that is the common goal of the parties. As a result, conspiracy has its own mens rea and actus reus, and a defendant can be charged with both the completed criminal act and conspiracy to commit that act (as opposed to attempt and solicitation, which "merge" with the criminal act if it is completed).

The mens rea of conspiracy under common law requires specific intent. Each party to the conspiracy must have intent to agree with the other parties. Further, the agreement must be to accomplish something that is illegal. Regardless of whether the crime is actually committed, persons who have agreed to work toward a common goal that is illegal are guilty of conspiracy.

The actus reus is perhaps the most difficult element to establish in a prosecution for conspiracy. There is seldom any concrete evidence, such as a contract, that will establish that the persons have taken steps to agree to a common criminal goal. Generally, the jury must rely on evidence of the actions of the parties to the conspiracy. The prosecution's description of the acts of these parties must convince the jury beyond a reasonable doubt that the parties had no other purpose than to conspire to commit a criminal act. Many statutes today have extended this burden of proving actus reus beyond the common law. Today, most statutes require at least one of the parties to perform some physical act that demonstrates his or her intent to be part of a conspiracy.

Under the Model Penal Code, the elements of conspiracy are much more specific. Proof of the actus reus can be shown in one of three ways. There must be evidence that the conspirators assisted in planning, soliciting, attempting, or committing the actual criminal offense that is the goal of the conspiracy. In contrast, the mens rea of conspiracy required in the Model Penal Code is much less stringent. There need only be evidence that each person accused entered the agreement "with the purpose of promoting or facilitating" a goal of criminal conduct.[19]

The crime of attempt.   Under statutes in all states, an attempt to commit a crime is considered criminal. An attempt takes place when the person has the mens rea (state of mind) to commit a particular crime and indicates a willingness to complete the crime. For some reason, however, the actus reus is never completed.[20] As a consequence, the person cannot be convicted of that particular crime. It is not in the interest of society's goals, however, to condone even attempts at crime. Moreover, sometimes injuries result from a failed attempt, for example, attempted murder. A would-be murderer should not go free simply because the victim was fortunate enough to live through a violent crime designed to produce death. Consequently, if someone takes material steps toward such a crime, attempt can be charged.

The question the courts must determine in cases of attempt is, How far must an individual go toward the commission of a crime before the individual is considered guilty of actually attempting the crime? Several tests have been employed in common law. Perhaps the most frequently applied today is that of proximity. The court considers how close the defendant was to completing the crime. The closer a defendant was, the less likely he or she would have turned away before completion. Adequate proximity to completion of the crime means that it is very likely that the defendant would have completed the crime if given the opportunity. This is point at which an attempt can be said to occur.

In a variation on this rule, the court examines the individual and determines whether that particular individual would be likely to commit the particular crime. The court may also examine whether the defendant had control over all of the necessary elements to commit the crime. Whatever specific questions are applied, the basic issue remains the same. Given sufficient opportunity, is it likely beyond a reasonable doubt that the person would have completed the crime?

Unquestionably, a person cannot be convicted of attempt if his or her actual goal was not criminal. Even if the individual believes that his or her conduct will constitute a crime, if in fact it does not, there can be no conviction of attempt. Similarly, if a person attempts to commit a crime but his or her actions in reality do not constitute a crime, there can be no conviction of attempt. However, a defendant who takes steps toward the commission of the crime and would have committed the crime except for some intervening fact or force can be convicted of attempt.

 APPLICATION 12.2 ─────────────────────────

Jeremy, frustrated with his studies, has decided to do away with his law instructor. He waits outside the school. When the instructor passes by, Jeremy throws a knife at his instructor and misses. The instructor, unaware of the event, proceeds about his business. In this instance, no crime was committed, nor could one have resulted from Jeremy's action of throwing the knife. Therefore, Jeremy could not be convicted of attempted murder. Assume, however, that the knife did strike the instructor, but unknown to Jeremy, the instructor was wearing a metal vest, which deflected the weapon. In this instance, Jeremy attempted the crime and completed all necessary steps to kill his instructor. Because of an intervening fact (the metal vest), however, Jeremy's crime was incomplete. Nevertheless, in this latter situation, Jeremy could be convicted of attempting the crime of murder. (An alternative charge might be assault and battery, which, in fact, was completed.)

Point for Discussion
Would it matter if Jeremy had known about the metal vest?

If the intended crime is completed, a person cannot be convicted of the offense of attempt as well as of the actual crime. It is considered that an attempt becomes part of the actual crime when it is complete.[21] Thus, the two are merged into one crime. The usual terminology is that the attempt is a "lesser included offense"; that is, it is included in the greater and more serious offense of the crime. If for some reason the crime cannot be proven, a person may still be charged with and, in many cases, convicted of attempt.

For the crime of attempt, the Model Penal Code requires that the actor do much more than simply prepare for criminal conduct. The actor must take what would be considered a "substantial step" toward completion of the crime. This substantial step is something that makes the crime more than a contemplation. At this point, the elements of the crime are within the control of the defendant and can be completed with the defendant's further actions.

The mens reas required of attempt under the Model Penal Code is more complex. The prosecution must show that the defendant had the intent to attempt the crime and must also prove any requirements of mens rea for commission of the crime itself. Thus, in a trial, the jury must look to the mens rea of the crime that the defendant attempted and determine whether all of the mens rea requirements were met. Then the jury must determine whether the defendant had the specific intent to actually commit the criminal act. In some situations, this may be redundant.

The Model Penal Code is somewhat more liberal than the common law regarding charges and conviction. In common law, one must be charged with attempt or the actual crime or both. If convicted of the crime, however, one cannot be convicted of attempt, and vice versa. Although the result under the Model Penal Code is the same, the required procedure is slightly different. The Code permits a person to be charged with only the crime. However, if the jury finds that the person did not complete the crime but did attempt it, the person can be convicted of attempt. There is no requirement that the individual be formally charged with attempt in addition to the charge for the actual crime.

The crime of solicitation.   Solicitation has been defined as the act of enticing, inviting, requesting, urging, or ordering someone to commit a crime.[22] It differs from conspiracy or attempt. In conspiracy, two or more persons work together to achieve a common goal of criminal conduct. The crime of attempt describes the acts under the control of an individual toward completion of a crime. Solicitation is a crime wherein an individual seeks to persuade another individual to commit a crime. The trend in common law states is to adopt the Model Penal Code view of solicitation. The Code allows conviction and punishment of one who solicits any criminal offense, no matter how minor. The traditional common law approach was to punish only solicitation of more serious offenses against society.

At common law, conviction can be had for anyone who attempts to communicate with another in such a way that the other person will be encouraged to commit a crime. It is not necessary that the other person receive the communication or commit the crime. Solicitation is based on the premise that it is wrong in and of itself to willfully encourage criminal conduct. The actus reus is any conduct that would demonstrate such encouragement.

Solicitation is considered a specific intent offense in common law. The person who solicits a crime by another must intend that the crime actually be committed. It is not required that the person who solicits understand that solicitation itself is considered criminal conduct. Rather, it need only be shown that the person knows that the conduct that is being encouraged is criminal.

The Model Penal Code definition of actus reus in solicitation is quite similar to the common law interpretation. The primary difference is that under the Model Penal Code, a person needs to intend and demonstrate the intent to communicate the encouragement. As with common law, it is not required that the intent actually be communicated to the other person.

The mens rea for solicitation in the Model Penal Code requires that the person be aware that the encouragement is for a criminal act. Further, to prosecute for solicitation, it must be proven that a person has the intent that would be required to actually commit the offense that is encouraged.

In addition to conviction for solicitation, in common law states, the accused may also be convicted of being an accessory before the fact. Under the Model Penal Code, a person cannot be convicted as an accessory or as a conspirator in addition to being convicted for solicitation.

Miscellaneous Offenses

Some crimes, though categorized in some states as felonies, by definition are distinctly inchoate in characteristics. Such acts directly enable a person to commit a crime. Like the crimes previously discussed, these acts are such an integral part of creating the opportunity for other criminal conduct that they become crimes in and of themselves. Common examples include the illegal possession of weapons or the possession of such large quantities of drugs that it is probable that the drugs will be distributed illegally. Another example of such an offense is burglary. Traditionally, burglary was an offense that consisted of forcibly entering the home of another at night with the intent of committing a felony within the residence. This definition has been somewhat modified in many states under present-day statutes. Today, definitions of burglary are much more general and often include any unpermitted entry (regardless of whether it requires force) into the property of another (regardless of whether it is the home, automobile, or other property) at any time of day with the intent to commit a felony within the property.[23] This sounds remarkably inchoate in its definition. Burglary is an act that creates the opportunity for felonious conduct.

In cases of burglary, it is no longer required that the intended felony actually occur. Society wants to discourage unpermitted entry into the property of another with additional criminal intent. Such unpermitted entry is a necessary precursor to the commission of a felony on the property. Thus, if burglary is punished, perhaps persons will be deterred from entering private property to commit felonies. In any event, such persons can be punished for any actions they take that would enable the felonious conduct.

The Model Penal Code also recognizes these offenses and punishes them. Generally, punishment for all inchoate offenses under the Model Penal Code includes a range of severity that approaches the penalty for the actual commission of the more serious offense that might follow a conspiracy, attempt, solicitation, burglary, or other inchoate offense. Consequently, the Model Penal Code does not recognize any offenses that are perhaps beyond the inchoate offense but are not quite completion of the more serious offense. Some common law states have such intermediate stages. Under the Model Penal Code, the definition of an inchoate offense includes all conduct leading to the moment the subsequent offense is actually completed.

Under common law, categories of homicide might include attempted murder, assault with intent to kill, and murder. Assault with intent to kill might describe a situation wherein a person actually inflicts deadly force on an individual but the individual survives. It is more than a mere attempt, but the actual murder was not achieved.

Under the Model Penal Code, a person may be charged with attempted murder or murder. The definition of attempt is broad enough—and the penalties allowed are severe enough—to include the situation where the accused comes within a breath of murder.

Felony Crimes

As the preceding discussion indicates, the common law jurisdictions and Model Penal Code jurisdictions regard the same basic types of conduct as criminal. The distinction between the two is generally in the way the crimes are formally defined. The following sections discuss some additional felony crimes that occur with some frequency. The definitions are based on basic principles of law, with the understanding that each state may have its own definitions and penalties.

Assault.   In a civil case, assault is considered to be action threatening an unpermitted physical contact. However, in the criminal sense, assault often includes actual physical contact and is synonymous with civil battery. Depending on the nature of the particular offense, assault is often a felony crime. Generally, an assault that is committed with a weapon or with the intent to do dangerous bodily harm or that results in serious bodily harm will be treated as a felony. When criminal laws differentiate assault from battery, assault is generally considered to be more consistent with the civil definition. Thus, criminal assault would be an act that causes fear of immediate physical harm through unpermitted physical contact.[24]

Battery.   Many times in criminal law, the terms *assault* and *battery* are interchangeable. When a distinction is made, battery is considered to be the unlawful contact with another person. Such contact can be direct or through an instrument such as a weapon.[25] Like assault, the extent of the contact and the actor's intent will often dictate whether the crime will be prosecuted as a felony or a misdemeanor.

Usually, the mens rea required for assault/battery is one of general intent. A person need only be aware that his or her conduct is likely to result in an unpermitted physical contact. Of course, if a more specific intent is present, that would also be sufficient, but the minimum requirement would be only a reasonable awareness.

Theft, robbery, and larceny.   In ordinary usage, many laypersons interchange the terms burglary, theft, and robbery. However, as previously indicated, burglary does not include the taking of another person's property, only the invasion of it. Similarly, theft and robbery are distinct terms, whereas theft and larceny are often synonymous in criminal law.

Theft.   Theft occurs when a party unlawfully obtains the property of another with the intent to dispossess that person of the property.[26] The intent required can be merely to dispossess, to convert the property to one's own uses, or to convey the property to another. As long as the intent is to deprive an owner of the use, possession, or ownership of property, the mens rea requirement is satisfied.

In many jurisdictions, the value of the property influences the severity of the punishment. The theft of more valuable property, usually in excess of a stated dollar amount, is considered grand larceny and is a felony. The theft of property that is valued below the stated dollar amount is considered to be petty (also known as *petit*) larceny and is usually considered to be a misdemeanor.

Robbery.   The most serious offense involving unlawfully taking property is robbery. To commit a robbery, one must deprive an owner of property by the use of force or threats of force. The robber must either use physical violence or demonstrate to the owner that unless the property is turned over, physical violence will be used to obtain the property.[27] Thus, robbery must be committed in the presence of the owner. If the owner were not present to perceive the force or threats, there would be no necessity for their use. Robbery includes situations where physical force or weapons are used or threatened against victims. Because robbery is considered to be a crime of violence, the penalties are generally more severe than those for larceny.

Homicide.   When a person is killed as the result of conduct or omission by another person, a homicide has been committed. If there is no legal justification or excuse for such conduct, a criminal homicide has been committed. Only criminal homicide can result in conviction and punishment. Legal justification or excuse includes situations where the actor's conduct is considered noncriminal, generally, because the required mens rea for a criminal homicide is not present.

There are various types of homicide. Most often they are described as manslaughter and murder. Manslaughter is usually considered a less serious offense than murder because it is death caused without malice aforethought—a mental state that includes the intent to inflict deadly force. Manslaughter is further broken down into two categories: voluntary and involuntary.

Voluntary manslaughter.   Voluntary manslaughter is applicable in situations where the death of another was intentional but where special circumstances existed.[28] An example of such a case is a crime of passion, where a person loses all ability to reason as a result of extreme provocation by the deceased. It must be established that the deceased did something so outrageous to provoke the defendant that it is understandable that the defendant lost the ability to reason and, in the heat of the moment, attacked the deceased. Common situations include injury to one's family or to the marital relationship. One point is clear. The provocation must have been of a type so extraordinary that a jury could consider the defendant's conduct reasonable. This does not mean that the charges against the defendant will be dropped. Rather, it explains why the defendant is not charged with murder.

If the defendant has time to consider the action before it is taken, a charge of voluntary manslaughter would be inappropriate. The key element that separates murder from voluntary manslaughter is that in the latter case, the defendant did not have time to consider the ramifications of the actions about to be taken. In murder, there is time for someone to consider and plan the death or injury that ultimately produces death of another. Thus, the longer the period of time that elapses between the provocation and the act of killing, the more likely the charge will be murder.

Involuntary manslaughter.   Involuntary manslaughter occurs when one person is responsible for the death of another because of gross and extreme negligence or recklessness and without the intent to kill or inflict bodily harm.[29] Such conduct is considered to show total disregard for the safety or well-being of others. In some states, death caused as the result of driving while intoxicated is considered to be involuntary manslaughter. However, many states have a separate statute for this, such as vehicular or motor vehicle homicide. Another example of involuntary manslaughter is hunting in or around a populated area. When negligence and recklessness are differentiated by statute, negligence is treated as extreme carelessness, whereas recklessness involves a total disregard for others. Although both are types of involuntary manslaughter, generally, the penalties are more severe for reckless homicide than for negligent homicide.

Reckless or negligent homicide may occur during the commission of another crime that is a misdemeanor (for example, death caused by a drunk driver or as the result of reckless driving), or it may occur as the result of some careless act not intended to be criminal. The latter often includes situations that are the result of circumstance, although created by negligence (for example, a person who target shoots in his or her backyard in a suburban area). Assume in such a case that a neighbor is hit and killed by a stray bullet. There was never any intent to commit a crime, and certainly no intent to kill the neighbor. Nevertheless, discharging deadly weapons in a populated area would be considered extremely careless.

Manslaughter under the Model Penal Code.   The Model Penal Code recognizes the same basic principles regarding manslaughter. Although it does not use the terms *voluntary* and *involuntary*, it grades the degree of the offense and the severity of the penalty in accordance with situations that are reckless or negligent. The Code places emphasis not on the actual provocation but rather on the actual emotional condition of the defendant at the time death was caused. If the defendant was in a mental state such that control was impossible, the death could be considered voluntary manslaughter. Under this application, there is no need to examine whether the defendant had time to cool off after the provocation. The entire question turns on the defendant's actual mental state at the time of the killing.

Murder.   As indicated previously, murder is a premeditated act committed with specific malicious intent. Contrary to what the community used term *with malice aforethought* would suggest, the actor need not have thought out a careful plan to kill with hatred. Rather, the term describes the state of mind of a person who is aware of what he or she is doing and who can make the choice not to act. Many states that apply this common law theory or murder break up the definition by varying states of mind.

The term *degree* is often used to indicate various categories of murder. Murder in the first degree is usually the most serious felony. It often requires that the actor have the preconceived intent to kill and carry out that intent to fruition. This differs from murder in the second degree, which often describes a situation where a person intends to inflict serious physical harm on the victim and death follows. Finally, there is murder as the result of recklessness that is so great that the actor had no reasonable basis to believe that the death of another would not result from the action. The risk of death is more than substantial: it is a near certainty that a person will die from the actor's conduct.

Felony Murder Rule.   Some states employ an additional category of murder known as the Felony Murder Rule. This rule has two basic requirements: (1) the actor must be engaged in the commission of a dangerous felony, and

(2) the acts pertaining to the felony must proximately cause the death of another.[30] Further, in some states, if the victim is injured but dies as a proximate result of those injuries within one year, the actor can be charged with murder, even though other circumstances may have contributed to the death.

 APPLICATION 12.3

Charles breaks into the home of an elderly woman where he physically and sexually assaults the woman and steals valuable personal property. He is caught and charged with robbery and sexual assault. Meanwhile, the woman is hospitalized for injuries and is then transferred to a convalescent home to recuperate. She is despondent after the assault and requires assistance with daily living activities, including feeding. One day, three months after the incident, the elderly woman is being fed by a nurse when the elderly woman chokes to death. The charges against Charles are amended to include felony murder because the woman died as a proximate result of the assault by Charles.

Point for Discussion
Can Charles be charged with the murder if he has already been convicted of the other crimes?

Assignment 12.3

> Using the example in Application 12.3, chart the chain of events that show why Charles is the proximate cause of the elderly woman's death.

Murder under the Model Penal Code. The Model Penal Code follows the same basic premise as common law when determining guilt in cases of murder. Murder that results from the intent to inflict fatal injuries is defined in much the same way as murder in the first degree under common law.[31] The Model Penal Code also provides for situations of serious bodily harm or great recklessness that produces death, although these two situations are considered an offense of the same severity under the Code. The primary difference is that the Model Penal Code contains no provision for the Felony Murder Rule. The reasoning is that the person should be charged with murder or manslaughter in addition to the felony rather than be charged with a combined single charge of felony and murder. It is reasoned that the actual guilt and mens rea can be more easily and fairly determined by this method.

Rape. In recent years, the crime of rape has received a great deal of notoriety for a variety of reasons. Although the crime of rape went largely unreported in the past, changes in the roles of women in our society along with rape shield statutes have contributed to an increasing number of reports of sexual assault. Previously, it was not uncommon for the entire sexual history of the victim to be disclosed at the trial of the defendant in an attempt to show that the victim somehow encouraged the defendant's conduct. However, a majority of states have enacted rape shield statutes that prevent such information from being introduced as evidence. Also, women are now coming forward with charges of acquaintance rape (date rape), which was virtually unheard of in the past. The government now recognizes that rape need not, and usually does not, occur between total strangers.

Rape (also known as a type of sexual assault in some jurisdictions) is the forcible act of sexual intercourse by a male against a female without consent of the female. It is a crime in all jurisdictions, and penalties range from a few years to life in prison, depending upon the circumstances. The act of rape or even consensual intercourse with a minor typically carries even heavier penalties. When consensual intercourse occurs between an adult and a minor (to whom the adult is not married), the crime of statutory rape has been committed. The presumption is that the minor is incapable of making a proper decision as to whether to consent to intercourse, and therefore, intercourse with a minor is criminal per se. The age at which a minor is presumed to have sufficient capacity to consent to intercourse varies among jurisdictions. Also, in some jurisdictions, the fact that the minor lied about his or her age is an adequate defense to the charge of statutory rape.

PUNISHMENT

Common law and the Model Penal Code have similar concepts of punishment. Under each, the general rule is that a greater degree of specific intent will result in a more severe range of punishment for the convicted defendant. With respect to the most extreme punishment—death—the Model Penal Code includes it but neither advocates nor discourages it. The provision for the death penalty is included as an acknowledgment that the death penalty is part of American criminal law at this time. The position of common law has varied on the issue of capital punishment. At this time, it is considered an acceptable form of punishment by the government for certain types of crime.

Other punishments typically include imprisonment, monetary fines, community service (time spent doing activities that benefit the community at large), and restitution (repayment to a victim for injury to his or her person or property). Whatever the punishment, one constant remains: the punishment must not be cruel or unusual for the crime committed according to the Eighth Amendment. For example, the death penalty has been determined to be cruel and unusual punishment for the crime of rape, while it is still permissible for other crimes, such as murder.

CASE

COKER v. GEORGIA

433 U.S. 584, 97 S.Ct.
2861, 53 L.Ed.2d 982
(1977).

Mr. Justice **WHITE** announced the judgment of the Court and filed an opinion in which Mr. Justice **STEWART**, Mr. Justice **BLACKMUN**, and Mr. Justice **STEVENS**, joined.

Georgia Code Ann. § 26-2001 (1972) provides that '(a) person convicted of rape shall be punished by death or by imprisonment for life, or by imprisonment for not less than one nor more than 20 years.' (The section defines rape as having 'carnal knowledge of a female, forcibly and against her will. Carnal knowledge in rape occurs when there is any penetration of the female sex organ by the male sex organ.') Punishment is determined by a jury in a separate sentencing proceeding in which at least one of the statutory aggravating circumstances must be found before the death penalty may be imposed. Petitioner Coker was convicted of rape and sentenced to death. Both the conviction and the sentence were affirmed by the Georgia Supreme Court. Coker was granted a writ of certiorari, 429 U.S. 815, 97 S.Ct. 56, 50 L.Ed.2d 75, limited to the single claim, rejected by the Georgia court, that the punishment of death for rape violates the Eighth Amendment, which proscribes 'cruel and unusual punishments' and which must be observed by the States as well as the Federal Government. Robinson v. California, 370 U.S. 660, 82 S.Ct. 1417, 8 L.Ed.2d 758 (1962).

I

While serving various sentences for murder, rape, kidnapping, and aggravated assault, petitioner escaped from the Ware Correctional Institution near Waycross, Ga., on September 2, 1974. At approximately 11 o'clock that night, petitioner entered the house of Allen and Elnita Carver through an unlocked kitchen door. Threatening the couple with a 'board,' he tied up Mr. Carver in the bathroom, obtained a knife from the kitchen, and

took Mr. Carver's money and the keys to the family car. Brandishing the knife and saying 'you know what's going to happen to you if you try anything, don't you,' Coker then raped Mrs. Carver. Soon thereafter, petitioner drove away in the Carver car, taking Mrs. Carver with him. Mr. Carver, freeing himself, notified the police; and not long thereafter petitioner was apprehended. Mrs. Carver was unharmed.

Petitioner was charged with escape, armed robbery, motor vehicle theft, kidnapping, and rape. Counsel was appointed to represent him. Having been found competent to stand trial, he was tried. The jury returned a verdict of guilty, rejecting his general plea of insanity. A sentencing hearing was then conducted in accordance with the procedures dealt with at length in Gregg v. Georgia, 428 U.S. 153, 96 S.Ct. 2909, 49 L.Ed.2d 859 (1976), where this Court sustained the death penalty for murder when imposed pursuant to the statutory procedures. Ga.Code § 26-3102 (Supp. 1976):

'Capital offenses; jury verdict and sentence.

'Where, upon a trial by jury, a person is convicted of an offense which may be punishable by death, a sentence of death shall not be imposed unless the jury verdict includes a finding of at least one statutory aggravating circumstance and a recommendation that such sentence be imposed. Where a statutory aggravating circumstance is found and a recommendation of death is made, the court shall sentence the defendant to death. Where a sentence of death is not recommended by the jury, the court shall sentence the defendant to imprisonment as provided by law. Unless the jury trying the case makes a finding of at least one statutory aggravating circumstance and recommends the death sentence in its verdict, the court shall not sentence the defendant to death, provided that no such finding of statutory aggravating circumstance shall be necessary in offenses of treason or aircraft hijacking. The provisions of this section shall not affect a sentence when the case is tried without a jury or when the judge accepts a plea of guilty.'

Ga.Code § 27-2302 (Supp.1976):

Recommendation to mercy.
'In all capital cases, other than those of homicide, when the verdict is guilty, with a recommendation to mercy, it shall be legal and shall be a recommendation to the judge of imprisonment for life. Such recommendation shall be binding upon the judge.'
Ga.Code § 27-2534.1 (Supp. 1976):
'Mitigating and aggravating circumstances; death penalty. . . .
'(b) In all cases of other offenses for which the death penalty may be authorized, the judge shall consider, or he shall include in his instructions to the jury for it to consider, any mitigating circumstances or aggravating circumstances otherwise authorized by law and any of the following statutory aggravating circumstances which may be supported by the evidence:
'(1) The offense of murder, rape, armed robbery, or kidnapping was committed by a person with a prior record of conviction for a capital felony, or the offense of murder was committed by a person who has a substantial history of serious assaultive criminal convictions.
'(2) The offense of murder, rape, armed robbery, or kidnapping was committed while the offender was engaged in the commission of another capital felony, or aggravated battery, or the offense of murder was committed while the offender was engaged in the commission of burglary or arson in the first degree. . . .
'(7) The offense of murder, rape, armed robbery or kidnapping was outrageously or wantonly vile, horrible or inhuman in that it involved torture, depravity of mind, or an aggravated battery to the victim. . . .
'(c) The statutory instructions as determined by the trial judge to be warranted by the evidence shall be given in charge and in writing to the jury for its deliberation. The jury, if its verdict be a recommendation of death, shall designate in writing, signed by the foreman of the jury, the aggravating circumstance or circumstances which it found beyond a reasonable doubt. In non-jury cases the judge shall make such designation. Except in cases of treason or aircraft hijacking, unless at least one of the statutory aggravating circumstances enumerated in section 27-2534.1(b) is so found, the death penalty shall not be imposed.' Ga.Code § 27-2537 (Supp.1976):

'Review of death sentences.
'(a) Whenever the death penalty is imposed, and upon the judgment becoming final in the trial court, the sentence shall be reviewed on the record by the Supreme Court of Georgia. The clerk of the trial court, within ten days after receiving the transcript, shall transmit the entire record and transcript to the Supreme Court of Georgia together with a notice prepared by the clerk and a report prepared by the trial judge. The notice shall set forth the title and docket number of the case, the name of the defendant and the name and address of his attorney, a narrative statement of the judgment, the offense, and the punishment prescribed. The report shall be in the form of a standard questionnaire prepared and supplied by the Supreme Court of Georgia.
'(b) The Supreme Court of Georgia shall consider the punishment as well as any errors enumerated by way of appeal.
'(c) With regard to the sentence, the court shall determine:
'(1) Whether the sentence of death was imposed under the influence of passion, prejudice, or any other arbitrary factor, and
'(2) Whether, in cases other than treason or aircraft hijacking, the evidence supports the jury's or judge's finding of a statutory aggravating circumstance as enumerated in section 27-2534.1(b), and
'(3) Whether the sentence of death is excessive or disproportionate to the penalty imposed in similar cases, considering both the crime and the defendant. . . .

The jury was instructed that it could consider as aggravating circumstances whether the rape had been committed by a person with a prior record of conviction for a capital felony and whether the rape had been committed in the course of committing another capital felony, namely, the armed robbery of Allen Carver. The court also instructed, pursuant to statute, that even if aggravating circumstances were present, the death penalty need not be imposed if the jury found they were out-weighed by mitigating circumstances, that is, circumstances not constituting justification or excuse for the offense in question, 'but which, in fairness and mercy, may be considered as extenuating or reducing the degree' of moral culpability or punishment. App. 300. The jury's verdict on the rape count was death by electrocution. Both aggravating circumstances on which the court instructed were found to be present by the jury.

Furman v. Georgia, 408 U.S. 238. 92 S.Ct. 2726, 33 L.Ed.2d 346 (1972), ... [makes] unnecessary the recanvassing of certain critical aspects of the controversy about the constitutionality of capital punishment. It is now settled that the death penalty is not invariably cruel and unusual punishment within the meaning of the Eighth Amendment; it is not inherently barbaric or an unacceptable mode of punishment for crime; neither is it always disproportionate to the crime for which it is imposed. It is also established the imposing capital punishment, at least for murder, in accordance with the procedures provided under the Georgia statutes saves the sentence from the infirmities which led the Court to invalidate the prior Georgia capital punishment statute in Furman v. Georgia, supra.

In sustaining the imposition of the death penalty in Gregg, however, the Court firmly embraced the holdings and dicta from prior cases, Furman v. Georgia, supra; Robinson v. California, 370 U.S. 660, 82 S.Ct. 1417, 8 L.Ed.2d 758 (1962); Trop v. Dulles, 356 U.S. 86, 78 S.Ct. 590, 2 L.Ed.2d 630 (1958); and Weems v. United States, 217 U.S. 349, 30 S.Ct. 544, 54 L.Ed. 793 (1910), to the effect that the Eighth Amendment bars not only those punishments that are 'barbaric' but also those that are 'excessive' in relation to the crime committed. Under Gregg [v.Ga. 428 U.S. 153 (1976)], a punishment is 'excessive' and unconstitutional if it (1) makes no measurable contribution to acceptable goals of punishment and hence is nothing more than the purposeless and needless imposition of pain and suffering; or (2) is grossly out of proportion to the severity of the crime. A punishment might fail the test on either ground. Furthermore, these Eighth Amendment judgments should not be, or appear to be, merely the subjective views of individual Justices; judgment should be informed by objective factors to the maximum possible extent. To this end, attention must be given to the public attitudes concerning a particular sentence history and precedent, legislative attitudes, and the response of juries reflected in their

sentencing decisions are to be consulted. In Gregg, after giving due regard to such sources, the Court's judgment was that the death penalty for deliberate murder was neither the purposeless imposition of severe punishment nor a punishment grossly disproportionate to the crime. But the court reserved the question of the constitutionality of the death penalty when imposed for other crimes. 428 U.S., at 187 n. 35, 96 S.Ct., at 2932.

III

That question, with respect to rape of an adult woman, is now before us. We have concluded that a sentence of death is grossly disproportionate and excessive punishment for the crime of rape and is therefore forbidden by the Eighth Amendment as cruel and unusual punishment, . . .

A

. . . At no time in the last 50 years have a majority of the States authorized death as a punishment for rape. In 1925, 18 States, the District of Columbia, and the Federal Government authorized capital punishment for the rape of an adult female. By 1971 just prior to the decision in Furman v. Georgia, that number had declined, but not substantially, to 16 States plus the Federal Government. Furman then invalidated most of the capital punishment statutes in this country, including the rape statutes, because, among other reasons, of the manner in which the death penalty was imposed and utilized under those laws. . . .

Georgia argues that 11 of the 16 States that authorized death for rape in 1972 attempted to comply with Furman by enacting arguably mandatory death penalty legislation and that it is very likely that, aside from Louisiana and North Carolina, these States simply chose to eliminate rape as a capital offense rather than to require death for each and every instance of rape. The argument is not without force; but 4 of the 16 States did not take the mandatory course and also did not continue rape of an adult woman as a capital offense. Further, as we have indicated, the legislatures of 6 of the 11 arguably mandatory States have revised their death penalty laws since Woodson and Roberts without enacting a new death penalty for rape. And this is to say nothing of 19 other States that enacted nonmandatory, post-Furman statutes and chose not to sentence rapists to death. . . .

It should be noted that Florida, Mississippi, and Tennessee also authorized the death penalty in *some* rape cases, but only where the victim was a child and the rapist an adult. The Tennessee statute has since been invalidated because the death sentence was mandatory. Collins v. State, 550 S.W.2d 643 (Tenn.1977). The upshot is that Georgia is the sole jurisdiction in the United States at the present time that authorizes a sentence of death when the rape victim is an adult woman, and only two other jurisdictions provide capital punishment when the victim is a child. . . .

The current judgment with respect to the death penalty for rape is not wholly unanimous among state legislatures, but it obviously weighs very heavily on the side of rejecting capital punishment as a suitable penalty for raping an adult woman.

B

It was also observed in Gregg that '(t)he jury . . . is a significant and reliable objective index of contemporary values because it is so directly involved.' 428 U.S., at 181, 96 S.Ct., at 2929, and that it is thus important to look to the sentencing decisions that juries have made in the course of assessing whether capital punishment is an appropriate penalty for the crime being tried. Of course, the jury's judgment is meaningful only where the jury has an appropriate measure of choice as to whether the death penalty is to be imposed. As far as execution for rape is concerned, this is now true only in Georgia and in Florida; and in the latter State, capital punishment is authorized only for the rape of children.

According to the factual submissions in this Court, out of all rape convictions in Georgia since 1973 and that total number has not been tendered 63 cases had been reviewed by the Georgia Supreme Court as of the time of oral argument; and of these, 6 involved a death sentence, 1 of which was set aside, leaving 5 convicted rapists now under sentence of death in the State of Georgia. Georgia juries have thus sentenced rapists to death six times since 1973. This obviously is not a negligible number; and the State argues that as a practical matter juries simply reserve the extreme sanction for extreme cases of rape and that recent experience surely does not prove that jurors consider the death penalty to be a disproportionate punishment for every conceivable instance of rape, no matter how aggravated. Nevertheless, it is true that in the vast majority of cases, at least 9 out of 10, juries have not imposed the death sentence.

IV

These recent events evidencing the attitude of state legislatures and sentencing juries do not wholly determine this controversy, for the Constitution contemplates that in the end our own judgment will be brought to bear on the question of the acceptability of the death penalty under the Eighth Amendment. Nevertheless, the legislative rejection of capital punishment for rape strongly confirms our own judgment, which is that death is indeed a disproportionate penalty for the crime of raping an adult woman.

We do not discount the seriousness of rape as a crime. It is highly reprehensible, both in a moral sense and in its almost total contempt for the personal integrity and autonomy of the female victim and for the latter's privilege of choosing those with whom intimate relationships are to be established. Short of homicide, it is the 'ultimate violation of self.' It is also a violent crime because it normally involves force, or the threat of force or intimidation, to overcome the will and the capacity of the victim to resist. Rape is very often accompanied by physical injury to the female and can also inflict mental and psychological damage. Because it undermines the community's sense of security, there is public injury as well.

***

Rape is without doubt deserving of serious punishment; but in terms of moral depravity and of the injury to the person and to the public, it does not compare with murder, which does involve the unjustified taking of human life. Although it may be accompanied by another crime, rape by definition does not include the death of or even the serious injury to another person. The murderer kills; the rapist, if no more than that, does not. Life is over for the victim of the murderer; for the rape victim, life may not be nearly so happy as it was, but it is not over and normally is not beyond repair. We have the abiding conviction that the death penalty, which 'is unique in its severity and irrevocability,' Gregg v. Georgia, 428 U.S., at 187, 96 S.Ct., at 2931, is an excessive penalty for the rapist who, as such, does not take human life.

This does not end the matter; for under Georgia law, death may not be imposed for any capital offense, including rape, unless the jury or judge finds one of the statutory aggravating circumstances and then elects to impose that sentence. Ga.Code § 26-3102 (1976 Supp); Gregg v. Georgia, supra, 428 U.S., at 165–166, 96 S.Ct., at 2921–2922. For the rapist to be executed in Georgia, it must therefore be found not only that he committed rape but also that one or more of the following aggravating circumstances were present: (1) that the rape was committed by a person with a prior record of conviction for a capital felony; (2) that the rape was committed while the offender was engaged in the commission of another capital felony, or aggravated battery; or (3) the rape 'was outrageously or wantonly vile, horrible or inhuman in that it involved torture, depravity of mind, or aggravated battery to the victim.' (There are other aggravating circumstances provided in the statute, . . . but they are not applicable to rape.) Here, the first two of these aggravating circumstances were alleged and found by the jury.

Neither of these circumstances, nor both of them together, change our conclusion that the death sentence imposed on Coker is a disproportionate punishment for rape. Coker had prior convictions for capital felonies rape, murder, and kidnapping but these prior convictions do not change the fact that the instant crime being punished is a rape not involving the taking of life.

It is also true that the present rape occurred while Coker was committing armed robbery, a felony for which the Georgia statutes authorize the death penalty. In Gregg v. Georgia, the Georgia Supreme Court refused to sustain a death sentence for armed robbery because, for one reason, death had been so seldom imposed for this crime in other cases that such a sentence was excessive and could not be sustained under the statute. As it did in this case, however, the Georgia Supreme Court apparently continues to recognize armed robbery as

a capital offense for the purpose of applying the aggravating-circumstances provisions of the Georgia Code. But Coker was tried for the robbery offense as well as for rape and received a separate life sentence for this crime; the jury did not deem the robbery itself deserving of the death penalty, even though accompanied by the aggravating circumstance, which was stipulated, that Coker had been convicted of a prior capital crime.

Where the accompanying capital crime is murder, it is most likely that the defendant would be tried for murder, rather than rape; and it is perhaps academic to deal with the death sentence for rape in such a circumstance. It is likewise unnecessary to consider the rape felony murder a rape accompanied by the death of the victim which was unlawfully but nonmaliciously caused by the defendant. Where the third aggravating circumstance mentioned in the text is present that the rape is particularly vile or involves torture or aggravated battery it would seem that the defendant could very likely be convicted, tried, and appropriately punished for this additional conduct.

We note finally that in Georgia a person commits murder when he unlawfully and with malice aforethought, either express or implied, causes the death of another human being. He also commits that crime when in the commission of a felony he causes the death of another human being, irrespective of malice. But even where the killing is deliberate, it is not punishable by death absent proof of aggravating circumstances. It is difficult to accept the notion, and we do not, that the rapist, with or without aggravating circumstances, should be punished more heavily than the deliberate killer as long as the rapist does not himself take the life of his victim. The judgment of the Georgia Supreme Court upholding the death sentence is reversed, and the case is remanded to that court for further proceedings not inconsistent with this opinion.

Case Question
Is the death penalty ever acceptable for a crime less than murder?

WHITE-COLLAR CRIME

Crime also exists in the workplace, and criminal responsibility for such crime has received increased attention in recent years. Although corporations generally are not specifically liable for criminal acts, it does not mean that liability is nonexistent. Although the corporation is considered a person under the law in terms of equality of rights, it is still a legal fiction. Because the corporation does not possess a mind, it is incapable of formulating the adequate mens rea to commit a criminal act. Only those who represent the corporation can do that. The law has come to recognize that the persons who represent the corporation are in fact the mind of the corporation and through them the corporation can be convicted of most criminal acts.

If a person is employed by a corporation and acts on its behalf, the corporation can be held responsible for those acts under the theory of respondent superior. As long as the act was performed within the scope of the person's employment and related directly to the corporation, the entity as well as the individual can be held responsible. Although a corporation cannot be imprisoned, it can be heavily fined or dissolved involuntarily.

Crimes frequently committed on behalf of corporations include tax law violations, securities law violations, burglary and theft (in the case of trade secrets), and damage to the property of competitors. All of these actions require some actual mental and physical conduct by an individual, but they directly or indirectly benefit the corporation. If it can be shown that the corporate representatives acted, encouraged these acts, or accepted the benefits of these acts, the corporation may be charged for the crime as well. In addition, the individuals may be held responsible as principals.

The Model Penal Code recognizes liability of business entities in much the same manner as the common law. The only real difference is that the Model Penal Code has a fairly narrow definition of the types of offenses for which a business entity may be held responsible. Specifically, for a business entity to be held responsible under the Code, the offense must be one that the legislature clearly intended to apply to corporations or one in which the criminal actions can be proven to be consistent with the purpose of the corporation.[32] In other cases, only the individual will be held responsible for the criminal acts.

In addition to those crimes for which a corporation or business entity might be held criminally liable, crimes can be committed against the entity by its fiduciaries. For example, a bank employee who over a period of time extracts funds from the bank for personal use has committed embezzlement, which essentially is theft of property. Other crimes include violation of securities laws to injure or destroy a competitor's business or to take unfair advantage of investors. In the 1980s, much publicity centered around Wall Street figures Michael Milken and Ivan Boesky who were convicted of obtaining huge profits in the securities market by violating securities laws designed to promote fairness among investors.

While white-collar crime often appears to be victimless because no clearly identifiable and individual injury is caused by the act, it is nevertheless a violation of law and is dealt with in much the same manner as other criminal conduct.

C A S E

KARR v. STATE OF ALASKA

660 P.2d 450
(Alaska 1983).

COATS, Judge.

Diana Karr embezzled $356,000 from Meyeres' Real Estate, Inc. between November 1979 and December 1981. Karr was charged with one count of embezzlement by an employee for the money she took prior to January 1, 1980. (Former AS 11.20.280 reads: Embezzlement by employee or servant. An officer, agent, clerk, employee, or servant who embezzles or fraudulently converts to his own use, or takes or secretes with intent to embezzle or fraudulently convert to his own use, money, property, or thing of another which may be the subject of larceny, and which has come into his possession or is under his care by virtue of his employment is guilty of embezzlement. If the property embezzled exceeds $100 in value, a person guilty of embezzlement is punishable by imprisonment in the penitentiary for not less than one year nor more than 10 years. If the property embezzled does not exceed the value of $100, a person guilty of embezzlement is punishable by imprisonment in a jail for not less than one month nor more than one year, or by a fine of not less than $25 nor more than $100.) [Karr] was charged with theft in the first degree, AS 11.46.120, for money she took after January 1, 1980, the effective date for the revised criminal code.

(AS 11.46.120 reads:

> Theft in the first degree. (a) A person commits the crime of theft in the first degree if he commits theft as defined in § 100 of this chapter and the value of the property or services is $25,000 or more. (b) Theft in the first degree is a class B felony.) After Karr pled nolo contendere to these charges, Judge James R. Blair sentenced her to serve ten years with five suspended and to pay $300,000 restitution. Karr was sentenced to five years on each count, and the sentences were made consecutive to each

other. The five-year sentence for embezzlement by employee was suspended, resulting in a sentence of ten years with five suspended.

Karr appeals her sentence to this court. We affirm.

Karr first contends that the sentence imposed was excessive. Karr is thirty-four years old and has no prior criminal record. She points to Austin v. State, 627 P.2d 657, 658 (Alaska App.1981), where we said, '[n]ormally a first offender should receive a more favorable sentence than the presumptive sentence for a second offender. It is clear this rule should be violated only in an exceptional case." Karr also argues that we should consider her offense as one crime, since her crime was charged as two offenses only because the new criminal code came into effect on January 1, 1980. Karr argues that an offender who embezzled only after January 1, 1980 would have been charged only with one count, theft in the first degree. She contends she should not be treated differently merely because she embezzled both before and after January 1, 1980.

The record is clear that Judge Blair did not treat Karr differently because she was convicted of two counts. Essentially Karr was sentenced to ten years with five years suspended for theft in the first degree for a number of different acts of embezzlement committed over a period of over two years. Karr's sentence is not excessive under Austin because this is an exceptional case. Judge Blair classified Karr's offense as a particularly serious offense for an embezzlement. See AS 12.55.155(c)(10). Karr embezzled $356,000. The record establishes that Karr had earned a position of trust with Bud Meyeres, who owned Meyeres' Real Estate, and then used that position to embezzle. This amount was taken over a period of two years and involved numerous individual acts of embezzlement. In Karr's position she had to be aware of the effects of her embezzlement: at the time of Karr's sentencing, Meyeres was sixty-seven years old, and his real estate business was in serious financial trouble due to the embezzlement. Meyeres indicated that for the foreseeable future he will have to work hard to try to salvage his real estate business. It is unlikely that he will ever be able to retire. This is clearly an aggravated case. The presumptive sentence for a second class B felony offender is four years. Karr's actual sentence of imprisonment exceeds that by one year. In reviewing a sentence to determine whether it exceeds the presumptive sentence for a second offender under Austin, our primary focus is on the amount of imprisonment actually imposed. See Tazruk v. State, 655 P.2D 788 (Alaska App.1982). Judge Blair imposed the consecutive five-year suspended sentence primarily to enforce the restitution order. Karr's probation cannot be revoked for failure to make restitution if she makes a good faith effort to pay restitution but is unable to do so. See AS 12.55.051. In the event it is revoked she is entitled to another sentence appeal. Due to the seriousness of the offense, we conclude that this is an exceptional case, and the sentence of ten years with five suspended is not excessive.

The amount of money which Karr embezzled is the major distinguishing factor which separates this case from former Alaska cases in which lesser sentences were imposed for similar offenses. See Fields v. State, 629 P.2D 46 (Alaska 1981); Huff v. State, 598 P.2D 928 (Alaska 1979); Amidon v. State, 565 P.2D 1248 (Alaska 1977).

Karr also argues that the trial judge should not have imposed a consecutive sentence. However, Karr's total sentence did not exceed the sentence which she could have received for one count of theft in the first degree. Where a consecutive sentence is imposed but the total sentence does not exceed the sentence which could be imposed on one count, a consecutive sentence is not improper. See Mutschler v. State, 560 P.2D 377, 381 (Alaska 1977).

Karr next argues that the amount of restitution which Judge Blair ordered was excessive. Judge Blair acknowledged that it would be impossible for Karr to pay such a large amount of restitution.

Karr argues that AS 12.55.045(a) is violated when a trial judge orders an amount of restitution which cannot be paid. AS 12.55.045(a) provides:

> The court may order a defendant convicted of an offense to make restitution as provided in this section or as otherwise authorized by law. In determining the amount and method of payment of restitution, the court shall take into account the financial resources of the defendant and the nature of the burden its payment will impose.

It is clear that it will be difficult for Karr to pay the whole $300,000 in restitution. She appears to have some assets and therefore may be able to pay some restitution now. During her period of incarceration it is unlikely that she will be able to make any restitution. It appears Judge Blair considered these factors, as well as the fact that Karr will probably have difficulty in obtaining future employment similar to her previous employment, when he predicted that full restitution would be impossible.

Due to the difficulty in predicting from this point in time what amount of restitution is reasonable for Karr to pay, we conclude that it was reasonable for Judge Blair to order a large amount of restitution. In so doing he did not violate AS 12.55.045(a). Karr does not argue that she did not steal at least this amount from Meyeres. By ordering restitution, Judge Blair can require Karr to attempt to undo some of the damage caused by her criminal acts. The court can only enforce the order to the extent that it is reasonable for Karr to make restitution. We conclude that the court did not err in ordering $300,000 restitution.

The sentence is AFFIRMED.

Case Question
What purpose is served by imposing a fine that can never be paid?

DEFENSES TO CHARGES OF CRIMINAL CONDUCT

For every act committed, there are explanations for why the act occurred. In cases of criminal acts, some explanations are sufficient to prevent conviction and punishment of the actor. Such explanations are known as defenses, and they are wide and varied. The following sections examine a number of defenses that accused persons frequently assert.

Common Defenses

Justifiable or excusable conduct. Traditionally, justifiable or excusable conduct was a defense that could be applied in criminal cases. In present-day law, conduct that is justifiable or excusable is not considered criminal conduct and thus does not provide a basis for arrest or prosecution. **Justifiable conduct** is an act that takes place under special circumstances such as defense of oneself or others.[33] **Excusable conduct** refers to acts that would be considered criminal but for the actor's status at the time of the act.[34] For example, when law enforcement officers or military personnel intrude onto another's property or perhaps even kill in the line of duty, their conduct that would otherwise be considered criminal is excused because they are supposedly doing so in the interest of the public welfare. Of course, this may not apply if such persons abuse their authority and commit these acts without basis.

Involuntary conduct. A defense to charges of criminal conduct always exists in situations where the actor's conduct was not voluntary. Obviously, involuntary conduct includes acts over which the actor has no physical control.[35] Examples would include acts performed while sleeping, during seizures, or as the result of a reflex. Whether acts performed while under the influence of hypnosis or prescribed medication are voluntary is still questionable.

The key to the defense of involuntary conduct is proving that the defendant was physically incapable of forming the required mens rea prior to committing the crime. The lower the degree of requirement, such as general intent or awareness, the more difficult it is to prove the act was involuntary. (With respect to strict liability, since intent is not a consideration, involuntariness would not be a defense.)

Duress. A similar defense is duress, in which a third party causes another person to act by exerting influence over that person. The actor has a mental choice between following or refusing the commands of the third person. If the situation is extreme, duress may be used as a defense on the basis that in reality, only one choice could be made. For example, if the actor is told to act or his or her children will be killed, duress would apply. Although the actor has technically been given an option, in practical terms, he or she has no choice. The court will examine the circumstances to determine just how reasonable a refusal to act would have been.

Mistake. Mistake is a common defense to accusations of criminal acts. Two types of mistake can be alleged. Mistake of fact occurs when the person commits the act while reasonably believing something that was not true.[36] Many cases have been reported of persons who leave a store or other public building and

Justifiable Conduct
Conduct by one who, under the circumstances, is considered to be innocent of otherwise criminal behavior.

Excusable Conduct
Conduct by one who, under the color of authority, is considered to be innocent of otherwise criminal behavior.

drive away in what they think is their car, but in fact, their key fits an identical car belonging to someone else. Although such persons did indeed steal the automobile, they are not guilty of auto theft. They reasonably believed they were driving their own car. Thus, they made a mistake of fact. Any mistake of fact must bear directly on the intent required for the particular crime.

Mistake of law is applied much more rarely. It is appropriate only where a person actually believed that his or her conduct was lawful under one statute, despite the existence of another statute that might indicate such conduct was unlawful. An example is persons who exercise their right to avoid a search of their property by police without a proper warrant when another law gives police the right to search property in emergencies. If such persons are not aware of the emergency and deny the police entry, they are exercising a legal right. If, for example, unbeknownst to these persons, a criminal is hiding in their basement, these persons have made an honest mistake of law in protecting their rights and cannot be prosecuted for something such as obstruction of justice.

The Model Penal Code acknowledges both mistakes of fact and mistakes of law. In cases of mistake of fact, the mistake must be something that is believed and is part of the state of mind of the actor.[37] The Code, in line with common law, generally holds that ignorance of the law is no excuse. It does, however, allow certain exceptions that are similar to the common law exceptions that create a valid defense. Examples of these exceptions include (1) the actor did not have reasonable access to the law, (2) the actor reasonably believed the conduct was lawful (as in the common law example above), and (3) the actor was relying on the statement of the government or a government official. A person's lawyer's advice that conduct was permissible is not a defense. Such a statement must come from someone in a government capacity.

Entrapment.   A defense that has gained some notoriety in recent years is entrapment, which alleges that law enforcement personnel created a situation that would lead a law-abiding citizen with no prior criminal intent into criminal activity. The police must plant the idea and lead a person into criminal conduct that the person would not otherwise be predisposed to commit. This is often used in cases of prostitution and drug dealing. It is absolutely necessary for the police to do no more than accept or enhance the criminal conduct. The opportunity and intent to complete the crime must be developed by the criminal without any significant influence by the police.

The Insanity Defense

Probably the most publicized defense in criminal law is the insanity defense. While substantive as well as procedural law varies on this defense among the jurisdictions, the defense has common denominators. In all cases where insanity is raised as a defense to charges of criminal conduct, the issues are ultimately reduced to whether a mental impairment existed and whether the impairment played a role in the defendant's conduct at the time of the crime.

The insanity defense standards applied in about one third of the states is the M'Naughten Rule, which in its original form dates back to 1843.[38] While the rule has been modified in some states, the basic tenet of the *M'Naughten* decision is that the mental impairment either (1) prevented the defendant from understanding the criminal nature and quality of the criminal act or (2) prevented the defendant from determining whether the act was legal or illegal. The difficulty with the M'Naughten Rule is that it requires a determination that the defendant was sane or insane, with no middle ground. Consequently, a majority of states have chosen other methods to determine the question of insanity as an influence on one charged with criminal conduct.

Some jurisdictions allow in place of or in addition to the M'Naughten Rule, the irresistible impulse theory. Under this premise, the defendant claims to have been unable to control his or her behavior as the result of mental impairment at the time of the alleged criminal conduct. The irresistible impulse theory rests on the basis that the defendant at the time of the crime was subjected to a sudden impulse that he or she did not have the capacity to control.

Finally, a number of states have adopted a defense standard similar to that used in federal prosecutions. In 1984, this defense was embodied in a statutory definition by the Congress:

> (a) Affirmative Defense: It is an affirmative defense to a prosecution under any Federal statute that, at the time of the commission of the acts constituting the offense, the defendant, as a result of a severe mental disease or defect, was unable to appreciate the nature and quality or the wrongfulness of his acts. Mental disease or defect does not otherwise constitute a defense.
> (b) Burden of Proof: The defendant has the burden of proving the defense of insanity by clear and convincing evidence.[39]

This recent statute has made it more difficult to prove insanity as a defense. In the past, insanity was seen as a way to avoid prosecution for the acts of an otherwise reasonable individual. The new statute requires extensive proof of mental disability. It must be shown that the disability was severe and that it prevented any ability to appreciate or understand the act itself and its consequences. An additional hurdle is that the burden is placed on the defendant. Usually, the burden is on the prosecution to show guilt beyond a reasonable doubt. Thus, any doubt created in the minds of the jury by the defense is sufficient to prevent conviction. Under the new insanity statute, however, the defendant must present clear and convincing evidence of the required elements.

The Model Penal Code is the approach the majority of the states take with regard to the insanity defense. The Code permits a defendant to raise the insanity defense, but the defense must prove that the defendant did not have the ability to "appreciate the criminality of his conduct" or "conform his conduct to the requirements of law."[40] This requirement parallels and strengthens the reasoning of the common law approach. Under this rule, the defendant has the burden of establishing that he or she had some cognitive inability to understand right from wrong and was unable to control his or her actions within legal bounds. The rule's significance is that ordinarily, the prosecution has the burden of proving the defendant guilty. However, when the insanity defense is raised, the burden is switched, and the defendant has the burden to present proof to meet the insanity defense standard of the jurisdiction.

Go to the subject index of the statutes for your particular state. Examine the statutes pertaining to homicide and determine whether the statute follows common law or the Model Penal Code. Then determine whether a statute or rule of evidence sets forth the requirements for pleading insanity as a defense to a crime.

ETHICAL NOTE

While most persons do not consider themselves to be criminals, neither do most consider themselves to be unethical. However, frequently, the same type of conduct that many engage in on a daily basis could be technically considered unethical, perhaps even criminal. For example, if you drive through a fast-food restaurant and upon arriving home discover the clerk gave you thirty-five cents more change than you were due, how likely is it that you will get back in your car and return the money to the restaurant? Most people would probably not return the money because of the amount of time required for such a small figure. But keeping the money is no more ethical or legal just because the amount is considered by most as insignificant. Much of the reason that criminal laws mirror ethical standards of society is the belief that violations of the standards should not be tolerated.

Question

Can you identify three situations that are not ethical but are entirely legal?

CHAPTER SUMMARY

This chapter has briefly examined some of the more frequently encountered crimes. The common thread that pervades all criminal conduct is that the defendant must be aware of the decision to act or not to act. This awareness may be merely that, or it may be a general intent, a specific intent, or awareness as defined by the Model Penal Code. Each statute that defines criminal conduct indicates expressly or by implication the level of awareness required. Further, the statute sets forth with some certainty the acts or omissions that constitute criminal conduct. In contrast, defenses are created largely by judicial law. In most cases, the courts have formulated what is an acceptable or unacceptable reason for what would otherwise be criminal conduct. This generally includes not only the core criminal act but also all acts that enable the crime to be committed or prevent the discovery of the crime or the actor. These ideas are present in both the common law and the Model Penal Code. The primary difference between the two is the manner in which they are applied.

It should also be noted that simply because criminal conduct occurs, conviction is not always in order. The circumstances of the crime and the motivation of the parties involved may excuse or justify the conduct, or they may defeat the necessary elements for commission of the crime, such as the absence of specific intent or insanity.

Further research into the criminal law of a particular jurisdiction should always involve an initial determination of whether the jurisdiction applies common law principles or the Model Penal Code. Once this determination has been made, the appropriate principles of mens rea and actus reus will apply. Thus, it is necessary to determine only the specifics of mens rea and actus reus that are required for the particular crime in question.

REVIEW QUESTIONS

1. What is a felony?
2. Explain the difference between actus reus and mens rea.
3. What types of acts are subject to strict criminal liability?
4. Identify the parties to crime under the Model Penal Code and under common law.
5. What is an inchoate offense?
6. What is the difference between theft and robbery?
7. What are the types of homicide, and how are they differentiated?
8. When can a corporation be held criminally liable?
9. How does justifiable conduct differ from excusable conduct?

CHAPTER TERMS

Actus Reus
Criminal Law
Excusable Conduct
Felony
Justifiable Conduct
Mens Rea
Misdemeanor

NOTES

1. *Lord Fitzgerald Seaton v. Seaton,* L.R. 13 Ap.Ca. 78 (1888).
2. William Statsky, *Legal Thesaurus/Dictionary* (St. Paul: West, 1982).
3.–5. Id.
6. Model Penal Code, Section 1.13(9).
7. *In re Michael,* 423 A.2d 1180 (R.I. 1981).
8. *United States v. Sterley,* 764 F.2d 530 (8th Cir. 1985).
9. *People v. Love,* 11 Cal.App. 3d Supp.1, 168 Cal. Rptr. 591 (1980).
10. Id.
11. 95 A.L.R.3d 248.
12. *People v. Levitt,* 156 Cal.App. 3d 500, 156 Cal. Rptr. 276 (1984).
13. Model Penal Code, Section 1.13; 2.02.
14. *People v. Bargy,* 71 Mich.App. 609, 248 N.W.3d 636 (1976); State v. Furr, 292 N.C. 711, 235 S.E.2d 193 (1977).
15. Id.
16. Model Penal Code, Section 242.3; 2.06.
17. William Statsky, *Legal Thesaurus.*
18. *Manner v. State,* 387 So.2d 1014 (Fla. App. 4th Dist. 1980).
19. Model Penal Code, Section 5.03.
20. *State v. Stewart,* 537 S.W.2d 579 (Mo.App. 1976).
21. *Pinkett v. State,* 30 Md.App. 458, 352 A.2d 358 (1976).
22. William Statsky, *Legal Thesaurus.*
23. *State v. Lora,* 213 Kan. 184, 515 P.2d 1086 (1973).
24. *Anderson v. State,* 61 Md.App. 436, 487 A.2d 294 (1985).
25. Id.
26. *Wilcox v. State,* 401 So.2d 789 (Ala.Crim.App.1980).
27. *Dunn v. State,* 161 Ind.App. 586, 316 N.E.2d 834 (1974).
28. *State v. Beach,* 329 S.W.2d 712 (Mo. 1959).
29. *Callahan v. State,* 343 So.2d 551 (Ala.Crim.App. 1977).
30. *Goldsby v. State,* 226 Miss. 1, 78 So.2d 762 (1955).
31. *Wooden v. Commonwealth,* 222 Va. 758, 284 S.E.2d 811 (1981).
32. Model Penal Code, Section 210.2.
33. Model Penal Code, Section 2.07.
34. *State v. Williams,* 545 S.W.2d 342 (Mo.App. 1976).
35. *Law v. State,* 21 Md.App. 13, 318 A.2d 859 (1974).
36. Model Penal Code, Section 3.09.
37. Model Penal Code, Section 3.04.
38. Daniel M'Naughten's Case, 10 Cl. & F.200, 8 Eng.Rep. 718 (H.L. 1843).
39. 18 U.S.C.A. Section 20.
40. Model Penal Code, Section 402.

CHAPTER 13

Criminal Procedure

CHAPTER OBJECTIVES

After reading this chapter, you should be able to

- *Explain the purpose of selective incorporation and list the rights adopted into the definition of due process through selective incorporation.*

- *Explain the concept of double jeopardy and when it does not apply even though the defendant has gone to trial.*

- *Discuss when a defendant has the right to counsel.*

- *Discuss the determination of bail.*

- *Discuss when an arrest warrant is not required.*

- *Compare grand jury proceedings and preliminary hearings.*

- *Explain the process of arraignment.*

Criminal procedure is one of the most rapidly changing areas of law in the United States today. It differs significantly from civil procedure. Of course, the obvious difference is that rules of civil procedure govern civil actions and rules of criminal procedure govern criminal prosecutions. In addition, criminal procedure comes into play long before the action is formally commenced against a defendant. Criminal procedure affects the prosecution from the moment a crime is suspected.

Criminal prosecutions take place in federal and state judicial systems, each of which has its own rules of procedure. However, all are ultimately governed by certain constitutional requirements. Through its various amendments, the U.S. Constitution protects all persons from unfair and unequal treatment during criminal prosecutions. The courts vigorously enforce the Constitution and require that all persons be treated fairly and equally. Therefore, although the rules may differ somewhat from jurisdiction to jurisdiction, the effect of the rules must be constitutionally permissible or the rules may be invalidated by the courts.

This chapter provides a limited introduction to the constitutional limitations on criminal procedure, the current status of criminal procedure, and the stages of a criminal prosecution. Keep in mind that since the law is subject to radical changes as the courts review various procedural rules and judge their constitutionality, only basic principles are discussed here, and even they may be subject to change.

CRIMINAL PROCEDURE AND THE CONSTITUTION

The Approach of the U.S. Supreme Court

Various amendments to the U.S. Constitution affect criminal rights. The Bill of Rights was adopted, in part, to protect individuals from being unfairly or unnecessarily penalized by the justice system.

Assignment 13.1

Identify each right in the following amendments that could play a role in a criminal prosecution. (These amendments are reprinted with original spelling and punctuation.)

- Amendment 4: The right of the people to be secure in their persons, houses, papers, and effects, against unreasonable searches and seizures, shall not be violated, and no Warrants shall issue, but upon probable cause, supported by Oath or affirmation, and particularly describing the place to be searched, and the persons or things to be seized.
- Amendment 5: No person shall be held to answer for a capital, or otherwise infamous crime, unless on a presentment or indictment of a Grand Jury, except in cases arising in the land or naval forces, or in the Militia, when in actual service in time of War or public danger; nor shall any person be subject for the same offense to be twice put

in jeopardy of life or limb; nor shall be compelled in any criminal case to be a witness against himself, nor be deprived of life, liberty, or property, without due process of law; nor shall private property be taken for public use, without just compensation.

- Amendment 6: In all criminal prosecutions, the accused shall enjoy the right to a speedy and public trial, by an impartial jury of the State and district wherein the crime shall have been committed, which district shall have been previously ascertained by law, and to be informed of the nature and cause of the accusation; to be confronted with the witnesses against him; to have the compulsory process for obtaining witnesses in his favor, and to have the Assistance of Counsel for his defense.
- Amendment 8: Excessive bail shall not be required, nor excessive fines imposed, nor cruel and unusual punishments inflicted.
- Amendment 14, Section 1: All persons born or naturalized in the United States, and subject to the jurisdiction thereof, are citizens of the United States and of the State wherein they reside. No State shall make or enforce any law which shall abridge the privileges or immunities of citizens of the United States; nor shall any State deprive any person of life, liberty, or property, without due process of law; nor deny to any person within its jurisdiction the equal protection of the laws.

Amendments 4, 5, 8, and 14 address virtually every aspect of criminal procedure, including but not limited to invasion of one's property for the purpose of searching for and seizure of criminal evidence, self-incrimination, and the grounds for capital offenses (where punishment can be death). The effects of these amendments on criminal procedure are discussed in subsequent sections.

The Fourteenth Amendment: Due Process

In recent years, the Fourteenth Amendment, passed in 1868, has played a controversial role in criminal procedure. The obvious interpretation is that all citizens are subject to federal law and, further, that no state may pass or interpret laws that would conflict with federal law or the specific rights listed in the amendment. For many years, this was the interpretation given by the U.S. Supreme Court.[1] In various decisions, the Court maintained that the Fourteenth Amendment guaranteed only fundamental rights necessary to justice and order. It did not interpret the amendment to mean that all states must follow with absolute certainty all other constitutional amendments when creating law. Rather, as long as their laws did not conflict with constitutional guarantees, the states were permitted to create laws in any manner they chose.

During the 1950s and 1960s, the Court's approach to the Fourteenth Amendment changed. At that time, the justices who had been appointed to the Court were, as a group, more liberal than at any time in the Court's history. In addition, there was a great deal of unrest in the United States. Many felt that the constitutional guarantees in the Bill of Rights were being ignored or violated at the state level. The result was a great many alleged discrimination claims against the state governments as well as civil disobedience by the citizens. In various parts of the country, individuals protesting against the alleged inequities of state laws engaged in riots and other actions. Protest marches were held, sit-ins were conducted, and various other measures were taken by individuals to protect what they perceived to be fundamental rights. In the South, civil rights volunteers came from various other parts of the country to help secure the freedom of blacks to vote, assemble, and be treated with equality in the way laws were applied. All around the United States, people began to stand up against local and state governments that they believed operated with indifference to the fundamental protections that were so important in the creation of the original Constitution and Bill of Rights.

Although the Supreme Court of the 1950s and 1960s was quite liberal in its thinking, it was unwilling to utilize the total integration approach.[2] This approach follows the theory that the Fourteenth Amendment effectively integrates the entire Constitution and its amendments into each state's laws. The actual result would be to replace the state constitutions with the federal Constitution or at least to add the federal Constitution and its amendments to all state constitutions. The states would have virtually no say in what rights would be afforded their citizens or how the citizens would be governed. All state laws would be virtually identical to federal laws.

Selective Incorporation

Process of expansion of the definition of due process to include certain guarantees enumerated in the Bill of Rights.

Due Process

That which is necessary to fundamental fairness in the American system of justice.

Selective incorporation.   Because the Court felt this invaded too much on the ability of state citizens to govern themselves without unnecessary federal government interference, it engaged in **selective incorporation.**[3] Previously, the Court had followed the rule that only the rights specifically stated in the Fourteenth Amendment were required to be followed explicitly by the states, including the right to **due process** (fundamental fairness) in the application of law before a person's life, liberty, or property could be seized. In simpler terms, an individual could not be sentenced to death or prison or have real or personal property taken by any state or federal government unless the person was treated fairly by the government. In addition, all persons were to be treated equally in the way laws were applied. For a time, this was sufficient. However, it became increasingly apparent that state and local governments did not always take a liberal view as to what constituted fundamental fairness in the way accused persons were treated and prosecuted.

To remedy this, the Court decided to more thoroughly and clearly define the term *due process*. In the past, it had been interpreted to mean essentially that which was fundamentally fair in a system of justice. However, the Court took the position that the states needed further clarification of the term. Because the Congress passed the Fourteenth Amendment, which required the states to give all citizens due process, the U.S. Supreme Court had the authority to interpret the amendment and, specifically, its language of due process. As noted earlier, the Court could do this by simply stating that all rights in the Bill of Rights were included in the definition of due process. However, since this was seen as too invasive, the Court opted instead to review case by case and determine whether a certain right in the Bill of Rights should be included in the definition of due process. If the Court determined that right was included, it would state with specificity how the right was to be protected at the state level.

Over the years, the process of selective incorporation has resulted in expansion of the definition of due process to include the Fourth, Fifth, Sixth, and Eighth Amendments. One by one, cases have come to the Supreme Court, where it was determined that the circumstances of treatment of the accused did not afford the accused fundamental fairness during investigation, arrest, and prosecution.[4]

The ultimate effect of selective incorporation is quite simple. Once the Supreme Court finds that a particular right is incorporated into the Fourteenth Amendment, any state laws that would affect this right must be fair and reasonable. The Court will invalidate state laws that affect protected federal constitutional rights.

Selective incorporation has been especially relevant to laws of criminal procedure, which guide criminal prosecutions and set forth what is considered fundamental to the criminal process. These laws ultimately affect the American theory of innocence until guilt is proven beyond any reasonable doubt by controlling the manner in which the accused is treated and evidence is obtained.

The following sections discuss the amendments to the U.S. Constitution that have been selectively incorporated into the Fourteenth Amendment. The reasoning behind the incorporation of each particular amendment and the effect of the amendment's incorporation on state laws are included. It is especially helpful to examine the cases in which the Court made these decisions, because the cases provide examples that actually occurred.

The Fourth Amendment: Search and Seizure

As early as 1914, the U.S. Supreme Court first held that evidence in a federal criminal prosecution that was obtained without a proper search warrant or probable cause would be inadmissible in court.[5] This was the beginning of the exclusionary rule, under which improperly obtained evidence is excluded from trial. Consequently, no matter how damaging, such evidence cannot be used to convict someone of a crime. The Supreme Court adopted this position with regard to the federal court system's criminal prosecutions.

The idea that the Fourth Amendment should be incorporated into the Fourteenth, thereby requiring states to apply the exclusionary rule, was first addressed in 1949 in *Wolf v. Colorado.*[6] At that time, the Court examined what the states had done on their own and found that some thirty states had considered the exclusionary rule used in federal cases but had chosen not to follow the rule in state criminal prosecutions. Rather, these states decided to develop their own methods to discourage police from unreasonable practices in obtaining evidence. In *Wolf,* the Court decided that since a majority of the states had rejected the exclusionary rule and were using means other than the exclusion of evidence to prevent unlawful searches and seizures, it should not forcibly impose the requirement on the states. Thus, the Court held that the states could adequately protect the rights of their citizens without a forced application of the exclusionary rule to guarantee rights under the Fourth Amendment. Therefore, the Fourth Amendment was not at this time incorporated into the Fourteenth Amendment definition of due process. Consequently, the states were not yet required to adopt

APPLICATION 13.1

College student A shares an apartment with college students B and C. Unknown to A, B and C sell cocaine. In accordance with state law, the police break into the apartment at night and find the cocaine. A, B, and C are all charged, prosecuted, and convicted, even though A is totally innocent. Under the exclusionary rule, police are required to follow certain standards of reasonableness in searches and seizures, designed, in part, to determine who is actually involved in criminal activity. However, with states not subject to the exclusionary rule, such requirements did not exist unless under state law.

Point for Discussion
Why do you think the Court originally chose not to force application of the exclusionary rule in state prosecutions?

the federal position on the exclusionary rule. The effect was that as long as the state law was followed, a person's property could be searched and seized and any evidence of criminal activity used against the individual in a prosecution.

Just twelve years after *Wolf v. Colorado,* the Supreme Court reconsidered the incorporation of the Fourth Amendment into the Fourteenth Amendment. In *Mapp v. Ohio,*[7] the Court reversed its prior holding (an extremely rare occurrence) and held that the federally developed exclusionary rule is the most appropriate way of protecting citizens from unreasonable searches and seizures. The Court further held that for a citizen to be afforded due process in a criminal prosecution (a right guaranteed in the Fourteenth Amendment), the Fourth Amendment protections must be adhered to, including the federal method of using the exclusionary rule. Consequently, the Fourth Amendment protections should be incorporated into the definition of the Fourteenth Amendment. Further, the states should be required to follow the exclusionary rule, which is the method of choice to enforce the Fourth Amendment rule of no unreasonable search and seizure.

A large part of the reason for the Court's reversal of its position was the fact that since the *Wolf* decision, many states had tried methods other than the exclusionary rule and had failed. Many of these states then turned to the exclusionary rule on their own. The Court in *Mapp v. Ohio* affirmed this as an acceptable method of protecting citizens' rights.

Exclusionary rule. With this decision, the Fourteenth Amendment began to be expanded to include the rights enunciated in other amendments. The results of the decision in *Mapp v. Ohio* are continuing even today. Since that time, the Court has reviewed many state laws to determine what is a reasonable search or seizure and what is unreasonable. Evidence obtained through the latter is prohibited under the exclusionary rule from being used as evidence at a trial.

Over the years, a great deal of concern has been expressed about the exclusionary rule, which was intended to deter or prevent law enforcement personnel from obtaining evidence by means that violate Fourth Amendment rights. The rationale was that individuals were not in a position to protect their rights against law enforcement agencies. Further, if these agencies were not encouraged in some way to honor the constitutional amendment against unreasonable search and seizure, our society could be reduced to a police state, which, in its most extreme form, might include random invasions of people's homes and property in search of evidence that might incriminate them.

However noble the intent of the exclusionary rule, the actual result is indisputable. Whenever evidence is obtained in a questionable manner, the person who benefits is the accused. Although our government follows the doctrine that an accused is innocent until proven guilty, in many such cases, the evidence excluded is so strong that it would undoubtedly result in a verdict of guilty by a jury. As a consequence of applying the exclusionary rule to protect a defendant's Fourth Amendment rights, many criminals have gone free or plea bargained for greatly reduced charges.

The Supreme Court has been faced with a double bind. Without the exclusionary rule, improper searches and seizures of innocent people's property can occur. With the exclusionary rule, known criminals can go free because of a technical, minor, or innocent violation of the rule. In 1984, the Court considered this dilemma in *United States v. Leon*.[8] In the *Leon* decision, the Supreme Court addressed at length the difficulty with enforcing a broad application of the exclusionary rule. The Court recognized that excluding evidence because of an improper search or seizure, no matter how small the infraction that caused it to be improper, resulted in preventing the jury from accurately determining innocence or guilt at a trial. When the exclusionary rule is applied, often the case is dismissed because little admissible evidence is available to support a conviction. At the very least, the jury is given only limited information with which to make its decision. The jurors are allowed to consider only properly obtained evidence. In fact, they generally do not know that additional evidence exists and has been excluded.

In *Leon*, the Court was faced with a situation where the police properly requested a search warrant. The judge properly reviewed the information to support the warrant and issued the warrant. The police exercised the search warrant and found evidence that was very incriminating. Only after the search occurred was it discovered that the warrant was improper. The police had requested a warrant on the basis of limited surveillance and the information of a person who had never before acted as an informant. Unless informants have a history of providing accurate information to law enforcement, their testimony usually requires much additional evidence before a judge will believe there is probable cause to suspect a crime and issue a search warrant. In this case, the defendant challenged the validity of the search warrant, and a higher judge found that it should never have been issued on such limited information.

The Supreme Court used the *Leon* decision to make a major exception to the exclusionary rule. Observing that the police had made every effort to follow the requirements to protect the Fourth Amendment rights of the defendant, the Court reasoned that since this was the entire goal of the exclusionary rule, it had been satisfied. The police had gone so far as to request permission of a judge to search for criminal evidence. Therefore, the goal of the rule had been met, and the citizen's rights had been protected. The Court refused to exclude the evidence (a large amount of illegal drugs), and the defendant was prosecuted. The Court stated that the exclusionary rule is designed to deter unreasonable practices by law enforcement personnel, not to remedy poor exercises of authority by judges.

The *Leon* decision is very important in the law of criminal procedure. It signals that the Court has shifted toward a more conservative view of what is necessary to protect the rights of citizens. The Court currently regards certain areas as private and subject to the protection of a citizen's Fourteenth Amendment rights by requiring satisfaction of the guarantees under the Fourth Amendment.

Probable Cause

More than mere suspicion of criminal activity.

Probable cause.   What a person considers to be private is that which cannot be searched or seized without **probable cause.** The Court has established a two-step test to be used in determining what is private property. First, it must be decided whether the person acted in such a way as to keep the property private from others. Second, it must be determined whether the person was reasonable in believing such property should be allowed to be kept private.[9]

Before law enforcement personnel can search or seize private property, they must have probable cause to believe a crime has been committed and/or that the owner of the property has been involved in criminal activity. There must also be probable cause to believe that a search of the property will result in evidence that will assist in proving this. Further, whenever possible, the law enforcement agency must seek approval of the search and seizure by obtaining a warrant from a judicial officer. The basis for the warrant must be probable cause. Although it is much debated, no absolute formula has ever been developed to determine what constitutes probable cause. Rather, probable cause falls within a range that, when examined by a neutral observer, would be considered "more than bare suspicion" but "less than evidence which would justify . . . conviction."[10]

If law enforcement personnel can support their suspicions and allegation of probable cause with outside information or other evidence that would create this degree of probability that the person or property is connected with criminal activity, a search warrant may be issued by a judge. If there is not time to request a search warrant, the officers may proceed with the search if there is probable cause to conduct it.[11] Because the officers are not considered to be as objective as a judicial officer, they are under a particularly heavy burden to show that their search was made with probable cause. To qualify as an exception to the warrant requirement, there must be an immediate danger that the property or person associated with the criminal activity will be lost unless an immediate search is conducted.

Warrants.   The type of property that may be searched has also been discussed by the courts. Generally, before a private residence can be searched, a warrant must be issued. If the property has been abandoned, a citizen has no expectation of privacy; therefore, no warrant is needed.[12] In addition, if the criminal activity or evidence can be observed by persons around or above the property, the property is considered to be in view of the public, and thus there is no expectation of privacy.[13] If an officer is lawfully upon another person's property for any reason and discovers criminal evidence in plain view, the property may be seized immediately (known as the plain view rule). Finally, if someone other than the resident has access to the residence and voluntarily allows officers entrance to the property, such entrance is treated as if permission had been given by the resident. Therefore, landlords, roommates, or guests have the power to admit police officers voluntarily to a residence for the purpose of searching for evidence of criminal activity.[14] In such situations, no warrant is necessary.

Police do need a warrant to invade private property by other than ordinary means. If, for example, a wiretap is going to be used to obtain the content of conversations in a residence or on a telephone line from a residence, a search warrant must be obtained, because the public would perceive a reasonable expectation of privacy in such a situation. However, devices that merely record the numbers called from a residence are not considered private, as the telephone company has access to this information at all times. Further, tracking devices on vehicles are permissible because the purpose is to track the vehicle in public. There can be no expectation of privacy about where one goes in public.

Vehicles.   Vehicles have created a whole new arena for questions about search and seizure. They are private property capable of concealing a great deal of other property. At the same time, they are transported in public, which means that the expectation of privacy is lower than that in a residence. The courts have held that looking into the vehicle from the outside is not a search and that if evidence of criminal activity is seen, there is no need for a warrant.[15]

If a car has been abandoned, there is no expectation of privacy. Therefore, no warrant is needed to examine the interior of the vehicle. The courts have also given officers the ability to search those areas of a car that are within reasonable reach of the owner when a stop is made.[16] The rationale is that the owner may be within reach of a weapon that could be used to assault the officers or to effect escape. The recent trend has been to approve searches of vehicles even when the suspect is no longer in the car or the car has been impounded. The basic requirement seems to be not that an emergency must exist but rather that the officer must have probable cause to believe that evidence or dangerous items may be in the car, its compartments, or containers within it or that the car is not in the possession of the police and is subject to removal from the jurisdiction. The regulation of police searches of automobiles is a rapidly evolving area of the law with many distinctions between states and federal government. Accordingly, it is important to know the law specific to your jurisdiction.

This is a brief examination of some of the areas that have been addressed by the courts in determining what constitutes a search under the Fourth Amendment. Because the amendment has been applied to the states, these rules must be followed by state as well as federal law enforcement officers. The theory is that these rules will afford citizens due process and fairness before their privacy is invaded or their property is searched or seized by the state government. The rules also help to ensure fairer criminal prosecutions by reducing the chances of improper convictions.

Arrest. The same basic warrant requirements that apply to search and seizure of property apply to arrest. In essence, an arrest is a search and seizure of the person. Thus, the person is entitled to the same fair treatment as his or her property would be afforded. Consequently, the courts prefer that arrest warrants be obtained upon a showing of probable cause before the arrest is made. Often criminal activity is discovered while it is occurring or immediately after it has occurred. In such cases, it is usually unreasonable to expect that the criminal will remain until a warrant is obtained. Therefore, most arrests are made on the basis of a probable cause determination by law enforcement officers. This determination is subject to judicial review, just as a search made without a warrant would be.

When an arrest based on probable cause has been made, the officer may search the arrested person and all areas within his or her reach.[17] The reason for this is that the arrestee may be carrying a weapon that could be used to harm the officer. If the officer recovers other evidence of criminal activity during the search, the evidence may also be seized. Even though it is not what the officer may have been searching for, it is considered to be fruits of crime. A suspect who carries evidence of criminal activity on his or her person and is subsequently lawfully arrested does not have a reasonable expectation of privacy regarding that property.

Even when a full-fledged arrest is not made, the officers are entitled to take minimum steps to protect their own safety. Occasionally, an officer will stop an individual on suspicion of some criminal activity, perhaps even a minor infraction, such as a traffic violation. Even on stopping such an individual, the officer has the right to frisk the individual for a concealed weapon if the officer has a reasonable suspicion that the suspect is armed or otherwise dangerous.[18] This is permitted to avoid disastrous circumstances that have occurred and still occur when an individual stopped for a minor infraction pulls out a weapon and kills an officer of the law.

As this far from exhaustive discussion illustrates, the law of search and seizure is quite complex. Further, this area of law changes continually as the Supreme Court seeks to mold specific rules regarding the expectation of privacy by individuals for themselves and their property. The Court must balance these expectations against what is necessary to promote law enforcement and the safety of the people as a whole. As long as this balancing continues, this area of criminal procedure will grow.

The Fifth Amendment: Double Jeopardy, Self-Incrimination

Practically speaking, the role of the Fifth Amendment in criminal procedure has been primarily confined to the issues of double jeopardy and self-incrimination, addressed individually, since they are wholly separate rights.

Double Jeopardy
Being placed on trial for the same crime twice.

Double jeopardy. **Double jeopardy** is the right of every citizen to be tried once, and only once, for a specific crime charged. The theory is that the government should prove guilt beyond a reasonable doubt at trial. If this cannot be accomplished, the presumption of innocence is sustained and questions of guilt are dismissed. Citizens cannot be subjected to multiple trials for the same crime each time the government believes it can produce new evidence or select a more critical jury.

The rule of double jeopardy was rather easily incorporated into the Fourteenth Amendment and applied to the states. The Fourteenth Amendment clearly states that there can be no deprivation of life or liberty without due process of law. It seems quite logical that to force someone to be tried over and over again for the same crime would not be an exercise of due process of law. The very notion of fair treatment to all citizens is contrary to the thought that a citizen could be singled out and charged repeatedly with a crime until the prosecution was successful.

The courts have clearly defined the point at which double jeopardy becomes an issue. A person is not considered to be in jeopardy of loss of life or limb (in modern terms, penalty, liberty, or life) until it is a real possibility that such a result will occur. After a person is charged with a crime and until the time of trial, there is a possibility that the charges will be dropped. After the trial begins, however, it is assumed that a verdict will be reached and a penalty may ensue. Therefore, a person is not in jeopardy until such time as the jury has been sworn in.[19] In a "bench" trial before a judge, and without a jury, double jeopardy attaches when the first witness is sworn. At this point, the defendant can be subjected to a second trial for the charge only if the first trial results in a mistrial.

Once the verdict is reached, it is considered final. Following this, if the accused person is acquitted (found not guilty), he or she cannot be charged and tried again for the identical crime. In addition, the person generally cannot later be charged for other possible charges arising out of the same incident.[20] Thus, if the prosecution is unsuccessful in trying a person for murder, it cannot then charge the person with manslaughter or assault. If the judge dismisses the case because of a lack of evidence that would support a finding of guilty, ordinarily there can be no second prosecution.[21]

Once a trial has commenced and jeopardy has attached, the person cannot be charged and tried again with a crime, with a few exceptions. If there is a dismissal or a mistrial is called for any reason other than a lack of evidence or if the defendant appeals a guilty verdict, the charges may be reinstated and the case tried again. The Supreme Court has refused to adopt the double jeopardy right as a means of escaping conviction on technicalities. Thus, if the prosecution has sufficient evidence to uphold a conviction, the case may be retried. Further, if the defendant appealed a conviction and is granted a new trial, there is a second chance for sentencing as well. As long as the sentence is justified by the crime, a judge in a second trial may impose a stricter sentence than was given in the first trial.

The double jeopardy rule puts a burden on the prosecution to be relatively sure of its case before presenting it to a jury. However, the defendant is faced with the decision of accepting a guilty verdict or taking a chance on a potentially more severe sentence in a new trial.

APPLICATION 13.2

John is charged with kidnapping, a capital crime for which the penalty may be death. He pleads innocent and goes on trial. At the conclusion of the trial he is found guilty and sentenced to life in prison. He appeals and succeeds. The appellate court awards a new trial. (Recall from Chapter 2 that appellate courts typically don't determine guilt or innocence. Rather, they determine the appropriateness of the conduct of the trial court and whether it precluded a fair and legal result.) At the new trial, John is again convicted and this time is given the death penalty.

Point for Discussion

Allowing a more serious penalty at a new trial seems to discourage an appeal of the first conviction. Why is this permitted?

Self-incrimination. Interpretations regarding what constitutes self-incrimination are much more pervasive than interpretations of double jeopardy. The primary issue has been at what point the right to refuse to give information that may be incriminating originates. Under the Fifth Amendment, no person may be forced to give information that may then be used to convict that person of a crime. For nearly the first 200 years of the amendment's history, the courts merely examined whether information had been given voluntarily. But during the past few decades, the courts have begun to give more attention to the circumstances surrounding communications with persons suspected or accused of a crime. The courts began to recognize that in some cases, a suspect or defendant might be influenced by the circumstances and in this way be compelled to give information that he or she would ordinarily withhold as his or her right not to take part in self-prosecution.

A landmark decision in this area of the law came in *Miranda v. Arizona*.[22] In that decision, the Supreme Court firmly stated that every person accused of a crime must be informed at the very outset that all further communications might be used in a prosecution. The result of that decision was the adoption of the Miranda rights, now read to all persons in this country at the time of interrogation and/or arrest. All accused individuals are advised that (1) they have the right to remain silent, (2) anything they say may be used against them in a court of law, (3) they have the right to an attorney, and (4) they may have an attorney appointed if they cannot afford one.

As with double jeopardy, it was a logical step to incorporate this aspect of the Fifth Amendment into the Fourteenth Amendment and thus require the states to adhere to it in their own laws. Since it would be impossible to provide due process of law to any individuals who are forced to testify against themselves at any stage of a criminal proceeding, such individuals must be allowed the opportunity to remain silent.

At first this may appear to be contrary to the purpose of criminal justice, which is to catch and punish persons committing crimes against society. However, the Constitution is designed to protect all of the people, including those persons who may be innocent but lack the ability to act in their own best interest. Persons who are not adept at giving testimony and for whom the circumstances would imply guilt should have the right to protect their innocence with silence and not be penalized for it.

The *Miranda* decision clearly established that the right against self-incrimination originates at the moment an individual is held for interrogation or is placed under arrest, whichever occurs first. Therefore, all persons detained are placed on notice that any utterance can be used against them. Anything a suspected criminal says while in custody, even if it is not said to a police officer, may be used against him or her in a prosecution. The right against self-incrimination is the right to remain silent. It is not the right to make statements to some persons and not to others. A statement made to officers or within the confines of a police facility are considered to be voluntary statements with the exception of confidential communication to one's attorney.

If the police wish to interrogate a prisoner, the questioning must be done in the fairest of circumstances. The police must either allow an attorney to be present on behalf of the accused or demonstrate that the prisoner waived the right to have an attorney present.[23] Evidence of this waiver must be documented. It must be clear that the prisoner knew and understood the reasons for having an attorney present and intelligently chose not to have an attorney present. Further, the police cannot set up circumstances that play upon the weaknesses of the accused to the point that there is no voluntary waiver. For example, if a prisoner is known to suffer from some mental incapacity, the police may not take advantage of this to further impair the prisoner's ability to make a decision regarding counsel.

A prisoner who is willing to answer questions or give a statement or confession may do so without the presence or advice of legal counsel. However, the courts will scrutinize the record to make sure such information was given voluntarily. Therefore, the police will generally ask prisoners to sign a written statement that they know and understand their rights. A prisoner will acknowledge in the statement that he or she waives the right to remain silent and the right to counsel. Subsequently, the Supreme Court has held that if a prisoner knows of the right to counsel (following Miranda warnings) and does not request counsel, the police may interrogate. Once a prisoner requests counsel, however, the police are under a heavier burden to show that any communications outside the presence of counsel were indeed voluntary.

The *Miranda* decision was actually one of several similar cases. The Court was presented with numerous appeals on the same issue, although the facts differed somewhat from case to case. However, the Court applied its opinion in *Miranda* to each of the cases individually.

CASE

MIRANDA v. STATE OF ARIZONA

384 U.S. 436, 86
S.Ct. 1602, 16 L.Ed.2d
694 (1966).

Mr. Chief Justice
WARREN
delivered the opinion
of the Court.

The cases before us raise questions which go to the roots of our concepts of American criminal jurisprudence: the restraints society must observe consistent with the Federal Constitution in prosecuting individuals for crime. More specifically, we deal with the admissibility of statements obtained from an individual who is subjected to custodial police interrogation and the necessity for procedures which assure that the individual is accorded his privilege under the Fifth Amendment to the Constitution not to be compelled to incriminate himself.

We dealt with certain phases of this problem recently in Escobedo v. State of Illinois, 378 U.S. 478, 84 S.Ct. 1758, 12 L.Ed.2d 977 (1964). There, as in the four cases before us, law enforcement officials took the defendant into custody and interrogated him in a police station for the purpose of obtaining a confession. The police did not effectively advise him of his right to remain silent or of his right to consult with his attorney. Rather, they confronted him with an alleged accomplice who accused him of having perpetrated a murder. When the defendant denied the accusation and said 'I didn't shoot Manuel, you did it,' they handcuffed him and took him to an interrogation room. There, while handcuffed and standing, he was questioned for four hours until he confessed. During this interrogation, the police denied his request to speak to his attorney, and they prevented his retained attorney, who had come to the police station, from consulting with him. At his trial, the State, over his objection, introduced the confession against him. We held that the statements thus made were constitutionally inadmissible.

This case has been the subject of judicial interpretation and spirited legal debate since it was decided two years ago. Both state and federal courts, in assessing its implications, have arrived at varying conclusions. . . . A wealth of scholarly material has been written tracing its ramifications and underpinnings. . . . Police and prosecutor have speculated on its range and desirability. . . . We granted certiorari in these cases, 382 U.S. 924, 925, 937, 86 S.Ct. 318, 320, 395, 15 L.Ed.2d 338, 339, 348, in order further to explore some facets of the problems, thus exposed, of applying the privilege against self-incrimination to in-custody interrogation, and to give concrete constitutional guidelines for law enforcement agencies and courts to follow.

We start here, as we did in Escobedo, with the premise that our holding is not an innovation in our jurisprudence, but is an application of principles long recognized and applied in other settings. We have undertaken a thorough re-examination of the Escobedo decision and the principles it announced, and we reaffirm it. That case was but an explication of basic rights that are enshrined in our Constitution—that 'No person shall be compelled in any criminal case to be a witness against himself,' and that 'the accused shall have the Assistance of Counsel'—rights which were put in jeopardy in that case through official overbearing. These precious rights were fixed in our Constitution only after centuries of persecution and struggle. And in the words of Chief Justice Marshall, they were secured 'for ages to come, and designed to approach immortality as nearly as human institutions can approach it,' Cohens v. Commonwealth of Virginia, 6 Wheat. 264, 387, 5 L.Ed. 257 (1821).

* * *

Our holding will be spelled out with some specificity in the pages which follow but briefly stated it is this: the prosecution may not use statements, whether exculpatory or inculpatory, stemming from custodial interrogation of the defendant unless it demonstrates the use of procedural safeguards effective to secure the privilege against self-incrimination. By custodial interrogation, we mean questioning initiated by law enforcement officers after a person has been taken into custody or otherwise deprived of his freedom of action in any significant way. (This is what we meant in Escobedo when we spoke of an investigation which had focused on an accused.) As for the procedural safeguards to be employed, unless other fully effective means are devised to inform accused persons of their right of silence and to assure a continuous opportunity to exercise it, the following measures are required. Prior to any questioning, the person must be warned that he has a right to remain silent, that any statement he does make may be used as evidence against him, and that he has a right to the presence of an attorney, either retained or appointed. The defendant may waive effectuation of these rights, provided the waiver is made voluntarily, knowingly and intelligently. If, however, he indicates in any manner and at any stage of the process that he wishes to consult with an attorney before speaking there can be no questioning. Likewise, if the individual is alone and indicates in any manner that he does not wish to be interrogated, the police may not question him. The mere fact that he may have answered some questions or volunteered some statements on his own does not deprive him of the right to refrain from answering any further inquiries until he has consulted with an attorney and thereafter consents to be questioned.

1.

The constitutional issue we decide in each of these cases is the admissibility of statements obtained from a defendant questioned while in custody or otherwise deprived of his freedom of action in any significant way. In each, the defendant was questioned by police officers, detectives, or a prosecuting attorney in a room in which he was cut off from the outside world. In none of these cases was the defendant given a full and effective warning of his rights at the outset of the interrogation process. In all the cases, the questioning elicited oral admissions, and in three of them, signed statements as well which were admitted at their trials. They all thus share salient features—incommunicado interrogation of individuals in a police-dominated atmosphere, resulting in self-incriminating statements without full warnings of constitutional rights.

An understanding of the nature and setting of this in-custody interrogation is essential to our

decisions today. The difficulty in depicting what transpires at such interrogations stems from the fact that in this country they have largely taken place incommunicado. From extensive factual studies undertaken in the early 1930s, including the famous Wickersham Report to Congress by a Presidential Commission, it is clear that police violence and the 'third degree' flourished at that time. . . . In a series of cases decided by this Court long after these studies, the police resorted to physical brutality—beatings, hanging, whipping— and to sustained and protracted questioning incommunicado in order to extort confessions. . . . The Commission on Civil Rights in 1961 found much evidence to indicate that 'some policemen still resort to physical force to obtain confessions,' 1961 Comm'n on Civil Rights Rep., Justice, pt. 5, 17. The use of physical brutality and violence is not, unfortunately, relegated to the past or to any part of the country. Only recently in Kings County, New York, the police brutally beat, kicked and placed lighted cigarette butts on the back of a potential witness under interrogation for the purpose of securing a statement incriminating a third party. People v. Portelli, 15 N.Y.2d 235, 257 N.Y.S.2d 931, 205 N.E.2d 857 (1965).

* * *

Again we stress that the modern practice of in-custody interrogation is psychologically rather than physically oriented. As we have stated before, 'Since Chambers v. State of Florida, 309 U.S. 227, 60 S.Ct. 472, 84 L.Ed. 716, this Court has recognized that coercion can be mental as well as physical, and that the blood of the accused is not the only hallmark of an unconstitutional inquisition.' Blackburn v. State of Alabama, 361 U.S. 199, 206, 80 S.Ct. 274, 279, 4 L.Ed.2d 242 (1960). Interrogation still takes place in privacy. Privacy results in secrecy and this in turn results in a gap in our knowledge as to what in fact goes on in the interrogation rooms. A valuable source of information about present police practices, however, may be found in various police manuals and texts which document procedures employed with success in the past, and which recommend various other effective tactics.

Even without employing brutality, . . . the very fact of custodial interrogation exacts a heavy toll on individual liberty and trades on the weakness of individuals. . . . Interrogation procedures may even give rise to a false confession. The most recent conspicuous example occurred in New York, in 1964, when a Negro of limited intelligence confessed to two brutal murders and a rape which he had not committed. When this was discovered, the prosecutor was reported as saying: 'Call it what you want—brain-washing, hypnosis, fright. They made him give an untrue confession. The only thing I don't believe is that Whitmore was beaten.' N.Y. Times, Jan. 28, 1965, p. 1, col. 5. In two other instances, similar events had occurred. N.Y. Times, Oct. 20, 1964, p. 22, col. 1; N.Y. Times, Aug. 25, 1965, p. 1, col. 1. In general, see Borchard, Convicting the Innocent (1932); Frank & Frank, Not Guilty (1957).

* * *

In the cases before us today, given this background, we concern ourselves primarily with this interrogation atmosphere and the evils it can bring. In No. 759, Miranda v. Arizona, the police arrested the defendant and took him to a special interrogation room where they secured a confession. In No. 760, Vignera v. New York, the defendant made oral admissions to the police after interrogation in the afternoon, and then signed an inculpatory statement upon being questioned by an assistant district attorney later the same evening. In No. 761, Westover v. United States, the defendant was handed over to the Federal Bureau of Investigation by local authorities after they had detained and interrogated him for a lengthy period, both at night and the following morning. After some two hours of questioning, the federal officers had obtained signed statements from the defendant. Lastly, in No. 584, California v. Stewart, the local police held the defendant five days in the station and interrogated him on nine separate occasions before they secured his inculpatory statement.

In these cases, we might not find the defendants' statements to have been involuntary in traditional terms. Our concern for adequate safeguards to protect precious Fifth Amendment rights is, of course, not lessened in the slightest. In each of the cases, the defendant was thrust into an unfamiliar atmosphere and run through menacing police interrogation procedures. The potentiality for compulsion is forcefully apparent, for example, in Miranda, where the indigent Mexican defendant was a seriously disturbed individual with pronounced sexual fantasies, and in Stewart,

in which the defendant was an indigent Los Angeles Negro who had dropped out of school in the sixth grade. To be sure, the records do not evince overt physical coercion or patent psychological ploys. The fact remains that in none of these cases did the officers undertake to afford appropriate safeguards at the outset of the interrogation to insure that the statements were truly the product of free choice.

It is obvious that such an interrogation environment is created for no purpose other than to subjugate the individual to the will of his examiner. This atmosphere carries its own badge of intimidation. To be sure, this is not physical intimidation, but it is equally destructive of human dignity. . . . The current practice of incommunicado interrogation is at odds with one of our Nation's most cherished principles—that the individual may not be compelled to incriminate himself. Unless adequate protective devices are employed to dispel the compulsion inherent in custodial surroundings, no statement obtained from the defendant can truly be the product of his free choice.

The question in these cases is whether the privilege is fully applicable during a period of custodial interrogation. In this Court, the privilege has consistently been accorded a liberal construction. Albertson v. Subversive Activities Control Board, 382 U.S. 70, 81, 86 S.Ct. 194, 200, 15 L.Ed.2d 165 (1965); Hoffman v. United States, 341 U.S. 479, 486, 71 S.Ct. 814, 818, 95 L.Ed.2d 1118 (1951); Arnstein v. McCarthy, 254 U.S. 71, 72–73, 41 S.Ct. 26, 65 L.Ed. 138 (1920); Counselman v. Hitchcock, 142 U.S. 547, 562, 12 S.Ct. 195, 197, 35 L.Ed. 1110 (1892). We are satisfied that all the principles embodied in the privilege apply to informal compulsion exerted by law-enforcement officers during in-custody questioning. An individual swept from familiar surroundings into police custody, surrounded by antagonistic forces, and subjected to the techniques of persuasion described above cannot be otherwise than under compulsion to speak. As a practical matter, the compulsion to speak in the isolated setting of the police station may well be greater than in courts or other official investigations, where there are often impartial observers to guard against intimidation or trickery. . . .

This question, in fact, could have been taken as settled in federal courts almost 70 years ago, when, in Bram v. United States, 168 U.S. 532, 542, 18 S.Ct. 183, 187, 42 L.Ed. 568 (1897), this Court held:

> 'In criminal trials, in the courts of the United States, wherever a question arises whether a confession is incompetent because not voluntary, the issue is controlled by that portion of the fifth amendment commanding that no person 'shall be compelled in any criminal case to be a witness against himself.'

In Bram, the Court reviewed the British and American history and case law and set down the Fifth Amendment standard for compulsion which we implement today:

> 'Much of the confusion which has resulted from the effort to deduce from the adjudged cases what would be a sufficient quantum of proof to show that a confession was or was not voluntary has arisen from a misconception of the subject to which the proof must address itself. The rule is not that, in order to render a statement admissible, the proof must be adequate to establish that the particular communications contained in a statement were voluntarily made, but it must be sufficient to establish that the making of the statement was voluntary; that is to say, that, from the causes which the law treats as legally sufficient to engender in the mind of the accused hope or fear in respect to the crime charged, the accused was not involuntarily impelled to make a statement when but for the improper influences he would have remained silent.' 168 U.S., at 549, 18 S.Ct. at 189. And see, id., at 542, 18 S.Ct. at 186.

* * *

The decisions of this Court have guaranteed the same procedural protection for the defendant whether his confession was used in a federal or state court. It is now axiomatic that the defendant's constitutional rights have been violated if his conviction is based, in whole or in part, on an involuntary confession, regardless of its truth or falsity. Rogers v. Richmond, 365 U.S. 534, 544, 81 S.Ct. 735, 741, 5 L.Ed.2d 760 (1961); Siang Sung Wan v. United States, 266 U.S. 1, 45 S.Ct. 1, 69 L.Ed. 131 (1924). This is so even if there is ample evidence aside from the confession to support the

conviction, e.g., Malinski v. People of State of New York, 324 U.S. 401, 404, 65 S.Ct. 781, 783, 89 L.Ed. 1029 (1945); Bram v. United States, 168 U.S. 532, 540–542, 18 S.Ct. 183, 185–186 (1897).

Today, . . . there can be no doubt that the Fifth Amendment privilege is available outside of criminal court proceedings and serves to protect persons in all settings in which their freedom of action is curtailed in any significant way from being compelled to incriminate themselves. We have concluded that without proper safeguards the process of in-custody interrogation of persons suspected or accused of crime contains inherently compelling pressures which work to undermine the individual's will to resist and to compel him to speak where he would not otherwise do so freely. In order to combat these pressures and to permit a full opportunity to exercise the privilege against self-incrimination, the accused must be adequately and effectively apprised of his rights and the exercise of those rights must be fully honored.

* * *

At the outset, if a person in custody is to be subjected to interrogation, he must first be informed in clear and unequivocal terms that he has the right to remain silent. For those unaware of the privilege, the warning is needed simply to make them aware of it—the threshold requirement for an intelligent decision as to its exercise. More important, such a warning is an absolute prerequisite in overcoming the inherent pressures of the interrogation atmosphere. It is not just the subnormal or woefully ignorant who succumb to an interrogator's imprecations, whether implied or expressly stated, that the interrogation will continue until a confession is obtained or that silence in the face of accusation is itself damning and will bode ill when presented to a jury. . . . Further, the warning will show the individual that his interrogators are prepared to recognize his privilege should he choose to exercise it.

The Fifth Amendment privilege is so fundamental to our system of constitutional rule and the expedient of giving an adequate warning as to the availability of the privilege so simple, we will not pause to inquire in individual cases whether the defendant was aware of his rights without a warning being given. Assessments of the knowledge the defendant possessed, based on information as to his age, education, intelligence, or prior contact with authorities, can never be more than speculation; . . . a warning is a clearcut fact. More important, whatever the background of the person interrogated, a warning at the time of the interrogation is indispensable to overcome its pressures and to insure that the individual knows he is free to exercise the privilege at that point in time.

The warning of the right to remain silent must be accompanied by the explanation that anything said can and will be used against the individual in court. This warning is needed in order to make him aware not only of the privilege, but also of the consequences of foregoing it. It is only through an awareness of these consequences that there can be any assurance of real understanding and intelligent exercise of the privilege. Moreover, this warning may serve to make the individual more acutely aware that he is faced with a phase of the adversary system—that he is not in the presence of persons acting solely in his interest.

The circumstances surrounding in-custody interrogation can operate very quickly to overbear the will of one merely made aware of his privilege by his interrogators. Therefore, the right to have counsel present at the interrogation is indispensable to the protection of the Fifth Amendment privilege under the system we delineate today. Our aim is to assure that the individual's right to choose between silence and speech remains unfettered throughout the interrogation process. A once-stated warning, delivered by those who will conduct the interrogation, cannot itself suffice to that end among those who most require knowledge of their rights. A mere warning given by the interrogators is not alone sufficient to accomplish that end. Prosecutors themselves claim that the admonishment of the right to remain silent without more 'will benefit only the recidivist and the professional.' Brief for the National District Attorneys Association as amicus curiae, p. 14. Even preliminary advice given to the accused by his own attorney can be swiftly overcome by the secret interrogation process. Cf. Escobedo v. State of Illinois, 378 U.S. 478, 485, n. 5, 84 S.Ct. 1758, 1762. Thus, the need for counsel to protect the Fifth Amendment privilege comprehends not merely a right to consult with counsel prior to questioning, but also to have counsel present during any questioning if the defendant so desires. The accused who does not

know his rights and therefore does not make a request may be the person who most needs counsel. As the California Supreme Court has aptly put it:

'Finally, we must recognize that the imposition of the requirement for the request would discriminate against the defendant who does not know his rights. The defendant who does not ask for counsel is the very defendant who most needs counsel. We cannot penalize a defendant who, not understanding his constitutional rights, does not make the formal request and by such failure demonstrates his helplessness. To require the request would be to favor the defendant whose sophistication or status had fortuitously prompted him to make it.' People v. Dorado, 62 Cal.2d 338, 351, 42 Cal.Rptr. 169, 177–178, 398 P.2d 361, 369–370, (1965) (Tobriner, J.).

In Carnley v. Cochran, 369 U.S. 506, 513, 82 S.Ct. 884, 889, 8 L.Ed.2d 70 (1962), we stated: '(I)t is settled that where the assistance of counsel is a constitutional requisite, the right to be furnished counsel does not depend on a request.' This proposition applies with equal force in the context of providing counsel to protect an accused's Fifth Amendment privilege in the face of interrogation. See Herman, The Supreme Court and Restrictions on Police Interrogation, 25 Ohio St.L.J. 449, 480 (1964). Although the role of counsel at trial differs from the role during interrogation, the differences are not relevant to the question whether a request is a prerequisite.

Accordingly we hold that an individual held for interrogation must be clearly informed that he has the right to consult with a lawyer and to have the lawyer with him during interrogation under the system for protecting the privilege we delineate today. As with the warnings of the right to remain silent and that anything stated can be used in evidence against him, this warning is an absolute prerequisite to interrogation. No amount of circumstantial evidence that the person may have been aware of this right will suffice to stand in its stead. Only through such a warning is there ascertainable assurance that the accused was aware of this right.

If an individual indicates that he wishes the assistance of counsel before any interrogation occurs, the authorities cannot rationally ignore or deny his request on the basis that the individual does not have or cannot afford a retained attorney. The financial ability of the individual has no relationship to the scope of the rights involved here. The privilege against self-incrimination secured by the Constitution applies to all individuals. The need for counsel in order to protect the privilege exists for the indigent as well as the affluent. In fact, were we to limit these constitutional rights to those who can retain an attorney, our decisions today would be of little significance. The cases before us as well as the vast majority of confession cases with which we have dealt in the past involve those unable to retain counsel. . . . While authorities are not required to relieve the accused of his poverty, they have the obligation not to take advantage of indigence in the administration of justice. . . . Denial of counsel to the indigent at the time of interrogation while allowing an attorney to those who can afford one would be no more supportable by reason or logic than the similar situation at trial and on appeal struck down in Gideon v. Wainwright, 372 U.S. 335, 83 S.Ct. 792, 9 L.Ed.2d 799 (1963), and Douglas v. People of State of California, 372 U.S. 353, 83 S.Ct. 814, 9 L.Ed.2d 811 (1963).

In order fully to apprise a person interrogated of the extent of his rights under this system then, it is necessary to warn him not only that he has the right to consult with an attorney, but also that if he is indigent, a lawyer will be appointed to represent him. Without this additional warning, the admonition of the right to consult with counsel would often be understood as meaning only that he can consult with a lawyer if he has one or has the funds to obtain one. The warning of a right to counsel would be hollow if not couched in terms that would convey to the indigent—the person most often subjected to interrogation—the knowledge that he too has a right to have counsel present. . . . As with the warnings of the right to remain silent and of the general right to counsel, only by effective and express explanation to the indigent of this right can there be assurance that he was truly in a position to exercise it. . . .

Case Question

With the mass media communicating the "right to remain silent" in criminal situations, why is it still required for police officers to give this warning?

The Sixth Amendment: Speedy Trial, Impartial Jury, Confrontation

Speedy trial by an impartial jury.   In the past, the Supreme Court has determined that a speedy trial is absolutely necessary to due process.[24] Therefore, a speedy trial must be included in the due process definition of the Fourteenth Amendment. However, the Court has just as adamantly refused to consider a standard test to determine whether a trial has or has not been provided quickly enough. The Court recognizes that different types of criminal cases require different amounts of preparation and investigation. Therefore, as long as the time for preparation is reasonable and trial is available, the Sixth Amendment right will have been honored.

The Court has established certain criteria for determining whether the Sixth Amendment right has been honored. When it is alleged that the right to a speedy trial has been violated, the Supreme Court has provided a four-factor test that judges may employ to determine whether the allegation is true. Judges should examine (1) the actual time of the delay from arrest to trial; (2) the reasons the government has cited as a basis for the delay; (3) whether the defendant, at any time prior to trial, requested a speedy trial; and (4) whether the delay caused any harm to the defendant. The harm can include problems for the defense, such as unavailability of witnesses after a long period of time, lengthened detention if no bail was granted, or any other detriment to the defendant that would have been avoided by a speedy trial.

The guarantee of a speedy trial takes effect only upon the actual indictment for a crime. Prior to the formal charge, the prosecution is free to investigate at length before determining that there is sufficient evidence to charge a defendant. Once this evidence has been accumulated, the prosecution is obligated to make the decision of whether to prosecute. If the decision is made not to prosecute, the investigation may continue, and charges may be brought later. It is required only that there be reason for the delay other than to impair the defendant's ability to obtain evidence to be used in defense.

 CASE

MAINE v. O'HARA

627 A.2d 1001
(ME 1993).

ROBERTS, Justice.

Roy O'Hara appeals from a judgment entered on a jury verdict in the Superior Court convicting him of manslaughter . . . Because the trial court denied O'Hara's request that prospective jurors be questioned further about their relationships with the State's law enforcement witnesses, we vacate the conviction.

At the end of June 1990, Roy O'Hara, a self-described novice with guns, was given a .38 caliber revolver by his wife's grandmother to protect those living in their Norway home from a neighbor who had made serious threats against members of the household. On the evening of July 3, 1990, several people, including Brad Glickman, were gathered in O'Hara's television room playing Nintendo and talking. Shortly after midnight a noise from the outside was heard. Fearing that it might be the neighbor, O'Hara cocked his gun and went outside to investigate. When his search revealed no intruder, O'Hara returned inside and began talking with Glickman. During the conversation, Glickman asked if he could see O'Hara's gun. As O'Hara was handing the gun to Glickman, it fired and the bullet struck Glickman in the chest. Glickman died a short time later.

After O'Hara was indicted for manslaughter, he filed a motion to suppress statements he made to the State Police investigator on the ground that they were involuntary, and to suppress his testimony before the grand jury on the ground that it was tainted by his prior involuntary statements. After a hearing, the court (Brodrick, J.) granted the motion to suppress as it related to the police interrogation, but denied the motion as it related to the grand jury testimony.

I.

At the trial of this case, during JURY selection, the court conducted a general VOIR DIRE in which it asked if any members of the JURY panel "have a familiarity with" any of the prospective witnesses in the case. Seven members of the panel responded in the affirmative that they were "familiar with" or "recognized" some of the law enforcement witnesses. The court then asked each of the seven potential jurors whether the fact that they "were familiar with" or "recognized" those witnesses would cause them to believe they would have any difficulty being impartial. Each of the jurors responded in the negative. Later, the court established that no juror had a family member who is currently engaged in law enforcement. The court also asked whether any members of the panel believed that law enforcement officers have greater credibility than lay witnesses. No affirmative responses were received. Finally, the court asked whether any of the prospective jurors could think of any reason, not addressed by the court, why they could not be fair and objective jurors. Again, no affirmative responses were received.

At the conclusion of its general voir dire, the court asked whether the parties had any challenges for cause. O'Hara challenged for cause the seven jurors who had indicated a familiarity with some law enforcement witnesses or, in the alternative, requested further questioning of those jurors regarding their precise relationships with those witnesses. The court denied O'Hara's challenges for cause, as well as his request for further questioning. O'Hara then used five of his nine peremptory challenges to strike potential jurors who had been the subject of his challenges for cause. At the conclusion of the jury selection, O'Hara objected to the jury as selected because of the denial of his request for further questioning.

The purpose of VOIR DIRE is "to detect bias and prejudice in prospective jurors" to ensure that the defendant is tried "by as fair and impartial a JURY as possible." State v. Lovely, 451 A.2d 900, 901 (ME 1982).

To that end, M.R.Crim.P. 24(a) provides:

The parties or their attorneys may conduct the examination of the prospective jurors unless the court elects to conduct an initial examination itself. If the court elects to conduct an initial examination, when that examination is completed the court shall permit the parties or their attorneys to address additional questions to the prospective jurors on any subject which has not been fully covered in the court's examination and which is germane to the jurors' qualifications.

O'Hara contends that the court erred in denying his request to question further the potential jurors concerning their relationships with the law enforcement witnesses. We agree. The mere fact that the jurors stated they could be fair, notwithstanding their familiarity with the law enforcement witnesses, is no substitute for knowing the precise relationship between each juror and each of the prospective witnesses. While it is true, as the State notes, that we have held that a personal, social, or familial relationship with a law enforcement officer will not by itself support a challenge for cause, see State v. Heald, 443 A.2d 954, 956 (Me. 1982), we have never held that such a relationship with a law enforcement officer expected to testify as a witness would not support a challenge for cause. When, as here, members of the jury panel have indicated a familiarity with law enforcement witnesses, the trial court must conduct or permit further questioning concerning the precise nature of potential jurors' relationships with those witnesses. Only after such further questioning will the court have an adequate factual basis to rule on a challenge of those jurors for cause. In effect, the court in this case permitted each juror to be the judge of his or her own qualifications. . .

The entry is:

Judgment vacated.

Remanded for further proceedings consistent with the opinion herein.

All concurring.

Case Question

What is the purpose of voir dire and how was that purpose thwarted in the trial of this case?

Assignment 13.2

Examine the following situation and determine whether the defendant received the right to a speedy trial: SITUATION: Anne has been charged with theft from her employer. She was charged in January and asked for a speedy trial. At the time of her arrest, all pertinent records had been turned over to the police by her employer. At a preliminary hearing, Anne's employer asked to examine the records. The state gave copies of the records to Anne's attorney on May 1. Trial was set for July 1. On June 15, the state prosecutor was arrested for drug use. A new prosecutor was appointed who asked for a continuance of the trial date, which was reset to August 15. On August 1, the judge in the case died of a heart attack, and a new judge was not assigned to the case until August 13. The new judge continued all cases for ninety days while she disposed of the case-load she already had. Anne's new trial date was November 15. On

November 15, a terrible snowstorm hit the area, and all court cases were delayed. Anne was given a new trial date of January 6.

The right to a trial by jury has been incorporated into the definition of due process along with the other provisions of the Sixth Amendment. However, it is subject to limitation. The accused is not guaranteed a trial by jury in what are considered to be petty offenses. What comprises a petty offense is defined by state law but usually includes cases in which no jail time (loss of liberty) is at risk. The number of jurors (six to twelve) has been left up to state law. Similarly, whether the conviction must be by a unanimous jury is also determined by state law. However, federal criminal prosecutions require a jury of twelve and a verdict by unanimous consent.

It is a further requirement of the Fifth Amendment that the jury be composed of impartial peers. Therefore, the defendant has the right to be judged free from bias such as racial, religious, or sexual discrimination by jurors. The voir dire process is used by the defendant and counsel to eliminate those jurors who would add such bias to influence their verdict.

Critical Stage

Stage of a criminal proceeding in which the presumed innocence of the accused is in jeopardy and therefore the accused is entitled to representation of counsel.

Right of confrontation.   Also included in the Sixth Amendment (and in the definition of what constitutes due process under the Fourteenth Amendment) is the right to confront one's accusers. It is inherent in American law that before a person can be convicted on the basis of statements made by others, the person must be given the opportunity to face and challenge the statements of his or her accusers. Because not every person accused of a crime can adequately confront his or her accuser, this has been determined to be a **critical stage** in the prosecution that requires assistance of counsel. This includes pretrial procedures, such as identification and confrontation upon testimony at trial. The rationale is that the defendant should be given every opportunity to expose errors or irregularities in testimony of witnesses for the prosecution.

 APPLICATION 13.3

Nate was charged with assault and battery on fellow student Carlos, who claimed that he and Nate argued and that Nate struck him several times. Nate contends that Carlos concocted the story in an attempt to have Nate disqualified from his position on the college student senate. (Carlos had placed second to Nate in a recent college election.) Nate wants to confront Carlos to challenge the details of Carlos's accusations.

Point for Discussion

In cases such as drug trials, where the witness fears retaliation, is it possible to allow the witness to remain unidentified to the defendant and still protect the right of confrontation?

Right to counsel.   Subsequent to *Miranda,* the Court held that for protection of several necessary rights (such as the right to not incriminate or assist in the prosecution against oneself), counsel must be available at all points in a prosecution where there is opportunity for unfairness or where untrustworthy evidence may be obtained. Later decisions have identified these stages of prosecution as interrogation or questioning, identification procedures, first court appearance where action may be taken against the defendant, preliminary hearing or grand jury, arraignment, trial, sentencing, and probation revocation hearings. Various rights in addition to those in the Fifth Amendment have been interpreted to require this as part of the due process guarantee in the Fourteenth Amendment. The result has been that each state must follow these requirements in its own state laws and prosecutions.

Unless there are compelling circumstances, any accused is entitled to have an attorney present at the time a witness is asked to identify the accused as the one who committed a crime. Compelling circumstances would include situations that make it unreasonable to wait for an attorney to be present. Additionally, if a witness is shown only photographs of potential defendants, neither the defendant nor defendant's counsel has the right to be present. The right to assistance of counsel is considered to be necessary to aid the defendant in adequately responding to charges of a witness. Because there is little room for unfairness or prejudice in identifying a photograph, disallowing the presence of the defendant or counsel at this procedure is considered to do no harm to due process.

 APPLICATION 13.4

A mugging crime was interrupted. The police detained the perpetrator at the scene. In this type of situation, it is permissible for the victim to make the identification at that time.

Point for Discussion
Why is availability of counsel not required at the crime scene identification?

The Supreme Court has also found that the right to assistance of counsel occurs only after the defendant has been charged with a crime and the prosecution has commenced.[25] Therefore, if a person is asked to take part in a lineup or other form of identification procedure prior to arrest, no right to assistance of counsel attaches. The point has been raised that most law enforcement agencies are encouraged to conduct identification procedures before charging the defendant and thus avoid the necessity of counsel. This is not seen as a particularly significant issue, however. First, the individual has the right to refuse to appear voluntarily in the lineup. Secondly, if the procedure is conducted in an unfair manner that unduly suggests the suspect to witnesses as the criminal, the suspect (subsequently the defendant) has the opportunity to allege this at trial. If proven, the evidence of the identification of the defendant will be inadmissible.

Often, without a witness to identify the defendant as the one who committed the crime, a prosecution is unsuccessful. Therefore, police have the incentive to ensure that lineups are fairly conducted even before a defendant is formally charged with a crime.

The Eighth Amendment: Bail, Cruel and Unusual Punishment

The Eighth Amendment has also been clearly drawn into the Fourteenth Amendment definition of due process. The issues involve that of bail and freedom from cruel and unusual punishment.

Bail.   The Supreme Court has specifically addressed the issue of bail, the term used to describe release from custody during the time between arrest and conviction. Generally, the court asks for some guarantee or assurance that the defendant will not flee or commit other crimes if released. This assurance is the type or amount of bail that is required.[26] The Eighth Amendment guarantee against excessive bail has been integrated into the Fourteenth Amendment and applied to the states in an attempt to prevent the unwarranted detention and deprivation of liberty of accused persons prior to trial.

Many jurisdictions have specified amounts of bail that are predetermined for misdemeanors. In many states, if a person is charged with a traffic violation, the person's permanent driver's license will be accepted as bail. The license is then returned if the accused is found innocent or is given another penalty upon conviction. If the charges are minor, a specific dollar amount may be posted with the police to obtain release until a hearing is conducted. In other cases, the persons charged must remain in custody until they have an opportunity to appear before a judge or magistrate. Usually, this is within a matter of hours or, at most, a few days. The judge will determine what is an appropriate assurance or, in some instances, may even release the persons on their word that they will reappear at the formal hearing on the charges against them. The latter is known as being released on one's own recognizance, or O.R. In serious cases, and when there is reason to believe the accused will commit other crimes or flee the jurisdiction, the court may deny bail entirely and detain the person until trial.

The Eighth Amendment states that bail will not be excessive. A person is considered innocent until proven guilty in this country. Therefore, until proven guilty at a trial, the rationale is that accused persons should be allowed to continue their lives, earn a living, and reside with their families. Just as the circumstances vary with every case, however, so do the considerations of what would be excessive bail. For minor offenses, it is relatively assured that most persons will appear at trial. Therefore, bail may be a predetermined amount for all persons charged with those offenses. For serious crimes where the penalty upon a finding of guilt may be severe, the temptation to avoid a trial and possible sentencing by fleeing the jurisdiction is much greater. Additionally, many of the accused in these cases have criminal backgrounds. Thus, the likelihood that they will continue to commit crime while on bail is much greater.

The Eighth Amendment has been drawn into the definition of the Fourteenth Amendment on the basis of the general concept of due process.[27] The Supreme Court has reasoned that pretrial detention because bail is not allowed, or because it is so excessive that it effectively prevents an accused person from posting it, could be a deprivation of liberty without due process of law (essentially, a sentence of imprisonment prior to a trial). Thus, the factors that are considered in determining bail and the amount of bail that is required should be directly related.

The function of the courts in determining bail is to set an amount that will reasonably assure the appearance of the accused at trial.[28] If the judge determines that this cannot be assured by a sum of money and that a person should not be released on bail, the judge must make a very clear statement in the court record of reasons that support this decision.[29] The presumption is that all persons should have an opportunity to be released on bail. Therefore, this can be denied only in compelling circumstances.

The courts must consider several factors when determining bail, including but not limited to the following:

1. The past criminal history of the accused.
2. The past bail history of the accused.
3. The accused's connections to the community (such as job, family, and home).
4. The danger posed to the community by the accused.
5. The likelihood the accused will flee from the jurisdiction.

If enough of these factors or other considerations convince the court that the accused is likely to commit crimes or flee the jurisdiction, the court is justified in denying bail entirely. This does not constitute an improper violation of the individual right to due process, because the government interest in protecting the public is considered to be greater. This goes back to the traditional balance that courts try to achieve: the good of the individual versus the good of the people.

More often, the court is faced with a case that falls into a gray area. Although some factors are present that raise concern about the accused's conduct on bail release, the evidence is not sufficient to warrant holding the accused in custody until trial. In such cases, the judicial officer must make a determination of what amount of bail is reasonable to assure that the accused will not commit crimes or flee the jurisdiction. The court must also consider what amount the accused can reasonably be expected to post as assurance that he or she will appear for trial.

In questions of bail, there is a wide berth for judicial discretion. The decision must be made on a case-by-case basis, and every individual accused presents a unique situation to the court. Therefore, for more serious crimes, there is generally no set rule for the amount of bail a court will require. The court must consider all the evidence before it on this question and exercise its best judgment. As long as a higher court can find that a determination of bail falls somewhere within a range of reasonableness, the initial determination of bail will not be altered.

Assignment 13.3

Contact your local law enforcement agency (e.g., police station) and inquire as to what charges carry automatic bail terms (e.g., driver's license for moving violations).

Cruel and unusual punishment.   This guarantee of the Eighth Amendment protects all citizens from punishment deemed to be excessive or inappropriate for the crime committed according to societal standards. What defines cruel and unusual has gone through dramatic change in our nation's history consistent with the changes in our society.

Essentially, the Supreme Court has defined due process to include the protection of the Eighth Amendment with regard to the imposition of sentence. However, the Court has been somewhat reluctant to state specifics with regard to what constitutes such punishment. The Court has gone so far as to prohibit "barbaric" punishment or punishment that is excessive for the crime. Further, it has upheld the death penalty, refusing to categorize it as cruel and unusual. Part of the rationale of the Court for its position on the death penalty is that the penalty is approved by a significant majority of the states. This, in turn, supposedly reflects the belief of a majority of people that capital punishment is acceptable and appropriate. While the death penalty continues to be a topic of debate at the state level and the subject of many protests, until these laws are changed to reflect a changing society, it is unlikely that the Court will reverse its position.

Figure 13.1 lists the constitutional guarantees in the Bill of Rights and highlights those guarantees that have been included in the definition of due process.

THE STAGES OF CRIMINAL PROCEDURE

An understanding of the rights of accused persons in the criminal process allows a much clearer sense of the reasons for the various stages through which an accused must pass. These stages are all designed with the intent that every citizen shall have every available opportunity to have his or her conduct judged fairly without undue influence or unfair criticism. The following discussion of the actual stages of criminal procedure uses many of the examples already used in the discussion of the rights of the accused to illustrate the role these rights play in the criminal process.

Pre-Arrest

Generally, before an arrest is made and a defendant is charged with a crime, the law enforcement agencies will attempt to obtain sufficient evidence to warrant the arrest and the conviction. In fact, a standard of all arrests is that the arresting officer had probable cause to believe the suspect had committed a crime.[30] Generally, probable cause is established through introduction of evidence that connects the accused to the crime.

Right to privacy.   Many times, after or during the commission of a crime, the police look for evidence that will lead them to the person or persons who committed the crime. However, the constitutional rights guaranteed by the Fourth Amendment prevent the police from rampantly searching among members of the public and their belongings. Such searching would violate all rights of privacy and notions of fairness. The police are entitled to obtain whatever evidence exists publicly, but before they may delve into private property and dwellings, they must establish that there is probable cause to believe evidence of a crime exists there.

I. Establishment of religion.
    Free exercise of speech.
    Free exercise of press.
    Peaceable assembly.
    Petition of government for redress of grievances.
II. Well-regulated militia.
    Keep and bear arms.
III. To exclude soldiers from homes in times of peace and in times of war except as prescribed by law.
IV. **To be secure against unreasonable search and seizure and that no warrants shall be issued without probable cause.**
V. No civilian shall be tried for capital crimes except upon grand jury indictment.
    No one shall be subjected to double jeopardy.
    No one shall be compelled to be a witness against himself.
    No one shall be deprived of life, liberty or property without due process of law.
    No private property shall be taken for public use without just compensation.
VI. **Right to a speedy and public trial by an impartial jury.**
    To be informed of the nature and cause of the accusation.
    To confront witnesses for the prosecution.
    To have compulsory process to obtain witnesses in one's favor.
    To have assistance of counsel in one's defense.
VII. Right to jury trial in common law actions valued greater than $20.
    Jury determinations of fact are subject only to appeal in accordance with rules of common law.
VIII. **No excessive bail.**
    No excessive fines.
    No cruel and unusual punishments.
IX. No rights in the Constitution shall be used to deny other rights.
X. Powers not delegated to the U.S. or prohibited by the Constitution are reserved to the states.

*Rights affecting criminal procedure are underlined. Rights that have been integrated into the definition of due process through selective incorporation are in boldface type.

FIGURE 13.1
Bill of Rights Constitutional Guarantees*

As indicated earlier in the chapter, items or occurrences in public view do not require probable cause, because it would be unreasonable for a person to consider such things private. Such items include things that are on private property but can be viewed from outside the property. It is also permissible to use the assistance of such items as binoculars. If the item only enhances natural ability, it is acceptable.

In addition, individuals do not have a right to privacy with regard to such matters as the phone numbers they have called. No one can reasonably expect that the phone company will not be allowed to know what numbers are called from a private telephone. Indeed, these records are necessary to the phone company's business. Therefore, since this is common knowledge to a third party, such as the phone company, individuals should not expect that no other third party could obtain the information. Thus, phone registers, which record the numbers called from a private phone, require no showing of probable cause. Nor do conversations made on public telephones. There can be no reasonable expectation of privacy in the use of public facilities.

Before the police may enter the private property of an individual, they must have probable cause to suspect a connection between the property and the crime committed. As stated earlier, the police must have more than mere suspicion. They must have access to other evidence or testimony that would indicate the likelihood of criminal activity. For example, the police may have information from informants who have had contact with the person or persons suspected of criminal activity and can provide specific information regarding their conduct (such as phone conversations about the crimes) or the exact location of criminal evidence. If the police have conducted surveillance of the persons or property and have discovered highly suspicious activities taking place, a court may find probable cause.

Search warrant.   If a court finds that there is probable cause to suspect that evidence of a crime exists in or on private property, it will issue an appropriate search warrant. Search warrants must be specific concerning the objective, location, and scope of the search.[31] If, for example, the warrant is issued to determine whether the suspects are discussing crimes on the telephone, only wiretaps on the telephones may be placed. If the warrant is issued to search the premises for evidence of a crime, only the premises can be searched, and no wiretaps would be allowed. The requirement that warrants be specific prevents unreasonable invasions of privacy by some overzealous law enforcement officers.

Plain view rule.   What happens if a search is being conducted for specific evidence and evidence of other criminal activity is discovered? This falls under the plain view rule. If police are lawfully on property (public, with consent, or with a search warrant) and discover evidence of any crime in plain view, that evidence can be used against its owners in a criminal prosecution.

Arrest warrant.   If the police can demonstrate to the court that there is enough criminal evidence to support a conviction, the court will issue an arrest warrant. When the warrant is issued, the police have the authority to take the defendant into custody and make initial criminal charges. At this point, the defendant's constitutional protection against being deprived of life or liberty without due process of law becomes a concern of law enforcement personnel.

In certain situations, no search or arrest warrant is required. In such special circumstances, police have the authority to stop, search, and, if necessary, make an arrest. If there is probable cause to believe that individuals are committing—or have in the immediate past committed—a crime, the police have the authority to stop these individuals. When the individuals are stopped, the police have the authority to pat them down and search areas within their reach to determine whether anything is available that the individuals could use to harm the officers. The police then have the option of questioning the persons and releasing them, or if probable cause exists, the persons can be placed under arrest, and the property in their immediate reach can be searched.

Grand Jury
A number of individuals (often more than twenty) who review the evidence to determine whether the defendant could be convicted of the crime if charged and tried.

Grand jury.   Another method used in federal criminal prosecutions and some states for prosecutions of serious crimes is the **grand jury,** which consists of twenty or more citizens who, for a period of approximately six months, hear evidence of criminal activity in various cases presented by the prosecution. The duty of the grand jury is to determine whether there is enough evidence to prosecute someone for a crime. A grand jury proceeding often occurs even before an initial arrest has been made.

Much of the evidence the grand jury hears has been obtained through government investigation, the use of various search warrants, and the testimony of informants or other persons with relevant information. Suspects have no absolute right to appear at grand jury proceedings or to introduce evidence. The purpose of such proceedings is solely to determine whether enough evidence exists that a jury <u>could</u> find a person guilty of criminal conduct.

If the grand jury finds that sufficient evidence exists to formally charge an individual with a crime, it will issue an indictment ("in-dite-ment"), which gives authority to arrest and charge the individual with the crime. An indictment operates in much the same fashion as an arrest warrant issued by a judge. After apprehension, the person is taken into custody and advised of his or her rights. At that point, the stages of actual prosecution begin.

Arrest and Interrogation

Arrestee's rights. Persons who are initially arrested must be advised of their basic rights upon arrest.[32] They must be told that they have the right to remain silent; that anything they say can and will be used against them in a court of law; that they have the right to an attorney; and that if they cannot afford an attorney, one will be appointed for them at no cost. Law enforcement agencies are making it a common practice to require all arrestees to sign a statement indicating that they have been notified of and understand their rights. These written statements have greatly reduced the number of arrestees who claim they were never advised of their rights or that the advisement came after they had incriminated themselves.

Interrogation. After an arrest, the law enforcement officers and prosecutors may question (interrogate) the accused about the crime with which he or she is charged. Identification proceedings, such as lineups, where the victims or witnesses to the crime are asked to identify the alleged criminal from a group of persons, may also take place.

The arrestee has the right to have an attorney present to ensure that identification proceedings are not conducted in a way that would unduly influence the victims or witnesses to name the accused.[33] For example, if the police have information from a witness that the suspect was of a particular race and present a lineup of persons of other races except for the actual suspect, the witness would have no choice but to indicate the actual suspect as the criminal. Such an identification proceeding is unfair. Lineups must be conducted in such a way that they truly test the ability of the witness to identify the criminal.

Many law enforcement agencies avoid the necessity of providing attorneys for all those who are suspected of criminal activity. Instead, the police ask the individual prior to arrest to answer questions voluntarily or to take part in an identification proceeding. If the individual voluntarily complies, the police have complete consent and do not have to advise the person of his or her rights or provide counsel. The individual does, however, have the right to obtain his or her own counsel or to refuse to cooperate. An exception occurs when a grand jury issues a subpoena to the individual. In that situation, the person is required to appear to be questioned but may avoid answering on the basis of the Fifth Amendment guarantee against self-incrimination.

Confession. A particular concern arises when an arrestee confesses to a crime. At this point, law enforcement personnel are under a particular duty to establish that the individual was not coerced in any way or misled into an involuntary confession. It must be established that the confession was given freely and without undue influence. Further, it must be shown that the individual understood the possible consequences of a confession.[34] Increasingly, law enforcement agencies are establishing that a confession was made in fair circumstances by videotaping it. This is relatively inexpensive compared to the cost of trying the issue of a confession in court. Also, when a confession is videotaped and the court can actually observe the circumstances under which it was made, a defendant is much less likely to claim that it was unfairly obtained unless such circumstances truly existed.

Bail

Shortly after arrest, the accused person is entitled to request release from custody prior to trial in exchange for bail. Bail—or bond, as it is sometimes called—is the amount paid to the court as an assurance that the suspect will not flee the jurisdiction or commit additional crimes prior to trial. It operates as an insurance policy against such conduct by the accused.

Many persons utilize the services of bail bondsmen. For a fee, the bondsman will issue a bond to the court stating that if the accused flees the jurisdiction or commits a crime while the prosecution is pending, the bondsman will be responsible for the entire amount of bail. The bondsman acts as a sort of insurance company that issues the policy for the accused. If the accused violates the terms of the bail release and flees or commits a crime, the bondsman has the right to be reimbursed by the accused.

A method utilized when larger amounts of bail are imposed is payment of 10 percent of the amount of bail. Many jurisdictions allow the accused to make this 10 percent payment. If the accused then violates the terms of the bail release, full payment is required, and the accused will be taken back into custody.

The decision of how much bail to require—or whether to grant release on bail at all—is generally left to the discretion of the judge. The judge has the duty to determine (1) what would be a reasonable amount to assure the court of the accused's good conduct and presence at future hearings and (2) what is within the means of the defendant to pay. Although these two factors are balanced against each other, the more important factor is, of course, the first.[35]

If the judge determines that no amount would be assurance that the accused will not leave the jurisdiction or commit other crimes, bail may be denied. To be justified, this usually requires substantial evidence that the accused has ignored court orders in the past or has engaged in other conduct that would indicate a likelihood that bail would be ignored.

Another option is to require no security at all in the form of bail for release. When this occurs, as previously mentioned, the person is released on his or her own recognizance. The judge makes a finding that the person's contacts to the community, such as family and work, are strong enough to prevent the person from fleeing the jurisdiction. Further, there must be evidence that the person is not likely to commit additional crimes. Release on one's own recognizance is issued most often when the charge is less serious or when it is the person's first criminal offense.

Once the issue of bail has been determined, the accused is either released or returned to the physical custody of law enforcement personnel. The next stage of prosecution is the preliminary hearing.

Preliminary Hearing and Arraignment

Shortly after arrest, a preliminary hearing is scheduled. At this time, the defendant and the prosecution appear for a decision by the judge of whether sufficient admissible evidence exists to warrant further prosecution. The prosecution introduces evidence of the defendant's guilt. The defendant has the opportunity to challenge the admissibility of this evidence under the exclusionary rule. Generally, the defendant is not allowed to introduce evidence of defense. The burden is on the prosecutor to prove that a finding of guilty is possible. The purpose of the preliminary hearing is simply to determine whether there is enough admissible evidence to meet this burden. Since no conviction can result at this stage, there is no need for a defense at this point.

If the court finds that insufficient evidence exists that would be admissible in court, the case will be dismissed and all charges will be dropped. In the event the court finds sufficient evidence to prosecute, the court will arrange an **arraignment** and schedule the case for trial. In less serious matters, the stages of bail, preliminary hearing, and arraignment may be combined into a single proceeding. In more complex cases, each side must prepare a presentation for the various issues, and the three stages are scheduled separately.

Arraignment
Stage of a criminal proceeding in which the accused is formally charged.

Arraignment follows the preliminary hearing. At this stage, defendants are informed of the actual charge of which they are accused and for which they will be tried, and the charge is recorded in the court files. Often this charge is related to, but different from, the charge for which the defendant was initially arrested. This occurs because some evidence may have been excluded by the court or because additional evidence has been accumulated since the time of arrest. Either of these developments may affect the ability of the prosecution to prove guilt on a particular charge. Thus, the charge may be modified. Another possibility is that during the preliminary hearing the judge will determine that there is insufficient evidence for one charge but adequate evidence for another. In that event, the judge will order that the latter be the basis for prosecution.

During arraignment, the defendant is formally advised of the crime charged. Bail may also be reviewed by the court at this time. It may be increased, decreased, or withdrawn, with the accused placed back into custody. Most importantly, the defendant pleads on the issue of guilt at the arraignment.

Typically, a defendant pleads one of three ways. If the plea is guilty, the defendant is making an admission of responsibility for the crime committed. Thus, there is no need for a trial to prove guilt, and the procedure moves directly to sentencing. If the plea is not guilty, the court will schedule a trial date. At trial, the prosecution will attempt to prove the guilt of the defendant beyond a reasonable doubt. The third type of plea sometimes accepted by a court is nolo contendere, also known as no contest. This plea means that the defendant will not plead guilty but will raise no defense to the claims of the prosecutor. In essence, the defendant takes the position, "I am not saying I am guilty or innocent, but I will not defend myself at trial or challenge a conviction."

As a result of a nolo contendere plea, the defendant has no recorded confession of guilt, but no trial is required for a finding of guilt. Sentencing occurs immediately after this plea, just as it would upon a plea of guilty. Many times, a defendant will plead nolo contendere in a situation where someone injured by the crime may bring a civil suit against the defendant in addition to the criminal charge. If a defendant pleads nolo contendere, the injured party in a civil trial cannot introduce an admission of guilt for the act that caused the injury. Thus, it may be in the defendant's interest to plead nolo contendere in the criminal suit to increase his or her chances of success as a defendant in a civil suit.

 APPLICATION 13.5

Luz and Felipe are involved in a car accident. Luz is ticketed for running a red light. Felipe sues Luz in a civil suit for the injuries he received in the accident and the property damage to his car. If Luz pleads guilty to the traffic ticket, Felipe can introduce her plea as evidence of her admitted guilt for the conduct that allegedly caused the accident. If Luz pleads no contest or challenges the ticket, claiming innocence (even if she is subsequently found guilty), no evidence of the ticket can be introduced in the civil suit. (In most jurisdictions the rules of evidence prohibit any disclosure of criminal activity unless it is a felony conviction with a minimum penalty [usually ten years]. However, if the defendant pleads guilty in a court to an act that is also the subject of litigation in another court, that admission of guilt can be introduced for the limited purpose of demonstrating that the defendant admits to the conduct.)

Point for Discussion
Why is a plea of no contest inadmissible?

Plea bargaining.   For a number of reasons, plea bargaining has become an integral part of the criminal process. Plea bargaining occurs when the prosecution agrees to a lesser charge or a reduced sentence in exchange for a plea of guilty by the defendant. The benefit to the defendant is that he or she will not have to stand trial and face the possibility of a more serious conviction and/or penalty. The government is saved the expense of a trial and, perhaps more importantly, is able to impose a penalty on the defendant in some degree. When the prosecution is required to go to trial, the burden of proof is so severe that there is always the possibility of acquittal.

Trial, Appeal, and Sentencing

The crucial stage of any prosecution is the trial. At this point, the trier of fact—usually the jury—will determine the guilt or innocence of the defendant based on the evidence of the prosecution. Guilt must be established beyond a reasonable doubt. In practical terms, this means that one who considers the situation logically and rationally must have no doubt that the defendant committed the crime with which he or she is charged. Guilt cannot be based on prejudice or bias or pure circumstance. There must be no other reasonable explanation than that the accused committed the crime.

This burden of proof is quite severe to ensure that innocent individuals will not be convicted because of questionable circumstances. In the American legal system, individuals are considered innocent until proven guilty. Furthermore, they cannot be compelled to testify about information that might incriminate them. Some defendants, regardless of innocence, simply are not effective witnesses in a criminal prosecution because they do not communicate well, and they do their defense more harm than good by attempting to tell their story to the trier of fact. For this reason, a defendant is not required to testify at trial. Further, a jury may not consider such a refusal to testify as evidence of guilt. The evidence of guilt must be established by the prosecutor.

If the trier of fact determines that the prosecution has met its burden, a conviction will result. If the burden is not met, the charges are dismissed, and the defendant is released from further proceedings. Upon dismissal, bail is returned to the defendant if its terms were not violated during the prosecution. Upon a conviction, bail may be returned, or it may be applied to a fine imposed as a penalty for a conviction.

After conviction, the court may sentence the defendant immediately, or sentencing may be scheduled for a later time. In some instances, a jury is asked to impose the sentence on the defendant. This usually occurs in very serious cases that require much thought and consideration of the circumstances of the crime, for example, a capital offense where the sentence could be death. The reasoning is that in such a serious matter, several of one's peers can determine just punishment as well as or better than a single judge. The prosecution and defense are both allowed to introduce evidence that will enable a fair sentence to be imposed based on all of the circumstances. Such factors include the state of mind of the defendant, such as malice or premeditation, and the extent of the criminal conduct, such as extreme violence. Other factors, such as intelligence, maturity, or likelihood of rehabilitation, may also affect sentencing.

If a defendant chooses to appeal, it is up to the trial court to determine whether the defendant will be released during the appeal. In more serious cases, the defendant is usually required to begin serving the sentence, because appeals can take a very long time. Further, after conviction and sentencing, a defendant may be very tempted to flee the jurisdiction. If an appeal is successful and the conviction is overturned, the defendant is not entitled to any compensation for time served or inconvenience caused by the prosecution of the crime. In most of these cases, a new trial is granted and the procedure starts over again. A defendant who is granted a new trial is treated as if the first trial never occurred. Therefore, the sentence can be greater or lesser if conviction is obtained a second time.

Assignment 13.4

Evaluate the following case and diagram the likely results under the various types of pleas: Rhonda is charged with motor vehicle homicide, a felony with a possible penalty of five years' imprisonment. A victim of the accident that resulted in Rhonda's being charged has died. The prosecutor has offered Rhonda a plea bargain agreement. Under the agreement, Rhonda would plead guilty to drunken driving and reckless driving. Her penalty would be two years in prison. A civil suit is also now pending against Rhonda for the death of the victim.

CASE

SMITH v. ARKANSAS

1997 WL 607109
(Ark. 1997).

CORBIN, Associate Justice.

Appellant Anthony David Smith appeals the JUDGMENT of the Marion County Circuit Court convicting him of the capital murder of his wife Christine Smith and sentencing him to life imprisonment without the possibility of parole. Our jurisdiction is pursuant to Ark. Sup.Ct. R. 1- 2(a)(2). Appellant raises two points for reversal, namely that the trial court erred in failing to grant his motion for mistrial due to the prosecutor's comments during opening statement on his right to remain silent. . . We find no error and affirm.

In the early morning hours of October 6, 1994, officers and medical personnel responded to a call from the Smith residence concerning a possible drowning. At the scene, they found thirty-two-year-old Christine Smith wet and lying on her back on a wooden deck next to the family's swimming pool. She had blood coming from the back of her head and out of her nose and mouth. Her body was sent to the Arkansas State Medical Examiner's Office for an autopsy, where it was determined that Mrs. Smith had died as the result of both a contact gunshot wound to the back of her head and strangulation. Appellant was subsequently arrested and convicted for the capital murder of his wife and sentenced to life imprisonment.

I. Prosecutor's Remarks on Appellant's Right to Remain Silent

For his first point for reversal, Appellant argues that the trial court erred in failing to declare a mistrial due to the following remarks made by the prosecutor in opening statement:

"The presentation of this case which you're going to hear about are the events, primarily, of the early morning of the 6th day of October, 1994. And the thing that you have to realize is that, from the start of this, Mr. Smith was the only person alive who was present. He's the only

person alive who was present on the scene. On that morning, he got an opportunity then and he will get an opportunity in this courtroom, through the tapes and the other evidence we'll introduce, to present what he claims happened.

The prosecutor then went on to recite what he expected the State's evidence would prove during the course of the trial, including the substance of a taped interview that Appellant gave to police that same day. At the conclusion of the prosecutor's opening statement, Appellant moved for a mistrial on the ground that the remarks amounted to an improper reference to his right to remain silent. The trial judge denied the motion because he did not believe the reference to be significant.

On appeal, Appellant contends that the prosecutor's remarks violated his rights under the Fifth Amendment to the United States Constitution to remain silent and not be compelled to be a witness against himself. Specifically, appellant argues that the remarks emphasized the fact that he was the only person present at the scene and intimated that only his personal testimony could rebut the evidence against him. We do not reach the merits of this argument because Appellant failed to make a contemporaneous objection below. To preserve a point for appeal, a proper objection must be asserted at the first opportunity after the matter to which objection has been made occurs. Asher v. State, 303 Ark. 202, 795 S.W.2d 350 (1990), cert. denied, 98 U.S. 1048, 111 S.Ct. 757, 112 L.Ed.2d 777 (1991). Where the allegation of error concerns a statement made by the prosecutor during argument, the defendant must make an immediate objection to the statement at issue in order to preserve the allegation for appeal. Wallace v. State, 53 Ark.App. 199, 920 S.W.2d 864 (1996):

In Dixon v. State, 310 Ark. 460, 839 S.W.2d 173 (1992), this court held that the appellant's motion for mistrial based upon improper comments made by the prosecutor during opening statement was untimely because it was not made until after the conclusion of appellant's opening statement. This court reasoned that it was proper to deny a motion for a mistrial when the request was not made at the first opportunity, even though the motion had been preceded by two defense objections sustained by the trial court. Id.

Here, the particular comments were made by the prosecutor in the middle of his opening statement. Appellant did not object or move for a mistrial at the time the statements were made; instead, he waited until the prosecutor had finished his entire opening statement before bringing the alleged error to the trial court's attention through his motion for mistrial. Accordingly, it was not error for the trial court to deny the motion as it was untimely made.

II. Exclusion of Expert Testimony

For his second point for reversal, Appellant argues that the trial court erred in excluding the testimony of Carl Rainey as an expert on the subject of firearms. Appellant contends that Rainey, who had years of experience in hunting and using firearms, should have been permitted to testify about this subject.

III. Rule 4-3(h)

In accordance with Rule 4-3(h) of the Arkansas Supreme Court Rules, the record has been reviewed for adverse rulings objected to by Appellant but not argued on appeal, and no such errors were found. For the aforementioned reasons, the JUDGMENT of conviction is affirmed. NEWBERN and THORNTON, JJ., dissent.

NEWBERN, Justice,
Dissenting.

The position taken by the majority in this case takes the contemporaneous-objection rule to a new and dizzying height. I assume the reason for the rule is to assure that an objection or, as in this case, motion for mistrial is made while the facts giving rise to the motion are fresh and the court is in the best possible position to rule on the matter at hand. I can understand the notion that a waiver had occurred in Dixon v. State, 310 Ark. 460, 839 S.W.2d 173 (1992), because the motion for a mistrial was made by the defendant after two objections had been dealt with during the opening statement of the prosecution and after the defendant's opening statement had occurred. It was almost as if the motion for a mistrial were an afterthought.

The holding in Butler Mfg. Co. v. Hughes, 292 Ark. 198, 729 S.W.2d 142 (1987), is that an objection must be made at the time an objectionable

statement occurs during closing argument "so that the trial judge may take such action as is necessary to alleviate any prejudicial effect on the jury." It apparently was our perception that in the case of a closing argument, which often involves reiteration of evidence in great detail, it would be most helpful to avoid confusion by clearing up possible misstatements as they occurred, rather than waiting until the conclusion of an argument which could be quite lengthy. Be that as it may, it is unnecessary to apply that rule to opening statements by counsel which usually amount to no more than an abbreviated prospective summation. In this case, there is no doubt in my mind that the Trial Court could have taken "such action as is necessary to alleviate any prejudicial effect on the jury" at the close of the prosecutor's opening statement, and it would have been no less effective than if taken the moment the objectional reference was made.

While I can tolerate, in the case of a closing argument, a rule that preaches the common courtesy usually accorded to a speaker of allowing him or her to finish a speech, I cannot do so with respect to an opening statement. That is especially so in a case such as this one where that which was said had the potential of casting a taint upon all of the remainder of the trial.

In this case, the mistrial motion came after the prosecution's opening statement in which it was said that "he [Smith] will get an opportunity in this courtroom, through the tapes and other evidence we'll introduce, to present what he claims happened." Unlike the Dixon case, no other objections had been considered, the defense had not made its opening statement, the matter was fresh before the court, and the motion was made. Not only should we consider the merits of the motion, we should reverse the conviction because of the egregious error in declining to grant the motion after the reference to the "opportunity in this courtroom" Smith would have to prove his innocence—a burden no accused need bear. Aaron v. State, 312 Ark. 19, 846 S.W.2d 655 (1993); Bailey v. State, 287 Ark. 183, 697 S.W.2d 110 (1985).

I respectfully dissent.

Case Question
Why is it important to make an objection as soon as the comment objected to is made?

CASE

STATE OF N.C. v. YORK

489 S.E.2d 380 (1997).

LAKE, Justice.

On 2 May 1994, defendant was indicted for first-degree murder and first-degree kidnapping. He was tried capitally to a jury at the 10 July 1995 Criminal Session of Superior Court, Jackson County, Judge J. Marlene Hyatt presiding. The jury found defendant guilty of first-degree kidnapping and guilty of first-degree murder by torture and under the felony murder rule. After a capital sentencing proceeding, the jury recommended a sentence of life imprisonment for the first-degree murder conviction. On 25 July 1995, Judge Hyatt sentenced defendant to a term of life imprisonment for the first-degree murder conviction and to a twelve-year consecutive term of imprisonment for the kidnapping conviction. On the same day, Judge Hyatt arrested judgment on the kidnapping conviction. Defendant appeals to this Court as of right from the first-degree murder conviction.

The State presented evidence tending to show that the defendant, Walter Thomas York, met one of the codefendants, Vickie Fox, when he was fourteen years old and in the eighth grade. Fox was twenty-six years old at the time. Defendant initially went to Fox's trailer, located in the Wike's Trailer Park, to party, drink beer and smoke marijuana. He became sexually involved with Fox and moved in with her soon thereafter. Defendant quit school and began looking for work to help pay the bills. Defendant was illiterate, and Fox took care of any paperwork he needed, such as filling out job applications. Although still married to her husband, Kenneth Fox, who lived in the trailer intermittently, Vickie Fox was sexually involved with several other young men in addition to defendant. She had a reputation for providing alcohol and other things to male college students.

At the time of the events giving rise to this case, as many as thirteen people were living in Fox's three-bedroom, single-wide trailer. Among the residents was the twenty-four-year-old victim, Tony Queen. Fox met Queen and became sexually

involved with him in late 1992. He moved into the trailer after defendant began living there.

On or about 17 March 1994, Vickie Fox's five-year-old daughter, Kendra, told codefendant Michelle Vinson that the victim, Tony Queen, had "messed" with her. When questioned by the defendant, Queen admitted that he had molested Kendra and that he had placed a bottle of soapy water in Vickie's son's crib. The defendant became enraged and hit Queen. That evening, several other residents beat the victim, forced him to drink soapy water and made him sleep in the hall. Over approximately the next two weeks, the residents of the trailer and sundry other acquaintances systematically tortured the victim as punishment for his actions. Although the testimony at trial was conflicting as to who performed the various acts, the torture included: repeated beating and kicking of the victim, shaving his head, scraping the word "faggot" on his arm, attempting to burn a tattoo containing Vickie's name off his arm with a soldering iron, hitting his penis with a billy stick, cutting his throat with a knife, burning his genitals and legs with a torch made from an aerosol can, and forcing him to ingest his own urine. Defendant had a primary role in either the direction or carrying out of the majority of these actions. The victim was restrained in the trailer by a dog collar when the residents were not present, although witnesses testified that Queen was told he could leave the trailer if he so desired.

During the course of this systematic treatment, the residents decided that they needed to stop beating Queen for a while so that his face could heal and he could cash his unemployment check for them. However, after a short while, the residents realized that Queen's face was too injured to heal quickly, so they forged his name and cashed the check themselves. On the night of Queen's death, the residents decided to use the money from Queen's check to go out to eat at Pizza Hut. They placed a dog collar on Queen, taped his feet, gagged his mouth with a cloth and tape, and locked him in a bedroom closet by placing a screwdriver in the door and then nailing the door shut. When they returned, Tony Queen was dead. Several of the residents placed Queen's body in the trunk of Kenneth Fox's car and drove to Toccoa, Georgia, where they dumped his body in the woods. One of the codefendants, Robert Trantham, led authorities to the body.

An autopsy indicated that the victim died as a result of gagging and positional asphyxia. The autopsy revealed that the position in which the victim was placed caused interference with the mechanics of breathing. Pneumonia present in the victim's left lung was also a likely contributor to the victim's death.

In his first assignment of error, defendant contends that the trial court committed plain error by allowing the hearsay testimony of State Bureau of Investigation (SBI) Agent Kevin West regarding blood tests conducted by a serologist at the SBI lab. At trial, Agent West testified that blood tests conducted by serologist Brenda Vissitte showed the presence of the victim's blood in various rooms of the trailer. The purpose of the testimony was to bolster the State's theory that the victim was tortured by establishing, through scientific evidence, that the victim was tortured throughout the trailer. Defendant asserts that the evidence was inadmissible hearsay and improper lay-opinion testimony because the State failed to establish Agent West's competency to analyze and report on the test results in the manner allowed at trial. As a result, defendant argues that the evidence was so prejudicial that he is entitled to a new trial.

We note at the outset that the State concedes the testimony in question was hearsay. However, defendant did not object at trial to the introduction of this evidence. The trial court's admission of this evidence is thus reviewable by this Court only under the plain error rule. State v. Ocasio, 344 N.C. 568, 577, 476 S.E.2d 281, 286 (1996); Plain error is error which was " 'so fundamental as to amount to a miscarriage of justice or which probably resulted in the jury reaching a different verdict than it otherwise would have reached.' " State v. Collins, 334 N.C. 54, 62, 431 S.E.2d 188, 193 (1993). Defendant has failed to establish such error. Blood tests from the crime scene were analyzed by two SBI serologists, Brenda Vissitte and Mark Boodee. The reports reached identical conclusions regarding the critical question of whose blood was present in the trailer. The testimony by Agent West, about which defendant complains, involved only the

results of the Vissitte report. Because the blood tests from the Boodee report were properly admitted and because their substance was identical to that of the Vissitte report about which Agent West testified, no plain error can be shown. This assignment of error is overruled.

In his next assignment of error, defendant asserts that the trial court committed plain error by allowing DNA testimony from SBI serologist Mark Boodee without requiring the State to establish a proper chain of custody for the items on which the analysis was conducted. Defendant argues that, because circumstances indicate something happened during handling to skew the DNA analysis and because the testimony was so prejudicial to defendant, defendant is entitled to a new trial.

A review of the record reveals that defendant failed to object at trial to the authenticity of the disputed evidence. Assignments of error based on improper authentication of exhibits introduced at trial will not be heard unless objection was made in a timely manner at trial. State v. Terry, 329 N.C. 191, 196, 404 S.E.2d 658, 661 (1991). Furthermore, the trial court's actions do not constitute plain error. The value of the DNA evidence was that it was intended to bolster the State's theory that the victim was tortured by showing that the victim's blood was present throughout the trailer. However, other evidence was introduced establishing that the victim was tortured throughout the trailer, including the results of the blood tests conducted by Vissitte, the testimony of codefendants who participated in the torture, and the statement of defendant himself. Thus, the trial court's admission of the DNA analysis cannot be said to have caused a different result in defendant's trial. This assignment of error is overruled.

Defendant next assigns error in the trial court's allowing Captain Jamison of the Jackson County Sheriff's Department to read during his testimony from notes he took of his interview with the defendant. Defendant argues that the "reading" of the notes, which were a typed version of misplaced, rough handwritten notes, was prejudicial because it led the jury to believe the notes were defendant's confession. This was exacerbated, defendant contends, by the State's reference to the statements made by the defendant in the interview as a "confession." Defendant maintains that he is entitled to a new trial as a result. We find defendant's contention to be without merit.

The State did not offer the notes in question as a confession of the defendant. Captain Jamison testified that he did not have the defendant review the notes, nor did he attempt to record the interview or make a verbatim transcript of his interview with the defendant. Captain Jamison conceded that the notes at issue were a typed facsimile of his original rough handwritten notes. The question then becomes whether the trial court properly allowed Captain Jamison's use of the notes during his testimony in order to refresh his present recollection.

In present recollection refreshed the evidence is the testimony of the witness at trial. . . . "Under present recollection refreshed the witness' memory is refreshed or jogged through the employment of a writing, diagram, smell or even touch," and he TESTIFIES from his memory so refreshed. State v. Corn, 307 N.C. 79, 83, 296 S.E.2d 261, 264 (1982). "Because of the independent origin of the testimony actually elicited, the stimulation of an actual present recollection is not strictly bounded by fixed rules but, rather, is approached on a case-by-case basis looking to the peculiar facts and circumstances present." State v. Smith, 291 N.C. [505,] 516, 231 S.E.2d [663,] 670-71 [(1977)].

The rule in Smith which we hold controls the resolution of this issue states, "Where the testimony of the witness purports to be from his refreshed memory but is clearly a mere recitation of the refreshing memorandum, such testimony is not admissible as present recollection refreshed and should be excluded by the trial judge." Id. at 518, 231 S.E.2d at 671. Thus, we must determine whether the spirit of the rule of present recollection refreshed has been violated by testimony which was not the product of a refreshed memory, but clearly nothing more than a recitation of the witness' notes.

The fact that a witness appears to read from a refreshing memorandum is not a per se VIOLATION under Gibson. Such an interpretation would elevate form above substance. What must be examined is whether the witness has an independent recollection of the event and is merely using the memorandum to refresh details or whether the witness is using the memorandum as a testimonial crutch for something beyond his recall.

A review of the particular facts and circumstances surrounding Captain Jamison's use of his notes during his testimony indicates that certainly the spirit of the present recollection refreshed rule was not violated in this case. Captain Jamison first testified from memory, and in particular detail, about the events surrounding the interview with the defendant. He reviewed the reading of the Miranda warnings to defendant by reference to a waiver form signed by the defendant, and Captain Jamison read without objection from that form in describing the beginning of the interview. Captain Jamison then was questioned about the specific contents of the conversation. At that point, he referred to the redraft of his notes made contemporaneously with the interview. Captain Jamison spoke in the second person throughout his testimony about the details of the interview, consistently prefacing his testimony with the phrase, "Thomas [defendant] stated." Further, Captain Jamison's recounting of the interview was interrupted by questions from the prosecutor, to which Jamison answered independently of his notes. This witness had extensive independent recall about the events surrounding the interview and the interview itself. It is thus evident from the full circumstances that this witness used his notes, much like his use of the waiver form, in order to specifically recall for the jury what occurred during his interview with defendant. Accordingly, we hold that the use of these notes in this instance was for the purpose of refreshing recollection to facilitate accurate testimony and as such did not violate the present recollection refreshed rule.

With respect to defendant's contention that the trial court erroneously allowed the State to refer to defendant's interview statements as a "confession" during opening statement and closing argument, we are not persuaded. Defendant made no objection to such reference. "[W]here a party does not object to a jury argument, the allegedly improper argument must be so prejudicial and grossly improper as to interfere with defendant's right to a fair trial in order for the trial court to be found in error for failure to intervene ex mero motu." State v. Fernandez, 346 N.C. 1, 25, 484 S.E.2d 350, 365 (1997). Although the statements at issue were not introduced into evidence as a confession, they were sufficiently self-incriminating to be so characterized in argument, and such characterization by the prosecution was not belabored or emphasized. As a result, we hold that the references were not so grossly improper as to amount to a denial of defendant's right to a fair trial. This assignment of error is overruled.

In his final assignment of error, defendant asserts that the trial court erroneously instructed the jury on the theory of acting in concert. Defendant contends there was insufficient evidence in this case to prove that each of the codefendants shared a common plan or scheme to intentionally inflict torture on the victim. Defendant also argues that the acting in concert instruction lessened the State's burden of proof by allowing the jury to convict the defendant without the particular mens rea for the crimes charged. We reject this contention.

The common thread running throughout this case was the desire of defendant and the other residents of Vickie Fox's trailer to inflict punishment on the victim for his admission to molesting Fox's daughter. The punishment was accomplished by repeated acts of brutality and torture, including persistent beating and kicking of the victim, . . .

Murder by torture and felony murder: In State v. Johnson, 317 N.C. 193, 344 S.E.2d 775 (1986), this Court held that premeditation and deliberation is not an element of the crime of first-degree murder perpetrated by means of torture. Id. at 203, 3n element of felony murder. Id. at 407, 226 S.E.2d at 669. Further, intent to kill is not an essential element of first-degree murder either by torture or under the felony murder rule. Johnson, 317 N.C. at 203, 344 S.E.2d at 781. Thus, the Sg in concert were met, and the trial court did not err in its jury instructions. This assignment of error is overruled.

For the foregoing reasons, we hold that defendant received a fair trial, free of prejudicial error.

NO ERROR.

END OF DOCUMEN. Govt. Works

Case Question

How is a charge of felony murder different from a charge of murder?

ETHICAL NOTE

A common question asked of criminal defense lawyers is, "How can you represent someone that you know is guilty?" This seems to be a concept that the general public has great difficulty in reconciling as ethical behavior. However, representation of the accused is a cornerstone right guaranteed to all citizens under the U.S. Constitution. In the American system of justice, certain principles prevail. Everyone is innocent until proven guilty by evidence in a court of law. Not by the media, or speculation, or circumstance, or even the accused's own lawyer. Secondly, it is not the function of a criminal defense lawyer to judge the client. Rather, it is to see that the client's defense is heard in the best light possible and to take all necessary measures to achieve a fair trial for the client. The criminal defense lawyer is assisted in this endeavor by the Bill of Rights. Consequently, the answer to the preceding question is frequently not one of the ethics of the lawyer but one of the general public. It is important to view anyone accused of criminal conduct objectively until such time as the evidence is fully reviewed. This was the goal of the framers of the Constitution who sought primarily to reverse the standard of guilty until proven innocent.

Question

Why should the standard of guilty until proven innocent be reversed?

CHAPTER SUMMARY

As this chapter has shown, the American legal system is committed to fairness to persons accused of criminal conduct, and every attempt is made to ensure that innocent persons are not convicted and punished. Much of the U.S. Constitution was written with this objective in mind, and it continues to be the basis for all aspects of criminal procedure.

Criminal procedure begins at the moment law enforcement authorities suspect criminal activity; often accused individuals are afforded constitutional protections before they are even aware that they are suspects. An example of such a protection is the requirement of probable cause before any search, seizure, or arrest can be made. Whenever possible, this probable cause must be determined by a judicial officer who can view the situation more objectively than a law enforcement officer.

After arrest, the Constitution continues to influence the proceedings through its mandates regarding bail, specific charges, right to counsel, and a speedy trial. In spite of all these protections, innocent persons have still been convicted. In the majority of these cases, however, the mistaken conviction occurred as a result of misconduct by witnesses or, in some instances, prosecutors. The system, when properly applied, provides greater protection from improper convictions than perhaps any other legal system in the world.

REVIEW QUESTIONS

1. Selective incorporation is designed to do what?
2. Which guarantees of the Bill of Rights are currently adopted into the definition of due process?
3. What is probable cause?
4. When does double jeopardy not apply after trial has begun?
5. At what stages does a defendant have the right to counsel?
6. When can bail be denied?
7. When is an arrest warrant not necessary?
8. What is the function of a grand jury?
9. What happens when there is no grand jury?
10. What takes place at the arraignment?

CHAPTER TERMS

Arraignment
Critical Stage
Due Process

Double Jeopardy
Grand Jury
Probable Cause

Selective Incorporation

NOTES

1. United States Constitution, Amendments 4, 5, 8, 14.
2. *Palko v. Connecticut,* 302 U.S. 319, 58 S.Ct. 149, 82 L.Ed. 288 (1937).
3. Id.
4. *Mapp v. Ohio,* 367 U.S. 643, 81 S.Ct. 1684, 6 L.Ed.2d 1081 (1961).
5. Id.
6. *Weeks v. United States,* 232 U.S. 383, 34 S.Ct. 341, 58 L.Ed. 652 (1914).

7. 338 U.S. 25, 69 S.Ct. 1359, 93 L.Ed. 1782 (1949).

8. See note 4.

9. 468 U.S. 897, 104 S.Ct. 3405, 82 L.Ed.2d 677 (1984).

10. *Katz v. United States,* 389 U.S. 347, 88 S.Ct. 507, 19 L.Ed.2d 576 (1967).

11. *Brinegar v. United States,* 338 U.S. 160, 69 S.Ct. 1302, 93 L.Ed. 1879 (1949).

12. *Vale v. Louisiana,* 399 U.S. 30, 90 S.Ct. 1969, 26 L.Ed.2d 409 (1970).

13. *Hester v. United States,* 265 U.S. 57, 44 S.Ct. 445, 68 L.Ed. 898 (1924).

14. *United States v. Dunn,* 480 U.S. 294, 107 S.Ct. 1134, 94 L.Ed.2d 326 (1987).

15. See note 10.

16. *New York v. Class,* 475 U.S. 106, 106 S.Ct. 960, 89 L.Ed.2d 81 (1986).

17. *New York v. Belton,* 453 U.S. 454, 101 S.Ct. 2860, 69 L.Ed.2d 768 (1981).

18. Id.

19. *Terry v. Ohio,* 392 U.S. 1, 88 S.Ct. 1868, 20 L.Ed.2d 889 (1968).

20. *Crist v. Bretz,* 437 U.S. 28, 98 S.Ct. 2156, 57 L.Ed.2d 24 (1978).

21. Id.

22. *Arizona v. Washington,* 434 U.S. 497, 98 S.Ct. 824, 54 L.Ed.2d 717 (1978).

23. 384 U.S. 436, 86 S.Ct. 1602, 16 L.Ed.2d 694 (1966).

24. *Brewer v. Williams,* 430 U.S. 387, 97 S.Ct. 1232, 51 L.Ed.2d 424 (1977).

25. *Barker v. Wingo,* 407 U.S. 514, 92 S.Ct. 2182, 33 L.Ed.2d 101 (1972).

26. Id.

27. See note 24.

28. *United States v. Salerno,* 481 U.S. 739, 107 S.Ct. 2095, 95 L.Ed.2d 697 (1987).

29. *Schilb v. Kuebel,* 404 U.S. 357, 92 S.Ct. 479, 30 L.Ed.2d 502 (1971).

30. See note 20.

31. See note 28.

32. See note 19.

33. *Marron v. United States,* 275 U.S. 192, 48 S.Ct. 74, 72 L.Ed. 231 (1927).

34. See note 23.

35. See note 24.

CHAPTER 14

Family Law

CHAPTER OBJECTIVES

After reading this chapter, you should be able to

- *Explain the requirements for a valid antenuptial agreement.*
- *List the requirements for marriage.*
- *Explain the purpose of legal annulment.*
- *Discuss the rights of parties who cohabit without marriage.*

- *Discuss the function of temporary orders.*
- *Explain how courts determine custody issues.*
- *Discuss the disadvantages of joint custody.*
- *Explain the concept of no-fault divorce.*

Family law is an area of American law that has experienced phenomenal growth in this century. Before the latter half of the twentieth century, divorce was a rare occurrence. In addition, a woman's role was perceived to be primarily that of a caretaker of the home and children, not of a worker in the public workplace. In the event of divorce, there was no question but that the husband would be solely responsible for the material needs of his wife and children. The relatively few divorces, social pressures, and the fact that the public was largely uneducated in matters of law resulted in few challenges to the fairness of court-ordered divorce settlements.

Over the years, the role of women changed in large part because of technological developments, the opening of the job market to women, and the growth of educational opportunities for women. Gradually, women began to live independently. This trend increased markedly during World War II, when for the first time, large numbers of women entered the nation's work force. In addition, our society became more mobile as families relocated away from the traditional extended family to find jobs. These societal changes were accompanied by an increased awareness of legal rights. And for the first time, specific laws were put into place that protected the rights of victims of domestic violence. As a consequence of all these developments, the option of dissolving a marriage became a more realistic choice for many. Multiple marriages in one lifetime became more likely, and as a result, more detailed laws on the total marriage relationship became necessary.

The changes in family law have ranged from defining and, in many states, abolishing common law marriage to regulating custody and visitation rights when parents live in different states. Aside from the fact that virtually everyone has some contact with family law during his or her lifetime, this area of law is having an increasing effect on the workplace. For example, some employers have the duty to report and withhold wages for payment of child support or maintenance (alimony), and job transfers or changes may be delayed while a divorced parent seeks changes in the visitation schedule or obtains court permission to remove a child from the state.

This chapter addresses the creation and dissolution of marriages and the relationships that result from terminated marriages. Its emphasis will be on the dissolution of marriages and the resulting relationships, since during a marriage, the parties are generally in accord with respect to marital concerns, such as child care and education. It is when discord occurs and cannot be resolved that the parties seek intermediary help from the legal system.

MARRIAGE AND ANNULMENT

Antenuptial Agreement

(prenuptial agreement) Agreement between parties who intend to marry that typically provides for the disposition of the property rights of the parties in the event the marriage ends by death or divorce.

Antenuptial (Prenuptial) Agreements

Antenuptial agreements (sometimes referred to as prenuptial agreements) are contracts entered into by parties who are going to be married. Such contracts provide for the division of property rights at the time the marital relationship between the parties ends. Originally, antenuptial agreements dealt only with property division upon the death of a spouse. Ordinarily, one spouse cannot entirely disinherit another spouse. If no provisions are made by will, the surviving spouse can elect under a special statute (one exists in each state) to receive a percentage of the estate. In a traditional antenuptial agreement, however, each of the spouses may agree by contract not to challenge the provisions of the other spouse's will. This is often done when one spouse possesses a great deal more wealth or when one of the spouses has children from a prior marriage and seeks to protect the children's inheritance.

More recently, antenuptial agreements have taken on an entirely new meaning. In a time where dissolution occurs frequently, some parties attempt to arrange in advance for an orderly distribution of debts and assets should the marriage be dissolved. No longer are these agreements reserved only for the wealthy. Rather, they are often a reasonable alternative for spouses who each have a career and the ability to contribute financially to the relationship. Many such couples have minor children from previous relationships whose interests must be protected. For these and other reasons, an antenuptial agreement often resolves the concerns that may prevent parties from getting married at all. The agreement allows the parties to continue their relationship with one less concern. Perhaps the agreement will never be utilized, but if it is, there is some reassurance in knowing that reasonable terms were arranged when each of the parties was acting logically with fairness to the other in mind.

Requirements for an enforceable agreement.   It has taken some time for the courts and legislature to determine the requirements for an enforceable antenuptial agreement with provisions for a dissolution of the marriage. The agreement is essentially a contract and must contain the necessary elements of any contract.[1] Most states also require the agreement to be in writing pursuant to the statute of frauds. An exception to the requirement of writing occurs when one party can demonstrate that he or she has significantly altered his or her position in a detrimental manner as a direct result of reliance on the other party's promises in an oral antenuptial agreement.[2]

 APPLICATION 14.1

A fiancé agrees to accept financial responsibility for a woman's unborn child and treat the child as his own. The woman, relying on the man's promise, marries the man and gives birth to and keeps the child. Even though there is no written agreement, the husband cannot later refuse to accept financial responsibility for the child, because the woman gave up her right to abort or to give the child up for adoption based on the husband's promise to support. (*T.V.T.*, 216 Va. 867, 224 S.E.2d 148 [1976].)

Point for Discussion
Would it matter if the man could prove he was not the natural father of the child?

In addition to the requirement of writing, consideration must be given for the promises of each party in the antenuptial agreement. Consideration is given by each party in exchange for the promises made in the terms of the contract and is easily satisfied. Traditionally, the promise of marriage by each party has served as consideration for the other party's agreement to the terms of the antenuptial contract. Finally, a valid antenuptial agreement must be made with the free will of both parties without duress or coercion, conditional upon divorce, and not be unconscionable either when made or implemented.

Challenging an agreement.   Mutual assent to the terms of the contract has been carefully examined in most cases where such a contract has been challenged. The court is concerned that unscrupulous persons would take advantage of the position of another and persuade the other person to enter an agreement that, in the event of divorce, would be inherently unfair (known as overreaching). Examples include parties who do not disclose the full measure of their assets and liabilities and parties who accumulate assets directly from the support of their spouse but in a dissolution action allege that the support did not occur or was not substantial.

 APPLICATION 14.2

Husband and wife enter into an antenuptial agreement before their marriage. The agreement provides that upon dissolution of the marriage, all existing assets or debts of either party will be shared equally, or that in the event of the death of one spouse, the assets and debts of that spouse will be assumed by the surviving spouse. A few years later, the parties divorce and the husband discovers for the first time that the wife actively concealed many thousands of dollars of debt that had come into existence before the marriage or the agreement. Since there was not full disclosure, the agreement may not be enforced, because under the fraudulent circumstances, the husband did not have the opportunity to discover what his liabilities might be under the agreement.

Point for Discussion
What if the wife did not take steps to actively conceal the information but simply did not volunteer the knowledge of her wealth?

As the preceding example illustrates, it is crucial that any antenuptial agreement contain full disclosure of assets and liabilities.[3] In addition, the agreement should contain provisions for some fair and reasonable economic settlement. The parties do not usually anticipate divorce and cannot anticipate what their accumulation of wealth will be at the time of a divorce. However, they can anticipate that each will contribute to the marriage, and assets should be divided in a manner fair to each based on that contribution.

Upholding an agreement.   A difficulty in dealing with the settlement provision is that courts will often not recognize an agreement that provides for a specific financial award, since such an agreement is seen as encouraging dissolution of the marriage in an attempt to obtain a monetary settlement.[4] The courts will, however, uphold agreements that provide for a fair distribution of assets to be determined by an objective third party, such as a court, in the event the parties should cease to share marital assets. This reassures the parties that they are not being taken advantage of. Such an agreement also does not include any anticipation of divorce that the court might see as encouraging the end of a marriage. To ensure an enforceable and fair agreement, each party should seek independent legal counsel before entering into an antenuptial agreement.

Assignment 14.1

Under the following circumstances, would the antenuptial agreements be more likely to be enforced or invalidated? Why?

1. Sherry and Eric marry. Sherry is quite wealthy and believes the same of Eric, who has a great deal of real estate holdings. Sherry later discovers that Eric owes back taxes in an amount of the approximate equivalent of three times the value of the property. The parties signed an agreement on their wedding day that split all assets into equal parts in the event of divorce.
2. Bette is an English literature student. She marries Ron, a wealthy corporate executive. In an antenuptial agreement, Bette agrees to waive any claim to Ron's premarital assets in the event of a divorce. Ron makes a similar agreement. Any assets accumulated after the marriage will be split equally. Prior to the marriage, Bette wrote a book and got a contract to have it published. However, she did not receive royalties until well after the wedding. After two years of marriage, the parties divorce. Ron's assets are essentially the same as before the marriage. The book has netted Bette $2 million in the last one and one-half years.

Requirements for Marriage

The process of getting married has become quite complex in the legal sense. In many states, two people wishing to marry cannot simply obtain a license at the justice of the peace and be married at the same time. Because marriage so deeply affects the lives of those involved and because many marriages do not, in fact, succeed, as well as for reasons of public health and various other concerns linked to citizen welfare, laws have been created to establish the best possible environment for the marriage. Every state has enacted laws that set forth certain requirements that must be met before a recognized marriage will exist.

Capacity and consent.   For a marriage to be valid, there must be capacity and consent.[5] As previously noted, capacity requires that the party be of legal age and not be declared legally incompetent. The party must be capable of making the decision to enter into such an agreement. Many states also have provisions for parental or court consent in the event a party to the marriage is not of legal age or has been legally determined to be incapable of appreciating the consequences and responsibilities of marriage. If there is capacity, it is also necessary that each party openly and voluntarily consent to the marriage.

Marriage license.   Each state has a licensure provision for marriages.[6] Before a legal marriage exists, the parties are directed to make application for a marriage license. The license is generally granted unless some factor exists that would prevent the marriage from being legal under state law. Examples of such factors include (1) the parties are family members who have a close blood relationship (each state indicates the degree of kinship that will prevent a marriage), (2) the parties are persons of the same sex (although attempts are being made to change this), (3) one or both parties lack legal capacity, and (4) one of the parties is already in an existing marriage.

Blood tests and a waiting period are also often required to obtain a marriage license. The purpose behind blood tests is twofold. First, it is presumed that each party to the marriage has the right to know whether the other carries any sexually transmitted disease that could place the party at risk. In light of the AIDS crisis in the United States, some states have amended their statutes to require an additional blood test or disclosure that would provide information regarding the presence of AIDS. The second reason for blood tests is that the parties should be informed if there is a conflict between their particular blood types that may make it difficult for them to have healthy children. Although medicine has advanced to the point that most problems can be treated effectively, the parties are still presumed to be entitled to this information.

The statutes that require a waiting period (usually a matter of a few days) discourage marriages that are entered into without sufficient thought to the consequences. Thus, requiring a brief delay between issuance of the license and the time when it can be validated by a judge or minister encourages the parties to consider the ramifications of their action.

Marriage vows.   Finally, the parties are ordinarily required to solemnize the marriage. This involves the exchange of vows (an agreement to marry) in the presence of one who is permitted to legally acknowledge the marriage.[7] Usually, this is a minister or a judge, who will then validate the license by certifying that the parties have indeed agreed to be married. At that time, the minister or judge and the parties will sign the license. Often, additional witnesses to the marriage are required to sign the license. If citizens of one state wish to marry but would not be permitted to do so in their own state, they may not simply go to another state for the purpose of marrying. Many states now have laws that declare a marriage invalid if it was entered into in another state for the purpose of avoiding the first state's laws. Thus, in some states, parties otherwise unable to legally marry can no longer cross a state line to be married. They must be able to show that they had valid reasons for conducting the marriage ceremony in another state.

Annulment

A legal **annulment** is a judicial declaration that a marriage never actually existed because the legal requirements for a valid marriage were not met.[8] This is to be distinguished from a religious annulment. The latter is granted by a church authority for reasons of and in accordance with religious procedures. A religious annulment has no legal meaning or effect. Accordingly, a legal annulment has no religious significance.

Legal annulments can be obtained for a variety of reasons. Whatever the basis for the annulment, one requirement is common to all. The reason that the marriage should be declared invalid must have existed at the time the parties entered into the marriage.[9] Therefore, if an annulment is sought on the basis that one or both of the parties was under the legal age or without sufficient mental capacity, the incapacity must have existed at the time the parties attempted a marriage. Other common reasons for annulment include close blood relationships, incest, or bigamy. The general rule is that an annulment may be granted if the reason for the annulment, had it been previously disclosed, would have legally prevented the parties from marrying.

If the party seeking the annulment has taken any steps toward accepting and acknowledging the marriage relationship, his or her request may be denied. The theory is that one who attempts to solemnize a marriage cannot then take the position that the marriage never existed.[10] This is very similar to the contractual defense of unclean hands, which holds that a party who helped create the circumstances for a breach of contract cannot then turn and allege that he or she has been injured because of the breach. Nevertheless, the courts may still grant an annulment if the reason is a serious one, such as bigamy or incest.

Less frequently encountered actions for annulment include actions based on frolic, duress, or fraud. If the parties married as some sort of joke or game and never truly intended a binding marriage, the court will grant an annulment. (As with most contractual agreements, intent is required for a valid marriage to exist. For example, a marriage by parties who were intoxicated at the time of the marriage and did not intend to actually marry would be invalid.)

If a party believes that he or she has no choice but to marry or alternatively suffer serious physical, financial, or other harm, a marriage of duress has taken place. Effectively, the party had no real choice in the matter, and the courts will likely find no real intent to marry. As a result, annulment is a very real possibility in such situations.

Annulment on the basis of fraud is one of the most difficult to establish. The party seeking the annulment must prove all of the necessary elements of fraud. In the case of marriage, the elements are (1) a misrepresentation of a fact essential to the marriage relationship must have been made, and (2) the party claiming fraud must have reasonably relied on the misrepresentation as truth when making the decision to marry. Examples of misrepresentations sufficient for an annulment based upon fraud include religious beliefs or ability to biologically parent children.

Although an annulment is a declaration that the marriage relationship never existed in the eyes of the law, it does not mean that no relationship existed. Therefore, the courts may apportion rights and duties regarding property,

Annulment
Court order that restores the parties to their positions prior to the marriage. The marriage of the parties is void and treated as if it never existed. Permissible in situations where a particular legal disability prevented the marriage from becoming valid.

assets, debts, and even children as if the annulment were an action for dissolution of marriage (divorce).[11] The purpose is to return the parties to their original position before the marriage. If the parties have contributed anything to the relationship or if there are children, the court will consider the rights under the same equitable grounds used in dissolving a marital relationship. Figure 14.1 is an example of an annulment law.

Common Law Marriage

A minority of states still allow marriages created by common law. Such marital relationships are created by agreement of the parties. However, the formal requisites of license and legal solemnization by vows are not observed. Even states that do not permit the creation of common law marriages will recognize a common law marriage validly established in another state.

Generally, no public record of a common law marriage is made. Contrary to popular belief, a common law marriage is not based on the length of time two parties live together. Rather, the courts usually examine the following in determining whether such a marriage exists:

1. Did the parties hold themselves out to the public as married?
2. Did the parties cohabit?
3. Did the parties file joint tax returns?
4. Does the conduct of the parties indicate an intent to be married?

If the evidence is insufficient to establish a common law marriage or the relationship was created in a state that does not recognize common law marriage, the parties still may have legal rights under principles that deal with cohabitation (discussed in greater detail in the section that addresses nonmarital relationships).

Assignment 14.2

Use the subject index to your state statutes or code to locate the appropriate laws that will answer the following questions. Examine the statutes and answer the questions.

1. Does the state recognize common law marriages created in the state?
2. Does the state recognize common law marriages created in other states that recognize common law marriages?
3. What are the requirements for a valid and legally formalized marriage?
4. What are the grounds (reasons) for an annulment proceeding?

Assignment 14.3

Prepare a chart that details the requirements for valid marriage and common law marriage (in jurisdictions where recognized).

FIGURE 14.1 McKinney's Consolidated Laws of New York Annotated Domestic Relations Law Chapter 14 of the Consolidated Laws Article 9—Action to Annul a Marriage or Declare it Void

§ 140. Action for judgment declaring nullity of void marriages or annulling voidable marriage

(a) Former husband or wife living. An action to declare the nullity of a void marriage upon the ground that the former husband or wife of one of the parties was living, the former marriage being in force, may be maintained by either of the parties during the life-time of the other, or by the former husband or wife.

(b) Party under age of consent. An action to annul a marriage on the ground that one or both of the parties had not attained the age of legal consent may be maintained by the infant, or by either parent of the infant, or by the guardian of the infant's person; or the court may allow the action to be maintained by any person as the next friend of the infant. But a marriage shall not be annulled under this subdivision at the suit of a party who was of the age of legal consent when it was contracted, or by a party who for any time after he or she attained that age freely cohabited with the other party as husband or wife.

(c) Party a mentally retarded person or mentally ill person. An action to annul a marriage on the ground that one of the parties thereto was a mentally retarded person may be maintained at any time during the life-time of either party by any relative of a mentally retarded person, who has an interest to avoid the marriage. An action to annul a marriage on the ground that one of the parties thereto was a mentally ill person may be maintained at any time during the continuance of the mental illness, or, after the death of the mentally ill person in that condition, and during the life of the other party to the marriage, by any relative of the mentally ill person who has an interest to avoid the marriage. Such an action may also be maintained by the mentally ill person at any time after restoration to a sound mind; but in that case, the marriage should not be annulled if it appears that the parties freely cohabited as husband and wife after the mentally ill person was restored to a sound mind. Where one of the parties to a marriage was a mentally ill person at the time of the marriage, an action may also be maintained by the other party at any time during the continuance of the mental illness, provided the plaintiff did not know of the mental illness at the time of the marriage. Where no relative of the mentally retarded person or mentally ill person brings an action to annul the marriage and the mentally ill person is not restored to sound mind, the court may allow an action for that purpose to be maintained at any time during the life-time of both the parties to the marriage, by any person as the next friend of the mentally retarded person or mentally ill person.

(d) Physical incapacity. An action to annul a marriage on the ground that one of the parties was physically incapable of entering into the marriage state may be maintained by the injured party against the party whose incapacity is alleged; or such an action may be maintained by the party who was incapable against the other party, provided the incapable party was unaware of the incapacity at the time of marriage, or if aware of such incapacity, did not know it was incurable. Such an action can be maintained only where an incapacity continues and is incurable, and must be commenced before five years have expired since the marriage.

(e) Consent by force, duress or fraud. An action to annul a marriage on the ground that the consent of one of the parties thereto was obtained by force or duress may be maintained at any time by the party whose consent was so obtained. An action to annul a marriage on the ground that the consent of one of the parties thereto was obtained by fraud may be maintained by the party whose consent was so obtained within the limitations of time for enforcing a civil remedy of the civil practice law and rules. Any such action may also be maintained during the life-time of the other party by the parent, or the guardian of the person of the party whose consent was so obtained, or by any relative of that party who has an interest to avoid the marriage, provided that in an action to annul a marriage on the ground of fraud the limitation prescribed in the civil practice law and rules has not run. But a marriage shall not be annulled on the ground of force or duress if it appears that, at any time before the commencement of the action, the parties thereto voluntarily cohabited as husband and wife; or on the ground of fraud, if it appears that, at any time before the commencement thereof, the parties voluntarily cohabited as husband and wife, with a full knowledge of the facts constituting the fraud.

(f) Incurable mental illness for five years. An action to annul a marriage upon the ground that one of the parties has been incurably mentally ill for a period of five years or more may be maintained by or on behalf of either of the parties to such marriage.

The Marriage Relationship

Today, most states have statutes that impose an equal duty on each spouse to aid and financially support the other spouse during the marriage. Thus, no longer is it the sole duty of the husband to provide financial support for the wife. The practical result is that in the event of a dissolution, the husband may also be entitled to financial support, and in most cases, maintenance (alimony) is no longer awarded for life unless special circumstances exist. (These specifics are discussed later in the section that deals with the question of maintenance.)

During the marriage, the spouses have an ongoing duty to provide support of at least that which is necessary to meet the needs of the parties.[12] Such necessities include food, shelter, and clothing. If one party has agreed to work outside the home while the other remains at home, that party also has a duty to provide items necessary to the couple's existence. Often what is considered necessary is largely influenced by the income of the spouses and what that income enables the parties to provide.

During the marriage, most states recognize the theory of marital debt. Thus, if one spouse assumes a debt, the other spouse is equally bound. This becomes particularly important if the parties subsequently terminate their relationship. The marital debts must be apportioned fairly while taking into account the ability of each party to satisfy the claims of outside creditors. (The subject of apportionment is addressed later in the section that deals with property and debt division.)

The primary rule regarding existing marriages is the policy of nonintervention. The courts generally refuse to become involved in settling marital disputes regarding the duties of the parties.[13] When third parties such as creditors become involved and debts are not being paid, the court may declare that both parties are jointly liable. Beyond this, the courts presume that the parties are meeting their obligations of support for one another as long as they continue to live together and maintain a marital residence.

If the parties cease living together and abandon the marital relationship, the courts may become involved in dictating the legal rights of each party before and after a formal dissolution of the marriage. Most states have enacted statutes that permit awards of support during a legal separation or while a divorce is pending. Because divorces can sometimes become quite drawn out, it may be necessary to provide for the well-being of the parties (and possibly any children) during the interim.

Effects of Tort and Criminal Law on Domestic Relations

An additional factor to be considered regarding the marital relationship is the effect of a marriage on tort and criminal law. Historically, one spouse was not permitted to bring a legal action against the other spouse for injuries inflicted during the marriage. The reasoning was that marital harmony would be disturbed if the courts entertained lawsuits by spouses against one another. Slowly, the realization came about that if injuries by one spouse to another were so serious as to warrant a lawsuit, marital disharmony more than likely already existed. Further, it seemed unfair that gross negligence or intentional misconduct would be excused if it only injured a family member. Thus, most states have now abolished the doctrine of interspousal tort immunity.[14] No longer are parties who cause injury to their spouses immune from legal action.

Third-party actions against the marriage. Other torts that affect the marital relationship include actions of third parties against the marriage. Such actions are generally quite difficult to prove, and most persons are reluctant to raise the issue. Two such torts are criminal conversation (an action by one spouse against a third party for adulterous conduct with the other spouse) and alienation of affection (an action by a spouse against a third party who has induced the other spouse to transfer his or her affections to that party).[15] Because these actions have been used as a means to threaten and as virtual extortion (blackmail), some states have abolished the statutes that permit them. In addition, as noted previously, the very nature of the actions inhibits a significant amount of actual prosecution of claims by the injured party.

Domestic violence. Unfortunately, the occurrence of **domestic violence** (violence perpetrated by one member of a household onto another member of the household) is all too prevalent in American society and law. In 1991, one study indicated 1.13 million reported cases of domestic violence. This does not even reflect the immeasurable number of unreported incidents. However, one benefit of the growing knowledge by individuals regarding their personal legal rights discussed at the outset of this chapter is the increased willingness of individuals to step forward in such matters. As a result, a body of law has been developed and continues to evolve in the area of domestic violence.

> **Domestic Violence**
> Acts of physical violence perpetrated by one member of a household onto another member of the household.

State legislatures, courts, and law enforcement agencies have begun to develop, implement, and enforce laws—although still in what some consider to be formative stages—designed to protect individuals against domestic violence (see Figure 14.2). While in the past such matters were dealt with through temporary restraining orders that the police may or may not have fully enforced, today there are specific statutes that give the police the necessary authority to intervene in matters of domestic violence.

Marital violence. A rapidly changing area of criminal law that affects the family involves marital violence. More than one half the states have now enacted statutes that permit an action of a wife for marital rape by her husband. However, many of these statutes require the parties to have been living apart at the time of the incident.[16] Additionally, because of the doctrine of nonintervention in the marital relationship, there has been little if any alternative for the spouse who has been violently abused by the other spouse. But states do have statutes permitting special intervention by police, and subsequently by the courts, where a reasonable belief exists that a spouse has committed a felony against his or her partner.

The statute in Figure 14.2 is just one example of an attempt to deal with the domestic violence issue through the legal system. In addition, many community and charitable organizations have established shelters, crisis intervention

FIGURE 14.2   Connecticut General Statutes Annotated Title 46B. Family Law Chapter 815E. Marriage

§ 46b-38a. Family violence prevention and response: Definitions

For the purposes of sections 46b-38a to 46b-38f, inclusive:

(1) "Family violence" means an incident resulting in physical harm, bodily injury or assault, or an act of threatened violence that constitutes fear of imminent physical harm, bodily injury or assault between family or household members. Verbal abuse or argument shall not constitute family violence unless there is present danger and the likelihood that physical violence will occur.

(2) "Family or household member" means (A) spouses, former spouses; (B) parents and their children; (C) persons eighteen years of age or older related by blood or marriage; (D) persons sixteen years of age or older other than those persons in subparagraph (C) presently residing together or who have resided together; and (E) persons who have a child in common regardless of whether they are or have been married or have lived together at any time.

(3) "Family violence crime" means a crime as defined in section 53a-24 which, in addition to its other elements, contains as an element thereof an act of family violence to a family member and shall not include acts by parents or guardians disciplining minor children unless such acts constitute abuse.

(4) "Institutions and services" means peace officers, service providers, mandated reporters of abuse, agencies and departments that provide services to victims and families and services designed to assist victims and families.

§ 46b-38b. Investigation of family violence crime by peace officer. Arrest, when. Assistance to victim. Guidelines. Education and training program

(a) Whenever a peace officer determines upon speedy information that a family violence crime, as defined in subdivision (3) of section 46b-38a, has been committed within his jurisdiction, he shall arrest the person or persons suspected of its commission and charge such person or persons with the appropriate crime. The decision to arrest and charge shall not (1) be dependent on the specific consent of the victim, (2) consider the relationship of the parties or (3) be based solely on a request by the victim.

(b) No peace officer investigating an incident of family violence shall threaten, suggest or otherwise indicate the arrest of all parties for the purpose of discouraging requests for law enforcement intervention by any party. Where complaints are received from two or more opposing parties, the officer shall evaluate each complaint separately to determine whether he should seek a warrant for an arrest.

(c) No peace officer shall be held liable in any civil action regarding personal injury or injury to property brought by any party to a family violence incident for an arrest based on probable cause.

(d) It shall be the responsibility of the peace officer at the scene of a family violence incident to provide immediate assistance to the victim. Such assistance shall include but not be limited to: (1) Assisting the victim to obtain medical treatment if such is required; (2) notifying the victim of the right to file an affidavit or warrant for arrest; and (3) informing the victim of services available and referring the victim to the commission on victim services. In cases where the officer has determined that no cause exists for an arrest, assistance shall include: (A) Assistance included in subdivisions (1) to (3), inclusive, of this subsection; and (B) remaining at the scene for a reasonable time until in the reasonable judgment of the officer the likelihood of further imminent violence has been eliminated.

(e) On or before October 1, 1986, each law enforcement agency shall develop, in conjunction with the division of criminal justice, and implement specific operational guidelines for arrest policies in family violence incidents. Such guidelines shall include but not be limited to: (1) Procedures for the conduct of a criminal investigation; (2) procedures for arrest and for victim assistance by peace officers; (3) education as to what constitutes speedy information in a family violence incident; (4) procedures with respect to the provision of services to victims; and (5) such other criteria or guidelines as may be applicable to carry out the purposes of subsection (e) of section 17-38a and sections 17-38g, 46b-1, 46b-15, 46b-38a to 46b-38f, inclusive, and 54-1g.

(f) The municipal police training council, in conjunction with the division of criminal justice, shall establish an education and training program for law enforcement officers, supervisors and state's attorneys on the handling of family violence incidents. Such training shall: (1) Stress the enforcement of criminal law in family violence cases and the use of community resources and include training for peace officers at both recruit and in-service levels; (2) include: (A) The nature, extent and causes of family violence; (B) legal rights of and remedies available to victims of family violence and persons accused of family violence; (C) services and facilities available to victims and batterers; (D) legal duties imposed on police officers to make arrests and to offer protection and assistance; (E) techniques for handling incidents of family violence that minimize the likelihood of injury to the officer and promote safety of the victim.

centers, hotlines, counseling, and other methods to effectively deal with the domestic violence that occurs in our society. As more cases are reported and the guilt often felt by victims of domestic violence is exposed as unfounded, this area of law and community support can be expected to grow dramatically in coming years.

In criminal law, certain principles affect the marriage relationship. A primary example is the testimonial privilege. Traditionally, a spouse could not testify against the other spouse during a criminal prosecution. But over time, the law has been modified, and most states now permit but cannot compel a spouse to testify against his or her partner. Because the spouse has the right to protect the confidentiality of the marriage relationship, testimony cannot be forced or ordered.

ENDING THE MARITAL RELATIONSHIP

Jurisdiction

When one or both of the parties to a marital relationship decide to end the marriage, a judicial declaration must be made before the marriage and its associated rights and duties will be terminated. The declaration must come from a court that has jurisdiction over the parties to the suit. Procedural rules in each state specify when the courts will accept jurisdiction over a marital dissolution action.

Many of the requirements in these statutes are similar throughout the states. Perhaps the most common is the requirement of residency. Although the length of residence varies, generally the states require the party commencing the action to have been a resident of the state for a specified period of time prior to initiating the action for dissolution. Parties may also obtain jurisdiction in a court if the marriage was formalized there or if the grounds for divorce occurred while the parties maintained their residence in the state (regardless of whether the time requirement has been met).[17]

When a party obtains a decree but the court does not have jurisdiction to decide matters involving the settlement of the marital estate (e.g., assets are located in another jurisdiction), the decree may be registered with a court that has jurisdiction over both of the parties and their property. That court may then proceed to determine the rights and obligations of each party. Under the U.S. Constitution, each state is obligated to give full faith and credit to the judgment of another state's decree. This means a state should honor and enforce the judgments of a court from another state.

A major jurisdictional issue in dissolution actions pertains to the authority of a court over the rights and duties concerning children of a marriage. Initially, the court that has jurisdiction to determine the rights, duties, and division of the assets of the marital estate also has authority to make findings regarding custody, visitation, and support of minor children. However, later adjustments to these findings, commonly termed modifications, may raise serious issues as to which court has authority. Fortunately, these issues have been settled in large part by the Uniform Reciprocal Enforcement of Support Act (URESA). Most states adhere to the Act, which states quite specifically what courts have jurisdiction over matters concerning children of divorced parties.

Grounds for Dissolution of a Marriage

Although requirements of jurisdiction vary, the acceptable grounds for a divorce set forth by state statute are typically very similar. Although slight variations may exist, the basic premise for **dissolution of marriage** remains the same in most states. There must be sufficient evidence of some type that will establish that the marital bond is irreparably broken.

Dissolution of Marriage

The end of the marriage relationship (also known as divorce).

The grounds most commonly set forth in state statutes as sufficient to establish the end of the marriage relationship include, but are not limited to, the following:[18]

1. Habitual drunkenness or drug abuse
2. Adultery
3. Physical cruelty
4. Mental cruelty
5. Abandonment
6. Insanity

Traditionally, the party who suffered because of the existence of one or more of these grounds brought an action for divorce. He or she would be required to give evidence of the grounds, and on that basis the divorce would be granted.

More recently adopted has been the concept of no-fault divorce, the grounds for which are called irreconcilable differences. It has been recognized for many years that parties would agree to a specific grounds for a divorce as a means to expedite the end of the legal relationship when the marriage itself had come to an end sometime before. Many times, parties who no longer wish to be married have various reasons other than the statutorily stated grounds. In addition, the time and expense associated with divorce to the individuals and courts alike have increased significantly. As a result, in the past several years, every state has adopted a no-fault statute in some form. Although the requirements of proof of a broken marriage differ from state to state, the premise remains the same. It is unnecessary to claim that one party unilaterally caused the break in the marital bond. Rather, the parties have reached a point where they are no longer interested in maintaining the marital relationship.[19] For this reason, the bond is broken, and the legality of the relationship can be dissolved.

In an attempt to prevent parties from entering into a no-fault divorce when conciliation could still be achieved, many statutes impose requirements of proof that the marital bond is irreparably broken. Such requirements include lengthy separations before a no-fault divorce will be granted. Parties should be given every opportunity to evaluate the situation carefully and be sure of their decision. However, those parties who have firmly made a decision to end the marriage evade these requirements by returning to the former method of privately agreeing to one or more grounds based on fault of a party so that the divorce may be granted immediately. Thus, although the statutes have assisted many in obtaining a divorce without laying blame, abuse of statutes by giving grounds of fault continues in some states where it is much more time consuming to obtain a divorce on grounds of no-fault than on fault of a party.

Legal Separation

As previously mentioned, many times a divorce is a long and complicated process. Also, many parties do not file for divorce immediately upon separation. This may be for religious reasons, or the parties may want time to consider the possibility of reconciliation or at least the potential for agreement to the terms of the divorce. During this period, the parties remain legally obligated to each other as well as for the support of their children. As a consequence, a special area of law has developed by statute and by judicial decision that governs the rights of the parties during this period of **legal separation.**

Courts are reluctant to recognize antenuptial agreements that provide specifically for divorce. However, when a physical separation has occurred or is about to occur, the courts will consider an antenuptial or separation agreement between the parties that discusses the parties' rights and duties prior to the divorce when the marriage still exists legally but marital assets and liabilities are no longer shared. The courts will generally examine the agreement for fairness, full disclosure, and availability of legal counsel to each party.[20]

Separation agreements include such issues as custody, visitation, and support of minor children; possession of the marital residence; responsibility for payments due on marital debts; and maintenance (alimony), where appropriate. If the terms are agreeable to the parties, they may also serve as the basis for the terms in the final divorce decree for matters of convenience to the parties. However, it is important to note that legal separations have no direct connection to dissolution proceedings, and each may take place without the other.

Legal Separation

Legal document that establishes the property rights of the parties without effecting a dissolution of the actual marriage relationship.

Assignment 14.4

> Prepare a chart that details the differences between dissolution, annulment, common law divorce, and legal separation.

Temporary Orders

Unfortunately, not all parties are willing to reach an agreement regarding property and other rights. In such instances, state statutes give a court authority to make temporary provisions during the period after commencement of a divorce but before a final decree is issued. These temporary orders provide terms that the parties must follow with respect to the marital obligations previously discussed.

In addition to issuing temporary orders, courts are often requested to issue **temporary restraining orders** and **preliminary injunctions,** granted in circumstances where the court is convinced that one spouse will injure the partner or harm, destroy, or dispose of marital property.[21] If the threat of harm is immediate, the spouse in danger of injury or harm to property can appear in court ex parte. An ex parte proceeding is conducted without giving the other party to the action the opportunity to be present and voice his or her position. Because these orders are based on one person's

Temporary Restraining Order

Court order that temporarily orders a party to act or refrain from acting in a particular manner until such time as the court has the opportunity to consider a more permanent ruling on the issue.

Preliminary Injunction

Court order that orders a party to act or refrain from acting in a particular manner for a specified period of time (often during the pendency of a legal proceeding).

version of the story, the court will usually issue the order only in compelling circumstances, and such orders are usually effective for only a short period of time as an emergency measure.

 APPLICATION 14.3 ──────────────────

Corazon wants to divorce Raphael. She has left him and has filed an action for divorce. Raphael has threatened Corazon, saying that he is going to physically harm her. Raphael has physically abused Corazon on several occasions in the past. In addition, Raphael has indicated to Corazon that he is going to withdraw all funds from their bank accounts, leaving her no means with which to support herself.

Corazon appears in court with her attorney and requests a temporary restraining order that will prohibit funds from being withdrawn from their bank accounts and will also prohibit Raphael from contacting her in any way. The judge accepts that there is reason to believe that Raphael will attempt to carry out his threats. A temporary restraining order is issued granting Corazon's requests. The order is effective for only ten days, however, after which time another hearing is scheduled and Raphael will have the opportunity to present his side of the story.

Point for Discussion
Is it possible for Raphael to also obtain a restraining order against Corazon?

After a temporary restraining order has been issued, it is served on the party who is restrained. Even if the restrained party cannot be located, the order is effective, and if it is violated, the party can be arrested.[22] Without such a rule, parties could simply avoid being served and in the interim destroy marital property or perhaps seriously injure their spouse. Given the alternatives, the safer course seems to be to give the order effect from the time it is issued.

Temporary restraining orders are usually issued for a very short period of time. Thus, a party who can show evidence that such an order was improperly issued can have the order revoked at the earliest opportunity. When a hearing is held, however, if sufficient evidence is presented to warrant continuance of the order, a preliminary injunction will be issued that remains in effect during the pendency of the dissolution proceedings.

A preliminary injunction contains virtually the same provisions as a temporary restraining order. However, the injunction will be effective until the final divorce decree is entered. At that time, if marital property will continue to be held jointly or if the physical danger still exists, a **permanent injunction** may be issued that will remain effective until an order of the court removes it. Many times, these orders are left in force forever.

Permanent Injunction
Court order that permanently orders a party to act or refrain from acting in a particular manner.

APPLICATION 14.4

After the temporary restraining order was issued, Corazon and Raphael both appeared in court. Raphael contested the order by denying that he had abused his wife or that he had made threats against her or the marital property. Corazon produced evidence that Raphael had indeed attempted to close their joint accounts. Further, she produced witnesses who testified that Raphael had physically abused her in their presence. The judge issued a temporary injunction that would remain effective until the final divorce decree was entered.

At the hearing for the final divorce and settlement of marital assets, Corazon produced witnesses who testified that Raphael was simply waiting until the divorce was final to "get Corazon." Also, the marital residence was to remain in Corazon's possession until it could be sold and the profits distributed. Part of the divorce settlement is that Raphael will receive the profits from the sale of the home and Corazon will receive other marital assets. Raphael introduced evidence that Corazon has indicated to others that she intends to do damage to the house in order to prolong its sale and decrease its value. The judge issues two permanent injunctions. One is against Raphael and enjoins (prohibits) him permanently from approaching Corazon in any way without her consent. The second injunction is against Corazon, who is enjoined from doing anything at all that might be construed as damaging marital property or interfering with Raphael's right to sell the house and receive the maximum profit possible.

Point for Discussion
What could happen if either of the parties violates the injunction against him/her?

CUSTODY

Custody over minor children is perhaps one of the most litigated areas of family law. *Custody* is the term used to describe the care, control, and education of a minor child. It is effective as long as the child is a minor or is still in high school. A synonymous term used in some jurisdictions is **parental rights.** For purposes of this discussion, the term *custody* will be used here. When the child reaches the age of majority under statute in the state where the child resides, custody ends, and the child is considered to be an adult.[23] Residence is determined by the child's permanent dwelling, not by where the child attends school or where the other parent whom the child visits may live. Generally, the state of residence of the custodial parent is the state of residence of the child.

Custody may not end at the age of majority for a mentally disabled child. In cases where the child is unable to accept responsibility for his or her actions, the parent may be appointed the permanent custodian.[24]

Custody (Parental Rights)
The right to oversee the care, education, and rearing of a child.

In the event of the death of the custodial parent, the presumption is that custody will be transferred to the other parent. The exception to this is if the surviving parent is not able to provide an acceptable environment for the child. In such circumstances, stepparents, grandparents, or other interested parties who can provide a suitable environment for the child may be appointed guardian.

Fortunately, the courts rarely have to deal with such cases. However, there are quite often decisions to be made by the courts when both parents are living and willing to provide a home for the child or children. Formerly, the mother almost always received custody of the children. No longer is this the case. Courts consider numerous factors to determine who is best able to care for and attend to the needs of the children.[25]

Under what is known as the tender years doctrine, which was followed for many years but is rapidly declining in this country, the mother was presumed to be the best alternative for custody of young children of "tender years"[26] (usually children who had not reached their teens). The only way a father could overcome this presumption and have a chance for custody was to prove that the mother was unfit or, at the very least, far less able than the father to care for the children.

In recent times, many fathers have taken an increasingly active role in the upbringing of their children. Additionally, various movements throughout the country for equal rights for men have supported fathers in their quest for custody. Furthermore, it is no longer the general rule that mothers stay at home to care for the children. Many mothers work and are away from the home just as a father would be. For all of these reasons, many courts have struck down the tender years doctrine in favor of a case-by-case evaluation of who will best serve the interests and needs of the child.[27]

Who Gets Custody?

What is the standard that must be proven to obtain custody of a child? Contrary to popular belief, it is not necessary to prove that the other party is unfit as a parent. Although the evidence may establish this in some cases, it is not the standard used by most courts. Rather, the courts look at what will be in the best interests of the child. Divorce is extremely difficult for children of all ages to deal with. That is not to say it may not be a better alternative than to continue the marriage. But divorce does mean that a child's world goes through dramatic changes that require adjustment. Consequently, the court examines several areas that affect the child's life and looks to the child's particular needs. The court then looks at the environment that each parent will offer the child. The environment that is most compatible with the child's needs is the one that is in the child's best interests. Thus, each parent may offer a suitable environment, but the parent that is better suited to meet the needs of the child should prevail.

As this suggests, the standard that a parent must prove is that it is in the best interests of the child that the parent be awarded custody. The factors that a court considers in making this determination may include, but are not limited to, the following:[28]

1. The ability of the parent to care for the child personally (as opposed to extensive child-care services).

2. The religion of the parent.
3. The ability of the parent to attend to any special needs of the child because of young age or disability.
4. Immoral conduct that would have a direct effect on the child (otherwise this is considered irrelevant).
5. Ability to give continuity to the child's current environment (such as home, school, and friends).
6. The availability of contact with members of the child's extended family.

None of the preceding factors is individually controlling, and the court will usually consider factors that are peculiar to each case when making its determination. The U.S. Supreme Court has determined that race or ethnic background cannot be used as the only determining factor in a custody case, although a court may consider race or ethnicity along with the other factors in a custody decision when it is relevant.[29]

An additional factor that is not controlling but may be given some weight is the desire of the child. The general rule is that a child may not be able to determine objectively what is in his or her best interests. However, as a child matures, courts are often more willing to consider the child's opinion. Many states have statutory provisions that expressly permit the judge to give weight to this factor after a child reaches a certain age.[30] Because the child is still a minor and is deemed legally incompetent to make such significant decisions, a court will rarely accept the child's wishes as the sole determining factor.

Joint Custody

Thus far, the discussion has been confined to the issue of single-parent custody, in which one parent has the primary responsibility for the care, control, and education of the child. The noncustodial parent has visitation rights but no legal right to take an active part in the decisions regarding the child's rearing.

Because the limitation on such input was unacceptable to many parents, the concept of joint custody was developed. A common misconception is that joint custody involves only shared physical custody of the child or children. Although this sometimes occurs in joint custody, it is not the primary purpose. The child may very well live permanently with one parent. Joint custody gives each parent the right to take an active part in the rearing of the child. The parents will discuss and agree upon matters of education, religion, and, in general, all major decisions that affect the child's life.[31]

A majority of states have enacted statutes that permit the courts to award joint custody. It is left to the discretion of the judges to determine on a case-by-case basis whether the circumstances are appropriate for joint custody or whether the child's interests would be better served by an award of individual custody to one parent and significant contact with the other parent.

In the best of circumstances, joint custody allows both parents to have input into all aspects of a child's upbringing. As a practical matter, however, it is often an untenable situation. Because of this, judges are often reluctant to grant joint custody unless the circumstances appear overwhelmingly in favor of it.

The problem that arises with joint custody is that in many situations it is contradictory to the divorce itself. The parties have sought a dissolution of their marriage because their relationship was one involving irreconcilable differences. Yet, in joint custody, the parties seek permission of the court to have the legal right to determine important matters, with each having an equal voice in the decision. Often the parties are so opposed to each other they are not willing to work together, even in the best interests of the child. The result is that the parties return to the same judge for mediation of their disputes on matters concerning the child. The purpose of joint custody is not achieved, the parents incur additional legal expenses, and the child is subjected to more disruption than ever. Thus, unless the parties seem to be genuinely interested and capable of working with each other, many courts are hesitant to grant joint custody.

Enforcement of Custody Orders

An increasingly common issue in child custody cases is that of court jurisdiction. With the expanding mobility of American society, it is no longer uncommon for parents to live in different states. Consequently, enforcement of child custody orders can rapidly develop into a costly and time-consuming battle for parents in conflict. In response, the Uniform Child Custody Jurisdiction Act (UCCJA) has been adopted, which sets up guidelines for determining jurisdiction and establishing cooperation among the states in the enforcement of custody orders. While not a cure, this uniform law has eliminated a great many of the problems and concerns that parents might face when they live in separate jurisdictions. Figure 14.3 gives the text of the Uniform Child Custody Jurisdiction Act.

Assignment 14.5

> Examine the UCCJA and determine the proper steps that a parent must take to register a custody order in a jurisdiction other than where it was originally granted.

CHILD SUPPORT

Although the obligation to provide support to a spouse may end with the dissolution of the marital relationship, support of children of the marriage continues as long as the court determines it is necessary. Generally, this is for the remainder of the child's minority or until high school graduation.[32] However, judges are increasingly coming to the view that parents, when able, should also contribute toward a child's college education.[33] The theory is that the child of divorced parents should be in a position similar to the child of nondivorced parents who has the benefit of family support. Additionally, support may be extended beyond a child's majority if the child has some physical or mental incapacity that prevents the child from becoming responsible for filling his or her own needs.

FIGURE 14.3   Uniform Child Custody Jurisdiction Act

---

§ 1. Purposes of Act; Construction of Provisions.—

(a) The general purposes of this Act are to:

(1) avoid jurisdictional competition and conflict with courts of other states in matters of child custody which have in the past resulted in the shifting of children from state to state with harmful effects on their well-being;

(2) promote cooperation with the courts of other states to the end that a custody decree is rendered in that state which can best decide the case in the interest of the child;

(3) assure that litigation concerning the custody of a child take place ordinarily in the state with which the child and his family have the closest connection and where significant evidence concerning his care, protection, training, and personal relationships is most readily available, and that courts of this state decline the exercise of jurisdiction when the child and his family have a closer connection with another state;

(4) discourage continuing controversies over child custody in the interest of greater stability of home environment and of secure family relationships for the child;

(5) deter abductions and other unilateral removals of children undertaken to obtain custody awards;

(6) avoid re-litigation of custody decisions of other states in this state insofar as feasible;

(7) facilitate the enforcement of custody decrees of other states;

(8) promote and expand the exchange of information and other forms of mutual assistance between the courts of this state and those of other states concerned with the same child; and

(9) make uniform the law of those states which enact it.

(b) This Act shall be construed to promote the general purposes stated in this section.

§ 2. Definitions.—As used in this Act:

(1) "contestant" means a person, including a parent, who claims a right to custody or visitation rights with respect to a child;

(2) "custody determination" means a court decision and court orders and instructions providing for the custody of a child, including visitation rights; it does not include a decision relating to child support or any other monetary obligation of any person;

(3) "custody proceeding" includes proceedings in which a custody determination is one of several issues, such as an action for divorce or separation, and includes child neglect and dependency proceedings;

(4) "decree" or "custody decree" means a custody determination contained in a judicial decree or order made in a custody proceeding, and includes an initial decree and a modification decree;

(5) "home state" means the state in which the child immediately preceding the time involved lived with his parents, a parent, or a person acting as parent, for at least 6 consecutive months, and in the case of a child less than 6 months old the state in which the child lived from birth with any of the persons mentioned. Periods of temporary absence of any of the named persons are counted as part of the 6-month or other period;

(6) "initial decree" means the first custody decree concerning a particular child;

(7) "modification decree" means a custody decree which modifies or replaces a prior decree, whether made by the court which rendered the prior decree or by another court;

(8) "physical custody" means actual possession and control of a child;

(9) "person acting as parent" means a person, other than a parent, who has physical custody of a child and who has either been awarded custody by a court or claims a right to custody; and

(10) "state" means any state, territory, or possession of the United States, the Commonwealth of Puerto Rico, and the District of Columbia.

§ 3. Jurisdiction.—

(a) A court of this State which is competent to decide child custody matters has jurisdiction to make a child custody determination by initial or modification decree if:

(1) this State (i) is the home state of the child at the time of commencement of the proceeding, or (ii) had been the child's home state within 6 months before commencement of the proceeding and the child is absent from this State because of his removal or retention by a person claiming his custody or for other reasons, and a parent or person acting as parent continues to live in this State; or

(2) it is in the best interest of the child that a court of this State assume jurisdiction because (i) the child and his parents, or the child and at least one contestant, have a significant connection with this State, and (ii) there is available in this State substantial evidence concerning the child's present or future care, protection, training, and personal relationships; or

(3) the child is physically present in this State and (i) the child has been abandoned or (ii) it is necessary in an emergency to protect the child because he has been subjected to or threatened with mistreatment or abuse or is otherwise neglected [or dependent]; or

---

FIGURE 14.3   Uniform Child Custody Jurisdiction Act (*Continued*)

---

(4)(i) it appears that no other state would have jurisdiction under prerequisites substantially in accordance with paragraphs (1), (2), or (3), or another state has declined to exercise jurisdiction on the ground that this State is the more appropriate forum to determine the custody of the child, and (ii) it is in the best interest of the child that this court assume jurisdiction.

(b) Except under paragraphs (3) and (4) of subsection (a), physical presence in this State of the child, or of the child and one of the contestants, is not alone sufficient to confer jurisdiction on a court of this State to make a child custody determination.

(c) Physical presence of the child, while desirable, is not a prerequisite for jurisdiction to determine his custody.

§ 4. Notice and Opportunity to be Heard.—Before making a decree under this Act, reasonable notice and opportunity to be heard shall be given to the contestants, any parent whose parental rights have not been previously terminated, and any person who has physical custody of the child. If any of these persons is outside this State, notice and opportunity to be heard shall be given pursuant to section 5.

§ 5. Notice to Persons Outside this State; Submission to Jurisdiction.—

(a) Notice required for the exercise of jurisdiction over a person outside this State shall be given in a manner reasonably calculated to give actual notice, and may be:

(1) by personal delivery outside this State in the manner prescribed for service of process within this State;

(2) in the manner prescribed by the law of the place in which the service is made for service of process in that place in an action in any of its courts of general jurisdiction;

(3) by any form of mail addressed to the person to be served and requesting a receipt; or

(4) as directed by the court [including publication, if other means of notification are ineffective].

(b) Notice under this section shall be served, mailed, or delivered, [or last published] at least [10, 20] days before any hearing in this State.

(c) Proof of service outside this State may be made by affidavit of the individual who made the service, or in the manner prescribed by the law of this State, the order pursuant to which the service is made, or the law of the place in which the service is made. If service is made by mail, proof may be a receipt signed by the addressee or other evidence of delivery to the addressee.

(d) Notice is not required if a person submits to the jurisdiction of the court.

§ 6. Simultaneous Proceedings in Other States.—

(a) A court of this State shall not exercise its jurisdiction under this Act if at the time of filing the petition a proceeding concerning the custody of the child was pending in a court of another state exercising jurisdiction substantially in conformity with this Act, unless the proceeding is stayed by the court of the other state because this State is a more appropriate forum or for other reasons.

(b) Before hearing the petition in a custody proceeding the court shall examine the pleadings and other information supplied by the parties under section 9 and shall consult the child custody registry established under section 16 concerning the pendency of proceedings with respect to the child in other states. If the court has reason to believe that proceedings may be pending in another state it shall direct an inquiry to the state court administrator or other appropriate official of the other state.

(c) If the court is informed during the course of the proceeding that a proceeding concerning the custody of the child was pending in another state before the court assumed jurisdiction it shall stay the proceeding and communicate with the court in which the other proceeding is pending to the end that the issue may be litigated in the more appropriate forum and that information be exchanged in accordance with sections 19 through 22. If a court of this State has made a custody decree before being informed of a pending proceeding in a court of another state it shall immediately inform that court of the fact. If the court is informed that a proceeding was commenced in another state after it assumed jurisdiction it shall likewise inform the other court to the end that the issues may be litigated in the more appropriate forum.

§ 7. Inconvenient Forum.—

(a) A court which has jurisdiction under this Act to make an initial or modification decree may decline to exercise its jurisdiction any time before making a decree if it finds that it is an inconvenient forum to make a custody determination under the circumstances of the case and that a court of another state is a more appropriate forum.

(b) A finding of inconvenient forum may be made upon the court's own motion or upon motion of a party or a guardian ad litem or other representative of the child.

(c) In determining if it is an inconvenient forum, the court shall consider if it is in the interest of the child that another state assume jurisdiction. For this purpose it may take into account the following factors, among others:

(1) if another state is or recently was the child's home state;

(2) if another state has a closer connection with the child and his family or with the child and one or more of the contestants;

FIGURE 14.3   Uniform Child Custody Jurisdiction Act (*Continued*)

---

(3) if substantial evidence concerning the child's present or future care, protection, training, and personal relationships is more readily available in another state;

(4) if the parties have agreed on another forum which is no less appropriate; and

(5) if the exercise of jurisdiction by a court of this State would contravene any of the purposes stated in section 1.

(d) Before determining whether to decline or retain jurisdiction the court may communicate with a court of another state and exchange information pertinent to the assumption of jurisdiction by either court with a view to assuring that jurisdiction will be exercised by the more appropriate court and that a forum will be available to the parties.

(e) If the court finds that it is an inconvenient forum and that a court of another state is a more appropriate forum, it may dismiss the proceedings, or it may stay the proceedings upon condition that a custody proceeding be promptly commenced in another named state or upon any other conditions which may be just and proper, including the condition that a moving party stipulate his consent and submission to the jurisdiction of the other forum.

(f) The court may decline to exercise its jurisdiction under this Act if a custody determination is incidental to an action for divorce or another proceeding while retaining jurisdiction over the divorce or other proceeding.

(g) If it appears to the court that it is clearly an inappropriate forum it may require the party who commenced the proceedings to pay, in addition to the costs of the proceedings in this State, necessary travel and other expenses, including attorneys' fees, incurred by other parties or their witnesses. Payment is to be made to the clerk of the court for remittance to the proper party.

(h) Upon dismissal or stay of proceedings under this section the court shall inform the court found to be the more appropriate forum of this fact, or if the court which would have jurisdiction in the other state is not certainly known, shall transmit the information to the court administrator or other appropriate official for forwarding to the appropriate court.

(i) Any communication received from another state informing this State of a finding of inconvenient forum because a court of this State is the more appropriate forum shall be filed in the custody registry of the appropriate court. Upon assuming jurisdiction the court of this State shall inform the original court of this fact.

§ 8. Jurisdiction Declined by Reason of Conduct.—

(a) If the petitioner for an initial decree has wrongfully taken the child from another state or has engaged in similar reprehensible conduct the court may decline to exercise jurisdiction if this is just and proper under the circumstances.

(b) Unless required in the interest of the child, the court shall not exercise its jurisdiction to modify a custody decree of another state if the petitioner, without consent of the person entitled to custody, has improperly removed the child from the physical custody of the person entitled to custody or has improperly retained the child after a visit or other temporary relinquishment of physical custody. If the petitioner has violated any other provision of a custody decree of another state the court may decline to exercise its jurisdiction if this is just and proper under the circumstances.

(c) In appropriate cases a court dismissing a petition under this section may charge the petitioner with necessary travel and other expenses, including attorneys' fees, incurred by other parties or their witnesses.

§ 9. Information under Oath to be Submitted to the Court.—

(a) Every party in a custody proceeding in his first pleading or in an affidavit attached to that pleading shall give information under oath as to the child's present address, the places where the child has lived within the last 5 years, and the names and present addresses of the persons with whom the child has lived during that period. In this pleading or affidavit every party shall further declare under oath whether:

(1) he has participated (as a party, witness, or in any other capacity) in any other litigation concerning the custody of the same child in this or any other state;

(2) he has information of any custody proceeding concerning the child pending in a court of this or any other state; and

(3) he knows of any person not a party to the proceedings who has physical custody of the child or claims to have custody or visitation rights with respect to the child.

(b) If the declaration as to any of the above items is in the affirmative the declarant shall give additional information under oath as required by the court. The court may examine the parties under oath as to details of the information furnished and as to other matters pertinent to the court's jurisdiction and the disposition of the case.

(c) Each party has a continuing duty to inform the court of any custody proceeding concerning the child in this or any other state of which he obtained information during this proceeding.

§ 10. Additional Parties.—If the court learns from information furnished by the parties pursuant to section 9 or from other sources that a person not a party to the custody proceeding has physical custody of the child or claims to have custody or visitation rights with respect to the child, it shall order that person to be joined as a party and to be duly notified of the pendency of the proceeding and of his joinder as a party. If the person joined as a party is outside this State he shall be served with process or otherwise notified in accordance with section 5.

FIGURE 14.3   Uniform Child Custody Jurisdiction Act (*Continued*)

---

§ 11. Appearance of Parties and the Child.—

[(a) The court may order any party to the proceeding who is in this State to appear personally before the court. If that party has physical custody of the child the court may order that he appear personally with the child.]

(b) If a party to the proceeding whose presence is desired by the court is outside this State with or without the child the court may order that the notice given under section 5 include a statement directing that party to appear personally with or without the child and declaring that failure to appear may result in a decision adverse to that party.

(c) If a party to the proceeding who is outside this State is directed to appear under subsection (b) or desires to appear personally before the court with or without the child, the court may require another party to pay to the clerk of the court travel and other necessary expenses of the party so appearing and of the child if this is just and proper under the circumstances.

§ 12. Binding Force and Res Judicata Effect of Custody Decree.—A custody decree rendered by a court of this State which had jurisdiction under section 3 binds all parties who have been served in this State or notified in accordance with section 5 or who have submitted to the jurisdiction of the court, and who have been given an opportunity to be heard. As to these parties the custody decree is conclusive as to all issues of law and fact decided and as to the custody determination made unless and until that determination is modified pursuant to law, including the provisions of this Act.

§ 13. Recognition of Out-of-State Custody Decrees.—The courts of this State shall recognize and enforce an initial or modification decree of a court of another state which had assumed jurisdiction under statutory provisions substantially in accordance with this Act or which was made under factual circumstances meeting the jurisdictional standards of the Act, so long as this decree has not been modified in accordance with jurisdictional standards substantially similar to those of this Act.

§ 14. Modification of Custody Decree of Another State.—

(a) If a court of another state has made a custody decree, a court of this State shall not modify that decree unless (1) it appears to the court of this State that the court which rendered the decree does not now have jurisdiction under jurisdictional prerequisites substantially in accordance with this Act or has declined to assume jurisdiction to modify the decree and (2) the court of this State has jurisdiction.

(b) If a court of this State is authorized under subsection (a) and section 8 to modify a custody decree of another state it shall give due consideration to the transcript of the record and other documents of all previous proceedings submitted to it in accordance with section 22.

§ 15. Filing and Enforcement of Custody Decree of Another State.—

(a) A certified copy of a custody decree of another state may be filed in the office of the clerk of any [District Court, Family Court] of this State. The clerk shall treat the decree in the same manner as a custody decree of the [District Court, Family Court] of this State. A custody decree so filed has the same effect and shall be enforced in like manner as a custody decree rendered by a court of this State.

(b) A person violating a custody decree of another state which makes it necessary to enforce the decree in this State may be required to pay necessary travel and other expenses, including attorneys' fees, incurred by the party entitled to the custody or his witnesses.

§ 16. Registry of Out-of-State Custody Decrees and Proceedings.—The clerk of each [District Court, Family Court] shall maintain a registry in which he shall enter the following:

(1) certified copies of custody decrees of other states received for filing;

(2) communications as to the pendency of custody proceedings in other states;

(3) communications concerning a finding of inconvenient forum by a court of another state; and

(4) other communications or documents concerning custody proceedings in another state which may affect the jurisdiction of a court of this State or the disposition to be made by it in a custody proceeding.

§ 17. Certified Copies of Custody Decree.—The Clerk of the [District Court, Family Court] of this State, at the request of the court of another state or at the request of any person who is affected by or has a legitimate interest in a custody decree, shall certify and forward a copy of the decree to that court or person.

§ 18. Taking Testimony in Another State.—In addition to other procedural devices available to a party, any party to the proceeding or a guardian ad litem or other representative of the child may adduce testimony of witnesses, including parties and the child, by deposition or otherwise in another state. The court on its own motion may direct that the testimony of a person be taken in another state and may prescribe the manner in which and the terms upon which the testimony shall be taken.

FIGURE 14.3   Uniform Child Custody Jurisdiction Act (*Continued*)

§ 19. Hearings and Studies in Another State; Orders to Appear.—

(a) A court of this State may request the appropriate court of another state to hold a hearing to adduce evidence, to order a party to produce or give evidence under other procedures of that state, or to have social studies made with respect to the custody of a child involved in proceedings pending in the court of this State; and to forward to the court of this State certified copies of the transcript of the record of the hearing, the evidence otherwise adduced, or any social studies prepared in compliance with the request. The cost of the services may be assessed against the parties or, if necessary, ordered paid by the [County, State].

(b) A court of this State may request the appropriate court of another state to order a party to custody proceedings pending in the court of this State to appear in the proceedings, and if that party has physical custody of the child, to appear with the child. The request may state that travel and other necessary expenses of the party and of the child whose appearance is desired will be assessed against another party or will otherwise be paid.

§ 20. Assistance to Courts of Other States.—

(a) Upon request of the court of another state the courts of this State which are competent to hear custody matters may order a person in this State to appear at a hearing to adduce evidence or to produce or give evidence under other procedures available in this State [or may order social studies to be made for use in a custody proceeding in another state]. A certified copy of the transcript of the record of the hearing or the evidence otherwise adduced [and any social studies prepared] shall be forwarded by the clerk of the court to the requesting court.

(b) A person within this State may voluntarily give his testimony or statement in this State for use in a custody proceeding outside this State.

(c) Upon request of the court of another state a competent court of this State may order a person in this State to appear alone or with the child in a custody proceeding in another state. The court may condition compliance with the request upon assurance by the other state that state travel and other necessary expenses will be advanced or reimbursed.

§ 21. Preservation of Documents for Use in Other States.—In any custody proceeding in this State the court shall preserve the pleadings, orders and decrees, any record that has been made of its hearings, social studies, and other pertinent documents until the child reaches [18, 21] years of age. Upon appropriate request of the court of another state the court shall forward to the other court certified copies of any or all such documents.

§ 22. Request for Court Records of Another State.—If a custody decree has been rendered in another state concerning a child involved in a custody proceeding pending in a court of this State, the court of this State upon taking jurisdiction of the case shall request of the court of the other state a certified copy of the transcript of any court record and other documents mentioned in section 21.

§ 23. International Application.—The general policies of this Act extend to the international area. The provisions of this Act relating to the recognition and enforcement of custody decrees of other states apply to custody decrees and decrees involving legal institutions similar in nature to custody institutions rendered by appropriate authorities of other nations if reasonable notice and opportunity to be heard were given to all affected persons.

[§ 24. Priority.—Upon the request of a party to a custody proceeding which raises a question of existence or exercise of jurisdiction under this Act the case shall be given calendar priority and handled expeditiously.]

§ 25. Severability.—If any provision of this Act or the application thereof to any person or circumstance is held invalid, its invalidity does not affect other provisions or applications of the Act which can be given effect without the invalid provision or application, and to this end the provisions of this Act are several.

If a child marries or becomes legally emancipated before the age of majority, the child will become fully independent. As a result, the parents will no longer be legally responsible for providing support for the child. On the other hand, if a parent dies and leaves no provision for the support of the child, the child is still entitled to a share of the parent's estate for support. The exception to this occurs when the parent leaves a will in which he or she specifically disinherits the child. If this occurs, the support may, in some states, be terminated, and the child becomes the sole responsibility of the surviving parent. However, as with matters of domestic law, the particular state's law should be examined in a situation before reaching any conclusions.

There is usually little contest over the obligation to provide support. Most parties accept that they are obligated to support their natural or adopted children. The real turmoil begins when the parties attempt to determine the amount of support to be contributed. If financially able, the noncustodial parent—whether the mother or the father—is responsible for periodically paying a specified amount to the custodial parent. The money is to be used for such needs of the child as food, shelter, clothing, and medical and educational expenses.

Unless the parties agree to an amount for support, a hearing will be held to determine the financial needs of the child based on information provided by the parties and the financial ability of the noncustodial parent to contribute toward the needs of the child. With this information, the court will make a decision as to what an appropriate amount would be and how often the amount should be paid.[34]

Child Support Guidelines

When determining the amount of child support, the court considers many independent factors that influence the amount of support that it will actually order. Many states have guidelines that provide formulas for calculation or factors that should be considered, including, but not limited to, the following:

1. The number of children (of this marriage or others) for whom the parent is obligated to provide support.
2. Whether one of the parents provides health insurance for the child.
3. The net income of each parent.
4. Any special medical or educational needs of the child.
5. The standard of living the child would have enjoyed had the divorce not occurred.[35]

It is assumed that an equitable share is contributed by the custodial parent who physically provides the food, shelter, clothing, and attention to other needs of the child.

A particularly helpful statute has been adopted in recent years that establishes child support guidelines (see Figure 14.4). These guidelines have been adopted in most states and provide a formula that courts can employ to determine the appropriate amount of child support, given the financial circumstances of the parties. However, these are only guidelines, and typically, a court has the authority to override them in cases involving special considerations.

Modification of Support

Once support has been awarded, it is due and payable until the child reaches the age of majority or the court orders a change in the amount of support payable. If support is being paid to a custodial parent for the care of more than

FIGURE 14.4   Nevada Revised Statutes Title 11. Domestic Relations. Chapter 125B. Obligation of Support. General Provisions

---

125B.070. Amount of payment: Definitions; review of formula by State Bar of Nevada.

1. As used in this section and NRS 125B.080, unless the context otherwise requires:

(a) "Gross monthly income" means the total amount of income from any source of a wage-earning employee or the gross income from any source of a self-employed person, after deduction of all legitimate business expenses, but without deduction for personal income taxes, contributions for retirement benefits, contributions to a pension or for any other personal expenses.

(b) "Obligation for support" means the amount determined according to the following schedule:

(1) For one child, 18 percent;

(2) For two children, 25 percent;

(3) For three children, 29 percent;

(4) For four children, 31 percent; and

(5) For each additional child, an additional 2 percent, of a parent's gross monthly income, but not more than $500 per month per child for an obligation for support determined pursuant to subparagraphs (1) to (4), inclusive, unless the court sets forth findings of fact as to the basis for a different amount pursuant to subsection 5 of NRS 125B.080.

2. On or before January 18, 1993, and on or before the third Monday in January every 4 years thereafter, the State Bar of Nevada shall review the formulas set forth in this section to determine whether any modifications are advisable and report to the legislature their findings and any proposed amendments.

125B.080. Formula for determining amount of support.

1. A court shall apply the appropriate formula set forth in paragraph (b) of subsection 1 of NRS 125B.070 to:

(a) Determine the required support in any case involving the support of children.

(b) Any request filed after July 1, 1987, to change the amount of the required support of children.

2. If the parties agree as to the amount of support required, the parties shall certify that the amount of support is consistent with the appropriate formula set forth in paragraph (b) of subsection 1 of NRS 125B.070. If the amount of support deviates from the formula, the parties must stipulate sufficient facts in accordance with subsection 9 which justify the deviation to the court, and the court shall make a written finding thereon. Any inaccuracy or falsification of financial information which results in an inappropriate award of support is grounds for a motion to modify or adjust the award.

3. If the parties disagree as to the amount of the gross monthly income of either party, the court shall determine the amount and may direct either party to furnish financial information or other records, including income tax returns for the preceding 3 years. Once a court has established an obligation for support by reference to a formula set forth in paragraph (b) of subsection 1 of NRS 125B.070, any subsequent modification or adjustment of that support must be based upon changed circumstances or as a result of a review conducted pursuant to NRS 125B.145.

4. Notwithstanding the formulas set forth in paragraph (b) of subsection 1 of NRS 125B.070, the minimum amount of support that may be awarded by a court in any case is $100 per month per child, unless the court makes a written finding that the obligor is unable to pay the minimum amount. Willful underemployment or unemployment is not a sufficient cause to deviate from the awarding of at least the minimum amount.

5. It is presumed that the basic needs of a child are met by the formulas set forth in paragraph (b) of subsection 1 of NRS 125B.070. This presumption may be rebutted by evidence proving that the needs of a particular child are not met by the applicable formula.

6. If the amount of the awarded support for a child is greater or less than the amount which would be established under the applicable formula, the court shall set forth findings of fact as to the basis for the deviation from the formula.

7. Expenses for health care which are not reimbursed, including expenses for medical, surgical, dental, orthodontic and optical expenses, must be borne equally by both parents in the absence of extraordinary circumstances.

8. If a parent who has an obligation for support is willfully underemployed or unemployed, to avoid an obligation for support of a child, that obligation must be based upon the parent's true potential earning capacity.

9. The court shall consider the following factors when adjusting the amount of support of a child upon specific findings of fact:

(a) The cost of health insurance;

(b) The cost of child care;

(c) Any special educational needs of the child;

(d) The age of the child;

(e) The responsibility of the parents for the support of others;

(f) The value of services contributed by either parent;

(g) Any public assistance paid to support the child;

(h) Any expenses reasonably related to the mother's pregnancy and confinement;

(i) The cost of transportation of the child to and from visitation if the custodial parent moved with the child from the jurisdiction of the court which ordered the support and the noncustodial parent remained;

(j) The amount of time the child spends with each parent;

(k) Any other necessary expenses for the benefit of the child; and

(l) The relative income of both parents.

one child, the noncustodial parent cannot automatically reduce the support when one of the children reaches the age of majority. Usually, a party is required to petition the court to review the original support order and modify it accordingly.

Modification of support may be granted in circumstances other than a child's reaching majority. Courts will periodically entertain petitions to modify support when there has been a substantial change in the general cost of supporting the child. If a divorce occurs when a child is very young, it may be necessary for the custodial parent to seek an increase in support at some time during the child's minority. After several years, as the child enters school, inflation and other factors may increase the cost of meeting the child's needs. It may be necessary for the custodial parent to seek an upward modification of the original order of support.

The status of the parents may change dramatically over a longer period of time. If one parent meets with long-term financial difficulty, a downward or upward modification may be in order. If the custodial parent enjoys tremendous financial gain, it may serve no purpose for the noncustodial parent to continue contributing to the child's support. The point is that many circumstances could occur that necessitate a change in the original order of support. However, most states limit the frequency with which such changes may be made and require that the circumstances that warrant such a change be substantial and long term.

Failure to Pay

If a party fails to adhere to an order of support, several things may take place. Usually, the first to occur is a legal action by the custodial parent against the parent obligated to pay support. The action is generally a request to hold the noncustodial parent in contempt of court for deliberately disobeying a court order to provide support for the minor child. In addition, many states have enacted or are considering procedures by which the licenses (drivers, business, professional, liquor, etc.) of parents failing to pay child support can be revoked. A parent who is unable to pay support on the date ordered should always attempt to modify rather than ignore the court order. In the eyes of the court, if the parent is able to pay the support but does not or is habitually late in paying, the court may enter an order of contempt.[36]

The results of a finding of contempt of court may be many and varied. The wages of the party may be garnished. The party may be fined. In extreme cases—usually where there has been ongoing contemptuous conduct—the party may be jailed for a period of time. Contrary to popular belief, a court will not deny visitation on the sole basis of failure to pay child support. Nor should a custodial parent ever expect a court to approve of deliberate denial of visitation rights based on a failure to pay support. The two issues are treated as totally separate. The reasoning of the court is that although failure to support may adversely affect a child, denial of visitation has no positive effect on the child. Rather, it only increases the adversity that the child must deal with. If a court does deny visitation, it is usually on the basis that the parent has abandoned all parental responsibility.

In the past, many actions to recover support were rendered virtually impossible because the noncustodial parent lived in another state. This made it very difficult for the court to exercise any control over the parent in terms of compelling payment of support. However, all states have now adopted the Uniform Reciprocal Enforcement of Support Act, a pact among all states to assist one another in enforcing support orders. An action may be filed in the state where the dependent resides. However, a public prosecutor in the state where the noncustodial parent resides may try the case there and enforce any orders of support or contempt. No longer can a noncustodial parent avoid support simply by moving beyond the jurisdictional and financial reach of the custodial parent.

Assignment 14.6

Examine the following situation and determine which facts the court would be likely to consider when making a determination about support.

SITUATION: Gerry and Judith were divorced after three years of marriage. At the time of the divorce, their only child was one year old. Judith worked part time for minimum wage. Gerry worked full time as a laborer. He was ordered to pay support of $150 per month. Two years after the divorce, Gerry married Tomoko. The couple immediately moved 1,200 miles away. They subsequently had three children in four years of marriage. They are currently involved in a divorce action. Tomoko is employed, and her income exceeds Gerry's by approximately 10 percent. However, if Tomoko continues to work full time, all three children will require day care at a cost of $900 per month.

In addition, Gerry's first wife Judith has filed an action for modification and an increase in support for their child. Her basis for the action is that in the past six years, the financial needs of a child in school have greatly increased and the cost of living has risen dramatically. Judith is now employed as a full-time store manager and has approximately the same income as Gerry.

Gerry has just been laid off from his job as a laborer. He is routinely laid off at this time of year for approximately two months because of a seasonal lag in the work available. Gerry does not expect this year to be any different. In fact, during the year he saves a portion of his salary to carry him through this period. However, if he must pay a large amount of support for the children he had with Tomoko and if the increase is awarded in Judith's modification action, he will have little to live on and will not be able to save for layoffs as he has done in the past. Further, he may not be able to pay support at all during the months he is laid off.

CASE ──

**WRIGHT v.
STOVALL**

1997 WL 607508
(Tenn. App. 1997).

Opinion
LILLARD.

This is a child CUSTODY case. The parties had
entered into a Marital Dissolution Agreement in
which they had JOINT CUSTODY of the minor
child. After the father's remarriage, both the
mother and father filed petitions seeking
CUSTODY. The father now appeals the trial court's
order awarding sole CUSTODY of the parties' child
to the mother. We affirm.

James O. Wright ("Father") and Kathy Wright
Stovall ("Mother") were married in 1989. Their
only child, Daniel Ryan Wright, was born in
August 1991. At the time of Daniel's birth, both
parties were working full-time. When Daniel was
born, Mother took off six weeks to care for him.
Father was employed as a chef at the Opryland
Hotel and worked unusually long hours, 5 a.m. to
11 p.m. Mother resumed her full-time job for
approximately four weeks. After that she worked
part-time in order to spend more time with the
parties' child. Mother was clearly the primary
care-giver during this period.

In June 1992, Mother told Father that she was
considering a divorce. Father immediately quit his
position at the hotel and became much more
involved in raising the child. One month later,
Father filed for a divorce, alleging irreconcilable
differences. The parties continued to live together
until the Final Decree of Divorce was entered in
January 1993. The divorce decree incorporated a
Marital Dissolution Agreement (MDA) that
provided for JOINT CUSTODY of the child with
Father designated as the primary physical custodian.
The MDA provided that Father would pay all of the
child's medical bills and Mother would pay $250 per
month in child support. After the divorce, Father
continued to reside in the marital residence and
Mother moved less than one mile away.

After the divorce decree was entered in
January, 1993, the parties alternated care of

Daniel. At that time Daniel spent slightly more
time in Mother's care, generally spending four
nights a week with Mother and three with Father.
However, under a fairly complicated schedule, the
amount of time spent with each parent was
roughly the same. Father testified as to a few
problems between the parties during this time,
such as miscommunications regarding Daniel's
care, but the record indicates that the problems
were minimal.

This arrangement continued until Father's
remarriage in July, 1994. Father's new wife, Lucy,
worked as a radio personality, which permitted
her to be at home during the workday, except for
one day per week. Mother testified that, after
Father's remarriage, the day-to-day activities
regarding Daniel became more difficult to work
out, with Father's new wife becoming overly
involved in the decision making. The parties began
to disagree about issues such as which pediatrician
to use and whether Daniel should be told that
Santa Claus was make-believe. Mother
complained that Father began excluding her from
decision making. She stated that Father explained
to her that he and Lucy were forming a new
"family unit;" Mother also was disturbed by Father
telling Daniel that he now had "two mothers."

In the Spring of 1995, Father received a back
injury which impacted his ability to work as a
chef. Thereafter, he and Lucy have depended on
her income as a radio personality for the family's
income.

In approximately April, 1995, Daniel was
exposed to chicken pox. Father's new wife Lucy
was pregnant, and had never had chicken pox.
Exposure to chicken pox would have been a
health risk to the unborn child, so the parties
agreed that Mother would have exclusive care of
Daniel until the risk of Lucy contracting chicken
pox had abated. This arrangement lasted for
approximately a month. After this, Mother
testified that Father insisted on a change in the
visitation schedule that decreased her time with
Daniel. The new visitation schedule included
Daniel attending day care on Thursdays, even
though Mother was off work on Thursdays and
could care for Daniel. When asked about his

insistence that Daniel spend Thursdays in day care instead of Mother's care, Father said only that he wanted Mother to "keep the agreement." Father acknowledged that he sought to gradually increase the time Daniel spent in the care of he and his new wife, Lucy, and decrease the time Daniel spent with Mother. Mother complained that Father had changed the document at Daniel's day care center listing persons the day care should notify if necessary, to list Father's wife Lucy first and Mother last. Father explained that he made this change because Lucy could respond more quickly in case of an emergency. Mother testified that Father told her that it was his right to use Daniel as a "legal hammer." Father denied this remark.

At this point Mother consulted an attorney and filed a petition in which she alleged that the problems which developed after Father's remarriage constituted a change in circumstances and sought primary physical CUSTODY. Mother testified that, after she filed the petition, she had separate conversations with Father and his wife Lucy. Mother testified that after these conversations she believed that the parties had, for the most part, worked things out to retain JOINT CUSTODY. Mother said that she told Father she wanted Daniel to reside primarily with her, and that Father told her he would consider it and pray about it. She testified that Father suggested that they simply use his attorney to document the agreed changes. Mother then stated that Father came to her house the following Sunday morning and picked up Daniel. About fifteen minutes after picking up Daniel, he returned alone to Mother's house and presented Mother with a proposed agreement under which Mother would receive "standard visitation;" every other weekend and one week night. Mother testified that Father told her that she had to "sign that piece of paper before I could see Daniel again." When she refused, she testified that he told her she would have to have her attorney set up a hearing date in order to see Daniel. She stated that she was not permitted to see Daniel for twelve days, until the trial court ordered that she be permitted visitation every weekend. Mother stated that, after the trial court ordered visitation, Father refused to permit Mother to speak with Daniel by telephone while Daniel was in Father's care. Thereafter, Father filed a counter-petition, asserting

that JOINT CUSTODY was no longer feasible and seeking sole CUSTODY.

At trial, the parties testified regarding their respective employment and ability to care for Daniel. At the time of trial, Father was working reduced hours due to his back injury, and he and Lucy were dependent on Lucy's income as a radio personality for their family finances. Husband testified that he anticipated once again being able to work full-time. He admitted having held eleven different chef positions at restaurants throughout Nashville over the past four years. Father emphasized that Lucy was at home during the workday and could care for Daniel instead of sending him to day care. Father admitted that he was currently dependent on Lucy's income and that he and Lucy had undergone marital counseling, although both he and Lucy said their marriage was healthy. Mother has also remarried, but her remarriage apparently had little impact on the relationship between the parties regarding Daniel. Mother's new husband, Danny Stovall, works full-time, including eight hours on Saturdays. Mother indicated that she is currently working two jobs, arriving home on Monday, Tuesday and Wednesday nights at approximately 8 p.m. At the time of the trial, Mother was pregnant with her first child with Mr. Stovall.

At trial, Mother proffered the testimony of a child psychologist, who opined that the visitation schedule in place at that time was damaging to Daniel, and that Daniel needed more time with Mother. The psychologist expressed the opinion that Daniel related to Mother as primary care giver. The psychologist did not, however, interview Father or observe Daniel in his presence.

At the conclusion of the trial, the trial court awarded sole CUSTODY of Daniel to Mother. The trial court set forth its findings and explained its reasoning as follows:

That the remarriage of [Father] and intervention of the step-mother and changing of schedules initiated by [Father] have caused the JOINT CUSTODY arrangement previously approved by the Court to become unworkable.

That until the arrangement became unworkable, both parties shared CUSTODY of the child, but [Mother] had more time with the child which pattern was acquiesced in by [Father].

That the court takes into consideration the tender years doctrine but concludes it to be only one consideration which the Court is to consider pursuant to statute.

That there is no evidence that either of the parties continues to have any lifestyle that would not be conducive and in the BEST INTEREST of the welfare of the child.

That there is no evidence presented to the Court that either of the parties now uses illegal drugs even though there is evidence that both did so in the past.

That the proof shows that the parties now have different lifestyles at the time of this hearing than the ones they had at the time of the divorce.

That, taking into consideration the testimony of all of the witnesses, their demeanor, their attitudes, their controlling natures and expert testimony presented, the Court finds that both of these parties are fit and proper parents.

That at this time, the Court finds that it is in the BEST INTEREST of the child and evidence so indicates that sole and absolute CUSTODY of the minor child shall be awarded to the Mother, ...

The trial court then set forth a visitation schedule in which Daniel resides primarily with Mother during the school year, and primarily with Father during the summer months. The trial court also included the following in its Order:

That the Respondent, James Otis Wright, Jr., and his current spouse, Lucy Wright, shall be ENJOINED AND RESTRAINED from attempting to alienate the affections of the minor child from the Petitioner [Mother].

Father now appeals the trial court's award of sole CUSTODY to Mother.

On appeal, Father first asserts that the trial court erred in finding that there was a material change in circumstances warranting a change in CUSTODY. Father also asserts that, even if there were a material change in circumstances, the preponderance of the evidence did not support the trial court's decision to award sole CUSTODY to Mother.

In child CUSTODY cases, appellate review is de novo upon the record, with a presumption of the correctness of the trial court's factual findings. Tenn.R.App.P. 13(d); Hass v. Knighton, 676 S.W.2d 554, 555 (Tenn.1984); Dalton v. Dalton, 858 S.W.2d 324, 327 (Tenn.App.1993).

Father asserts first that the trial court erred in determining that there was a material change in circumstances justifying a change in CUSTODY.

In essence, Father asserts that the parties should return to a JOINT CUSTODY arrangement. However, in his counter-petition before the trial court, Father asserted that JOINT CUSTODY "is no longer workable or feasible, nor is it in the BEST INTEREST of the minor child of the parties." At trial, Father testified that the JOINT CUSTODY arrangement in place since the divorce decree had not worked. Mother testified that the JOINT CUSTODY arrangement had not worked since Father's remarriage.

At trial, Mother testified about a number of incidents which she alleged indicated that JOINT CUSTODY had not worked since Father's remarriage. These included Lucy's over-involvement in the parties' decisions regarding Daniel, Father's unilateral changes to the visitation schedule to reduce Mother's time with Daniel, and Father's insistence that Daniel spend time in day care on days Mother was available to care for him. Mother also complained of instances which she alleged indicated that Father sought to have Lucy replace her as Daniel's mother, such as placing Lucy first on the day care's list of persons to notify, and telling Daniel that he had "two mothers." Mother further cited Father's refusal to allow her to see Daniel without a court order and, after the trial court ordered visitation, his refusal to permit her to speak with Daniel by telephone.

Where the parties have agreed upon JOINT CUSTODY and the arrangement later becomes unworkable, this is a sufficient change of circumstances to warrant a re-evaluation of the CUSTODY arrangement. See Dalton v. Dalton, 858 S.W.2d 324, 326 (Tenn.App.1993); Dodd v. Dodd, 737 S.W.2d 286, 290 (Tenn.App.1987). The practical problems of JOINT CUSTODY have been repeatedly acknowledged by this court, especially if there is hostility between the two parents. See Winchester v. Winchester, No. 02A01-9604-CH-00092, 1997 WL 61508 (Tenn.App. Feb. 14, 1997); Jones v. Jones, No. 01-A-01-9601-CV00038, 1996 WL 512030 (Tenn.App. Sept. 11, 1996).

Father notes that the Marital Dissolution Agreement entered into by the parties states that the minor child will reside primarily with him. However, the proof established that, until Father insisted on a new visitation schedule that decreased Mother's time with Daniel, the child spent virtually equal amounts of time with each parent, spending slightly more time with Mother.

This Court has repeatedly emphasized the importance of stability for children involved in divorce. See Williams v. Williams, No. 01A01-9610-CV-00468, 1997 WL 272458, Tenn.App. May 23, 1997); Contreras v. Ward, 831 S.W.2d 288, 290 (Tenn.App.1991) (quoting Sartoph v. Sartoph, 31 Md.App. 58, 354 A.2d 467, 473 (Md. 1976)) ("In short, when all goes well with children, stability, not change, is in their BEST INTERESTS."). However, the testimony indicates that Daniel's current situation is unstable, with significant conflict between his parents. To succeed, JOINT CUSTODY "require[s] a harmonious and cooperative relationship between both parents." Dodd v. Dodd, 737 S.W.2d at 290. Both parties testified that JOINT CUSTODY had become unworkable, although each saw the other as the problem. The psychologist hired by Mother testified that Daniel's behavior worsened as the conflicts between his parents increased. The record contained sufficient evidence to support the trial court's decision to re-evaluate the CUSTODY arrangement.

After it is determined that a material change in circumstances has occurred, sufficient to warrant a re-evaluation of the CUSTODY arrangements, the trial court must perform a comparative fitness analysis to make a CUSTODY determination. See Williams. The trial court's findings in making a comparative fitness analysis were cursory in this case:

That, taking into consideration the testimony of all of the witnesses, their demeanor, their attitudes, their controlling natures and expert testimony presented, the Court finds that both of these parties are fit and proper parents.

That at this time, the Court finds that it is in the BEST INTEREST of the child and evidence so indicates that sole and absolute CUSTODY of the minor child shall be awarded to the Mother. . . .

The trial court also included in its order the following injunctive relief:

That the Respondent, James Otis Wright, Jr., and his current spouse, Lucy Wright, shall be ENJOINED AND RESTRAINED from attempting to alienate the affection of the minor child from the Petitioner [Mother].

Many factors are taken into account in making the comparative fitness analysis. See Tenn. Code

Ann. s 36-6-106. In this case, Daniel clearly loves both parents. Both parents have provided him with necessities. During Daniel's infancy, Mother was clearly the primary care giver. However, since the divorce, the time spent with each parent has been roughly equal, with Daniel spending slightly more time with Mother. Mother proffered the testimony of the psychologist, who testified that Daniel related to Mother as the primary care giver and was distressed at the prospect of leaving Mother to go to Father's house. However, the psychologist had not interviewed Father or seen how Daniel and Father relate to each other.

Both parents have remarried. Mother and her new husband were expecting a child at the time of trial. Father and Lucy had a 6-month old son. Father and Lucy have obtained some marital counseling, but both testified that their marriage is healthy. Father and Lucy are currently dependent on Lucy's income, due to Father's back injury, but there is no indication that they are unable to provide for Daniel. Lucy's work enables her to be at home much of the time, where she could care for Daniel. Father's job history is somewhat unstable, with numerous job changes. At the time of trial, Father was working only part-time, because of his injury, but anticipated going back to work full-time. There was no proof as to his work schedule when he returns to full-time work.

Mother's job history is stable, with continued employment at Tennessee Christian Medical Center. However, at the time of trial, Mother was working two jobs, arriving home at 8 p.m. on Monday, Tuesday and Wednesday nights. Her husband also worked long hours. The record did not indicate whether this would continue after the Stovalls' baby was born.

Looking at these factors alone, the question regarding CUSTODY is quite close. However, it should be noted that the trial court, in addition to awarding CUSTODY, enjoined Father and Lucy from "attempting to alienate the affections of the minor child" from Mother. In Varley v. Varley, 934 S.W.2d 659 (Tenn.App.1996), this Court affirmed an award of CUSTODY to the father, primarily because of the mother's "blatant attempt to alienate the affections of the children from their father." Varley, 934 S.W.2d at 667. The father testified that the children had been told that "Dad's bad" and had hit and yelled at the father, with tacit encouragement from the mother and her family. In addition, the mother had encouraged the children's relationship with her paramour, Mr. Ligon, while discouraging their relationship with their father. The Court stated:

The record also suggests that the children have been encouraged to develop a positive relationship with Mr. Ligon, which is not to be impugned except to the extent that such is detrimental to the children's relationship with their own father.

Id. at 667. The Court then observed:

We believe it [is] in the BEST INTEREST of these children that they maintain a loving and nurturing relationship with both parents. In light of the record, we do not believe that such can be accomplished by an award of CUSTODY to Wife at this time.

Id. at 668. Therefore, where one parent has attempted to alienate the affections of the child from the other parent, and has attempted to substitute a third person for the other parent, this mitigates in favor of an award of CUSTODY to the other parent, in order to preserve the child's relationship with both parents.

In this case, the record supports the trial court's implicit finding that Father had engaged in attempts to alienate Daniel's affections from Mother, and to have Lucy in effect supplant Mother instead of being simply a loving stepparent. The record is undisputed that Father insisted that Daniel stay in day care on Thursdays, when Mother was off work and could care for him. For a time, Father refused to permit Mother to see Daniel, until court-ordered visitation was imposed. Father refused to permit Mother to speak with Daniel by telephone, and attempted to explain this by stating that the calls were distressing to Daniel. After his remarriage, Father told Daniel that he had "two mothers" and asked Daniel's day care to contact Lucy before contacting Mother, purportedly because Lucy could get there more quickly. As stated in Varley, it is in Daniel's BEST INTEREST to "maintain a loving and nurturing relationship with both parents," and we agree with the trial court's implicit finding that this is BEST accomplished by awarding CUSTODY of Daniel to Mother. The award of sole CUSTODY to Mother is therefore affirmed.

Mother seeks attorney's fees on appeal. We do not find an award of attorney's fees appropriate in this case, and so decline Mother's request.

The decision of the trial court is affirmed. Costs are taxed to the Appellant, for which execution may issue if necessary.

FARMER and LEWIS, JJ., concur.

Case Question

In addition to shared physical custody, what constitutes "joint custody"?

 CASE

**JAYCEE B. v.
SUPERIOR COURT**

42 Cal.App.4th 718, 49
Cal.Rptr.2d 694.

I. Introduction

The facts of this surrogacy case would seem to be the most extraordinary to date. A married couple sought to have a child by gestational surrogacy. (See generally Johnson v. Calvert (1993) 5 Cal.4th 84, 19 Cal.Rptr.2d 494, 851 P.2d 776.) Gestational surrogacy means that the husband's sperm is artificially united with the egg of his wife and the resulting embryo is implanted in another woman's uterus, who then carries the child to term. (See Johnson, supra, 5 Cal.4th at

p. 87, 19 Cal.Rptr.2d 494, 851 P.2d 776; see also In re Marriage of Moschetta (1994) 25 Cal.App.4th 1218, 1222, 30 Cal.Rptr.2d 893.) The child is usually the genetic offspring of the married couple, but not the birth mother. We say "usually" because that is not quite what has been alleged to have happened here.

In this case, pursuant to a written contract between four people—a husband, wife, another woman and her husband—a sperm and an egg from anonymous donors were artificially united and implanted in the uterus of the other woman, with the intention that the offspring would be legally the child of the married couple. Unlike "usual" gestational surrogacy, here the child is not genetically related to the intended parents.

This case is also unusual in how it comes to this court. Unlike Johnson and Moschetta, it does not involve the so-called surrogate mother reneging on an agreement and seeking to establish her own parental rights vis-a-vis the child. Rather, about a month before the birth of the child, the married couple separated and dissolution proceedings soon followed. The child was born and the hospital released the child to the wife—the intended mother under the contract. Several months later the wife, in the dissolution action, brought an order to show cause proceeding seeking pendente lite child support, that is, temporary child support pending final adjudication of the matter, from the husband who was the intended father under the contract.

The husband was willing to stipulate that he had signed the contract, but he vigorously disputed the jurisdiction of the family law court to award even temporary support. He claimed the family court could not make such an award because it had not yet been established that the child here was indeed a "child of the marriage." (See Fam.Code, § 2010 ["In a proceeding for dissolution of marriage . . . the court has jurisdiction to inquire into and render any judgment and make orders that are appropriate concerning . . . [¶] . . . [¶] (b) The custody of minor children of the marriage. [¶] (c) The support of children for whom support may be ordered, including children born after the filing of the initial petition. . . ."].)

The trial judge agreed with the husband and ruled the court had no jurisdiction to make a temporary child support order. Essentially, he reasoned that the wife's remedy was first to get an order from the probate court decreeing the child had been adopted. The judge did not address the point raised by the wife's counsel that a probate court could not force the husband to sign adoption papers. However, he acknowledged he was putting the wife in a "Catch-22" situation: requiring her to first establish that the husband was the father of the child before she could obtain an order forcing him to contribute to the child's support.

The trial judge also recognized the case was one of first impression, and that the child might have rights independent of those of the married couple. And he recognized the effect of his decision was to put the economic burden on the wife to challenge his decision by petition for extraordinary writ, so

he appointed independent counsel for the minor. The trial judge then continued the matter to give the minor's counsel time to file the petition.

That petition was filed about two weeks ago. We then invited informal responses from both spouses and the trial court. The wife, of course, sides with the minor, arguing the family law court has jurisdiction. The husband argues there is no legal basis for establishing his paternity, and until a probate court action establishes some type of parentage, there is no jurisdiction for the family law court to award temporary support.

As we now explain, the petition must be granted. We need not—and do not—decide at this juncture whether the child is legally the husband's daughter. It is enough to hold that the wife has made a sufficient showing that the child will be when the question is ultimately settled, by (depending on how far up the ladder this case goes) the trial court, this court, or our Supreme Court. Under facts as were stipulated to by the parties at the hearing, the family law court has jurisdiction to make an order forcing the husband to pay temporary child support until the issue of his parenthood is finally decided.

We therefore issue the requested writ, and direct the family law court to determine an appropriate child support order given the circumstances of the parties. (See Fam.Code, § 3600 ["During the pendency of any proceeding for dissolution of marriage . . . or in any proceeding where there is at issue the support of a minor child or a child for whom support is authorized under Section 3901 . . . the court may order . . . either or both parents to pay any amount necessary for the support of the child, as the case may be."]; Fam.Code, § 3901 [defining duration of duty of support imposed by § 3900]; Fam.Code, § 3900 ["Subject to this division, the father and mother of a minor child have an equal responsibility to support their child in the manner suitable to the child's circumstances."].)

II. Additional Facts

While the introduction to this opinion covers the essential facts, here is a more detailed rendering of the events leading to this writ petition.

John and Luanne were married in May 1989. On March 30, 1995, John filed a petition for dissolution of marriage. He alleged that the couple separated in September 1994, and there were no minor children.

> Because of the procedural posture of the case we must tell the story as it unfolds in the pleadings, rather than in direct chronological order.

Luanne filed her response April 20, 1995. Instead of agreeing with John that there were no minor children, she asserted that the "[p]arties" were "expecting a child by way of surrogate contract" and that the doctor indicated the birth would be about May 5. Luanne attached a copy of the surrogacy contract to her response.

The surrogacy contract was signed by John, Luanne, a woman named Pamela, and Pamela's husband, Randy. Under the terms of the contract, Pamela was to be "implanted with the embryo(s) created with donated genetic material, unrelated to any of the parties. The child [was] to be taken into the home of the Intended Father and Intended Mother and raised by them as their child, without interference by the Surrogate [Pamela] or her husband, and without retention or assertion by the Surrogate and her husband of any parental rights." Among other terms, the contract provided that if the "Intended Mother" died prior to the child's birth, the child would be placed with the "Intended Father," and vice versa. If both intended parents died before the child's birth, the surrogate and her husband were to place the child into the custody of the guardians or intended guardians of the intended parents' children in accordance with the terms of their will.

The contract made reference to Johnson v. Calvert, supra, 5 Cal.4th 84, 19 Cal.Rptr.2d 494, 851 P.2d 776, but recited that the Johnson decision had "not been specifically extended" to these facts. "As such," the document went on, "the parties understand that parentage and custody issues have not been fully settled, and no warranties have been or can be made as to the ultimate cost, liability or obligation of the parties which may result from judicial process arising out of this Agreement."

The date the contract was signed by John and Luanne is not apparent, as neither filled in the line marked "DATED" by their signatures. Pamela and her husband signed the agreement August 25, 1994.

On October 12, 1995, Luanne filed an order to show cause seeking, among other things, sole custody of, and child support for, Jaycee, who had been born April 26, 1995. On that day John filed a responsive declaration opposing the requests for custody and support because the family court lacked jurisdiction.

While this case is obviously one of first impression, it involves a "Catch-22" or chicken-and-egg problem which is familiar to the courts, and which our Supreme Court has already solved, albeit in decisions more resembling Sense and Sensibility than Cells and Surrogacy.

The present case is the functional equivalent of a paternity action, where a mother who is the caretaker of a child seeks court-ordered support from a man but for whose actions the child would never have come into existence. As in a classic paternity action, this case involves the conundrum of a court's authority to order a man to pay child support before it is authoritatively adjudicated that he is the child's father: If jurisdiction depends on first establishing the fact of parentage by final decree, then there can be no jurisdiction to award support prior to such an adjudication. (And, of course, if the paternity defendant really is the father of the child, it means that he escapes his duty to support the child for the duration of the litigation over the parentage issue.)

The precise quantum of proof necessary to show the probable existence of the legal relationship of paternity and marriage upon which a temporary support order could be predicated has been a somewhat troublesome matter, at least as revealed in the late 19th century marriage case of Hite v. Hite. In Hite, a man who was sued for divorce denied he was ever married to the plaintiff. The three-justice lead opinion concluded the trial judge did not intend to hold there was a "preponderance in favor of the fact of marriage," but did so without much discussion of the facts which led them to so conclude. Accordingly, the court reversed a pendente lite alimony and suit money order. (Hite, supra, 124 Cal. at p. 395, 57 P. 227 (lead opn. of Temple, J.).)

Chief Justice Beatty concurred separately to emphasize the point made in the majority opinion (see id. at p. 392, 57 P. 227), that a mere prima facie case—that is, one where the decision would be made without the defendant being able to tell his side of the story—would not be sufficient. (See id. at pp. 396-397, 57 P. 227 (conc. opn. of Beatty, C.J.).) His point was that the defendant had made a "complete denial of the facts alleged by plaintiff as constituting a marriage," and "until that issue [was] tried and determined by final judgment the plaintiff ha[d] no claim upon [the defendant] as his wife." (Ibid.) Justice Harrison also concurred separately. Even though he agreed with the lead opinion, he wrote to emphasize that where the fact of the marriage was denied, the defendant should be entitled to "a hearing and an opportunity to controvert the showing made by the plaintiff upon her application for [pendente lite] alimony as at the final hearing of the action. . . ." (Id. at p. 400, 57 P. 227 (conc. opn. of Harrison, J.).)

On the quantum of evidence point Justice Garoutte attacked the lead opinion as enunciating a rule "opposed to the great weight of authority," including Sharon v. Sharon, supra, 75 Cal. 1, 45, 16 P. 345, decided 11 years earlier, which had indicated a prima facie case would do. (Hite, supra, 124 Cal. at pp. 403–404, 57 P. 227 (dis. opn. of Garoutte, J.).) He then took issue with the majority on their own terms, arguing that the evidence presented by the plaintiff really did establish the existence of the marriage by a preponderance of the evidence. (Id. at p. 405, 57 P. 227 (dis. opn. of Garoutte, J.).)

While Justice Traynor in Carbone did not quite say the proof necessary to establish paternity for purposes of a pendente lite order was the Hite case's "preponderance of the evidence," he did hint strongly in that direction by citing the opinion and stating the rule for marriage cases was proof by a preponderance of the evidence. (See Carbone, supra, 18 Cal.2d at p. 772, 117 P.2d 872.) Interestingly enough, though, another panel of our own court, in a paternity action where the mother sought to discover financial information from an alleged father, indicated it was enough that there be a "prima facie showing of paternity" to compel financial records other than tax returns. (Thomas B. v. Superior Court (1985) 175 Cal.App.3d 255, 258, 220 Cal.Rptr. 577.) In Thomas B. this court stated that in an action to establish parentage there were four component parts, the first of which was "a prima facie showing of paternity for purposes of pendente lite support." (Id. at p. 265, 220 Cal.Rptr. 577.) The phrase was repeated by another panel of this court again in Sherry H. v. Thomas B. (1988)

203 Cal.App.3d 1500, 250 Cal.Rptr. 830, which stated that a pendente lite attorney fee award in a paternity case could be justified "as a form of interim support," thus allowing resort to the defendant's personal financial records. (Id. at pp. 1503–1504, 250 Cal.Rptr. 830.)

In the paternity and marriage cases previously discussed, the result turned on the resolution of a factual dispute. A man was or was not the father of a child (Carbone); a marriage had or had not taken place (Hite). The problem faced by the court was not one where the basic facts were settled, but the legal significance of those facts was at issue; rather, the most basic facts were unsettled at the time the moving party applied for a support order.

A 1935 case, Bancroft v. Bancroft, supra, 9 Cal.App.2d 464, 50 P. 2d 465, was quick to pick up on the distinction between a dispute over a basic jurisdictional fact (like whether there was a marriage in the first place), and the legal significance of an event (like whether an earlier divorce decree was valid) which might bear on the existence of a legal relationship. In the latter case, the admission of the basic jurisdictional fact was enough to establish the legal relationship upon which a support order could be based, even though a court might later hold that the relationship did not exist.

Bancroft was a marriage case where the plaintiff sought temporary alimony. She alleged she was married to the defendant; the defendant admitted he had participated in a marriage ceremony with her in 1913, but denied that they were ever legally married because the plaintiff had never been properly divorced from a previous husband. (See id. at pp. 465-466, 50 P.2d 465.) Taking his cue from Hite, the defendant challenged a $20 per week support order on the theory that the plaintiff had to prove the marriage by a preponderance of the evidence before she could receive even temporary support. (Ibid.)

The appellate court rejected the defendant's contention by distinguishing the Hite case. In Hite, the defendant had denied the fact of marriage; since the fact of marriage had not been established by a preponderance of the evidence, the plaintiff was not allowed pendente lite support. (See Bancroft, supra, 9 Cal.App.2d at p. 467, 50 P.2d 465.) But in the Bancroft case, the defendant had not denied the fact of the marriage. Rather, "[a]ll that he did was to deny the legal effect of this marriage for the reason that the plaintiff was under a supposed disability that prevented her from entering into a lawful marriage with him." (Ibid., emphasis added.) Because the fact of the marriage had been established, the trial court in the Bancroft case "was fully justified" in concluding that the plaintiff had established her marriage "by a preponderance of the evidence," so there was no error in making the temporary support order. (Id. at p. 469, 50 P.2d 465.)

In this case, as in Bancroft, the dispute does not concern the fact of an agreement, but its legal effect. As his attorney told the court, John was willing to stipulate that he signed the contract. The critical question thus becomes whether the surrogacy contract is sufficient to show—by a preponderance of the evidence—that John is Jaycee's father, taking into account that the adjudication of parenthood need not be "so conclusively established" as it would be for purposes of a final adjudication of the matter. (Id. at p. 468, 50 P.2d 465; see also Carbone, supra, 18 Cal.2d at p. 772, 117 P.2d 872 [evidence to support pendente lite paternity order need not be "so complete" or "so extensive" as to constitute a final determination].)

In essence, the question becomes one of law, not fact. At the same time, we must bear in mind that we are not going to decide the ultimate issue in this writ proceeding brought merely to ascertain whether there is jurisdiction to award child support. We must deal in legal probabilities in much the same way that trial courts do when they decide applications for preliminary injunctions. Given the admission he signed the surrogacy agreement, is it likely that John will ultimately be held to be the father?

We turn for the answer, as we did in Moschetta, supra, 25 Cal.App.4th at p. 1228, 30 Cal.Rptr.2d 893, to the only surrogacy decision of our state Supreme Court, Johnson v. Calvert, supra, 5 Cal.4th 84, 19 Cal.Rptr.2d 494, 851 P.2d 776.

Johnson was a gestational surrogacy case where, unlike the present situation, the "intended" parents were also the genetic parents. The dispute was between those intended parents and the woman who gave birth to the child. Our Supreme Court first demonstrated that under the Uniform Parentage Act both the intended

(genetic) mother and the birth mother could establish parentage. (See Johnson, supra, 5 Cal.4th at p. 92, 19 Cal.Rptr.2d 494, 851 P.2d 776.) The court next established there was no preference for either method of showing parenthood under the act, blood tests showing a genetic relationship or the fact of giving birth. Having set up a tie under the terms of the Act, the Supreme Court broke the tie by looking to the "parties' intentions as manifested in the surrogacy agreement." (Id. at p. 93, 19 Cal.Rptr.2d 494, 851 P.2d 776.)

As our exegesis of Johnson in Moschetta tried to show, the court did not go so far as to hold the surrogacy agreement was "enforceable per se." (See Moschetta, supra, 25 Cal.App.4th at p. 1230, 30 Cal.Rptr.2d 893). Rather, such a contract was "a proper basis on which to ascertain the intent" of the parties. (Ibid., original emphasis.)

The remarkable thing about this case is that, unless a court is to hold that the surrogate Pamela is the natural mother of the child, Jaycee has no legal parents at all. Her genetic parents are anonymous and will probably not be held to be her natural parents. (See Fam.Code, § 7613, subd. (b).) And Pamela, the so-called surrogate mother who could establish parenthood under the Uniform Parentage Act, never contemplated keeping the child.

> This statute provides that the donor of semen provided to a licensed physician for use in artificial insemination of a woman other than the donor's wife is treated in law as if he were not the father of the child. We are hard pressed to think of any reason a woman in an analogous situation should be treated differently.

Holding that Pamela, the birth mother, is the natural mother (and thereby, by extension, holding that John cannot be the father) is unlikely to comport with the ultimate result in this case. As our Supreme Court pointed out in Johnson, to rule that the birth mother in a gestational surrogacy arrangement is the natural mother is to burden her with "responsibilities" she never contemplated and is directly "contrary to her expectations." (Johnson, supra, 5 Cal.4th at p. 94, 19 Cal.Rptr.2d 494, 851 P.2d 776.) We decline— particularly at this early stage of the litigation—to reach a result contrary to her and all the parties' expressed intentions. The Johnson court underscored the importance of intentions on page 94 of the opinion, where it quoted from a law review article which advocated their presumptive importance. (Ibid., quoting Shultz, Reproductive Technology and Intent-Based Parenthood: An Opportunity for Gender Neutrality (1990) Wis.L.Rev. 297, 323 [" 'intentions that are voluntarily chosen, deliberate, express and bargained-for ought presumptively to determine legal parenthood' " (fn. omitted)].)

Pamela is not like a natural mother who gives her child up for adoption, but at the last moment the prospective adoptive parents back out. She carried a child that would not have been conceived but for the contract with the intended parents.

While the precise question of gestational surrogacy where the intended parents are not genetically related to the child was not directly before it, the Johnson court did foresee such a possibility. On pages 94 and 95 of the opinion, the court noted there might be an "extremely rare situation in which neither the gestator nor the woman who provided the ovum for fertilization is willing to assume custody of the child after birth." That is quite literally the situation before us now. And what was the Supreme Court's answer? To look to the intention of the parties.

"In what we must hope will be the extremely rare situation in which neither the gestator nor the woman who provided the ovum for fertilization is willing to assume custody of the child after birth, a rule recognizing the intending parents as the child's legal, natural parents should best promote certainty and stability for the child." (Johnson, supra, 5 Cal.4th at pp. 94-95, 19 Cal.Rptr.2d 494, 851 P.2d 776.)

As indicated above, the primary issue that will need to be decided is whether Jaycee is John's child so that he will be obligated to support her under Family Code section 3900. Given the Supreme Court's statement about the importance of looking to the intention of the parties in a situation where neither "mother" (as the term is employed in the Uniform Parentage Act) wants the child, the most likely legal result based on the undisputed fact of John's signing the surrogacy agreement is that John will be held to be Jaycee's father. While we need not finally decide the issue now, it is enough that

John admits he signed the surrogacy agreement which, for all practical purposes, caused Jaycee's conception every bit as much as if he had caused her birth the old fashioned way. As the Supreme Court said in Johnson, "But for their acted-on intention, the child would not exist." (Id. at p. 93, 19 Cal.Rptr.2d 494, 851 P.2d 776.) As we pointed out in Moschetta, the child "would never have been born" except for the surrogacy agreement. (Moschetta, supra, 25 Cal.App.4th at p. 1235, 30 Cal.Rptr.2d 893.)

To take our cue from Carbone and Bancroft, we do not "so conclusively establish" that John is Jaycee's parent under Family Code section 3900 at this juncture in the litigation. But there is enough in the existing law as declared in the Johnson case that we can firmly say that John's signing the surrogacy agreement does show, "by a preponderance of the evidence," that he will likely be held to be Jaycee's father. The family law court has as much jurisdiction to make a pendente lite support order in this case as the courts did in Carbone and Bancroft.

IV. Disposition

[3] Peremptory writs in the first instance are not favored. (See Alexander v. Superior Court (1993) 5 Cal.4th 1218, 1222-1223, 23 Cal.Rptr.2d 397, 859 P.2d 96.) The "accelerated procedure" described in Palma v. U.S. Industrial Fasteners, Inc. (1984) 36 Cal.3d 171, 203 Cal.Rptr. 626, 681 P.2d 893 of inviting informal responses to the petition and then acting on the petition, is the " 'exception; it should not become routine. Generally, that procedure should be adopted only when petitioner's entitlement to relief is so obvious that no purpose could reasonably be served by plenary consideration.' " (Alexander, supra, 5 Cal.4th at p. 1223, 23 Cal.Rptr.2d 397, 859 P.2d 96, quoting Ng v. Superior Court (1992) 4 Cal.4th 29, 35, 13 Cal.Rptr.2d 856, 840 P.2d 961.)

[4] Then again, as Ng pointed out, "unusual urgency," otherwise described as "compelling temporal urgency" (see Ng, supra, 4 Cal.4th at p. 35, 13 Cal.Rptr.2d 856, 840 P.2d 961) can justify the accelerated procedure, as long as the law and facts mandating the relief sought are "entirely clear." (Ibid.)

First, we obviously have extreme urgency: a child needs support. It is important to note the time pressure under which we receive this writ. To issue an alternative writ and require the additional briefing which the normal procedure calls for could delay resolution of the narrow issue before us for several months, and those are several months in which Jaycee will be without the benefit of a support order and during which the parties will be uncertain about whether a support order can even be obtained.

Second, while the entitlement to the relief is not "entirely" clear, the entitlement is as reasonably clear as one might hope for in a case of first impression. Given the language on pages 94 and 95 of the Johnson opinion which contemplates pretty much the exact situation before us, it seems that the law is clear enough that John will probably be ultimately held to be Jaycee's father. Whether, after a full and complete study of the subject, the court having the last word on the subject ultimately agrees, is not relevant at the moment.

Finally, there is a clear fail-safe mechanism built into the procedural posture of the case as it now stands. Further considerations relating to the problem of who is Jaycee's parent under Family Code section 3900 may still be presented at the order to show cause hearing. Our ruling today is an extremely narrow one: we merely hold that the fact John signed the surrogacy agreement in the circumstances of this case is enough to give

the family court jurisdiction to hear the order to show cause. John may still separately appeal from any order made if he is aggrieved by it, and then this court, or the Supreme Court, will contemplate the subject in more leisurely circumstances. (See Carbone, supra, 18 Cal.2d at p. 772, 117 P.2d 872 ["The application is determined upon a record of its own and results in an appealable judgment independent of the final judgment in the action."].) On top of that, he will also be able to appeal any final adjudication that he is Jaycee's father.

Let a peremptory writ issue directing the family law court to hold a hearing forthwith on Luanne's order to show cause for temporary child support and issue an appropriate child support order. To prevent frustration of the relief granted, this opinion shall be final as to this court five days from the date of filing. (Cal.Rules of Court, rule 24(d).)

Once again, the need for legislation in the surrogacy area is apparent. (See Moschetta, supra, 25 Cal.App.4th at p. 1235, 30 Cal.Rptr.2d 893.) We reiterate our previous call for legislative action. CROSBY and WALLIN, JJ., concur.

Case Question
How does the "intended mother" gain parental rights in a surrogacy proceeding such as this?

 CASE

IN RE MARRIAGE OF FALAT

201 Ill.App.3d 320,
147 Ill.Dec. 33, 559
N.E.2d 33 (1990).

Justice **MANNING** delivered the opinion of the court.

Respondent, Donald P. Falat, appeals from an order of the circuit court of Cook County which denied his motion to strike and dismiss Loretta Joyce Falat's petition to increase child support. He further appeals from an order of the court increasing child support for adult children.

On February 6, 1979, a judgment for dissolution of marriage was entered dissolving the marriage of Loretta Joyce Falat ("Joyce Falat") and Donald Falat. The judgment included a separation agreement between the parties which established that child support for their two minor children, David and Karen, is to be paid by the husband in the amount of $410 per month, based on a $25,000 gross annual salary for the husband and $10,000 gross annual salary for the wife. It was further agreed that:

"Husband's obligation for payment of child support shall cease upon any one of the following events:

(a) Emancipation of the child;

(b) The child reaching the age of eighteen (18) years of age, however, said obligation for payment of child support shall continue if after reaching the age of eighteen, said child shall be enrolled as a full-time student in high school or college, and in such event, Husband's obligation to pay child support shall cease upon completion of four-year course of college education.

* * *

On February 6, 1986, Joyce Falat filed a petition for rule to show cause and for modification of the judgment for dissolution of marriage, requesting an increase in child support. A hearing on the petition was commenced on June 16, 1986, before the Honorable William Peterson. During the hearing, Donald Falat testified that his gross income for 1985 was about $39,000 and copies of three paystubs reflecting his income through March 31, 1986, as $12,626 were received into evidence. Donald Falat also submitted an affidavit of his expenses. Joyce Falat testified regarding her income and expenses and the income and expenses of her children at the time of the divorce and at the time of the hearing. The petition for rule to show cause was resolved on August 13, 1986, when an agreed order was entered by Judge Peterson, providing for the husband and wife to each pay 50% of the college educational expenses of the children. . . . Donald Falat filed a motion to strike and dismiss the petition to increase child support on the basis that the court lacked jurisdiction to grant an increase to adult children. This motion was denied by the trial court on March 18, 1987. A hearing on Joyce Falat's petition to increase child support was held on August 21, 1987. Joyce Falat testified at the hearing. However, Donald Falat did not attend the hearing, nor was he required to attend since the court had previously stated that "further testimony of Donald Falat is not required." A court reporter was present at the August 21, 1987, hearing; however, the court reporter lost the notes of that hearing. Donald Falat initially filed his proposed report of proceedings on November 20, 1987. After the passing of a significant period of time, on February 2, 1988, Joyce Falat was granted leave to file instanter a responsive report of proceedings. On that same date, the trial court refused "to certify a report of proceedings due to a lack of memory as to this

case." On April 7, 1988, Donald Falat requested the trial court to certify Joyce Falat's proposed report of proceedings as to what occurred during the August 21, 1987, proceedings. The report of proceedings was certified by the trial judge on that date.

Joyce Falat stated in the report of proceedings that at the August 21, 1987, hearing she tendered an affidavit dated August 21, 1987, setting forth her monthly income and expenses and an affidavit dated June 16, 1986, prepared by Donald Falat which had been furnished to the court at a prior hearing. Donald Falat's paystub for the period ending March 31, 1986, was also tendered to the court.

* * *

Joyce Falat further testified at the August 21, 1987, hearing that the $410 per month child support was agreeable to her at the time of the dissolution of marriage since at that time the children were minors, ages 11 and 13. However, now they are 19 and 20 years of age and attending college. She also testified that an increase of child support is needed due to inflation and the increased expenses of the children in general, utilities and food. She stated that Karen and David earned $10,022 and $4,620 respectively in 1986.

* * *

Thereafter, the trial court modified the child support to $550 per month retroactive to February 6, 1986, for the period of February 6, 1986, to June 1, 1987. The court then proceeded to set child support at $475 per month.

On appeal the respondent argues that the trial court erred in entering an order increasing child support for adult children who were neither mentally or physically disabled and the funds were not necessary for the childrens' education. Respondent further argues that the petitioner failed to sustain her burden of showing a substantial change in circumstances since the dissolution of marriage to justify an increase in child support and the ability of the respondent to pay. We agree with the orders of the trial court.

We will initially address respondent's argument that in the present case the trial court lacked jurisdiction to grant an increase of child support to adult children who were neither physically or mentally disabled nor were the funds necessary for the childrens' education. This contention is without merit since a trial court has jurisdiction to consider future child support needs in a dissolution of marriage proceeding and it is not required to expressly retain jurisdiction in order to preside over such proceedings. (In re Marriage of Geis (1987), 159 Ill.App.3d 975, 111 Ill.Dec. 717, 982, 512 N.E.2d 1354; In re Marriage of Petramale (1981), 102 Ill.App.3d 1049, 58 Ill.Dec. 537, 430 N.E.2d 569.) The general rule is that the obligation of a parent to support his children terminates when the child reaches majority. (In re Marriage of Holderrieth (1989), 181 Ill.App.3d 199, 206, 129 Ill.Dec. 896, 536 N.E.2d 946.) However, section 510(c) of the Marriage and Dissolution of Marriage Act ("the Act") specifically provides that "unless otherwise agreed in writing or expressly provided in the judgment, provisions for the support of a child are terminated by emancipation of the child, except as otherwise provided herein . . ." (Ill.Rev.Stat.1987, ch. 40, par. 510(c).) The legislative purpose behind the adoption of section 510(c) is to allow the parties to a dissolution proceeding to remain liable for the support of children beyond emancipation. Finley v. Finley (1980), 81 Ill.2d 317, 326, 43 Ill.Dec. 12, 410 N.E.2d 12.

The record in the case at bar reveals that the respondent expressly agreed to remain obligated to pay child support if the children were enrolled as full-time students in high school or college. Settlement agreements as they relate to child support are looked upon favorably by Illinois courts and such agreements will not be set aside absent clear and convincing evidence that the agreement was entered as a result of coercion, fraud, duress or the agreement is contrary to public policy or morals. (In re Marriage of Holderrieth (1989), 181 Ill.App.3d 199, 206, 129 Ill.Dec. 896, 536 N.E.2d 946; Stutler v. Stutler (1978), 61 Ill.App.3d 201, 204, 18 Ill.Dec. 377, 377 N.E.2d 862.) Additionally, we have specifically held that the circuit court does have the authority to modify a child support provision in a dissolution of marriage judgment that was entered in accordance with a settlement agreement. Ill.Rev. Stat.1987, ch. 40, pars. 502(f), 510(a); In re Marriage of Geis, 159 Ill.App.3d at 982, 111 Ill.Dec. 717, 512 N.E.2d 1354; Powers v. Powers (1979), 69 Ill.App.3d 485, 26 Ill.Dec. 452, 388 N.E.2d 76.

It is undisputed in the present case that the parties intended to pay child support past the age of majority, and we have frequently held that it is within the broad discretion of the trial court to determine the necessity for child support and the amount granted, and its decision will not be set aside unless it is contrary to the manifest weight of the evidence. (In re Marriage of Geis, 159 Ill.App.3d at 982, 111 Ill.Dec. 717, 512 N.E.2d 1354; In re Marriage of Mitchell (1981), 103 Ill.App.3d 242, 249, 58 Ill.Dec. 684, 430 N.E.2d 716.) Moreover, it is well settled that the modification of a child support award is within the sound discretion of the trial court and that decision will not be reversed on appeal absent an abuse of discretion. In re Marriage of Morrisroe (1987), 155 Ill.App.3d 765, 770–71, 108 Ill.Dec. 303, 508 N.E.2d 464; In re Marriage of Winters (1987), 160 Ill.App.3d 277, 285, 111 Ill.Dec. 734, 512 N.E.2d 1371; In re Marriage of Milburn (1986), 144 Ill.App.3d 76, 80, 98 Ill.Dec. 234, 494 N.E.2d 161; Schmerold v. Schmerold (1980), 88 Ill.App.3d 348, 43 Ill.Dec. 629, 410 N.E.2d 629.

Section 513 of the Act provides that in determining the amount of child support to assess, the circuit court must consider the child's financial resources, the financial resources of both parents, and the standard of living the child would have enjoyed but for the dissolution of the marriage. (Ill.Rev.Stat.1987, ch. 40, par. 513; In re Marriage of Harsy (1990), 193 Ill.App.3d 415, 423, 140 Ill. Dec. 344, 549 N.E.2d 995.) The trial court will also consider the physical, emotional and educational needs of the child. (Ill.Rev.Stat.1985, ch. 40, par. 505; In re Marriage of Morrisroe, 155 Ill.App.3d at 771, 108 Ill.Dec. 303, 508 N.E.2d 464; In re Marriage of Milburn (1986), 144 Ill.App.3d 76, 79–80, 98 Ill. Dec. 234, 494 N.E.2d 161.) Respondent argues that the increase in child support was not necessary for the children's education since an agreed order was entered for the husband and wife to each pay 50% of the college educational expenses of the children. Petitioner argues that although the parties were ordered to pay educational expenses, the court did not order the parties to share the living and other expenses of the children while attending college. Section 513 of the Act authorizes the trial court to make provisions for the education and maintenance of children after they have attained the age of majority and section 505 of the Act allows the court to order the payments to be made out of income. (In re Marriage of Coram (1980), 86 Ill.App.3d 845, 850–51, 42 Ill.Dec. 40, 408 N.E.2d 418.) Educational expenses entitle a mother to receive reasonable living expenses in addition to the cost of tuition and books when the children are residing at home while attending college. In re Marriage of Pauley (1982), 104 Ill.App.3d 559 N.E. 2d 33.

The Act further grants the trial court the authority to modify any judgment regarding child support upon a showing of a substantial and material change in circumstances. (Ill.Rev.Stat.1987, ch. 40, par. 510(a); In re Marriage of Eisenstein (1988), 172 Ill.App.3d 264, 269, 122 Ill.Dec. 237, 526 N.E.2d 496; In re Marriage of Morrisroe, 155 Ill.App.3d at 770, 108 Ill.Dec. 303, 508 N.E.2d 464.) Respondent contends that the petitioner failed to sustain her burden of showing a substantial change in circumstances since the dissolution of marriage to justify an increase in child support and the ability of the respondent to pay. Moreover, under the terms of the settlement agreement he agreed to continue child support while the children attended college, not increase child support for his adult children. In marriage dissolution proceedings, a court is not bound by the agreements between the parties providing for the support of children. (Blisset v. Blisset (1988), 123 Ill.2d 161, 167, 121 Ill.Dec. 931, 526 N.E.2d 125; Ill.Rev.Stat.1987, ch. 40, par. 502(b).) Moreover, section 502(f) of the Act prohibits parties to an agreement from limiting or precluding the modification of child support. (Ill.Rev.Stat. 1987, ch. 40 par. 502 (f). Additionally, the Act provides that a trial court "may order parents owing a duty of support to pay an amount reasonable and necessary for the support of the children." Ill.Rev.Stat.1987, ch. 40 par. 505.

The trial court is only justified in increasing child support upon a showing that the needs of the children and the earnings of the supporting parent have increased since the judgment granting child support was entered. (Addington v. Addington (1977), 48 Ill.App.3d 859, 863, 6 Ill.Dec. 622, 363 N.E.2d 151; In re Marriage of Milburn, 144 Ill.App.3d at 81, 98 Ill.Dec. 234, 494 N.E.2d 161.) Once the respondent's increased ability to pay has been demonstrated, the petitioner may establish increased needs of the children based on the fact that the children have grown older and the cost of living has risen. (In re Marriage of Milburn, 144 Ill.App.3d at 81, 98 Ill.Dec. 234, 494 N.E.2d 161; Addington, 48 Ill.App.3d at 863, 6 Ill.Dec. 622, 363 N.E.2d 151.) Moreover, the trial court may presume that the expenses associated with the raising of children are increased each year. In re Marriage of Loomis (1987), 153 Ill.App. 3d 404, 406, 106 Ill.Dec. 219, 505 N.E.2d 766.

In the present case, the court was provided with the incomes of Joyce Falat, David Falat and the children at the time of the dissolution of marriage and for 1986. Donald Falat's income increased from $25,000 to approximately $50,000 in 1986. Joyce Falat's income increased from $10,000 to $24,000 in 1986. David Falat's income increased from zero to $4,900 in 1986 and Karen Falat's income increased from zero to $10,022 in 1986. Donald Falat's 1986 income was based upon a paystub tendered to the court for the period ending March 31, 1986. Information regarding the parties' income and expenses was originally tendered and authenticated when the trial began on June 16, 1986. This information was again tendered to the trial court at the August 21, 1987, hearing. Specifically, at that hearing, Joyce Falat's attorney tendered an affidavit dated August 21, 1987, stating her monthly income and expenses. He also tendered an affidavit prepared by Donald Falat dated June 16, 1986, indicating his income and expenses. Additionally, at the August 21, 1987, hearing a paystub for Donald Falat for the period ending March 31, 1986, was tendered to the trial court upon its request. During the August 21, 1987, hearing the trial court attempted to obtain current information by asking the respondent's attorney, "What is the husband's income now?" The response provided was "That is for the petitioner to show. I'm standing on the evidence." Just prior to this exchange, when the trial court asked the respondent if he had any evidence that he wished to present, the respondent's attorney stated, "Your Honor, I am not offering any evidence on behalf of respondent."

* * *

The evidence indicated that the respondent agreed to the continuation of child support past the age of majority. Therefore, both parties intended that the children would receive support if they attended college. Moreover, the evidence revealed Donald Falat's ability to pay increased child support taking into consideration inter alia the 100% increase in his income since the original award of child support, the petitioner's income and her testimony regarding the increased need for child support due to increased expenses of the children, inflation, increased costs associated with utilities and food. Furthermore, there is nothing in the record to demonstrate that the trial court did not consider the relevant factors, as set forth in the Act, that were reasonable and necessary to determine whether an increase in child support should be granted. Therefore, the evidence supports petitioner's assertion of a substantial change in circumstances since the original dissolution judgment to support an increase in child support and based upon the facts of this case, we conclude that the trial court did not abuse its discretion in granting an increase in child support.

For the foregoing reasons, the orders of the circuit court of Cook County are affirmed.

AFFIRMED.

Case Question

Because a minor of married parents cannot force the parents to contribute to a college education, why is it acceptable to force payment by a noncustodial divorced parent?

VISITATION

When one parent is awarded custody of the child, the noncustodial parent is usually given specific visitation rights. In some cases, the rights are characterized as reasonable visitation. However, this tends to leave the visitation to the discretion of the custodial parent in determining what is reasonable. Often the parents will dispute over this term, since what is reasonable visitation to one may be unreasonable visitation to the other. Ultimately, many parties return to court to have a judge make the determination. Therefore, the preferred choice is to set forth specific times and sometimes arrangements (when travel is involved) for visitation.

Every parent is deemed to possess a constitutional right to share the companionship of his or her child.[37] Unless the parent's conduct would endanger the child, this right cannot be abridged. However, if the parent's conduct might endanger the child, the court may limit or place conditions on the visitation. Common conditions include requiring visitation to be confined to a specific place or requiring visitation to be supervised by a third party to ensure the safety and well-being of the child. Extreme situations may result in a court's denial of visitation for a period of time to protect the welfare of the child.

Many states have statutory guidelines that judges attempt to follow to ensure each parent time and the opportunity to share special holidays and other occasions with the child. It must be understood that a visitation schedule sets forth the minimum rights of the noncustodial parent. If the two parents agree to additional or different times for visitation, this is entirely appropriate. If problems arise, however, the court will generally not enforce such agreements but will usually follow only the scheduled visitation plan.

Penalties may result in cases where a visitation schedule is set forth in a court order and the custodial parent interferes with visitation. Interference includes such things as refusing visitation, not having the children available for visitation when the noncustodial parent arrives, directly influencing the children to avoid visitation, or engaging in other conduct that interferes with the noncustodial parent's constitutional right to share companionship with the children.

When such conduct occurs, the noncustodial parent has the right to bring an action against the custodial parent for contempt of court. The allegation is generally that the custodial parent willfully ignored or interfered with a court order of visitation. A court is not likely to be tolerant of such conduct. Penalties range from monetary fines to jail sentences. In continuing and extreme cases, the court may view the conduct as adverse to the best interests of the child and may order a change of custody.

PROPERTY AND DEBT DIVISION

The states follow two schools of thought with respect to **property settlement** in the case of divorce. Some states are separate property states; others are community property states. The theory that a state follows will dictate the rights of the parties seeking a divorce. In cases where the parties were formally married, lived, or divorced in different states, the court will usually look to the law of the state where the parties resided when the property was acquired.

Property Settlement
Agreement as to the property rights and obligations of co-owners/ co-debtors, such as parties to a marriage.

Separate Property

Separate property states take the position that all property individually owned prior to the marriage is individual property and not jointly owned marital property.[38] In addition, property acquired during the marriage through gift, inheritance, or personal earnings without contribution by the other spouse is individual property. In a divorce action, parties are awarded their individual property respectively, and the court determines how marital property should be distributed.

In a complete application of the separate property theory, a nonemployed spouse may be entitled to virtually nothing at the conclusion of the divorce. Because this effect is not fair, based on each spouse's contribution to the marital relationship, many courts have modified the rule to result in a more equitable application. While a state may still adhere to the theory of separate property, the court has a duty to equitably distribute property obtained during the marriage. Such property may have been purchased solely with the earnings of one spouse. If, however, the other spouse cared for the home and otherwise supported and enabled the first spouse to earn the money to purchase the property, such property is considered the result of a joint effort. In this way, the court can fairly consider certain property to be marital property and distribute it equally.

Community Property

Community property states take a different approach to the disposition of the property of spouses. In such states, property acquired during the marriage through personal earnings is presumed to be marital property.[39] Also included is property individually owned before the marriage that a party contributed to the marriage. When a spouse can establish that certain property was never comingled or otherwise shared with the other spouse as marital property would be, such property is not included as community property.

After the court has determined what, if any, separate property exists, it attempts to equitably divide the community property. The court considers the contribution of each partner to the marriage and then attempts to make a fairly equal division of the property. Circumstances must be rather compelling before a court is permitted to make a significantly unbalanced distribution of the parties' assets.

Pensions and Employee Benefit Programs

If a spouse was employed and received an interest in a pension or benefit plan during the marriage, under either type of property state, the other spouse may have a claim to a portion of the amount to be received under the plan. Determination of what is equitable is a perplexing problem for most courts. In many cases, the divorce occurs many years before the benefits are to be received. In addition, it is difficult to determine what an equitable share of an earned pension or benefit program would be, since the spouse has not earned the maximum pension or benefit possible. A final problem is that the parties remain somewhat bound to each other even through retirement. Many courts prefer to make a valuation of each party's interest and have one party buy out the other party's interest at the time of the dissolution. In this way, the parties' ties to each other can be completely and permanently severed, thus lessening the possibilities for future legal disputes.

It should be noted that to establish division of pension and retirement funds in a way that will be recognized by the Internal Revenue Service, a Qualified Domestic Relations Order (QDRO) must be issued (in addition to the other documents, such as property settlement agreement and Decree of Dissolution of Marriage) that details the rights and obligations of the parties with respect to these matters.

Marital Debts

The manner in which individual and marital debts are determined and distributed is substantially the same as with property. The same tests are applied to determine whether debts were incurred as part of the marital relationship or on behalf of the individual. Similarly, the courts attempt an equitable distribution of responsibility for such debts. However, debts incurred during a marriage have an additional aspect that property usually does not—the claims of third parties.

While parties may agree—or a court may determine—that certain debts are individual rather than marital, great legal expense can arise from claims of third parties that the debt is joint. For example, as long as the parties are joint owners of a credit card, any property purchased with the credit card is a joint debt. Even if a debt is taken on individually, if it is done during the marriage, there is a presumption that the debt benefited both parties.

Another facet of this problem arises when the divorce is final and responsibility for debts has been distributed equitably between the two spouses. If one spouse fails to honor the responsibility, the third party can claim and collect the debt from the other spouse. Although this may appear unfair at first, it should be remembered that the creditor was not even involved in the distribution of the debts. Therefore, the creditor is not bound by any court order as to who should bear responsibility. Since this situation arises fairly often, it is very important that all decrees contain a provision that entitles a spouse to collect reimbursement when he or she pays a debt that was to have been the responsibility of the other spouse.

MAINTENANCE (ALIMONY OR SPOUSAL SUPPORT)

Awards of maintenance or spousal support (formerly called alimony) are becoming an increasingly rare occurrence. The reasons are numerous. Previously, in a pure application of separate property, the wife often did not receive a significant share of marital assets. Today, all states (whether they are community property or separate property states) attempt to provide a more equitable distribution. In addition, women now actively participate in the work force and have greater opportunities than ever before to become self-sufficient.

At present, a court might award maintenance to a spouse who is unable to secure employment sufficient to meet reasonable necessary expenses or to a child for whom care by one other than the parent during working hours would not be appropriate.[40] An example of the former is a spouse who has not worked for many years and, for all practical purposes, would not be able to reenter the work force at a level that would provide independent financial support. An example of the latter is a child who suffers from physical or emotional conditions that necessitate skilled care at a cost greater than what the parent could earn if he or she were required to work full-time outside the home.

As these examples suggest, the trend of the courts is to award maintenance only in compelling circumstances. Although many situations are not as clearly defined as those described, often a spouse requires some form of assistance before he or she can be restored to an independent earning capacity. For example, a spouse may have been away from the work force but would be capable of reentering with some retraining, or the parties may have several young children who will be entering school in the reasonably near future. In such situations, short-term maintenance would be appropriate. The court may award maintenance for a specified period of time to supplement the income of the other spouse.

Today, the goal of the court is to give a spouse sufficient time and resources to prepare for financial independence. Thus, the spouse required to pay maintenance is not burdened with lifetime support of a former spouse, and the spouse receiving maintenance is not suddenly thrust into the world unequipped to provide for such basic expenses as food and shelter. Maintenance is awarded only for a period of time that is deemed reasonably sufficient to enable the receiving spouse to achieve independence.

The amount and duration of maintenance are generally left to the discretion of the court, which will consider such factors as the earning power and the reasonable needs of each party. Also considered is the amount of time necessary to prepare the spouse receiving maintenance to successfully return to the work force.[41] If the age and educational level of this spouse effectively prevent a return to the workforce, permanent maintenance may be considered. The same is true of a situation in which the parties have an incapacitated child.

If either party dies, maintenance automatically terminates. If the intent is that the receiving party should continue to be entitled in the event of death of the payor, it should be so stipulated in the court order approving maintenance.

If the financial status of either party changes significantly during the period of maintenance payments, a modification may be requested. A formal petition must be filed with the court setting forth the reasons that would justify adjustment of the maintenance order. It is then within the discretion of the court to determine whether the modification is warranted. Significant changes in circumstances include a substantial decrease in the earning power of the payor spouse or a substantial increase in the earning power of the recipient spouse. Remarriage or cohabitation of the recipient spouse also may be considered sufficient grounds to terminate maintenance.

Failure to pay maintenance is remedied by a request to hold the wrongful party in contempt of court. The procedure and penalties are basically the same. The court will hear the petition, and penalties will ensue if grounds exist to find that a party has willfully ignored the order of maintenance.

Assignment 14.7

Examine the following situations and indicate whether a court would be likely to grant maintenance and, if so, whether maintenance would be permanent or temporary. Give reasons to support your answer.

SITUATION 1. Gladys and Edgar have been married for 27 years. Before their marriage, Gladys taught kindergarten. After their marriage, Edgar provided the sole source of income, and Gladys cared for their home and four children. They are now divorcing. Edgar's income is moderate and would probably not adequately support two households. The children are grown and live away from home. Gladys is 52 years of age.

SITUATION 2. Louellen and Dennis have been married for 39 years. Louellen quit teaching high school math 30 years ago. Since then, Dennis has provided all financial support for himself and Louellen. Louellen is now 61 years of age. Dennis, who is 58, will be eligible to retire next year. If he is required to support Louellen, he would not be able to do so on his pension alone.

NONMARITAL RELATIONSHIPS

As previously indicated, most states do not recognize the creation of a common law marriage. Nevertheless, many couples do cohabit without the formal requisites of marriage. Although they share in the acquisition of property and debts, when they decide to terminate their relationship, they do not have the specific legal rights of persons who are dissolving a legal marriage.

Although previous courts had issued decisions addressing various aspects of this particular situation, the landmark opinion was issued in *Marvin v. Marvin*,[42] in which the court fully addressed the issues associated with the dissolution of nonmarital cohabitation. Courts in several other states have cited the decision with approval and have used it as persuasive authority to adopt the position taken by the court in the *Marvin* decision.[43]

 CASE

MARVIN v. MARVIN

18 Cal. 3d 660, 134
Cal.Rptr. 815, 557 P.2d
106 (1976).

En banc
1. The factual setting of this appeal.
. . . Plaintiff avers that in October of 1964 she and defendant "entered into an oral agreement" that while "that parties lived together they would combine their efforts and earnings and would share equally any and all property accumulated as a result of their efforts whether individual or combined." Furthermore, they agreed to "hold themselves out to the general public as husband and wife" and that "plaintiff would further render her services as a companion, homemaker, housekeeper and cook to . . . defendant.

Shortly thereafter, plaintiff agreed to "give up her lucrative career as an entertainer [and] singer in order to "devote her full time to defendant . . . as a companion, homemaker, housekeeper and cook"; in return defendant agreed to "provide for all of plaintiff's financial support and needs for the rest of her life."

Plaintiff alleges that she lived with defendant from October of 1964 through May of 1970 and fulfilled her obligations under the agreement. During this period the parties as a result of their efforts and earnings acquired in defendant's name

substantial real and personal property, including motion picture rights worth over $1 million. In May of 1970, however, defendant compelled plaintiff to leave his household. He continued to support plaintiff until November of 1971, but thereafter refused to provide further support.

On the basis of these allegations plaintiff asserts two causes of action. The first, for declaratory relief, asks the court to determine her contract and property rights; the second seeks to impose a constructive trust upon one half of the property acquired during the course of the relationship.

Defendant demurred unsuccessfully, and then answered the complaint. Following extensive discovery and pretrial proceedings, the case came to trial. Defendant renewed his attack on the complaint by a motion to dismiss. . . .

After hearing argument the court granted defendant's motion and entered judgment for the defendant. Plaintiff moved to set aside the judgment and asked leave to amend her complaint to allege that she and defendant reaffirmed their agreement after defendant's divorce was final. The trial court denied plaintiff's motion, and she appealed from the judgment.
2. Plaintiff's complaint states a cause of action for breach of an express contract.

In *Trutalli v. Meraviglia* (1932) 215 Cal. 698, 12 P.2d. 430, we established the principle that nonmarital partners may lawfully contract concerning the ownership of property acquired during the relationship. We reaffirmed this principle in *Vallera v. Vallera* (1943) 21 Cal.2d 681, 685, 134 P.2d 761, 763, stating that "If a man and woman [who are not married] live together as husband and wife under an agreement to pool their earnings and share equally in their joint accumulations, equity will protect the interests of each in such property."

In the case before us plaintiff, basing here cause of action in contract upon these precedents, maintains that the trial court erred in denying her a trial on the merits of her contention. . . .

Numerous . . . cases have upheld enforcement of agreements between nonmarital partners in factual settings essentially indistinguishable from the present case. *In re Marriage of Foster* (1947) 42 Cal.App.3d 577, 117 Cal.Rptr. 49; . . . *Ferguson v. Schuenemann* (1959) 167 Cal.App.2d 413, 334 P.2d. 668; . . . *Ferraro v. Ferraro* (1956) 146 Cal.App.2d 849, 304 P.2d 168.

We conclude that the judicial barriers that may stand in the way of a policy based upon the fulfillment of the reasonable expectations of the parties to a nonmarital relationship should be removed. As we have explained, the courts now hold that express agreements will be enforced unless they rest on an unlawful meretricious consideration. We add that in the absence of an express agreement, the courts may look to a variety of other remedies in order to protect the parties' lawful expectations.

We do not seek to resurrect the doctrine of common law marriage, which was abolished in California by statute in 1895. (See Norman v. Thomson (1898) 121 Cal. 620, 628, 54 P. 143; Estate of Abate (1958) 166 Cal.App.2d 282, 292, 333 P.2d 200.) Thus we do not hold that plaintiff and defendant were 'married,' nor do we extend to plaintiff the rights which the Family Law Act grants valid or putative spouses; we hold only that she has the same rights to enforce contracts and to assert her equitable interest in property acquired through her effort as does any other unmarried person.

The courts may inquire into the conduct of the parties to determine whether that conduct demonstrates an implied contract, implied agreement of partnership or joint venture (see Estate of Thornton (1972) 81 Wash.2d 72, 499 P.2d 864), or some other tacit understanding between the parties. . . . Finally, a nonmarital partner may recover in quantum meruit for the reasonable value of household services rendered less the reasonable value of support received if he can show that he rendered services with the expectation of monetary reward. (See Hill v. Estate of Westbrook, supra, 39 Cal.2d 458, 462, 247 P.2d 19.)

Our opinion does not preclude the evolution of additional equitable remedies to protect the expectations of the parties to a nonmarital relationship in cases in which existing remedies prove inadequate; the suitability of such remedies may be determined in later cases in light of the factual setting in which they arise.

Since we have determined that plaintiff's complaint states a cause of action for breach of an express contract, and, as we have explained, can be amended to state a cause of action independent of allegations of express contract, we must conclude that the trial court erred in granting defendant a judgment on the pleadings.

Case Question

What if the reason the relationship broke up had been infertility?

Some courts have rejected the *Marvin* decision on the basis that it too closely resembles recognition of common law marriage, and they are not willing to adopt a position that so closely parallels it. In a time when cohabitation is an increasingly frequent occurrence, however, methods may have to be developed to determine the legal rights of the parties involved.

ETHICAL NOTE

Legal ethics play a very important role in the law of domestic relations. It is not uncommon for only one party to retain counsel in situations involving dissolution, marital property, or interests regarding children. In such situations, the attorney is under an ethical obligation to make it clear to the other party that a lawyer cannot represent both sides of a legal issue. To do so would constitute a conflict of interest. Consequently, it is quite common that a property settlement or other document of settlement of legal issues contain a clause that identifies who is represented by the attorney.

In an uncontested dissolution of marriage where there are few matters to be determined, such as division of property, the parties may elect to use one attorney to minimize the cost. However, this does not change the position of the attorney. Ethically, the attorney can represent only one of the parties. The other party who chooses to agree to the terms presented must do so independently and without the advice or counsel of the attorney. Further, that party must always retain the right to seek legal advice on the matter from another attorney. In this way, the initial attorney cannot be considered to be attempting to represent the best interest of two parties on opposite sides of a conflict.

Question

Is an attorney for one spouse ethically correct in explaining the terms of a property settlement agreement to the other spouse and then accepting that spouse's signature on the agreement?

CHAPTER SUMMARY

The law surrounding domestic relations is constantly changing to better meet the needs of our current society. As society changes, so must the laws to provide fair treatment to persons in relationships that have legal implications. Like a stone thrown into a pond, domestic relations law creates an ever-widening circle that touches many other aspects of society. It currently affects virtually every area of society, including psychology and social work in matters involving children; the health care industry in matters involving provision of insurance or continued health care for a spouse or child; business in matters of child support, maintenance, and pension or profit-sharing plans; and the banking industry in matters of distribution of assets. A better understanding of the basic principles of domestic relations can greatly enhance the effectiveness with which these related fields can deal with the parties involved in a domestic relations lawsuit.

Relevant in all domestic relations cases are the status of the parties and the circumstances of the particular case. Questions to be answered include, but are not limited to, the following:

1. Was there a valid marriage? If not, does either of the parties have rights with respect to the other?
2. If there was a valid marriage, how have economic conditions of the parties changed since the marriage, and what role did each party play in those changes?
3. Were there children from the marriage? If so, what are their ages or special needs, and what custody, visitation, and support arrangement will best serve the interests of the children?

4. If the marital relationship is broken, which is the best alternative—annulment, legal separation, or dissolution?
5. How can the assets and debts of the parties be fairly distributed?

These and many other questions like them must be addressed in most domestic relations cases. Even when a marriage has been previously dissolved and some subsequent dispute arises between the parties, many of the same questions will affect the outcome of the dispute.

As knowledge increases among the general population, so does exposure of the ills of the population. One of the most significant problems that has come to light is the degree of domestic violence occurring in our society. In response to this, laws are now in place and more are being developed to deal with domestic violence.

REVIEW QUESTIONS

1. Are antenuptial agreements legally enforceable?
2. What is necessary for a valid marriage?
3. When can a marriage be legally annulled?
4. What rights are available to persons who cohabit but do not marry, in the event the relationship ends?
5. How does a legal separation differ from the dissolution of a marriage?
6. What relief is available to the parties after dissolution is sought but before it is granted?
7. What standard do the courts apply when determining custody?
8. What is joint custody?
9. What is the difficulty with joint custody?
10. What are no-fault grounds for dissolution?

CHAPTER TERMS

Annulment
Antenuptial Agreement
  (Prenuptial Agreement)
Custody (Parental Rights)

Dissolution of Marriage
Domestic Violence
Legal Separation
Permanent Injunction

Preliminary Injunction
Property Settlement
Temporary Restraining Order

NOTES

1. *In re Estate of Cummings*, 493 Pa. 11, 425 A.2d 340 (1981).
2. 81 A.L.R.3d. 453.
3. Id.
4. Mobilia, "Ante-nuptial agreements anticipating divorce: How effective are they?" 70 *Massachusetts Law Review* 82 10 (June 1985).
5. 55 C.J.S., Marriage, Section 10.
6. Id., Sections 24, 25.
7. Id., Sections 28–31.
8. Id., Section 48.
9. *McDonald v. McDonald*, 6 Cal.2d 457, 58 P.2d 163 (1936).
10. *Wirth v. Wirth*, 175 Misc. 342, 23 N.Y.S.2d 289 (1940).
11. 81 A.L.R.3d. 281.
12. *Jackson v. Jackson*, 276 F.2d 501 (D.C.Cir. 1960).

13. *Maschauer v. Downs,* 53 App.D.C. 142, 289 Fed. 540 (1923).
14. 41 Am.Jur.2d., Husband and Wife, Section 522.
15. Federal Rules of Evidence, 28 U.S.C.A. Rule 501.
16. 23 *Journal of Family Law* 454 (April 1985).
17. 51 A.L.R.3d 223.
18. Id.
19. 24 Am.Jur.2d, Divorce and Separation, Section 29.
20. *Glendening v. Glendening,* 206 A.2d 824 (D.C. App. 1965).
21. Uniform Marriage and Divorce Act, Section 304(b) (2).
22. 24 Am.Jur.2d., Divorce and Separation, Section 328.
23. 75 A.L.R.3d.
24. 48 A.L.R.4th 919.
25. Id.
26. Id.
27. 70 A.L.R.3d 262.
28. 24 Am.Jur.2d., Divorce and Separation, Sections 974, 975.
29. Id.
30. Id.
31. 17 A.L.R.4th 1013.
32. *Perla v. Perla,* 58 So.2d 689 (Fla. 1952).
33. Smith, "Education support obligations of noncustodial parents," 36 *Rutgers Law Review* 588 (September 1984).
34. Comment, "Battling inconsistency and inadequacy: Child support guidelines in the states," *Harvard Women's Law Journal* 197 (Spring 1988).
35. See note 21, Section 102(5); 309.
36. 23 Am.Jur.2d, Desertion and Non-support, Section 128, et seq.
37. *In re J.S. & C.,* 129 N.J.Super. 486, 324 A.2d 90 (1974).
38. 24 Am.Jur.2d., Divorce and Separation, Section 866.
39. Id.; 20 Am.Jur. 2d, Sections 321–370.
40. 97 A.L.R.3d 740.
41. See note 38, Section 584.
42. Monroe, "Marvin v. Marvin: Five years later," 65 *Marquette Law Review* 389 (Spring 1982).
43. *Marvin v. Marvin,* 18 Cal.3d 660, 134 Cal.Rptr. 815, 557 P.2d 106 (1976).

CHAPTER 15

The Legal Professional's Role and Ethical Obligations

CHAPTER OBJECTIVES

After reading this chapter, you should be able to

- *Discuss the role of the trial, appellate, and administrative law judge.*

- *Explain the functions of a lawyer in the practice of law.*

- *Distinguish a paralegal from a lawyer.*

- *Discuss the limitation on the work of a paralegal.*

- *Identify and define the roles of the members of the legal support staff.*

- *Discuss who is bound by the rule of confidentiality.*

- *Explain the ethical rule of independent judgment.*

ROLE OF THE LEGAL PROFESSIONAL

As our society and culture increase in complexity, so does the legal system designed to maintain order among the population. The growth of the structure of the American legal system has resulted in the evolution of various legal professions. The goal of this chapter is to introduce you to the various professions and fields of employment associated with the American legal system. The chapter also examines the ethical and legal obligations of legal professionals.

Initially, the legal professions consisted primarily of judges and lawyers. Today, they consist of several types of judges, court clerks, law clerks, court officers, lawyers, paralegals/legal assistants, legal investigators, legal secretaries, and general accounting and clerical staff. Most of these positions have developed during the twentieth century as a result of the great increases in population, technology, transportation, and communication systems. To illustrate some of these changes, let's use the example of the filing of a court document. In 1850, the lawyer handwrote the document using a fountain pen and ink. He then carried it himself to the courthouse and often presented it personally to the judge. Today, that same document may be discussed by the lawyer and legal assistant; researched by the lawyer, legal assistant (paralegal), or **law clerk;** dictated by machine; placed on a computer file by the clerical staff (if not generated originally on the computer); and subsequently transmitted electronically to the parties to suit and the court. At the court, the document is registered by a clerk and may be recorded on computer before being placed in the file for the particular case. The clerk or an assistant to the judge would then establish a time for a hearing and notify all parties by telephone, mail, or electronic transmission, such as a fax. Some law firms even have a direct communication system set up between their own computer and the courts' computer.

It seems as though the method of 1850 was simpler and more efficient. Given the status of the legal system at the time, perhaps it was. However, with the phenomenal technological developments that respond to the ever-increasing number of cases on file in the courts, the current system is incredibly efficient. The following discussion examines the various roles of legal professionals as well as the ethical demands on these professionals. While no specific job description in the law office other than that of the lawyer and the paralegal will be dealt with, all legal workers are important members of the support team that permits the legal professional to accomplish the goals of his or her job.

Law Clerk
Lawyer or law student who conducts legal research and writing but does not represent individual clients as a licensed attorney.

Judges

Jurist (Judge)
Judicial officer who presides over cases in litigation within the court system.

Jurists—commonly called **judges**—are individuals who resolve disputes between parties who have different interpretations of the law. It is the duty of a judge to objectively evaluate the circumstances of the parties. The judge determines which legal standards are most appropriate. In the absence of a jury (bench trial or appellate review), the judge applies the law to the facts of the case and issues a ruling. In a jury trial, the judge presides over the proceedings to ensure that the law is applied properly and that the evidence is presented in accordance with rules of evidence and procedure.

Before trial, a judge issues rulings on various procedural issues, such as discovery, motions, selection of jury, and instructions. The judge also has the responsibility to determine which law will be applied to the case.

The American legal system has many different kinds of judges: federal and state appellate judges, trial judges, and magistrates; municipal judges and various levels of hearing officers; and administrative law judges. All have the essential duty to interpret and apply the law within the limitations of their particular role as an officer of the court. However, significant differences in the function of judges lie in the distinction between appellate, trial, and administrative judges.

Appellate judges.   Appellate judges review cases that have been previously ruled on in the trial court. The goal of an appellate judge is to ensure that the correct law was applied fairly and consistently. If it is the opinion of the appellate court that the lower court exceeded or improperly used its authority (discretion), the appellate court concludes that there was an abuse of discretion. The court then issues a ruling as to what should occur next in the case. (More information on appellate procedures can be found in Chapters 2 and 5.)

Usually, several appellate judges review a case together as a panel. This collective wisdom reduces the possibility of error or personal bias on a legal issue. Because it is the duty of appellate judges to ensure proper, fair, and consistent application of law for a jurisdiction, the position of appellate judges requires a great deal of knowledge of legal principles. As with other legal professionals, appellate judges often have the assistance of law clerks (discussed later in the chapter).

Typically, the appellate panel will issue a written opinion after consideration of a case (and possibly after hearing a short argument by each party). The opinion not only will give the judgment but also will indicate the support or nonsupport of each judge. If the entire membership of an appellate court—rather than a panel of a few members—issues a joint decision, such decision is known as an en banc opinion. Typically, joint decisions are reserved for issues of great significance. A judge who agrees with the result but not with the reasoning of the other appellate judges may issue a concurrent opinion. A judge on the panel who disagrees with the result but is in the minority may issue a dissenting opinion. Concurrent and dissenting opinions are valuable for the light they may shed on how future cases may be dealt with, but the majority opinion is the controlling precedent that lower courts generally look to for guidance in future cases. The majority opinion also dictates the outcome of the particular case on appeal.

Trial judges.   To properly perform their duties, trial judges must maintain current knowledge of the law at all times. Because of the large volume of litigation, many courts assign trial judges to specific categories of cases. This not only creates a more organized and efficient court system, it also allows the trial judge the opportunity to develop expertise in certain areas of law. However, many less congested courts still have judges of general jurisdiction who hear cases of all types.

Changes in case law begin with the trial judge. At some point, a judge will take the position that a precedent is no longer appropriate. The judge may follow new statutory or administrative legal standards or indicate that societal standards dictate a change in the legal standards applicable to a situation. The judge has the option of applying existing precedent. When the case reaches conclusion (and possibly earlier in certain situations), a party dissatisfied with the result may challenge the trial court judgment before an appellate court. In some jurisdictions, including federal, a series of appeals can be taken before increasingly powerful courts (discussed further in Chapter 2). On appeal, the higher court affirms or reverses the position of the trial court and establishes future precedent. Consequently, the trial judge plays a crucial role in the establishment of legal standards.

Administrative Law Judge

Judicial officer assigned to preside over cases between individuals or entities and government administrative agencies.

Administrative law judge.   The **administrative law judge** functions in a totally different arena from that of the appellate or trial judge. The duties of administrative law judges are confined to hearing cases involving the conduct of administrative agencies and the effects of that conduct on the individual or entity who challenges the agency action.

The administrative law judge (also known as a.l.j.) is presumed to be an objective judicial authority who rules exclusively on issues of administrative law. The a.l.j. determines such issues as whether a party is subject to the authority of the agency and whether a party's conduct is in accordance with administrative rules and regulations. Typically, administrative cases are initially filed with the agency rather than in the courts. Appeals of an administrative decision are generally made to the trial court level in the judicial system. This is a limited instance when the trial court exercises appellate rather than original jurisdiction. (Additional information on the administrative process is found in Chapter 4.)

Each type of judicial officer plays an extremely important role in the American legal system. Whether hearing evidence at trial or reviewing another judge's application of law, the input of a judge as an objective observer with knowledge of legal standards is necessary to the effective operation of the American system of government.

 APPLICATION 15.1

1. Conrad sues Justin for breach of contract. Conrad wins at trial and is awarded $15,000. Justin appeals on the basis that Conrad improperly introduced at trial information about past lawsuits against Justin. Justin contends that the information unduly influenced the jury. The panel of appellate judges considers the case and determines that the past lawsuits were irrelevant and immaterial and should have been disallowed. It does not rule on the question of breach of contract. The appellate panel orders a new trial.

2. Andy and Keiko are involved in a lawsuit to increase visitation rights with the children of their former marriages. Each testifies as to why the current visitation rights are appropriate or unsatisfactory. The judge reviews the case, applies the precedent, and renders a verdict.
3. Sara wants to start her own radio station. She applies to the F.C.C. for a license and is denied. Sara challenges the decision. An administrative law judge hears the evidence of the F.C.C. in support of its denial. The judge also hears Sara's evidence as to why she should receive the license. The judge sides with the agency, and Sara does not receive the license. (Sara now has the option of appealing the a.l.j. decision in the judicial system.)

Point for Discussion
What are the similarities between the various types of judges?

Lawyers

Because of the increasing complexity of the American legal system, **lawyers (attorneys)** function not only as advocates for clients but also as counselors and liaisons between the lay public and the courts, legislatures, and executive branches. Lawyers are required to complete certain coursework and meet standards for licensure to practice law. Most states require that prior to licensure, the lawyer must graduate from an accredited law school and pass an examination (bar exam) in the licensing state or in another state. The exam tests the legal knowledge and analytical ability of the lawyer.

Although the definition of the practice of law varies from state to state, certain components of the definition are fairly standard. Most jurisdictions give the lawyer, when licensed to practice law, the generally exclusive privilege to give legal advice and to advocate on the behalf of clients.

Lawyer/Attorney
Individual who has completed the necessary requirements of education and training and who has been licensed to practice law in a jurisdiction.

Legal advice and analysis. The giving of legal advice requires special analytical ability by the lawyer. A lawyer is responsible for examining the law applicable to a situation and informing a client as to the likely outcome of the case. Based on the information, received, the client can take appropriate further action. Often, the lawyer will recommend specific further action.

Legal analysis requires the lawyer to be able to select all applicable legal standards, break them down, compare the elements to the client's circumstances, and predict the influence of the legal standards. Such analytical ability is a skill, and because clients often determine future conduct affecting their rights based on the lawyer's recommendation, the process of giving legal advice is licensed by the state and prohibited for anyone not having a proper license.

Advocacy. The second function of a licensed attorney is advocacy—the process of representing the legal rights and interests of another person within the confines of legal proceedings in one of the branches of government. While in business, it is not uncommon to have an agent represent one's interests in such areas as negotiations, sales, and purchases, a license to practice law is required to represent the interests of another person in court and other legal proceedings. Advocacy frequently has a long-term effect on a person's legal rights and thus is monitored closely by the government through licensure and law practice requirements.

Practicing law without a license.   When an individual undertakes the practice of law without a license to do so, a statutory violation occurs and criminal proceedings may be instituted. In recent years, there has been an increasing awareness of this issue as certain professions have begun to cross over. For example, is a CPA who gives advice to a client about tax laws giving legal advice or accounting advice? Is a real estate broker who draws up a purchase agreement and advises a client to sign giving advice about the client's business concerns (sale of property) or legal advice? These are just two examples of the many gray areas that have developed along with the evolution of the legal system. Thus far, the courts have by and large dealt with such situations on a case-by-case basis. They examine the law involved, the other areas affected (such as accounting or property), the expectations of the party receiving information, and the extent of the advice given by the professional. After reviewing all of these and any other relevant information, the court will determine whether the unauthorized practice of law has occurred.

 CASE

STATE v. BUYERS SERVICE COMPANY, INC.

292 S.C. 426, 357 S.E. 2d 15 (1987).

PER CURIAM:

In this action the circuit court issued a declaratory judgment that Buyers Service Company, Inc. (Buyers Service) has illegally engaged in the practice of law. Additionally, Buyers Service was enjoined from performing future acts deemed to constitute the practice of law. We affirm in part and reverse in part.

Facts

Buyers Service is a commercial title company which also assists homeowners in purchasing residential real estate. Its principal place of business is Hilton Head Island.

The State brought this action alleging Buyers Service has engaged in the unauthorized practice of law by: (1) providing reports, opinions or certificates as to the status of titles to real estate and mortgage liens; (2) preparing documents affecting title to real property; (3) handling real estate closings; (4) recording legal documents at the courthouse; and (5) advertising to the public that it may handle conveyancing and real estate closings.

Buyers Service's clients are usually prospective home purchasers referred by local real estate agents. Its general procedures for handling a real estate transaction are as follows:

After a client is referred, Buyers Service receives an executed contract of sale from the realtor. If the sale involves a mortgage, the buyer makes an application to a local lender. If the lender approves the loan, it notifies Buyers Service and sends a letter of commitment to the buyer stating the terms. Buyers Service then orders the loan package from the lender. This consists of a set of instructions, a note and mortgage, truth in lending statement, HUD-1 Statement, miscellaneous affidavits regarding employment, and other forms. The documents arrive in various degrees of completion depending upon the particular lender. Buyers Service fills in the mortgagor-mortgagee on the mortgage, the grantor-grantee on the deed, consideration, the legal description and other blank spaces.

Buyers Service sends the completed forms to the purchaser for his examination and signature. Thereafter, the lender examines the loan package and funds the loan. Buyers Service deposits the loan proceeds check in its escrow account and disburses the funds according to the HUD-1 Statement and the closing instructions. Buyers Service also prepares settlement statements after loans are closed.

When a title search is necessary, Buyers Service sends an employee to the courthouse to abstract the title. The purchaser pays $50 for this service. The abstract is reviewed by a non-attorney employee who determines if the seller has fee simple title to the property. Buyers Service gives purchasers a fact sheet describing three ways to hold fee simple title in South Carolina. If a purchaser has questions, an employee of Buyers Service elaborates. The purchasers then tell Buyers Service how they wish to hold title.

Subsequent to the commencement of the litigation, Buyers Service retained an attorney to review its closing documents. The attorney, whose name and charges appear on the settlement sheet, receives $35 for this service. Buyers Service pays this fee and passes it on to the purchaser. There is no direct contact between the attorney and the purchaser.

Buyers Service conducts closings without any attorney present. The majority are handled by mail. For these, Buyers Service sends written instructions to the parties as to the manner of signing the legal documents. When the purchaser comes to Buyers Service's office for the closing, an employee supervises the signing of the legal documents. If the purchaser has any questions, the employee answers them or refers the purchaser to the mortgage lender.

Buyers Service has legal instruments hand-carried or mailed to the courthouse for recording. It sends a form instruction letter with each set of documents but does not take responsibility for ensuring proper recording, which it maintains is the responsibility of the clerk of court.

The circuit court's order enjoins Buyers Service from the following activities:

"1. Providing reports, opinions or certificates as to the status of real estate titles to persons other than attorneys licensed to practice law in the State of South Carolina and seeking separate compensation for performing title work in connection with [Buyers Service's] title insurance business.

2. Preparing deeds, mortgages, notes and other legal instruments related to transfer of real property or mortgage loans.

3. Giving legal advice during the closing of real estate transfers or real estate mortgage loan transactions.

4. Advertising to the general public that the Defendant is a full-service closing company and may handle complete real estate closings, practice law, or perform any activity constituting the practice of law."

Both Buyers Service and the State have appealed.

Discussion
This court in In re Duncan, 83 S.C. 186, 189, 65 S.E. 210, 211 (1909) held the practice of law includes ". . . conveyancing, the preparation of legal instruments of all kinds, and, in general, all advice to clients, and all action for them in matters connected with the law." See also State v. Wells, 191 S.C. 468, 5 S.E. 2d 181 (1939); Matter of Easler, 275 S.C. 400, 272 S.E. 2d 32 (1980). Additionally, S.C. Code Ann. § 40-5-320 (1986) strictly prohibits corporations from the practice of law.

A. Preparation of Instruments
Buyers Service contends the circuit court erred in holding it may not prepare deeds, notes and other instruments related to mortgage loans and transfers of real property. It argues the forms are standard and require no creative drafting. The State counters that preparation of instruments falls within the definition of the practice of law of In re

Duncan, and that Buyers Service acts as more than a mere scrivener in the process. We agree.

The practice of law is not confined to litigation, but extends to activities in other fields which entail specialized legal knowledge and ability. Often, the line between such activities and permissible business conduct by non-attorneys is unclear. However, courts of other jurisdictions considering the issue of whether preparation of instruments involves the practice of law have held that it does.

In Pioneer Title Ins. & Trust Co. v. State Bar of Nev., 74 Nev. 186, 326 P.2d 408 (1958) escrow agents were enjoined from preparation of instruments necessary to effectuate real estate sales transactions. The court reasoned that preparation of instruments, even with preprinted forms, involves more than a mere scrivener's duties. By necessity, the agents pass upon the legal sufficiency of the instruments to accomplish the contractual agreement of the parties. See also Arkansas Bar Ass'n v. Block, 230 Ark. 430, 323 S.W.2d 912, cert. denied, 361 U.S. 836, 80 S.Ct. 87, 4 L.Ed.2d 76 (1959).

The reason preparation of instruments by lay persons must be held to constitute the unauthorized practice of law is not for the economic protection of the legal profession. Rather, it is for the protection of the public from the potentially severe economic and emotional consequences which may flow from erroneous advice given by persons untrained in the law. This principle was stated by the Supreme Court of Washington in Bennion, Van Camp, Hagen & Ruhl v. Kassler Escrow, Inc., 96 Wash.2d 443, 635 P.2d 730 (1981). There, the legislature had enacted a statute authorizing escrow agents to perform services such as selection, preparation and completion of instruments in real estate transactions. The court previously had held these activities to constitute the unauthorized practice of law. See Washington State Bar Ass'n v. Great W. Union Fed. Sav. & Loan Ass'n, 91 Wash.2d 48, 586 P.2d 870 (1978). The statute was held unconstitutional on the ground it violated the court's exclusive power to regulate the practice of law:

The statute fails to consider who is to determine whether such agents and employees of banks, etc., are possessed of the requisite skill, competence and ethics. Only the Supreme Court has the power to make that determination through a bar examination, yearly Continuing Legal Education requirements, and the Code of Professional Responsibility. The public is also protected against unethical attorneys by a client's security fund maintained by the Washington State Bar Association.

635 P.2d at 734.

Similar protections are afforded to the public in South Carolina through this Court's regulation of attorneys' competency and conduct.

As noted in the statement of facts, Buyers Service has retained attorneys to review the closing documents. This does not save its activities from constituting the unauthorized practice of law. In State Bar of Ariz. v. Arizona Land Title & Trust Co., 90 Ariz. 76, 366 P.2d 1, reheard, 91 Ariz. 293, 371 P.2d 1020 (1962), a title company employed staff counsel to prepare legal instruments. The court cited the Arizona prohibition against a corporation's practice of law similar to that in S.C. Code Ann. § 40-5-320 (1986). The court then noted the conflicts of interest inherent in such an arrangement, reasoning that the adverse interests in real estate transactions make it extremely difficult for the attorney to maintain a proper professional posture toward each party.

We agree and hold the circuit court properly enjoined Buyers Service from the preparation of deeds, mortgages, notes and other legal instruments related to mortgage loans and transfers of real property.

B. Title Abstracts

Buyers Service next contends the circuit court erred in holding that preparation of title abstracts for persons other than attorneys constitutes the unauthorized practice of law. As noted in the statement of facts, the buyer pays Buyers Service $50 for title searches. However, the resulting title abstract is furnished not to the buyer, but to the mortgagee to certify that fee simple title will be vested in the buyer.

The State argues that even though the buyer does not see the title abstract, he nevertheless relies upon it to determine if he receives good, marketable title. That is, because the buyer knows a title search has been conducted, he reasonably assumes title is good if nothing adverse is reported. We agree.

The same principles which render the preparation of instruments the practice of law apply equally to the preparation of title abstracts. In Beach Abstract & Guar. Co. v. Bar Ass'n of Ark., 230 Ark. 494, 326 S.W.2d 900 (1959), the court relied upon its earlier holding in Arkansas Bar Ass'n v. Block, supra, in holding that title examination, when done for another, constitutes the practice of law. The court rejected the title insurance company's arguments that the examinations were performed only incidentally to its own business and that no separate fee was charged.

We affirm the circuit court's injunction which provides Buyers Service may conduct title examinations and prepare abstracts only for the benefit of attorneys. The examination of titles requires expert legal knowledge and skill. For the protection of the public such activities, if conducted by lay persons, must be under the supervision of a licensed attorney.

C. Real Estate Closings

The terms of the circuit court's injunction permit Buyers Service to continue its practice of handling real estate and mortgage loan closings with the restriction that no legal advice be given to the parties during the closing sessions.

The State contends instructing clients in the manner in which to execute legal documents is itself the practice of law and requires a legal knowledge of statutes and case law. See, e.g., S.C. Code Ann. §§ 27-7-10 and 30-5-30 (1976). We agree.

Courts of other jurisdictions have recognized dangers in allowing lay persons to handle real estate closings. See, e.g., Bowers v. Transamerica Title Ins. Co., 100 Wash.2d 581, 675 P.2d 193 (1983); Coffee County Abstract and Title Co. v. State ex rel. Norwood, 445 So.2d 852 (Ala.1984); Conway-Bogue Realty Inv. Co. v. Denver Bar Ass'n, 135 Colo. 398, 312 P.2d 998 (1957); Oregon State Bar v. Security Escrows, Inc., 233 Or. 80, 377 P.2d 334 (1962); New Jersey State Bar Ass'n v. Northern N.J. Mortgage Assocs., 32 N.J. 430, 161 A.2d 257 (1960).

While some of these cases hold that lay persons may conduct closings, they note that giving advice as to the effect of the various instruments required to be executed constitutes the unauthorized practice of law. Thus, in Coffee County Abstract and Title Co., supra, the title company was permitted to conduct real estate closings with the restriction that no legal advice or opinions be given. Chief Justice Torbert, concurring, gave instructions as to how such a closing should be handled: "If the parties to the transaction raise a legal question at the closing, the title company should stop the proceeding and instruct them to consult their attorneys." 445 So.2d at 857.

We agree this approach, in theory, would protect the public from receiving improper legal advice. However, there is in practice no way of assuring that lay persons conducting a closing will adhere to the restrictions. One handling a closing might easily be tempted to offer a few words of explanation, however innocent, rather than risk losing a fee for his or her employer.

We are convinced that real estate and mortgage loan closings should be conducted only under the supervision of attorneys, who have the ability to furnish their clients legal advice should the need arise and fall under the regulatory rules of this court. Again, protection of the public is of paramount concern.

D. Recording Instruments

The circuit court's order permits Buyers Service to continue its practice of mailing or hand-carrying instruments to the courthouse for recording. The State contends this activity is the practice of law. We agree.

We do not consider the physical transportation or mailing of documents to the courthouse to be the practice of law. However, when this step takes place as part of a real estate transfer it falls under the definition of the practice of law as formulated by this court in In re Duncan, supra. It is an aspect of conveyancing and affects legal rights. The appropriate sequence of recording is critical in order to protect a purchaser's title to property.

We conclude that instructions to the Clerk of Court or Register of Mesne Conveyances as to the manner of recording, if given by a lay person for the benefit of another, must be given under the supervision of an attorney.

Both parties' remaining exceptions relating to evidentiary rulings are without merit, and we affirm pursuant to Supreme Court Rule 23.

AFFIRMED IN PART AND REVERSED IN PART.

NESS, C.J., GREGORY and FINNEY, JJ., and

RICHTER, Acting Associate J., concur.
CHANDLER, J., not participating.

Case Question

Is it legal to draw up any document for another person if you are not a lawyer?

Assignment 15.1

> Identify two other professions in which advice may be given that has legal rights involved or affected.

Paralegals

The concept of the paralegal (legal assistant) has been recognized as a formal profession in this country only during the past thirty years or so. At the outset, note that the terms *paralegal* and *legal assistant* are used synonymously in some regions, while in others, a distinct difference in the level of education and training is noted by the specific term used. For the purposes of this text, the term **paralegal** is considered synonymous with that of **legal assistant**.

As stated, the paralegal profession is relatively young. Although lawyering is an old profession, the concept of a trained assistant who functions in a capacity other than clerical is essentially new. Taking the signal from medical and dental professions who have employed professional assistants for many years, the legal profession, too, has recognized the utility of someone trained in specific legal support areas.

While no uniformly accepted definition of paralegal exists, certain standards have been developed. Essentially, a paralegal is someone with training and knowledge in the law who should be able to perform all functions generally performed by an attorney with the exception of giving legal advice and advocacy. (In some jurisdictions, even limited advocacy is permitted.) While the typical perception of an attorney is someone who is in court all of the time, the reality is quite different. Attorneys have historically performed many daily functions that are now also within the parameters of the paralegal job description (see Table 15.1).

Many paralegals are still being employed to conduct, in addition to true paralegal duties, a degree of work that is clerical in nature. This is waning, however, because of the economic benefits of having a trained paralegal perform paralegal functions. Because the tasks performed by a paralegal are tradition-

Paralegal/Legal Assistant

One who has legal training and education and performs tasks in the law office that were traditionally performed by the attorney, with the exception of advocacy and giving of legal advice. In some geographical areas, these terms are used interchangeably, while in others, they imply distinct levels of professional ability.

DUTY/SKILL	Attorney	Paralegal	
Legal advice and representation (client contract, settlement negotiation, depositions, trial, and all situations involving advisement or advocacy)	X		**TABLE 15.1** Comparison of Duties of Attorneys and Paralegals*
Client interview and subsequent meetings	X	X	
Legal research	X	X	
Draft pleadings/motions	X	X	
Obtain evidence	X	X	
Interview witnesses	X	X	
Draft demand letters and settlement documents	X	X	
Select and prepare jury instructions	X	X	
Abstract depositions	X	X	
Trial notebook and general case management	X	X	
Draft contracts and corporate documents	X	X	

*With proper attorney supervision, the qualified paralegal can perform all of the functions indicated in the table and all other tasks required in the law office that do not involve legal advice or advocacy. Some paralegals also make excellent law office administrators, especially helpful in firms that do not employ a full-time administrator.

ally those performed by attorneys, it has been established that a paralegal's professional services may be billed to clients. This principle was a major achievement in establishing paralegals as legal professionals in their own right. A key element in paralegal functions and billing is that paralegal work must be performed under the supervision of a licensed attorney.

 CASE

MISSOURI v. JENKINS

491 U.S. 274, 109 S.Ct. 2463, 105 L.Ed.2d 229 (1989).

Justice **BRENNAN** delivered the opinion of the Court.

This is the attorney's fee aftermath of major school desegregation litigation in Kansas City, Missouri. We granted certiorari, 488 U.S. 888, 109 S.Ct. 218, 102 L.Ed.2d 209 (1988), to resolve two questions relating to fees litigation under 90 Stat. 2641, as amended, 42 U.S.C. § 1988. She obtained this figure in the following fashion:

I've gotten my figures from the Court Administrator which he indicated for each day that the trial would take just for the use of the courtroom facilities, the personnel would be—and first he said approximately $800. And then he called me back to say it was $782 per day. And I can't help but think that's a fairly accurate figure. And in light of the figure I've heard in other matters tried in other counties which are billable to the County of Middlesex, I think that comes within the parameter of ["reasonableness" set forth in the Appellate Division's interlocutory order]. Because in some instances in criminal trials where there's a number of Sheriff's officers involved, it runs to some three, four, $500 an hour to try a case. And I think that $782 has to be considered reasonable.

None of the parties has contested the accuracy of the per diem expense.

Where authorized, as here, the allowance of costs is generally committed to the court's discretion. Fortugno Realty Co. v. Shiavone-Bonomo Corp., 39 N.J. 382, 396, 189 A.2d 7 (1963); Hirsch v. Tushill, Ltd., Inc., 110 N.J. 644, 646, 542 A.2d 897 cents Y (1988). We find no abuse of discretion in fixing court costs occasioned by counsels' default.

The order allowing costs and counsel fees is modified and, as modified, affirmed. The matter is remanded to the trial court for further proceedings consistent with this opinion.

* * *

[S]hould the fee award compensate the work of paralegals and law clerks by applying the market rate for their work?

I

This litigation began in 1977 as a suit by the Kansas City Missouri School District (KCMSD), the school board, and the children of two school board members, against the State of Missouri and other defendants. The plaintiffs alleged that the State, surrounding school districts, and various federal agencies had caused and perpetuated a system of racial segregation in the schools of the Kansas City metropolitan area. They sought various desegregation remedies. KCMSD was subsequently realigned as a nominal defendant, and a class of present and future KCMSD students was certified as plaintiffs. After lengthy proceedings, including a trial that lasted 7½ months during 1983 and 1984, the District Court found the State of Missouri and KCMSD liable, while dismissing the suburban school districts and the federal defendants. It ordered various intradistrict remedies, to be paid for by the State and KCMSD, including $260 million in capital improvements and a magnet-school plan costing over $200 million. See Jenkins v. Missouri, 807 F.2d 657 (CA8 1986) (en banc), cert. denied, 484 U.S. 816 (1987); Jenkins v. Missouri, 855 F.2d 1295 (CA8 1988), cert. granted, 490 U.S. 1034, 109 S.Ct.

The plaintiff class has been represented, since 1979, by Kansas City lawyer Arthur Benson and, since 1982, by the NAACP Legal Defense and Educational Fund, Inc. (LDF). Benson and the LDF requested attorney's fees under the Civil Rights Attorney's Fees Awards Act of 1976, 42 U.S.C. § 1988. Benson and his associates had devoted 10,875 attorney hours to the litigation, as well as 8,108 hours of paralegal and law clerk time. For the LDF the corresponding figures were 10,854 hours for attorneys and 15,517 hours for paralegals and law clerks. Their fee applications deleted from these totals 3,628 attorney hours and 7,046 paralegal hours allocable to unsuccessful claims against the suburban school districts. With additions for postjudgment monitoring and for preparation of the fee application, the District Court awarded Benson a total of approximately $1.7 million and the LDF $2.3 million. App. to Pet. for Cert. A22–A43.

Section 1988 provides in relevant part: "In any action or proceeding to enforce a provision of sections 1981, 1982, 1983, 1985, and 1986 of this title, title IX of Public Law 92-318 [20 U.S.C. § 1681 et seq.], or title VI of the Civil Rights Act of 1964 [42 U.S.C. s 2000d et seq.], the court, in its discretion, may allow the prevailing party, other than the United States, a reasonable attorney's fee as part of the costs."

In calculating the hourly rate for Benson's fees the court noted that the market rate in Kansas City for attorneys of Benson's qualifications was in the range of $125 to $175 per hour, and found that "Mr. Benson's rate would fall at the higher end of this range based upon his expertise in the area of civil rights." Id., at A26. It calculated his fees on the basis of an even higher hourly rate of $200, however, because of three additional factors: the preclusion of other employment, the undesirability of the case, and the delay in payment for Benson's services. Id., at A26–A27. The court also took account of the delay in payment in setting the rates for several of Benson's associates by using current market rates rather than those applicable at the time the services were rendered. Id., at A28–A30. For the same reason, it calculated the fees for the LDF attorneys at current market rates. Id., at A33.

Both Benson and the LDF employed numerous paralegals, law clerks (generally law students working part time), and recent law graduates in this litigation. The court awarded fees for their work based on Kansas City market rates for those categories. As in the case of the attorneys, it used current rather than historic market rates in order to compensate for the delay in payment. It therefore awarded fees based on hourly rates of $35 for law clerks, $40 for paralegals, and $50 for recent law graduates. Id., at A29–A31, A34.

* * *

III

Missouri's second contention is that the District Court erred in compensating the work of law clerks and paralegals (hereinafter collectively "paralegals") at the market rates for their services, rather than at their cost to the attorney. While Missouri agrees that compensation for the cost of these personnel should be included in the fee award, it suggests that an hourly rate of $15—which it argued below corresponded to their salaries, benefits, and overhead—would be appropriate, rather than the market rates of $35 to $50. According to Missouri, § 1988 does not authorize billing paralegals' hours at market rates, and doing so produces a "windfall" for the attorney.

The Courts of Appeals have taken a variety of positions on this issue. Most permit separate billing of paralegal time. . . . Some courts, on the other hand, have considered paralegal work "out-of-pocket expense," recoverable only at cost to the attorney. See, e.g., Northcross v. Board of Education of Memphis City Schools, 611 F.2d 624, 639 (CA6 1979), cert. denied, 447 U.S. 911, 100 S.Ct. 3000, 64 L.Ed.2d 862 (1980). . . . At least one Court of Appeals has refused to permit any recovery of paralegal expense apart from the attorney's hourly fee. Abrams v. Baylor College of Medicine, 805 F.2d 528, 535 (CA5 1986).

We begin with the statutory language, which provides simply for "a reasonable attorney's fee as part of the costs." 42 U.S.C. § 1988. Clearly, a

"reasonable attorney's fee" cannot have been meant to compensate only work performed personally by members of the bar. Rather, the term must refer to a reasonable fee for the work product of an attorney. Thus, the fee must take into account the work not only of attorneys, but also of secretaries, messengers, librarians, janitors, and others whose labor contributes to the work product for which an attorney bills her client; and it must also take account of other expenses and profit. The parties have suggested no reason why the work of paralegals should not be similarly compensated, nor can we think of any. We thus take as our starting point the self-evident proposition that the "reasonable attorney's fee" provided for by statute should compensate the work of paralegals, as well as that of attorneys. The more difficult question is how the work of paralegals is to be valuated in calculating the overall attorney's fee.

The statute specifies a "reasonable" fee for the attorney's work product. In determining how other elements of the attorney's fee are to be calculated, we have consistently looked to the marketplace as our guide to what is "reasonable." In Blum v. Stenson, 465 U.S. 886, 104 S.Ct. 1541, 79 L.Ed.2d 891 (1984), for example, we rejected an argument that attorney's fees for nonprofit legal service organizations should be based on cost. We said: "The statute and legislative history establish that 'reasonable fees' under § 1988 are to be calculated according to the prevailing market rates in the relevant community. . . ." Id., at 895, 104 S.Ct., at 1547. See also, e.g., Delaware Valley, 483 U.S., at 732, 107 S.Ct., at 3090 (O'CONNOR, J., concurring) (controlling question concerning contingency enhancements is "how the market in a community compensates for contingency"); Rivera, 477 U.S., at 591, 106 S.Ct. at 2703 (REHNQUIST, J., dissenting) (reasonableness of fee must be determined "in light of both the traditional billing practices in the profession, and the fundamental principle that the award of a 'reasonable' attorney's fee under § 1988 means a fee that would have been deemed reasonable if billed to affluent plaintiffs by their own attorneys"). A reasonable attorney's fee under § 1988 is one calculated on the basis of rates and practices prevailing in the relevant market, i.e., "in line with those [rates] prevailing in the community for similar services by lawyers of reasonably comparable skill, experience, and reputation," Blum, supra, 465 U.S., at 896, n. 11, 104 S.Ct., at 1547, n. 11, and one that grants the successful civil rights plaintiff a "fully compensatory fee," Hensley v. Eckerhart, 461 U.S. 424, 435, 103 S.Ct. 1933, 1940, 76 L.Ed.2d

40 (1983), comparable to what "is traditional with attorneys compensated by a fee-paying client." S.Rep. No. 94-1011, p. 6 (1976), U.S.Code Cong. & Admin.News 1976, pp. 5908, 5913.

Case Question
What type of paralegal services could not reasonably be billed to the client?

Support Personnel

In addition to employing the lawyer and paralegal, most law firms and government and corporate legal departments employ a variety of positions to provide necessary support services. While not exhaustive, several of these positions are described in the following table. Please note that the descriptions are general.

BILLING CLERK	Manages day-to-day accounts, billing clients, incoming and outgoing funds.
FILING CLERK	Maintains files, opens new files, closes completed files, maintains organization and confidentiality of files.
LAW CLERK	Performs basic legal research and writing functions.
LAW OFFICE ADMINISTRATOR	Manages the business affairs of the organization, personnel issues, etc.
LEGAL SECRETARY	Performs all necessary clerical functions for the organization.
LEGAL INVESTIGATOR	Assists the lawyers and paralegals in the collection of admissible evidence and supporting information for case files.
LIBRARIAN	Maintains the law library, updates existing materials, and sees that contents are kept current through ordering new materials, etc.
RECEPTIONIST	Responsible for registering visitors, scheduling, telephone routing, and other clerical support.

These are just a few of the people necessary to make the legal profession operate in an organized and efficient manner. All work is done under the supervision of an attorney, and it is the legal responsibility of the lawyer to see that each works within the constraints of the ethical standards imposed on all licensed attorneys.

Assignment 15.2

Create a flowchart and demonstrate how each of the jobs described on the previous page affects a client's representation.

ETHICAL RESPONSIBILITIES OF THE LEGAL PROFESSIONAL

Although lawyer jokes are plentiful and prosecution of members of the bar for criminal acts generally makes the news, the story has another side. The practice of law is one of the very few professions that maintain a comprehensive set of legal and ethical standards that can result in professional discipline and, occasionally, criminal prosecution if violated. In addition to being required to take an examination to practice law, lawyers are required to pass an exam on ethics. Every state has an office where ethical violations of attorneys can be reported.

Why the emphasis on ethics of lawyers? Since individuals often put their legal rights in the hands of lawyers, the result may mean freedom or imprisonment, no judgment or a verdict that will bankrupt a defendant. Often, the stakes are very high. As a result, lawyers have the ultimate responsibility to handle a client's affairs properly or not to handle them. In our ever-increasingly complicated legal system, plethora of legal standards, litigation explosion, and age of technology, lawyers have an overwhelming task to represent clients well. Ethical standards give lawyers and clients alike some guidance in this pursuit.

The American Bar Association Model Rules of Professional Conduct is the essential standard of attorney ethics. The rules—or rules similar in nature—are followed in the states and federal courts as the required standards of conduct for attorneys. Following is a summary of some of the duties of a lawyer under the Rules.

1. Lawyers have the duty to maintain the confidentiality of client communications.

 APPLICATION 15.2

A client meets with his lawyer to discuss possible settlement of a custody case. The client informs the lawyer about certain personal habits that the lawyer believes will affect the client's ability to properly parent the child. None of the habits are illegal. The lawyer is not at liberty to disclose the information to the court or the opposing counsel.

Points for Discussion
1. What do you think the lawyer should do?
2. When a child's welfare is possibly at stake, why does the rule still apply?

2. Lawyers have the duty to act competently.

APPLICATION 15.3

Elena is hired fresh out of law school by a large firm. She studies and takes the bar exam. On the day she is licensed to practice law, her employer says, "I want you to try the Smithson case next Monday. It's a jury trial and will be good experience." Elena's response is "Could I see a trial first?" Elena does not feel competent to conduct a trial independently, as she has never even witnessed one. She should not conduct the trial, because she reasonably believes she is not competent to do so.

Point for Discussion
What should Elena do to obtain competence?

3.   Lawyers have the duty to avoid conflicts of interest.

 APPLICATION 15.4

Otto works for Harland and Pavlov. At meetings of the lawyers of the firm, he takes part in a discussion on strategy for one of the other lawyer's clients, Dean Morino. About six months later, Otto accepts a position with the firm of Richards and Epps. At that time, he submits a list of the case files from his former job in which he had any contact whatsoever. Richards and Epps marks all files in which it was opposing counsel, including the Dean Morino file. By doing this, Otto can recognize any files at the new firm that he should not be involved with because of the possibility of his privileged information on the files at his former place of employment.

Points for Discussion
1. What is accomplished by giving a list of all files?
2. Can't Otto just remember not to work on them?

4.   Lawyers have the duty to represent clients zealously.

 APPLICATION 15.5

Review Application 15.2. If the lawyer honestly believes that the client should not have custody, the lawyer should consider withdrawing from the case if those beliefs are going to influence the lawyer's representation of the client to the best of the lawyer's ability.

Point for Discussion
Why aren't lawyers withdrawing from cases all the time?

5.   Lawyers have the duty to exercise independent professional judgment.

APPLICATION 15.6

A young lawyer starting a practice meets a young doctor who is also just starting out. The two decide to go into business together to construct a new building. They agree that as soon as each has $100,000 to contribute, they will build a professional office building. The doctor is doing very well. The lawyer is having a hard time building a client base. The doctor agrees to refer patients who are injured in accidents for a per-client fee of $100. If the lawyer accepts the referrals, his judgment may be clouded by the monetary benefits of all the referrals. For this reason, lawyers typically are prevented from engaging with nonlawyers in business dealings that require legal expertise.

Point for Discussion
What are the possible negative results of this example?

Assignment 15.3

Create a situation in which each of the foregoing ethical standards comes into question. Be prepared to discuss your answers.

As the preceding examples illustrate, the practice of law is more than performing a job description. The lawyer and the subordinate staff have numerous responsibilities to conduct themselves in a way that protects the interests of the client even when doing so supersedes the interests of the attorney.

 CASE

KOHN v. SCHIAPPA

281 N.J.Super. 235,
656 A.2d 1322 (1995).

As a general rule, an attorney, like other tortfeasors, will be held liable to clients who are foreseeably and proximately harmed by his or her negligence. In a legal malpractice action, damages are typically measured by that amount which the client would have recovered, but for the attorney's negligence. Lieberman v. Employers Ins. of Wausau, 84 N.J. 325, 342, 419 A.2d 417 (1980). This requires proof of the viability and worth of the negligently lost claim.

This method of establishing damages has been frequently characterized as involving a "suit within a suit." See e.g. Gautam, supra, 215 N.J.Super. at 397-398, 521 A.2d 1343 (citing Lieberman v. Employers Ins. of Wausau, supra, 84 N.J. at 342, 419 A.2d 417; Coggen, "Attorney Negligence . . . A Suit Within a Suit," 60 W.Va.L.Rev. 225, 233 (1958); Annotation, Attorney-Negligence-Damages, 45 A.L.R.2d 62, 63-67 (1956)).

In Gautam, supra, the plaintiffs claimed that their attorney had negligently handled their medical malpractice action. In addition to the lost value of the medical malpractice claim, plaintiffs claimed the right to recover for the severe emotional distress purportedly suffered by them as well. Rejecting this contention, the appellate division articulated a general rule that, "emotional distress damages should not be awarded in legal malpractice cases at least in the absence of egregious or extraordinary circumstances." Id. at 399, 521 A.2d 1343 (emphasis added).

Although guided by public policy considerations, the court appeared to be influenced by the economic nature of the lawyer-client relationship as well as the underlying claim itself, and concluded that damages should be limited to recompensing a party solely for the economic losses sustained. Id. at 399-400, 521 A.2d 1343. While "the outer-most boundaries of the law dealing with emotional distress damages are not yet visible, we are thoroughly satisfied that there is no warrant for allowing recovery under the facts of this case." Id. at 400, 521 A.2d 1343 (emphasis added) (citation omitted).

Plaintiffs argue that Gautam is not controlling because their claim is not predicated upon an economic loss. Instead, they contend that the improper disclosure of privileged information has severely damaged their emotional and mental well being, and urge that their circumstances be deemed "extraordinary" as contemplated by Gautam.

Since no economic "claim" was impaired by counsel's alleged negligence, the "suit within a suit" framework typically utilized in adjudicating legal malpractice actions, has no application. Consequently, without the ability to seek redress for emotional distress damages, negligent counsel would have virtual immunity for any malpractice committed when retained for non-economic purposes. The unfairness of such a result is quickly manifest given the wide variety of attorney-client relationships other than adoption proceedings, which are not predicated upon economic interests. Drafting a living will, contested child custody or visitation disputes, criminal defense work, as well as numerous pursuits in the general equity courts are but a few examples. In such instances one would be unable to quantify any economic loss. On the other hand, severe mental and emotional distress, resulting from the loss of custody or visitation rights, or wrongful incarceration, is readily foreseeable.

Federal and sister jurisdictions analyzing the reach of Gautam, have also authorized emotional distress claims in such contexts. In Lawson v. Nugent, 702 F.Supp. 91 (D.N.J.1988), the United States District Court, applying New Jersey law, permitted the plaintiff to assert and prove emotional distress caused by his attorney's negligent representation in a criminal proceeding. The defendant there, as here, urged that Gautam precluded such damages under New Jersey law. In an exhaustive and comprehensive analysis of New Jersey law, Judge Lifland acknowledged a liberal and expansive trend regarding the viability of emotional distress claims. Noting that plaintiff's underlying attorney-client relationship was predicated upon a liberty, rather than a pecuniary interest, the judge distinguished Gautam and concluded that damages for emotional distress were recoverable. Id. at 93. See also, Snyder v. Baumecker, 708 F.Supp. 1451, 1464 (D.N.J. 1989) (emotional distress damages from loss of liberty recoverable, following Lawson, supra).

The plaintiff alleged that but for the attorney's negligence, he would only have served forty months in a correctional facility, instead of 5 years. Id. at 92.

In support of this trend, the court reviewed, among other things, Ayers v. Jackson Tp., 106 N.J. 557, 525 A.2d 287 (1987) (fear of cancer by residents who alleged exposure to toxic waste may provide a basis for a claim of emotional distress); Saunderlin v. E.I. DuPont Co., 102 N.J. 402, 508 A.2d 1095 (1986) (fear of cancer attributable to exposure to work place asbestos may provide a basis for a claim of emotional distress where injury is demonstrable by objective medical evidence); Procanik by Procanik v. Cillo, 97 N.J. 339, 478 A.2d 755 (1984) (allowing emotional distress damages to parents of impaired child in medical malpractice action); Evers v. Dollinger, 95 N.J. 399, 471 A.2d 405 (1984) (negligent delay of surgery may cause emotional distress where delay exacerbated patient's disease).

Likewise, in Henderson v. Domingue, 626 So.2d 555, 559 (La.App. 3rd Cir. 1993), writ denied, 630 So.2d 799 (La.1994), a legal malpractice action predicated on counsel's failure to prosecute a United States Tax Court action, plaintiff's serious aggravation, his grave concern and embarrassment, and the damage suffered to his credit reputation, caused the court to affirm a damage award for mental anguish. See also, Smith v. Superior Court, 10 Cal.App.4th 1033, 13 Cal.Rptr.2d 133, 137-38 (1992) (while mere negligence will not support a recovery for mental suffering where the defendant's tortious conduct has resulted in only economic injury, "where a plaintiff sufficiently alleges intentional or affirmative misconduct by an attorney or noneconomic injury resulting from an attorney's professional negligence, recovery of emotional distress damages is permitted") (emphasis added); and see, McDaniel v. Gile, 230 Cal.App.3d 363, 373-75, 281 Cal.Rptr. 242 (1991) (emotional distress damages available in action predicated on attorney's malfeasance of criminal defense, resulting in incarceration).

In doing so, the court distinguished an earlier decision to the contrary. Compare, Richards v. Cousins, 550 So.2d 1273 (La.App. 4th Cir.), writ denied, 552 So.2d 397 (La.1989).

Permitting recovery for emotional distress in legal malpractice actions has also attracted the attention of the commentators. See e.g., Joseph J. Kelleher, "An Attorney's Liability for the Negligent Infliction of Emotional Distress," 58 Fordham L.Rev. 1309 (1990); D. Dusty Rhoades & Laura W. Morgan, "Recovery of Emotional Distress Damages in Attorney Malpractice Actions," 45 S.C.L.Rev. 837, 841 (1994), (noting the emergence of a general trend allowing recovery for emotional distress damages "when the direct damage interferes with a personal interest of the client, such as liberty or family.").

While Gautam held that "damages should be limited to recompensing the injured party for his economic loss," 215 N.J.Super. at 399, 521 A.2d 1343, that court was not asked to consider, nor did it address, whether damages for emotional distress were recoverable in cases involving non-economic claims where the "suit within a suit" framework is inapplicable. Consequently, it cannot be said that Gautam forecloses a plaintiff from alleging severe emotional distress where the underlying representation was for noneconomic purposes. Indeed, recognizing that exceptions to any hard and fast rule would undoubtedly evolve, the court cautioned:

> [E]ven if emotional distress damages were recoverable in legal malpractice actions, such awards would be impermissible in the absence of medical evidence establishing substantial bodily injury or severe and demonstrable psychiatric sequelae proximately caused by the tortfeasor's misconduct.

[Gautam, supra, 215 N.J.Super. at 399, 521 A.2d 1343.]

While the burden thus imposed is a formidable one, it cannot be held at this stage of the proceedings that plaintiffs will be unable to meet it.

In this matter, plaintiffs retained defendant to handle a formal adoption, not to seek recovery for an economic loss. Indeed, other than the retainer, there were no pecuniary interests involved. If plaintiffs are precluded from asserting and proving the mental anguish and distress purportedly caused by counsel's wrongful disclosure of confidential information, then they are, for all intents and purposes, remediless. Based upon the foregoing, I am satisfied that affording virtual immunity to negligent attorneys who are retained for non-economic purposes is contrary to the public interest and therefore not sound public policy. Accordingly, defendant's motion for summary judgment is denied.

Plaintiffs shall submit the appropriate order.

Case Question
What two things must be shown to establish damages in an action for malfeasance by an attorney?

CASE

IN RE DISCIPLINARY PROCEEDINGS AGAINST SYLVAN

202 Wis.2d 123, 549
N.W.2d 249 (Wis. 1996).

Attorney Sylvan was admitted to practice law in Wisconsin in 1959 and practiced in Menomonee Falls. He has not been the subject of a prior disciplinary proceeding but has been suspended from the practice of law since June, 1994 for failure to comply with continuing legal education requirements. Because of his failure to file an answer to the Board's complaint, the referee, Attorney Jean DiMotto, granted the Board's motion for default and made findings of fact based on the Board's complaint.

Attorney Sylvan was retained in January, 1992 to probate the estate of a client's mother. That estate consisted of solely owned property in the amount of approximately $353,000, in the form of certificates of deposit, savings bonds, a treasury note, a demand note, a checking account, a life insurance policy and miscellaneous stock. Attorney Sylvan commenced informal probate and after filing the general inventory did nothing in the estate for more than a year. The probate court notified him in June, 1993 that four items were needed to close the estate: the judgment on claims, a closing certificate for fiduciaries, receipts and a statement to close. The court stated that if the estate were not closed promptly, it would issue an order to show cause. Soon after receiving that letter from the court, Attorney Sylvan assured the personal representative that there would be no difficulty getting everything completed to close the estate promptly.

When the estate was not closed six months later, the court issued an order to show cause, and on the return date Attorney Sylvan filed the receipts and the closing certificate and obtained a two-month extension to furnish the remaining two items. When nothing was done over the next three months and Attorney Sylvan failed to appear at the adjourned return date on the order to show cause, the court removed him as attorney for the estate and appointed a successor, who promptly closed the estate, charging $150 to do so.

After filing the application for informal probate, Attorney Sylvan did not communicate with or respond to the inquiries of the personal representative for extended periods of time, despite numerous attempts by the personal representative to contact him by telephone. As a result, the personal representative experienced needless concern and anxiety.

The probate of the estate was simple and uncomplicated in view of the nature of the assets and the number and identity of the beneficiaries. Moreover, the personal representative handled liquidation and distribution of the assets to the beneficiaries. Also, Attorney Sylvan did not prepare or file the estate tax returns. Yet, Attorney Sylvan, who kept no time records for the work he performed in the probate, charged and received fees of $10,598, representing three percent of the estate's asset value, despite a statutory proscription of percentage fees in probate, Wis.Stat. § 851.40(2)(e). The referee found that the maximum reasonable fee to which an experienced attorney would be entitled for the probate of this estate is $2500.

Wis.Stat. § 851.40 (1993-94) provides, in part: Basis for attorney fees.

(2) Any personal representative, heir, beneficiary under a will or other interested party may petition the court to review any attorney's fee which is subject to sub. (1). If the decedent died intestate or the testator's will contains no provision concerning attorney fees, the court shall consider the following factors in determining what is just and reasonable attorney's fee:

(e) The sufficiency of assets properly available to pay for the services, except that the value of the estate may not be the controlling factor.

When the Board requested a response to the personal representative's grievance, Attorney Sylvan did not respond. He also did not respond to a second letter from the Board. When the grievance was referred to the district professional responsibility committee for investigation, Attorney Sylvan met with the investigator and admitted that he had received the Board's inquiries but gave no reason for not responding to them or cooperating with the Board.

The referee concluded that Attorney Sylvan's failure to probate the estate with reasonable diligence and promptness violated SCR 20:1.3; his failure to keep the personal representative reasonably informed of the status of the probate and reply to reasonable requests for information violated SCR 20:1.4(a); his charging an excessive and unreasonable fee violated SCR 20:1.5(a) and, because it was contrary to statute, also violated SCR 20:8.4(f). Finally, Attorney Sylvan's failure to cooperate with the Board's investigation violated SCR 21.03(4) and 22.07(2).

SCR 20:1.3 provides: Diligence A lawyer shall act with reasonable diligence and promptness in representing a client.

SCR 20:1.4 provides, in pertinent part: Communication (a) A lawyer shall keep a client reasonably informed about the status of a matter and promptly comply with reasonable requests for information.

SCR 20:1.5 provides, in pertinent part: Fees (a) A lawyer's fee shall be reasonable. The factors to be considered in determining the reasonableness of a fee include the following: (1) the time and labor required, the novelty and difficulty of the questions involved, and the skill requisite to perform the legal service properly; (2) the likelihood, if apparent to the client, that the acceptance of the particular employment will preclude other employment by the lawyer; (3) the fee customarily charged in the locality for similar legal services; (4) the amount involved and the results obtained; (5) the time limitations imposed by the client or by the circumstances; (6) the nature and length of the professional relationship with the client; (7) the experience, reputation, and ability of the lawyer or lawyers performing the services; and (8) whether the fee is fixed or contingent.

SCR 20:8.4 provides, in pertinent part: Misconduct. It is professional misconduct for a lawyer to:

(f) violate a statute, supreme court rule, supreme court order or supreme court decision regulating the conduct of lawyers;

SCR 21.03 provides, in pertinent part: General principles.

(4) Every attorney shall cooperate with the board and the administrator in the investigation, prosecution and disposition of grievances and complaints filed with or by the board or administrator.

As discipline for that misconduct, the referee recommended a 60-day license suspension.

In addition to the suspension, the referee recommended that Attorney Sylvan be required to make restitution to the estate in the amount of $8,098, the amount by which his fee exceeded a reasonable fee for his work in the matter. The referee also recommended that Attorney Sylvan be required to pay the costs of this proceeding.

We adopt the referee's findings of fact and conclusions of law and determine that Attorney Sylvan's professional misconduct, viewed in light of his conduct in the course of this proceeding, warrant the 60-day license suspension recommended by the referee. In addition, he is required to make restitution to the estate as the referee recommended.

IT IS ORDERED that the license of Attorney Ronald W. Sylvan to practice law in Wisconsin is suspended for a period of 60 days, effective the date of the order.

IT IS FURTHER ORDERED that within 60 days of the date of this order Ronald W. Sylvan make restitution in the amount of $8,098 as set forth in the referee's report.

IT IS FURTHER ORDERED that within 60 days of the date of this order Ronald W. Sylvan pay to the Board of Attorneys Professional Responsibility the costs of this proceeding, provided that if the costs are not paid within the time specified and absent a showing to this court of his inability to pay the costs within that time, the license of Ronald W. Sylvan to practice law in Wisconsin shall remain suspended until further order of the court.

IT IS FURTHER ORDERED that Ronald W. Sylvan comply with the provisions of SCR 22.26 concerning the duties of a person whose license to practice law in Wisconsin has been suspended.

Case Question
What constitutes reasonable diligence?

CHAPTER SUMMARY

This chapter has discussed the various roles of professionals within the American legal system. The judge acts as mediator and trier of law. Specifically, the appellate judge determines whether fair treatment was afforded the parties and whether the law was properly applied. The trial judge determines which law is applicable to a case and sees that the law is applied fairly and consistently. The trial judge also resolves disputes between the parties during the pretrial and trial process. The administrative law judge provides an informed view as to the appropriateness of administrative agency action.

The role of the lawyer is changing. No longer does the attorney handle all aspects of the litigation process. Rather, the lawyer today primarily practices law, that is, gives legal advice and advocates. Many lawyers delegate other duties to the trained paralegal—the new legal professional. The paralegal functions as an extension of the lawyer and performs tasks traditionally completed by lawyers. The paralegal is supervised by the lawyer, as are the other members of the legal staff.

Although ethical behavior of attorneys has always been a required standard of the practice of law, it has gained attention in an atmosphere of increasing litigation and numbers of lawyers practicing. Among the standards all lawyers are required to adhere to are confidentiality, competence, avoidance of conflicts of interest, zealous representation, and independent professional judgment.

This chapter is by no means exhaustive on the subject of legal professionals and legal ethics. Rather, the information here serves to create an awareness of the responsibilities of the key players in the American legal system.

REVIEW QUESTIONS

1. Explain the role and duties of various types of judges.
2. Define the two primary functions of a lawyer in the practice of law.
3. How is a paralegal different from a lawyer?
4. Explain the role of the modern paralegal.
5. What is the requirement of all work performed by a paralegal?
6. Identify and define the roles of the members of the legal support staff.
7. To whom does the standard of confidentiality apply?
8. Give an example of a conflict of interest by an attorney.
9. What does the term *zealous representation* mean?
10. What is the rule of independent judgment?

CHAPTER TERMS

Administrative Law Judge
Jurist (Judge)

Law Clerk
Lawyer/Attorney

Paralegal/Legal Assistant

The Constitution of the United States

PREAMBLE

We the People of the United States, in Order to form a more perfect Union, establish Justice, insure domestic Tranquility, provide for the common defence, promote the general Welfare, and secure the Blessings of Liberty to ourselves and our Posterity, do ordain and establish this Constitution for the United States of America.

ARTICLE I

Section 1. All legislative Powers herein granted shall be vested in a Congress of the United States, which shall consist of a Senate and House of Representatives.

Section 2. The House of Representatives shall be composed of Members chosen every second Year by the People of the several States, and the Electors in each State shall have the Qualifications requisite for Electors of the most numerous Branch of the State Legislature.

No Person shall be a Representative who shall not have attained to the Age of twenty five Years, and been seven Years a Citizen of the United States, and who shall not, when elected, be an Inhabitant of that State in which he shall be chosen.

Representatives and direct Taxes shall be apportioned among the several States which may be included within this Union, according to their respective Numbers, which shall be determined by adding to the whole Number of free Persons, including those bound to Service for a Term of Years, and excluding Indians not taxed, three fifths of all other Persons. The actual Enumeration shall be made within three years after the first Meeting of the Congress of the United States, and within every subsequent Term of ten Years, in such Manner as they shall by Law direct. The Number of Representatives shall not exceed one for every thirty Thousand, but each State shall have at Least one Representative; and until such enumeration shall be made, the State of New Hampshire shall be entitled to chuse three, Massachusetts eight, Rhode Island and Providence Plantations one, Connecticut five, New York six, New Jersey four, Pennsylvania eight, Delaware one, Maryland six, Virginia ten, North Carolina five, South Carolina five, and Georgia three.

When vacancies happen in the Representation from any State, the Executive Authority thereof shall issue Writs of Election to fill such Vacancies.

The House of Representatives shall chuse their Speaker and other Officers; and shall have the sole Power of Impeachment.

Section 3. The Senate of the United States shall be composed of two Senators from each State, chosen by the Legislature thereof, for six Years; and each Senator shall have one Vote.

Immediately after they shall be assembled in Consequence of the first Election, they shall be divided as equally as may be into three Classes. The Seats of the Senators of the first Class shall be vacated at the Expiration of the second Year, of the second Class at the Expiration of the fourth Year, and of the third Class at the Expiration of the sixth Year, so that one third may be chosen every second Year; and if Vacancies happen by Resignation, or otherwise, during the Recess of the Legislature of any State, the Executive thereof may make temporary Appointments until the next Meeting of the Legislature, which shall then fill such Vacancies.

No Person shall be a Senator who shall not have attained to the Age of thirty Years, and been nine Years a Citizen of the United States, and who shall not, when elected, be an Inhabitant of that State for which he shall be chosen.

The Vice President of the United States shall be President of the Senate, but shall have no Vote, unless they be equally divided.

The Senate shall chuse their other Officers, and also a President pro tempore, in the Absence of the Vice President, or when he shall exercise the Office of President of the United States.

The Senate shall have the sole Power to try all Impeachments. When sitting for that Purpose, they shall be on Oath or Affirmation. When the President of the United States is tried, the Chief Justice shall preside: And no Person shall be convicted without the Concurrence of two thirds of the Members present.

Judgment in Cases of Impeachment shall not extend further than to removal from Office, and disqualification to hold and enjoy any Office of honor, Trust, or Profit under the United States: but the Party convicted shall nevertheless be liable and subject to Indictment, Trial, Judgment, and Punishment, according to Law.

Section 4. The Times, Places and Manner of holding Elections for Senators and Representatives, shall be prescribed in each State by the Legislature thereof; but the Congress may at any time by Law make or alter such Regulations, except as to the Places of chusing Senators.

The Congress shall assemble at least once in every Year, and such Meeting shall be on the first Monday in December, unless they shall by Law appoint a different Day.

Section 5. Each House shall be the Judge of the Elections, Returns, and Qualifications of its own Members, and a Majority of each shall constitute a Quorum to do Business; but a smaller Number may adjourn from day to day, and may be authorized to compel the Attendance of absent Members, in such Manner, and under such Penalties as each House may provide.

Each House may determine the Rules of its Proceedings, punish its Members for disorderly Behavior, and, with the Concurrence of two thirds, expel a Member.

Each House shall keep a Journal of its Proceedings, and from time to time publish the same, excepting such Parts as may in their Judgment require Secrecy; and the Yeas and Nays of the Members of either House on any question shall, at the Desire of one fifth of those Present, be entered on the Journal.

Neither House, during the Session of Congress, shall, without the Consent of the other, adjourn for more than three days, nor to any other Place than that in which the two Houses shall be sitting.

Section 6. The Senators and Representatives shall receive a Compensation for their Services, to be ascertained by Law, and paid out of the Treasury of the United States. They shall in all Cases, except Treason, Felony and Breach of the Peace, be privileged from Arrest during their Attendance at the Session of their respective Houses, and in going to and returning from the same; and for any Speech or Debate in either House, they shall not be questioned in any other Place.

No Senator or Representative shall, during the Time for which he was elected, be appointed to any civil Office under the Authority of the United States, which shall have been created, or the Emoluments whereof shall have been increased during such time; and no Person holding any Office under the United States, shall be a Member of either House during his Continuance in Office.

Section 7. All Bills for raising Revenue shall originate in the House of Representatives; but the Senate may propose or concur with Amendments as on other Bills.

Every Bill which shall have passed the House of Representatives and the Senate, shall, before it become a Law, be presented to the President of the United States; If he approve he shall sign it, but if not he shall return it, with his Objections to the House in which it shall have originated, who shall enter the Objections at large on their Journal, and proceed to reconsider it. If after such Reconsideration two thirds of that House shall agree to pass the Bill, it shall be sent together with the Objections, to the other House, by which it shall likewise be reconsidered, and if approved by two thirds of that House, it shall become a Law. But in all such Cases the Votes of both Houses shall be determined by Yeas and Nays, and the Names of the Persons voting for and against the Bill shall be entered on the Journal of each House respectively. If any Bill shall not be returned by the President within ten Days (Sundays excepted) after it shall have been presented to him, the Same shall be a Law, in like Manner as if he had signed it, unless the Congress by their Adjournment prevent its Return in which Case it shall not be a Law.

Every Order, Resolution, or Vote, to which the Concurrence of the Senate and House of Representatives may be necessary (except on a question of Adjournment) shall be presented to the President of the United States; and before the Same shall take Effect, shall be approved by him, or being disapproved by him, shall be repassed by two thirds of the Senate and House of Representatives, according to the Rules and Limitations prescribed in the Case of a Bill.

Section 8. The Congress shall have Power To lay and collect Taxes, Duties, Imposts and Excises, to pay the Debts and provide for the common Defence and general Welfare of the United States; but all Duties, Imposts and Excises shall be uniform throughout the United States;

To borrow Money on the credit of the United States;

To regulate Commerce with foreign Nations, and among the several States, and with the Indian Tribes;

To establish an uniform Rule of Naturalization, and uniform Laws on the subject of Bankruptcies throughout the United States;

To coin Money, regulate the Value thereof, and of foreign Coin, and fix the Standard of Weights and Measures;

To provide for the Punishment of counterfeiting the Securities and current Coin of the United States;

To establish Post Offices and post Roads;

To promote the Progress of Science and useful Arts, by securing for limited Times to Authors and Inventors the exclusive Right to their respective Writings and Discoveries;

To constitute Tribunals inferior to the supreme Court;

To define and punish Piracies and Felonies committed on the high Seas, and Offenses against the Law of Nations;

To declare War, grant Letters of Marque and Reprisal, and make Rules concerning Captures on Land and Water;

To raise and support Armies, but no Appropriation of Money to that Use shall be for a longer Term than two Years;

To provide and maintain a Navy;

To make Rules for the Government and Regulation of the land and naval Forces;

To provide for calling forth the Militia to execute the Laws of the Union, suppress Insurrections and repel Invasions;

To provide for organizing, arming, and disciplining, the Militia, and for governing such Part of them as may be employed in the Service of the United States, reserving to the States respectively, the Appointment of the Officers, and the Authority of training the Militia according to the discipline prescribed by Congress;

To exercise exclusive Legislation in all Cases whatsoever, over such District (not exceeding ten Miles square) as may, by Cession of particular States, and the Acceptance of Congress, become the Seat of the Government of the United States, and to exercise like Authority over all Places purchased by the Consent of the Legislature of the State in which the Same shall be, for the Erection of Forts, Magazines, Arsenals, dock-Yards, and other needful Buildings;—And

To make all Laws which shall be necessary and proper for carrying into Execution the foregoing Powers, and all other Powers vested by this Constitution in the Government of the United States, or in any Department or Officer thereof.

Section 9. The Migration or Importation of such Persons as any of the States now existing shall think proper to admit, shall not be prohibited by the Congress prior to the Year one thousand eight hundred and eight, but a Tax or duty may be imposed on such Importation, not exceeding ten dollars for each Person.

The privilege of the Writ of Habeas Corpus shall not be suspended, unless when in Cases of Rebellion or Invasion the public Safety may require it.

No Bill of Attainder or ex post facto Law shall be passed.

No Capitation, or other direct, Tax shall be laid, unless in Proportion to the Census or Enumeration herein before directed to be taken.

No Tax or Duty shall be laid on Articles exported from any State.

No Preference shall be given by any Regulation of Commerce or Revenue to the Ports of one State over those of another: nor shall Vessels bound to, or from, one State be obliged to enter, clear, or pay Duties in another.

No Money shall be drawn from the Treasury, but in Consequence of Appropriations made by Law; and a regular Statement and Account of the Receipts and Expenditures of all public Money shall be published from time to time.

No Title of Nobility shall be granted by the United States: And no Person holding any Office of Profit or Trust under them, shall, without the Consent of the Congress, accept of any present, Emolument, Office, or Title, of any kind whatever, from any King, Prince, or foreign State.

Section 10. No State shall enter into any Treaty, Alliance, or Confederation; grant Letters of Marque and Reprisal; coin Money; emit Bills of Credit; make any Thing but gold and silver Coin a Tender in Payment of Debts; pass any Bill of Attainder, ex post facto Law, or Law impairing the Obligation of Contracts, or grant any Title of Nobility.

No State shall, without the Consent of the Congress, lay any Imposts or Duties on Imports or Exports, except what may be absolutely necessary for executing it's inspection Laws: and the net Produce of all Duties and Imposts, laid by any State on Imports or Exports, shall be for the Use of the Treasury of the United States, and all such Laws shall be subject to the Revision and Controul of the Congress.

No State shall, without the Consent of Congress, lay any Duty of Tonnage, keep Troops, or Ships of War in time of Peace, enter into any Agreement or Compact with another State, or with a foreign Power, or engage in War, unless actually invaded, or in such imminent Danger as will not admit of delay.

ARTICLE II

Section 1. The executive Power shall be vested in a President of the United States of America. He shall hold his Office during the Term of four Years, and, together with the Vice President, chosen for the same Term, be elected, as follows:

Each State shall appoint, in such Manner as the Legislature thereof may direct, a Number of Electors, equal to the whole Number of Senators and Representatives to which the State may be entitled in the Congress; but no Senator or Representative, or Person holding an Office of Trust or Profit under the United States, shall be appointed an Elector.

The Electors shall meet in their respective States, and vote by Ballot for two Persons, of whom one at least shall not be an Inhabitant of the same State with themselves. And they shall make a List of all the Persons voted for, and of the Number of Votes for each; which List they shall sign and certify, and transmit sealed to the Seat of the Government of the United States, directed to the President of the Senate. The President of the Senate shall, in the Presence of the Senate and House of Representatives, open all the Certificates, and the Votes shall then be counted. The Person having the greatest Number of Votes shall be the President, if such Number be a Majority of the whole Number of Electors appointed; and if there be more than one who have such Majority, and have an equal Number of Votes, then the House of Representatives shall immediately chuse by Ballot one of them for President; and if no Person have a Majority, then from the five highest on the List the said House shall in like Manner chuse the President. But in chusing the President, the Votes shall be taken by States, the Representation from each State having one Vote; A quorum for this Purpose shall consist of a Member or Members from two thirds of the States, and a Majority of all the States shall be necessary to a Choice. In every Case, after the Choice of the President, the Person having the greater Number of Votes of the Electors shall be the Vice President. But if there should remain two or more who have equal Votes, the Senate shall chuse from them by Ballot the Vice President.

The Congress may determine the Time of chusing the Electors, and the Day on which they shall give their Votes; which Day shall be the same throughout the United States.

No person except a natural born Citizen, or a Citizen of the United States, at the time of the Adoption of this Constitution, shall be eligible to the Office of President; neither shall any Person be eligible to that Office who shall not have attained to the Age of thirty five Years, and been fourteen Years a Resident within the United States.

In Case of the Removal of the President from Office, or of his Death, Resignation or Inability to discharge the Powers and Duties of the said Office, the same shall devolve on the Vice President, and the Congress may by Law provide for the Case of Removal, Death, Resignation or Inability, both of the President and Vice President, declaring what Officer shall then act as President, and such Officer shall act accordingly, until the Disability be removed, or a President shall be elected.

The President shall, at stated Times, receive for his Services, a Compensation, which shall neither be increased nor diminished during the Period for which he shall have been elected, and he shall not receive within that Period any other Emolument from the United States, or any of them.

Before he enter on the Execution of his Office, he shall take the following Oath or Affirmation: "I do solemnly swear (or affirm) that I will faithfully execute the Office of President of the United States, and will to the best of my Ability, preserve, protect and defend the Constitution of the United States."

Section 2. The President shall be Commander in Chief of the Army and Navy of the United States, and of the Militia of the several States, when called into the actual Service of the United States; he may require the Opinion, in writing, of the principal Officer in each of the executive Departments, upon any Subject relating to the Duties of their respective Offices, and he shall have Power to grant Reprieves and Pardons for Offenses against the United States, except in Cases of Impeachment.

He shall have Power, by and with the Advice and Consent of the Senate to make Treaties, provided two thirds of the Senators present concur; and he shall nominate, and by and with the Advice and Consent of the Senate, shall appoint Ambassadors, other public Ministers and Consuls, Judges of the supreme Court, and all other Officers of the United States, whose Appointments are not herein otherwise provided for, and which shall be established by Law; but the Congress may by Law vest the Appointment of such inferior Officers, as they think proper, in the President alone, in the Courts of Law, or in the Heads of Departments.

The President shall have Power to fill up all Vacancies that may happen during the Recess of the Senate, by granting Commissions which shall expire at the End of their next Session.

Section 3. He shall from time to time give to the Congress Information of the State of the Union, and recommend to their Consideration such Measures as he shall judge necessary and expedient; he may, on extraordinary Occasions, convene both Houses, or either of them, and in Case of Disagreement between them, with Respect to the Time of Adjournment, he may adjourn them to such Time as he shall think proper; he shall receive Ambassadors and other public Ministers; he shall take Care that the Laws be faithfully executed, and shall Commission all the Officers of the United States.

Section 4. The President, Vice President and all civil Officers of the United States, shall be removed from Office on Impeachment for, and Conviction of, Treason, Bribery, or other high Crimes and Misdemeanors.

ARTICLE III

Section 1. The judicial Power of the United States, shall be vested in one supreme Court, and in such inferior Courts as the Congress may from time to time ordain and establish. The Judges, both of the supreme and inferior Courts, shall hold their Offices during good Behaviour, and shall, at stated Times, receive for their Services a Compensation, which shall not be diminished during their Continuance in Office.

Section 2. The judicial Power shall extend to all Cases, in Law and Equity, arising under this Constitution, the Laws of the United States, and Treaties made, or which shall be made, under their Authority;—to all Cases affecting Ambassadors, other public Ministers and Consuls;—to all Cases of admiralty and maritime Jurisdiction;—to Controversies to which the United States shall be a Party;—to Controversies between two or more States;—between a State and Citizens of another State;—between Citizens of different States;—between Citizens of the same State claiming Lands under Grants of different States, and between a State, or the Citizens thereof, and foreign States, Citizens or Subjects.

In all Cases affecting Ambassadors, other public Ministers and Consuls, and those in which a State shall be a Party, the supreme Court shall have original Jurisdiction. In all the other Cases before mentioned, the supreme Court shall have appellate Jurisdiction, both as to Law and Fact, with such Exceptions, and under such Regulations as the Congress shall make.

The Trial of all Crimes, except in Cases of Impeachment, shall be by Jury; and such Trial shall be held in the State where the said Crimes shall have been committed; but when not committed within any State, the Trial shall be at such Place or Places as the Congress may by Law have directed.

Section 3. Treason against the United States, shall consist only in levying War against them, or, in adhering to their Enemies, giving them Aid and Comfort. No Person shall be convicted of Treason unless on the Testimony of two Witnesses to the same overt Act, or on Confession in open Court.

The Congress shall have Power to declare the Punishment of Treason, but no Attainder of Treason shall work Corruption of Blood, or Forfeiture except during the Life of the Person attained.

ARTICLE IV

Section 1. Full Faith and Credit shall be given in each State to the public Acts, Records, and judicial Proceedings of every other State. And the Congress may by general Laws prescribe the Manner in which such Acts, Records and Proceedings shall be proved, and the Effect thereof.

Section 2. The Citizens of each State shall be entitled to all Privileges and Immunities of Citizens in the several States.

A Person charged in any State with Treason, Felony, or other Crime, who shall flee from Justice, and be found in another State, shall on Demand of the executive Authority of the State from which he fled, be delivered up, to be removed to the State having Jurisdiction of the Crime.

No Person held to Service or Labour in one State, under the Laws thereof, escaping into another, shall, in Consequence of any Law or Regulation therein, be discharged from such Service or Labour, but shall be delivered up on Claim of the Party to whom such Service or Labour may be due.

Section 3. New States may be admitted by the Congress into this Union; but no new State shall be formed or erected within the Jurisdiction of any other State; nor any State be formed by the Junction of two or more States, or Parts of States, without the Consent of the Legislatures of the States concerned as well as of the Congress.

The Congress shall have Power to dispose of and make all needful Rules and Regulations respecting the Territory or other Property belonging to the United States; and nothing in this Constitution shall be so construed as to Prejudice any Claims of the United States, or of any particular State.

Section 4. The United States shall guarantee to every State in this Union a Republican Form of Government, and shall protect each of them against Invasion; and on Application of the Legislature, or of the Executive (when the Legislature cannot be convened) against domestic Violence.

ARTICLE V

The Congress, whenever two thirds of both Houses shall deem it necessary, shall propose Amendments to this Constitution, or, on the Application of the Legislatures of two thirds of the several States, shall call a Convention for proposing Amendments, which, in either Case, shall be valid to all Intents and Purposes, as part of this Constitution, when ratified by the Legislatures of three fourths of the several States, or by Conventions in three fourths thereof, as the one or the other Mode of Ratification may be pro-

posed by the Congress; Provided that no Amendment which may be made prior to the Year One thousand eight hundred and eight shall in any Manner affect the first and fourth Clauses in the Ninth Section of the first Article; and that no State, without its Consent, shall be deprived of its equal Suffrage in the Senate.

ARTICLE VI

All Debts contracted and Engagements entered into, before the Adoption of this Constitution shall be as valid against the United States under this Constitution, as under the Confederation.

This Constitution, and the Laws of the United States which shall be made in Pursuance thereof; and all Treaties made, or which shall be made, under the Authority of the United States, shall be the supreme Law of the Land; and the Judges in every State shall be bound thereby, any Thing in the Constitution or Laws of any State to the Contrary notwithstanding.

The Senators and Representatives before mentioned, and the Members of the several State Legislatures, and all executive and judicial Officers, both of the United States and of the several States, shall be bound by Oath or Affirmation, to support this Constitution; but no religious Test shall ever be required as a Qualification to any Office or public Trust under the United States.

ARTICLE VII

The Ratification of the Conventions of nine States shall be sufficient for the Establishment of this Constitution between the States so ratifying the Same.

AMENDMENT I [1791]

Congress shall make no law respecting an establishment of religion, or prohibiting the free exercise thereof; or abridging the freedom of speech, or of the press; or the right of the people peaceably to assembly, and to petition the Government for a redress of grievances.

AMENDMENT II [1791]

A well regulated Militia, being necessary to the security of a free State, the right of the people to keep and bear Arms, shall not be infringed.

AMENDMENT III [1791]

No Soldier shall, in time of peace be quartered in any house, without the consent of the Owner, nor in time of war, but in a manner to be prescribed by law.

AMENDMENT IV [1791]

The right of the people to be secure in their persons, houses, papers, and effects, against unreasonable searches and seizures, shall not be violated, and no Warrants shall issue, but upon probable cause, supported by Oath or affirmation, and particularly describing the place to be searched, and the persons or things to be seized.

AMENDMENT V [1791]

No person shall be held to answer for a capital, or otherwise infamous crime, unless on a presentment or indictment of a Grand Jury, except in cases arising in the land or naval forces, or in the Militia, when in actual service in time of War or public danger; nor shall any person be subject for the same offence to be twice put in jeopardy of life or limb; nor shall be compelled in any criminal case to be a witness against himself, nor be deprived of life, liberty, or property, without due process of law; nor shall private property be taken for public use, without just compensation.

AMENDMENT VI [1791]

In all criminal prosecutions, the accused shall enjoy the right to a speedy and public trial, by an impartial jury of the State and district wherein the crime shall have been committed, which district shall have been previously ascertained by law, and to be informed of the nature and cause of the accusation; to be confronted with the witnesses against him; to have compulsory process for obtaining witnesses in his favor, and to have the Assistance of Counsel for his defence.

AMENDMENT VII [1791]

In Suits at common law, where the value in controversy shall exceed twenty dollars, the right of trial by jury shall be preserved, and no fact tried by jury, shall be otherwise re-examined in any Court of the United States, than according to the rules of the common law.

AMENDMENT VIII [1791]

Excessive bail shall not be required, nor excessive fines imposed, nor cruel and unusual punishments inflicted.

AMENDMENT IX [1791]

The enumeration in the Constitution, of certain rights, shall not be construed to deny or disparage others retained by the people.

AMENDMENT X [1791]

The powers not delegated to the United States by the Constitution, nor prohibited by it to the States, are reserved to the States respectively, or to the people.

AMENDMENT XI [1798]

The Judicial power of the United States shall not be construed to extend to any suit in law or equity, commenced or prosecuted against one of the United States by Citizens of another State, or by Citizens or Subjects of any Foreign State.

AMENDMENT XII [1804]

The Electors shall meet in their respective states, and vote by ballot for President and Vice-President, one of whom, at least, shall not be an inhabitant of the same state with themselves; they shall name in their ballots the person voted for as President, and in distinct ballots the person voted for as Vice-President, and they shall make distinct lists of all persons voted for as President, and of all persons voted for as Vice-President, and of the number of votes for each, which lists they shall sign and certify, and transmit sealed to the seat of the government of the United States, directed to the President of the Senate;—The President of the Senate shall, in the presence of the Senate and House of Representatives, open all the certificates and the votes shall then be counted;—The person having the greatest number of votes for President, shall be the President, if such number be a majority of the whole number of Electors appointed; and if no person have such majority, then from the persons having the highest numbers not exceeding three on the list of those voted for as President, the House of Representatives shall choose immediately, by ballot, the President. But in choosing the President, the votes shall be taken by states, the representation from each state having one vote; a quorum for this purpose shall consist of a member or members from two-thirds of the states, and a majority of all states shall be necessary to a choice. And if the House of Representatives shall not choose a President whenever the right of choice shall devolve upon them, before the fourth day of March next following, then the Vice-President shall act as President, as in the case of the death or other constitutional disability of the President.—The person having the greatest number of votes as Vice-President, shall be the Vice-President, if such number be a majority of the whole number of Electors appointed, and if no person have a majority, then from the two highest numbers on the list, the Senate shall choose the Vice-President; a quorum for the purpose shall consist of two-thirds of the whole number of Senators, and a majority of the whole number shall be necessary to a choice. But no person constitutionally ineligible to the office of President shall be eligible to that of Vice-President of the United States.

AMENDMENT XIII [1865]

Section 1. Neither slavery nor involuntary servitude, except as a punishment for crime whereof the party shall have been duly convicted, shall exist within the United States, or any place subject to their jurisdiction.

Section 2. Congress shall have power to enforce this article by appropriate legislation.

AMENDMENT XIV [1868]

Section 1. All persons born or naturalized in the United States, and subject to the jurisdiction thereof, are citizens of the United States and of the State wherein they reside. No State shall make or enforce any law which shall abridge the privileges or immunities of citizens of the United States; nor shall any State deprive any person of life, liberty, or property, without due process of law; nor deny to any person within its jurisdiction the equal protection of the laws.

Section 2. Representatives shall be apportioned among the several States according to their respective numbers, counting the whole number of persons in each State, excluding Indians not taxed. But when the right to vote at any election for the choice of electors for President and Vice President of the United States, Representatives in Congress, the Executive and Judicial officers of a State, or the members of the Legislature thereof, is denied to any of the male inhabitants of such State, being twenty-one years of age, and citizens of the United States, or in any way abridged, except for participation in rebellion, or other crime, the basis of representation therein shall be reduced in the proportion which the number of such male citizens shall bear to the whole number of male citizens twenty-one years of age in such State.

Section 3. No person shall be a Senator or Representative in Congress, or elector of President and Vice President, or hold any office, civil or military, under the United States, or under any State, who having previously taken an oath, as a member of Congress, or as an officer of the United States, or as a member of any State legislature, or as an executive or judicial officer of any State, to support the Constitution of the United States, shall have engaged in insurrection or rebellion against the same, or given aid or comfort to the enemies thereof. But Congress may by a vote of two-thirds of each House, remove such disability.

Section 4. The validity of the public debt of the United States, authorized by law, including debts incurred for payment of pensions and bounties for services in suppressing insurrection or rebellion, shall not be questioned. But neither the United States nor any State shall assume or pay any debt or obligation incurred in aid of insurrection or rebellion against the United States, or any claim for the loss or emancipation of any slave; but all such debts, obligations and claims shall be held illegal and void.

Section 5. The Congress shall have power to enforce, by appropriate legislation, the provisions of this article.

AMENDMENT XV [1870]

Section 1. The right of citizens of the United States to vote shall not be denied or abridged by the United States or by any State on account of race, color, or previous condition of servitude.

Section 2. The Congress shall have power to enforce this article by appropriate legislation.

AMENDMENT XVI [1913]

The Congress shall have power to lay and collect taxes on incomes, from whatever source derived, without apportionment among the several States, and without regard to any census or enumeration.

AMENDMENT XVII [1913]

[1] The Senate of the United States shall be composed of two Senators from each State, elected by the people thereof, for six years; and each Senator shall have one vote. The electors in each State shall have the qualifications requisite for electors of the most numerous branch of the State legislatures.

[2] When vacancies happen in the representation of any State in the Senate, the executive authority of such State shall issue writs of election to fill such vacancies: *Provided,* That the legislature of any State may empower the executive thereof to make temporary appointments until the people fill the vacancies by election as the legislature may direct.

[3] This amendment shall not be so construed as to affect the election or term of any Senator chosen before it becomes valid as part of the Constitution.

AMENDMENT XVIII [1919]

Section 1. After one year from the ratification of this article the manufacture, sale, or transportation of intoxicating liquors within, the importation thereof into, or the exportation thereof from the United States and all territory subject to the jurisdiction thereof for beverage purposes is hereby prohibited.

Section 2. The Congress and the several States shall have concurrent power to enforce this article by appropriate legislation.

Section 3. This article shall be inoperative unless it shall have been ratified as an amendment to the Constitution by the legislatures of the several States, as provided in the Constitution, within seven years from the date of the submission hereof to the States by the Congress.

AMENDMENT XIX [1920]

[1] The right of citizens of the United States to vote shall not be denied or abridged by the United States or by any State on account of sex.

[2] Congress shall have power to enforce this article by appropriate legislation.

AMENDMENT XX [1933]

Section 1. The terms of the President and Vice President shall end at noon on the 20th day of January, and the terms of Senators and Representatives at noon on the 3d day of January, of the years in which such terms would have ended if this article had not been ratified; and the terms of their successors shall then begin.

Section 2. The Congress shall assemble at least once in every year, and such meeting shall begin at noon on the 3d day of January, unless they shall by law appoint a different day.

Section 3. If, at the time fixed for the beginning of the term of the President, the President elect shall have died, the Vice President elect shall become President. If the President shall not have been chosen before the time fixed for the beginning of his term, or if the President elect shall have failed to qualify, then the Vice President elect shall act as President until a President shall have qualified; and

the Congress may by law provide for the case wherein neither a President elect nor a Vice President elect shall have qualified, declaring who shall then act as President, or the manner in which one who is to act shall be selected, and such person shall act accordingly until a President or Vice President shall have qualified.

Section 4. The Congress may by law provide for the case of the death of any of the persons from whom the House of Representatives may choose a President whenever the right of choice shall have devolved upon them, and for the case of the death of any of the persons from whom the Senate may choose a Vice President whenever the right of choice shall have devolved upon them.

Section 5. Sections 1 and 2 shall take effect on the 15th day of October following the ratification of this article.

Section 6. This article shall be inoperative unless it shall have been ratified as an amendment to the Constitution by the legislatures of three-fourths of the several States within seven years from the date of its submission.

AMENDMENT XXI [1933]

Section 1. The eighteenth article of amendment to the Constitution of the United States is hereby repealed.

Section 2. The transportation or importation into any State, Territory, or possession of the United States for delivery or use therein of intoxicating liquors, in violation of the laws thereof, is hereby prohibited.

Section 3. This article shall be inoperative unless it shall have been ratified as an amendment to the Constitution by conventions in the several States, as provided in the Constitution, within seven years from the date of the submission hereof to the States by the Congress.

AMENDMENT XXII [1951]

Section 1. No person shall be elected to the office of the President more than twice, and no person who has held the office of President, or acted as President, for more than two years of a term to which some other person was elected President shall be elected to the office of President more than once. But this Article shall not apply to any person holding the office of President when this Article was proposed by the

Congress, and shall not prevent any person who may be holding the office of President, or acting as President, during the term within which this Article becomes operative from holding the office of President or acting as President during the remainder of such term.

Section 2. This article shall be inoperative unless it shall have been ratified as an amendment to the Constitution by the legislatures of three-fourths of the several States within seven years from the date of its submission to the States by the Congress.

AMENDMENT XXIII [1961]

Section 1. The District constituting the seat of Government of the United States shall appoint in such manner as the Congress may direct:

A number of electors of President and Vice President equal to the whole number of Senators and Representatives in Congress to which the District would be entitled if it were a State, but in no event more than the least populous state; they shall be in addition to those appointed by the states, but they shall be considered, for the purposes of the election of President and Vice President, to be electors appointed by a state; and they shall meet in the District and perform such duties as provided by the twelfth article of amendment.

Section 2. The Congress shall have power to enforce this article by appropriate legislation.

AMENDMENT XXIV [1964]

Section 1. The right of citizens of the United States to vote in any primary or other election for President or Vice President, for electors for President or Vice President, or for Senator or Representative in Congress, shall not be denied or abridged by the United States, or any State by reason of failure to pay any poll tax or other tax.

Section 2. The Congress shall have power to enforce this article by appropriate legislation.

AMENDMENT XXV [1967]

Section 1. In case of the removal of the President from office or of his death or resignation, the Vice President shall become President.

Section 2. Whenever there is a vacancy in the office of the Vice President, the President shall nominate a Vice President who shall take office upon confirmation by a majority vote of both Houses of Congress.

Section 3. Whenever the President transmits to the President pro tempore of the Senate and the Speaker of the House of Representatives his written declaration that he is unable to discharge the powers and duties of his office, and until he transmits to them a written declaration to the contrary, such powers and duties shall be discharged by the Vice President as Acting President.

Section 4. Whenever the Vice President and a majority of either the principal officers of the executive departments or of such other body as Congress may by law provide, transmit to the President pro tempore of the Senate and the Speaker of the House of Representatives their written declaration that the President is unable to discharge the powers and duties of his office, the Vice President shall immediately assume the powers and duties of the office as Acting President.

Thereafter, when the President transmits to the President pro tempore of the Senate and the Speaker of the House of Representatives his written declaration that no inability exists, he shall resume the powers and duties of his office unless the Vice President and a majority of either the principal officers of the executive department or of such other body as Congress may by law provide, transmit within four days to the President pro tempore of the Senate and the Speaker of the House of Representatives their written declaration and the President is unable to discharge the powers and duties of his office. Thereupon Congress shall decide the issue, assembling within forty-eight hours for that purpose if not in session. If the Congress, within twenty-one days after receipt of the latter written declaration, or, if Congress is not in session, within twenty-one days after Congress is required to assemble, determines by two-thirds vote of both Houses that the President is unable to discharge the powers and duties of his office, the Vice President shall continue to discharge the same as Acting President; otherwise, the President shall resume the powers and duties of his office.

AMENDMENT XXVI [1971]

Section 1. The right of citizens of the United States, who are eighteen years of age or older, to vote shall not be denied or abridged by the United States or by any State on account of age.

Section 2. The Congress shall have power to enforce this article by appropriate legislation.

APPENDIX B

The Model Business Corporation Act

§ 1. Short Title*

This Act shall be known and may be cited as the ".....† Business Corporation Act."

§ 2. Definitions

As used in this Act, unless the context otherwise requires, the term:

(a) "Corporation" or "domestic corporation" means a corporation for profit subject to the provisions of this Act, except a foreign corporation.

(b) "Foreign corporation" means a corporation for profit organized under laws other than the laws of this State for a purpose or purposes for which a corporation may be organized under this Act.

(c) "Articles of incorporation" means the original or restated articles of incorporation or articles of consolidation and all amendments thereto including articles of merger.

(d) "Shares" means the units into which the proprietary interests in a corporation are divided.

(e) "Subscriber" means one who subscribes for shares in a corporation, whether before or after incorporation.

(f) "Shareholder" means one who is a holder of record of shares in a corporation. If the articles of incorporation or the by-laws so provide, the board of directors may adopt by resolution a procedure whereby a shareholder of the corporation may certify in writing to the corporation that all or a portion of the shares registered in the name of such shareholder are held for the account of a specified person or persons. The resolution shall set forth (1) the classification of shareholder who may certify, (2) the purpose or purposes for which the certification may be made, (3) the form of certification and information to be contained therein, (4) if the certification is with respect to a record date or closing of the stock transfer books within which the certification must be received by the corporation and (5) such other provisions with respect to the procedure as are deemed necessary or desirable. Upon receipt by the corporation of a certification complying with the procedure, the persons specified in the certification shall be deemed, for the purpose or purposes set forth in the certification, to be the holders of record of the number of shares specified in place of the shareholder making the certification.

(g) "Authorized shares" means the shares of all classes which the corporation is authorized to issue.

(h) "Employee" includes officers but not directors. A director may accept duties which make him also an employee.

(i) "Distribution" means a direct or indirect transfer of money or other property (except its own shares) or incurrence of indebtedness, by a corporation to or for the benefit of any of its shareholders in respect of any of its shares, whether by dividend or by purchase, redemption or other acquisition of its shares, or otherwise.

---

*[By the Editor] The Model Business Corporation Act prepared by the Committee on Corporate Laws (Section of Corporation, Banking and Business Law) of the American Bar Association was originally patterned after the Illinois Business Corporation Act of 1933. It was first published as a complete act in 1950. In subsequent years several revisions, addenda and optional or alternative provisions were added. The Act was substantially revised and renumbered in 1969.

This Act should be distinguished from the Model Business Corporation Act promulgated in 1928 by the Commissioners on Uniform State Laws under the name "Uniform Business Corporation Act" and renamed Model Business Corporation Act in 1943. This Uniform Act was withdrawn in 1957.

The Model Business Corporation Act has been influential in the codification of corporation statutes in more than 35 states. However, there is no state that has totally adopted it in its current form. Moreover, since the Model Act itself has been substantially modified from time to time, there is considerable variation among the statutes of the states that used this Act as a model.
†Insert name of State.

§ 3. Purposes

Corporations may be organized under this Act for any lawful purpose or purposes, except for the purpose of banking or insurance.

§ 4. General Powers

Each corporation shall have power:

(a)   To have perpetual succession by its corporate name unless a limited period of duration is stated in its articles of incorporation.

(b)   To sue and be sued, complain and defend, in its corporate name.

(c)   To have a corporate seal which may be altered at pleasure, and to use the same by causing it, or a facsimile thereof, to be impressed or affixed or in any other manner reproduced.

(d)   To purchase, take, receive, lease, or otherwise acquire, own, hold, improve, use and otherwise deal in and with, real or personal property, or any interest therein, wherever situated.

(e)   To sell, convey, mortgage, pledge, lease, exchange, transfer and otherwise dispose of all or any part of its property and assets.

(f)   To lend money and use its credit to assist its employees.

(g)   To purchase, take, receive, subscribe for, or otherwise acquire, own, hold, vote, use, employ, sell, mortgage, lend, pledge, or otherwise dispose of, and otherwise use and deal in and with, shares or other interests in, or obligations of, other domestic or foreign corporations, associations, partnerships or individuals, or direct or indirect obligations of the United States or of any other government, state, territory, governmental district or municipality or of any instrumentality thereof.

(h)   To make contracts and guarantees and incur liabilities, borrow money at such rates of interest as the corporation may determine, issue its notes, bonds, and other obligations, and secure any of its obligations by mortgage or pledge of all or any of its property, franchises and income.

(i)   To lend money for its corporate purposes, invest and reinvest its funds, and take and hold real and personal property as security for the payment of funds so loaned or invested.

(j)   To conduct its business, carry on its operations and have offices and exercise the powers granted by this Act, within or without this State.

(k)   To elect or appoint officers and agents of the corporation, and define their duties and fix their compensation.

(l)   To make and alter by-laws, not inconsistent with its articles of incorporation or with the laws of this State, for the administration and regulation of the affairs of the corporation.

(m)   To make donations for the public welfare or for charitable, scientific or educational purposes.

(n)   To transact any lawful business which the board of directors shall find will be in aid of governmental policy.

(o)   To pay pensions and establish pension plans, pension trusts, profit sharing plans, stock bonus plans, stock option plans and other incentive plans for any or all of its directors, officers and employees.

(p)   To be a promoter, partner, member, associate, or manager of any partnership, joint venture, trust or other enterprise.

(q)   To have and exercise all powers necessary or convenient to effect its purposes.

§ 5. Indemnification of Directors and Officers

(a)   As used in this section:

(1)   "Director" means any person who is or was a director of the corporation and any person who, while a director of the corporation, is or was serving at the request of the corporation as a director, officer, partner, trustee, employee or agent of another foreign or domestic corporation, partnership, joint venture, trust, other enterprise or employee benefit plan.

(2)   "Corporation" includes any domestic or foreign predecessor entity of the corporation in a merger, consolidation or other transaction in which the predecessor's existence ceased upon consummation of such transaction.

(3)   "Expenses" include attorneys' fees.

(4)   "Official capacity" means

(A)   when used with respect to a director, the office of director in the corporation, and

(B)   when used with respect to a person other than a director, as contemplated in subsection (i), the elective or appointive office in the corporation held by the officer or the employment or agency relationship undertaken by the employee or agent in behalf of the corporation,

but in each case does not include service for any other foreign or domestic corporation or any partnership, joint venture, trust, other enterprise, or employee benefit plan.

(5) "Party" includes a person who was, is, or is threatened to be made, a named defendant or respondent in a proceeding.
(6) "Proceeding" means any threatened, pending or completed action, suit or proceeding, whether civil, criminal, administrative or investigative.

(b) A corporation shall have power to indemnify any person made a party to any proceeding by reason of the fact that he is or was a director if

(1) he conducted himself in good faith; and
(2) he reasonably believed

(A) in the case of conduct in his official capacity with the corporation, that his conduct was in its best interests, and
(B) in all other cases, that his conduct was at least not opposed to its best interests; and

(3) in the case of any criminal proceeding, he had no reasonable cause to believe his conduct was unlawful.

Indemnification may be made against judgments, penalties, fines, settlements and reasonable expenses, actually incurred by the person in connection with the proceeding; except that if the proceeding was by or in the right of the corporation, indemnification may be made only against such reasonable expenses and shall not be made in respect of any proceeding in which the person shall have been adjudged to be liable to the corporation. The termination of any proceeding by judgment, order, settlement, conviction, or upon a plea of nolo contendere or its equivalent, shall not, of itself, be determinative that the person did not meet the requisite standard of conduct set forth in this subsection (b).

(c) A director shall not be indemnified under subsection (b) in respect of any proceeding charging improper personal benefit to him, whether or not involving action in his official capacity, in which he shall have been adjudged to be liable on the basis that personal benefit was improperly received by him.

(d) Unless limited by the articles of incorporation,

(1) a director who has been wholly successful, on the merits or otherwise, in the defense of any proceeding referred to in subsection (b) shall be indemnified against reasonable expenses incurred by him in connection with the proceeding; and
(2) a court of appropriate jurisdiction, upon application of a director and such notice as the court shall require, shall have authority to order indemnification in the following circumstances:

(A) if it determines a director is entitled to reimbursement under clause (1), the court shall order indemnification, in which case the director shall also be entitled to recover the expenses of securing such reimbursement; or
(B) if it determines that the director is fairly and reasonably entitled to indemnification in view of all the relevant circumstances, whether or not he has met the standard of conduct set forth in subsection (b) or has been adjudged liable in the circumstances described in subsection (c), the court may order such indemnification as the court shall deem proper, except that indemnification with respect to any proceeding by or in the right of the corporation or in which liability shall have been adjudged in the circumstances described in subsection (c) shall be limited to expenses.

A court of appropriate jurisdiction may be the same court in which the proceeding involving the director's liability took place.

(e) No indemnification under subsection (b) shall be made by the corporation unless authorized in the specific case after a determination has been made that indemnification of the director is permissible in the circumstances because he has met the standard of conduct set forth in subsection (b). Such determination shall be made:

(1) by the board of directors by a majority vote of a quorum consisting of directors not at the time parties to the proceeding; or
(2) if such a quorum cannot be obtained, then by a majority vote of a committee of the board, duly designated to act in the matter by a majority vote of the full board (in which designation directors who are parties may participate), consisting solely of two or more directors not at the time parties to the proceeding; or
(3) by special legal counsel, selected by the board of directors or a committee thereof by vote as set

forth in clauses (1) or (2) of this subsection (e), or, if the requisite quorum of the full board cannot be obtained therefor and such committee cannot be established, by a majority vote of the full board (in which selection directors who are parties may participate); or

(4) by the shareholders.

Authorization of indemnification and determination as to reasonableness of expenses shall be made in the same manner as the determination that indemnification is permissible, except that if the determination that indemnification is permissible is made by special legal counsel, authorization of indemnification and determination as to reasonableness of expenses shall be made in a manner specified in clause (3) in the preceding sentence for the selection of such counsel. Shares held by directors who are parties to the proceeding shall not be voted on the subject matter under this subsection (e).

(f) Reasonable expenses incurred by a director who is a party to a proceeding may be paid or reimbursed by the corporation in advance of the final disposition of such proceeding upon receipt by the corporation of

(1) a written affirmation by the director of his good faith belief that he has met the standard of conduct necessary for indemnification by the corporation as authorized in this section, and

(2) a written undertaking by or on behalf of the director to repay such amount if it shall ultimately be determined that he has not met such standard of conduct, and after a determination that the facts then known to those making the determination would not preclude indemnification under this section. The undertaking required by clause (2) shall be an unlimited general obligation of the director but need not be secured and may be accepted without reference to financial ability to make repayment. Determinations and authorizations of payments under this subsection (f) shall be made in the manner specified in subsection (e).

(g) No provision for the corporation to indemnify or to advance expenses to a director who is made a party to the proceeding, whether contained in the articles of incorporation, the by-laws, a resolution of shareholders or directors, an agreement or otherwise (except as contemplated by subsection (j)), shall be valid unless consistent with this section or, to the extent that indemnity hereunder is limited by the arti-

cles of incorporation, consistent therewith. Nothing contained in this section shall limit the corporation's power to pay or reimburse expenses incurred by a director in connection with his appearance as a witness in a proceeding at a time when he has not been made a named defendant or respondent in the proceeding.

(h) For purposes of this section, the corporation shall be deemed to have requested a director to serve an employee benefit plan whenever the performance by him of his duties to the corporation also imposes duties on, or otherwise involves services by, him to the plan or participants or beneficiaries of the plan; excise taxes assessed on a director with respect to an employee benefit plan pursuant to applicable law shall be deemed "fines"; and action taken or omitted by him with respect to an employee benefit plan in the performance of his duties for a purpose reasonably believed by him to be in the interest of the participants and beneficiaries of the plan shall be deemed to be for a purpose which is not opposed to the best interests of the corporation.

(i) Unless limited by the articles of incorporation,

(1) an officer of the corporation shall be indemnified as and to the same extent provided in subsection (d) for a director and shall be entitled to the same extent as a director to seek indemnification pursuant to the provisions of subsection (d);

(2) a corporation shall have the power to indemnify and to advance expenses to an officer, employee or agent of the corporation to the same extent that it may indemnify and advance expenses to directors pursuant to this section; and

(3) a corporation, in addition, shall have the power to indemnify and to advance expenses to an officer, employee or agent who is not a director to such further extent, consistent with law, as may be provided by its articles of incorporation, by-laws, general or specific action of its board of directors, or contract.

(j) A corporation shall have power to purchase and maintain insurance on behalf of any person who is or was a director, officer, employee or agent of the corporation, or who, while a director, officer, employee or agent of the corporation, is or was serving at the request of the corporation as a director, officer, partner, trustee, employee or agent of another foreign or domestic corporation, partnership, joint venture, trust, other enterprise or employee benefit plan, against any liability asserted against him and incurred by him in any such capacity or arising out of his status as such, whether or not the corporation would have the power to indemnify him against such liability under the provisions of this section.

(k)   Any indemnification of, or advance of expenses to, a director in accordance with this section, if arising out of a proceeding by or in the right of the corporation, shall be reported in writing to the shareholders with or before the notice of the next shareholders' meeting.

§ 6. Power of Corporation to Acquire Its Own Shares

A corporation shall have the power to acquire its own shares. All of its own shares acquired by a corporation shall, upon acquisition, constitute authorized but unissued shares, unless the articles of incorporation provide that they shall not be reissued, in which case the authorized shares shall be reduced by the number of shares acquired.

If the number of authorized shares is reduced by an acquisition, the corporation shall, not later than the time it files its next annual report under this Act with the Secretary of State, file a statement of cancellation showing the reduction in the authorized shares. The statement of cancellation shall be executed in duplicate by the corporation by its president or a vice president and by its secretary or an assistant secretary, and verified by one of the officers signing such statement, and shall set forth:

(a)   The name of the corporation.

(b)   The number of acquired shares cancelled, itemized by classes and series.

(c)   The aggregate number of authorized shares, itemized by classes and series, after giving effect to such cancellation.

Duplicate originals of such statement shall be delivered to the Secretary of State. If the Secretary of State finds that such statement conforms to law, he shall, when all fees and franchise taxes have been paid as in this Act prescribed:

(1)   Endorse on each of such duplicate originals the word "Filed," and the month, day and year of the filing thereof.
(2)   File one of such duplicate originals in his office.
(3)   Return the other duplicate original to the corporation or its representative.

§ 7. Defense of Ultra Vires

No act of a corporation and no conveyance or transfer of real or personal property to or by a corporation shall be invalid by reason of the fact that the corporation was without capacity or power to do such act or to make or receive such conveyance or transfer, but such lack of capacity or power may be asserted:

(a)   In a proceeding by a shareholder against the corporation to enjoin the doing of any act or the transfer of real or personal property by or to the corporation. If the unauthorized act or transfer sought to be enjoined is being, or is to be, performed or made pursuant to a contract to which the corporation is a party, the court may, if all of the parties to the contract are parties to the proceeding and if it deems the same to be equitable, set aside and enjoin the performance of such contract, and in so doing may allow to the corporation or to the other parties to the contract, as the case may be, compensation for the loss or damage sustained by either of them which may result from the action of the court in setting aside and enjoining the performance of such contract, but anticipated profits to be derived from the performance of the contract shall not be awarded by the court as a loss or damage sustained.

(b)   In a proceeding by the corporation, whether acting directly or through a receiver, trustee, or other legal representative, or through shareholders in a representative suit, against the incumbent or former officers or directors of the corporation.

(c)   In a proceeding by the Attorney General, as provided in this Act, to dissolve the corporation, or in a proceeding by the Attorney General to enjoin the corporation from the transaction of unauthorized business.

§ 8. Corporate Name

The corporate name:

(a)   Shall contain the word "corporation," "company," "incorporated" or "limited," or shall contain an abbreviation of one of such words.

(b)   Shall not contain any word or phrase which indicates or implies that it is organized for any purpose other than one or more of the purposes contained in its articles of incorporation.

(c)   Shall not be the same as, or deceptively similar to, the name of any domestic corporation existing

under the laws of this State or any foreign corporation authorized to transact business in this State, or a
name the exclusive right to which is, at the time, reserved in the manner provided in this Act, or the
name of a corporation which has in effect a registration of its corporate name as provided in this Act, except that this provision shall not apply if the applicant
files with the Secretary of State either of the following: (1) the written consent of such other corporation
or holder of a reserved or registered name to use the
same or deceptively similar name and one or more
words are added to make such name distinguishable
from such other name, or (2) a certified copy of a final
decree of a court of competent jurisdiction establishing the prior right of the applicant to the use of such
name in this State.

A corporation with which another corporation,
domestic or foreign, is merged, or which is formed by
the reorganization or consolidation of one or more
domestic or foreign corporations or upon a sale, lease
or other disposition to or exchange with, a domestic
corporation of all or substantially all the assets of another corporation, domestic or foreign, including its
name, may have the same name as that used in this
State by any of such corporations if such other corporation was organized under the laws of, or is authorized to transact business in, this State.

§ 9. Reserved Name
The exclusive right to the use of a corporate name
may be reserved by:

(a)   Any person intending to organize a corporation
under this Act.

(b)   Any domestic corporation intending to change
its name.

(c)   Any foreign corporation intending to make application for a certificate of authority to transact business in this State.

(d)   Any foreign corporation authorized to transact
business in this State and intending to change its name.

(e)   Any person intending to organize a foreign corporation and intending to have such corporation
make application for a certificate of authority to transact business in this State.

The reservation shall be made by filing with the
Secretary of State an application to reserve a specified
corporate name, executed by the applicant. If the
Secretary of State finds that the name is available for

corporate use, he shall reserve the same for the exclusive use of the applicant for a period of one hundred and twenty days.

The right to the exclusive use of a specified corporate name so reserved may be transferred to any
other person or corporation by filing in the office of
the Secretary of State a notice of such transfer, executed by the applicant for whom the name was reserved, and specifying the name and address of the
transferee.

§ 10. Registered Name
Any corporation organized and existing under the
laws of any state or territory of the United States may
register its corporate name under this Act, provided
its corporate name is not the same as, or deceptively
similar to, the name of any domestic corporation existing under the laws of this State, or the name of any
foreign corporation authorized to transact business in
this State, or any corporate name reserved or registered under this Act.

Such registration shall be made by:

(a)   Filing with the Secretary of State (1) an application
for registration executed by the corporation by an officer thereof, setting forth the name of the corporation,
the state or territory under the laws of which it is incorporated, the date of its incorporation, a statement that it
is carrying on or doing business, and a brief statement of
the business in which it is engaged, and (2) a certificate
setting forth that such corporation is in good standing
under the laws of the state or territory wherein it is organized, executed by the Secretary of State of such state
or territory or by such other official as may have custody
of the records pertaining to corporations, and

(b)   Paying to the Secretary of State a registration fee
in the amount of .... for each month, or fraction
thereof, between the date of filing such application
and December 31st of the calendar year in which such
application is filed.

Such registration shall be effective until the close of
the calendar year in which the application for registration is filed.

§ 11. Renewal of Registered Name
A corporation which has in effect a registration of its
corporate name, may renew such registration from year
to year by annually filing an application for renewal setting forth the facts required to be set forth in an original application for registration and a certificate of good

standing as required for the original registration and by paying a fee of .... A renewal application may be filed between the first day of October and the thirty-first day of December in each year, and shall extend the registration for the following calendar year.

§ 12. Registered Office and Registered Agent

Each corporation shall have and continuously maintain in this State:

(a)   A registered office which may be, but need not be, the same as its place of business.

(b)   A registered agent, which agent may be either an individual resident in this State whose business office is identical with such registered office, or a domestic corporation, or a foreign corporation authorized to transact business in this State, having a business office identical with such registered office.

§ 13. Change of Registered Office or Registered Agent

A corporation may change its registered office or change its registered agent, or both, upon filing in the office of the Secretary of State a statement setting forth:

(a)   The name of the corporation.

(b)   The address of its then registered office.

(c)   If the address of its registered office is to be changed, the address to which the registered office is to be changed.

(d)   The name of its then registered agent.

(e)   If its registered agent is to be changed, the name of its successor registered agent.

(f)   That the address of its registered office and the address of the business office of its registered agent, as changed, will be identical.

(g)   That such change was authorized by resolution duly adopted by its board of directors.

Such statement shall be executed by the corporation by its president, or a vice president, and verified by him, and delivered to the Secretary of State. If the Secretary of State finds that such statement conforms to the provisions of this Act, he shall file such statement in his office, and upon such filing the change of address of the registered office, or the appointment of a new registered agent, or both, as the case may be, shall become effective.

Any registered agent of a corporation may resign as such agent upon filing a written notice thereof, executed in duplicate, with the Secretary of State, who shall forthwith mail a copy thereof to the corporation at its registered office. The appointment of such agent shall terminate upon the expiration of thirty days after receipt of such notice by the Secretary of State.

If a registered agent changes his or its business address to another place within the same .... ,* he or it may change such address and the address of the registered office of any corporation of which he or it is registered agent by filing a statement as required above except that it need be signed only by the registered agent and need not be responsive to (e) or (g) and must recite that a copy of the statement has been mailed to the corporation.

§ 14. Service of Process on Corporation

The registered agent so appointed by a corporation shall be an agent of such corporation upon whom any process, notice or demand required or permitted by law to be served upon the corporation may be served.

Whenever a corporation shall fail to appoint or maintain a registered agent in this State, or whenever its registered agent cannot with reasonable diligence be found at the registered office, then the Secretary of State shall be an agent of such corporation upon whom any such process, notice, or demand may be served. Service on the Secretary of State of any such process, notice, or demand shall be made by delivering to and leaving with him, or with any clerk having charge of the corporation department of his office, duplicate copies of such process, notice or demand. In the event any such process, notice or demand is served on the Secretary of State, he shall immediately cause one of the copies thereof to be forwarded by registered mail, addressed to the corporation at its registered office. Any service so had on the Secretary of State shall be returnable in not less than thirty days.

The Secretary of State shall keep a record of all processes, notices and demands served upon him under this section, and shall record therein the time of such service and his action with reference thereto.

Nothing herein contained shall limit or affect the right to serve any process, notice or demand required or permitted by law to be served upon a corporation in any other manner now or hereafter permitted by law.

---

*Supply designation of jurisdiction, such as county, etc., in accordance with local practice.

§ 15. Authorized Shares

Each corporation shall have power to create and issue the number of shares stated in its articles of incorporation. Such shares may be divided into one or more classes with such designations, preferences, limitations, and relative rights as shall be stated in the articles of incorporation. The articles of incorporation may limit or deny the voting rights of or provide special voting rights for the shares of any class to the extent not inconsistent with the provisions of this Act.

Without limiting the authority herein contained, a corporation, when so provided in its articles of incorporation, may issue shares of preferred or special classes:

(a)   Subject to the right of the corporation to redeem any of such shares at the price fixed by the articles of incorporation for the redemption thereof.

(b)   Entitling the holders thereof to cumulative, noncumulative or partially cumulative dividends.

(c)   Having preference over any other class or classes of shares as to the payment of dividends.

(d)   Having preference in the assets of the corporation over any other class or classes of shares upon the voluntary or involuntary liquidation of the corporation.

(e)   Convertible into shares of any other class or into shares of any series of the same or any other class, except a class having prior or superior rights and preferences as to dividends or distribution of assets upon liquidation.

§ 16. Issuance of Shares of Preferred or Special Classes in Series

If the articles of incorporation so provide, the shares of any preferred or special class may be divided into and issued in series. If the shares of any such class are to be issued in series, then each series shall be so designated as to distinguish the shares thereof from the shares of all other series and classes. Any or all of the series of any such class and the variations in the relative rights and preferences as between different series may be fixed and determined by the articles of incorporation, but all shares of the same class shall be identical except as to the following relative rights and preferences, as to which there may be variations between different series:

(A)   The rate of dividend.

(B)   Whether shares may be redeemed and, if so, the redemption price and the terms and conditions of redemption.

(C)   The amount payable upon shares in the event of voluntary and involuntary liquidation.

(D)   Sinking fund provisions, if any, for the redemption or purchase of shares.

(E)   The terms and conditions, if any, on which shares may be converted.

(F)   Voting rights, if any.

If the articles of incorporation shall expressly vest authority in the board of directors, then, to the extent that the articles of incorporation shall not have established series and fixed and determined the variations in the relative rights and preferences as between series, the board of directors shall have authority to divide any or all of such classes into series and, within the limitations set forth in this section and in the articles of incorporation, fix and determine the relative rights and preferences of the shares of any series so established.

In order for the board of directors to establish a series, where authority so to do is contained in the articles of incorporation, the board of directors shall adopt a resolution setting forth the designation of the series and fixing and determining the relative rights and preferences thereof, or so much thereof as shall not be fixed and determined by the articles of incorporation.

Prior to the issue of any shares of a series established by the resolution adopted by the board of directors, the corporation shall file in the office of the Secretary of State a statement setting forth:

(a)   The name of the corporation.

(b)   A copy of the resolution establishing and designating the series, and fixing and determining the relative rights and preferences thereof.

(c)   The date of adoption of such resolution.

(d)   That such resolution was duly adopted by the board of directors.

Such statement shall be executed in duplicate by the corporation by its president or a vice president and by its secretary or an assistant secretary, and verified by one of the officers signing such statement, and shall be delivered to the Secretary of State. If the Secretary of State finds that such statement conforms to law, he shall, when all franchise taxes and fees have been paid as in this Act prescribed:

(1)   Endorse on each of such duplicate originals the word "Filed," and the month, day, and year of the filing thereof.

(2)   File one of such duplicate originals in his office.

(3)   Return the other duplicate original to the corporation or its representative.

Upon the filing of such statement by the Secretary of State, the resolution establishing and designating the series and fixing and determining the relative rights and preferences thereof shall become effective and shall constitute an amendment of the articles of incorporation.

§ 17. Subscriptions for Shares

A subscription for shares of a corporation to be organized shall be irrevocable for a period of six months, unless otherwise provided by the terms of the subscription agreement or unless all of the subscribers consent to the revocation of such subscription.

Unless otherwise provided in the subscription agreement, subscriptions for shares, whether made before or after the organization of a corporation, shall be paid in full at such time, or in such installments and at such times, as shall be determined by the board of directors. Any call made by the board of directors for payment on subscriptions shall be uniform as to all shares of the same class or as to all shares of the same series, as the case may be. In case of default in the payment of any installment or call when such payment is due, the corporation may proceed to collect the amount due in the same manner as any debt due the corporation. The by-laws may prescribe other penalties for failure to pay installments or calls that may become due, but no penalty working a forfeiture of a subscription, or of the amounts paid thereon, shall be declared as against any subscriber unless the amount due thereon shall remain unpaid for a period of twenty days after written demand has been made therefor. If mailed, such written demand shall be deemed to be made when deposited in the United States mail in a sealed envelope addressed to the subscriber at his last post-office address known to the corporation, with postage thereon prepaid. In the event of the sale of any shares by reason of any forfeiture, the excess of proceeds realized over the amount due and unpaid on such shares shall be paid to the delinquent subscriber or to his legal representative.

§ 18. Issuance of Shares

Subject to any restrictions in the articles of incorporation:

(a)   Shares may be issued for such consideration as shall be authorized by the board of directors establishing a price (in money or other consideration) or a minimum price or general formula or method by which the price will be determined; and

(b)   Upon authorization by the board of directors, the corporation may issue its own shares in exchange for or in conversion of its outstanding shares, or distribute its own shares, pro rata to its shareholders or the shareholders of one or more classes or series, to effectuate stock dividends or splits, and any such transaction shall not require consideration; provided, that no such issuance of shares of any class or series shall be made to the holders of shares of any other class or series unless it is either expressly provided for in the articles of incorporation, or is authorized by an affirmative vote or the written consent of the holders of at least a majority of the outstanding shares of the class or series in which the distribution is to be made.

§ 19. Payment for Shares

The consideration for the issuance of shares may be paid, in whole or in part, in money, in other property, tangible or intangible, or in labor or services actually performed for the corporation. When payment of the consideration for which shares are to be issued shall have been received by the corporation, such shares shall be nonassessable.

Neither promissory notes nor future services shall constitute payment or part payment for the issuance of shares of a corporation.

In the absence of fraud in the transaction, the judgment of the board of directors or the shareholders, as the case may be, as to the value of the consideration received for shares shall be conclusive.

§ 20. Stock Rights and Options

Subject to any provisions in respect thereof set forth in its articles of incorporation, a corporation may create and issue, whether or not in connection with the issuance and sale of any of its shares or other securities, rights or options entitling the holders thereof to purchase from the corporation shares of any class or classes. Such rights or options shall be evidenced in such manner as the board of directors shall approve and, subject to the provisions of the articles of incorporation, shall set forth the terms upon which, the time or times within which and the price or prices at which such shares may be purchased from the corporation upon the exercise of any such right or option. If such rights or options are to be issued to directors, officers or employees as such of the corporation or of any subsidiary thereof, and not to the shareholders generally, their issuance shall be approved by the affirmative vote of the holders of a majority of the shares entitled to vote thereon or shall be authorized by and consistent with a plan approved or ratified by such a vote of shareholders. In the absence of fraud in the transaction, the judgment of the board of directors as to the adequacy of the consideration received for such rights or options shall be conclusive.

§ 21. Determination of Amount of Stated Capital
[Repealed in 1979].

§ 22. Expenses of Organization, Reorganization and Financing
The reasonable charges and expenses of organization or reorganization of a corporation, and the reasonable expenses of and compensation for the sale or underwriting of its shares, may be paid or allowed by such corporation out of the consideration received by it in payment for its shares without thereby rendering such shares assessable.

§ 23. Shares Represented by Certificates and Uncertified Shares
The shares of a corporation shall be represented by certificates or shall be uncertificated shares. Certificates shall be signed by the chairman or vice-chairman of the board of directors or the president or a vice president and by the treasurer or an assistant treasurer or the secretary or an assistant secretary of the corporation, and may be sealed with the seal of the corporation or a facsimile thereof. Any of or all the signatures upon a certificate may be a facsimile. In case any officer, transfer agent or registrar who has signed or whose facsimile signature has been placed upon such certificate shall have ceased to be such officer, transfer agent or registrar before such certificate is issued, it may be issued by the corporation with the same effect as if he were such officer, transfer agent or registrar at the date of its issue.

Every certificate representing shares issued by a corporation which is authorized to issue shares of more than one class shall set forth upon the face or back of the certificate, or shall state that the corporation will furnish to any shareholder upon request and without charge, a full statement of the designations, preferences, limitations, and relative rights of the shares of each class authorized to be issued, and if the corporation is authorized to issue any preferred or special class in series, the variations in the relative rights and preferences between the shares of each such series so far as the same have been fixed and determined and the authority of the board of directors

to fix and determine the relative rights and preferences of subsequent series.

Each certificate representing shares shall state upon the face thereof:

(a)   That the corporation is organized under the laws of this State.

(b)   The name of the person to whom issued.

(c)   The number and class of shares, and the designation of the series, if any, which such certificate represents.

(d)   The par value of each share represented by such certificate, or a statement that the shares are without par value.

No certificate shall be issued for any share until such share is fully paid.

Unless otherwise provided by the articles of incorporation or by-laws, the board of directors of a corporation may provide by resolution that some or all of any or all classes and series of its shares shall be uncertificated shares, provided that such resolution shall not apply to shares represented by a certificate until such certificate is surrendered to the corporation. Without a reasonable time after the issuance or transfer of uncertificated shares, the corporation shall send to the registered owner thereof a written notice containing the information required to be set forth or stated on certificates pursuant to the second and third paragraphs of this section. Except as otherwise expressly provided by law, the rights and obligations of the holders of uncertificated shares and the rights and obligations of the holders of certificates representing shares of the same class and series shall be identical.

§ 24. Fractional Shares
A corporation may (1) issue fractions of a share, either represented by a certificate or uncertificated, (2) arrange for the disposition of fractional interests by those entitled thereto, (3) pay in money the fair value of fractions of a share as of a time when those entitled to receive such fractions are determined, or (4) issue scrip in registered or bearer form which shall entitle the holder to receive a certificate for a full share or an uncertificated full share upon the surrender of such scrip aggregating a full share. A certificate for a fractional share or an uncertificated fractional share shall, but scrip shall not unless otherwise provided therein, entitle the holder to exercise voting rights, to receive dividends thereon, and

to participate in any of the assets of the corporation in the event of liquidation. The board of directors may cause scrip to be issued subject to the condition that it shall become void if not exchanged for certificates representing full shares or uncertificated full shares before a specified date, or subject to the condition that the shares for which scrip is exchangeable may be sold by the corporation and the proceeds thereof distributed to the holders of scrip, or subject to any other conditions which the board of directors may deem advisable.

§ 25. Liability of Subscribers and Shareholders
A holder of or subscriber to shares of a corporation shall be under no obligation to the corporation or its creditors with respect to such shares other than the obligation to pay to the corporation the full consideration for which such shares were issued or to be issued.

Any person becoming an assignee or transferee of shares or of a subscription for shares in good faith and without knowledge or notice that the full consideration therefor has not been paid shall not be personally liable to the corporation or its creditors for any unpaid portion of such consideration.

An executor, administrator, conservator, guardian, trustee, assignee for the benefit of creditors, or receiver shall not be personally liable to the corporation as a holder of or subscriber to shares of a corporation but the estate and funds in his hands shall be so liable.

No pledgee or other holder of shares as collateral security shall be personally liable as a shareholder.

§ 26. Shareholders' Preemptive Rights
The shareholders of a corporation shall have no preemptive right to acquire unissued shares of the corporation, or securities of the corporation convertible into or carrying a right to subscribe to or acquire shares, except to the extent, if any, that such right is provided in the articles of incorporation.

§ 26A. Shareholders' Preemptive Rights [Alternative]
Except to the extent limited or denied by this section or by the articles of incorporation, shareholders shall have a preemptive right to acquire unissued shares or securities convertible into such shares or carrying a right to subscribe to or acquire shares.

Unless otherwise provided in the articles of incorporation,

(a) No preemptive right shall exist.

(1) to acquire any shares issued to directors, officers or employees pursuant to approval by the affirmative vote of the holders of a majority of the shares entitled to vote thereon or when authorized by and consistent with a plan theretofore approved by such a vote of shareholders; or

(2) to acquire any shares sold otherwise than for money.

(b) Holders of shares of any class that is preferred or limited as to dividends or assets shall not be entitled to any preemptive right.

(c) Holders of shares of common stock shall not be entitled to any preemptive right to shares of any class that is preferred or limited as to dividends or assets or to any obligations, unless convertible into shares of common stock or carrying a right to subscribe to or acquire shares of common stock.

(d) Holders of common stock without voting power shall have no preemptive right to shares of common stock with voting power.

(e) The preemptive right shall be only an opportunity to acquire shares or other securities under such terms and conditions as the board of directors may fix for the purpose of providing a fair and reasonable opportunity for the exercise of such right.

§ 27. By-Laws
The initial by-laws of a corporation shall be adopted by its board of directors. The power to alter, amend or repeal the by-laws or adopt new by-laws, subject to repeal or change by action of the shareholders, shall be vested in the board of directors unless reserved to the shareholders by the articles of incorporation. The by-laws may contain any provisions for the regulation and management of the affairs of the corporation not inconsistent with law or the articles of incorporation.

§ 27A. By-Laws and Other Powers in Emergency [Optional]
The board of directors of any corporation may adopt emergency by-laws, subject to repeal or change by action of the shareholders, which shall, notwithstanding any different provision elsewhere in this Act or in the articles of incorporation or by-laws, be operative during any emergency in the conduct of the business of the corporation resulting from an attack on the United States or any nuclear or atomic disaster. The emergency by-laws may make any provision that may

be practical and necessary for the circumstances of the emergency, including provisions that:

(a)   A meeting of the board of directors may be called by any officer or director in such manner and under such conditions as shall be prescribed in the emergency by-laws;

(b)   The director or directors in attendance at the meeting, or any greater number fixed by the emergency by-laws, shall constitute a quorum; and

(c)   The officers or other persons designated on a list approved by the board of directors before the emergency, all in such order of priority and subject to such conditions, and for such period of time (not longer than reasonably necessary after the termination of the emergency) as may be provided in the emergency by-laws or in the resolution approving the list shall, to the extent required to provide a quorum at any meeting of the board of directors, be deemed directors for such meeting.

The board of directors, either before or during any such emergency, may provide, and from time to time modify, lines of succession in the event that during such an emergency any or all officers or agents of the corporation shall for any reason be rendered incapable of discharging their duties.

The board of directors, either before or during any such emergency, may, effective in the emergency, change the head office or designate several alternative head offices or regional offices, or authorize the officers so to do.

To the extent not inconsistent with any emergency by-laws so adopted, the by-laws of the corporation shall remain in effect during any such emergency and upon its termination the emergency by-laws shall cease to be operative.

Unless otherwise provided in emergency by-laws, notice of any meeting of the board of directors during any such emergency may be given only to such of the directors as it may be feasible to reach at the time and by such means as may be feasible at the time, including publication or radio.

To the extent required to constitute a quorum at any meeting of the board of directors during any such emergency, the officers of the corporation who are present shall, unless otherwise provided in emergency by-laws, be deemed, in order of rank and within the same rank in order of seniority, directors for such meeting.

No officer, director or employee acting in accordance with any emergency by-laws shall be liable except for willful misconduct. No officer, director or employee shall be liable for any action taken by him

in good faith in such an emergency in furtherance of the ordinary business affairs of the corporation even though not authorized by the by-laws then in effect.

§ 28. Meetings of Shareholders

Meetings of shareholders may be held at such place within or without this State as may be stated in or fixed in accordance with the by-laws. If no other place is stated or so fixed, meetings shall be held at the registered office of the corporation.

An annual meeting of the shareholders shall be held at such time as may be stated in or fixed in accordance with the by-laws. If the annual meeting is not held within any thirteen-month period the Court of .... may, on the application of any shareholder, summarily order a meeting to be held.

Special meetings of the shareholders may be called by the board of directors, the holders of not less than one-tenth of all the shares entitled to vote at the meeting, or such other persons as may be authorized in the articles of incorporation or the by-laws.

§ 29. Notice of Shareholders' Meetings

Written notice stating the place, day and hour of the meeting and, in case of a special meeting, the purpose or purposes for which the meeting is called, shall be delivered not less than ten nor more than fifty days before the date of the meeting, either personally or by mail, by or at the direction of the president, the secretary, or the officer or persons calling the meeting, to each shareholder of record entitled to vote at such meeting. If mailed, such notice shall be deemed to be delivered when deposited in the United States mail addressed to the shareholder at his address as it appears on the stock transfer books of the corporation, with postage thereon prepaid.

§ 30. Closing of Transfer Books and Fixing Record Date

For the purpose of determining shareholders entitled to notice of or to vote at any meeting of shareholders or any adjournment thereof, or entitled to receive payment of any dividend, or in order to make a determination of shareholders for any other proper purpose, the board of directors of a corporation may provide that the stock transfer books shall be closed for a stated period but not to exceed, in any case, fifty days. If the stock transfer books shall be closed for the purpose of determining shareholders entitled to notice of or to vote at a meeting of shareholders, such books shall be closed for at least ten days immediately preceding such meeting. In lieu of closing the stock transfer books, the by-laws, or in the absence of an applicable by-law the board of directors, may fix in advance a date as the record date for any such determination of shareholders, such date in any case to be not more than fifty days and, in case of a meeting of shareholders, not less than ten days prior to the date on which the particular action, requiring such determination of shareholders, is to be taken. If the stock transfer books are not closed and no record date is fixed for the determination of shareholders entitled to notice of or to vote at a meeting of shareholders, or shareholders entitled to receive payment of a dividend, the date on which notice of the meeting is mailed or the date on which the resolution of the board of directors declaring such dividend is adopted, as the case may be, shall be the record date for such determination of shareholders. When a determination of shareholders entitled to vote at any meeting of shareholders has been made as provided in this section, such determination shall apply to any adjournment thereof.

§ 31. Voting Record

The officer or agent having charge of the stock transfer books for shares of a corporation shall make a complete record of the shareholders entitled to vote at such meeting or any adjournment thereof, arranged in alphabetical order, with the address of and the number of shares held by each. Such record shall be produced and kept open at the time and place of the meeting and shall be subject to the inspection of any shareholder during the whole time of the meeting for the purposes thereof.

Failure to comply with the requirements of this section shall not affect the validity of any action taken at such meeting.

An officer or agent having charge of the stock transfer books who shall fail to prepare the record of shareholders, or produce and keep it open for inspection at the meeting, as provided in this section, shall be liable to any shareholder suffering damage on account of such failure, to the extent of such damage.

§ 32. Quorum of Shareholders

Unless otherwise provided in the articles of incorporation, a majority of the shares entitled to vote, represented in person or by proxy, shall constitute a quorum at a meeting of shareholders, but in no event shall a quorum consist of less than one-third of the shares entitled to vote at the meeting. If a quorum is present, the affirmative vote of the majority of the shares represented at the meeting and entitled to vote on the subject matter shall be the act of the shareholders, unless the vote of a greater number or voting by classes is required by this Act or the articles of incorporation or by-laws.

§ 33. Voting of Shares

Each outstanding share, regardless of class, shall be entitled to one vote on each matter submitted to a vote at a meeting of shareholders, except as may be otherwise provided in the articles of incorporation. If the articles of incorporation provide for more or less than one vote for any share, on any matter, every reference in this Act to a majority or other proportion of shares shall refer to such a majority or other proportion of votes entitled to be cast.

Shares held by another corporation if a majority of the shares entitled to vote for the election of directors of such other corporation is held by the corporation, shall not be voted at any meeting or counted in determining the total number of outstanding shares at any given time.

A shareholder may vote either in person or by proxy executed in writing by the shareholder or by his duly authorized attorney-in-fact. No proxy shall be valid after eleven months from the date of its execution, unless otherwise provided in the proxy.

[Either of the following prefatory phrases may be inserted here: "The articles of incorporation may provide that" or "Unless the articles of incorporation otherwise provide"] . . . at each election of directors every shareholder entitled to vote at such election shall have the right to vote, in person or by proxy, the number of shares owned by him for as many persons as there are directors to be elected and for whose election he has a right to vote, or to cumulate his votes by giving one candidate as many votes as the number of such directors multiplied by the number of his shares shall equal, or by distributing such votes on the same principle among any number of such candidates.

Shares standing in the name of another corporation, domestic or foreign, may be voted by such officer, agent or proxy as the by-laws of such other corporation may prescribe, or, in the absence of such provision, as the board of directors of such other corporation may determine.

Shares held by an administrator, executor, guardian or conservator may be voted by him, either in person or by proxy, without a transfer of such shares into his name. Shares standing in the name of a trustee may be voted by him, either in person or by proxy, but no trustee shall be entitled to vote shares held by him without a transfer of such shares into his name.

Shares standing in the name of a receiver may be voted by such receiver, and shares held by or under the control of a receiver may be voted by such receiver without the transfer thereof into his name if authority so to do be contained in an appropriate order of the court by which such receiver was appointed.

A shareholder whose shares are pledged shall be entitled to vote such shares until the shares have been transferred into the name of the pledgee, and thereafter the pledgee shall be entitled to vote the shares so transferred.

On and after the date on which written notice of redemption of redeemable shares has been mailed to the holders thereof and a sum sufficient to redeem such shares has been deposited with a bank or trust company with irrevocable instruction and authority to pay the redemption price to the holders thereof upon surrender of certificates therefor, such shares shall not be entitled to vote on any matter and shall not be deemed to be outstanding shares.

§ 34. Voting Trusts and Agreements Among Shareholders

Any number of shareholders of a corporation may create a voting trust for the purpose of conferring upon a trustee or trustees the right to vote or otherwise represent their shares, for a period of not to exceed ten years, by entering into a written voting trust agreement specifying the terms and conditions of the voting trust, by depositing a counterpart of the agreement with the corporation at its registered office, and by transferring their shares to such trustee or trustees for the purposes of the agreement. Such trustee or trustees shall keep a record of the holders of voting trust certificates evidencing a beneficial interest in the voting trust, giving the names and addresses of all such holders and the number and class of the shares in respect of which the voting trust certificates held by each are issued, and shall deposit a copy of such record with the corporation at its registered office. The counterpart of the voting trust agreement and the copy of such record so deposited with the corporation shall be subject to the same right of examination by a shareholder of the corporation, in person or by agent or attorney, as are the books and records of the corporation, and such counterpart and such copy of such record shall be subject to examination by any holder of record of voting trust certificates, either in person

or by agent or attorney, at any reasonable time for any proper purpose.

Agreements among shareholders regarding the voting of their shares shall be valid and enforceable in accordance with their terms. Such agreements shall not be subject to the provisions of this section regarding voting trusts.

§ 35. Board of Directors

All corporate powers shall be exercised by or under authority of, and the business and affairs of a corporation shall be managed under the direction of, a board of directors except as may be otherwise provided in this Act or the articles of incorporation. If any such provision is made in the articles of incorporation, the powers and duties conferred or imposed upon the board of directors by this Act shall be exercised or performed to such extent and by such person or persons as shall be provided in the articles of incorporation. Directors need not be residents of this State or shareholders of the corporation unless the articles of incorporation or by-laws so require. The articles of incorporation or by-laws may prescribe other qualifications for directors. The board of directors shall have authority to fix the compensation of directors unless otherwise provided in the articles of incorporation.

A director shall perform his duties as a director, including his duties as a member of any committee of the board upon which he may serve, in good faith, in a manner he reasonably believes to be in the best interests of the corporation, and with such care as an ordinarily prudent person in a like position would use under similar circumstances. In performing his duties, a director shall be entitled to rely on information, opinions, reports or statements, including financial statements and other financial data, in each case prepared or presented by:

(a)   one or more officers or employees of the corporation whom the director reasonably believes to be reliable and competent in the matters presented,

(b)   counsel, public accountants or other persons as to matters which the director reasonably believes to be within such person's professional or expert competence, or

(c)   a committee of the board upon which he does not serve, duly designated in accordance with a provision of the articles of incorporation or the by-laws, as to matters within its designated authority, which committee the director reasonably believes to merit confidence, but he shall not be considered to be acting in good faith if he has knowledge concerning the matter in question that would cause such reliance to be unwarranted. A person who so performs his duties shall have no liability by reason of being or having been a director of the corporation.

A director of a corporation who is present at a meeting of its board of directors at which action on any corporate matter is taken shall be presumed to have assented to the action taken unless his dissent shall be entered in the minutes of the meeting or unless he shall file his written dissent to such action with the secretary of the meeting before the adjournment thereof or shall forward such dissent by registered mail to the secretary of the corporation immediately after the adjournment of the meeting. Such right to dissent shall not apply to a director who voted in favor of such action.

§ 36. Number and Election of Directors
The board of directors of a corporation shall consist of one or more members. The number of directors shall be fixed by, or in the manner provided in, the articles of incorporation or the by-laws, except as to the number constituting the initial board of directors, which number shall be fixed by the articles of incorporation. The number of directors may be increased or decreased from time to time by amendment to, or in the manner provided in, the articles of incorporation or the by-laws, but no decrease shall have the effect of shortening the term of any incumbent director. In the absence of a by-law providing for the number of directors, the number shall be the same as that provided for in the articles of incorporation. The names and addresses of the members of the first board of directors shall be stated in the articles of incorporation. Such persons shall hold office until the first annual meeting of shareholders, and until their successors shall have been elected and qualified. At the first annual meeting of shareholders and at each annual meeting thereafter the shareholders shall elect directors to hold office until the next succeeding annual meeting, except in case of the classification of directors as permitted by this Act. Each director shall hold office for the term for which he is elected and until his successor shall have been elected and qualified.

§ 37. Classification of Directors
When the board of directors shall consist of nine or more members, in lieu of electing the whole number of directors annually, the articles of incorporation may provide that the directors be divided into either two or three classes, each class to be as nearly equal in number as possible, the term of office of directors of the first class to expire at the first annual meeting of shareholders after their election, that of the second class to expire at the second annual meeting after their election, and that of the third class, if any, to expire at the third annual meeting after their election. At each annual meeting after such classification the number of directors equal to the number of the class whose term expires at the time of such meeting shall be elected to hold office until the second succeeding annual meeting, if there be two classes, or until the third succeeding annual meeting, if there be three classes. No classification of directors shall be effective prior to the first annual meeting of shareholders.

§ 38. Vacancies
Any vacancy occurring in the board of directors may be filled by the affirmative vote of a majority of the remaining directors though less than a quorum of the board of directors. A director elected to fill a vacancy shall be elected for the unexpired term of his predecessor in office. Any directorship to be filled by reason of an increase in the number of directors may be filled by the board of directors for the term of office continuing only until the next election of directors by the shareholders.

§ 39. Removal of Directors
At a meeting of shareholders called expressly for that purpose, directors may be removed in the manner provided in this section. Any director or the entire board of directors may be removed, with or without cause, by a vote of the holders of a majority of the shares then entitled to vote at an election of directors.

In the case of a corporation having cumulative voting, if less than the entire board is to be removed, no one of the directors may be removed if the votes cast against his removal would be sufficient to elect him if then cumulatively voted at an election of the entire board of directors, or, if there be classes of directors, at an election of the class of directors of which he is a part.

Whenever the holders of the shares of any class are entitled to elect one or more directors by the provisions of the articles of incorporation, the provisions of this section shall apply, in respect to the removal of a director or directors so elected, to the vote of the holders of the outstanding shares of that class and not to the vote of the outstanding shares as a whole.

§ 40. Quorum of Directors

A majority of the number of directors fixed by or in the manner provided in the by-laws or in the absence of a by-law fixing or providing for the number of directors, then of the number stated in the articles of incorporation, shall constitute a quorum for the transaction of business unless a greater number is required by the articles of incorporation or the by-laws. The act of the majority of the directors present at a meeting at which a quorum is present shall be the act of the board of directors, unless the act of a greater number is required by the articles of incorporation or the by-laws.

§ 41. Director Conflicts of Interest

No contract or other transaction between a corporation and one or more of its directors or any other corporation, firm, association or entity in which one or more of its directors are directors or officers or are financially interested, shall be either void or voidable because of such relationship or interest or because such director or directors are present at the meeting of the board of directors or a committee thereof which authorizes, approves or ratifies such contract or transaction or because his or their votes are counted for such purpose, if:

(a)   the fact of such relationship or interest is disclosed or known to the board of directors or committee which authorizes, approves or ratifies the contract or transaction by a vote or consent sufficient for the purpose without counting the votes or consents of such interested directors; or

(b)   the fact of such relationship or interest is disclosed or known to the shareholders entitled to vote and they authorize, approve or ratify such contract or transaction by vote or written consent; or

(c)   the contract or transaction is fair and reasonable to the corporation.

Common or interested directors may be counted in determining the presence of a quorum at a meeting of the board of directors or a committee thereof which authorizes, approves or ratifies such contract or transaction.

§ 42. Executive and Other Committees

If the articles of incorporation or the by-laws so provide, the board of directors, by resolution adopted by a majority of the full board of directors, may designate from among its members an executive committee and one or more other committees each of which, to the

extent provided in such resolution or in the articles of incorporation or the by-laws of the corporation, shall have and may exercise all the authority of the board of directors, except that no such committee shall have authority to (i) authorize distributions, (ii) approve or recommend to shareholders actions or proposals required by this Act to be approved by shareholders, (iii) designate candidates for the office of director, for purposes of proxy solicitation or otherwise, or fill vacancies on the board of directors or any committee thereof, (iv) amend the by-laws, (v) approve a plan of merger not requiring shareholder approval, (vi) authorize or approve the reacquisition of shares unless pursuant to a general formula or method specified by the board of directors, or (vii) authorize or approve the issuance or sale of, or any contract to issue or sell, shares or designate the terms of a series of a class of shares, provided that the board of directors, having acted regarding general authorization for the issuance or sale of shares, or any contract therefor, and, in the case of a series, the designation thereof, may, pursuant to a general formula or method specified by the board by resolution or by adoption of a stock option or other plan, authorize a committee to fix the terms of any contract for the sale of the shares and to fix the terms upon which such shares may be issued or sold, including, without limitation, the price, the dividend rate, provisions for redemption, sinking fund, conversion, voting or preferential rights, and provisions for other features of a class of shares, or a series of a class of shares, with full power in such committee to adopt any final resolution setting forth all the terms thereof and to authorize the statement of the terms of a series for filing with the Secretary of State under this Act.

   Neither the designation of any such committee, the delegation thereto of authority, nor action by such committee pursuant to such authority shall alone constitute compliance by any member of the board of directors, not a member of the committee in question, with his responsibility to act in good faith, in a manner he reasonably believes to be in the best interests of the corporation, and with such care as an ordinarily prudent person in a like position would use under similar circumstances.

§ 43. Place and Notice of Directors' Meetings; Committee Meetings

Meetings of the board of directors, regular or special, may be held either within or without this State.

   Regular meetings of the board of directors or any committee designated thereby may be held with or without notice as prescribed in the by-laws. Special meetings of the board of directors or any committee designated thereby shall be held upon such notice as is prescribed in the by-laws. Attendance of a director at a meeting shall constitute a waiver of notice of such meeting, except where a director attends a meeting for the express purpose of objecting to the transaction of any business because the meeting is not lawfully called or convened. Neither the business to be transacted at, nor the purpose of, any regular or special meeting of the board of directors or any committee designated thereby need be specified in the notice or waiver of notice of such meeting unless required by the by-laws.

Except as may be otherwise restricted by the articles of incorporation or by-laws, members of the board of directors or any committee designated thereby may participate in a meeting of such board or committee by means of a conference telephone or similar communications equipment by means of which all persons participating in the meeting can hear each other at the same time and participation by such means shall constitute presence in person at a meeting.

§ 44. Action by Directors Without a Meeting

Unless otherwise provided by the articles of incorporation or by-laws, any action required by this Act to be taken at a meeting of the directors of a corporation, or any action which may be taken at a meeting of the directors or of a committee, may be taken without a meeting if a consent in writing, setting forth the action so taken, shall be signed by all of the directors, or all of the members of the committee, as the case may be. Such consent shall have the same effect as a unanimous vote.

§ 45. Distributions to Shareholders

Subject to any restrictions in the articles of incorporation, the board of directors may authorize and the corporation may make distributions, except that no distribution may be made if, after giving effect thereto, either:

(a)   the corporation would be unable to pay its debts as they become due in the usual course of its business; or

(b)   the corporation's total assets would be less than the sum of its total liabilities and (unless the articles of incorporation otherwise permit) the maximum amount that then would be payable, in any liquidation, in respect of all outstanding shares having preferential rights in liquidation.

Determinations under subparagraph (b) may be based upon (i) financial statements prepared on the basis of accounting practices and principles that are reasonable in the circumstances, or (ii) a fair valuation or other method that is reasonable in the circumstances.

In the case of a purchase, redemption or other acquisition of a corporation's shares, the effect of a distribution shall be measured as of the date money or other property is transferred or debt is incurred by the corporation, or as of the date the shareholder ceases to be a shareholder of the corporation with respect to such shares, whichever is earlier. In all other cases, the effect of a distribution shall be measured as of the date of its authorization if payment occurs 120 days or less following the date of authorization, or as of the date of payment if payment occurs more than 120 days following the date of authorization.

Indebtedness of a corporation incurred or issued to a shareholder in a distribution in accordance with this Section shall be on a parity with the indebtedness of the corporation to its general unsecured creditors except to the extent subordinated by agreement.

§ 46. Distributions from Capital Surplus
[Repealed in 1979].

§ 47. Loans to Employees and Directors

A corporation shall not lend money to or use its credit to assist its directors without authorization in the particular case by its shareholders, but may lend money to and use its credit to assist any employee of the corporation or of a subsidiary, including any such employee who is a director of the corporation, if the board of directors decides that such loan or assistance may benefit the corporation.

§ 48. Liability of Directors in Certain Cases

In addition to any other liabilities, a director who votes for or assents to any distribution contrary to the provisions of this Act or contrary to any restrictions contained in the articles of incorporation, shall, unless he complies with the standard provided in this Act for the performance of the duties of directors, be liable to the corporation, jointly and severally with all other directors so voting or assenting, for the amount of such dividend which is paid or the value of such distribution in excess of the amount of such distribution which could have been made without a violation of the provisions of this Act or the restrictions in the articles of incorporation.

Any director against whom a claim shall be asserted under or pursuant to this section for the making of a distribution and who shall be held liable thereon, shall be entitled to contribution from the shareholders who accepted or received any such distribution, knowing such distribution to have been made in violation of this Act, in proportion to the amounts received by them.

Any director against whom a claim shall be asserted under or pursuant to this section shall be entitled to contribution from any other director who voted for or assented to the action upon which the claim is asserted and who did not comply with the standard provided in this Act for the performance of the duties of directors.

§ 49. Provisions Relating to Actions by Shareholders

No action shall be brought in this State by a shareholder in the right of a domestic or foreign corporation unless the plaintiff was a holder of record of shares or of voting trust certificates therefor at the time of the transaction of which he complains, or his shares or voting trust certificates thereafter devolved upon him by operation of law from a person who was a holder of record at such time.

In any action hereafter instituted in the right of any domestic or foreign corporation by the holder or holders of record of shares of such corporation or of voting trust certificates therefor, the court having jurisdiction, upon final judgment and a finding that the action was brought without reasonable cause, may require the plaintiff or plaintiffs to pay to the parties named as defendant the reasonable expenses, including fees of attorneys, incurred by them in the defense of such action.

In any action now pending or hereafter instituted or maintained in the right of any domestic or foreign corporation by the holder or holders of record of less than five per cent of the outstanding shares of any class of such corporation or of voting trust certificates therefor, unless the shares or voting trust certificates so held have a market value in excess of twenty-five thousand dollars, the corporation in whose right such action is brought shall be entitled at any time before final judgment to require the plaintiff or plaintiffs to give security for the reasonable expenses, including fees of attorneys, that may be incurred by it in connection with such action or may be incurred by other parties named as defendant for which it may become legally liable. Market value shall be determined as of the date that the plaintiff institutes the action or, in the case of an intervenor, as of the date that he becomes a party to the action. The amount of such security may from time to time be increased or

decreased, in the discretion of the court, upon showing that the security provided has or may become inadequate or is excessive. The corporation shall have recourse to such security in such amount as the court having jurisdiction shall determine upon the termination of such action, whether or not the court finds the action was brought without reasonable cause.

§ 50. Officers

The officers of a corporation shall consist of a president, one or more vice presidents as may be prescribed by the by-laws, a secretary, and a treasurer, each of whom shall be elected by the board of directors at such time and in such manner as may be prescribed by the by-laws. Such other officers and assistant officers and agents as may be deemed necessary may be elected or appointed by the board of directors or chosen in such other manner as may be prescribed by the by-laws. Any two or more offices may be held by the same person, except the offices of president and secretary.

All officers and agents of the corporation, as between themselves and the corporation, shall have such authority and perform such duties in the management of the corporation as may be provided in the by-laws, or as may be determined by resolution of the board of directors not inconsistent with the by-laws.

§ 51. Removal of Officers

Any officer or agent may be removed by the board of directors whenever in its judgment the best interests of the corporation will be served thereby, but such removal shall be without prejudice to the contract rights, if any, of the person so removed. Election or appointment of an officer or agent shall not of itself create contract rights.

§ 52. Books and Records: Financial Reports to Shareholders; Examination of Records

Each corporation shall keep correct and complete books and records of account and shall keep minutes of the proceedings of its shareholders and board of directors and shall keep at its registered office or principal place of business, or at the office of its transfer agent or registrar, a record of its shareholders, giving the names and addresses of all shareholders and the number and class of the shares held by each. Any books, records and minutes may be in written form or in any other form capable of being converted into written form within a reasonable time.

Any person who shall have been a holder of record of shares or of voting trust certificates therefor at least six months immediately preceding his demand or shall be the holder of record of, or the holder of record of voting trust certificates for, at least five percent of all the outstanding shares of the corporation, upon written demand stating the purpose thereof, shall have the right to examine, in person, or by agent or attorney, at any reasonable time or times, for any proper purpose its relevant books and records of account, minutes, and record of shareholders and to make extracts therefrom.

Any officer or agent who, or a corporation which, shall refuse to allow any such shareholder or holder of voting trust certificates, or his agent or attorney, so to examine and make extracts from its books and records of account, minutes, and record of shareholders, for any proper purpose, shall be liable to such shareholder or holder of voting trust certificates in a penalty of ten percent of the value of the shares owned by such shareholder, or in respect of which such voting trust certificates are issued, in addition to any other damages or remedy afforded him by law. It shall be a defense to any action for penalties under this section that the person suing therefor has within two years sold or offered for sale any list of shareholders or of holders of voting trust certificates for shares of such corporation or any other corporation or has aided or abetted any person in procuring any list of shareholders or of holders of voting trust certificates for any such purpose, or has improperly used any information secured through any prior examination of the books and records of account, or minutes, or record of shareholders or of holders of voting trust certificates for shares of such corporation or any other corporation, or was not acting in good faith or for a proper purpose in making his demand.

Nothing herein contained shall impair the power of any court of competent jurisdiction, upon proof by a shareholder or holder of voting trust certificates of proper purpose, irrespective of the period of time during which such shareholder or holder of voting trust certificates shall have been a shareholder of record or a holder of record of voting trust certificates, and irrespective of the number of shares held by him or represented by voting trust certificates held by him, to compel the production for examination by such shareholder or holder of voting trust certificates of the books and records of account, minutes and record of shareholders of a corporation.

Each corporation shall furnish to its shareholders annual financial statements, including at least a balance sheet as of the end of each fiscal year and a statement of income for such fiscal year, which shall be prepared on the basis of generally accepted accounting principles, if the corporation prepares financial statements for such fiscal year on that basis for any purpose, and may be consolidated statements of the corporation and one or more of its subsidiaries. The financial statements shall be mailed by the corporation to each of its shareholders within 120 days after the close of each fiscal year and, after such mailing and upon written request, shall be mailed by the corporation to any shareholder (or holder of a voting trust certificate for its shares) to whom a copy of the most recent annual financial statements has not previously been mailed. In the case of statements audited by a public accountant, each copy shall be accompanied by a report setting forth his opinion thereon; in other cases, each copy shall be accompanied by a statement of the president or the person in charge of the corporation's financial accounting records (1) stating his reasonable belief as to whether or not the financial statements were prepared in accordance with generally accepted accounting principles and, if not, describing the basis of presentation, and (2) describing any respects in which the financial statements were not prepared on a basis consistent with those prepared for the previous year.

§ 53. Incorporators
One or more persons, or a domestic or foreign corporation, may act as incorporator or incorporators of a corporation by signing and delivering in duplicate to the Secretary of State articles of incorporation for such corporation.

§ 54. Articles of Incorporation
The articles of incorporation shall set forth:

(a)   The name of the corporation.

(b)   The period of duration, which may be perpetual.

(c)   The purpose or purposes for which the corporation is organized which may be stated to be, or to include, the transaction of any or all lawful business for which corporations may be incorporated under this Act.

(d)   The aggregate number of shares which the corporation shall have authority to issue and, if such shares are to be divided into classes, the number of shares of each class.

(e)   If the shares are to be divided into classes, the designation of each class and a statement of the preferences, limitations and relative rights in respect of the shares of each class.

(f)   If the corporation is to issue the shares of any preferred or special class in series, then the designation of each series and a statement of the variations in the relative rights and preferences as between series insofar as the same are to be fixed in the articles of incorporation, and a statement of any authority to be vested in the board of directors to establish series and fix and determine the variations in the relative rights and preferences as between series.

(g)   If any preemptive right is to be granted to shareholders, the provisions therefor.

(h)   The address of its initial registered office, and the name of its initial registered agent at such address.

(i)   The number of directors constituting the initial board of directors and the names and addresses of the persons who are to serve as directors until the first annual meeting of shareholders or until their successors be elected and qualify.

(j)   The name and address of each incorporator.

In addition to provisions required therein, the articles of incorporation may also contain provisions not inconsistent with law regarding:

(1)   the direction of the management of the business and the regulation of the affairs of the corporation;
(2)   the definition, limitation and regulation of the powers of the corporation, the directors, and the shareholders, or any class of the shareholders, including restrictions on the transfer of shares;
(3)   the par value of any authorized shares or class of shares;
(4)   any provision which under this Act is required or permitted to be set forth in the by-laws.

It shall not be necessary to set forth in the articles of incorporation any of the corporate powers enumerated in this Act.

§ 55. Filing of Articles of Incorporation
Duplicate originals of the articles of incorporation shall be delivered to the Secretary of State. If the Secretary of State finds that the articles of incorporation conform to law, he shall, when all fees have been paid as in this Act prescribed:

(a)   Endorse on each of such duplicate originals the word "Filed," and the month, day and year of the filing thereof.

(b)   File one of such duplicate originals in his office.

(c)   Issue a certificate of incorporation to which he shall affix the other duplicate original.

The certificate of incorporation, together with the duplicate original of the articles of incorporation affixed thereto by the Secretary of State, shall be returned to the incorporators or their representative.

§ 56. Effect of Issuance of Certificate of Incorporation
Upon the issuance of the certificate of incorporation, the corporate existence shall begin, and such certificate of incorporation shall be conclusive evidence that all conditions precedent required to be performed by the incorporators have been complied with and that the corporation has been incorporated under this Act, except as against this State in a proceeding to cancel or revoke the certificate of incorporation or for involuntary dissolution of the corporation.

§ 57. Organization Meeting of Directors
After the issuance of the certificate of incorporation an organization meeting of the board of directors named in the articles of incorporation shall be held, either within or without this State, at the call of a majority of the directors named in the articles of incorporation, for the purpose of adopting by-laws, electing officers and transacting such other business as may come before the meeting. The directors calling the meeting shall give at least three days' notice thereof by mail to each director so named, stating the time and place of the meeting.

§ 58. Right to Amend Articles of Incorporation
A corporation may amend its articles of incorporation, from time to time, in any and as many respects as may be desired, so long as its articles of incorporation as amended contain only such provisions as might be lawfully contained in original articles of incorporation at the time of making such amendment, and, if a change in shares or the rights of shareholders, or an exchange, reclassification or cancellation of shares or rights of shareholders is to be made, such provisions as may be necessary to effect such change, exchange, reclassification or cancellation.

In particular, and without limitation upon such general power of amendment, a corporation may amend its articles of incorporation, from time to time, so as:

(a)   To change its corporate name.

(b)   To change its period of duration.

(c)   To change, enlarge or diminish its corporate purposes.

(d)   To increase or decrease the aggregate number of shares, or shares of any class, which the corporation has authority to issue.

(e)   To provide, change or eliminate any provision with respect to the par value of any shares or class of shares.

(f)   To exchange, classify, reclassify or cancel all or any part of its shares, whether issued or unissued.

(g)   To change the designation of all or any part of its shares, whether issued or unissued, and to change the preferences, limitations, and the relative rights in respect of all or any part of its shares, whether issued or unissued.

(h)   To change the shares of any class, whether issued or unissued [sic] into a different number of shares of the same class or into the same or a different number of shares of other classes.

(i)   To create new classes of shares having rights and preferences either prior and superior or subordinate and inferior to the shares of any class then authorized, whether issued or unissued.

(j)   To cancel or otherwise affect the right of the holders of the shares of any class to receive dividends which have accrued but have not been declared.

(k)   To divide any preferred or special class of shares, whether issued or unissued, into series and fix and determine the designations of such series and the variations in the relative rights and preferences as between the shares of such series.

(l)   To authorize the board of directors to establish, out of authorized but unissued shares, series of any preferred or special class of shares and fix and determine the relative rights and preferences of the shares of any series so established.

(m)   To authorize the board of directors to fix and determine the relative rights and preferences of the authorized but unissued shares of series theretofore established in respect of which either the relative rights and preferences have not been fixed and determined or the relative rights and preferences theretofore fixed and determined are to be changed.

(n)   To revoke, diminish, or enlarge the authority of the board of directors to establish series out of authorized but unissued shares of any preferred or special class and fix and determine the relative rights and preferences of the shares of any series so established.

(o)   To limit, deny or grant to shareholders of any class the preemptive right to acquire additional shares of the corporation, whether then or thereafter authorized.

§ 59. Procedure to Amend Articles of Incorporation

Amendments to the articles of incorporation shall be made in the following manner:

(a)   The board of directors shall adopt a resolution setting forth the proposed amendment and, if shares have been issued, directing that it be submitted to a vote at a meeting of shareholders, which may be either the annual or a special meeting. If no shares have been issued, the amendment shall be adopted by resolution of the board of directors and the provisions for adoption by shareholders shall not apply. If the corporation has only one class of shares outstanding, an amendment solely to change the number of authorized shares to effectuate a split of, or stock dividend in, the corporation's own shares, or solely to do so and to change the number of authorized shares in proportion thereto, may be adopted by the board of directors; and the provisions for adoption by shareholders shall not apply, unless otherwise provided by the articles of incorporation. The resolution may incorporate the proposed amendment in restated articles of incorporation which contain a statement that except for the designated amendment the restated articles of incorporation correctly set forth without change the corresponding provisions of the articles of incorporation as theretofore amended, and that the restated articles of incorporation together with the designated amendment supersede the original articles of incorporation and all amendments thereto.

(b)   Written notice setting forth the proposed amendment or a summary of the changes to be effected thereby shall be given to each shareholder of record entitled to vote thereon within the time and in the manner provided in this Act for the giving of notice of meetings of shareholders. If the meeting be an annual meeting, the proposed amendment of such summary may be included in the notice of such annual meeting.

(c)   At such meeting a vote of the shareholders entitled to vote thereon shall be taken on the proposed amendment. The proposed amendment shall be adopted upon receiving the affirmative vote of the holders of a majority of the shares entitled to vote thereon, unless any class of shares is entitled to vote thereon as a class, in which event the proposed amendment shall be adopted upon receiving the affirmative vote of the holders of a majority of the shares of each class of shares entitled to vote thereon as a class and of the total shares entitled to vote thereon.

Any number of amendments may be submitted to the shareholders, and voted upon by them, at one meeting.

§ 60. Class Voting on Amendments

The holders of the outstanding shares of a class shall be entitled to vote as a class upon a proposed amendment, whether or not entitled to vote thereon by the provisions of the articles of incorporation, if the amendment would:

(a)   Increase or decrease the aggregate number of authorized shares of such class.

(b)   Effect an exchange, reclassification or cancellation of all or part of the shares of such class.

(c)   Effect an exchange, or create a right of exchange, of all or any part of the shares of another class into the shares of such class.

(d)   Change the designations, preferences, limitations or relative rights of the shares of such class.

(e)   Change the shares of such class into the same or a different number of shares of the same class or another class or classes.

(f)   Create a new class of shares having rights and preferences prior and superior to the shares of such class, or increase the rights and preferences or the number of authorized shares, of any class having rights and preferences prior or superior to the shares of such class.

(g)   In the case of a preferred or special class of shares, divide the shares of such class into series and fix and determine the designation of such series and the variations in the relative rights and preferences between the shares of such series, or authorize the board of directors to do so.

(h)   Limit or deny any existing preemptive rights of the shares of such class.

(i)   Cancel or otherwise affect dividends on the shares of such class which have accrued but have not been declared.

§ 61. Articles of Amendment

The articles of amendment shall be executed in duplicate by the corporation by its president or a vice president and by its secretary or an assistant secretary, and verified by one of the officers signing such articles, and shall set forth:

(a)   The name of the corporation.

(b)   The amendments so adopted.

(c)   The date of the adoption of the amendment by the shareholders, or by the board of directors where no shares have been issued.

(d)   The number of shares outstanding, and the number of shares entitled to vote thereon, and if the shares of any class are entitled to vote thereon as a class, the designation and number of outstanding shares entitled to vote thereon of each such class.

(e)   The number of shares voted for and against such amendment, respectively, and, if the shares of any class are entitled to vote thereon as a class, the number of shares of each such class voted for and against such amendment, respectively, or if no shares have been issued, a statement to that effect.

(f)   If such amendment provides for an exchange, reclassification or cancellation of issued shares, and if the manner in which the same shall be effected is not set forth in the amendment, then a statement of the manner in which the same shall be effected.

§ 62. Filing of Articles of Amendment

Duplicate originals of the articles of amendment shall be delivered to the Secretary of State. If the Secretary of State finds that the articles of amendment conform to law, he shall, when all fees and franchise taxes have been paid as in this Act prescribed:

(a)   Endorse on each of such duplicate originals the word "Filed," and the month, day and year of the filing thereof.

(b)   File one of such duplicate originals in his office.

(c)   Issue a certificate of amendment to which he shall affix the other duplicate original.

The certificate of amendment, together with the duplicate original of the articles of amendment affixed thereto by the Secretary of State, shall be returned to the corporation or its representative.

§ 63. Effect of Certificate of Amendment
Upon the issuance of the certificate of amendment by the Secretary of State, the amendment shall become effective and the articles of incorporation shall be deemed to be amended accordingly.

No amendment shall affect any existing cause of action in favor of or against such corporation, or any pending suit to which such corporation shall be a party, or the existing rights of persons other than shareholders; and, in the event the corporate name shall be changed by amendment, no suit brought by or against such corporation under its former name shall abate for that reason.

§ 64. Restated Articles of Incorporation
A domestic corporation may at any time restate its articles of incorporation as theretofore amended, by a resolution adopted by the board of directors.

Upon the adoption of such resolution, restated articles of incorporation shall be executed in duplicate by the corporation by its president or a vice president and by its secretary or assistant secretary and verified by one of the officers signing such articles and shall set forth all of the operative provisions of the articles of incorporation as theretofore amended together with a statement that the restated articles of incorporation correctly set forth without change the corresponding provisions of the articles of incorporation as theretofore amended and that the restated articles of incorporation supersede the original articles of incorporation and all amendments thereto.

Duplicate originals of the restated articles of incorporation shall be delivered to the Secretary of State. If the Secretary of State finds that such restated articles of incorporation conform to law, he shall, when all fees and franchise taxes have been paid as in this Act prescribed:

(1) Endorse on each of such duplicate originals the word "Filed," and the month, day and year of the filing thereof.
(2) File one of such duplicate originals in his office.
(3) Issue a restated certificate of incorporation, to which he shall affix the other duplicate original.

The restated certificate of incorporation, together with the duplicate original of the restated articles of incorporation affixed thereto by the Secretary of State, shall be returned to the corporation or its representative.

Upon the issuance of the restated certificate of incorporation by the Secretary of State, the restated articles of incorporation shall become effective and shall supersede the original articles of incorporation and all amendments thereto.

§ 65. Amendment of Articles of Incorporation in Reorganization Proceedings
Whenever a plan of reorganization of a corporation has been confirmed by decree or order of a court of competent jurisdiction in proceedings for the reorganization of such corporation, pursuant to the provisions of any applicable statute of the United States relating to reorganizations of corporations, the articles of incorporation of the corporation may be amended, in the manner provided in this section, in as many respects as may be necessary to carry out the plan and put it into effect, so long as the articles of incorporation as amended contain only such provisions as might be lawfully contained in original articles of incorporation at the time of making such amendment.

In particular and without limitation upon such general power of amendment, the articles of incorporation may be amended for such purpose so as to:

(A) Change the corporate name, period of duration or corporate purposes of the corporation;

(B) Repeal, alter or amend the by-laws of the corporation;

(C) Change the aggregate number of shares or shares of any class, which the corporation has authority to issue;

(D) Change the preferences, limitations and relative rights in respect of all or any part of the shares of the corporation, and classify, reclassify or cancel all or any part thereof, whether issued or unissued;

(E) Authorize the issuance of bonds, debentures or other obligations of the corporation, whether or not convertible into shares of any class or bearing warrants or other evidences of optional rights to purchase or subscribe for shares of any class, and fix the terms and conditions thereof; and

(F) Constitute or reconstitute and classify or reclassify the board of directors of the corporation, and appoint directors and officers in place of or in addition to all or any of the directors or officers then in office.

Amendments to the articles of incorporation pursuant to this section shall be made in the following manner:

(a)   Articles of amendment approved by decree or order of such court shall be executed and verified in duplicate by such person or persons as the court shall designate or appoint for the purpose, and shall set forth the name of the corporation, the amendments of the articles of incorporation approved by the court, the date of the decree or order approving the articles of amendment, the title of the proceedings in which the decree or order was entered, and a statement that such decree or order was entered by a court having jurisdiction of the proceedings for the reorganization of the corporation pursuant to the provisions of an applicable statute of the United States.

(b)   Duplicate originals of the articles of amendment shall be delivered to the Secretary of State. If the Secretary of State finds that the articles of amendment conform to law, he shall, when all fees and franchise taxes have been paid as in this Act prescribed:

(1)   Endorse on each of such duplicate originals the word "Filed," and the month, day and year of the filing thereof.

(2)   File one of such duplicate originals in his office.

(3)   Issue a certificate of amendment to which he shall affix the other duplicate original.

The certificate of amendment, together with the duplicate original of the articles of amendment affixed thereto by the Secretary of State, shall be returned to the corporation or its representative.

Upon the issuance of the certificate of amendment by the Secretary of State, the amendment shall become effective and the articles of incorporation shall be deemed to be amended accordingly, without any action thereon by the directors or shareholders of the corporation and with the same effect as if the amendments had been adopted by unanimous action of the directors and shareholders of the corporation.

§ 66. Restriction on Redemption or Purchase of Redeemable Shares
[Repealed in 1979].

§ 67. Cancellation of Redeemable Shares by Redemption or Purchase
[Repealed in 1979].

§ 68. Cancellation of Other Reacquired Shares
[Repealed in 1979].

§ 69. Reduction of Stated Capital in Certain Cases
[Repealed in 1979].

§ 70. Special Provisions Relating to Surplus and Reserves
[Repealed in 1979].

§ 71. Procedure for Merger
Any two or more domestic corporations may merge into one of such corporations pursuant to a plan of merger approved in the manner provided in this Act.

The board of directors of each corporation shall, by resolution adopted by each such board, approve a plan of merger setting forth:

(a)   The names of the corporations proposing to merge, and the name of the corporation into which they propose to merge, which is hereinafter designated as the surviving corporation.

(b)   The terms and conditions of the proposed merger.

(c)   The manner and basis of converting the shares of each corporation into shares, obligations or other securities of the surviving corporation or of any other corporation or, in whole or in part, into cash or other property.

(d)   A statement of any changes in the articles of incorporation of the surviving corporation to be effected by such merger.

(e)   Such other provisions with respect to the proposed merger as are deemed necessary or desirable.

§ 72. Procedure for Consolidation
Any two or more domestic corporations may consolidate into a new corporation pursuant to a plan of consolidation approved in the manner provided in this Act.

The board of directors of each corporation shall, by a resolution adopted by each such board, approve a plan of consolidation setting forth:

(a)   The names of the corporations proposing to consolidate, and the name of the new corporation into which they propose to consolidate, which is hereinafter designated as the new corporation.

(b)   The terms and conditions of the proposed consolidation.

(c)   The manner and basis of converting the shares of each corporation into shares, obligations or other securities of the new corporation or of any other corporation or, in whole or in part, into cash or other property.

(d)   With respect to the new corporation, all of the statements required to be set forth in articles of incorporation for corporations organized under this Act.

(e)   Such other provisions with respect to the proposed consolidation as are deemed necessary or desirable.

§ 72A. Procedure for Share Exchange

All the issued or all the outstanding shares of one or more classes of any domestic corporation may be acquired through the exchange of all such shares of such class or classes by another domestic or foreign corporation pursuant to a plan of exchange approved in the manner provided in this Act.

The board of directors of each corporation shall, by resolution adopted by each such board, approve a plan of exchange setting forth:

(a)   The name of the corporation the shares of which are proposed to be acquired by exchange and the name of the corporation to acquire the shares of such corporation in the exchange, which is hereinafter designated as the acquiring corporation.

(b)   The terms and conditions of the proposed exchange.

(c)   The manner and basis of exchanging the shares to be acquired for shares, obligations or other securities of the acquiring corporation or any other corporation, or, in whole or in part, for cash or other property.

(d)   Such other provisions with respect to the proposed exchange as are deemed necessary or desirable. The procedure authorized by this section shall not be deemed to limit the power of a corporation to acquire all or part of the shares of any class of classes of a corporation through a voluntary exchange or otherwise by agreement with the shareholders.

§ 73. Approval by Shareholders

(a)   The board of directors of each corporation in the case of a merger or consolidation, and the board of directors of the corporation the shares of which are to be acquired in the case of an exchange, upon approving such plan of merger, consolidation or exchange, shall, by resolution, direct that the plan be submitted to a vote at a meeting of its shareholders, which may be either an annual or a special meeting. Written no-

tice shall be given to each shareholder of record, whether or not entitled to vote at such meeting, not less than twenty days before such meeting, in the manner provided in this Act for the giving of notice of meetings of shareholders, and, whether the meeting be an annual or a special meeting, shall state that the purpose or one of the purposes is to consider the proposed plan of merger, consolidation or exchange. A copy or a summary of the plan of merger, consolidation or exchange, as the case may be, shall be included in or enclosed with such notice.

(b)   At each such meeting, a vote of the shareholders shall be taken on the proposed plan. The plan shall be approved upon receiving the affirmative vote of the holders of a majority of the shares entitled to vote thereon of each such corporation, unless any class of shares of any such corporation is entitled to vote thereon as a class, in which event, as to such corporation, the plan shall be approved upon receiving the affirmative vote of the holders of a majority of the shares of each class of shares entitled to vote thereon as a class and of the total shares entitled to vote thereon. Any class of shares of any such corporation shall be entitled to vote as a class if any such plan contains any provision which, if contained in a proposed amendment to articles of incorporation, would entitle such class of shares to vote as a class and, in the case of an exchange, if the class is included in the exchange.

(c)   After such approval by a vote of the shareholders of each such corporation, and at any time prior to the filing of the articles of merger, consolidation or exchange, the merger, consolidation or exchange may be abandoned pursuant to provisions therefor, if any, set forth in the plan.

(d)   (1)Notwithstanding the provisions of subsections (a) and (b), submission of a plan of merger to a vote at a meeting of shareholders of a surviving corporation shall not be required if:

(i) the articles of incorporation of the surviving corporation do not differ except in name from those of the corporation before the merger,

(ii) each holder of shares of the surviving corporation which were outstanding immediately before the effective date of the merger is to hold the same number of shares with identical rights immediately after,

(iii) the number of voting shares outstanding immediately after the merger, plus the number of voting shares issuable on conversion of other securities issued by virtue of the terms of the merger and on exercise of rights and warrants so issued, will not exceed by more than 20 percent the number of voting shares outstanding immediately before the merger, and

(iv) the number of participating shares outstanding immediately after the merger, plus the number of participating shares issuable on conversion of other securities issued by virtue of the terms of the merger and on exercise of rights and warrants so issued, will not exceed by more than 20 percent the number of participating shares outstanding immediately before the merger.

(2) As used in this subsection:

(i) "voting shares" means shares which entitle their holders to vote unconditionally in elections of directors;

(ii) "participating shares" means shares which entitle their holders to participate without limitation in distribution of earnings or surplus.

§ 74. Articles of Merger, Consolidation or Exchange

(a) Upon receiving the approvals required by Sections 71, 72 and 73, articles of merger or articles of consolidation shall be executed in duplicate by each corporation by its president or a vice president and by its secretary or an assistant secretary, and verified by one of the officers of each corporation signing such articles, and shall set forth:

(1) The plan of merger or the plan of consolidation;

(2) As to each corporation, either (i) the number of shares outstanding, and, if the shares of any class are entitled to vote as a class, the designation and number of outstanding shares of each such class, or (ii) a statement that the vote of shareholders is not required by virtue of subsection 73(d);

(3) As to each corporation the approval of whose shareholders is required, the number of shares voted for and against such plan, respectively, and, if the shares of any class are entitled to vote as a class, the number of shares of each such class voted for and against such plan, respectively.

(b)   Duplicate originals of the articles of merger, consolidation or exchange shall be delivered to the Secretary of State. If the Secretary of State finds that such articles conform to law, he shall, when all fees and franchise taxes have been paid as in this Act prescribed:

(1) Endorse on each of such duplicate originals the word "Filed," and the month, day and year of the filing thereof.

(2) File one of such duplicate originals in his office.

(3) Issue a certificate of merger, consolidation or exchange to which he shall affix the other duplicate original.

(c) The certificate of merger, consolidation or exchange together with the duplicate original of the articles affixed thereto by the Secretary of State, shall be returned to the surviving, new or acquiring corporation, as the case may be, or its representative.

§ 75. Merger of Subsidiary Corporation

Any corporation owning at least ninety per cent of the outstanding shares of each class of another corporation may merge such other corporation into itself without approval by a vote of the shareholders of either corporation. Its board of directors shall, by resolution, approve a plan of merger setting forth:

(A)   The name of the subsidiary corporation and the name of the corporation owning at least ninety per cent of its shares, which is hereinafter designated as the surviving corporation.

(B)   The manner and basis of converting the shares of the subsidiary corporation into shares, obligations or other securities of the surviving corporation or of any other corporation or, in whole or in part, into cash or other property.

A copy of such plan of merger shall be mailed to each shareholder of record of the subsidiary corporation.

Articles of merger shall be executed in duplicate by the surviving corporation by its president or a vice president and by its secretary or an assistant secretary, and verified by one of its officers signing such articles, and shall set forth:

(a)   The plan of merger;

(b)   The number of outstanding shares of each class of the subsidiary corporation and the number of such shares of each class owned by the surviving corporation; and

(c)   The date of the mailing to shareholders of the subsidiary corporation of a copy of the plan of merger.

On and after the thirtieth day after the mailing of a copy of the plan of merger to shareholders of the subsidiary corporation or upon the waiver thereof by the holders of all outstanding shares duplicate originals of the articles of merger shall be delivered to the Secretary of State. If the Secretary of State finds that such articles conform to law, he shall, when all fees and franchise taxes have been paid as in this Act prescribed:

(1) Endorse on each of such duplicate originals the word "Filed," and the month, day and year of the filing thereof,

(2) File one of such duplicate originals in his office, and

(3) Issue a certificate of merger to which he shall affix the other duplicate original.

The certificate of merger, together with the duplicate original of the articles of merger affixed thereto by the Secretary of State, shall be returned to the surviving corporation or its representative.

§ 76. Effect of Merger, Consolidation or Exchange

Upon the issuance of the certificate of merger or the certificate of consolidation by the Secretary of State, the merger or consolidation shall be effected.

When such merger or consolidation has been effective:

(a) The several corporations parties to the plan of merger or consolidation shall be a single corporation, which, in the case of a merger, shall be that corporation designated in the plan of merger as the surviving corporation, and, in the case of a consolidation, shall be the new corporation provided for in the plan of consolidation.

(b) The separate existence of all corporations parties to the plan of merger or consolidation, except the surviving or new corporation, shall cease.

(c) Such surviving or new corporation shall have all the rights, privileges, immunities and powers and shall be subject to all the duties and liabilities of a corporation organized under this Act.

(d) Such surviving or new corporation shall thereupon and thereafter possess all the rights, privileges, immunities, and franchises, of a public as well as of a private nature, of each of the merging or consolidating corporations; and all property, real, personal and mixed, and all debts due on whatever account, including subscriptions to shares, and all other choses in action, and all and every other interest of or belonging to or due to each of the corporations so merged or consolidated, shall be taken and deemed to be transferred to and vested in such single corpora-

tion without further act or deed; and the title to any real estate, or any interest therein, vested in any of such corporations shall not revert or be in any way impaired by reason of such merger or consolidation.

(e) Such surviving or new corporation shall thenceforth be responsible and liable for all the liabilities and obligations of each of the corporations so merged or consolidated; and any claim existing or action or proceeding pending by or against any of such corporations may be prosecuted as if such merger or consolidation had not taken place, or such surviving or new corporation may be substituted in its place. Neither the rights of creditors nor any liens upon the property of any such corporation shall be impaired by such merger or consolidation.

(f) In the case of a merger, the articles of incorporation of the surviving corporation shall be deemed to be amended to the extent, if any, that changes in its articles of incorporation are stated in the plan of merger; and, in the case of a consolidation, the statements set forth in the articles of consolidation and which are required or permitted to be set forth in the articles of incorporation of corporations organized under this Act shall be deemed to be the original articles of incorporation of the new corporation.

§ 77. Merger, Consolidation or Exchange of Shares Between Domestic and Foreign Corporations

One or more foreign corporations and one or more domestic corporations may be merged or consolidated in the following manner, if such merger or consolidation is permitted by the laws of the state under which each such foreign corporation is organized:

(a) Each domestic corporation shall comply with the provisions of this Act with respect to the merger or consolidation, as the case may be, of domestic corporations and each foreign corporation shall comply with the applicable provisions of the laws of the state under which it is organized.

(b) If the surviving or new corporation, as the case may be, is to be governed by the laws of any state other than this State, it shall comply with the provisions of this Act with respect to foreign corporations if it is to transact business in this State, and in every case it shall file with the Secretary of State of this State:

(1) An agreement that it may be served with process in this State in any proceeding for the enforcement of any obligation of any domestic corporation which is a party to such merger or

consolidation and in any proceeding for the enforcement of the rights of a dissenting shareholder of any such domestic corporation against the surviving or new corporation;

(2)   An irrevocable appointment of the Secretary of State of this State as its agent to accept service of process in any such proceeding; and

(3)   An agreement that it will promptly pay to the dissenting shareholders of any such domestic corporation the amount, if any, to which they shall be entitled under the provisions of this Act with respect to the rights of dissenting shareholders.

The effect of such merger or consolidation shall be the same as in the case of the merger or consolidation of domestic corporations, if the surviving or new corporation is to be governed by the laws of this State. If the surviving or new corporation is to be governed by the laws of any state other than this State, the effect of such merger or consolidation shall be the same as in the case of the merger or consolidation of domestic corporations except insofar as the laws of such other state provide otherwise.

At any time prior to the filing of the articles of merger or consolidation, the merger or consolidation may be abandoned pursuant to provisions therefor, if any, set forth in the plan of merger or consolidation.

§ 78. Sale of Assets in Regular Course of Business and Mortgage or Pledge of Assets

The sale, lease, exchange, or other disposition of all, or substantially all, the property and assets of a corporation in the usual and regular course of its business and the mortgage or pledge of any or all property and assets of a corporation whether or not in the usual and regular course of business may be made upon such terms and conditions and for such consideration, which may consist in whole or in part of cash or other property, including shares, obligations or other securities of any other corporation, domestic or foreign, as shall be authorized by its board of directors; and in any such case no authorization or consent of the shareholders shall be required.

§ 79. Sale of Assets Other Than in Regular Course of Business

A sale, lease, exchange, or other disposition of all, or substantially all, the property and assets, with or without the good will, of a corporation, if not in the usual and regular course of its business, may be made upon such terms and conditions and for such consideration, which may consist in whole or in part of cash or other property, including shares, obligations or other securities of any other corporation, domestic or foreign, as may be authorized in the following manner:

(a)   The board of directors shall adopt a resolution recommending such sale, lease, exchange, or other disposition and directing the submission thereof to a vote at a meeting of shareholders, which may be either an annual or a special meeting.

(b)   Written notice shall be given to each shareholder of record, whether or not entitled to vote at such meeting, not less than twenty days before such meeting, in the manner provided in this Act for the giving of notice of meetings of shareholders, and, whether the meeting be an annual or a special meeting, shall state that the purpose, or one of the purposes is to consider the proposed sale, lease, exchange, or other disposition.

(c)   At such meeting the shareholders may authorize such sale, lease, exchange, or other disposition and may fix, or may authorize the board of directors to fix, any or all of the terms and conditions thereof and the consideration to be received by the corporation therefor. Such authorization shall require the affirmative vote of the holders of a majority of the shares of the corporation entitled to vote thereon, unless any class of shares is entitled to vote thereon as a class, in which event such authorization shall require the affirmative vote of the holders of a majority of the shares of each class of shares entitled to vote as a class thereon and of the total shares entitled to vote thereon.

(d)   After such authorization by a vote of shareholders, the board of directors nevertheless, in its discretion, may abandon such sale, lease, exchange, or other disposition of assets, subject to the rights of third parties under any contracts relating thereto, without further action or approval by shareholders.

§ 80. Right of Shareholders to Dissent and Obtain Payment for Shares

(a)   Any shareholder of a corporation shall have the right to dissent from, and to obtain payment for his shares in the event of, any of the following corporate actions:

(1)   Any plan of merger or consolidation to which the corporation is a party, except as provided in subsection (c);

(2)   Any sale or exchange of all or substantially all of the property and assets of the corporation not

made in the usual or regular course of its business, including a sale in dissolution, but not including a sale pursuant to an order of a court having jurisdiction in the premises or a sale for cash on terms requiring that all or substantially all of the net proceeds of sale be distributed to the shareholders in accordance with their respective interests within one year after the date of sale;

(3) Any plan of exchange to which the corporation is a party as the corporation the shares of which are to be acquired;

(4) Any amendment of the articles of incorporation which materially and adversely affects the rights appurtenant to the shares of the dissenting shareholder in that it:

(i) alters or abolishes a preferential right of such shares;

(ii) creates, alters or abolishes a right in respect of the redemption of such shares, including a provision respecting a sinking fund for the redemption or repurchase of such shares;

(iii) alters or abolishes a preemptive right of the holder of such shares to acquire shares or other securities;

(iv) excludes or limits the right of the holder of such shares to vote on any matter, or to cumulate his votes, except as such right may be limited by dilution through the issuance of shares or other securities with similar voting rights; or

(5) Any other corporate action taken pursuant to a shareholder vote with respect to which the articles of incorporation, the bylaws, or a resolution of the board of directors directs that dissenting shareholders shall have a right to obtain payment for their shares.

(b) (1) A record holder of shares may assert dissenters' rights as to less than all of the shares registered in his name only if he dissents with respect to all the shares beneficially owned by any one person, and discloses the name and address of the person or persons on whose behalf he dissents. In that event, his rights shall be determined as if the shares as to which he has dissented and his other shares were registered in the names of different shareholders.

(2) A beneficial owner of shares who is not the record holder may assert dissenters' rights with respect to shares held on his behalf, and shall be treated as a dissenting shareholder under the

terms of this section and section 81 if he submits to the corporation at the time of or before the assertion of these rights a written consent of the record holder.

(c) The right to obtain payment under this section shall not apply to the shareholders of the surviving corporation in a merger if a vote of the shareholders of such corporation is not necessary to authorize such merger.

(d) A shareholder of a corporation who has a right under this section to obtain payment for his shares shall have no right at law or in equity to attack the validity of the corporate action that gives rise to his right to obtain payment, nor to have the action set aside or rescinded, except when the corporate action is unlawful or fraudulent with regard to the complaining shareholder or to the corporation.

§ 81. Procedures for Protection of Dissenters' Rights

(a) As used in this section:

(1) "Dissenter" means a shareholder or beneficial owner who is entitled to and does assert dissenters' rights under section 80, and who has performed every act required up to the time involved for the assertion of such rights.

(2) "Corporation" means the issuer of the shares held by the dissenter before the corporate action, or the successor by merger or consolidation of that issuer.

(3) "Fair value" of shares means their value immediately before the effectuation of the corporate action to which the dissenter objects, excluding any appreciation or depreciation in anticipation of such corporate action unless such exclusion would be inequitable.

(4) "Interest" means interest from the effective date of the corporate action until the date of payment, at the average rate currently paid by the corporation on its principal bank loans, or, if none, at such rate as is fair and equitable under all the circumstances.

(b) If a proposed corporate action which would give rise to dissenters' rights under section 80(a) is submitted to a vote at a meeting of shareholders, the notice of meeting shall notify all shareholders that they have or may have a right to dissent and obtain payment for their shares by complying with the terms of this section, and shall be accompanied by a copy of sections 80 and 81 of this Act.

(c)   If the proposed corporate action is submitted to a vote at a meeting of shareholders, any shareholder who wishes to dissent and obtain payment for his shares must file with the corporation, prior to the vote, a written notice of intention to demand that he be paid fair compensation for his shares if the proposed action is effectuated, and shall refrain from voting his shares in approval of such action. A shareholder who fails in either respect shall acquire no right to payment for his shares under this section or section 80.

(d)   If the proposed corporate action is approved by the required vote at a meeting of shareholders, the corporation shall mail a further notice to all shareholders who gave due notice of intention to demand payment and who refrained from voting in favor of the proposed action. If the proposed corporate action is to be taken without a vote of shareholders, the corporation shall send to all shareholders who are entitled to dissent and demand payment for their shares a notice of the adoption of the plan of corporate action. The notice shall (1) state where and when a demand for payment must be sent and certificates of certificated shares must be deposited in order to obtain payment, (2) inform holders of uncertificated shares to what extent transfer of shares will be restricted from the time that demand for payment is received, (3) supply a form for demanding payment which includes a request for certification of the date on which the shareholder, or the person on whose behalf the shareholder dissents, acquired beneficial ownership of the shares, and (4) be accompanied by a copy of sections 80 and 81 of this Act. The time set for the demand and deposit shall be not less than 30 days from the mailing of the notice.

(e)   A shareholder who fails to demand payment, or fails (in the case of certificated shares) to deposit certificates, as required by a notice pursuant to subsection (d) shall have no right under this section or section 80 to receive payment for his shares. If the shares are not represented by certificates, the corporation may restrict their transfer from the time of receipt of demand for payment until effectuation of the proposed corporate action, or the release of restrictions under the terms of subsection (f). The dissenter shall retain all other rights of a shareholder until these rights are modified by effectuation of the proposed corporate action.

(f)   (1) Within 60 days after the date set for demanding payment and depositing certificates, if the corporation has not effectuated the proposed corporate action and remitted payment for shares pursuant to paragraph (3), it shall return any certificates that have been deposited, and release uncertificated shares from any transfer restrictions imposed by reason of the demand for payment.

(2)   When uncertificated shares have been released from transfer restrictions, and deposited certificates have been returned, the corporation may at any later time send a new notice conforming to the requirements of subsection (d), with like effect.

(3)   Immediately upon effectuation of the proposed corporate action, or upon receipt of demand for payment if the corporate action has already been effectuated, the corporation shall remit to dissenters who have made demand and (if their shares are certificated) have deposited their certificates the amount which the corporation estimates to be the fair value of the shares, with interest if any has accrued. The remittance shall be accompanied by:

(i)   the corporation's closing balance sheet and statement of income for a fiscal year ending not more than 16 months before the date of remittance, together with the latest available interim financial statements;

(ii)   a statement of the corporation's estimate of fair value of the shares; and

(iii)   a notice of the dissenter's right to demand supplemental payment, accompanied by a copy of sections 80 and 81 of this Act.

(g)   (1) If the corporation fails to remit as required by subsection (f), or if the dissenter believes that the amount remitted is less than the fair value of his shares, or that the interest is not correctly determined, he may send the corporation his own estimate of the value of the shares or of the interest, and demand payment of the deficiency.

(2)   If the dissenter does not file such an estimate within 30 days after the corporation's mailing of its remittance, he shall be entitled to no more than the amount remitted.

(h)   (1) Within 60 days after receiving a demand for payment pursuant to subsection (g), if any such demands for payment remain unsettled, the corporation shall file in an appropriate court a petition requesting that the fair value of the shares and interest thereon be determined by the court.

(2) An appropriate court shall be a court of competent jurisdiction in the county of this state where the registered office of the corporation is located. If, in the case of a merger or consolidation or exchange of shares, the corporation is a foreign corporation without a registered office in this state, the petition shall be filed in the county where the registered office of the domestic corporation was last located.

(3) All dissenters, wherever residing, whose demands have not been settled shall be made parties to the proceeding as in an action against their shares. A copy of the petition shall be served on each such dissenter; if a dissenter is a nonresident, the copy may be served on him by registered or certified mail or by publication as provided by law.

(4) The jurisdiction of the court shall be plenary and exclusive. The court may appoint one or more persons as appraisers to receive evidence and recommend a decision on the question of fair value. The appraisers shall have such power and authority as shall be specified in the order of their appointment or in any amendment thereof. The dissenters shall be entitled to discovery in the same manner as parties in other civil suits.

(5) All dissenters who are made parties shall be entitled to judgment for the amount by which the fair value of their shares is found to exceed the amount previously remitted, with interest.

(6) If the corporation fails to file a petition as provided in paragraph (1) of this subsection, each dissenter who made a demand and who has not already settled his claim against the corporation shall be paid by the corporation the amount demanded by him, with interest, and may sue therefor in an appropriate court.

(i) (1) The costs and expenses of any proceeding under subsection (h), including the reasonable compensation and expenses of appraisers appointed by the court, shall be determined by the court and assessed against the corporation, except that any part of the costs and expenses may be apportioned and assessed as the court may deem equitable against all or some of the dissenters who are parties and whose action in demanding supplemental payment the court finds to be arbitrary, vexatious, or not in good faith.

(2) Fees and expenses of counsel and of experts for the respective parties may be assessed as the court may deem equitable against the corporation and in favor of any or all dissenters if the corporation failed to comply substantially with the requirements of this section, and may be assessed against either the corporation or a dissenter, in favor of any other party, if the court finds that the party against whom the fees and expenses are assessed acted arbitrarily, vexatiously, or not in good faith in respect to the rights provided by this Section and Section 80.

(3) If the court finds that the services of counsel for any dissenter were of substantial benefit to other dissenters similarly situated, and should not be assessed against the corporation, it may award to these counsel reasonable fees to be paid out of the amounts awarded to the dissenters who were benefitted.

(j) (1) Notwithstanding the foregoing provisions of this section, the corporation may elect to withhold the remittance required by subsection (f) from any dissenter with respect to shares of which the dissenter (or the person on whose behalf the dissenter acts) was not the beneficial owner on the date of the first announcement to news media or to shareholders of the terms of the proposed corporate action. With respect to such shares, the corporation shall, upon effectuating the corporate action, state to each dissenter its estimate of the fair value of the shares, state the rate of interest to be used (explaining the basis thereof), and offer to pay the resulting amounts on receiving the dissenter's agreement to accept them in full satisfaction.

(2) If the dissenter believes that the amount offered is less than the fair value of the shares and interest determined according to this section, he may within 30 days after the date of mailing of the corporation's offer, mail the corporation his own estimate of fair value and interest, and demand their payment. If the dissenter fails to do so, he shall be entitled to no more than the corporation's offer.

(3) If the dissenter makes a demand as provided in paragraph (2), the provisions of subsections (h) and (i) shall apply to further proceedings on the dissenter's demand.

§ 82. Voluntary Dissolution by Incorporators

A corporation which has not commenced business and which has not issued any shares, may be voluntarily dissolved by its incorporators at any time in the following manner:

(a)　Articles of dissolution shall be executed in duplicate by a majority of the incorporators, and verified by them, and shall set forth:

(1)　The name of the corporation.

(2)　The date of issuance of its certificate of incorporation.

(3)　That none of its shares has been issued.

(4)　That the corporation has not commenced business.

(5)　That the amount, if any, actually paid in on subscriptions for its shares, less any part thereof disbursed for necessary expenses, has been returned to those entitled thereto.

(6)　That no debts of the corporation remain unpaid.

(7)　That a majority of the incorporators elect that the corporation be dissolved.

(b)　Duplicate originals of the articles of dissolution shall be delivered to the Secretary of State. If the Secretary of State finds that the articles of dissolution conform to law, he shall, when all fees and franchise taxes have been paid as in this Act prescribed:

(1)　Endorse on each of such duplicate originals the word "Filed," and the month, day and year of the filing thereof.

(2)　File one of such duplicate originals in his office.

(3)　Issue a certificate of dissolution to which he shall affix the other duplicate original.

The certificate of dissolution, together with the duplicate original of the articles of dissolution affixed thereto by the Secretary of State, shall be returned to the incorporators or their representative. Upon the issuance of such certificate of dissolution by the Secretary of State, the existence of the corporation shall cease.

§ 83. Voluntary Dissolution by Consent of Shareholders

A corporation may be voluntarily dissolved by the written consent of all of its shareholders.

Upon the execution of such written consent, a statement of intent to dissolve shall be executed in duplicate by the corporation by its president or a vice president and by its secretary or an assistant secretary, and verified by one of the officers signing such statement, which statement shall set forth:

(a)　The name of the corporation.

(b)　The names and respective addresses of its officers.

(c)　The names and respective addresses of its directors.

(d)　A copy of the written consent signed by all shareholders of the corporation.

(e)　A statement that such written consent has been signed by all shareholders of the corporation or signed in their names by their attorneys thereunto duly authorized.

§ 84. Voluntary Dissolution by Act of Corporation

A corporation may be dissolved by the act of the corporation, when authorized in the following manner:

(a)　The board of directors shall adopt a resolution recommending that the corporation be dissolved, and directing that the question of such dissolution be submitted to a vote at a meeting of shareholders, which may be either an annual or a special meeting.

(b)　Written notice shall be given to each shareholder of record entitled to vote at such meeting within the time and in the manner provided in this Act for the giving of notice of meetings of shareholders, and, whether the meeting be an annual or special meeting, shall state that the purpose, or one of the purposes, of such meeting is to consider the advisability of dissolving the corporation.

(c)　At such meeting a vote of shareholders entitled to vote thereat shall be taken on a resolution to dissolve the corporation. Such resolution shall be adopted upon receiving the affirmative vote of the holders of a majority of the shares of the corporation entitled to vote thereon, unless any class of shares is entitled to vote thereon as a class, in which event the resolution shall be adopted upon receiving the affirmative vote of the holders of a majority of the shares of each class of shares entitled to vote thereon as a class and of the total shares entitled to vote thereon.

(d)   Upon the adoption of such resolution, a statement of intent to dissolve shall be executed in duplicate by the corporation by its president or a vice president and by its secretary or an assistant secretary, and verified by one of the officers signing such statement, which statement shall set forth:

(1)   The name of the corporation.
(2)   The names and respective addresses of its officers.
(3)   The names and respective addresses of its directors.
(4)   A copy of the resolution adopted by the shareholders authorizing the dissolution of the corporation.
(5)   The number of shares outstanding, and, if the shares of any class are entitled to vote as a class, the designation and number of outstanding shares of each such class.
(6)   The number of shares voted for and against the resolution, respectively, and, if the shares of any class are entitled to vote as a class, the number of shares of each such class voted for and against the resolution, respectively.

§ 85. Filing of Statement of Intent to Dissolve

Duplicate originals of the statement of intent to dissolve, whether by consent of shareholders or by act of the corporation, shall be delivered to the Secretary of State. If the Secretary of State finds that such statement conforms to law, he shall, when all fees and franchise taxes have been paid as in this Act prescribed:

(a)   Endorse on each of such duplicate originals the word "Filed," and the month, day and year of the filing thereof.

(b)   File one of such duplicate originals in his office.

(c)   Return the other duplicate original to the corporation or its representative.

§ 86. Effect of Statement of Intent to Dissolve

Upon the filing by the Secretary of State of a statement of intent to dissolve, whether by consent of shareholders or by act of the corporation, the corporation shall cease to carry on its business, except insofar as may be necessary for the winding up thereof,

but its corporate existence shall continue until a certificate of dissolution has been issued by the Secretary of State or until a decree dissolving the corporation has been entered by a court of competent jurisdiction as in this Act provided.

§ 87. Procedure after Filing of Statement of Intent to Dissolve

After the filing by the Secretary of State of a statement of intent to dissolve:

(a)   The corporation shall immediately cause notice thereof to be mailed to each known creditor of the corporation.

(b)   The corporation shall proceed to collect its assets, convey and dispose of such of its properties as are not to be distributed in kind to its shareholders, pay, satisfy and discharge its liabilities and obligations and do all other acts required to liquidate its business and affairs, and, after paying or adequately providing for the payment of all its obligations, distribute the remainder of its assets, either in cash or in kind, among its shareholders according to their respective rights and interests.

(c)   The corporation, at any time during the liquidation of its business and affairs, may make application to a court of competent jurisdiction within the state and judicial subdivision in which the registered office or principal place of business of the corporation is situated, to have the liquidation continued under the supervision of the court as provided in this Act.

§ 88. Revocation of Voluntary Dissolution Proceedings by Consent of Shareholders

By the written consent of all of its shareholders, a corporation may, at any time prior to the issuance of a certificate of dissolution by the Secretary of State, revoke voluntary dissolution proceedings theretofore taken, in the following manner:

Upon the execution of such written consent, a statement of revocation of voluntary dissolution proceedings shall be executed in duplicate by the corporation by its president or a vice president and by its secretary or an assistant secretary, and verified by one of the officers signing such statement, which statement shall set forth:

(a)   The name of the corporation.

(b)   The names and respective addresses of its officers.

(c)   The names and respective addresses of its directors.

(d)   A copy of the written consent signed by all shareholders of the corporation revoking such voluntary dissolution proceedings.

(e)   That such written consent has been signed by all shareholders of the corporation or signed in their names by their attorneys thereunto duly authorized.

§ 89. Revocation of Voluntary Dissolution Proceedings by Act of Corporation

By the act of the corporation, a corporation may, at any time prior to the issuance of a certificate of dissolution by the Secretary of State, revoke voluntary dissolution proceedings theretofore taken, in the following manner:

(a)   The board of directors shall adopt a resolution recommending that the voluntary dissolution proceedings be revoked, and directing that the question of such revocation be submitted to a vote at a special meeting of shareholders.

(b)   Written notice, stating that the purpose or one of the purposes of such meeting is to consider the advisability of revoking the voluntary dissolution proceedings, shall be given to each shareholder of record entitled to vote at such meeting within the time and in the manner provided in this Act for the giving of notice of special meetings of shareholders.

(c)   At such meeting a vote of the shareholders entitled to vote thereat shall be taken on a resolution to revoke the voluntary dissolution proceedings, which shall require for its adoption the affirmative vote of the holders of a majority of the shares entitled to vote thereon.

(d)   Upon the adoption of such resolution, a statement of revocation of voluntary dissolution proceedings shall be executed in duplicate by the corporation by its president or a vice president and by its secretary or an assistant secretary, and verified by one of the officers signing such statement, which statement shall set forth:

(1)   The name of the corporation.
(2)   The names and respective addresses of its officers.
(3)   The names and respective addresses of its directors.

(4)   A copy of the resolution adopted by the shareholders revoking the voluntary dissolution proceedings.
(5)   The number of shares outstanding.
(6)   The number of shares voted for and against the resolution, respectively.

§ 90. Filing of Statement of Revocation of Voluntary Dissolution Proceedings

Duplicate originals of the statement of revocation of voluntary dissolution proceedings, whether by consent of shareholders or by act of the corporation, shall be delivered to the Secretary of State. If the Secretary of State finds that such statement conforms to law, he shall, when all fees and franchise taxes have been paid as in this Act prescribed:

(a)   Endorse on each of such duplicate originals the word "Filed," and the month, day and year of the filing thereof.

(b)   File one of such duplicate originals in his office.

(c)   Return the other duplicate original to the corporation or its representative.

§ 91. Effect of Statement of Revocation of Voluntary Dissolution Proceedings

Upon the filing by the Secretary of State of a statement of revocation of voluntary dissolution proceedings, whether by consent of shareholders or by act of the corporation, the revocation of the voluntary dissolution proceedings shall become effective and the corporation may again carry on its business.

§ 92. Articles of Dissolution

If voluntary dissolution proceedings have not been revoked, then when all debts, liabilities and obligations of the corporation have been paid and discharged, or adequate provision has been made therefor, and all of the remaining property and assets of the corporation have been distributed to its shareholders, articles of dissolution shall be executed in duplicate by the corporation by its president or a vice president and by its secretary or an assistant secretary, and verified by one of the officers signing such statement, which statement shall set forth:

(a)   The name of the corporation.

(b)   That the Secretary of State has theretofore filed a statement of intent to dissolve the corporation, and the date on which such statement was filed.

(c)   That all debts, obligations and liabilities of the corporation have been paid and discharged or that adequate provision has been made therefor.

(d)   That all the remaining property and assets of the corporation have been distributed among its shareholders in accordance with their respective rights and interests.

(e)   That there are no suits pending against the corporation in any court, or that adequate provision has been made for the satisfaction of any judgment, order or decree which may be entered against it in any pending suit.

§ 93. Filing of Articles of Dissolution
Duplicate originals of such articles of dissolution shall be delivered to the Secretary of State. If the Secretary of State finds that such articles of dissolution conform to law, he shall, when all fees and franchise taxes have been paid as in this Act prescribed:

(a)   Endorse on each of such duplicate originals the word "Filed," and the month, day and year of the filing thereof.

(b)   File one of such duplicate originals in his office.

(c)   Issue a certificate of dissolution to which he shall affix the other duplicate original.

The certificate of dissolution, together with the duplicate original of the articles of dissolution affixed thereto by the Secretary of State, shall be returned to the representative of the dissolved corporation. Upon the issuance of such certificate of dissolution the existence of the corporation shall cease, except for the purpose of suits, other proceedings and appropriate corporate action by shareholders, directors and officers as provided in this Act.

§ 94. Involuntary Dissolution
A corporation may be dissolved involuntarily by a decree of the .... court in an action filed by the Attorney General when it is established that:

(a)   The corporation has failed to file its annual report within the time required by this Act, or has failed to pay its franchise tax on or before the first day of August of the year in which such franchise tax becomes due and payable; or

(b)   The corporation procured its articles of incorporation through fraud; or

(c)   The corporation has continued to exceed or abuse the authority conferred upon it by law; or

(d)   The corporation has failed for thirty days to appoint and maintain a registered agent in this State; or

(e)   The corporation has failed for thirty days after change of its registered office or registered agent to file in the office of the Secretary of State a statement of such change.

§ 95. Notification to Attorney General
The Secretary of State, on or before the last day of December of each year, shall certify to the Attorney General the names of all corporations which have failed to file their annual reports or to pay franchise taxes in accordance with the provisions of this Act, together with the facts pertinent thereto. He shall also certify, from time to time, the names of all corporations which have given other cause for dissolution as provided in this Act, together with the facts pertinent thereto. Whenever the Secretary of State shall certify the name of a corporation to the Attorney General as having given any cause for dissolution, the Secretary of State shall concurrently mail to the corporation at its registered office a notice that such certification has been made. Upon the receipt of such certification, the Attorney General shall file an action in the name of the State against such corporation for its dissolution. Every such certificate from the Secretary of State to the Attorney General pertaining to the failure of a corporation to file an annual report or pay a franchise tax shall be taken and received in all courts as prima facie evidence of the facts therein stated. If, before action is filed, the corporation shall file its annual report or pay its franchise tax, together with all penalties thereon, or shall appoint or maintain a registered agent as provided in this Act, or shall file with the Secretary of State the required statement of change of registered office or registered agent, such fact shall be forthwith certified by the Secretary of State to the Attorney General and he shall not file an action against such corporation for such cause. If, after action is filed, the corporation shall file its annual report or pay its franchise tax, together with all penalties thereon, or shall appoint or maintain a registered agent as provided in this Act, or shall file with the Secretary of State the required statement of change of registered office or registered agent, and shall pay the costs of such action, the action for such cause shall abate.

§ 96. Venue and Process
Every action for the involuntary dissolution of a corporation shall be commenced by the Attorney General either in the .... court of the county in which the

registered office of the corporation is situated, or in the .... court of .... county. Summons shall issue and be served as in other civil actions. If process is returned not found, the Attorney General shall cause publication to be made as in other civil cases in some newspaper published in the county where the registered office of the corporation is situated, containing a notice of the pendency of such action, the title of the court, the title of the action, and the date on or after which default may be entered. The Attorney General may include in one notice the names of any number of corporations against which actions are then pending in the same court. The Attorney General shall cause a copy of such notice to be mailed to the corporation at its registered office within ten days after the first publication thereof. The certificate of the Attorney General of the mailing of such notice shall be prima facie evidence thereof. Such notice shall be published at least once each week for two successive weeks, and the first publication thereof may begin at any time after the summons has been returned. Unless a corporation shall have been served with summons, no default shall be taken against it earlier than thirty days after the first publication of such notice.

§ 97. Jurisdiction of Court to Liquidate Assets and Business of Corporation

The .... courts shall have full power to liquidate the assets and business of a corporation:

(a)   In an action by a shareholder when it is established:

(1)   That the directors are deadlocked in the management of the corporate affairs and the shareholders are unable to break the deadlock, and that irreparable injury to the corporation is being suffered or is threatened by reason thereof; or

(2)   That the acts of the directors or those in control of the corporation are illegal, oppressive or fraudulent; or

(3)   That the shareholders are deadlocked in voting power, and have failed, for a period which includes at least two consecutive annual meeting dates, to elect successors to directors whose terms have expired or would have expired upon the election of their successors; or

(4)   That the corporate assets are being misapplied or wasted.

(b)   In an action by a creditor:

(1)   Then the claim of the creditor has been reduced to judgment and an execution thereon returned unsatisfied and it is established that the corporation is insolvent; or

(2)   When the corporation has admitted in writing that the claim of the creditor is due and owing and it is established that the corporation is insolvent.

(c)   Upon application by a corporation which has filed a statement of intent to dissolve, as provided in this Act, to have its liquidation continued under the supervision of the court.

(d)   When an action has been filed by the Attorney General to dissolve a corporation and it is established that liquidation of its business and affairs should precede the entry of a decree of dissolution.

Proceedings under clause (a), (b) or (c) of this section shall be brought in the county in which the registered office or the principal office of the corporation is situated.

It shall not be necessary to make shareholders parties to any such action or proceeding unless relief is sought against them personally.

§ 98. Procedure in Liquidation of Corporation by Court

In proceedings to liquidate the assets and business of a corporation the court shall have power to issue injunctions, to appoint a receiver or receivers pendente lite, with such powers and duties as the court, from time to time, may direct, and to take such other proceedings as may be requisite to preserve the corporate assets wherever situated, and carry on the business of the corporation until a full hearing can be had.

After a hearing had upon such notice as the court may direct to be given to all parties to the proceedings and to any other parties in interest designated by the court, the court may appoint a liquidating receiver or receivers with authority to collect the assets of the corporation, including all amounts owing to the corporation by subscribers on account of any unpaid portion of the consideration for the issuance of shares. Such liquidating receiver or receivers shall have authority, subject to the order of the court, to sell, convey and dispose of all or any part of the assets of the corporation wherever situated, either at public or private sale. The assets of the corporation or the proceeds resulting from a sale, conveyance or other disposition thereof shall be applied to the expenses of such liquidation and to the payment of the liabilities and obligations of the corporation, and any remaining assets or proceeds shall be distributed among its shareholders according to their respective rights and interests. The order appointing such liquidating receiver or receivers shall state their powers and duties. Such powers and duties may be increased or diminished at any time during the proceedings.

The court shall have power to allow from time to time as expenses of the liquidation compensation to the receiver or receivers and to attorneys in the proceeding, and to direct the payment thereof out of the assets of the corporation or the proceeds of any sale or disposition of such assets.

A receiver of a corporation appointed under the provisions of this section shall have authority to sue and defend in all courts in his own name as receiver of such corporation. The court appointing such receiver shall have exclusive jurisdiction of the corporation and its property, wherever situated.

§ 99. Qualifications of Receivers

A receiver shall in all cases be a natural person or a corporation authorized to act as receiver, which corporation may be a domestic corporation or a foreign corporation authorized to transact business in this State, and shall in all cases give such bond as the court may direct with such sureties as the court may require.

§ 100. Filing of Claims in Liquidation Proceedings

In proceedings to liquidate the assets and business of a corporation the court may require all creditors of the corporation to file with the clerk of the court or with the receiver, in such form as the court may prescribe, proofs under oath of their respective claims. If the court requires the filing of claims it shall fix a date, which shall be not less than four months from the date of the order, as the last day for the filing of claims, and shall prescribe the notice that shall be given to creditors and claimants of the date so fixed. Prior to the date so fixed, the court may extend the time for the filing of claims. Creditors and claimants failing to file proofs of claim on or before the date so fixed may be barred, by order of court, from participating in the distribution of the assets of the corporation.

§ 101. Discontinuance of Liquidation Proceedings

The liquidation of the assets and business of a corporation may be discontinued at any time during the liquidation proceedings when it is established that cause for liquidation no longer exists. In such event the court shall dismiss the proceedings and direct the receiver to redeliver to the corporation all its remaining property and assets.

§ 102. Decree of Involuntary Dissolution

In proceedings to liquidate the assets and business of a corporation, when the costs and expenses of such proceedings and all debts, obligations and liabilities of the corporation shall have been paid and discharged and all of its remaining property and assets distributed to its shareholders, or in case its property and assets are not sufficient to satisfy and discharge such costs, expenses, debts and obligations, all the property and assets have been applied so far as they will go to their payment, the court shall enter a decree dissolving the corporation, whereupon the existence of the corporation shall cease.

§ 103. Filing of Decree of Dissolution

In case the court shall enter a decree dissolving a corporation, it shall be the duty of the clerk of such court to cause a certified copy of the decree to be filed with the Secretary of State. No fee shall be charged by the Secretary of State for the filing thereof.

§ 104. Deposit with State Treasurer of Amount Due Certain Shareholders

Upon the voluntary or involuntary dissolution of a corporation, the portion of the assets distributable to a creditor or shareholder who is unknown or cannot be found, or who is under disability and there is no person legally competent to receive such distributive portion, shall be reduced to cash and deposited with the State Treasurer and shall be paid over to such creditor or shareholder or to his legal representative upon proof satisfactory to the State Treasurer of his right thereto.

§ 105. Survival of Remedy after Dissolution

The dissolution of a corporation either (1) by the issuance of a certificate of dissolution by the Secretary of State, or (2) by a decree of court when the court has not liquidated the assets and business of the corporation as provided in this Act, or (3) by expiration of its period of duration, shall not take away or impair any remedy available to or against such corporation, its directors, officers, or shareholders, for any right or claim existing, or any liability incurred, prior to such dissolution if action or other proceeding thereon is commenced within two years after the date of such dissolution. Any such action or proceeding by or against the corporation may be prosecuted or defended by the corporation in its corporate name. The shareholders, directors and officers shall have power to take such corporate or other action as shall be appropriate to protect such remedy, right or claim. If such corporation was dissolved by the expiration of its period of duration, such corporation may amend its articles of incorporation at any time during such period of two years so as to extend its period of duration.

§ 106. Admission of Foreign Corporation

No foreign corporation shall have the right to transact business in this State until it shall have procured a certificate of authority so to do from the Secretary of State. No foreign corporation shall be entitled to procure a certificate of authority under this Act to transact in this State any business which a corporation organized under this Act is not permitted to transact. A foreign corporation shall not be denied a certificate of authority by reason of the fact that the laws of the state or country under which such corporation is organized governing its organization and internal affairs differ from the laws of this State, and nothing in this Act contained shall be construed to authorize this State to regulate the organization or the internal affairs of such corporation.

Without excluding other activities which may not constitute transacting business in this State, a foreign corporation shall not be considered to be transacting business in this State, for the purposes of this Act, by reason of carrying on in this State any one or more of the following activities:

(a)   Maintaining or defending any action or suit or any administrative or arbitration proceeding, or effecting the settlement thereof or the settlement of claims or disputes.

(b)   Holding meetings of its directors or shareholders or carrying on other activities concerning its internal affairs.

(c)   Maintaining bank accounts.

(d)   Maintaining offices or agencies for the transfer, exchange and registration of its securities, or ap-

pointing and maintaining trustees or depositaries with relation to its securities.

(e)   Effecting sales through independent contractors.

(f)   Soliciting or procuring orders, whether by mail or through employees or agents or otherwise, where such orders require acceptance without this State before becoming binding contracts.

(g)   Creating as borrower or lender, or acquiring, indebtedness or mortgages or other security interests in real or personal property.

(h)   Securing or collecting debts or enforcing any rights in property securing the same.

(i)   Transacting any business in interstate commerce.

(j)   Conducting an isolated transaction completed within a period of thirty days and not in the course of a number of repeated transactions of like nature.

§ 107. Powers of Foreign Corporation

A foreign corporation which shall have received a certificate of authority under this Act shall, until a certificate of revocation or of withdrawal shall have been issued as provided in this Act, enjoy the same, but no greater, rights and privileges as a domestic corporation organized for the purposes set forth in the application pursuant to which such certificate of authority is issued; and, except as in this Act otherwise provided, shall be subject to the same duties, restrictions, penalties and liabilities now or hereafter imposed upon a domestic corporation of like character.

§ 108. Corporate Name of Foreign Corporation

No certificate of authority shall be issued to a foreign corporation unless the corporate name of such corporation:

(a)   Shall contain the word "corporation," "company," "incorporated," or "limited," or shall contain an abbreviation of one of such words, or such corporation shall, for use in this State, add at the end of its name one of such words or an abbreviation thereof.

(b)   Shall not contain any word or phrase which indicates or implies that it is organized for any purpose other than one or more of the purposes contained in its articles of incorporation or that it is authorized or empowered to conduct the business of banking or insurance.

(c) Shall not be the same as, or deceptively similar to, the name of any domestic corporation existing under the laws of this State or any foreign corporation authorized to transact business in this State, or a name the exclusive right to which is, at the time, reserved in the manner provided in this Act, or the name of a corporation which has in effect a registration of its name as provided in this Act except that this provision shall not apply if the foreign corporation applying for a certificate of authority files with the Secretary of State any one of the following:

(1) a resolution of its board of directors adopting a fictitious name for use in transacting business in this State which fictitious name is not deceptively similar to the name of any domestic corporation or of any foreign corporation authorized to transact business in this State or to any name reserved or registered as provided in this Act, or

(2) the written consent of such other corporation or holder of a reserved or registered name to use the same or deceptively similar name and one or more words are added to make such name distinguishable from such other name, or

(3) a certified copy of a final decree of a court of competent jurisdiction establishing the prior right of such foreign corporation to the use of such name in this State.

§ 109. Change of Name by Foreign Corporation

Whenever a foreign corporation which is authorized to transact business in this State shall change its name to one under which a certificate of authority would not be granted to it on application therefor, the certificate of authority of such corporation shall be suspended and it shall not thereafter transact any business in this State until it has changed its name to a name which is available to it under the laws of this State or has otherwise complied with the provisions of this Act.

§ 110. Application for Certificate of Authority

A foreign corporation, in order to procure a certificate of authority to transact business in this State, shall make application therefor to the Secretary of State, which application shall set forth:

(a) The name of the corporation and the state or county under the laws of which it is incorporated.

(b) If the name of the corporation does not contain the word "corporation," "company," "incorporated," or "limited," or does not contain an abbreviation of one of such words, then the name of the corporation with the word or abbreviation which it elects to add thereto for use in this State.

(c) The date of incorporation and the period of duration of the corporation.

(d) The address of the principal office of the corporation in the state or country under the laws of which it is incorporated.

(e) The address of the proposed registered office of the corporation in this State, and the name of its proposed registered agent in this State at such address.

(f) The purpose or purposes of the corporation which it proposes to pursue in the transaction of business in this State.

(g) The names and respective addresses of the directors and officers of the corporation.

(h) A statement of the aggregate number of shares which the corporation has authority to issue, itemized by classes and series, if any, within a class.

(i) A statement of the aggregate number of issued shares, itemized by class and by series, if any, within each class.

(j) An estimate, expressed in dollars, of the value of all property to be owned by the corporation for the following year, wherever located, and an estimate of the value of the property of the corporation to be located within the State during such year, and an estimate, expressed in dollars of the gross amount of business which will be transacted by the corporation during such year, and an estimate of the gross amount thereof which will be transacted by the corporation at or from places of business in this State during such year.

(k) Such additional information as may be necessary or appropriate in order to enable the Secretary of State to determine whether such corporation is entitled to a certificate of authority to transact business in this State and to determine and assess the fees and franchise taxes payable as in this Act prescribed.

Such application shall be made on forms prescribed and furnished by the Secretary of State and shall be executed in duplicate by the corporation by its president or a vice president and by its secretary or an assistant secretary, and verified by one of the officers signing such application.

§ 111. Filing of Application for Certificate of Authority

Duplicate originals of the application of the corporation for a certificate of authority shall be delivered to the Secretary of State, together with a copy of its articles of incorporation and all amendments thereto, duly authenticated by the proper officer of the state or country under the laws of which it is incorporated.

If the Secretary of State finds that such application conforms to law, he shall, when all fees and franchise taxes have been paid as in this Act prescribed:

(a)   Endorse on each of such documents the word "Filed," and the month, day and year of the filing thereof.

(b)   File in his office one of such duplicate originals of the application and the copy of the articles of incorporation and amendments thereto.

(c)   Issue a certificate of authority to transact business in this State to which he shall affix the other duplicate original application.

The certificate of authority, together with the duplicate original of the application affixed thereto by the Secretary of State, shall be returned to the corporation or its representative.

§ 112. Effect of Certificate of Authority

Upon the issuance of a certificate of authority by the Secretary of State, the corporation shall be authorized to transact business in this State for those purposes set forth in its application, subject, however, to the right of this State to suspend or to revoke such authority as provided in this Act.

§ 113. Registered Office and Registered Agent of Foreign Corporation

Each foreign corporation authorized to transact business in this State shall have and continuously maintain in this State:

(a)   A registered office which may be, but need not be, the same as its place of business in this State.

(b)   A registered agent, which agent may be either an individual resident in this State whose business office is identical with such registered office, or a do-mestic corporation, or a foreign corporation authorized to transact business in this State, having a business office identical with such registered office.

§ 114. Change of Registered Office or Registered Agent of Foreign Corporation

A foreign corporation authorized to transact business in this State may change its registered office or change its registered agent, or both, upon filing in the office of the Secretary of State a statement setting forth:

(a)   The name of the corporation.

(b)   The address of its then registered office.

(c)   If the address of its registered office be changed, the address to which the registered office is to be changed.

(d)   The name of its then registered agent.

(e)   If its registered agent be changed, the name of its successor registered agent.

(f)   That the address of its registered office and the address of the business office of its registered agent, as changed, will be identical.

(g)   That such change was authorized by resolution duly adopted by its board of directors.

Such statement shall be executed by the corporation by its president or a vice president, and verified by him, and delivered to the Secretary of State. If the Secretary of State finds that such statement conforms to the provisions of this Act, he shall file such statement in his office, and upon such filing the change of address of the registered office, or the appointment of a new registered agent, or both, as the case may be, shall become effective.

Any registered agent of a foreign corporation may resign as such agent upon filing a written notice thereof, executed in duplicate, with the Secretary of State, who shall forthwith mail a copy thereof to the corporation at its principal office in the state or country under the laws of which it is incorporated. The appointment of such agent shall terminate upon the expiration of thirty days after receipt of such notice by the Secretary of State.

If a registered agent changes his or its business address to another place within the same .... *, he or it may change such address and the address of the registered office of any corporation of which he or it

---

*Supply designation of jurisdiction, such as county, etc., in accordance with local practice.

is registered agent by filing a statement as required above except that it need be signed only by the registered agent and need not be responsive to (e) or (g) and must recite that a copy of the statement has been mailed to the corporation.

§ 115. Service of Process on Foreign Corporation

The registered agent so appointed by a foreign corporation authorized to transact business in this State shall be an agent of such corporation upon whom any process, notice or demand required or permitted by law to be served upon the corporation may be served.

Whenever a foreign corporation authorized to transact business in this State shall fail to appoint or maintain a registered agent in this State, or whenever any such registered agent cannot with reasonable diligence be found at the registered office, or whenever the certificate of authority of a foreign corporation shall be suspended or revoked, then the Secretary of State shall be an agent of such corporation upon whom any such process, notice, or demand may be served. Service on the Secretary of State of any such process, notice or demand shall be made by delivering to and leaving with him, or with any clerk having charge of the corporation department of his office, duplicate copies of such process, notice or demand. In the event any such process, notice or demand is served on the Secretary of State, he shall immediately cause one of such copies thereof to be forwarded by registered mail, addressed to the corporation at its principal office in the state or country under the laws of which it is incorporated. Any service so had on the Secretary of State shall be returnable in not less than thirty days.

The Secretary of State shall keep a record of all processes, notices and demands served upon him under this section, and shall record therein the time of such service and his action with reference thereto.

Nothing herein contained shall limit or affect the right to serve any process, notice or demand, required or permitted by law to be served upon a foreign corporation in any other manner now or hereafter permitted by law.

§ 116. Amendment to Articles of Incorporation of Foreign Corporation

Whenever the articles of incorporation of a foreign corporation authorized to transact business in this State are amended, such foreign corporation shall, within thirty days after such amendment becomes ef-

fective, file in the office of the Secretary of State a copy of such amendment duly authenticated by the proper officer of the state or country under the laws of which it is incorporated; but the filing thereof shall not of itself enlarge or alter the purpose or purposes which such corporation is authorized to pursue in the transaction of business in this State, nor authorize such corporation to transact business in this State under any other name than the name set forth in its certificate of authority.

§ 117. Merger of Foreign Corporation Authorized to Transact Business in This State

Whenever a foreign corporation authorized to transact business in this State shall be a party to a statutory merger permitted by the laws of the state or country under the laws of which it is incorporated, and such corporation shall be the surviving corporation, it shall, within thirty days after such merger becomes effective, file with the Secretary of State a copy of the articles of merger duly authenticated by the proper officer of the state or country under the laws of which such statutory merger was effected; and it shall not be necessary for such corporation to procure either a new or amended certificate of authority to transact business in this State unless the name of such corporation be changed thereby or unless the corporation desires to pursue in this State other or additional purposes than those which it is then authorized to transact in this State.

§ 118. Amended Certificate of Authority

A foreign corporation authorized to transact business in this State shall procure an amended certificate of authority in the event it changes its corporate name, or desires to pursue in this State other or additional purposes than those set forth in its prior application for a certificate of authority, by making application therefor to the Secretary of State.

The requirements in respect to the form and contents of such application, the manner of its execution, the filing of duplicate originals thereof with the Secretary of State, the issuance of an amended certificate of authority and the effect thereof, shall be the same as in the case of an original application for a certificate of authority.

§ 119. Withdrawal of Foreign Corporation

A foreign corporation authorized to transact business in this State may withdraw from this State upon procuring from the Secretary of State a certificate of withdrawal. In order to procure such certificate of withdrawal, such foreign corporation shall deliver to the Secretary of State an application for withdrawal, which shall set forth:

(a) The name of the corporation and the state or country under the laws of which it is incorporated.

(b) That the corporation is not transacting business in this State.

(c) That the corporation surrenders its authority to transact business in this State.

(d) That the corporation revokes the authority of its registered agent in this State to accept service of process and consents that service of process in any action, suit or proceeding based upon any cause of action arising in this State during the time the corporation was authorized to transact business in this State may thereafter be made on such corporation by service thereof on the Secretary of State.

(e) A post-office address to which the Secretary of State may mail a copy of any process against the corporation that may be served on him.

(f) A statement of the aggregate number of shares which the corporation has authority to issue, itemized by class and series, if any, within each class, as of the date of such application.

(g) A statement of the aggregate number of issued shares, itemized by class and series, if any, within each class, as of the date of such application.

(h) Such additional information as may be necessary or appropriate in order to enable the Secretary of State to determine and assess any unpaid fees or franchise taxes payable by such foreign corporation as in this Act prescribed.

The application for withdrawal shall be made on forms prescribed and furnished by the Secretary of State and shall be executed by the corporation by its president or a vice president and by its secretary or an assistant secretary, and verified by one of the officers signing the application, or, if the corporation is in the hands of a receiver or trustee, shall be executed on behalf of the corporation by such receiver or trustee and verified by him.

§ 120. Filing of Application for Withdrawal
Duplicate originals of such application for withdrawal shall be delivered to the Secretary of State. If the Secretary of State finds that such application con-

forms to the provisions of this Act, he shall, when all fees and franchise taxes have been paid as in this Act prescribed:

(a) Endorse on each of such duplicate originals the word "Filed," and the month, day and year of the filing thereof.

(b) File one of such duplicate originals in his office.

(c) Issue a certificate of withdrawal to which he shall affix the other duplicate original.

The certificate of withdrawal, together with the duplicate original of the application for withdrawal affixed thereto by the Secretary of State, shall be returned to the corporation or its representative. Upon the issuance of such certificate of withdrawal, the authority of the corporation to transact business in this State shall cease.

§ 121. Revocation of Certificate of Authority
The certificate of authority of a foreign corporation to transact business in this State may be revoked by the Secretary of State upon the conditions prescribed in this section when:

(a) The corporation has failed to file its annual report within the time required by this Act, or has failed to pay any fees, franchise taxes or penalties prescribed by this Act when they have become due and payable; or

(b) The corporation has failed to appoint and maintain a registered agent in this State as required by this Act; or

(c) The corporation has failed, after change of its registered office or registered agent, to file in the office of the Secretary of State a statement of such change as required by this Act; or

(d) The corporation has failed to file in the office of the Secretary of State any amendment to its articles of incorporation or any articles of merger within the time prescribed by this Act; or

(e) A misrepresentation has been made of any material matter in any application, report, affidavit, or other document submitted by such corporation pursuant to this Act.

No certificate of authority of a foreign corporation shall be revoked by the Secretary of State unless (1) he shall have given the corporation not less than sixty days' notice thereof by mail addressed to its registered office in this State, and (2) the corporation shall fail prior to revocation to file such annual report, or pay such fees, franchise taxes or penalties, or file the required statement of change of registered agent or registered office, or file such articles of amendment or articles of merger, or correct such misrepresentation.

§ 122. Issuance of Certificate of Revocation

Upon revoking any such certificate of authority, the Secretary of State shall:

(a) Issue a certificate of revocation in duplicate.

(b) File one of such certificates in his office.

(c) Mail to such corporation at its registered office in this State a notice of such revocation accompanied by one of such certificates.

Upon the issuance of such certificate of revocation, the authority of the corporation to transact business in this State shall cease.

§ 123. Application to Corporations Heretofore Authorized to Transact Business in This State

Foreign corporations which are duly authorized to transact business in this State at the time this Act takes effect, for a purpose or purposes for which a corporation might secure such authority under this Act, shall, subject to the limitations set forth in their respective certificates of authority, be entitled to all the rights and privileges applicable to foreign corporations procuring certificates of authority to transact business in this State under this Act, and from the time this Act takes effect such corporations shall be subject to all the limitations, restrictions, liabilities, and duties prescribed herein for foreign corporations procuring certificates of authority to transact business in this State under this Act.

§ 124. Transacting Business Without Certificate of Authority

No foreign corporation transacting business in this State without a certificate of authority shall be permitted to maintain any action, suit or proceeding in any court of this State, until such corporation shall have obtained a certificate of authority. Nor shall any action, suit or proceeding be maintained in any court of this State by any successor or assignee of such corporation on any right, claim or demand arising out of the transaction of business by such corporation in this State, until a certificate of authority shall have been obtained by such corporation or by a corporation which has acquired all or substantially all of its assets.

The failure of a foreign corporation to obtain a certificate of authority to transact business in this State shall not impair the validity of any contract or act of such corporation, and shall not prevent such corporation from defending any action, suit or proceeding in any court of this State.

A foreign corporation which transacts business in this State without a certificate of authority shall be liable to this State, for the years or parts thereof during which it transacted business in this State without a certificate of authority, in an amount equal to all fees and franchise taxes which would have been imposed by this Act upon such corporation had it duly applied for and received a certificate of authority to transact business in this State as required by this Act and thereafter filed all reports required by this Act, plus all penalties imposed by this Act for failure to pay such fees and franchise taxes. The Attorney General shall bring proceedings to recover all amounts due this State under the provisions of this Section.

§ 125. Annual Report of Domestic and Foreign Corporations

Each domestic corporation, and each foreign corporation authorized to transact business in this State, shall file, within the time prescribed by this Act, an annual report setting forth:

(a) The name of the corporation and the state or country under the laws of which it is incorporated.

(b) The address of the registered office of the corporation in this State, and the name of its registered agent in this State at such address, and, in case of a foreign corporation, the address of its principal office in the state or country under the laws of which it is incorporated.

(c) A brief statement of the character of the business in which the corporation is actually engaged in this State.

(d) The names and respective addresses of the directors and officers of the corporation.

(e) A statement of the aggregate number of shares which the corporation has authority to issue, itemized by class and series, if any, within each class.

(f) A statement of the aggregate number of issued shares, itemized by class and series, if any, within each class.

(g)   A statement, expressed in dollars, of the value of all the property owned by the corporation, wherever located, and the value of the property of the corporation located within this State, and a statement, expressed in dollars, of the gross amount of business transacted by the corporation for the twelve months ended on the thirty-first day of December preceding the date herein provided for the filing of such report and the gross amount thereof transacted by the corporation at or from places of business in this State. If, on the thirty-first day of December preceding the time herein provided for the filing of such report, the corporation had not been in existence for a period of twelve months, or in the case of a foreign corporation had not been authorized to transact business in this State for a period of twelve months, the statement with respect to business transacted shall be furnished for the period between the date of incorporation or the date of its authorization to transact business in this State, as the case may be, and such thirty-first day of December. If all the property of the corporation is located in this State and all of its business is transacted at or from places of business in this State, then the information required by this subparagraph need not be set forth in such report.

(h)   Such additional information as may be necessary or appropriate in order to enable the Secretary of State to determine and assess the proper amount of franchise taxes payable by such corporation.

Such annual report shall be made on forms prescribed and furnished by the Secretary of State, and the information therein contained shall be given as of the date of the execution of the report, except as to the information required by subparagraphs (g) and (h) which shall be given as of the close of business on the thirty-first day of December next preceding the date herein provided for the filing of such report. It shall be executed by the corporation by its president, a vice president, secretary, an assistant secretary, or treasurer, and verified by the officer executing the report, or, if the corporation is in the hands of a receiver or trustee, it shall be executed on behalf of the corporation and verified by such receiver or trustee.

§ 126. Filing of Annual Report of Domestic and Foreign Corporations

Such annual report of a domestic or foreign corporation shall be delivered to the Secretary of State between the first day of January and the first day of March of each year, except that the first annual report of a domestic or foreign corporation shall be filed between the first day of January and the first day of March of the year next succeeding the calendar year in which its certificate of incorporation or its certificate of authority, as the case may be, was issued by the Secretary of State. Proof to the satisfaction of the Secretary of State that prior to the first day of March such report was deposited in the United States mail in a sealed envelope, properly addressed, with postage prepaid, shall be deemed a compliance with this requirement. If the Secretary of State finds that such report conforms to the requirements of this Act, he shall file the same. If he finds that it does not so conform, he shall promptly return the same to the corporation for any necessary corrections, in which event the penalties hereinafter prescribed for failure to file such report within the time hereinabove provided shall not apply, if such report is corrected to conform to the requirements of this Act and returned to the Secretary of State within thirty days from the date on which it was mailed to the corporation by the Secretary of State.

§ 127. Fees, Franchise Taxes and Charges to be Collected by Secretary of State

The Secretary of State shall charge and collect in accordance with the provisions of this Act:

(a)   Fees for filing documents and issuing certificates.

(b)   Miscellaneous charges.

(c)   License fees.

(d)   Franchise taxes.

§ 128. Fees for Filing Documents and Issuing Certificates

The Secretary of State shall charge and collect for:

(a)   Filing articles of incorporation and issuing a certificate of incorporation, ... dollars.

(b)   Filing articles of amendment and issuing a certificate of amendment, ... dollars.

(c)   Filing restated articles of incorporation, ... dollars.

(d)   Filing articles of merger or consolidation and issuing a certificate of merger or consolidation, ... dollars.

(e)   Filing an application to reserve a corporate name, ... dollars.

(f)   Filing a notice of transfer of a reserved corporate name, ... dollars.

(g)   Filing a statement of change of address of registered office or change of registered agent or both, ... dollars.

(h)   Filing a statement of the establishment of a series of shares, ... dollars.

(i)   Filing a statement of intent to dissolve, ... dollars.

(j)   Filing a statement of revocation of voluntary dissolution proceedings, ... dollars.

(k)   Filing articles of dissolution, ... dollars.

(l)   Filing an application of a foreign corporation for a certificate of authority to transact business in this State and issuing a certificate of authority, ... dollars.

(m)   Filing an application of a foreign corporation for an amended certificate of authority to transact business in this State and issuing an amended certificate of authority, ... dollars.

(n)   Filing a copy of an amendment to the articles of incorporation of a foreign corporation holding a certificate of authority to transact business in this State, ... dollars.

(o)   Filing a copy of articles of merger of a foreign corporation holding a certificate of authority to transact business in this State, ... dollars.

(p)   Filing an application for withdrawal of a foreign corporation and issuing a certificate of withdrawal, ... dollars.

(q)   Filing any other statement or report, except an annual report, of a domestic or foreign corporation, ... dollars.

§ 129. Miscellaneous Charges

The Secretary of State shall charge and collect:

(a)   For furnishing a certified copy of any document, instrument, or paper relating to a corporation, ... cents per page and .... dollars for the certificate and affixing the seal thereto.

(b)   At the time of any service of process on him as resident agent of a corporation, ... dollars, which amount may be recovered as taxable costs by the party to the suit or action causing such service to be made if such party prevails in the suit or action.

§ 130. License Fees Payable by Domestic Corporations

The Secretary of State shall charge and collect from each domestic corporation license fees, based upon the number of shares which it will have authority to issue or the increase in the number of shares which it will have authority to issue, at the time of:

(a)   Filing articles of incorporation;

(b)   Filing articles of amendment increasing the number of authorized shares; and

(c)   Filing articles of merger or consolidation increasing the number of authorized shares which the surviving or new corporation, if a domestic corporation, will have the authority to issue above the aggregate number of shares which the constituent domestic corporations and constituent foreign corporations authorized to transact business in this State had authority to issue.

The license fees shall be at the rate of .... cents per share up to and including the first 10,000 authorized shares, ... cents per share for each authorized share in excess of 10,000 shares up to and including 100,000 shares, and .... cents per share for each authorized share in excess of 100,000 shares.

The license fees payable on an increase in the number of authorized shares shall be imposed only on the increased number of shares, and the number of previously authorized shares shall be taken into account in determining the rate applicable to the increased number of authorized shares.

§ 131. License Fees Payable by Foreign Corporations

The Secretary of State shall charge and collect from each foreign corporation license fees, based upon the proportion represented in this State of the number of shares which it has authority to issue or the increase in the number of shares which it has authority to issue, at the time of:

(a)   Filing an application for a certificate of authority to transact business in this State;

(b)   Filing articles of amendment which increased the number of authorized shares; and

(c)   Filing articles of merger or consolidation which increased the number of authorized shares which the surviving or new corporation, if a foreign corporation, has authority to issue above the aggregate number of shares which the constituent domestic corporations and constituent foreign corporations authorized to transact business in this State had authority to issue.

The license fees shall be at the rate of .... cents per share up to and including the first 10,000 authorized shares represented in this State, ... cents per share for each authorized share in excess of 10,000 shares up to and including 100,000 shares represented in this State, and .... cents per share for each authorized share in excess of 100,000 shares represented in this State.

The license fees payable on an increase in the number of authorized shares shall be imposed only on the increased number of such shares represented in this State, and the number of previously authorized shares represented in this State shall be taken into account in determining the rate applicable to the increased number of authorized shares.

The number of authorized shares represented in this State shall be that proportion of its total authorized shares which the sum of the value of its property located in this State and the gross amount of business transacted by it at or from places of business in this State bears to the sum of the value of all of its property, wherever located, and the gross amount of its business, wherever transacted. Such proportion shall be determined from information contained in the application for a certificate of authority to transact business in this State until the filing of an annual report and thereafter from information contained in the latest annual report filed by the corporation.

§ 132. Franchise Taxes Payable by Domestic Corporations

The Secretary of State shall charge and collect from each domestic corporation an initial franchise tax at the time of filing its articles of incorporation at the rate of one-twelfth of one-half of the license fee payable by such corporation under the provisions of this Act at the time of filing its articles of incorporation, for each calendar month, or fraction thereof, between the date of the issuance of the certificate of incorporation by the Secretary of State and the first day of July of the next succeeding calendar year.

The Secretary of State shall charge and collect from each domestic corporation an annual franchise tax, payable in advance for the period from July 1 in each year to July 1 in the succeeding year, beginning July 1 in the calendar year in which such corporation is required to file its first annual report under this Act, (Alternative 1: at the rate of .... per cent of the amount represented in this State of the stated capital

of the corporation, as determined in accordance with accounting practices and principles that are reasonable in the circumstances, as disclosed by the latest report filed by the corporation with the Secretary of State) (Alternative 2: at the rate of .... cents per share up to and including the first 10,000 issued and outstanding shares, and .... cents per share for each issued and outstanding share in excess of 10,000 shares up to and including 100,000 shares, and .... cents per share for each issued and outstanding share in excess of 100,000 shares).

[If Alternative 2 is enacted, the following paragraph should be deleted.]

The amount represented in this State of the stated capital of the corporation shall be that proportion of its stated capital which the sum of the value of its property located in this State and the gross amount of business transacted by it at or from places of business in this State bears to the sum of the value of all of its property, wherever located, and the gross amount of its business, wherever transacted.

§ 133. Franchise Taxes Payable by Foreign Corporations

The Secretary of State shall charge and collect from each foreign corporation authorized to transact business in this State an initial franchise tax at the time of filing its application for a certificate of authority at the rate of one-twelfth of one-half of the license fee payable by such corporation under the provisions of this Act at the time of filing such application, for each month, or fraction thereof, between the date of the issuance of the certificate of authority by the Secretary of State and the first day of July of the next succeeding calendar year.

The Secretary of State shall charge and collect from each foreign corporation authorized to transact business in this State an annual franchise tax, payable in advance for the period from July 1 in each year to July 1 in the succeeding year, beginning July 1 in the calendar year in which such corporation is required to file its first annual report under this Act, (Alternative 1: at the rate of .... per cent of the amount represented in this State of the stated capital of the corporation, as determined in accordance with accounting practices and principles that are reasonable in the circumstances, as disclosed by the latest annual report filed by the corporation with the Secretary of State) (Alternative 2: at a rate of .... cents per share up to and including the first 10,000 issued and outstanding shares represented in this State, and .... cents per share for each issued and outstanding share in excess of 10,000 shares up to and including 100,000 shares represented in this State, and .... cents per share for each issued and outstanding share in excess of 100,000 shares represented in this State).

[If Alternative 2 is enacted, the following paragraph should be deleted.]

The amount represented in this State of the stated capital of the corporation shall be that proportion of its stated capital which the sum of the value of its property located in this State and the gross amount of business transacted by it at or from places of business in this State bears to the sum of the value of all of its property, wherever located, and the gross amount of its business, wherever transacted.

§ 134. Assessment and Collection of Annual Franchise Taxes

It shall be the duty of the Secretary of State to collect all annual franchise taxes and penalties imposed by, or assessed in accordance with, this Act.

Between the first day of March and the first day of June of each year, the Secretary of State shall assess against each corporation, domestic and foreign, required to file an annual report in such year, the franchise tax payable by it for the period from July 1 of such year to July 1 of the succeeding year in accordance with the provisions of this Act, and, if it has failed to file its annual report within the time prescribed by this Act, the penalty imposed by this Act upon such corporation for its failure so to do; and shall mail a written notice to each corporation against which such tax is assessed, addressed to such corporation at its registered office in this State, notifying the corporation (1) of the amount of franchise tax assessed against it for the ensuing year and the amount of penalty, if any, assessed against it for failure to file its annual report; (2) that objections, if any, to such assessment will be heard by the officer making the assessment on or before the fifteenth day of June of such year, upon receipt of a request from the corporation; and (3) that such tax and penalty shall be payable to the Secretary of State on the first day of July next succeeding the date of the notice. Failure to receive such notice shall not relieve the corporation of its obligation to pay the tax and any penalty assessed, or invalidate the assessment thereof.

The Secretary of State shall have power to hear and determine objections to any assessment of franchise tax at any time after such assessment and, after hearing, to change or modify any such assessment. In the event of any adjustment of franchise tax with respect to which a penalty has been assessed for failure to file an annual report, the penalty shall be adjusted in accordance with the provisions of this Act imposing such penalty.

All annual franchise taxes and all penalties for failure to file annual reports shall be due and payable on the first day of July of each year. If the annual franchise tax assessed against any corporation subject to the provisions of this Act, together with all penalties assessed thereon, shall not be paid to the Secretary of State on or before the thirty-first day of July of the year in which such tax is due and payable, the Secretary of State shall certify such fact to the Attorney General on or before the fifteenth day of November of such year, whereupon the Attorney General may institute an action against such corporation in the name of this State, in any court of competent jurisdiction, for the recovery of the amount of such franchise tax and penalties, together with the cost of suit, and prosecute the same to final judgment.

For the purpose of enforcing collection, all annual franchise taxes assessed in accordance with this Act, and all penalties assessed thereon and all interest and costs that shall accrue in connection with the collection thereof, shall be a prior and first lien on the real and personal property of the corporation from and including the first day of July of the year when such franchise taxes become due and payable until such taxes, penalties, interest, and costs shall have been paid.

§ 135. Penalties Imposed Upon Corporations

Each corporation, domestic or foreign, that fails or refuses to file its annual report for any year within the time prescribed by this Act shall be subject to a penalty of ten per cent of the amount of the franchise tax assessed against it for the period beginning July 1 of the year in which such report should have been filed. Such penalty shall be assessed by the Secretary of State at the time of the assessment of the franchise tax. If the amount of the franchise tax as originally assessed against such corporation be thereafter adjusted in accordance with the provisions of this Act, the amount of the penalty shall be likewise adjusted to ten per cent of the amount of the adjusted franchise tax. The amount of the franchise tax and the amount of the penalty shall be separately stated in any notice to the corporation with respect thereto.

If the franchise tax assessed in accordance with the provisions of this Act shall not be paid on or before the thirty-first day of July, it shall be deemed to be delinquent, and there shall be added a penalty of one per cent for each month or part of month that the same is delinquent, commencing with the month of August.

Each corporation, domestic or foreign, that fails or refuses to answer truthfully and fully within the time prescribed by this Act interrogatories propounded by the Secretary of State in accordance with the provisions of this Act, shall be deemed to be guilty of a misdemeanor and upon conviction thereof may be fined in any amount not exceeding five hundred dollars.

§ 136. Penalties Imposed Upon Officers and Directors

Each officer and director of a corporation, domestic or foreign, who fails or refuses within the time prescribed by this Act to answer truthfully and fully interrogatories propounded to him by the Secretary of State in accordance with the provisions of this Act, or who signs any articles, statement, report, application or other document filed with the Secretary of State which is known to such officer or director to be false in any material respect, shall be deemed to be guilty of a misdemeanor, and upon conviction thereof may be fined in any amount not exceeding .... dollars.

§ 137. Interrogatories by Secretary of State

The Secretary of State may propound to any corporation, domestic or foreign, subject to the provisions of this Act, and to any officer or director thereof, such interrogatories as may be reasonably necessary and proper to enable him to ascertain whether such corporation has complied with all the provisions of this Act applicable to such corporation. Such interrogatories shall be answered within thirty days after the mailing thereof, or within such additional time as shall be fixed by the Secretary of State, and the answers thereto shall be full and complete and shall be made in writing and under oath. If such interrogatories be directed to an individual they shall be answered by him, and if directed to a corporation they shall be answered by the president, vice president, secretary or assistant secretary thereof. The Secretary of State need not file any document to which such interrogatories relate until such interrogatories be answered as herein provided, and not then if the answers thereto disclose that such document is not in conformity with the provisions of this Act. The Secretary of State shall certify to the Attorney General, for such action as the Attorney General may deem appropriate, all interrogatories and answers thereto which disclose a violation of any of the provisions of this Act.

§ 138. Information Disclosed by Interrogatories

Interrogatories propounded by the Secretary of State and the answers thereto shall not be open to public inspection nor shall the Secretary of State disclose any facts or information obtained therefrom except insofar as his official duty may require the same to be made public or in the event such interrogatories or the answers thereto are required for evidence in any criminal proceedings or in any other action by this State.

§ 139. Powers of Secretary of State

The Secretary of State shall have the power and authority reasonably necessary to enable him to administer this Act efficiently and to perform the duties therein imposed upon him.

§ 140. Appeal from Secretary of State

If the Secretary of State shall fail to approve any articles of incorporation, amendment, merger, consolidation or dissolution, or any other document required by this Act to be approved by the Secretary of State before the same shall be filed in his office, he shall, within ten days after the delivery thereof to him, give written notice of his disapproval to the person or corporation, domestic or foreign, delivering the same, specifying the reasons therefor. From such disapproval such person or corporation may appeal to the .... court of the county in which the registered office of such corporation is, or is proposed to be, situated by filing with the clerk of such court a petition setting forth a copy of the articles or other document sought to be filed and a copy of the written disapproval thereof by the Secretary of State; whereupon the matter shall be tried de novo by the court, and the court shall either sustain the action of the Secretary of State or direct him to take such action as the court may deem proper.

If the Secretary of State shall revoke the certificate of authority to transact business in this State of any foreign corporation, pursuant to the provisions of this Act, such foreign corporation may likewise appeal to the .... court of the county where the registered office of such corporation in this State is situated, by filing with the clerk of such court a petition setting forth a copy of its certificate of authority to transact business in this State and a copy of the notice of revocation given by the Secretary of State; whereupon the matter shall be tried de novo by the court, and the court shall either sustain the action of the Secretary of State or direct him to take such action as the court may deem proper.

Appeals from all final orders and judgments entered by the .... court under this section in review of any ruling or decision of the Secretary of State may be taken as in other civil actions.

§ 141. Certificates and Certified Copies to be Received in Evidence

All certificates issued by the Secretary of State in accordance with the provisions of this Act, and all copies of documents filed in his office in accordance with the provisions of this Act when certified by him, shall be taken and received in all courts, public offices, and official bodies as prima facie evidence of the facts therein stated. A certificate by the Secretary of State under the great seal of this State, as to the existence or non-existence of the facts relating to corporations shall be taken and received in all courts, public offices, and official bodies as prima facie evidence of the existence or non-existence of the facts therein stated.

§ 142. Forms to be Furnished by Secretary of State

All reports required by this Act to be filed in the office of the Secretary of State shall be made on forms which shall be prescribed and furnished by the Secretary of State. Forms for all other documents to be filed in the office of the Secretary of State shall be furnished by the Secretary of State on request therefor, but the use thereof, unless otherwise specifically prescribed in this Act, shall not be mandatory.

§ 143. Greater Voting Requirements

Whenever, with respect to any action to be taken by the shareholders of a corporation, the articles of incorporation require the vote or concurrence of the holders of a greater proportion of the shares, or of any class or series thereof, than required by this Act with respect to such action, the provisions of the articles of incorporation shall control.

§ 144. Waiver of Notice

Whenever any notice is required to be given to any shareholder or director of a corporation under the provisions of this Act or under the provisions of the articles of incorporation or by-laws of the corporation, a waiver thereof in writing signed by the person or persons entitled to such notice, whether before or after the time stated therein, shall be equivalent to the giving of such notice.

§ 145. Action by Shareholders Without a Meeting

Any action required by this Act to be taken at a meeting of the shareholders of a corporation, or any action which may be taken at a meeting of the shareholders, may be taken without a meeting if a consent in writing, setting forth the action so taken, shall be signed by all of the shareholders entitled to vote with respect to the subject matter thereof.

Such consent shall have the same effect as a unanimous vote of shareholders, and may be stated as such in any articles or document filed with the Secretary of State under this Act.

§ 146. Unauthorized Assumption of Corporate Powers

All persons who assume to act as a corporation without authority so to do shall be jointly and severally liable for all debts and liabilities incurred or arising as a result thereof.

§ 147. Application to Existing Corporations

The provisions of this Act shall apply to all existing corporations organized under any general act of this State providing for the organization of corporations for a purpose or purposes for which a corporation might be organized under this Act, where the power has been reserved to amend, repeal or modify the act under which such corporation was organized and where such act is repealed by this Act.

§ 148. Application to Foreign and Interstate Commerce

The provisions of this Act shall apply to commerce with foreign nations and among the several states only insofar as the same may be permitted under the provisions of the Constitution of the United States.

§ 149. Reservation of Power

The .... * shall at all times have power to prescribe such regulations, provisions and limitations as it may deem advisable, which regulations, provisions and limitations shall be binding upon any and all corporations subject to the provisions of this Act, and the .... * shall have power to amend, repeal or modify this Act at pleasure.

§ 150. Effect of Repeal of Prior Acts

The repeal of a prior act by this Act shall not affect any right accrued or established, or any liability or penalty

*Insert name of legislative body.

incurred, under the provisions of such act, prior to the repeal thereof.

§ 151. Effect of Invalidity of Part of this Act

If a court of competent jurisdiction shall adjudge to be invalid or unconstitutional any clause, sentence, paragraph, section or part of this Act, such judgment or decree shall not affect, impair, invalidate or nullify the remainder of this Act, but the effect thereof shall be confined to the clause, sentence, paragraph, section or part of this Act so adjudged to be invalid or unconstitutional.

§ 152. Exclusivity of Certain Provisions [Optional]

In circumstances to which section 45 and related sections of this Act are applicable, such provisions supersede the applicability of any other statutes of this state with respect to the legality of distributions.

§ 153. Repeal of Prior Acts (Insert appropriate provisions) ....

SPECIAL COMMENTS—CLOSE CORPORATIONS

In view of the increasing importance of close corporations, both for the small family business and for the larger undertakings conducted by some small number of other corporations, this liberalizing trend has now been followed by the 1969 Amendments to the Model Act. The first sentence of section 35, providing that the business of the corporation shall be managed by a board of directors, was supplemented by a new clause "except as may be otherwise provided in the articles of incorporation." This permits the shareholders to take over and exercise the functions of the directors by appropriate provision to that effect in the articles, or to allocate functions between the directors and shareholders in such manner as may be desired. Taken with other provisions of the Model Act, which are here enumerated for convenience, this rounds out the adaptability of the Model Act for all the needs of a close corporation:

(1) By section 4(*l*) the by-laws may make any provision for the regulation of the affairs of the corporation that is not inconsistent with the articles or the laws of the incorporating state.

(2) By section 15 shares may be divided into several classes and the articles may limit or deny the voting rights of or provide special voting rights for the shares of any class to the extent not inconsistent with the Model Act. The narrow limits of this exception are revealed by section 33 which provides that each outstanding share, regardless of class, shall be entitled to one vote on each matter submitted to a vote at a meeting of the shareholders "except as may be otherwise provided in the articles of incorporation," thus expressly authorizing more than one vote per share or less than one vote per share, either generally or in respect to particular matters.

(3) By section 16 item (F) the shares of any preferred or special class may be issued in series and there may be variations between different series in numerous respects, including specifically the matter of voting rights, if any.

(4) By section 32 the articles may reduce a quorum of shareholders to not less than one-third of the shares entitled to vote, or leave the quorum at the standard of a majority or, as confirmed by section 143, increase the number to any desired point.

(5) By section 34 agreements among shareholders regarding the voting of their shares are made valid and enforceable in accordance with their terms without limitation in time. These could relate to the election or compensation of directors or officers or the creation of various types of securities for new financing or the conduct of business of various kinds or dividend policy or mergers and consolidations or other transactions without limit.

(6) The flexibility permitted by the revision of section 35 in the distribution or reallocation of authority among directors and stockholders has already been mentioned.

(7) Under section 36 the number of directors may be fixed by the by-laws at one or such greater number as may best serve the interests of the shareholders and that number may be increased or decreased from time to time by amendment to, or in the manner provided in, the articles or the by-laws, subject to any limiting provision adopted pursuant to law, such as an agreed requirement for a unanimous vote by directors for any such change or a requirement that amendments to the by-laws be made by shareholder vote. Similarly, under section 53, the incorporation may be effected by a single incorporator or by more as may be desired.

(8) By section 37 directors may be classified. While this relates to directors classified in such manner that the term of office of a specified proportion terminates in each year, the Model Act does not forbid the election of separate directors by separate classes of stock.

(9) Section 40 permits the articles or the by-laws to require more than a majority of the directors to constitute a quorum for the transaction of business and also permits the articles or by-laws to require the act of a greater number than a majority of those present at a meeting where a quorum is present before any specified business may be transacted. Or a unanimous vote of all directors may be required. This may be utilized to confer a right of veto on any designated class in order to protect its special interests.

(10) By section 50 the authority and duties of the respective officers and agents of the corporation may be tailored and prescribed in the by-laws, or consistently with the by-laws, in such manner as the needs of the shareholders may indicate.

(11) By section 54 the articles may include any desired provision for the regulation of the internal affairs of the corporation, including, in particular, "any provision restricting the transfer of shares." This expressly validates agreements for prior offering of shares to the corporation or other shareholders. All such restrictions must, of course, be clearly shown on the stock certificate as required by the Uniform Commercial Code. A similarly broad provision for the contents of the by-laws is contained in section 27.

(12) By sections 60, 73 and 79, respectively, a class vote may be required for an amendment to the articles, for any merger or consolidation or for a sale of assets other than in the regular course of business.

(13) Section 143 permits the articles to require, for any particular action by the shareholders, the vote or concurrence of the holders of a greater proportion of the shares, or of any class or series thereof, than the Model Act itself requires.

(14) Section 44 permits action by directors without a meeting and section 145 permits the same for shareholders, while section 144 contains a broad provision on waiver of notice. Thus the formality of meetings may, where desired, be eliminated in whole or in part, except for the annual meeting required by section 28.

Under these provisions protection may be afforded for a great diversity of interests. By way of illustration, the shares may be divided into different classes with different voting rights and each class may be permitted to elect a different director. Or some classes may be permitted to vote on certain transactions, but not all. Even more drastically, some classes may be denied all voting rights whatever. Thus a family could provide for equal participation in the profits of the venture, but restrict the power of management to selected members. The advantages of having a known group of business associates may be safeguarded by restrictions on the transfer of shares. Most commonly this takes the form of a requirement for *pro rata* offering to the other shareholders before selling to an outsider. Or the other shareholders may be given an option, in the event of death or a proposed transfer, to buy the stock *pro rata*. The same option may be given to the corporation. The purchase price may be fixed by any agreed formula, such as adjusted book value or some multiple of recent earnings. Or stockholder agreements may be used to assure that, at least for a limited number of years, all shares will be voted for certain directors and officers, or in a certain way on other corporate matters. Cumulative voting may be provided for, by which each shareholder has a number of votes equal to the number of his shares multiplied by the number of directors to be elected, with the privilege of casting all of his votes for a single candidate, or dividing them as he may wish. This helps minorities obtain representation on the board of directors. Thus the holder of one-fourth of the shares voting, plus one share, is sure of electing one of three directors. The preemptive right is another important protection in the case of close corporations, since it assures each stockholder a right to maintain his proportionate interest. Still more definite protection is afforded by provisions in the articles that prohibit particular transactions except with the assent of a specified percentage of all outstanding shares or of each class of shares. Much the same protection can sometimes be obtained by requiring a specially large quorum for the election of directors, or a specially large vote, or even unanimous vote, by directors for the authorization of particular transactions. Quite the opposite situation exists if one of the participants is to be an inactive investor, for whom non-voting preferred stock, with its prior right to a return from earnings, may be sufficient. But even here he may require a veto power over major transactions, such as the issuance of debt, the issuance of additional preferred shares or mergers or consolidations. Or the preferred shareholders may be given as a class the right to elect one or more of the directors, particularly in the event that dividends should be in arrears.

These possibilities are listed merely as illustrations and not in any sense as exhausting the variations permissible under the Model Act.

APPENDIX C

The Uniform Partnership Act

(Adopted in 49 States [all of the states except Louisiana], the District of Columbia, the Virgin Islands, and Guam. The adoptions by Alabama and Nebraska do not follow the official text in every respect, but are substantially similar, with local variations.)

The Act consists of 7 Parts as follows:

I. Preliminary Provisions
II. Nature of Partnership
III. Relations of Partners to Persons Dealing with the Partnership
IV. Relations of Partners to One Another
V. Property Rights of a Partner
VI. Dissolution and Winding Up
VII. Miscellaneous Provisions

An Act to make uniform the Law of Partnerships
Be it enacted, etc.:

PART I
PRELIMINARY PROVISIONS
§ 1. Name of Act
This act may be cited as Uniform Partnership Act.

§ 2. Definition of Terms
In this act, "Court" includes every court and judge having jurisdiction in the case.

"Business" includes every trade, occupation, or profession.

"Person" includes individuals, partnerships, corporations, and other associations.

"Bankrupt" includes bankrupt under the Federal Bankruptcy Act or insolvent under any state insolvent act.

"Conveyance" includes every assignment, lease, mortgage, or encumbrance.

"Real property" includes land and any interest or estate in land.

§ 3. Interpretation of Knowledge and Notice
(1) A person has "knowledge" of a fact within the meaning of this act not only when he has actual knowledge thereof, but also when he has knowledge of such other facts as in the circumstances shows bad faith.
(2) A person has "notice" of a fact within the meaning of this act when the person who claims the benefit of the notice:
  (a) States the fact to such person, or
  (b) Delivers through the mail, or by other means of communication, a written statement of the fact to such person or to a proper person at his place of business or residence.

§ 4. Rules of Construction
(1) The rule that statutes in derogation of the common law are to be strictly construed shall have no application to this act.
(2) The law of estoppel shall apply under this act.
(3) The law of agency shall apply under this act.
(4) This act shall be so interpreted and construed as to effect its general purpose to make uniform the law of those states which enact it.
(5) This act shall not be construed so as to impair the obligations of any contract existing when the act goes into effect, nor to affect any action or proceedings begun or right accrued before this act takes effect.

§ 5. Rules for Cases Not Provided for in this Act.
In any case not provided for in this act the rules of law and equity, including the law merchant, shall govern.

PART II
NATURE OF PARTNERSHIP

§ 6. Partnership Defined

(1) A partnership is an association of two or more persons to carry on as co-owners a business for profit.

(2) But any association formed under any other statute of this state, or any statute adopted by authority, other than the authority of this state, is not a partnership under this act, unless such association would have been a partnership in this state prior to the adoption of this act; but this act shall apply to limited partnerships except in so far as the statutes relating to such partnerships are inconsistent herewith.

§ 7. Rules for Determining the Existence of a Partnership

In determining whether a partnership exists, these rules shall apply:

(1) Except as provided by Section 16 persons who are not partners as to each other are not partners as to third persons.

(2) Joint tenancy, tenancy in common, tenancy by the entireties, joint property, common property, or part ownership does not of itself establish a partnership, whether such co-owners do or do not share any profits made by the use of the property.

(3) The sharing of gross returns does not of itself establish a partnership, whether or not the persons sharing them have a joint or common right or interest in any property from which the returns are derived.

(4) The receipt by a person of a share of the profits of a business is prima facie evidence that he is a partner in the business, but no such inference shall be drawn if such profits were received in payment:

  (a) As a debt by installments or otherwise,
  (b) As wages of an employee or rent to a landlord,
  (c) As an annuity to a widow or representative of a deceased partner,
  (d) As interest on a loan, though the amount of payment varies with the profits of the business.
  (e) As the consideration for the sale of a good-will of a business or other property by installments or otherwise.

§ 8. Partnership Property

(1) All property originally brought into the partnership stock or subsequently acquired by purchase or otherwise, on account of the partnership, is partnership property.

(2) Unless the contrary intention appears, property acquired with partnership funds is partnership property.

(3) Any estate in real property may be acquired in the partnership name. Title so acquired can be conveyed only in the partnership name.

(4) A conveyance to a partnership in the partnership name, though without words of inheritance, passes the entire estate of the grantor unless a contrary intent appears.

PART III
RELATIONS OF PARTNERS TO PERSONS DEALING WITH THE PARTNERSHIP

§ 9. Partner Agent of Partnership as to Partnership Business

(1) Every partner is an agent of the partnership for the purpose of its business, and the act of every partner, including the execution in the partnership name of any instrument, for apparently carrying on in the usual way the business of the partnership of which he is a member binds the partnership, unless the partner so acting has in fact no authority to act for the partnership in the particular matter, and the person with whom he is dealing has knowledge of the fact that he has no such authority.

(2) An act of a partner which is not apparently for the carrying on of the business of the partnership in the usual way does not bind the partnership unless authorized by the other partners.

(3) Unless authorized by the other partners or unless they have abandoned the business, one or more but less than all the partners have no authority to:

  (a) Assign the partnership property in trust for creditors or on the assignee's promise to pay the debts of the partnership,
  (b) Dispose of the good-will of the business,
  (c) Do any other act which would make it impossible to carry on the ordinary business of a partnership,
  (d) Confess a judgment,
  (e) Submit a partnership claim or liability to arbitration or reference.

(4) No act of a partner in contravention of a restriction on authority shall bind the partnership to persons having knowledge of the restriction.

§ 10. Conveyance of Real Property of the Partnership

(1) Where title to real property is in the partnership name, any partner may convey title to such property by a conveyance executed in the partnership name; but the partnership may recover such property unless the partner's act binds the partnership under the provisions of paragraph (1) of section 9, or unless such property has been conveyed by the grantee or a person claiming through such grantee to a holder for value without knowledge that the partner, in making the conveyance, has exceeded his authority.

(2) Where title to real property is in the name of the partnership, a conveyance executed by a partner, in his own name, passes the equitable interest of the partnership, provided the act is one within the authority of the partner under the provisions of paragraph (1) of section 9.

(3) Where title to real property is in the name of one or more but not all the partners, and the record does not disclose the right of the partnership, the partners in whose name the title stands may convey title to such property, but the partnership may recover such property if the partners' act does not bind the partnership under the provisions of paragraph (1) of section 9, unless the purchaser or his assignee, is a holder for value, without knowledge.

(4) Where the title to real property is in the name of one or more or all the partners, or in a third person in trust for the partnership, a conveyance executed by a partner in the partnership name, or in his own name, passes the equitable interest of the partnership, provided the act is one within the authority of the partner under the provisions of paragraph (1) of section 9.

(5) Where the title to real property is in the names of all the partners a conveyance executed by all the partners passes all their rights in such property.

§ 11. Partnership Bound by Admission of Partner

An admission or representation made by any partner concerning partnership affairs within the scope of his authority as conferred by this act is evidence against the partnership.

§ 12. Partnership Charged with Knowledge of or Notice to Partner

Notice to any partner of any matter relating to partnership affairs, and the knowledge of the partner act-ing in the particular matter, acquired while a partner or then present to his mind, and the knowledge of any other partner who reasonably could and should have communicated it to the acting partner, operate as notice to or knowledge of the partnership, except in the case of a fraud on the partnership committed by or with the consent of that partner.

§ 13. Partnership Bound by Partner's Wrongful Act

Where, by any wrongful act or omission of any partner acting in the ordinary course of the business of the partnership or with the authority of his co-partners, loss or injury is caused to any person, not being a partner in the partnership, or any penalty is incurred, the partnership is liable therefor to the same extent as the partner so acting or omitting to act.

§ 14. Partnership Bound by Partner's Breach of Trust

The partnership is bound to make good the loss:

(a) Where one partner acting within the scope of his apparent authority receives money or property of a third person and misapplies it; and

(b) Where the partnership in the course of its business receives money or property of a third person and the money or property so received is misapplied by any partner while it is in the custody of the partnership.

§ 15. Nature of Partner's Liability

All partners are liable

(a) Jointly and severally for everything chargeable to the partnership under sections 13 and 14.

(b) Jointly for all other debts and obligations of the partnership; but any partner may enter into a separate obligation to perform a partnership contract.

§ 16. Partner by Estoppel

(1) When a person, by words spoken or written or by conduct, represents himself, or consents to another representing him to any one, as a partner in an existing partnership or with one or more persons not actual partners, he is liable to any such person to whom such representation has been made, who has, on the faith of such representation, given credit to the actual or apparent partnership, and if he has made such rep-

resentation or consented to its being made in a public manner he is liable to such person, whether the representation has or has not been made or communicated to such person so giving credit by or with the knowledge of the apparent partner making the representation or consenting to its being made.

(a) When a partnership liability results, he is liable as though he were an actual member of the partnership.

(b) When no partnership liability results, he is liable jointly with the other persons, if any, so consenting to the contract or representation as to incur liability, otherwise separately.

(2) When a person has been thus represented to be a partner in an existing partnership, or with one or more persons not actual partners, he is an agent of the persons consenting to such representation to bind them to the same extent and in the same manner as though he were a partner in fact, with respect to persons who rely upon the representation. Where all the members of the existing partnership consent to the representation, a partnership act or obligation results; but in all other cases it is the joint act or obligation of the person acting and the persons consenting to the representation.

§ 17. Liability of Incoming Partner

A person admitted as a partner into an existing partnership is liable for all the obligations of the partnership arising before his admission as though he had been a partner when such obligations were incurred, except that this liability shall be satisfied only out of partnership property.

PART IV
RELATIONS OF PARTNERS TO ONE ANOTHER
§ 18. Rules Determining Rights and Duties of Partners

The rights and duties of the partners in relation to the partnership shall be determined, subject to any agreement between them, by the following rules:

(a) Each partner shall be repaid his contributions, whether by way of capital or advances to the partnership property and share equally in the profits and surplus remaining after all liabilities, including those to partners, are satisfied; and must contribute towards the losses, whether of capital or otherwise, sustained by the partnership according to his share in the profits.

(b) The partnership must indemnify every partner in respect of payments made and personal liabilities reasonably incurred by him in the ordinary and proper conduct of its business, or for the preservation of its business or property.

(c) A partner, who in aid of the partnership makes any payment or advance beyond the amount of capital which he agreed to contribute, shall be paid interest from the date of the payment or advance.

(d) A partner shall receive interest on the capital contributed by him only from the date when repayment should be made.

(e) All partners have equal rights in the management and conduct of the partnership business.

(f) No partner is entitled to remuneration for acting in the partnership business, except that a surviving partner is entitled to reasonable compensation for his services in winding up the partnership affairs.

(g) No person can become a member of a partnership without the consent of all the partners.

(h) Any difference arising as to ordinary matters connected with the partnership business may be decided by a majority of the partners; but no act in contravention of any agreement between the partners may be done rightfully without the consent of all the partners.

§ 19. Partnership Books

The partnership books shall be kept, subject to any agreement between the partners, at the principal place of business of the partnership, and every partner shall at all times have access to and may inspect and copy any of them.

§ 20. Duty of Partners to Render Information

Partners shall render on demand true and full information of all things affecting the partnership to any partner or the legal representative of any deceased partner or partner under legal disability.

§ 21. Partner Accountable as a Fiduciary

(1) Every partner must account to the partnership for any benefit, and hold as trustee for it any profits derived by him without the consent of the

other partners from any transaction connected with the formation, conduct, or liquidation of the partnership or from any use by him of its property.

(2) This section applies also to the representatives of a deceased partner engaged in the liquidation of the affairs of the partnership as the personal representatives of the last surviving partner.

§ 22. Right to an Account

Any partner shall have the right to a formal account as to partnership affairs:

(a) If he is wrongfully excluded from the partnership business or possession of its property by his co-partners,

(b) If the right exists under the terms of any agreement,

(c) As provided by section 21,

(d) Whenever other circumstances render it just and reasonable.

§ 23. Continuation of Partnership Beyond Fixed Term

(1) When a partnership for a fixed term or particular undertaking is continued after the termination of such term or particular undertaking without any express agreement, the rights and duties of the partners remain the same as they were at such termination, so far as is consistent with a partnership at will.

(2) A continuation of the business by the partners or such of them as habitually acted therein during the term, without any settlement or liquidation of the partnership affairs, is prima facie evidence of a continuation of the partnership.

PART V
PROPERTY RIGHTS OF A PARTNER

§ 24. Extent of Property Rights of a Partner

The property rights of a partner are (1) his rights in specific partnership property, (2) his interest in the partnership, and (3) his right to participate in the management.

§ 25. Nature of a Partner's Right in Specific Partnership Property

(1) A partner is co-owner with his partners of specific partnership property holding as a tenant in partnership.

(2) The incidents of this tenancy are such that:

(a) A partner, subject to the provisions of this act and to any agreement between the partners, has an equal right with his partners to possess specific partnership property for partnership purposes; but he has no right to possess such property for any other purpose without the consent of his partners.

(b) A partner's right in specific partnership property is not assignable except in connection with the assignment of rights of all the partners in the same property.

(c) A partner's right in specific partnership property is not subject to attachment or execution, except on a claim against the partnership. When partnership property is attached for a partnership debt the partners, or any of them, or the representatives of a deceased partner, cannot claim any right under the homestead or exemption laws.

(d) On the death of a partner his right in specific partnership property vests in the surviving partner or partners, except where the deceased was the last surviving partner, when his right in such property vests in his legal representative. Such surviving partner or partners, or the legal representative of the last surviving partner, has no right to possess the partnership property for any but a partnership purpose.

(e) A partner's right in specific partnership property is not subject to dower, curtesy, or allowances to widows, heirs, or next of kin.

§ 26. Nature of Partner's Interest in the Partnership

A partner's interest in the partnership is his share of the profits and surplus, and the same is personal property.

§ 27. Assignment of Partner's Interest

(1) A conveyance by a partner of his interest in the partnership does not of itself dissolve the partnership, nor, as against the other partners in the absence of agreement, entitle the assignee, during the continuance of the partnership, to interfere in the management or administration of the partnership business or affairs, or to require any information or account of partnership transactions, or to inspect the partnership books; but it merely entitles the assignee to receive in accor-

dance with his contract the profits to which the assigning partner would otherwise be entitled.

(2) In case of a dissolution of the partnership, the assignee is entitled to receive his assignor's interest and may require an account from the date only of the last account agreed to by all the partners.

§ 28. Partner's Interest Subject to Charging Order

(1) On due application to a competent court by any judgment creditor of a partner, the court which entered the judgment, order, or decree, or any other court, may charge the interest of the debtor partner with payment of the unsatisfied amount of such judgment debt with interest thereon; and may then or later appoint a receiver of his share of the profits, and of any other money due or to fall due to him in respect of the partnership, and make all other orders, directions, accounts and inquiries which the debtor partner might have made, or which the circumstances of the case may require.

(2) The interest charged may be redeemed at any time before foreclosure, or in case of a sale being directed by the court may be purchased without thereby causing a dissolution:

   (a) With separate property, by any one or more of the partners, or
   (b) With partnership property, by any one or more of the partners with the consent of all the partners whose interests are not so charged or sold.

(3) Nothing in this act shall be held to deprive a partner of his right, if any, under the exemption laws, as regards his interest in the partnership.

PART VI
DISSOLUTION AND WINDING UP
§ 29. Dissolution Defined

The dissolution of a partnership is the change in the relation of the partners caused by any partner ceasing to be associated in the carrying on as distinguished from the winding up of the business.

§ 30. Partnership not Terminated by Dissolution

On dissolution the partnership is not terminated, but continues until the winding up of partnership affairs is completed.

§ 31. Causes of Dissolution
Dissolution is caused:
(1) Without violation of the agreement between the partners,

   (a) By the termination of the definite term or particular undertaking specified in the agreement,
   (b) By the express will of any partner when no definite term or particular undertaking is specified,
   (c) By the express will of all the partners who have not assigned their interests or suffered them to be charged for their separate debts, either before or after the termination of any specified term or particular undertaking,
   (d) By the expulsion of any partner from the business bona fide in accordance with such a power conferred by the agreement between the partners;

(2) In contravention of the agreement between the partners, where the circumstances do not permit a dissolution under any other provision of this section, by the express will of any partner at any time;
(3) By any event which makes it unlawful for the business of the partnership to be carried on or for the members to carry it on in partnership;
(4) By the death of any partner;
(5) By the bankruptcy of any partner or the partnership;
(6) By decree of court under section 32.

§ 32. Dissolution by Decree of Court
(1) On application by or for a partner the court shall decree a dissolution whenever:

   (a) A partner has been declared a lunatic in any judicial proceeding or is shown to be of unsound mind,
   (b) A partner becomes in any other way incapable of performing his part of the partnership contract,
   (c) A partner has been guilty of such conduct as tends to affect prejudicially the carrying on of the business,
   (d) A partner wilfully or persistently commits a breach of the partnership agreement, or otherwise so conducts himself in matters relating to the partnership business that it is not reasonably practicable to carry on the business in partnership with him,

(e)   The business of the partnership can only be carried on at a loss,

(f)   Other circumstances render a dissolution equitable.

(2)   On the application of the purchaser of a partner's interest under sections 28 or 29 [should read 27 or 28];

(a)   After the termination of the specified term or particular undertaking,

(b)   At any time if the partnership was a partnership at will when the interest was assigned or when the charging order was issued.

§ 33. General Effect of Dissolution on Authority of Partner

Except so far as may be necessary to wind up partnership affairs or to complete transactions begun but not then finished, dissolution terminates all authority of any partner to act for the partnership,

(1)   With respect to the partners,

(a)   When the dissolution is not by the act, bankruptcy or death of a partner; or

(b)   When the dissolution is by such act, bankruptcy or death of a partner, in cases where section 34 so requires.

(2)   With respect to persons not partners, as declared in section 35.

§ 34. Rights of Partner to Contribution from Co-partners After Dissolution

Where the dissolution is caused by the act, death or bankruptcy of a partner, each partner is liable to his copartners for his share of any liability created by any partner acting for the partnership as if the partnership had not been dissolved unless

(a)   The dissolution being by act of any partner, the partner acting for the partnership had knowledge of the dissolution, or

(b)   The dissolution being by the death or bankruptcy of a partner, the partner acting for the partnership had knowledge or notice of the death or bankruptcy.

§ 35. Power of Partner to Bind Partnership to Third Persons After Dissolution

(1)   After dissolution a partner can bind the partnership except as provided in Paragraph (3).

(a)   By any act appropriate for winding up partnership affairs or completing transactions unfinished at dissolution;

(b)   By any transaction which would bind the partnership if dissolution had not taken place, provided the other party to the transaction

(I)   Had extended credit to the partnership prior to dissolution and had no knowledge or notice of the dissolution; or

(II)   Though he had not so extended credit, had nevertheless known of the partnership prior to dissolution, and, having no knowledge or notice of dissolution, the fact of dissolution had not been advertised in a newspaper of general circulation in the place (or in each place if more than one) at which the partnership business was regularly carried on.

(2)   The liability of a partner under paragraph (1b) shall be satisfied out of partnership assets alone when such partner had been prior to dissolution

(a)   Unknown as a partner to the person with whom the contract is made; and

(b)   So far unknown and inactive in partnership affairs that the business reputation of the partnership could not be said to have been in any degree due to his connection with it.

(3)   The partnership is in no case bound by any act of a partner after dissolution

(a)   Where the partnership is dissolved because it is unlawful to carry on the business, unless the act is appropriate for winding up partnership affairs; or

(b)   Where the partner has become bankrupt; or

(c)   Where the partner has no authority to wind up partnership affairs; except by a transaction with one who

(I)   Had extended credit to the partnership prior to dissolution and had no knowledge or notice of his want of authority; or

(II)   Had not extended credit to the partnership prior to dissolution, and, having no knowledge or notice of his want of authority, the fact of his want of authority has not been advertised in the manner provided for advertising the fact of dissolution in paragraph (1bII).

(4) Nothing in this section shall affect the liability under Section 16 of any person who after dissolution represents himself or consents to another representing him as a partner in a partnership engaged in carrying on business.

§ 36. Effect of Dissolution on Partner's Existing Liability

(1) The dissolution of the partnership does not of itself discharge the existing liability of any partner.

(2) A partner is discharged from any existing liability upon dissolution of the partnership by an agreement to that effect between himself, the partnership creditor and the person or partnership continuing the business; and such agreement may be inferred from the course of dealing between the creditor having knowledge of the dissolution and the person or partnership continuing the business.

(3) Where a person agrees to assume the existing obligations of a dissolved partnership, the partners whose obligations have been assumed shall be discharged from any liability to any creditor of the partnership who, knowing of the agreement, consents to a material alteration in the nature or time of payment of such obligations.

(4) The individual property of a deceased partner shall be liable for all obligations of the partnership incurred while he was a partner but subject to the prior payment of his separate debts.

§ 37. Right to Wind Up

Unless otherwise agreed the partners who have not wrongfully dissolved the partnership or the legal representative of the last surviving partner, not bankrupt, has the right to wind up the partnership affairs; provided, however, that any partner, his legal representative or his assignee, upon cause shown, may obtain winding up by the court.

§ 38. Rights of Partners to Application of Partnership Property

(1) When dissolution is caused in any way, except in contravention of the partnership agreement, each partner, as against his co-partners and all persons claiming through them in respect of their interests in the partnership, unless otherwise agreed, may have the partnership property applied to discharge its liabilities, and the surplus applied to pay in cash the net amount owing to the respective partners. But if disso-

lution is caused by expulsion of a partner, bona fide under the partnership agreement and if the expelled partner is discharged from all partnership liabilities, either by payment or agreement under section 36(2), he shall receive in cash only the net amount due him from the partnership.

(2) When dissolution is caused in contravention of the partnership agreement the rights of the partners shall be as follows:

(a) Each partner who has not caused dissolution wrongfully shall have,
  (I) All the rights specified in paragraph (1) of this section, and
  (II) The right, as against each partner who has caused the dissolution wrongfully, to damages for breach of the agreement.

(b) The partners who have not caused the dissolution wrongfully, if they all desire to continue the business in the same name, either by themselves or jointly with others, may do so, during the agreed term for the partnership and for that purpose may possess the partnership property, provided they secure the payment by bond approved by the court, or pay to any partner who has caused the dissolution wrongfully, the value of his interest in the partnership at the dissolution, less any damages recoverable under clause (2a II) of the section, and in like manner indemnify him against all present or future partnership liabilities.

(c) A partner who has caused the dissolution wrongfully shall have:
  (I) If the business is not continued under the provisions of paragraph (2b) all the rights of a partner under paragraph (1), subject to clause (2aII), of this section,
  (II) If the business is continued under paragraph (2b) of this section the right as against his co-partners and all claiming through them in respect of their interests in the partnership, to have the value of his interest in the partnership, less any damages caused to his co-partners by the dissolution, ascertained and paid to him in cash, or the payment secured by bond approved by the

court, and to be released from all existing liabilities of the partnership; but in ascertaining the value of the partner's interest the value of the good-will of the business shall not be considered.

§ 39. Rights Where Partnership is Dissolved for Fraud or Misrepresentation

Where a partnership contract is rescinded on the ground of the fraud or misrepresentation of one of the parties thereto, the party entitled to rescind is, without prejudice to any other right, entitled,

(a) To a lien on, or right of retention of, the surplus of the partnership property after satisfying the partnership liabilities to third persons for any sum of money paid by him for the purchase of an interest in the partnership and for any capital or advances contributed by him; and

(b) To stand, after all liabilities to third persons have been satisfied, in the place of the creditors of the partnership for any payments made by him in respect of the partnership liabilities; and

(c) To be indemnified by the person guilty of the fraud or making the representation against all debts and liabilities of the partnership.

§ 40. Rules for Distribution

In settling accounts between the partners after dissolution, the following rules shall be observed, subject to any agreement to the contrary:

(a) The assets of the partnership are:

   (I) The partnership property,
   (II) The contributions of the partners necessary for the payment of all the liabilities specified in clause (b) of this paragraph.

(b) The liabilities of the partnership shall rank in order of payment, as follows:

   (I) Those owing to creditors other than partners,
   (II) Those owing to partners other than for capital and profits,
   (III) Those owing to partners in respect of capital,
   (IV) Those owing to partners in respect of profits.

(c) The assets shall be applied in the order of their declaration in clause (a) of this paragraph to the satisfaction of the liabilities.

(d) The partners shall contribute, as provided by section 18(a) the amount necessary to satisfy the liabilities; but if any, but not all, of the partners are insolvent, or, not being subject to process, refuse to contribute, the other partners shall contribute their share of the liabilities, and, in the relative proportions in which they share the profits, the additional amount necessary to pay the liabilities.

(e) An assignee for the benefit of creditors or any person appointed by the court shall have the right to enforce the contributions specified in clause (d) of this paragraph.

(f) Any partner or his legal representative shall have the right to enforce the contributions specified in clause (d) of this paragraph, to the extent of the amount which he has paid in excess of his share of the liability.

(g) The individual property of a deceased partner shall be liable for the contributions specified in clause (d) of this paragraph.

(h) When partnership property and the individual properties of the partners are in possession of a court for distribution, partnership creditors shall have priority on partnership property and separate creditors on individual property, saving the rights of lien or secured creditors as heretofore.

(i) Where a partner has become bankrupt or his estate is insolvent the claims against his separate property shall rank in the following order:

   (I) Those owing to separate creditors,
   (III) Those owing to partnership creditors,
   (III) Those owing to partners by way of contribution.

§ 41. Liability of Persons Continuing the Business in Certain Cases

(1) When any new partner is admitted into an existing partnership, or when any partner retires and assigns (or the representative of the deceased partner assigns) his rights in partnership property to two or more of the partners, or to one or more of the partners and one or more third persons, if the business is continued without liquidation of the partnership affairs, creditors of the first or dissolved partnership are also creditors of the partnership so continuing the business.

(2) When all but one partner retire and assign (or the representative of a deceased partner assigns) their rights in partnership property to the remaining

partner, who continues the business without liquidation of partnership affairs, either alone or with others, creditors of the dissolved partnership are also creditors of the person or partnership so continuing the business.

(3) When any partner retires or dies and the business of the dissolved partnership is continued as set forth in paragraphs (1) and (2) of this section, with the consent of the retired partners or the representative of the deceased partner, but without any assignment of his right in partnership property, rights of creditors of the dissolved partnership and of the creditors of the person or partnership continuing the business shall be as if such assignment had been made.

(4) When all the partners or their representatives assign their rights in partnership property to one or more third persons who promise to pay the debts and who continue the business of the dissolved partnership, creditors of the dissolved partnership are also creditors of the person or partnership continuing the business.

(5) When any partner wrongfully causes a dissolution and the remaining partners continue the business under the provisions of section 38(2b), either alone or with others, and without liquidation of the partnership affairs, creditors of the dissolved partnership are also creditors of the person or partnership continuing the business.

(6) When a partner is expelled and the remaining partners continue the business either alone or with others, without liquidation of the partnership affairs, creditors of the dissolved partnership are also creditors of the person or partnership continuing the business.

(7) The liability of a third person becoming a partner in the partnership continuing the business, under this section, to the creditors of the dissolved partnership shall be satisfied out of partnership property only.

(8) When the business of a partnership after dissolution is continued under any conditions set forth in this section the creditors of the dissolved partnership, as against the separate creditors of the retiring or deceased partner or the representative of the deceased partner, have a prior right to any claim of the retired partner or the representative of the deceased partner against the person or partnership continuing the business, on account of the retired or deceased partner's interest in the dissolved partnership or on account of any consideration promised for such interest or for his right in partnership property.

(9) Nothing in this section shall be held to modify any right of creditors to set aside any assignment on the ground of fraud.

(10) The use by the person or partnership continuing the business of the partnership name, or the name of a deceased partner as part thereof, shall not of itself make the individual property of the deceased partner liable for any debts contracted by such person or partnership.

§ 42. Rights of Retiring or Estate of Deceased Partner When the Business is Continued

When any partner retires or dies, and the business is continued under any of the conditions set forth in section 41 (1, 2, 3, 5, 6), or section 38(2b) without any settlement of accounts as between him or his estate and the person or partnership continuing the business, unless otherwise agreed, he or his legal representative as against such persons or partnership may have the value of his interest at the date of dissolution ascertained, and shall receive as an ordinary creditor an amount equal to the value of his interest in the dissolved partnership with interest, or, at his option or at the option of his legal representative, in lieu of interest, the profits attributable to the use of his right in the property of the dissolved partnership; provided that the creditors of the dissolved partnership as against the separate creditors, or the representative of the retired or deceased partner, shall have priority on any claim arising under this section, as provided by section 41(8) of this act.

§ 43. Accrual of Actions

The right to an account of his interest shall accrue to any partner, or his legal representative, as against the winding up partners or the surviving partners or the person or partnership continuing the business, at the date of dissolution, in the absence of any agreement to the contrary.

PART VII
MISCELLANEOUS PROVISIONS
§ 44. When Act Takes Effect
This act shall take effect on the ____ day of ____ one thousand nine hundred and ____ .

§ 45. Legislation Repealed
All acts or parts of acts inconsistent with this act are hereby repealed.

The Uniform Limited Partnership Act

*(Adopted August 5, 1976, by the National Conference of Commissioners on Uniform State Laws, it is intended to replace the existing Uniform Limited Partnership Act (Appendix D). It has been adopted in 36 States: Alabama, Arizona, Arkansas, California, Colorado, Connecticut, Delaware, Florida, Idaho, Illinois, Iowa, Kansas, Maryland, Massachusetts, Michigan, Minnesota, Mississippi, Missouri, Montana, Nebraska, Nevada, New Jersey, North Carolina, North Dakota, Ohio, Oklahoma, Oregon, Rhode Island, South Carolina, South Dakota, Texas, Virginia, Washington, West Virginia, Wisconsin, and Wyoming.

The Act consists of 11 Articles as follows:

1. General Provisions
2. Formation; Certificate of Limited Partnership
3. Limited Partners
4. General Partners
5. Finance
6. Distributions and Withdrawal
7. Assignment of Partnership Interests
8. Dissolution
9. Foreign Limited Partnership
10. Derivative Actions
11. Miscellaneous

ARTICLE 1
GENERAL PROVISIONS
§ 101. Definitions
As used in this Act, unless the context otherwise requires:

---

*At its annual conference in August 1985, the National Conference of Commissioners on Uniform State Laws approved amendments to the "Revised Uniform Partnership Act." This printing includes these amendments.

(1) "Certificate of limited partnership" means the certificate referred to in Section 201, and the certificate as amended or restated.

(2) "Contribution" means any cash, property, services rendered, or a promissory note or other binding obligation to contribute cash or property or to perform services, which a partner contributes to a limited partnership in his capacity as a partner.

(3) "Event of withdrawal of a general partner" means an event that causes a person to cease to be a general partner as provided in Section 402.

(4) "Foreign limited partnership" means a partnership formed under the laws of any state other than this State and having as partners one or more general partners and one or more limited partners.

(5) "General partner" means a person who has been admitted to a limited partnership as a general partner in accordance with the partnership agreement and named in the certificate of limited partnership as a general partner.

(6) "Limited partner" means a person who has been admitted to a limited partnership as a limited partner in accordance with the partnership agreement.

(7) "Limited partnership" and "domestic limited partnership" mean a partnership formed by two or more persons under the laws of this State and having one or more general partners and one or more limited partners.

(8) "Partner" means a limited or general partner.

(9) "Partnership agreement" means any valid agreement, written or oral, of the partners as to the affairs of a limited partnership and the conduct of its business.

(10) "Partnership interest" means a partner's share of the profits and losses of a limited partnership

and the right to receive distributions of partnership assets.

(11) "Person" means a natural person, partnership, limited partnership (domestic or foreign), trust, estate, association, or corporation.

(12) "State" means a state, territory, or possession of the United States, the District of Columbia, or the Commonwealth of Puerto Rico.

§ 102. Name

The name of each limited partnership as set forth in its certificate of limited partnership:

(1) shall contain without abbreviation the words "limited partnership";

(2) may not contain the name of a limited partner unless (i) it is also the name of a general partner or the corporate name of a corporate general partner, or (ii) the business of the limited partnership had been carried on under that name before the admission of that limited partner;

(3) may not be the same as, or deceptively similar to, the name of any corporation or limited partnership organized under the laws of this State or licensed or registered as a foreign corporation or limited partnership in this State; and

(4) may not contain the following words [here insert prohibited words].

§ 103. Reservation of Name

(a) The exclusive right to the use of a name may be reserved by:

(1) any person intending to organize a limited partnership under this Act and to adopt that name;

(2) any domestic limited partnership or any foreign limited partnership registered in this State which, in either case, intends to adopt that name;

(3) any foreign limited partnership intending to register in this State and adopt that name; and

(4) any person intending to organize a foreign limited partnership and intending to have it register in this State and adopt that name.

(b) The reservation shall be made by filing with the Secretary of State an application, executed by the applicant, to reserve a specified name. If the Secretary of State finds that the name is available for use by a domestic or foreign limited partnership, he [or she] shall reserve the name for the exclusive use of the applicant for a period of 120 days. Once having so reserved a name, the same applicant may not again reserve the same name until more than 60 days after the expiration of the last 120-day period for which that applicant reserved that name. The right to the exclusive use of a reserved name may be transferred to any other person by filing in the office of the Secretary of State a notice of the transfer, executed by the applicant for whom the name was reserved and specifying the name and address of the transferee.

§ 104. Specified Office and Agent

Each limited partnership shall continuously maintain in this State:

(1) an office, which may but need not be a place of its business in this State, at which shall be kept the records required by Section 105 to be maintained; and

(2) an agent for service of process on the limited partnership, which agent must be an individual resident of this State, a domestic corporation, or a foreign corporation authorized to do business in this State.

§ 105. Records to be Kept

(a) Each limited partnership shall keep at the office referred to in Section 104(1) the following:

(1) a current list of the full name and last known business address of each partner separately identifying the general partners (in alphabetical order) and the limited partners (in alphabetical order);

(2) a copy of the certificate of limited partnership and all certificates of amendment thereto, together with executed copies of any powers of attorney pursuant to which any certificate has been executed;

(3) copies of the limited partnership's federal, state and local income tax returns and reports, if any, for the three most recent years;

(4) copies of any then effective written partnership agreements and of any financial statements of the limited partnership for the three most recent years; and

(5) unless contained in a written partnership agreement, a writing setting out:

(i) the amount of cash and a description and statement of the agreed value of the other property or services contributed by each partner and which each partner has agreed to contribute;

    (ii) the times at which or events on the happening of which any additional contributions agreed to be made by each partner are to be made;

    (iii) any right of a partner to receive, or of a general partner to make, distributions to a partner which include a return of all or any part of the partner's contribution; and

    (iv) any events upon the happening of which the limited partnership is to be dissolved and its affairs wound up.

(b) Records kept under this section are subject to inspection and copying at the reasonable request at the expense of any partner during ordinary business hours.

§ 106. Nature of Business

A limited partnership may carry on any business that a partnership without limited partners may carry on except [here designate prohibited activities].

§ 107. Business Transactions of Partner with Partnership

Except as provided in the partnership agreement, a partner may lend money to and transact other business with the limited partnership and, subject to other applicable law, has the same rights and obligations with respect thereto as a person who is not a partner.

ARTICLE 2
FORMATION; CERTIFICATE OF LIMITED PARTNERSHIP

§ 201. Certificate of Limited Partnership

(a) In order to form a limited partnership, a certificate of limited partnership must be executed and filed in the office of the Secretary of State. The certificate shall set forth:

    (1) the name of the limited partnership;

    (2) the address of the office and the name and address of the agent for service of process required to be maintained by Section 104;

    (3) the name and the business address of each general partner;

    (4) the latest date upon which the limited partnership is to dissolve; and

    (5) any other matters the general partners determine to include therein.

(b) A limited partnership is formed at the time of the filing of the certificate of limited partnership in the office of the Secretary of State or at any later time specified in the certificate of limited partnership if, in either case, there has been substantial compliance with the requirements of this section.

§ 202. Amendment to Certificate

(a) A certificate of limited partnership is amended by filing a certificate of amendment thereto in the office of the Secretary of State. The certificate shall set forth:

    (1) the name of the limited partnership;

    (2) the date of filing the certificate; and

    (3) the amendment to the certificate.

(b) Within 30 days after the happening of any of the following events, an amendment to a certificate of limited partnership reflecting the occurrence of the event or events shall be filed:

    (1) the admission of a new general partner;

    (2) the withdrawal of a general partner; or

    (3) the continuation of the business under Section 801 after an event of withdrawal of a general partner.

(c) A general partner who becomes aware that any statement in a certificate of limited partnership was false when made or that any arrangements or other facts described have changed, making the certificate inaccurate in any respect, shall promptly amend the certificate.

(d) A certificate of limited partnership may be amended at any time for any other proper purpose the general partners determine.

(e) No person has any liability because an amendment to a certificate of limited partnership has not been filed to reflect the occurrence of any event referred to in subsection (b) of this section if the amendment is filed within the 30-day period specified in subsection (b).

(f) A restated certificate of limited partnership may be executed and filed in the same manner as a certificate of amendment.

§ 203. Cancellation of Certificate

A certificate of limited partnership shall be cancelled upon the dissolution and the commencement of winding up of the partnership or at any other time there are no limited partners. A certificate of cancellation shall be filed in the office of the Secretary of State and set forth:

(1) the name of the limited partnership;

(2) the date of filing of its certificate of limited partnership;

(3) the reason for filing the certificate of cancellation;

(4) the effective date (which shall be a date certain) of cancellation if it is not to be effective upon the filing of the certificate; and

(5) any other information the general partners filing the certificate determine.

§ 204. Execution of Certificates

(a) Each certificate required by this Article to be filed in the office of the Secretary of State shall be executed in the following manner:

    (1) an original certificate of limited partnership must be signed by all general partners,

    (2) a certificate of amendment must be signed by at least one general partner and by each other general partner designated in the certificate as a new general partner; and

    (3) a certificate of cancellation must be signed by all general partners.

(b) Any person may sign a certificate by an attorney-in-fact, but a power of attorney to sign a certificate relating to the admission of a general partner must specifically describe the admission.

(c) The execution of a certificate by a general partner constitutes an affirmation under the penalties of perjury that the facts stated therein are true.

§ 205. Execution by Judicial Act

If a person required by Section 204 to execute any certificate fails or refuses to do so, any other person who is adversely affected by the failure or refusal, may petition the [designate the appropriate court] to direct the execution of the certificate. If the court finds that it is proper for the certificate to be executed and that any person so designated has failed or refused to execute the certificate, it shall order the Secretary of State to record an appropriate certificate.

§ 206. Filing in Office of Secretary of State

(a) Two signed copies of the certificate of limited partnership and of any certificates of amendment or cancellation (or of any judicial decree of amendment or cancellation) shall be delivered to the Secretary of State. A person who executes a certificate as an agent or fiduciary need not exhibit evidence of his [or her] authority as a prerequisite to filing. Unless the Secretary of State finds that any certificate does not conform to law, upon receipt of all filing fees required by law he [or she] shall:

    (1) endorse on each duplicate original the word "Filed" and the day, month, and year of the filing thereof;

    (2) file one duplicate original in his [or her] office; and

    (3) return the other duplicate original to the person who filed it or his [or her] representative.

(b) Upon the filing of a certificate of amendment (or judicial decree of amendment) in the office of the Secretary of State, the certificate of limited partnership shall be amended as set forth therein, and upon the effective date of a certificate of cancellation (or a judicial decree thereof), the certificate of limited partnership is cancelled.

§ 207. Liability for False Statement in Certificate

If any certificate of limited partnership or certificate of amendment or cancellation contains a false statement, one who suffers loss by reliance on the statement may recover damages for the loss from:

(1) any person who executes the certificate, or causes another to execute it on his behalf, and knew, and any general partner who knew or should have known, the statement to be false at the time the certificate was executed; and

(2) any general partner who thereafter knows or should have known that any arrangement or other fact described in the certificate has changed, making the statement inaccurate in any respect within a sufficient time before the statement was relied upon reasonably to have enabled that general partner to cancel or amend the certificate, or to file a petition for its cancellation or amendment under Section 205.

§ 208. Scope of Notice

The fact that a certificate of limited partnership is on file in the office of the Secretary of State is notice that the partnership is a limited partnership and the persons designated therein as general partners are general partners, but it is not notice of any other fact.

ARTICLE 3
LIMITED PARTNERS

§ 301. Admission of Additional Limited Partners

(a) A person becomes a limited partner:

(1) at the time the limited partnership is formed; or

(2) at any later time specified in the records of the limited partnership for becoming a limited partner.

(b) After the filing of a limited partnership's original certificate of limited partnership, a person may be admitted as an additional limited partner:

(1) in the case of a person acquiring a partnership interest directly from the limited partnership, upon compliance with the partnership agreement or, if the partnership agreement does not so provide, upon the written consent of all partners; and

(2) in the case of an assignee of a partnership interest of a partner who has the power, as provided in Section 704, to grant the assignee the right to become a limited partner, upon the exercise of that power and compliance with any conditions limiting the grant or exercise of the power.

§ 302. Voting

Subject to Section 303, the partnership agreement may grant to all or to a specified group of the limited partners the right to vote (on a per capita or any other basis) upon any matter.

§ 303. Liability to Third Parties

(a) Except as provided in subsection (d), a limited partner is not liable for the obligations of a limited partnership unless he [or she] is also a general partner or, in addition to the exercise of his [or her] rights and powers as a limited partner, he [or she] participates in the control of the business. However, if the limited partner participates in the control of the business, he [or she] is liable only to persons who transact business with the limited partnership reasonably believing, based upon the limited partner's conduct, that the limited partner is a general partner.

(b) A limited partner does not participate in the control of the business within the meaning of subsection (a) solely by doing one or more of the following:

(1) being a contractor for or an agent or employee of the limited partnership or of a general partner or being an officer, director, or shareholder of a general partner that is a corporation;

(2) consulting with and advising a general partner with respect to the business of the limited partnership;

(3) acting as surety for the limited partnership or guaranteeing or assuming one or more specific obligations of the limited partnership;

(4) taking any action required or permitted by law to bring or pursue a derivative action in the right of the limited partnership;

(5) requesting or attending a meeting of partners;

(6) proposing, approving, or disapproving, by voting or otherwise, one or more of the following matters:

(i) the dissolution and winding up of the limited partnership;

(ii) the sale, exchange, lease, mortgage, pledge, or other transfer of all or substantially all of the assets of the limited partnership;

(iii) the incurrence of indebtedness by the limited partnership other than in the ordinary course of its business;

(iv) a change in the nature of the business;

(v) the admission or removal of a general partner;

(vi) the admission or removal of a limited partner;

(vii) a transaction involving an actual or potential conflict of interest between a general partner and the limited partnership or the limited partners;

(viii) an amendment to the partnership agreement or certificate of limited partnership; or

(ix) matters related to the business of the limited partnership not otherwise enumerated in this subsection (b), which the partnership agreement states in writing may be subject to the approval or disapproval of limited partners;

(7) winding up the limited partnership pursuant to Section 803; or

(8) exercising any right or power permitted to limited partners under this Act and not specifically enumerated in this subsection (b).

(c) The enumeration in subsection (b) does not mean that the possession or exercise of any other powers by a limited partner constitutes participation by him [or her] in the business of the limited partnership.

(d) A limited partner who knowingly permits his [or her] name to be used in the name of the limited partnership, except under circumstances permitted by Section 102(2), is liable to creditors who extend credit to the limited partnership without actual knowledge that the limited partner is not a general partner.

§ 304. Person Erroneously Believing Himself [or Herself] Limited Partner

(a) Except as provided in subsection (b), a person who makes a contribution to a business enterprise and erroneously but in good faith believes that he [or she] has become a limited partner in the enterprise is not a general partner in the enterprise and is not bound by its obligations by reason of making the contribution, receiving distributions from the enterprise, or exercising any rights of a limited partner, if, on ascertaining the mistake, he [or she]:

  (1) causes an appropriate certificate of limited partnership or a certificate of amendment to be executed and filed; or

  (2) withdraws from future equity participation in the enterprise by executing and filing in the office of the Secretary of State a certificate declaring withdrawal under this section.

(b) A person who makes a contribution of the kind described in subsection (a) is liable as a general partner to any third party who transacts business with the enterprise (i) before the person withdraws and an appropriate certificate is filed to show withdrawal, or (ii) before an appropriate certificate is filed to show that he [or she] is not a general partner, but in either case only if the third party actually believed in good faith that the person was a general partner at the time of the transaction.

§ 305. Information

Each limited partner has the right to:

  (1) inspect and copy any of the partnership records required to be maintained by Section 105; and

  (2) obtain from the general partners from time to time upon reasonable demand (i) true and full

information regarding the state of the business and financial condition of the limited partnership, (ii) promptly after becoming available, a copy of the limited partnership's federal, state, and local income tax returns for each year, and (iii) other information regarding the affairs of the limited partnership as is just and reasonable.

ARTICLE 4
GENERAL PARTNERS

§ 401. Admission of Additional General Partners

After the filing of a limited partnership's original certificate of limited partnership, additional general partners may be admitted as provided in writing in the partnership agreement or, if the partnership agreement does not provide in writing for the admission of additional general partners, with the written consent of all partners.

§ 402. Events of Withdrawal

Except as approved by the specific written consent of all partners at the time, a person ceases to be a general partner of a limited partnership upon the happening of any of the following events:

  (1) the general partner withdraws from the limited partnership as provided in Section 602;

  (2) the general partner ceases to be a member of the limited partnership as provided in Section 702;

  (3) the general partner is removed as a general partner in accordance with the partnership agreement;

  (4) unless otherwise provided in writing in the partnership agreement, the general partner: (i) makes an assignment for the benefit of creditors; (ii) files a voluntary petition in bankruptcy; (iii) is adjudicated a bankrupt or insolvent; (iv) files a petition or answer seeking for himself [or herself] any reorganization, arrangement, composition, readjustment, liquidation, dissolution or similar relief under any statute, law, or regulation; (v) files an answer or other pleading admitting or failing to contest the material allegations of a petition filed against him [or her] in any proceeding of this nature; or (vi) seeks, consents to, or acquiesces in the appointment of a trustee, receiver, or liquidator of the general partner or of all or any substantial part of his [or her] properties;

  (5) unless otherwise provided in writing in the partnership agreement, [120] days after the

commencement of any proceeding against the general partner seeking reorganization, arrangement, composition, readjustment, liquidation, dissolution or similar relief under any statute, law, or regulation, the proceeding has not been dismissed, or if within [90] days after the appointment without his [or her] consent or acquiescence of a trustee, receiver, or liquidator of the general partner or of all or any substantial part of his [or her] properties, the appointment is not vacated or stayed or within [90] days after the expiration of any such stay, the appointment is not vacated;

(6) in the case of a general partner who is a natural person,

    (i) his [or her] death; or

    (ii) the entry of an order by a court of competent jurisdiction adjudicating him [or her] incompetent to manage his [or her] person or his [or her] estate;

(7) in the case of a general partner who is acting as a general partner by virtue of being a trustee of a trust, the termination of the trust (but not merely the substitution of a new trustee);

(8) in the case of a general partner that is a separate partnership, the dissolution and commencement of winding up of the separate partnership;

(9) in the case of a general partner that is a corporation, the filing of a certificate of dissolution, or its equivalent, for the corporation or the revocation of its charter; or

(10) in the case of an estate, the distribution by the fiduciary of the estate's entire interest in the partnership.

§ 403. General Powers and Liabilities

(a) Except as provided in this Act or in the partnership agreement, a general partner of a limited partnership has the rights and powers and is subject to the restrictions of a partner in a partnership without limited partners.

(b) Except as provided in this Act, a general partner of a limited partnership has the liabilities of a partner in a partnership without limited partners to persons other than the partnership and the other partners. Except as provided in this Act or in the partnership agreement, a general partner of a limited partnership has the liabilities of a partner in a partnership without limited partners to the partnership and to the other partners.

§ 404. Contributions by General Partner

A general partner of a limited partnership may make contributions to the partnership and share in the profits and losses of, and in distributions from, the limited partnership as a general partner. A general partner also may make contributions to and share in profits, losses, and distributions as a limited partner. A person who is both a general partner and a limited partner has the rights and powers, and is subject to the restrictions and liabilities, of a general partner and, except as provided in the partnership agreement, also has the powers, and is subject to the restrictions, of a limited partner to the extent of his [or her] participation in the partnership as a limited partner.

§ 405. Voting

The partnership agreement may grant to all or certain identified general partners the right to vote (on a per capita or any other basis), separately or with all or any class of the limited partners, on any matter.

ARTICLE 5
FINANCE

§ 501. Form of Contribution

The contribution of a partner may be in cash, property, or services rendered, or a promissory note or other obligation to contribute cash or property or to perform services.

§ 502. Liability for Contribution

(a) A promise by a limited partner to contribute to the limited partnership is not enforceable unless set out in a writing signed by the limited partner.

(b) Except as provided in the partnership agreement, a partner is obligated to the limited partnership to perform any enforceable promise to contribute cash or property or to perform services, even if he [or she] is unable to perform because of death, disability, or any other reason. If a partner does not make the required contribution of property or services, he [or she] is obligated at the option of the limited partnership to contribute cash equal to that portion of the value, as stated in the partnership records required to be kept pursuant to Section 105, of the stated contribution which has not been made.

(c) Unless otherwise provided in the partnership agreement, the obligation of a partner to make a contribution or return money or other property paid or distributed in violation of this Act may be compromised only by consent of all partners.

Notwithstanding the compromise, a creditor of a limited partnership who extends credit, or otherwise acts in reliance on that obligation after the partner signs a writing which, reflects the obligation, and before the amendment or cancellation thereof to reflect the compromise, may enforce the original obligation.

§ 503. Sharing of Profits and Losses

The profits and losses of a limited partnership shall be allocated among the partners, and among classes of partners, in the manner provided in writing in the partnership agreement. If the partnership agreement does not so provide in writing, profits and losses shall be allocated on the basis of the value, as stated in the partnership records required to be kept pursuant to Section 105, of the contributions made by each partner to the extent they have been received by the partnership and have not been returned.

§ 504. Sharing of Distributions

Distributions of cash or other assets of a limited partnership shall be allocated among the partners and among classes of partners in the manner provided in writing in the partnership agreement. If the partnership agreement does not so provide in writing, distributions shall be made on the basis of the value, as stated in the partnership records required to be kept pursuant to Section 105, of the contributions made by each partner to the extent they have been received by the partnership and have not been returned.

ARTICLE 6
DISTRIBUTIONS AND WITHDRAWAL

§ 601. Interim Distributions

Except as provided in this Article, a partner is entitled to receive distributions from a limited partnership before his [or her] withdrawal from the limited partnership and before the dissolution and winding up thereof to the extent and at the times or upon the happening of the events specified in the partnership agreement.

§ 602. Withdrawal of General Partner

A general partner may withdraw from a limited partnership at any time by giving written notice to the other partners, but if the withdrawal violates the partnership agreement, the limited partnership may recover from the withdrawing general partner damages for breach of the partnership agreement and offset the damages against the amount otherwise distributable to him [or her].

§ 603. Withdrawal of Limited Partner

A limited partner may withdraw from a limited partnership at the time or upon the happening of events specified in writing in the partnership agreement. If the agreement does not specify in writing the time or the events upon the happening of which a limited partner may withdraw or a definite time for the dissolution and winding up of the limited partnership, a limited partner may withdraw upon not less than six months' prior written notice to each general partner at his [or her] address on the books of the limited partnership at its office in this State.

§ 604. Distribution Upon Withdrawal

Except as provided in this Article, upon withdrawal any withdrawing partner is entitled to receive any distribution to which he [or she] is entitled under the partnership agreement and, if not otherwise provided in the agreement, he [or she] is entitled to receive, within a reasonable time after withdrawal, the fair value of his [or her] interest in the limited partnership as of the date of withdrawal based upon his [or her] right to share in distributions from the limited partnership.

§ 605. Distribution in Kind

Except as provided in the partnership agreement, a partner, regardless of the nature of his [or her] contribution, has no right to demand and receive any distribution from a limited partnership in any form other than cash. Except as provided in writing in the partnership agreement, a partner may not be compelled to accept a distribution of any asset in kind from a limited partnership to the extent that the percentage of the asset distributed to him [or her] exceeds a percentage of the asset which is equal to the percentage in which he [or she] shares in distributions from the limited partnership.

§ 606. Right to Distribution

At the time a partner becomes entitled to receive a distribution, he [or she] has the status of, and is entitled to all remedies available to, a creditor of the limited partnership with respect to the distribution.

§ 607. Limitations on Distribution

A partner may not receive a distribution from a limited partnership to the extent that, after giving effect to the distribution, all liabilities of the limited partnership, other than liabilities to partners on account of their partnership interests, exceed the fair value of the partnership assets.

§ 608. Liability Upon Return of Contribution

(a) If a partner has received the return of any part of his [or her] contribution without violation of the partnership agreement or this Act, he [or she] is liable to the limited partnership for a period of one year thereafter for the amount of the returned contribution, but only to the extent necessary to discharge the limited partnership's liabilities to creditors who extended credit to the limited partnership during the period the contribution was held by the partnership.

(b) If a partner has received the return of any part of his [or her] contribution in violation of the partnership agreement or this Act, he [or she] is liable to the limited partnership for a period of six years thereafter for the amount of the contribution wrongfully returned.

(c) A partner receives a return of his [or her] contribution to the extent that a distribution to him [or her] reduces his [or her] share of the fair value of the net assets of the limited partnership below the value, as set forth in the partnership records required to be kept pursuant to Section 105, of his contribution which has not been distributed to him [or her].

ARTICLE 7
ASSIGNMENT OF PARTNERSHIP INTERESTS

§ 701. Nature of Partnership Interest
A partnership interest is personal property.

§ 702. Assignment of Partnership Interest
Except as provided in the partnership agreement, a partnership interest is assignable in whole or in part. An assignment of a partnership interest does not dissolve a limited partnership or entitle the assignee to become or to exercise any rights of a partner. An assignment entitles the assignee to receive, to the extent assigned, only the distribution to which the assignor would be entitled. Except as provided in the partnership agreement, a partner ceases to be a partner upon assignment of all his [or her] partnership interest.

§ 703. Rights of Creditor
On application to a court of competent jurisdiction by any judgment creditor of a partner, the court may charge the partnership interest of the partner with payment of the unsatisfied amount of the judgment with interest. To the extent so charged, the judgment creditor has only the rights of an assignee of the partnership interest. This Act does not deprive any partner of the benefit of any exemption laws applicable to his [or her] partnership interest.

§ 704. Right of Assignee to Become Limited Partner

(a) An assignee of a partnership interest, including an assignee of a general partner, may become a limited partner if and to the extent that (i) the assignor gives the assignee that right in accordance with authority described in the partnership agreement, or (ii) all other partners consent.

(b) An assignee who has become a limited partner has, to the extent assigned, the rights and powers, and is subject to the restrictions and liabilities, of a limited partner under the partnership agreement and this Act. An assignee who becomes a limited partner also is liable for the obligations of his [or her] assignor to make and return contributions as provided in Articles 5 and 6. However, the assignee is not obligated for liabilities unknown to the assignee at the time he [or she] became a limited partner.

(c) If an assignee of a partnership interest becomes a limited partner, the assignor is not released from his [or her] liability to the limited partnership under Sections 207 and 502.

§ 705. Power of Estate of Deceased or Incompetent Partner
If a partner who is an individual dies or a court of competent jurisdiction adjudges him [or her] to be incompetent to manage his [or her] person or his [or her] property, the partner's executor, administrator, guardian, conservator, or other legal representative may exercise all the partner's rights for the purpose of settling his [or her] estate or administering his [or her] property, including any power the partner had to give an assignee the right to become a limited partner. If a partner is a corporation, trust, or other entity and is dissolved or terminated, the powers of that partner may be exercised by its legal representative or successor.

ARTICLE 8
DISSOLUTION

§ 801. Nonjudicial Dissolution
A limited partnership is dissolved and its affairs shall be wound up upon the happening of the first to occur of the following:

(1) at the time specified in the certificate of limited partnership;

(2) upon the happening of events specified in writing in the partnership agreement;

(3) written consent of all partners;

(4) an event of withdrawal of a general partner unless at the time there is at least one other general partner and the written provisions of the partnership agreement permit the business of the limited partnership to be carried on by the remaining general partner and that partner does so, but the limited partnership is not dissolved and is not required to be wound up by reason of any event of withdrawal, if, within 90 days after the withdrawal, all partners agree in writing to continue the business of the limited partnership and to the appointment of one or more additional general partners if necessary or desired; or

(5) entry of a decree of judicial dissolution under Section 802.

§ 802. Judicial Dissolution

On application by or for a partner the [designate the appropriate court] court may decree dissolution of a limited partnership whenever it is not reasonably practicable to carry on the business in conformity with the partnership agreement.

§ 803. Winding Up

Except as provided in the partnership agreement, the general partners who have not wrongfully dissolved a limited partnership or, if none, the limited partners, may wind up the limited partnership's affairs; but the [designate the appropriate court] court may wind up the limited partnership's affairs upon application of any partner, his [or her] legal representative, or assignee.

§ 804. Distribution of Assets

Upon the winding up of a limited partnership, the assets shall be distributed as follows:

(1) to creditors, including partners who are creditors, to the extent permitted by law, in satisfaction of liabilities of the limited partnership other than liabilities for distributions to partners under Section 601 or 604;

(2) except as provided in the partnership agreement, to partners and former partners in satisfaction of liabilities for distributions under Section 601 or 604; and

(3) except as provided in the partnership agreement, to partners first for the return of their contribu-

tions and secondly respecting their partnership interests, in the proportions in which the partners share in distributions.

ARTICLE 9
FOREIGN LIMITED PARTNERSHIPS
§ 901. Law Governing

Subject to the Constitution of this State, (i) the laws of the state under which a foreign limited partnership is organized govern its organization and internal affairs and the liability of its limited partners, and (ii) a foreign limited partnership may not be denied registration by reason of any difference between those laws and the laws of this State.

§ 902. Registration

Before transacting business in this State, a foreign limited partnership shall register with the Secretary of State. In order to register, a foreign limited partnership shall submit to the Secretary of State, in duplicate, an application for registration as a foreign limited partnership, signed and sworn to by a general partner and setting forth:

(1) the name of the foreign limited partnership and, if different, the name under which it proposes to register and transact business in this State;

(2) the State and date of its formation;

(3) the name and address of any agent for service of process on the foreign limited partnership whom the foreign limited partnership elects to appoint; the agent must be an individual resident of this State, a domestic corporation, or a foreign corporation having a place of business in, and authorized to do business in, this State;

(4) a statement that the Secretary of State is appointed the agent of the foreign limited partnership for service of process if no agent has been appointed under paragraph (3) or, if appointed, the agent's authority has been revoked or if the agent cannot be found or served with the exercise of reasonable diligence;

(5) the address of the office required to be maintained in the state of its organization by the laws of that state or, if not so required, of the principal office of the foreign limited partnership;

(6) the name and business address of each general partner; and

(7) the address of the office at which is kept a list of the names and addresses of the limited partners

and their capital contributions, together with an undertaking by the foreign limited partnership to keep those records until the foreign limited partnership's registration in this State is cancelled or withdrawn.

§ 903. Issuance of Registration
(a) If the Secretary of State finds that an application for registration conforms to law and all requisite fees have been paid, he [or she] shall:

  (1) endorse on the application the word "Filed," and the month, day and year of the filing thereof;
  (2) file in his [or her] office a duplicate original of the application; and
  (3) issue a certificate of registration to transact business in this State.

(b) The certificate of registration, together with a duplicate original of the application, shall be returned to the person who filed the application or his [or her] representative.

§ 904. Name
A foreign limited partnership may register with the Secretary of State under any name, whether or not it is the name under which it is registered in its state of organization, that includes without abbreviation the words "limited partnership" and that could be registered by a domestic limited partnership.

§ 905. Changes and Amendments
If any statement in the application for registration of a foreign limited partnership was false when made or any arrangements or other facts described have changed, making the application inaccurate in any respect, the foreign limited partnership shall promptly file in the office of the Secretary of State a certificate, signed and sworn to by a general partner, correcting such statement.

§ 906. Cancellation of Registration
A foreign limited partnership may cancel its registration by filing with the Secretary of State a certificate of cancellation signed and sworn to by a general partner. A cancellation does not terminate the authority of the Secretary of State to accept service of process on the foreign limited partnership with respect to [claims for relief] [causes of action] arising out of the transactions of business in this State.

§ 907. Transaction of Business Without Registration
(a) A foreign limited partnership transacting business in this State may not maintain any action, suit, or proceeding in any court of this State until it has registered in this State.
(b) The failure of a foreign limited partnership to register in this State does not impair the validity of any contract or act of the foreign limited partnership or prevent the foreign limited partnership from defending any action, suit, or proceeding in any court of this State.
(c) A limited partner of a foreign limited partnership is not liable as a general partner of the foreign limited partnership solely by reason of having transacted business in this State without registration.
(d) A foreign limited partnership, by transacting business in this State without registration, appoints the Secretary of State as its agent for service of process with respect to [claims for relief] [causes of action] arising out of the transaction of business in this State.

§ 908. Action by [Appropriate Official]
The [designate the appropriate official] may bring an action to restrain a foreign limited partnership from transacting business in this State in violation of this Article.

ARTICLE 10
DERIVATIVE ACTIONS
§ 1001. Right of Action
A limited partner may bring an action in the right of a limited partnership to recover a judgment in its favor if general partners with authority to do so have refused to bring the action or if an effort to cause those general partners to bring the action is not likely to succeed.

§ 1002. Proper Plaintiff
In a derivative action, the plaintiff must be a partner at the time of bringing the action and (i) must have been a partner at the time of the transaction of which he [or she] complains or (ii) his [or her] status as a partner must have devolved upon him [or her] by operation of law or pursuant to the terms of the partnership agreement from a person who was a partner at the time of the transaction.

§ 1003. Pleading

In a derivative action, the complaint shall set forth with particularity the effort of the plaintiff to secure initiation of the action by a general partner or the reasons for not making the effort.

§ 1004. Expenses

If a derivative action is successful, in whole or in part, or if anything is received by the plaintiff as a result of a judgment, compromise or settlement of an action or claim, the court may award the plaintiff reasonable expenses, including reasonable attorney's fees, and shall direct him [or her] to remit to the limited partnership the remainder of those proceeds received by him [or her].

ARTICLE 11
MISCELLANEOUS

§ 1101. Construction and Application

This Act shall be so applied and construed to effectuate its general purpose to make uniform the law with respect to the subject of this Act among states enacting it.

§ 1102. Short Title

This Act may be cited as the Uniform Limited Partnership Act.

§ 1103. Severability

If any provision of this Act or its application to any person or circumstance is held invalid, the invalidity does not affect other provisions or applications of the Act which can be given effect without the invalid provision or application, and to this end the provisions of this Act are severable.

§ 1104. Effective Date, Extended Effective Date and Repeal

Except as set forth below, the effective date of this Act is ____ and the following acts [list existing limited partnership acts] are hereby repealed:

(1) The existing provisions for execution and filing of certificates of limited partnerships and amendments thereunder and cancellations thereof continue in effect until [specify time required to create central filing system], the extended effective date, and Sections 102, 103, 104, 105, 201, 202, 203, 204 and 206 are not effective until the extended effective date.

(2) Section 402, specifying the conditions under which a general partner ceases to be a member of a limited partnership, is not effective until the extended effective date, and the applicable provisions of existing law continue to govern until the extended effective date.

(3) Sections 501, 502 and 608 apply only to contributions and distributions made after the effective date of this Act.

(4) Section 704 applies only to assignments made after the effective date of this Act.

(5) Article 9, dealing with registration of foreign limited partnerships, is not effective until the extended effective date.

(6) Unless otherwise agreed by the partners, the applicable provisions of existing law governing allocation of profits and losses (rather than the provisions of Section 503), distributions to a withdrawing partner (rather than the provisions of Section 604), and distribution of assets upon the winding up of a limited partnership (rather than the provisions of Section 804) govern limited partnerships formed before the effective date of this Act.

§ 1105. Rules for Cases Not Provided for in This Act

In any case not provided for in this Act the provisions of the Uniform Partnership Act govern.

§ 1106. Savings Clause

The repeal of any statutory provision by this Act does not impair, or otherwise affect, the organization or the continued existence of a limited partnership existing at the effective date of this Act, nor does the repeal of any existing statutory provision by this Act impair any contract or affect any right accrued before the effective date of this Act.

APPENDIX E

Understanding and Locating Legal Citations

The purpose of this appendix is to familiarize you with common legal citations and their meaning. With the assistance of the following information, you should be able to locate a legal authority in the library by determining the content of the citation. For a more comprehensive approach to legal research, consult the appropriate authority.

A legal citation is a reference to the name and location of a legal document. Although there are as many and as varied books and papers in a library containing legal authorities as there are in any other type of library, locating authorities through the use of a systematic method of arranging information about the authority makes the process virtually painless.

To help one to understand the typical organization of legal authorities, almost all such authorities are somehow arranged or indexed by subject. The information contained in a standard citation is generally uniform for the type of authority. For example, all published judicial opinions are maintained in what are known as reports or reporters. Each jurisdiction publishes its appellate judicial opinions in a designated "official report." Quite often the opinion is also published in what commercial firms call a reporter. Because this is such a common practice, many jurisdictions have ceased their own publication and adopted the commercial publication as the official location for judicial opinions.

In a citation of judicial authority, the reader is usually given the official location (report), followed by a secondary location (reporter) of the opinion (if one exists). Additional information included is a direct or indirect reference to the source (court that delivered the opinion), year of the opinion, and the last name of the first plaintiff and first defendant listed in the case (it is not uncommon for there to be

multiple plaintiffs or defendants in a suit). A typical case citation might appear as follows: *State v. Markowitz*, 333 Ark. 44, 111 S.W.2d 555 (1953).

A breakdown of the citation would render the following information:

Names of Parties to Suit: (1) State of Arkansas (because the case is reported in the Arkansas Reports and one of the parties is the "State"), (2) Markowitz.

Official Publication: Arkansas Reports *Volume Number* (appears on binding of book): 333 *Page Number:* 44

Unofficial Publication: SouthWestern Reporter Second Series *Volume Number:* 111 *Page Number:* 555

Year of the Decision: 1953

Court Rendering the Decision: Supreme Court of Arkansas

The rendering court is identified by the fact that the only court that publishes its opinions in the Arkansas Reports is the Supreme Court of Arkansas. Thus, it would be redundant to mention the fact that the case published in the Arkansas Report is a case of the Arkansas Supreme Court. In some situations, however, the different opinions published in a report or reporter come from a variety of courts and therefore must be specifically identified, for example, *Frey v. U.S.*, 666 F.2d 11 (11th Cir. 1991).

Names of Parties: (1) Frey, (2) United States of America.

Official Publication: Federal Reporter Second Series *Volume:* 666 *Page:* 11

Year of the Decision: 1991

Court Rendering the Decision: 11th Circuit Court of Appeals.

The rendering court is identified in this citation because the Federal Reporter contains the decisions of all U.S. Circuit Courts of Appeals. To determine whether the opinion you are reading would have authority in your jurisdiction, you need to know whether the opinion was handed down by a court within the same jurisdiction. If, for example, you were involved in a suit in the 5th Circuit, the 11th Circuit opinion would not have to be followed by the 5th Circuit. Recall from the discussion of the federal court structure that all U.S. Circuit Courts of Appeals are in equal standing. You would thus want to first attempt to find authority from your own jurisdiction. For this reason, the court is mentioned or indirectly referenced (through the name of the reporter) in the citation. Authority from another jurisdiction may be persuasive but is not mandatory.

With respect to the volume and page numbers, the arrangement is simple and uniform. In a case (judicial opinion) citation, the volume number always immediately precedes the abbreviated name of the reporter. When you locate the reporter in the library, you will see that the volume number of each book is clearly printed on the binding. The page number where the opinion begins always immediately follows the abbreviated name of the reporter in the citation. If there is more than one set of numbers, such as "56 Ill.2d 119, 123," the second number refers to the exact page where the reference is made. For example, if you were reading a case and in the opinion the judge referred to a precedent case and a quotation is given, you should see in the citation not only the location of the case but also the exact page of the opinion where the quotation is found.

Note that citations do not always appear in proper and complete form. Generally, however, enough essential information is given to enable you to locate the case. Upon finding the opinion, the information that may have been omitted can usually be found on the first page of the case, for example, a judicial opinion itself. Occasionally, when referring to precedent, the year or court of the decision will be omitted. However, armed with the names of the parties and the volume, page, and reporter numbers, it is easy to locate the case and obtain the other information.

Citations of legislative law generally contain essentially the same information as judicial opinions. Although there are some slight variations on the arrangement of the citation, they are not so great as to prevent one from locating an unfamiliar authority.

Recall that the discussion of legislative law in Chapter 3 noted that the laws are arranged by general subject. While each jurisdiction determines which subject headings will be used, the methodol-

ogy remains virtually identical. All the statutes are grouped under general subject headings, which are arranged alphabetically and numbered consecutively. Usually, the first heading (often one beginning with the letter "A," such as Agriculture) will be assigned number one. This numbering continues on in sequence until all of the headings have been assigned numbers.

The next step in organizing the statutes is to assign a specific number to each individual law under a subject heading. If a law is repealed, the number of that law is never used again because of the potential for confusion between a repealed law and a new law. Because statutes are constantly modified, the process of organizing is ongoing. New statute numbers are continually added, and occasionally, even new subject headings are used. Because of the prohibitive cost of completely reprinting the statutes each year, the repealed, amended, and new statutes are usually placed in cumulative annual pocket parts or supplements—paperback books placed next to or inside the cover of the book where the subject heading is located. The changes are printed each year and added to the prior year(s) in the supplements until such time as new volumes of the statutes are printed and the supplements are incorporated into them.

When attempting to locate a statute by its citation, certain information should always be present: the name of the statutory publication, the number representing the subject, and the number representing the specific statute. Proper form dictates that the year of the publication should also be included, but the year is sometimes omitted in everyday practice. The symbol § represents Section and in statutory citations is used to signify the numbers representing the section of the statute. Multiple sections are signified by a double symbol (§§). If more than one series of numbers appear together but are separated by a hyphen, (e.g., § 23-4446), the first number represents the subject and is followed by the number that represents the specific statute, for example, Or. Rev. Stat. § 33-1441 (1991). Breakdown of the citation would render the following information:

Statutory Publication: Oregon Revised Statutes

Subject: #33

Specific Statute: #1441

Year of Publication (not necessarily year of statute): 1991

Sometimes the subject number appears before the name of the statutory publication, for example, 28 U.S.C. § 1441 (1986).

Breakdown of the citation:

Statutory Publication: United States Code
Subject: #28
Specific Statute: #1441
Year of Publication: 1986

Some courts include the word *title, chapter,* or *paragraph* or some other similar descriptive term or terms in the citation. If such words or terms are followed in descending order, they will produce the same information. For example, if the citation includes the terms *chapter* and *paragraph*, it makes sense that the broader term *chapter* would refer to the subject and the narrower term *paragraph* would refer to the specific statute.

Some courts actually break their statutory publication into separate codes, with subjects and specific statutes located within a code. For example, the "Code of Procedure" might contain the individual procedural laws arranged by rules of civil procedure, criminal procedure, evidence, and appellate procedure. This method is just one variation on the basic theme of arranging statutes by subject. Consequently, if you have the citation, you should be able to decipher from it the name of the publication, the number representing the general subject, the number representing the specific statute, and the year of publication. Any additional information in the citation is usually present to make this task even simpler by giving more specific descriptions of the location, such as R. Civ.Pro., which indicates that the statute is within the Rules of Civil Procedure.

The year of the citation publication, while sometimes omitted, is actually very important, since the statutes are published every several years. Even supplements are published only annually as a general rule. Because the same statute may be modified (amended), it is important to locate the version that is the subject of discussion. The statute in effect at the time of the incident resulting in a lawsuit is not the same as the statute at the time the suit goes to trial. Generally, the law in effect at the time of the incident is controlling, and consequently, locating the correct version is crucial. Additionally, you can become very frustrated if you go to the correct subject and statutory number only to find no sign of the statute's existence. A quick reference to the year of publication (which is either on the binding or inside the front cover) will eliminate this problem. You may be looking at a publication that preceded the statute or that was printed after the statute was repealed or moved to a different subject. When looking for current law, it is also important to always check any subsequent publications and supplements for any changes. When conducting formal legal research, updating services should be consulted for any changes in the law since the last publication date. For the purposes of this discussion, however, your objective is confined to locating the opinion or statute by referring to the citation.

Glossary

abandoned property   Personal property that has been deliberately left in a location without the intention to retrieve it.

acceptance   Final step necessary to form a legal contract. A demonstration of agreement to all of the terms of the contract that has been offered.

actus reus   Element of physical conduct necessary to commit a criminal act.

administrative agency   Government office enabled by the legislature and overseen by the executive branch. The purpose of such agencies is to apply certain specified laws created by the legislature.

administrative branch   Administrative agencies created pursuant to legislation and overseen by the executive branch to administer and define statutes.

administrative law   Regulations and decisions issued by administrative agencies that explain and detail statutes.

administrative law judge   Judicial officer assigned to preside over cases between individuals or entities and government administrative agencies.

Administrative Procedure Act   Congressional enactment applied to all federal administrative agencies requiring them to follow certain procedures in the issuance of administrative law.

adverse possession   When title to real property is acquired without purchase or voluntary transfer of title. Ordinarily, one who obtains title by adverse possession must openly and continuously exercise possession and control over the entire property inconsistent with the interest of the current owner and all others who claim rights to the property for a period of time specified by statute.

affirm   Approve. When an appellate court affirms the result in the original court, that result is approved and can be enforced.

agency   Relationship in which one party, known as the agent, acts on behalf of another party, known as the principal. In a valid agency relationship, the agent can legally bind the principal; e.g. an agent can enter into a contract on behalf of a principal.

ancillary jurisdiction   Authority of a court over issues in a case subject to the court's authority on grounds unrelated to the issues.

annulment   Legal relationship declared invalid in which the parties to the relationship are treated as if the relationship never existed, e.g., marriage.

antenuptial agreement   Agreement between parties prior to a marriage that states the terms for distribution of assets and liabilities in the event the marriage relationship ends.

appellate jurisdiction   Authority of one court to review the actions in another court for the purpose of identifying an abuse of discretion. See *Discretion*

arraignment   Stage of a criminal proceeding in which the accused is formally charged.

articles of incorporation   Document filed with the state at the time of incorporation to state the purpose of the corporation and define the corporate structure.

assignment   A grant of rights to a third party an original party is entitled to under a contract.

assumption of risk   Defense to negligence on the basis that the plaintiff knew of, appreciated, and voluntarily encountered the danger of the defendant's conduct.

attorney   Individual who has completed the necessary requirements of education and training to receive a license to practice law in a jurisdiction.

bailment   Temporary relinquishment of control over one's personal property to a third party.

bench trial   Trial in which the judge determines which law will be applicable and applies the law to the facts of the case.

bilateral contract   Contractual agreement between two or more persons in which each party promises to deliver performance in exchange for the performance of the other.

bill   Proposed law presented to the legislature for consideration.

bylaws   Document of a corporation that details the methods of operation, such as officers and duties, chain of command, and general corporate procedures.

case law   Law that is created judicially when a legal principle of common law is extended to a similar situation.

cases   Judicial opinions that are common law or case law and that interpret statutory and administrative law.

civil law   Law that governs the private rights of individuals, legal entities, and government. See *Criminal Law*

Code of Federal Regulations   Publication that contains all current administrative regulations.

codification   Process of incorporating newly passed legislation into existing publication of statutes.

common law   Judicially created legal principles or standards. The judiciary has the authority to create law in situations where none currently exists.

comparative negligence   Degree of plaintiff's own negligent conduct that was responsible for plaintiff's injury.

compensatory damages   An award of money payable to the injured party for the reasonable cost of the injuries.

complaint   (also known as petition) Document that apprises the court and the defendant of the nature of the cause of action by the plaintiff.

concurrent jurisdiction   When more than one court has authority to hear a case.

contract   Legally binding agreement that obligates two or more parties to do something they were not already obligated to do or refrain from doing something to which the parties were legally entitled.

contractual capacity   Ability to enter into and be bound by a legal contract, which ability has not been diminished by age of minority or adjudicated incompetence.

contributory negligence   Doctrine that maintains that a plaintiff who, in any way, contributes to his/her injury cannot recover from a negligent defendant.

consideration   That which one party provides to another party as inducement to enter into a contractual agreement. The benefit a party receives as the result of entering a contract with another party.

corporation   Entity legally recognized as independent of its owners, known as shareholders. A corporation can sue or be sued in its own name regarding its own rights and liabilities.

criminal law   Law created and enforced by the legislature for the health, welfare, safety, and general good of the public.

criminal procedure   Law created to assist in the fair and efficient enforcement of criminal law.

critical stage   Stage of a criminal proceeding in which the presumed innocence of the accused is in jeopardy and thus the accused is entitled to representation of counsel.

damage   Financial, physical, or emotional injury.

deposition   Written or oral questions submitted to a party or witness in a lawsuit in which the answers are given orally and under oath, then transcribed into writing.

defendant   Party against whom a lawsuit is instituted.

delegation   Transfer of one's contractual obligations to a third person.

delegation doctrine   Principle that Congress may not assign its authority to create statutory law, nor may any other government entity assume such authority.

discovery Court-supervised exchange of evidence and other relevant information between parties to a lawsuit.

discretion Limits of authority. Abuse of discretion occurs when one's authority is exceeded or improperly used; e.g., abuse of discretion by a judge or jury is grounds for appeal.

dissolution of marriage End of a marriage relationship.

diversity of citizenship Method of achieving federal jurisdiction over a matter. It is necessary that all parties be diverse; i.e., no plaintiff and defendant can be domiciled in the same state. The second requirement of diversity of citizenship is that the amount in dispute between the parties be in excess of the minimum amount stated by federal statute.

double jeopardy Being placed on trial for the same crime twice.

due process That which is necessary to fundamental fairness in the American system of justice.

enabling act Congressional enactment that creates the authority in the executive to organize and oversee an administrative agency.

equity Functional legal remedy sought when money damages would be inadequate as a method of compensating the injured party. Actions in equity ask the court to order performance or nonperformance of certain acts.

estate All material assets of an individual or legal entity, including liquid assets (cash or items that can readily be converted to cash) and nonliquid assets.

evidence Testimony, documentation, or tangible items admissible in court to support a party's claims or defenses in a lawsuit.

exclusive jurisdiction Authority of a court to hear a case, which authority is superior to all other courts.

excusable behavior Behavior by one who, under the color of authority, is considered to be innocent of otherwise criminal behavior.

exhaustion of remedies Requirement that anyone having a dispute with an administrative agency must first follow all available procedures to resolve the dispute within the agency before taking the issue before the judiciary.

federal court A court that is part of the United States courts.

federal question Method of achieving jurisdiction of the federal courts over a dispute between parties. It is necessary that a significant part of the dispute arise from the Constitution or a federal law.

fee simple Absolute ownership of property in American law.

felony Serious crime punishable by imprisonment in excess of one year and/or other significant penalties.

fixture Item of personal property that has been so affixed to real property that it cannot be removed without damage to the real property. A fixture is personal property that essentially becomes part of the real property.

forced share Legal right of a surviving spouse to receive a certain percentage of the estate of the deceased spouse, superior to the terms of a will or other rights of inheritance by heirs.

forum non conveniens (inconvenient forum) Applied when a court with jurisdiction over a matter determines that another court, which also has jurisdiction, would be the more appropriate forum.

freehold estate Interest in real property that involves certain rights of ownership. See *Nonfreehold estate*

grand jury A number of individuals (usually more than 20) who review the evidence to determine whether defendant could be convicted of the crime if charged and tried.

in personam jurisdiction Authority of a court over an individual and all of his/her assets.

in rem jurisdiction Authority of a court over a person's real or personal property.

intentional tort Act that the actor knows or should know with substantial certainty will cause harm to another.

interrogatories Questions submitted by one party in a lawsuit to the opposing party. Said questions must pertain to the dispute between the parties and must be answered within a specific time and under oath. A method of discovery.

intestate succession　　Method of distributing an estate of one who died without a valid will.

joint custody　　Sharing of responsibility for upbringing of children of the joint custodians. In some cases, joint custody also involves shared physical custody of the children.

joint tenancy　　Form of multiple property ownership in which the property owners have fee simple and share four unities. Each owner shares in the right of survivorship.

judge　　Judicial officer who presides over cases in litigation within a court system.

judiciary　　Appointed or elected officials (judges, magistrates, justices of the peace) who preside in the courts over disputes among citizens and the government.

jurisdiction　　(1) Authority of a court over parties and subject of a dispute. (2) Geographical boundaries of the area and citizens over which a court has authority.

justifiable behavior　　Behavior by one who, under the circumstances, is considered to be innocent of otherwise criminal behavior.

law clerk　　Lawyer, law student, or paralegal who conducts legal research and writing and various other duties but who does not represent individual clients as a licensed attorney.

lawyer　　See *attorney.*

legal analysis　　Process of examining precedent in detail to predict its effect on future similar circumstances.

legal separation　　Legal document that establishes the property rights of the parties without effecting a dissolution of the actual marriage relationship.

legal standard　　Law created by one of the three sources of government, including the legislature, executive branch or the judiciary.

legislative branch　　Members of a congress elected by the citizens of a jurisdiction to represent their interests, e.g., senator or representative.

liability　　Legal responsibility resulting from an act or failure to act when there was a legal obligation to do so.

life estate　　Right to possess and use real property for the duration of one's life, with limited ownership rights.

limited partnership　　Partnership of two or more persons in which the limited partner can be held liable for partnership debts only to the extent of his or her investment and cannot take part in general management and operation of the partnership business.

lobbyist　　Individual representing interested parties who meets with legislators about proposed laws.

long-arm jurisdiction　　Authority of the government of one jurisdiction to reach into another jurisdiction for the purpose of exercising control over a particular citizen.

lost property　　Property unintentionally left by the owner in a place no longer known to the owner.

maintenance　　Financial assistance from a divorced spouse to the other divorced spouse to be used for necessary living expenses and income.

material evidence　　Evidence necessary to a fair and informed decision by the trier of fact.

mens rea　　Mental state required as an element necessary to commit a criminal act.

misdemeanor　　Criminal offense punishable by a fine or imprisonment of less than one year.

mislaid property　　Property that was intentionally placed by the owner and later forgotten.

modern balance　　Goal of lawmaking authorities to balance the need for consistency and stability against the need for a flexible and adaptive government.

motion　　Formal request by a party to a lawsuit for court-ordered action/nonaction.

naturalist theory　　Philosophy that all persons know inherently the difference between right and wrong.

negligence　　Act or failure to act toward another when (1) a duty was owed to the other person; (2) the act or failure to act was less than a reasonable person would have done under the circumstances; (3) the act or failure to act was the direct cause of injury to the other person; and

(4) the injury caused measurable financial, physical, or emotional damage to the other person.

negotiable instrument   Document recognized by law as an exchange for legal tender and that meets all legal requirements, including that the document be (1) written, (2) signed, (3) for a specified amount, (4) payable on a certain date or on demand, (5) written with words that indicate whether the document is payable to a stated person (bearer), (6) required that no additional acts are to be performed before payment.

nonfreehold estate   Interest in real property that is limited in duration and involves the right of possession but not ownership. See *Freehold Estate*

note   Negotiable instrument that involves two parties: the "payor" promises to pay an amount to the "payee" on a specified date.

offer   A party presents an agreement for acceptance or rejection by a second party, which agreement includes all necessary requirements and elements of a legal contract.

original jurisdiction   Authority of a court to rule in a lawsuit from commencement through the conclusion of trial.

overrule   Judicial action that states that a legal standard previously recognized is no longer effective as law. Distinguished from reversal (see below).

par value   Legal value of stock (percentages of ownership) in a corporation. Par value is determined by the board of directors of the corporation.

paralegal/legal assistant   One who has legal training and education and performs tasks in the law office traditionally performed by the attorney, with the exception of advocacy and giving of legal advice. In some geographical areas, these terms are used interchangeably, while in others, they imply distinct levels of professional ability.

partnership   Agreement of two or more parties to engage in business or enterprise, with profits and losses shared among all parties.

pendant jurisdiction   Occurs when a case involves multiple issues and the court in which the case is filed has actual authority over some but not all of the issues, in which case, the court has the option to exercise authority over those issues it could not ordinarily decide, thus exercising pendant jurisdiction.

per capita   Distribution in equal shares, with each person representing one share.

per stirpes   Distribution in equal shares to one level or class of persons; if a member of this level or class is deceased, the member's heirs divide the share.

permanent injunction   Court order that permanently orders a party to act or refrain from acting in a particular manner.

personal property   Movable items that are not land or permanently affixed to land. Personal property includes tangible (physical) and intangible items, such as rights of ownership in property held by others, e.g., bank accounts, or rights of ownership in legal entities, e.g. stock. It does not include rights to bring legal action against others, commonly known as a chose in action.

positivist theory   Political belief that there should be a superior government entity not subject to question or challenge.

precedent   Existing legal standards that courts look to for guidance when making a determination of a legal issue.

preliminary injunction   Court order that orders a party to act or refrain from acting in a particular manner for a specified period of time.

probable cause   Legal concept of suspicion supported by facts necessary before a search or arrest can be conducted by law enforcement officers.

probate   Process of paying creditors and distributing the estate of one who is deceased. Probate courts also often administer the estates of living persons who are incapable of managing their own affairs.

procedural law   Law used to guide parties fairly and efficiently through the legal system.

promoter   One who is hired as a fiduciary to recruit investors in a proposed corporation.

property settlement agreement   Agreement as to the property rights and obligations of co-owners/co-debtors, such as parties to a marriage.

proximate cause   Direct cause sufficient to produce a result. No other intervening force can occur independently and prior to the result that is also sufficient to produce the result.

quasi in rem jurisdiction   Authority of a court to alter a person's interest and/or ownership in real or personal property.

real property   Land or anything permanently affixed to land and no longer movable.

reasonable conduct   That action or nonaction that is appropriate under the circumstances when all risks and benefits are taken into account.

reasonable man   One similar in age, intelligence, and experience to the party alleged to be at fault who perceives and appreciates all dangers and benefits of action or nonaction and who acts in the most careful manner.

recision   Legal termination of a contract prior to its completion. Cancellation.

relevant evidence   Evidence that tends to establish an essential fact in the dispute.

remand   Action of one court that returns a case to the court where it originated, e.g., following a reversal or improper transfer.

removal   Transfer of a case to federal court that was originally filed in state court.

request for production   Written request from one party in a lawsuit to the opposing party that seeks to copy and/or inspect documentary evidence relevant to the dispute. A method of discovery.

res ipsa loquitur   "The thing speaks for itself." Method of proving negligence when (1) the injury would not ordinarily have occurred without negligence, (2) the instrument causing injury was in the exclusive control of the defendant, and (3) the plaintiff in no way contributed to the injury.

respondeat superior   Liability of an employer for the acts of an employee who caused damage to a third party while acting within the scope of employment.

reverse   The action of an appellate court used to invalidate a decision by a court of original jurisdiction. The parties to the lawsuit are affected accordingly.

right of survivorship   Characteristic associated with multiple property ownership in which the ownership interest transfers automatically to co-owners upon death.

session law   Published statutes passed during a specific session of the legislature.

shareholder   One who owns stock representing an ownership interest in a corporation.

slip law   Individual statute not yet published with other statutes.

slip opinion   Individual court opinion that is not yet published with other opinions.

sociological theory   Doctrine that follows the principle that government should adapt laws to reflect the current needs and beliefs of society.

sole proprietorship   Individual ownership of a business entity. The individual is personally liable for debts of the business.

specific performance   Court order to complete performance as stated in a contract. Allowed in certain cases of equity where the performance is unique and cannot be imitated or compensated by the payment of money.

stare decisis   "Let the decision stand." Method used by the judiciary when applying precedent to current situations.

statute of frauds   Statutory law that specifies what contracts must be in writing before they will be enforced.

statutory law   A statute. Law that is created by the legislature.

strict liability   Liability without fault. Applied in situations where the intention or neglect of the party is immaterial. The mere performance of the act or omission will result in liability.

subject matter jurisdiction   Authority of a court to determine the actual issue between the parties.

substantive law   Law that creates and resolves the issue between the parties. Legal standard that guides conduct and is applied to determine whether or not conduct was legally appropriate.

summary judgment   Determination prior to trial of the rights and obligations of the parties. This is granted only when there is no significant fact left to be decided on the basis of the evidence. The greatest weight of the evidence supports only one result.

temporary restraining order   Court order that orders a party to act or refrain from acting in a particular manner for a short time until the court has the opportunity to consider a more permanent ruling.

tenancy in common   Form of multiple ownership of property in which each tenant (owner) shares with the other(s) an undivided interest in the property.

tenancy by entirety   Form of multiple ownership of property between spouses that includes right of survivorship.

testate succession   Method of distributing the estate of a deceased person in accordance with the terms of a valid will.

third-party beneficiary   One who, as the result of gift or collateral agreement, is entitled to the contractual performance owed another.

tort   Civil wrong by a party, other than breach of contract, that results in injury to the private rights or interests of another party.

traditional balance   Goal of the judiciary to allow maximum personal freedom without detracting from the welfare of the general public.

trial court   Court of original jurisdiction with authority to hear evidence of parties and render a verdict.

unilateral contract   Contractual agreement in which one party makes a promise to perform upon receiving the actual performance of the other party.

venue   Proper individual court within a jurisdiction to determine a dispute between parties.

veto   Presidential power to invalidate law passed by a majority of Congress (2/3 majority of each house needed to override).

Index